W9-DFW-536

DATE DUE

Sociology

SECOND EDITION

Sociology

A Brief Introduction

ALEX THIO
OHIO UNIVERSITY

HarperCollinsCollegePublishers

Acquisitions Editor:	Alan McClare
Developmental Editor:	Phil Herbst
Project Editor:	Ellen MacElree
Design Supervisor:	Paul Agresti
Text Design Adaptation:	Paul Agresti
Cover Design:	Molly Heron
Cover Illustration:	Molly Heron
Photo Researcher:	Rosemary Hunter
Production Manager/Assistant:	Willie Lane/Sunaina Sehwani
Compositor:	Black Dot Graphics
Printer and Binder:	R. R. Donnelley & Sons Company
Cover Printer:	The Lehigh Press, Inc.

For permission to use copyrighted material, grateful acknowledgment is made to the copyright holders on pp. 431–432, which are hereby made part of this copyright page.

Sociology: A Brief Introduction, Second Edition

Library of Congress Cataloging-in-Publication Data
Thio, Alex.
   Sociology : a brief introduction / Alex Thio. — 2nd ed.
      p.   cm.
   Includes bibliographical references and indexes.
   ISBN 0-06-501359-X (student ed.) 0-06-502345-5 (instructor's ed.)
   1. Sociology.   I. Title.
HM51.T53   1994
301—dc20   93-33285
                                                                          CIP

93 94 95 96 9 8 7 6 5 4 3 2 1

CONTENTS IN BRIEF

CONTENTS IN DETAIL

This new edition of *Sociology: A Brief Introduction* is a major revision. I have, however, continued to present the essentials of sociology without a loss of substance or concreteness. In pruning away those topics that are not essential for learning about sociological issues, I have concentrated on major areas in depth but with enough lively details to maintain student interest. Although this text is relatively short, it provides instructors and students with the full range of sociological analyses and issues. To ensure that students learn a great deal from this brief text, I have retained most of the successful features of my full-length book. I have also tried to convey the sense of excitement that I feel about sociology.

Many students seem to assume that sociology is merely common sense—that there is nothing new in sociology, or that whatever is there they have known all along. To help students recognize how much their unexamined assumptions affect the way they view the world, I begin each chapter with a set of popular myths and the realities behind them that have been uncovered through sociological research. These myths and realities are further discussed, along with many others, throughout the text. Students will find some of their firmest assumptions challenged, and that should lead to increased interest in the materials of the course.

The discussion in each chapter also begins with a real-life vignette that is designed to dramatize the central theme of the chapter, showing how abstract sociological principles reflect underlying realities and illuminate them.

New to This Edition

This text has been thoroughly revised and updated. All the real-life vignettes are new, portraying current events in our fast-changing world. There are consider-

ably more tables and figures than in the previous edition. And the subject of education is now combined in a single chapter with science and health. This edition is packed with new topics, of which only the most significant are listed below.

Chapter 1: The Essence of Sociology
- Jane Addams is included as one of the founders of American sociology. (She has long been ignored in textbooks, despite her rare distinction of being the only sociologist to have won the Nobel Prize.)
- A new section on the feminist perspective in sociology.

Chapter 2: Culture
- A new section on American pop culture.

Chapter 3: Social Structure
- A new section containing a sociological analysis of the reasons for Japan's emergence as an economic giant.

Chapter 4: Groups and Organizations
- A new discussion on female styles of managing business organizations.

Chapter 5: Socialization
- Updated information on the effect of environment on intelligence.
- An entirely new section on the processes of socialization: learning how to think, feel, and see oneself, which replaces the psychological theories of personality development. This section incorporates new information on emotional socialization.
- A new section on the influence of gender and class on adolescent peer groups.

■ Updated information on the effects of television on socialization.

Chapter 6: Deviance and Control
■ An updated section on rape, emphasizing date rape, especially on college campuses.

■ A cross-cultural analysis of homicide.

■ A new section on control theory, including the new "shaming theory."

■ A new section on the feminist theory of deviance.

■ These added sociological theories replace the biological and psychological theories.

■ A new section on the war on drugs.

Chapter 7: Social Stratification
■ A new section on poverty, welfare, and homelessness.

■ A new section on the feminization of poverty.

■ A new section on global stratification.

■ New data on the widening gap between the rich and the poor.

■ A new section on how to achieve social equality.

Chapter 8: Racial and Ethnic Minorities
■ A new section on affirmative action and its critics.

■ New data on the victimization of African-Americans by stereotypes and legal harassment.

■ Updated information on bilingual education involving Hispanic-Americans.

■ New material on the problems of "glass ceiling" and "model minority" faced by Asian-Americans.

Chapter 9: Gender and Age
■ Updated information on gender discrimination in employment.

■ A new section on gender bias in religion.

■ A new section on gender bias in sports.

■ An updated section on the presentation of gender roles in the mass media.

■ A new section on elder abuse.

Chapter 10: The Family
■ New data on sex myths.

■ A new section on the battle over abortion.

■ A new section on marriage choice.

■ A new section on stepfamilies.

■ Updated information on staying single and the changing American family.

Chapter 11: Religion
■ A significantly updated section on religious fundamentalism.

■ New sections each on New Age and Islam.

■ A new section on religious television.

Chapter 12: Politics and the Economy
■ A new section on the power to declare war.

■ Updated information on political participation.

■ A new section on the revolutions in Eastern Europe and the former Soviet Union.

■ Updated information on terrorism.

■ New data on the postindustrial world.

■ Updated sections on capitalist and socialist economies

■ A new section on the American economy today.

■ New data on the surge in temporary employment.

Chapter 13: Education, Science, and Health
■ Significantly updated information on AIDS.

■ A new section on the changing medical profession.

■ A new section on the right to die.

Chapter 14: Population, Ecology, and Urbanization
■ A new section on the latest U.S. census.

■ Significantly updated information on environmental pollution.

■ A new section on saving the environment.

■ A new section on the growth of suburban cities.

■ A new section on the recent changes in American cities.

Chapter 15: Collective Behavior and Social Change
■ A new section, "Is the United States in Decline?"

■ New information on the demassification of society.

Organization

The book covers all the essential topics for an introductory sociology course. The first chapter introduces students to the essence of sociology, showing them how to think sociologically and how to do sociology. Major sociological perspectives and research methods are presented here. Chapters 2 through 5 examine the social bases of human behavior—culture, social structure, groups and organizations, and socialization. These are followed by a chapter on deviant behavior, as an illustration of how even seemingly personal actions are socially motivated. Chapters 7 through 9 analyze various forms of human inequality. They include the inequality between rich and poor, between dominant and minority groups, between males and females, and between old and young. Chapters 10 through 13 deal with major social institutions—the family, religion, politics, economics, education, science, and medicine. In the final two chapters, I discuss those aspects of society that change most visibly. They are population, ecology, urbanization, collective behavior (including social movements), and social change.

Features

SCHOLARSHIP AND READABILITY

This book offers a unique blend of scholarship and readability. I have tried not to gloss over complex sociological issues but to confront them head-on. Although I have taken great care to be fair and accurate in discussing the various theoretical and empirical studies, I have also critiqued them, evaluated them, or related them to other studies. Further, I have applied the major sociological perspectives—introduced in the first chapter—throughout the text, wherever they can throw light on a specific subject. It has been my goal to make complex sociological ideas easy for students to follow. To achieve this, I have written simply and directly, avoiding the use of long and complicated sentences, but without any condescension.

CURRENT RESEARCH

I have taken special care to present the most recent findings from the sociological literature. Sociology is a fast-growing field. In recent years it has produced an abundance of new concepts and data, reflecting the significant changes that have recently taken place in American society. Thus many references cited in this text are as recent as 1992 and 1993. I have also discussed, with a sociological interpretation, numerous current events reported in first-class newspapers and newsmagazines.

PEDAGOGICAL AIDS

In order to ensure that students get the most out of this course, I have developed a comprehensive system of pedagogical aids. The overall goal of these teaching devices is to motivate students and facilitate learning. Students are encouraged to think about the materials by themselves or by discussing important issues in class. It is frequently through such active involvement, as opposed to passive acceptance of what one reads, that students really begin to sharpen their thinking skills. Then the understanding and absorption of ideas presented in the text will come easily.

Chapter Vignettes Along with a chapter outline and a myths and realities box, each chapter opens with a thought-provoking story. This is intended to fix the student's mind on the main themes of the chapter.

Illustrations and Captions The photographs have been selected to illuminate key ideas throughout the text. The captions have been purposely written to recapitulate those key ideas. Together, the photos and captions reinforce the student's comprehension and retention of the material.

Questions for Discussion and Review In every chapter there are questions at the end of each main section. Instructors can use them as a springboard for lively discussions in class. Students can use them to review the main ideas that have just been discussed, before moving on to the next topic. However the questions are used, students will learn more as active thinkers than as passive recipients of facts and ideas.

Chapter Summaries Each chapter ends with a full summary in a question-and-answer format. The standard form of summary in an introductory text tends to turn students into passive consumers of knowledge. In contrast, the question-and-answer format encourages students to become actively involved, by inviting them to join the author in thinking about important issues. Students who have actively thought about what they have read will more easily understand and remember it later.

Key Terms The most important words are identified in the text with boldface type and are defined when they are introduced. They are listed and defined again at the end of each chapter, with a page cross-reference to facilitate study. All key terms are also defined in full in the Glossary at the end of the book.

Suggested Readings In line with the currentness of the material in the text, the most up-to-date books for further reading are listed at the end of each chapter. These sources enable students to seek additional knowledge about the subject matter of each chapter. Most books are readily available in school libraries.

Supplements

Accompanying this text is a useful support package for instructors and students.

SOCIETIES: A MULTI-CULTURAL READER

A collection of 38 relatively brief articles, all related to cross-cultural issues, has been assembled by Peter Morrill of Bronx Community College. There are two to three readings for each chapter in the text. The great variety of topics covered will help students appreciate cultural diversity within the United States and will also illustrate how ways of life in other societies can differ from the familiar world they know. Each reading begins with a short introduction that relates the material to key concepts in the text and ends with a short set of study questions.

INSTRUCTOR'S MANUAL

Prepared by Peter Morrill of Bronx Community College, this manual provides chapter outlines, learning objectives, a complete summary of chapter topics, and an extensive set of classroom discussion questions keyed to main topics. Each chapter also includes demonstrations, projects, and applications that are designed to develop the thinking skills of students. The *Instructor's Manual* ends with an exten-

sive list of audiovisual aids and their sources. The goal of the manual is to enable instructors to show students how to think effectively about sociological topics. In addition, students are helped not only to master the material of the course but also to take an active role in learning it.

TEST BANK

The *Test Bank,* also prepared by Peter Morrill, contains over 1100 multiple-choice, short-answer, and essay questions. The *Test Bank* is available as a printed manual and on Testmaster. Testmaster is Harper-Collins' computerized test-generating system. It produces customized tests and allows instructors to scramble questions and add new ones. Testmaster is available for use with IBM PC and compatibles, and the Macintosh.

STUDY GUIDE

A *Study Guide,* also prepared by Professor Morrill, is a substantial book in its own right. Each chapter opens with an outline of the chapter in the text, a list of learning objectives, a detailed review of the material designed to get the student deep into the particulars of the chapter, and numerous questions and answers to check the student's knowledge.

SUPERSHELL STUDENT TUTORIAL SOFTWARE

Prepared by Peter Morrill, this computerized student tutorial guide is designed to help students retain the key concepts and ideas they have read. This versatile drill-and-practice software contains questions for each chapter in the text which provide students with immediate feedback. Questions are referenced to the pages in the text where relevant information is presented. Students may print out narrative chapter outlines or consult an easy-to-use tutorial guide. In addition, a flash card program is included to drill students on the terms in the text's glossary.

Acknowledgments

I am grateful to the many instructors all over the country who have adopted the previous edition of this book. I would also like to thank many colleagues at various universities and colleges for reviewing the manuscript of this edition. Their criticisms and suggestions have enabled me to continue writing a textbook that is both challenging and interesting to students. The reviewers include: Tim Britton, Lenoir Community College; Mary L. Cain, Our Lady of the Lake University; Alline DeVore, Kingsborough Community College; Patricia Dorman, Boise State University; Ralph Faris, Community College of Philadelphia; Thesalonia Ford, St. Louis Community College; Gerald Freeman, Broom Community College; Mark Geller, Rutgers University; David Jaffe, SUNY-New Paltz; Michael Kimmel, University of California-Berkeley; Diane Levy, University of Wilmington; Charles Mulford, Iowa State University; Daniel Polak, Hudson Valley Community College; Earl Schaeffer, Columbus State Community College; and Jeff Weaver, Defiance College.

I am particularly thankful to Peter Morrill of Bronx Community College. His tireless pursuit of appropriate articles for *Societies* and his work on the *Study Guide, Test Bank,* and the *Instructor's Manual* have contributed immensely to the text's support package.

I owe a special debt to several people at Harper-Collins. Alan McClare, the sociology editor, has over the years made me feel that it is a pleasure to write textbooks for HarperCollins. The meticulous editorial supervision of Philip Herbst, the development editor, has greatly enhanced the quality of this revised text. Ellen MacElree, the project editor, has efficiently guided the production of the book. Julie Conway, supplements editor, has assembled an effective teaching and learning package.

Finally, I am grateful to my wife and children for their understanding and patience. They have made it possible for me to take a lot of pleasure, without much guilt, in writing this book.

ALEX THIO

ABOUT THE AUTHOR

Alex Thio is Professor of Sociology at Ohio University. Born of Chinese parentage in Penang, Malaysia, he grew up in a multicultural environment. He acquired fluency in Mandarin (modern standard Chinese), two Chinese dialects (Fukienese and Hakka), Malay, and Indonesian. He also picked up a smattering of English and Dutch.

After attending primary school in Malaysia and high school in Indonesia, he came to the United States and put himself through college in Missouri. Later, he did graduate work in sociology at the State University of New York at Buffalo, where he completed his doctorate while working as a research and teaching assistant.

Dr. Thio regularly teaches courses on introductory sociology, social problems, criminology, and deviance. In addition to teaching, he enjoys writing. Aside from this text, he is author of the popular texts *Deviant Behavior* and *Sociology: An Introduction,* both of which are published by HarperCollins, and has written many articles.

He lives with his wife Jane and daughters Diane and Julie in Athens, Ohio. His hobbies include reading, movies, traveling, and sailing.

Sociology

1

THE ESSENCE
OF SOCIOLOGY

n April 29, 1992, several hours after a nearly all-white jury acquitted four white police officers of illegally beating black motorist Rodney King, riots erupted in South-Central Los Angeles. The violence started with some young blacks throwing stones and bottles at passing cars. Before long, the mob swelled. Two white motorists were pulled out of their cars and beaten. Many other drivers panicked, jumping from cars and fleeing as fast as they could. Some rioters smashed or torched the abandoned vehicles. Others turned their destructive attention to liquor stores, gas stations, and small shops. Soon huge flames and black smoke engulfed the area. People of all races, mostly poor, looted stores, manically carrying out armfuls of items large and small as if they had won prizes on a TV game show. The sound of gunfire also rattled throughout the neighborhood. Lasting more than 48 hours, the L.A. riots left 44 dead, some 2000 wounded, and about $1 billion in stolen goods and charred ruins (Mathews, 1992b).

The Rodney King verdict had obviously triggered the riots because it was seen as an outrageous miscarriage of justice. In fact, the black community's rage had long been building, as numerous instances of police abuse against African-Americans had occurred. But African-Americans were not the only participants in the riots. They were joined by many Hispanics and even some whites—including men, women, and children. Why did these people, who were far from being personally outraged by the King verdict, participate in the riots? Their behavior can be attributed to what sociologists call "the emergent norm" that encourages members of a crowd to engage in the same activity without necessarily having the same feeling, attitude, or belief (see Chapter 15: Collective Behavior and Social Change).

But how does this emergent norm come about in the first place? Are there some unique characteristics of a crowd that produce this norm? Do all human groups influence our behavior in the same way as a crowd does? These questions are important because they deal with the world in which we live. And there are many other important questions about that world: Why are some marriages successful while others end in divorce? Are we born with our personalities already built into us? How will a college education affect your income? Is the American work ethic losing its steam? Are men naturally more aggressive than women? Apart from having more money, are rich people different from everyone else? Do cities make people callous and rude? Sociology can help us find answers to questions like these. As the scientific study of human social behavior, **sociology** can show us how people act and react, what the characteristics of groups and societies are, and how these social units affect people.

Thus, the subject matter of sociology is familiar. It is, as Peter Berger (1963) said, "the very world in which we have lived all our lives." But sociology casts a new light on this world, offering a unique view on human life. In this chapter, we examine that view as well as the history of sociology, its major perspectives, and its research methods.

The Study of Social Life

Virtually everybody has something to say about human social behavior. Because it is the stuff of everyday life, many people think they know all about it. But, as Otto Larsen (1981) noted, "Living in a family or working in an organization does not automatically make one a sociologist any more than swimming in the sea makes one an oceanographer or being an animal breeder makes one a geneticist." Sociologists have a special way of looking at human behavior and special tools for studying it.

THE SOCIOLOGICAL IMAGINATION

When sociologists examine people and their behavior, they focus on how people are influenced by other people and by society. No matter how personal our experiences are, they are influenced by **social forces**—forces that arise from the society of which we are a part. Social forces exist outside the individual, in the form of social relationships such as those we share with our friends, relatives, and people in educational, economic, religious, and other institutions. C. Wright Mills (1959b) referred to the ability to see the impact of social forces on individuals, especially on their private lives, as the **sociological imagination.** This imagination is the essence of the sociological perspective.

Consider the case of suicide. It is reasonable to assume that those who kill themselves are frustrated and unhappy, since happy people rarely want to die. But suicide cannot be explained simply by saying that people who commit suicide are frustrated and unhappy. This explanation does not tell us why, for example, Protestants have higher rates of suicide than Catholics. There is no evidence that Protestants as a group are more unhappy than Catholics. How, then, do we account for the different suicide rates of these two groups?

The sociological perspective leads us to look not at the individual personalities of those who commit suicide, but at social forces. When French sociologist Emile Durkheim (1951) examined suicide in the late nineteenth century, he detailed variations in the rates of suicide among various countries and groups. These rates constitute social, not individual, facts, and, to explain them, Durkheim turned to social forces. Among the forces he explored was **social integration,** the degree to which people are tied to a social group. When there is either excessive or inadequate social integration, suicide rates are likely to be high.

In the past, when elderly Eskimos committed suicide, the cause was usually extreme social integration. Obedient to the values and customs of their society, they did what they were expected by others to do: killing themselves when they could no longer contribute to the economy of their community. Similarly, Hindu widows used to follow the tradition of

their society by ceremoniously throwing themselves onto the funeral pyres of their husbands. These ritual suicides were called *suttee* (literally, "good women"). Those elderly Eskimos and Hindu widows apparently felt pressured to commit suicide. If they refused to kill themselves, they might be stigmatized as "selfish" or "bad women."

On the other hand, a lack of social integration can also be found in high suicide rates. Divorced and widowed people, for example, are more likely than married people to be isolated from others and to receive little affection or moral support when they are frustrated. In other words, the divorced and the widowed are more likely to experience inadequate social integration. As a result, they are also more likely than married people to commit suicide. Similarly, Protestants traditionally have been less integrated into their church community than Catholics. Whereas the Catholic church emphasizes salvation through the community and binds its members to the church through its doctrines and rituals, Protestant churches emphasize individual salvation and individual responsibility. When feeling extremely miserable, Protestants tend to rely more on themselves—rather than on friends and others—to lighten their miseries. This individualism may underlie the higher rate of suicide found among Protestants. The reason is that, by relying on oneself to solve one's own emotional problem, one tends to be too emotional and subjective to find a viable solution.

Suicide is an extreme, exceptional act, but all around us we can see ordinary actions that are also molded by social forces. If your family had only half its actual income, would you be reading this book today? Would you be in college? Would your ambitions be the same? The distribution of income in the United States is a social fact. Your family's position in that distribution is one of your social characteristics. And this characteristic influences your way of living and your chances in life—such as the likelihood that you will attend college. What career are you planning for yourself? If you had been born in 1900, the chances that you would be a farmer would be much greater than they are now. Suppose you were an Egyptian citizen today; your chances of becoming a business executive would be much less than they are for you as an American. Our private worlds can never be totally sealed off from the larger world of society. The technology and economy of the United States; its customs, ideals, and beliefs; its government and politics—all these are social characteristics and represent social forces that help shape our lives.

No matter how personal our experiences seem, they are influenced by the social forces of our society. Sociologist Emile Durkheim explored how a social force known as social integration could reduce the likelihood of suicide. Top: As an indication of strong social integration, people are closely tied to a social group. Such people are less likely to commit suicide, because when deeply frustrated they receive a great deal of affection, care, and help from others. Bottom: When social integration is lacking, isolated individuals tend more to commit suicide because they do not get help from others to lighten their problem.

We cannot account for social forces by simply adding up the characteristics of individuals any more than we can describe water by listing the characteristics of its components. When hydrogen and oxygen form water, the water has characteristics different from either hydrogen or oxygen. When people form a sports team, the team develops characteristics (such as teamwork, solidarity, and camaraderie) that are not found in any one of its members. So, too, any social group is more than just the sum of its parts. It has characteristics that are not found in separate individuals but that arise only when these individuals in-

teract. The sociological perspective directs our attention to these social characteristics and the social forces that create them. The sociological imagination grasps the significance of these forces in our lives.

SOCIOLOGY AND COMMON SENSE

To some people, sociology appears to be the laborious study of the obvious, an expensive way to discover what everybody already knows. To these people sociology is merely common sense. But is it? Consider the following statements:

1. Because mental ability declines with age, older people are less productive than younger ones.
2. Since we have the highest divorce rate in the world, marriage must be losing its appeal in the United States.
3. Religion and science do not mix. Religion cannot encourage the development of science.
4. Persistent poverty can easily cause a revolution.
5. Unlike the Japanese, Americans do not work hard, because they are more interested in having fun.
6. Armed robbery is more dangerous to the victim than unarmed robbery.
7. Most of the young people who join cults are different from their conventional peers. They, at the very least, have some problems with their parents.
8. Because Big Business dominates the United States, most Americans work in large companies with more than 1000 employees each.
9. Severe prejudice and discrimination always make minorities poor.
10. College men who have little or no sexual experience are more likely to rape their dates than those who have a lot of sexual experience.

How many of these statements do you believe to be true? Research has shown that every one of them is false. Here are the facts:

1. On most measures of productivity, older workers are as productive as younger ones, despite some decline in the older workers' perception and reactive speed (Chapter 9: Gender and Age).
2. We have one of the highest rates of marriage in the world. Even divorced Americans are likely, eventually, to remarry. To most Americans, divorce means rejection only of a specific partner, not of marriage in general (Chapter 10: The Family).
3. Religion may play an important part in the development of science, as it did in seventeenth-century England (Chapter 13: Education, Science, and Health).
4. Revolutions are more likely to occur when living conditions are improving than when they remain consistently bad (Chapter 12: Politics and the Economy).
5. Most Americans work hard, but they try to enjoy themselves more on the job as well as off (Chapter 2: Culture).

6. Unarmed robbery is more dangerous than armed robbery. An unarmed robber is more likely to hurt the victim because the victim is more inclined to resist the weaponless robber (Chapter 6: Deviance and Control).
7. The young people who join cults are mostly normal and come from warm, loving families (Chapter 11: Religion).
8. Most Americans work in small firms, especially those with fewer than 100 employees (Chapter 12: Politics and the Economy).
9. In the United States, West Indian blacks, whose ancestors came from the Caribbean, have suffered as much discrimination as a minority, but they have achieved greater educational, economic, and political success than whites (Chapter 8: Racial and Ethnic Minorities).
10. Sexually active men are more likely to rape their dates (Chapter 6: Deviance and Control).

These and other sociological findings may surprise you because they appear to contradict common sense. Of course, not every finding in sociology is surprising. In fact, some confirm what you have known all along. You should not be surprised, therefore, to learn from sociology that there is more joblessness among blacks than whites or that there are more poor people than rich people in prison. But many other commonsense ideas have turned out to be false, like the above examples. By systematically checking commonsense ideas with reliable facts, sociology can tell us which popular beliefs are myths and which are realities.

Sociology can also help clarify the confusion that sometimes arises from common sense. You may have read that "birds of a feather flock together" but also that "opposites attract." You may have heard the encouraging message that "absence makes the heart grow fonder," but you may still remember the discouraging warning, "out of sight, out of mind." When confronted with such conflicting commonsense ideas, how can we tell which are correct and which are false? We can get the answer from sociological research. It has shown, for example, that the effect of someone's absence on another depends on the strength of the initial relationship. If two people have loved each other deeply like Romeo and Juliet, absence would make their hearts grow fonder, but a high school romance tends to disintegrate, because such relationships are usually not deep and serious enough to begin with (Kohn, 1988).

In short, it is not true that sociology is only

common sense. If it were, you wouldn't want to study sociology at all. Why would you waste your time trying to learn something you already knew? Sociology is made up of more than commonsense ideas because it requires that ideas be systematically checked against evidence. Common sense requires only a willingness to believe what it tells us. It, therefore, cannot tell us whether those beliefs have any basis in fact. But sociology can. This is one of the reasons why sociology is exciting. It often shows us that what has long been familiar—or just "common sense"—may turn out to be unfamiliar or uncommon. Thus, the distinction between sociology and common sense is clear. While common sense gives us familiar and untested ideas, sociology offers factually supported ideas as well as the excitement of discovering something new about ourselves.

SOCIOLOGY AS A SCIENCE

The goal of science is to find order in apparent chaos. Scientists search for a pattern in what, on the surface, may look like random variations. They look for regularity, something that appears over and over, across time and space. Observation is given the last word in this search. It is true that scientists, like everyone else, have preconceived ideas, beliefs, and values, and they use logic and intuition to understand the world. But scientific methods require scientists to put aside existing views of what the world should be like and to rely, above all, on observation.

When scientists discover a pattern in the world, they describe it in a **hypothesis,** a tentative statement of what the pattern is, of how various events are related to one another. Then they test the hypothesis against systematic observations, producing evidence for or against it. Hypotheses, however, must be related to one another in order to explain a broader range of phenomena. A set of logically related hypotheses that explains the relationship among various phenomena is called a **theory.** A good theory will apply to a wide range of existing observations and suggest testable predictions about what can be observed in the future.

Suppose we are investigating the causes of revolutions. We find that the American Revolution was a struggle against a distant ruler that resulted in the establishment of a democracy. We also find that the Russian Revolution was an uprising against a ruling class that produced a new but still undemocratic government. Despite these differences, we come across some similarities between the two revolutions. In both, the people had experienced a foretaste of liberty. They knew their conditions could be improved. They were enraged by the discrepancy between what was and what they felt ought to be. From these similarities, we could devise the hypothesis that revolutions are caused by a discrepancy between expectations and reality. If we test this hypothesis against systematic observations of other revolutions and find that the evidence consistently supports our hypothesis, then we have a theory of revolution.

We would, however, have proven our theory to be only tentatively rather than absolutely true. A scientific theory is always open to revision in the light of new evidence. Scientific findings are always subject to verification or refutation by other scientists. If the findings cannot be duplicated by other scientists, they are suspect. Scientists routinely check whether their findings confirm or contradict those of their colleagues. This procedure increases the chances that mistakes, oversights, or biases will be detected. It ensures the objectivity of science.

QUESTIONS FOR DISCUSSION AND REVIEW
1. How does the sociological imagination clarify the role of the social forces that shape the experiences of individuals?
2. How does sociology differ from common sense?

The Development of Sociology

Sociology has a very short history. Of course, centuries before Christ was born, people such as Plato and Socrates had thought and argued about social behavior. But most of them did not make systematic observations to test their speculations against reality. They were social philosophers, not sociologists. The field of sociology emerged in the nineteenth century, when European social philosophers began to use scientific methods.

Two factors combined to convert some philosophers into sociologists: the social upheavals of nineteenth-century Europe and the advancement of the natural sciences. The Western world was radically altered during the nineteenth century, as the Industrial Revolution brought new industries and technologies and new ways of living. Almost overnight, societies that had long been rural and stable became industrialized, urbanized, and chaotic. They confronted problems such as the exploitation of factory workers, the migration of people from farms to cities, congestion and poverty in the cities, crowded and squalid housing, broken families, and rising crime. Meanwhile, the political order of Europe had been shaken up. In the aftermath of the French Revolution, many people began to question the legitimacy of their monarchies and the authority of their churches, demanding greater freedom for the individual. Many social philosophers felt challenged to find solutions to their societies' new problems and to understand how and why such radical change could occur. At the same time, the natural sciences were highly respected, because they were providing ways to both explain and control aspects of the physical world. Some social philosophers looked on natural science as a model for how they might go about understanding and controlling the social world.

As sociology developed, these two urges—to improve the world and to apply scientific methods to the study of society—continued to motivate sociologists.

Auguste Comte (1798–1857) was the first to argue for the need for scientific knowledge about society. He is regarded as the father of sociology.

THE PIONEERS OF SOCIOLOGY

The nineteenth-century French philosopher Auguste Comte (1798–1857) is sometimes called the father of sociology. He coined the word "sociology" in 1838 to refer to the scientific study of society. Comte believed that every society goes through three stages of development: religious, metaphysical, and scientific. According to Comte, reliance on superstition and speculation characterizes the religious and metaphysical stages, and neither is adequate for understanding society or for solving society's problems. What is needed, he argued, is scientific knowledge about society based on social facts, just as scientific knowledge about the physical world is based on physical facts. He envisioned a science of society with two branches: *statics,* the study of the organization that allows societies to endure, and *dynamics,* the study of the processes by which societies change. During the scientific stage, Comte believed, sociologists would develop a scientific knowledge of society and would guide society in a peaceful, orderly evolution.

Herbert Spencer (1820–1903) did not assign such an exalted role to sociologists. This nineteenth-century Englishman had a different view of how society works. He believed that a society can be compared to a living organism. Each part of an animal—its heart, lungs, brains, and so on—has its own function to perform, yet all the parts are interdependent, so that a change in one part affects all the

others. Moreover, each part contributes to the survival and health of the animal as a whole. If one organ becomes diseased, others adapt to the crisis, working harder to ensure the animal's survival. Similarly, in Spencer's view, each part of a society performs its own function and contributes to the survival and stability of the whole. The family, religion, the government, industry—all are parts of one "organism," society.

Spencer concluded that society, if left alone, corrects its own problems. It tends naturally toward health and stability. Social problems work themselves out through the natural process of "survival of the fittest." The phrase implies that rich, powerful, or otherwise successful people—the "fittest"—deserve to enjoy their wealth, power, or success because they have been "selected" by nature to be what they are. On the other hand, poor, weak, or otherwise unsuccessful individuals—the "unfit"—should be left to fend for themselves, because nature has doomed them to failure. If government interferes with this natural process by helping the unfit, society will suffer because the efforts of its successful people will be wasted. According to Spencer, the best thing government can do about social problems is to leave them alone. The fate of society, in his view, is governed by laws of nature. If nature is left to do its job without government interference, society will not only survive but evolve to become better.

But where Spencer saw harmony and stability,

Karl Marx (1818-1883) observed underlying conflict, exploitation, and the seeds of revolution. According to Marx, a German who spent much of his life writing in England, Spencer's stable, interdependent society was a myth. The primary feature of society, Marx claimed, is not stability and interdependence but conflict and competition. Every society, past and present, is marked by social conflict.

In particular, Marx claimed that the primary feature of society is **class conflict.** There is a class of capitalists, the bourgeoisie, who own the means of production, and an exploited class of laborers, the proletariat, who do not own the means of production. These two classes, he said, are inevitably locked in conflict. The laborers, far from being naturally unfit, are destined to overthrow the capitalists and establish a classless society in which everyone will work according to ability and receive according to need.

Marx did not believe, as Spencer did, that the differences between laborers and capitalists are determined by natural selection. On the contrary, Marx believed that they are determined by the economic system. In fact, he argued, the economic system determines a society's religious beliefs, its values, and the nature of its educational system, government, and other institutions. And again unlike Spencer, he urged people not to let society evolve on its own but to change it.

Despite their differences, both Marx and Spencer, like Comte, recognized the value of science in the study of society. But they did not actually use scientific methods. They argued about how society worked and how its troubles might be eased. Nevertheless, they did not conduct scientific observations, much less experiments. It was Emile Durkheim (1858-1917) who pioneered the systematic application of scientific methods to sociology. His ideas about suicide, which we discussed earlier, were not based on speculation. In his study of suicide, he made a research plan. Then he collected a large mass of statistical data on suicide in various European countries. Finally, he analyzed the data in order to discover the causes of suicide. He not only used systematic observation but also argued that sociologists should consider only what they could observe and should look at "social facts as things." They should not look, he said, to "the notions" of people in order to explain society. People's subjective experiences should not be a concern of sociologists.

In contrast, the German sociologist Max Weber (1864-1920) believed that sociologists must go be-

Emile Durkheim (1858-1917) pioneered the systematic application of scientific principles to sociology. He was the first to use statistical methods to test hypotheses.

yond what people do, beyond what can be observed directly. He argued that individuals always interpret the meaning of their own behavior and act according to these interpretations. Sociologists must therefore find out how people feel or what they think about their own behavior. To do this, according to Weber, sociologists should adopt a method he called **Verstehen**—sympathetic understanding of their subjects. By mentally putting themselves into their subjects' position, sociologists could obtain an "interpretive understanding" of the meanings of particular behavior. Then, he said, they should test this understanding through careful observation.

AMERICAN SOCIOLOGY

By the turn of the twentieth century, sociology had made its way from Europe to the United States. Like their European predecessors, the first American sociologists tried to understand and solve the problems of their time, problems such as crime and delinquency, broken homes, slums, and racial unrest. But they dealt with social problems differently. The Europeans were more interested in developing large-scale social theories. So they examined the fundamental issues of social order and social change, trying to discover the causes of social problems as a whole. In contrast, the Americans were more pragmatic. They were more inclined to focus on specific problems, such as prostitution or juvenile delinquency, and to treat each problem separately. To study and solve these problems, they developed scientific, quantitative methods (Ross, 1991).

A good example of those Americans was Jane Addams (1860-1935), one of the most outstanding founders of American sociology. In Chicago, she set up and then directed a center for research and social thought, which she named Hull House. Most of the sociologists working at Hull House were women. They often exchanged ideas and interests with the predominantly male sociologists at the University of Chicago. The chief goal of Hull House was to apply sociological knowledge to solving social problems. The male sociologists at the University of Chicago also had the same goal, but they were not as successful as the Hull House sociologists.

In doing their projects, Addams and her colleagues would first identify a certain problem, then gather data documenting the nature of the problem, formulate a social-action policy based on the data, and finally organize citizens and lobby political and community leaders to eliminate or alleviate the problem. They dealt with a wide array of social ills, including poverty, worker exploitation, child labor, juvenile delinquency, unjust laws, and difficulties faced by working women and the elderly. A new research technique called "mapping" was used. It involved seeking information on an urban population's demographic characteristics (such as age, sex, occupations, wages, and housing conditions) and then presenting the geographic distribution of those characteristics on a map. By applying research in this way, Addams was able to play a significant role in establishing many government programs—most notably Social Security, the Children's Bureau, the Immigrant Bureau, Workers' Compensation—and various government regulations affecting health and safety standards. In 1931, Addams was awarded the Nobel Peace Prize (Deegan, 1988; Ross, 1991).

For about 40 years, from 1900, most American sociologists focused on studying and solving social problems. But then their reformist fervor began to cool. Some turned their attention to general theories of society. The idea grew that sociology should be a *basic science,* seeking knowledge only, not an *applied science,* putting knowledge to use. Moreover, many people believed that sociology must be objective and free of values. There was no room then in sociology for a commitment to reform society in order to bring it into conformity with certain values. From about 1940 to 1960, sociology was dominated by the attempt to develop scientific methods that could be applied to the study of societies and social behavior. During these two decades, sociologists developed increasingly sophisticated research techniques.

In the 1960s, however, the ideal of objective, value-free knowledge came under fire in just about all fields, including sociology. Renewed awareness of poverty and years of social unrest—marked by race riots, student revolts, and controversy about the Vietnam War—put pressure on sociologists to attack society's ills once again. Meanwhile, attitudes toward the major theoretical perspectives in sociology were also shifting. The conflict perspective, which emphasizes social conflict as a constant fact of social life, was becoming popular at the expense of the functionalist perspective, which stresses the persistence of social order.

American sociology has thus developed into a diverse discipline. Today, it is both a basic and an applied science, and sociologists use both objective and subjective methods. The soaring number of sociologists—from only about 3000 in the 1960s to about 20,000 today—has further splintered sociology into numerous specialties, such as mathematical sociology, historical Marxism, phenomenology, ethnomethodology, sociobiology, network analysis, organizational research, clinical sociology, and race and ethnic relations. Each of these specialties has itself differentiated into many subspecialties. The specialty

Jane Addams (1860-1935) conducted scientific research on social problems with the aim of eliminating or alleviating them. She was the only sociologist ever to have received a Nobel prize.

of race relations, for example, has broken down into studies of blacks, Hispanics, Asians, and other specific minorities in the United States (Blalock, 1984; Collins, 1986; Gans, 1989). Underlying all this diversity are certain theoretical perspectives that sociologists employ to study and understand social behavior. We will examine four major ones in the next section.

QUESTIONS FOR DISCUSSION AND REVIEW

1. How did Karl Marx's understanding of nineteenth-century European society differ from that of Herbert Spencer and Max Weber?
2. What are some of the ways in which the development of American sociology differed from the work of European sociologists?

Sociological Perspectives

Sociologists, like just about everyone else, use different levels of analysis. They can look at the "big picture," at one small piece of it, or at something in between. On the lowest level of analysis, we find very specific explanations, such as an analysis of the social causes of alcoholism or of the customs of hazing in fraternities. At a middle level of analysis, sociologists develop theories that are broad enough to take in a whole class of activities or events but specific enough to be tested by observation or experiment. Thus we find, for example, theories about the causes of numerous kinds of crime and delinquency. The early European sociologists, however, often developed yet another kind of analysis: they offered a broad vision of what society fundamentally is like or how it works. Their views provided the basis for today's models of society, or **theoretical perspectives.** These perspectives are merely "orienting strategies" (Wagner and Berger, 1985). They show us how to view society and what kinds of questions we should ask about social behavior. Therefore, unlike the more specific theories, they cannot be validated as either true or false. They can only orient or direct us toward what is assumed to be the real nature of society.

Four major theoretical perspectives are used by sociologists today: the functionalist perspective, the conflict perspective, the symbolic interactionist perspective, and the feminist perspective. All four emphasize the influence of social forces on human behavior. But each perspective offers a different view of which social forces are most important.

THE FUNCTIONALIST PERSPECTIVE

Both Spencer and Durkheim provided ideas that inspired the **functionalist perspective.** According to this perspective, which is often called *functionalism,* each part of society—the family, the school, the economy, or the state—contributes something. Each performs certain functions for the society as a whole. Moreover, all the parts are interdependent. The family, for example, depends on the school to educate its children, and the school, in turn, depends on the family or the state to provide financial support. The state, in turn, depends on the family and school to help children grow up to become law-abiding, tax-paying citizens. Out of these interdependent parts of society comes a stable social order, the structure. If something happens to disrupt this social order, its parts will adjust in a way that produces a new stability. Suppose the economy were in bad shape, with high rates of inflation and unemployment. The family would adjust, perhaps by spending less and saving more. The school would probably offer fewer programs and emphasize vocational training. The state might try to cut its budget. As a result, there would be a new social order.

However, what holds the society together, enabling all its parts to produce social order? The answer, according to functionalists, is **social consensus,** a condition in which most members of the society agree on what would be good for everybody and cooperate to achieve it. Durkheim assumed that social consensus can come about in the form of either mechanical or organic solidarity.

Mechanical solidarity is a type of social cohesion that develops when people do similar work and have similar beliefs and values. It exists in relatively simple, traditional societies. An example of such societies is one in which almost everyone works at farming and believes in the same gods. In contrast, **organic solidarity** is a type of social cohesion that arises when the people in a society perform a wide variety of specialized jobs and therefore have to depend on one another. Organic solidarity is characteristic of complex, industrialized societies. The people in an American city, for example, are likely to hold many very different types of jobs, to have grown up with different family customs, to hold varying beliefs and values. There are bankers, teachers, engineers, plumbers, and many other businesses, professions, and occupations. Among these people there will probably be atheists and Christians, Jews and Muslims, reactionaries and radicals, and everything in between. Thus, mechanical solidarity among the city's people is not likely to be strong. They cannot be bound together by conformity to the same ideas and ideals. But they can be more easily bound together by their need for each other. The banker needs the worker who deposits and borrows money, and both need the storekeeper, who needs the trucker who delivers food, who needs the mechanic and gas station attendant, and so on. The complex ties of dependence seem virtually endless. These people are bound together by organic solidarity.

During the 1940s and 1950s, the functionalist perspective became widely accepted by American sociologists. But in its move from Europe to the United States, functionalism had been altered somewhat. Originally, it was used to help explain the society as a whole—to clarify how its order and stability were maintained. But American sociologists have been more interested in discovering the functions of specific types of human behavior.

The most prominent among these American sociologists is Robert Merton (1957). He classified functions into two types: manifest and latent. **Manifest functions** are those that are intended and seem obvious; **latent functions** are unintended and often unrecognized. The manifest function of going to college, for example, is to get an education, but going to college also has the latent function of enabling many students to find their future spouses. Another latent function of going to college is to force you to learn the valuable lesson of negotiating your way through bureaucratic mazes in order to get things done. After four years of learning to master preregistration, parking permits, financial aid forms, major and general education requirements, course schedules, add-and-drop policies, and dormitory preference forms, you will find it easier to work in even the most formidable business bureaucracy (Galles, 1989).

To study a social phenomenon, we need only common sense to know its manifest functions. Such knowledge is obvious or superficial. But the search for its latent functions requires sociological understanding, which reveals its deeper, underlying reality. Analyses of latent functions, then, can be interesting. Let us, for example, take a look at a functional analysis of the Persian Gulf War. Guided by common sense, many Americans paid attention to the manifest functions of the war. Those who opposed the war essentially pointed out its destructive nature—the loss of lives and property—and those who supported the war saw the fighting as evil but necessary for stopping Iraqi aggression against Kuwait. But the war also had its latent functions.

First, it enhanced social solidarity among countries on either side of the war by focusing attention on fighting a common enemy. Arabs in the Middle East who supported Iraq felt strongly united against the United States and its allies. The United States, in turn, joined forces with various nations, including the traditionally anti-American Russia and Syria. Second, the Gulf War, like other wars, stimulated scientific and technological development. The war served

The automobile enables people to go from one place to another. This is its manifest, or intended and obvious, function. One latent, or less recognized, function, especially of a shiny, expensive car, is to serve as a status symbol, making the car's owner feel a sense of pride.

as a live laboratory for testing new high-tech weapons. Before the war, it was uncertain, for example, whether Tomahawk cruise missiles and stealth fighter-bombers could fly undetected and hit their targets with pinpoint accuracy. Because the high-tech weapons were guided by computer systems, knowledge gained from their use in the war benefited the computer industry. Finally, the war brought pressures for democratic reforms in Kuwait, Saudi Arabia, and other Gulf states that have long been governed by kings or sheiks. Kuwait's autocratic ruler, for example, promised democratic reforms. He has acknowledged that without popular support from his subjects in exile, his tiny nation could have vanished quickly.

Throughout this book we will see many examples of the usefulness of functionalism, but by itself it cannot lead to a complete picture of social events. It has also been criticized for focusing on the positive functions of an event such as war and ignoring its negative functions. Similarly, when applied to analysis of society, functionalism has been criticized for being inherently conservative as well. In effect, it justifies the status quo. By emphasizing what every current aspect of society does for its citizens, functionalism encourages people to dismiss social change as "dysfunctional" (harmful), even though change may, in fact, produce a better society.

THE CONFLICT PERSPECTIVE

The conflict perspective produces a picture of society strikingly different from that offered by functionalism. Whereas functionalism emphasizes society's stability, the **conflict perspective** portrays society as always changing and always marked by conflict. Functionalists tend to focus on social order, to view social change as harmful, and to assume that the social order is based largely on people's willing cooperation. Implicitly, functionalism defends the status quo. In contrast, proponents of the conflict perspective are inclined to concentrate on social conflict, to see social change as beneficial, and to assume that the social order is forcibly imposed by the powerful on the weak. They criticize the status quo.

The conflict perspective originated largely from Karl Marx's writings on the class conflict between capitalists and the proletariat. For decades American sociologists tended to ignore Marx and the conflict perspective because the functionalist perspective dominated their view of society. Then came the turbulent 1960s, and the conflict perspective gained popularity among American sociologists. Generally, they have defined conflict more broadly than Marx did. Whereas Marx believed that conflict between *economic* classes was the key force in society, conflict theorists today define social conflict to mean conflict between any unequal groups or societies. Thus, they examine conflict between whites and blacks, men and women, one religious group and another, one society and another, and so on. They emphasize that groups or societies will have conflicting interests and values and thus will compete with each other. Because of this perpetual competition, society or the world is always changing.

The conflict perspective leads sociologists to ask such questions as: Which groups are more powerful and which are weaker? How do powerful groups benefit from the existing social order, and how are weaker groups hurt? Looking at the Gulf War, conflict theorists might emphasize that the war reflected the unequal positions of its major participants. Militarily powerful Iraq invaded weaker Kuwait, and the United States, more powerful than Iraq, drove that country out of Kuwait. Moreover, the war reflected an exploitation of the masses by the ruling elite. Iraq's Saddam Hussein, the ruthless ruler of a poverty-stricken country, expected his takeover of Kuwait, which is a rich country, to gain popularity from the Arab masses in poor, Middle Eastern countries. Military leaders in the United States expected to become heroes, and business leaders hoped to reap profits from the sales of military weapons. But it was mostly the poor, working-class, and minority Americans who were sent to the Gulf to fight and risk their lives.

In short, while the functionalist perspective focuses on the benefits of the Gulf War, the conflict perspective emphasizes the exploitation of the poor masses by their powerful rulers. Note that those who disagree with the conflict perspective have criticized it for overemphasizing social conflict and other negative aspects of society while ignoring the order, stability, and other positive aspects of society.

THE SYMBOLIC INTERACTIONIST PERSPECTIVE

Both functionalist and conflict perspectives tend to focus on abstract concepts and the large social issues of order and conflict. In contrast, the **symbolic interactionist perspective**, also called symbolic interactionism, directs our attention to the details of everyday life and the interaction between individuals.

Conflict theorists see society as always changing and marked by conflict and competition. Conflict between ethnic or racial groups is not uncommon. Here black demonstrators boycott a Korean-owned grocery store in Brooklyn, New York. The boycott began after a black woman was allegedly assaulted by employees of the store.

We can trace its origins to Max Weber's argument that people act according to their interpretation of the meaning of their social world. But it was George Herbert Mead (1863–1931), an American philosopher, who introduced symbolic interactionism to American sociology in the 1920s.

According to symbolic interactionism, people assign meanings to each other's words and actions. Their actions and attitudes, then, are not determined by some action in and of itself. Instead, they act according to their subjective interpretation of the action. When you speak to a friend, an observer can easily give an objective report of the words you have said. But your friend's response will depend not on the list of words you spoke but on his or her interpretation of the entire interaction, and your friend's response is at the same time influencing what you are saying. If your friend perceives by the way you speak that you are intelligent, this interpretation may make your friend respect and admire you and, perhaps, respond more positively to what you are saying. If you, in turn, catch this interpretation, you may feel proud and speak more confidently. In short, the exchange is a symbolic interaction. It is an interaction between individuals that is governed by their interpretation of the meaning of symbols. In this case, the symbols are primarily spoken words. But a symbol can be anything—an object, a sound, a gesture—that points to something beyond itself. The marks on this paper are symbols because they point to something—they mean something—beyond black squiggles.

The symbolic interactionist perspective implies two things. First, people do not respond directly to physical "things." Rather, they respond to their own interpretations of them. Second, because people constantly make interpretations—of the world in general, of other people, of themselves and their own interpretations—and then act according to them, human behavior is fluid, always changing. How we act is constantly being altered by how we interpret other people's actions and their reactions to our own behavior.

Symbolic interactionists therefore pay very close attention to how, exactly, people act and try to determine what meanings people are giving to their own actions and to those of others. Looking at the Gulf War, symbolic interactionists might focus on how George Bush's and Saddam Hussein's interpretations of each other's actions led to the war.

Before the Iraqi invasion of Kuwait, Bush regarded Saddam as a potential force for stability in the Middle East. Bush therefore refrained from strongly criticizing Saddam for using chemical weapons against Iran and for spreading poison gas on Iraq's Kurdish minority. A week before the Iraqi invasion of Kuwait, the U.S. ambassador in Iraq assured Saddam that President Bush wanted to seek better relations with Iraq and that the United States would not intervene in Saddam's border dispute with Kuwait while urging that violence not be used. All this presumably was taken by Saddam as a green light to invade Kuwait. The invasion outraged Bush, who threatened Saddam with war if he did not withdraw from

Kuwait. But Saddam shrugged off the threat, apparently believing that Americans' Vietnam experience would deter them from going to war against Iraq. Even when he finally realized that Bush would carry out his threat, Saddam still did not pull out of Kuwait. He was hoping for a "victorious defeat." As an Arab diplomat who has dealt personally with the Iraqi dictator on dozens of occasions explained, "If there is no war and Saddam withdraws, then he looks like a coward, an idiot, who's lost everything. He is thinking, 'If I go to war, there is a chance that I will survive it, and at least I will be looked on by the Arabs as a hero who went against the whole world because of right and justice'" (Dickey, 1991). Saddam expected to lose the war and be forced out of Kuwait, but he still considered the war his triumph for having fought and survived against the mighty United States and its allies. Thinking that Saddam did not appreciate the awesomeness of the military power arrayed against him, Bush finally decided to show it to him by starting the war.

In contrast with the relatively abstract concerns of the functionalist and conflict perspectives, symbolic interactionism directs our attention to the concrete details of human life as seen through the eyes of the individuals. It has been criticized, however, for ignoring the larger issues of societal stability and change. It has been faulted, as it were, for examining the trees so closely that it fails to show us what the forest looks like. Moreover, it has been criticized for ignoring the influence of social institutions, groups, and societies on individual interactions.

THE FEMINIST PERSPECTIVE

The preceding three perspectives are largely derived from men's experiences as if women—the other half of humanity—did not exist. Without specifically taking women into account, the three perspectives inevitably present a distorted view of the social world in which both men and women participate. Even when women are taken into account, the three perspectives also offer a distorted picture of the female world. Because women's social lives differ significantly from men's, perspectives based on the male experience can accurately portray men's world, but not women's. To understand women—and to help understand the world in which both men and women live—we turn to the **feminist perspective**, which views social life and human experience from the standpoint of women.

The feminist perspective sees women as "different from, less privileged than, and subordinate to" men (Lengermann and Niebrugge-Brandtley, 1992). This suggests three things about women vis-a-vis men. (1) Women's experiences are *different* from those of men. There is a diversity of feminist views on what the gender differences are. But most agree that bearing and caring for infants, being gentle rather than tough, and being peaceful rather than violent toward others are among the socially learned characteristics that distinguish some women from men. To feminists, these feminine values are at least equal, if not superior, to traditional masculine values. They deserve to be respected—recognized as valuable alternatives to rather than as undesirable departures from male values. But men tend to have different views, so that (2) women's position in most situations is *unequal* to that of men. Compared with men, women have less power, freedom, respect, money, or opportunities for a happy life. This gender inequality comes from the widely held sexist belief that women are inferior to men. It may also originate from the need of capitalism to enhance profits by turning women into wives, housewives, and mothers. In these roles, women serve as unpaid caregivers for husbands and children in order to ensure a productive work force, and also serve as consumers of goods and services for the household. Worse yet, (3) women are *oppressed*—restrained, subordinated, controlled, molded, or abused—by men. This is the essence of **patriarchy**—"a system of domination in which men exercise power over women" (Kimmel, 1992). The oppression may involve overt physical violence against women, such as rape, wife abuse, incest, unnecessary caesareans, and forced sterilization (directed largely at working class women and women of color). It may entail more subtle forms of violence such as unpaid household drudgery, underpaid wage work, sexual harassment in the workplace, and the standards of fashion and beauty that reduce women to men's sexual playthings (Lengermann and Niebrugge-Brantley, 1992).

In distinguishing women's lives from men's, feminists expose the limitations of the three perspectives discussed earlier. First, consider functionalism. It presents social life as a collage of different people consensually coming together, each playing a separate and distinct role, say, as a wage earner or a nurturant parent but not both. This view of compartmentalized roles may reflect men's lives but not those of women, who are forced to merge their roles of both wage earners and nurturant mothers in modern

The feminist perspective in sociology sees women as being different from men and unequal to them in social position. It also emphasizes the traditional subordination of women to men, including the abuse women sometimes receive from men in a patriarchy. The above art by Barbara Kruger is part of Liz Claiborne, Inc.'s Women's Work program

society or as both farmers and housewives in traditional society. As for conflict theory, it tends to see the weaker group, such as the poor or racial minorities, as helpless victims likely to vent frustration through violent and destructive acts, such as the recent riots in Los Angeles after the Rodney King verdict. This view may hold true for men but not women. Women are generally less violent than men as shown by their lower rates of murder, assault, and other violent crimes. Women also have other positive values (such as nurture, sensitivity, and community)

that are superior to those of men (toughness, braggadocio, and victory). These power-centered patriarchal values tend to cause loneliness among men, depriving them of emotionally rich, tender, or loving relationships with women, children, and male friends. But with their feeling-centered values, women can turn the world into a more gentle, humane, and happy one (French, 1985). Finally, symbolic interactionism is also less relevant to women than men. Its emphasis on the importance of the self suggests that, when people are interpreting others' actions toward them, they are primarily self-centered, more attuned to their own than others' needs and demands. This may hold true for men, but not necessarily for women. Women's interpretations of others' actions are more other-centered, more capable of understanding and accommodating others' wishes.

Let us analyze the Gulf War from the feminist perspective. The war, like other violent action, is a product of the patriarchal value of toughness. As the leader of a patriarchal society, Saddam considered himself a brave man, not afraid to go to war against the United States and its many allies. Several months before the war, he even scorned the United States for not having the "stomach" for another war after its defeat in Vietnam. Even when he later saw the war and his defeat as inevitable, he continued to talk tough: "I know I am going to lose, but at least I will have the death of a hero." Similarly, President Bush, also the leader of a patriarchal society, exhibited his bravado by telling the American soldiers in Saudi Arabia that "we are going to kick Saddam's butt." This was reminiscent of what he did earlier after the U.S. invasion of Panama. He boasted that no one could call him "timid"—he had at last proven himself a "macho man" (Ehrenreich, 1990). A major cause of war, then, is the widespread and deeply rooted patriarchal belief that the ultimate test of a man's masculinity involves being tough, brave, or aggressive toward his enemy (Enloe, 1983; 1989).

In sum, the feminist perspective reveals the basic differences between women and men as well as the limitations of conventional, male-centered theories about social life. It further suggests that the feminist insight can shed light on various human—not only women's—experiences as illustrated by the preceding analysis of the Gulf War.

But the feminist perspective has been criticized for exaggerating the prevalence of male power over women to make it appear as if each and every man had the power. A recent spate of books about men argue that men as a group may have power over women but most men do not *feel* powerful. These critics point out that many men only appear to have power. The men's plight is compared to that of a chauffeur. He is in the driver's seat, so he may appear to have the power. Actually he does not have the power because someone else is giving the orders. But the critics do not realize that in the analogy that someone else is also a man, thus revealing the ubiquity and inescapability of patriarchy (Kimmel, 1992). Being men, those critics would not acknowledge the truth that patriarchy gives every man many "unearned advantages" of being male over women (such as having better jobs, higher salaries, or greater likelihood of being in some leadership position) in the same way as racism gives every white many unearned advantages of being white over blacks and other minorities. Acknowledging this male privilege is threatening to men because it means that they are actually less worthy or less deserving (because of being less intelligent, less diligent, or less competent) than they appear to be for having a better life than women (McIntosh, 1993).

Nonetheless, the feminist perspective is not perfect. It tends to focus only on the oppressive nature of patriarchal society, thereby glossing over the irony that the same male-dominated society may have produced many positive *female* values, such as sensitivity and compassion. Another weakness of the feminist perspective is that much of the perspective "has been constructed from the particular experiences of white, middle-class, (heterosexual) women," which differ greatly from those of minority, poor, or lesbian women (Andersen, 1993). A number of black or lesbian feminists have analyzed how patriarchy oppresses women of color, poverty, or same-sex orientation much more than white middle-class heterosexual women (Rich, 1982; Andersen and Collins, 1992). But all these efforts have not produced a feminist theory that can apply simultaneously to those different groups of women. The reason is that race, class, and heterosexism (prejudice and discrimination against homosexuals) may be more powerful than gender and gender-related phenomena such as patriarchy in influencing women's (and men's) lives. This is why in their lives white middle-class heterosexual women seem to have more in common with white middle-class men than with women of a different race, class, or sexual orientation. Race, class, and heterosexism may be more powerful in another way: being able to strengthen or weaken the impact of patriarchy on women. As has been mentioned, patriarchy oppresses minority, poor, or lesbian women far more than white middle-class heterosexual women.

AN INTEGRATED VIEW

By itself, each of the four perspectives can produce a distorted picture of society (see Table 1.1). In effect,

TABLE 1.1 *How the Four Perspectives Differ*

	SUBJECT UNDER FOCUS	NATURE OF SOCIETY	MAINTAINENCE OF SOCIAL ORDER
Functionalist perspective	Social order or stability	Consists of inter-dependent groups pursuing common goals	Through social consensus, whereby people agree to cooperate in order to contribute to social order
Conflict perspective	Social conflict or change	Made up of conflicting groups, each pursuing its own interest	Through coercion, social order is imposed by the powerful on the weak
Symbolic interactionist perspective	Interaction between individuals	Composed of individuals whose actions depend on interpreting each other's behavior	Through constant negotiations between individuals trying to understand each other's actions and reactions
Feminist perspective	Women's position in society	Made up of men and women, with the former dominating the latter	Through oppression, whereby men maintain their dominance over women

each gives us a view from just one angle. The four perspectives are not entirely incompatible. To some extent, they are like different perspectives on a house. Looked at from the front, the house has a door, windows, and a chimney on top. From the back, it has a door and a chimney on top but fewer windows. From the side it has no doors, but it has windows and a chimney on top. From the top, it has no doors or windows, but it has a chimney in the middle. It is the same house, but it looks very different, depending on one's perspective. Similarly, whether we see functions, conflict, interaction, or patriarchy depends on from where we are looking. However, if we overemphasize any one perspective, we are likely to miss something about the complex reality of our social world. Each of these perspectives is useful because we cannot take everything about the complex social world into account at once. We need some vantage point. Each perspective tells us what to look for, and each brings some aspect of society and human behavior into sharper focus. Combined, though, these perspectives can enrich our sociological knowledge of the world.

As we will see in later chapters, the usefulness of each perspective depends on what we are studying, and the four perspectives are not equally helpful in understanding every phenomenon. But often each does have something to contribute to our understanding of the same subject. If we are studying the interaction between white and black Americans, or between upper- and lower-class people, each perspective can be useful. Functionalist and conflict perspectives can lead us to analyses that clarify how the interaction is affected by larger social forces, such as racial prejudice and social inequality. Symbolic interactionism can give us a richer, more detailed view of specific interactions and an understanding of why people influenced by the same social forces behave in different ways. The feminist perspective can reveal how the exercise of power over women reinforces oppression against black and poor Americans—minorities as powerless as women. Sometimes the four perspectives are complementary, sometimes they give contradictory views, but we need to evaluate the merits of each.

QUESTIONS FOR DISCUSSION AND REVIEW
1. What is a "theoretical perspective," and what are the main features of the four perspectives sociologists use today?
2. How do the basic assumptions of the conflict perspective differ from those of structural functionalism?

3. Is any one of the four sociological perspectives better than the others?

Major Research Methods

From these sociological perspectives, we can draw many ideas about how social forces shape our lives. Yet these ideas are merely idle guesswork unless they are backed up by scientific facts. This is one important reason why sociologists conduct scientific research to collect data. Social research, however, is not only for checking the presumed validity of existing theories about people and society. It is also for producing information that describes our lives and for developing new theories that explain how our lives are influenced by various social forces. Thus the production of sociological knowledge depends heavily on social research. It involves the use of four basic methods: survey, observation, experiment, and analysis of existing data.

SURVEY

Of the four research methods, the **survey,** which involves asking questions about opinions, beliefs, or behavior, is most frequently used by sociologists. Suppose we want to know whether from 1970 to 1990 the percentage of college students having premarital intercourse changed. We could take a survey, and we would find that the percentage had increased. Or suppose a theory suggests that students' social class and geographical background (say, urban, rural, or suburban) are related to their sexual behavior. Survey data could be collected to determine whether this might be true.

Sampling   To take a survey, we first select a **population,** the people whom we want to study. We can choose a population of any size, but all its members must have something in common. Thus a population may consist of all Americans above the age of 100, or all U.S. congresswomen, or all the students at a large university, or all U.S. citizens, or all the people in the world.

If a population is relatively small, all its members can be approached and interviewed. But if a population is very large, it could cost too much time and money to contact all its members. In such a case, a **sample** of the population, a small number of people taken from the whole population, must be selected. The sample, however, must accurately represent the entire population from which it is drawn. Otherwise the information obtained from the sample cannot be generalized to the population. Failure to heed this may produce misleading conclusions.

A famous case in point was the attempt to predict the outcome of the presidential election in 1936. A popular magazine of that era, *Literary Digest,* selected a large sample of people from telephone directories and automobile registration lists and then asked them whom they would vote for. An overwhelming majority replied that they would choose the Republican candidate, Alfred Landon, over his Democratic opponent, Franklin Roosevelt. So the editors of the magazine concluded that Landon was going to have a landslide victory. But it turned out that Landon was overwhelmingly defeated. Meanwhile, a young man named George Gallup, who had chosen a much smaller but far more representative sample of all the voters, correctly predicted the election's outcome. The *Literary Digest's* incorrect prediction was due to the selection of a sample that did not represent the entire voting population. The sample included only middle-and upper-class people, who could afford telephones and automobiles during those Depression years and who, being largely Republicans, tended to vote for the Republican candidate. The less well-off, who later voted for the winning Democratic candidate, were excluded from the sample.

The *Literary Digest* apparently assumed that since they contacted a huge number of people (10 million), they could accurately predict the election. They did not realize, as Gallup did, that it is not the size but the representativeness of the sample that ensures accuracy. A sample as large as the *Literary Digest's* can be misleading if it is not representative of the population, but a sample as small as Gallup's (only 300,000) can be accurate if it adequately represents that population. In fact, because of today's increased sophistication in sampling, as few as 1500 people can constitute a representative sample of the U.S. population. A representative sample, then, is extremely important for getting correct information on the population as a whole. But how do sociologists go about finding a representative sample?

If a sample is to be representative, all members of the population must have the same chance of getting selected for the sample. The selection in effect must be random, which is why a representative sample is often called a **random sample.** A crude way to select a random sample is to throw the names of

an entire population into a hat, mix them up, and then pull out as many names as needed for a sample. This method may be too cumbersome to use if the size of the population is very large. There are more sophisticated and convenient techniques for drawing random samples from large populations. The most commonly used are systematic and stratified sampling.

Systematic sampling involves the use of a system, such as selecting every tenth or hundredth person in the population. We must still make sure that all the members of the population have the same chance of falling into our sample. If every tenth person is taken, then each person in the population has a one-tenth chance of being sampled. But the sample would not be representative of, say, a student population if we talk to every tenth student walking into a library, or passing by a street corner, or entering a bar. This is because not all the students are equally likely to go to these places at the time when the survey is taken. Some students may have more than a one-tenth chance of being selected, while others have less than a one-tenth chance. In fact, numerous students would have a zero chance of being included in the sample if they have never gone to those places. To make the sample accurately represent the student population, we should take, say, every tenth name in a list—such as a student directory—where all the students' names can be found.

Stratified sampling is used when the population can be divided into various strata or categories, such as males and females or rural, urban, and suburban residents. To draw a stratified sample, we have to know what percentage of the population falls into each of the categories used and then select a random sample in which each category is represented in exactly the same proportion as in the population. Suppose we know that the population of a city is 52 percent female and 48 percent male; then our stratified sample should also be 52 percent female and 48 percent male.

Types of Surveys   Once a random sample is selected, we can ask its members about their opinions, attitudes, or behavior. This is usually done by using self-administered questionnaires, personal interviews, or telephone surveys.

In using *self-administered questionnaires,* the researcher simply gives or sends the people in the sample a list of questions and asks them to fill in the answers themselves. Usually the list consists of true-false and multiple-choice questions. The respondents

How important is a college education today—very important, fairly important, or not too important?

"We spent a lot of money educating him, so if you want Junior's opinion, you'll have to pay for it."

are asked to answer "yes," "no," or "don't know" or to check one of the answers, such as "single," "married," "divorced," or "widowed." There are several advantages to this method. First, it costs the researcher relatively little time and money. Second, since the respondents are assured of their anonymity and fill out the questionnaires in privacy, they may answer the questions more honestly. Third, because they answer the same set of questions, all the respondents can easily be compared with one another as to their attitudes and reported behavior. Such comparison may enable us to know why some people do a certain thing while others do not.

The mailed survey has a big problem, though. Some people will not return the questionnaires. The usual way to tackle this nonresponse problem is to send the subjects a follow-up letter or telephone them and ask them to please fill out the questionnaires. What if this and other remedies do not work and the amount of nonresponse remains substantial? Then the researcher must find out if there is a significant difference in age, education, or some other characteristic between respondents and nonrespondents. If there is no difference, the study may be continued. If there is one, the project may have to be

scrapped—or modified by using some other survey method, such as personal interviews.

Personal interviews may get greater response from the subjects than does the mailed survey. Fewer people would refuse to cooperate when approached in person than they would when solicited by mail. Personal interviews may be either structured or unstructured. In **structured interviews,** the researcher uses the same kind of questionnaire employed in the mailed survey, with the obvious exception that the interviewer reads the questions to the subject and obtains answers on the spot. Because all the respondents are asked exactly the same questions in exactly the same way and are provided with exactly the same choice of answers, the researcher can compare the subjects with one another on the basis of which answers they choose. Explanations of their attitudes and behavior could then be found. The standardization of questions and answers, however, cannot deal with the great diversity among people and the subtle complexity of human attitudes. Thus, respondents with different views are often forced to give the same answer. Some respondents may complain that it is impossible for them to answer the questions with the answers provided in the questionnaire because none of the answers adequately reflects their personal views. Even among those respondents who do not complain, many may simply unthinkingly pick the standardized answers just to get rid of the interviewer.

The researcher could get out of this problem by using an **unstructured interview.** In this kind of interview, open-ended questions are asked—respondents are allowed to answer freely, in their own words. Usually the interviewer starts off by asking a general question, such as "What do you think about political corruption?" Various respondents would interpret this question in varying ways and so would respond differently. Some may focus on the definition of "political corruption"; others may concentrate on the consequences of political corruption; still others may concern themselves with how to fight political corruption, and so on. The different points raised by different respondents would further lead the interviewer to pursue various issues in different directions. Consequently, the interview with each of the respondents may become a unique case. The interviewer may find that no two answers are alike, because different respondents express themselves differently and mean different things even if they use the same words. All this makes it difficult to compare the answers of many different respondents, which in turn makes it hard to find the causes of whatever is under investigation. Nevertheless, an unstructured interview can produce rich data and deep insights, helping us to gain a profound understanding of the subject.

Whether structured or unstructured, personal interviews can cost much time and money. A complex study may require a bureaucracy with a swarm of administrators, field supervisors, interviewers, and sometimes even public relations personnel. Interviewers must not only be paid for the hours spent in the field but also reimbursed for travel expenses. Interviews are often lengthy, and the interviewer may have to travel a long distance (Bailey, 1987). In addition, the interviewer "may drive several miles to a respondent's home, find no one there, return to the research office, and drive back the next day—possibly finding no one there again" (Babbie, 1989).

It is much more convenient to use *telephone surveys,* which have jokingly been called the telephone polls. For many years, the telephone has been used merely to encourage respondents to return their mailed questionnaires. In the past, researchers stayed away from telephone surveys because they could produce a biased sample by excluding poor people, who did not own telephones, from the studies. Although today 97 percent of American households have telephones (Babbie, 1989), biases can slip in. If researchers interview only those subjects who could be reached on the first try, the results may not be accurate. One reason is that some people answer the phone more often than others—women, for example, answer the phone 70 percent of the time (Budiansky, 1988). To avoid such a sampling bias, researchers simply have to make a determined effort to reach everyone on their list of randomly selected subjects by calling as many times as necessary. Telephone interviewing has recently become very popular in survey research and is routinely used in many public opinion polls. An even more convenient method, computer-assisted telephone interviewing, has become increasingly popular. The U.S. Census Bureau and commercial survey firms are already using it.

Telephone surveys have certain disadvantages by comparison with face-to-face interviews. Because the interviewer cannot look the respondents in the eye, respondents are less motivated and can more easily end the interview by simply hanging up. Another problem is that people are more distrustful when answering questions from a stranger they cannot see. They may suspect that the stranger has a hidden interest, perhaps posing as an interviewer in order to sell magazine subscriptions.

OBSERVATION

It is obvious from the preceding section that in surveys we depend on others to tell us what has happened. By contrast, in observation we rely on ourselves to go where the action is—and watch what is happening. There are two ways to observe an ongoing activity. In **detached observation,** we observe as outsiders, from a distance, without getting involved. As detached observers, we may watch children playing in a schoolyard or bring them into a room and then watch them from behind a one-way mirror. Detached observation has the advantage of making it less likely that the subjects will be affected by the observer. But it has at least one disadvantage: the detached observer has difficulty perceiving and understanding subtle communication among the subjects. The detached observer behind a one-way mirror might not see some important facial expressions. The detached observer of a religious cult might never understand the emotions attached to particular symbols.

The second type of observation avoids this

*Detached observation is one method of gathering data.
From behind a one-way mirror, researchers unobtru-
sively note interactions among preschool children.
Since the subjects can be themselves, they behave as
they would under normal circumstances, not changing
their behavior to please the observer. This enhances
the validity of the study's results.*

problem. In **participant observation,** researchers
take part in the activities of the group they are studying. Sometimes they conceal their identity as researchers when they join the group they are to observe. This enhances the chances that the subjects,
not knowing they are being studied, will act naturally. If the subjects knew they were being observed,
they might change their behavior. As members of the
group, the researchers have the opportunity to observe practically everything, including whatever secret activities are hidden from outsiders. As a result,
the researchers could discover some surprising facts

about their subjects. Consider, for example, the following case of participant observation involving the
concealment of the researcher's identity.

Most people assume that if men engage in homosexual acts, they must be homosexuals. If you entertain this assumption, you may be surprised to
learn the results from Laud Humphreys's (1970) research. Humphreys concealed his identity as a researcher by offering to serve as a lookout for men engaging in homosexual activity in public restrooms, so
that the police would not arrest them. Without being
suspected of being an outsider, Humphreys also succeeded in secretly jotting down his subjects' automobile license plate numbers, which he used to trace
their addresses. A year later, he disguised himself, vis-
ited those men at their homes, and found that they
were mostly conservative lower-class married men.
They had sought the homosexual experience as a
means of releasing tension, they considered themselves straight and masculine. Humphreys has been
severely criticized for being unethical in his use of
deception. He has argued, though, that had he not
concealed his identity, it would have been impossible
for him to get scientifically accurate information because his subjects would have behaved differently or
would have refused to be studied.

Many sociologists do identify themselves as researchers to the people they study. They do not
worry that their true identity will change their subjects' behavior. They are not overly concerned that
subjects would hide secrets from them. Usually they
strive to minimize these problems by not getting too
deeply involved with their subjects while simultaneously establishing a good rapport with them. This is
not easy to accomplish, though. Nevertheless, such
efforts have paid off, as can be indicated by some sociological insights that have emerged from their
works. Herbert Gans (1982a), for example, became a
participant observer in a poor Italian neighborhood
in Boston in the late 1950s. On the surface the neighborhood looked like a badly organized slum. Yet Gans
discovered that it was a well-organized community
where the residents enjoyed close social relationships
with one another. Other writers holding the stereotyped notion of the poor neighborhood as a slum
would have called it an urban jungle. But Gans, appropriately enough, referred to its dwellers as urban
villagers.

Whether it is carried out with detachment, with
participation as a disguised member, or with participation as a known researcher, observation has the advantage of providing firsthand experience with natur-

al, real-life situations. The wealth of findings derived from this experience are useful for developing new theories. Gans's data, for example, can be used to suggest the theory that many slums are actually well-organized communities. This very advantage, however, is also a disadvantage. Because rich findings from observation techniques are largely relevant to one particular case study but not generalizable to other cases, they may not be used for testing theories. To test theories, sociologists usually use surveys, which we have discussed, or experiments.

EXPERIMENT

Actually, a theory can be tested only indirectly, not directly. It must be translated into a hypothesis or a series of related hypotheses that are directly testable—more specific statements that can be demonstrated to be either true or false. To test a hypothesis, researchers first specify what they assume to be the independent and dependent variables. Then they create a situation in which they can determine whether the *independent variable* causes the *dependent variable.* They are, in effect, conducting an **experiment,** a research operation in which the researcher manipulates variables so that their influence can be determined. Two researchers (Prerost and Brewer, 1980), for example, wanted to test the hypothesis that human crowding (independent variable) reduces humor appreciation (dependent variable). They assumed that if we find ourselves in a crowded situation, we tend to feel uncomfortable, which in turn will make it hard for us to laugh. Thus, to create a crowded condition, the experimenters put six college students in a relatively small room. They also put six other students in a larger room—a less crowded situation. Both groups were asked to rate 36 written jokes for funniness on a seven-point scale from 0 for "not funny at all" to 6 for "extremely funny." The researchers found what they had hypothesized: students under the cramped condition gave the jokes a lower rating than did those with more elbow room.

Quite often sociologists design controls to ensure that a hidden third variable is not producing the apparent effect of the independent variable. To do this, they generally select two groups of people who are similar in all respects except for the way they are treated in the experiment. One group, called the **experimental group,** is exposed to the independent variable; the second, called the **control group,** is

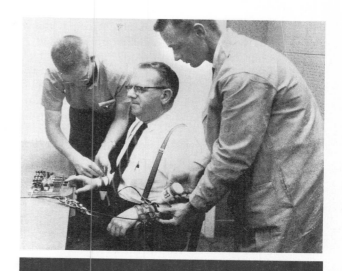

The laboratory experiment poses the problem of observing people in an artificial setting that can color their responses. In Stanley Milgram's famous experiment on obedience to authority, he devised an elaborate simulation to overcome the artificiality of the setting. The subject, who activated an electric shock machine, believed that he was causing the other person to scream with pain. Actually, the machine was a fake, and the man who was screaming, shown here being attached to the machine, was acting.

not. If the researchers find that the experimental group differs from the control group with respect to the dependent variable, they may reasonably conclude that the independent variable is the cause of this effect.

Robert Rosenthal (1973) and his colleague Lenore Jacobson, for example, wanted to test the theory of the self-fulfilling prophecy, which says that an expectation can create behavior that leads to the fulfillment of the expectation. In applying this theory to the classroom, they hypothesized that teachers' expectations influence students' performance. That is, if a teacher considers certain students unintelligent and expects them to do poorly in class, the students will do poorly. If the teacher regards other students as intelligent and expects them to perform well, they will perform well. To test this hypothesis, Rosenthal and Jacobson gave all the children in an elementary school an IQ test. Then, *without looking at the test results,* they randomly chose a small number of children and told their teachers—falsely—that these children had scored very high on the test. The intention was to make the teachers expect these supposedly "bright" children to show remarkable success later in the year. Thus the experimental group consisted of these "bright" children, who were exposed to high teacher expectations; the control group included the rest of the pupils. Eight months later, the researchers went back to the school and gave all the children another test. They found that the experimental group did perform better than the control group. They concluded that teacher expectations (the independent variable) were indeed the cause of student performance (the dependent variable).

You may notice that the experiments just discussed were carried out in the classroom, that is, in the field. In these *field experiments,* the subjects could behave naturally. But it is still possible for the experimenter to unconsciously influence the subjects and make them behave unnaturally. This is what happened to one of the most famous field experiments in social science. It was carried out by Elton Mayo in the 1930s at the Hawthorne plant of Western Electric Company in Chicago (Roethlisberger and Dickson, 1939).

Mayo wanted to find out what kinds of incentives and work conditions would encourage workers to work harder. He first systematically changed the lighting, lunch hours, coffee breaks, methods of payment (salary versus piece rate), and the like. He was then surprised to find that no matter what changes were made, the workers increased their productivity. When the light was made brighter, they worked harder than before; but when it was made dimmer, they *also* worked harder. When they were given two or three coffee breaks, they increased their output; when they were not allowed any coffee break, they continued to increase their output. Mayo later discovered that the increased productivity was actually due to all the attention the workers were getting from the researcher. They felt that they were not mere cogs in a machine but instead respected for their work; hence, they reciprocated by working harder. The impact of the researcher's presence on subjects' behavior is now known as the **Hawthorne effect.** Social scientists today strive to avoid it by using hidden cameras and tape recorders, or by using various means to prevent subjects from knowing they are being observed.

The Hawthorne effect is particularly threatening to *laboratory experiments.* Unlike the field experiment, which is carried out in a natural setting, the laboratory experiment is conducted under the artificial condition of a lab, where subjects are always aware of being observed. A number of researchers have nevertheless managed to make their laboratory experiments as realistic as real-life situations. Stanley Milgram (1974), for example, told his subjects that he was running a test on the effects of punishment on learning. In fact, he was conducting an experiment on obedience to authority. After asking each of his subjects to assist in the experiment by taking the role of "teacher," Milgram introduced him or her to another subject playing the role of "student." Actually this "student" was Milgram's research associate. Then Milgram told the teacher to punish the student with an electric shock every time the student gave the wrong answer to a question. Whenever the subject (teacher) obeyed Milgram's command by pressing the shock machine, he or she heard the student screaming with pain. In reality, the shock machine was a fake and the student was faking, but all the subjects were led to believe that everything they did or heard was real. They trembled, sweated, and showed other signs of stress when "punishing" the student. Still, a large majority carried out Milgram's order, administering what they believed was great pain. This led Milgram to conclude that ordinary people will follow orders if they come from a legitimate authority, in the same way as the Germans did when told by their Nazi leaders to commit atrocities against the Jews.

The realism of Milgram's experiment should not blind us to the disadvantages of experiments as a whole. What happens inside a laboratory will not necessarily happen in the real world outside, where a multitude of other variables are at work. Moreover, most of the larger, important sociological issues cannot be studied through experiments. We cannot create and then study a race riot, a revolution, or a war. Nevertheless, compared with other methods, experiments give researchers more leeway to control and manipulate variables. As a result, by using experiments, they are better able to determine the relationship among variables.

ANALYZING EXISTING DATA

So far we have discussed methods for collecting data from scratch. Sometimes it is unnecessary to gather new information because there are a lot of "old" data available which have been collected by someone else. Sometimes it is simply impossible to conduct an interview, observation, or experiment because the people we want to study are long dead. Thus sociologists often turn to analysis of existing data.

Secondary Analysis In **secondary analysis** we search for new knowledge in the data collected earlier by another researcher or some public agency. Usually the original investigator has gathered the data for a specific purpose, and the secondary analyst uses them for something else. Suppose we want to study religious behavior by means of secondary analysis. We might get our data from an existing study of voting behavior conducted by a political scientist. This kind of research typically provides information on the voters' religion along with education, income, gender, and other social characteristics. The political scientist may try to find out from this research whether, among other things, men are more likely than women to vote in a presidential election and whether the more religious are more politically active than the less religious. As secondary analysts, we can find out from the same data whether women attend church more often than men. In the last two decades the opportunities for secondary analysis have multiplied many times over. Various research centers throughout the world have developed a network of data archives whereby they collect and exchange data sets. Because these data sets are stored in computers, they can easily be reproduced and sold for broad circulation and use (Babbie, 1989).

Data suitable for secondary analysis are also available from government agencies. The use of these data has a long tradition. In his classic analysis of suicide in the 1890s, Emile Durkheim relied on official statistics. Finding from the statistics that Protestant countries, regions, and states had higher suicide rates than Catholic ones, Durkheim was able to conclude that many suicides result from a lack of social integration—assuming that Protestantism, a more individualist religious system, makes it harder for unhappy people to get moral support from others. Today many American sociologists employ statistics compiled by the U.S. Bureau of the Census for information on standards of living, migration, differences in incomes of ethnic and racial groups, birth and death rates, and a host of other facts about our society. The Federal Bureau of Investigation, the National Center for Health Statistics, and the Department of Labor are among the other government agencies that provide important statistics. In addition, survey agencies such as the National Opinion Research Center, the Gallup poll, and other public opinion polls publish very useful information. The sources are practically endless.

Sociologists can save a lot of time and effort by using the information they need from these storehouses of existing data, but secondary analysis has at least two disadvantages. First, the available data may not be completely relevant to the subject being investigated because they have been assembled for different purposes. Data on the median U.S. income, for example, are often given for households, not individuals. If we want to compare the standard of living over the last 20 years, these data can be misleading: they are likely to show an abnormally higher standard of living in recent years because the size of households has been shrinking and the number of two-income families has been expanding. Moreover, secondary data sometimes are not sufficiently accurate and reliable—and some investigators may not be sufficiently sensitized to such problems. Official statistics on crime, for example, overreport lower-class crimes and underreport crimes committed by members of the middle and upper classes.

Content Analysis The data for secondary analysis are usually quantitative, presented in the form of numbers, percentages, and other statistics, such as the *percentage* of women as compared to the *percentage* of men attending church once a week or the Protestants' suicide *rate* (number of suicides for every 100,000 people) as opposed to the Catholics' suicide *rate*. But some of the existing information is qualitative, in the form of words or ideas. This can be found in virtually all kinds of human communication—books, magazines, newspapers, movies, TV programs, speeches, letters, songs, laws, and so on. To study human behavior from these materials, sociologists often resort to **content analysis,** searching for specific words or ideas and then turning them into numbers.

How can we carry out "this marvelous social alchemy" (Bailey, 1987) that transforms verbal documents into quantitative data? Suppose we want to know whether public attitudes toward sex have indeed changed significantly in the last 20 years. We may find the answer from comparing popular novels of today with those of the past to see if one is more erotic than the other. To save time, we will select and study only a representative sample rather than all the novels of the two periods. Before analyzing each book, we will also choose a random sample of pages or paragraphs rather than the whole volume. Then we should decide what words will reflect the nature of eroticism. After we settle on a list of words such as "love," "kiss," and "embrace" to serve as indicators of eroticism, we will comb the selected pages for them.

Finally, we will count the number of times those words appear on an average page, and the number will be used as the measure of how erotic the novel is. In repeating the same process with other novels, we will see which ones are more erotic.

This method of examining the *manifest content*—the visible aspects—of a communication is almost like child's play. It merely scratches the surface of the communication, thereby missing its deeper and richer meaning. Thus, in regard to the novels, we should also analyze their *latent content*—underlying meanings—by reading them in their entirety and making an overall judgment of how erotic they are. The problem with this method, however, is that it is more subjective than the analysis of manifest content. Consequently, what is erotic to one researcher may not be so to another. Furthermore, investigators, operating without any clear-cut guidelines, may be inconsistent in interpreting the latent content. They may consider a love scene in some passage erotic but not so a similar love scene on another page, may regard explicit language of sex as erotic but not subtle language of love, and so on.

As a whole, content analysis has the big advantage of saving the researcher much time and money. Anybody can do a content analysis, as the materials are available in any school or public library. Even if we botch up a study, it is easier to redo it than is true with other methods. Other methods usually cost too much or are impossible to redo because the event under study no longer exists. A second advantage of content analysis is its unique suitability for historical research. It is like a time machine enabling us to visit people of another time. If we analyze the newspapers published in the last century, we can find out how the people of that period lived, which we cannot do

with the other research methods. Finally, content analysis has the distinct advantage of being *unobtrusive*—the analyst cannot have any effect on the subject being studied. There is no way for a content analyst to influence, say, a novel, because it has already been written. On the other hand, the basic disadvantage of content analysis is its lack of validity. **Validity** is the extent to which a study measures what it is supposed to measure—popularly known as accuracy. As we have just suggested, the coding or interpretation of a communication does not necessarily reflect its true meaning, because the analysis of manifest content tends to be superficial and the analysis of latent content is likely to be subjective (Babbie, 1989).

Psychiatrist Thomas Szasz once observed that when you get up in the morning and put on a shirt, "if you button the first buttonhole to the second button, then it doesn't matter how careful you are the rest of the way." So it is with sociology. If the research is sloppy—if the sample is unrepresentative, the control inadequate, the observation biased, or the secondary data unreliable—then all the brilliant analyses in the world will not make things right. The details of research studies, however, mostly fall beyond the scope of this text, and in the remaining chapters we will emphasize their conclusions.

QUESTIONS FOR DISCUSSION AND REVIEW
1. Why do sociologists use surveys more than other kinds of research methods?
2. How does detached observation differ from participant observation?
3. Why does the Hawthorne effect threaten the validity of many laboratory experiments?
4. Where do sociologists find the data they use in secondary and content analysis?

CHAPTER REVIEW

1. *What is unique about the way sociologists look at human behavior?* They view human behavior, even personal experiences, as being influenced by social forces. This focus on the influence of social forces constitutes the sociological perspective. *How does sociology differ from common sense?* While common sense gives familiar and untested ideas, sociology provides scientific facts and scientifically supported ideas.

2. *Plato and Socrates discussed social issues. Were they sociologists?* No, they were social philosophers, who thought and argued about the nature of the world but did not test their ideas against systematic observation. *What led to the transformation of social philosophy into sociology?* Seized with the desire to solve social problems and impressed with the contributions from the natural sciences, some nineteenth-century social philosophers tried to apply the scientific method to the study of society in the hope

of curing social ills. This attempt to replace philosophical speculation with the scientific method of systematic observation transformed social philosophy into sociology.

3. *What did Spencer mean when he said society is like a living organism?* In Spencer's view, each part of society, like each organ of an animal, performs its own function. If one part of society has problems, the other parts will adapt to the situation, ensuring the survival of the entire society. *What did Marx mean by class conflict?* Marx was referring to the struggle between the class of capitalists, who own the means of production, and the proletariat, who perform the labor. *What is the difference between Verstehen and Durkheim's objective approach?* Verstehen requires sociologists to adopt an attitude of understanding or empathy toward their subjects in order to understand how people interpret their own behavior, whereas Durkheim, who pioneered the application of scientific methods to sociology, argued that sociologists should deal solely with observable aspects of human behavior.

4. *How did the early American sociologists differ from their European predecessors?* The European sociologists were primarily interested in explaining the nature of society as a whole—the causes of social stability and change. In the United States, interest shifted to the study of specific social problems. Later, American sociologists emphasized the search for sociological knowledge rather than its application to social problems, but their interest in social reform grew again during the 1960s. *What is the nature of modern sociology?* Modern sociology is a diverse discipline, one that is both a basic and an applied science and that uses both objective and subjective methods of investigation.

5. *What are the basic ideas of the functionalist perspective?* It focuses on social order and assumes that the various parts of a society are interdependent, forming a social structure in which each part serves a function that helps ensure the survival of the whole. *How does the conflict perspective differ from functionalism?* Whereas functionalism focuses on social order and stability, the conflict perspective emphasizes social conflict and change, showing how one group dominates another. *What is a symbolic interaction?* It is an interaction between individuals that is governed by their interpretations of each other's actions. *What are the basic ideas of the feminist perspective?* Women are different from, unequal to, and oppressed by men. Without taking these ideas into account, male-centered perspectives distort the nature of social life.

6. *What research methods do sociologists use?* There are four major methods: survey, which gathers information on a population through interviews or questionnaires; *observation*, which provides first-hand experience of the subject being studied; *experiment,* which allows the researcher to manipulate variables; and *secondary and content analyses,* which use existing data.

KEY TERMS

Class conflict Marx's term for the struggle between capitalists, who own the means of production, and the proletariat, who do not (p. 9).

Conflict perspective A theoretical perspective that focuses on conflict and change in society, particularly conflict between a dominant and a subordinate group, and emphasizes that conflict is a constant fact of social life (p. 13).

Content analysis The analysis of a communication by searching for its specific words or ideas and then turning them into numbers (p. 25).

Control group The subjects in an experiment who are not exposed to the independent variable (p. 23).

Detached observation A method of observation in which the researcher stands apart from the subjects (p. 21).

Experiment A research operation in which the researcher manipulates variables so that their influence can be determined (p. 23).

Experimental group The subjects in an experiment who are exposed to the independent variable (p. 23).

Feminist perspective A theoretical perspective that views social life and human experience from the standpoint of women (p. 15).

Functionalist perspective A theoretical perspective that focuses on social order, which is assumed to be based on the positive functions performed by the interdependent parts of society (p. 11).

Hawthorne effect The unintended effect of the researcher's presence on the subjects' behavior (p. 24).

Hypothesis A tentative statement about how various events are related to one another (p. 7).

Latent function A function that is unintended and thus often unrecognized (p. 12).

Manifest function A function that is intended and thus seems obvious (p. 12).

Mechanical solidarity A form of social cohesion that develops when people do similar work and have similar beliefs and values; characteristic of simple, traditional societies (p. 11).

Organic solidarity A form of social cohesion that develops when the differences among occupations make people depend on each other; characteristic of complex, industrialized societies (p. 11).

Participant observation A method of observation in which the researcher takes part in the activities of the group being studied (p. 22).

Patriarchy A system of domination in which men exercise power over women (p. 15).

Population The entire group of people to be studied (p. 18).

Random sample A sample drawn in such a way that all members of the population had an equal chance of being selected (p. 19).

Sample A relatively small number of people selected from a larger population (p. 18).

Secondary analysis The analysis of existing data that have been collected by somebody else (p. 25).

Social consensus Condition in which most members of society agree on what is good for everybody to have and cooperate to achieve it (p. 11).

Social forces Forces that arise from the society of which we are a part (p. 4).

Social integration The degree to which people are tied to a social group (p. 4).

Sociological imagination C. Wright Mills's term for the ability to see the impact of social forces on individuals, especially on their private lives (p. 4).

Sociology The scientific study of human social behavior (p. 3).

Stratified sampling The process of drawing a random sample in which various categories of people are represented in proportions equal to their presence in the population (p. 19).

Structured interview An interview in which the researcher asks standardized questions that require respondents to choose from among several standardized answers (p. 20).

Survey A research method that involves asking questions about opinions, beliefs, or behavior (p. 18).

Symbolic interactionist perspective A theoretical perspective that focuses on the interaction between individuals and is based on the assumption that their subjective interpretations of each other's actions influence their interaction (p. 13).

Systematic sampling The process of drawing a random sample systematically, rather than haphazardly (p. 19).

Theoretical perspective A set of broad assumptions about the nature of a subject that cannot be proven true or false (p. 11).

Theory A set of logically related hypotheses that explains the relationship among various phenomena (p. 7).

Unstructured interview An interview in which open-ended questions are asked and the respondent is allowed to answer freely (p. 21).

Validity The extent to which a study measures what it is supposed to measure; popularly known as accuracy (p. 26).

Verstehen Weber's term for the subjective method, which requires sociologists to adopt an attitude of understanding or empathy toward their subjects (p. 9).

SUGGESTED READINGS

Andersen, Margaret L. 1993. *Thinking About Women: Sociological Perspectives on Sex and Gender,* 3rd ed. New York: Macmillan. A sociological perspective on the lives of women, a useful counterbalance to most sociological studies, which claim to deal with people in general but in fact focus on men only.

Berger, Bennett M. 1990. *Authors of Their Own Lives: Intellectual Autobiographies of Twenty American Sociologists.* Berkeley: University of California Press. An interesting collection of stories on how sociologists get their ideas about social behavior.

Borgatta, Edgar F., and Karen S. Cook (eds.). 1988. *The Future of Sociology.* Newbury Park, Calif.: Sage. An analysis of the trends in many different subfields of sociology, ranging from age and aging to political sociology.

Gans, Herbert J. (ed.). 1990. *Sociology in America.* Newbury Park, Calif.: Sage. A collection of essays analyzing today's sociology and its influences on American society.

Ross, Dorothy. 1991. *The Origins of American Social Science.* New York: Cambridge University Press. Shows how the early American sociologists, along with economists and political scientists, sought to model their new discipline on the natural sciences.

2

CULTURE

MYTHS AND REALITIES

Myth: Americans have given up the work ethic. They are more interested in having fun than in working hard.

Reality: Americans now work harder than before, having increased their work week from 40.6 hours fifteen years ago to 46.8 hours today. While working harder, though, they also try to enjoy themselves more—on the job and off.

Myth: Laws can effectively control our behavior.

Reality: Without the strong backing from popular beliefs, laws are difficult to enforce.

Myth: If you praise Chinese for having done an excellent job, they would not say "thank you." Instead, they would say "Oh, no, I've done poorly." This means that they are inscrutable.

Reality: Chinese are not inscrutable. Like people in other societies, they simply respond to the dictates of their culture, which places a high value on humility.

Myth: All over the world it is natural for people to nod their heads to mean yes and shake them to mean no.

Reality: In the United States, we, of course, nod our heads to mean yes and shake them to mean no. But in Bulgaria, head nodding means no, and head shaking means yes. Body language varies from one culture to another.

Myth: Language, aside from being useful for communication, is only a tool for people to express their thoughts.

Reality: Language is more than that. It can determine, or at least influence, how we think. It can be a source of our thoughts.

Myth: There is "moral decay" on today's prime-time television, subverting family values by, for example, encouraging young women to have babies out of wedlock.

Reality: Most of the popular prime-time TV shows render support to traditional family values by featuring heterosexual, monogamous couples and their children with a lot of familial love.

Myth: In India, the Hindus refrain from killing cows for food, simply because they consider the animals sacred.

Reality: The reason has to do with more than the Hindu belief in the sacredness of cows. India's peasant economy depends heavily on the cows performing various services, without which massive numbers of people would starve to death.

atoru Seo works in Toyota's Motomachi plant in Toyota City, Japan. He earns $75,000 a year. But since most things cost much more in Japan than in the United States, the standard of living for Seo—and other Japanese workers—is considerably lower. He lives with his wife and three children in a small house, which has a tiny kitchen, a postage-stamp garden, and no central heating. Nevertheless, Seo works very hard. Like most Japanese, he works six days a week, putting in about six weeks more each year than his American counterparts, 14 weeks more than West Germans, and 17 weeks more than Swedes. He rarely takes his allotted vacation. He keeps plugging away for his company even when he suffers back pain, wrist ailments, and other invisible injuries. Working excessively, Seo risks becoming a victim of *karoshi* (death by overwork), which has happened to thousands of workers in Japan in recent years (Schor, 1991; Chipello and Templin, 1992).

Why do Seo and other Japanese work so hard? The reason has much to do with Japan's group-oriented culture, which considers groups more important than individuals. Thus Japanese work hard because they are socially pressured to do so—or out of a sense of obligation to their company. They are not as likely as Americans to work hard because they want to or out of a desire for self-fulfillment. Not surprisingly, as indicated by a poll, 11 percent of the Japanese respondents said that if they had their choice they would not work, a preference chosen by only 4 percent of the American respondents (Lehner, 1992).

What, then, is culture, which can influence people's work and attitudes about work? **Culture** is a design for living or, more precisely, a complex whole consisting of objects, values, and other characteristics that people have acquired as members of society. It is obvious from this definition that when sociologists talk about cultures, they are not talking about sophistication or about knowledge of the opera, literature, or other fine arts. Only a small portion of a population is sophisticated, but all members of a society possess a culture. Neither is culture the same as society, although the two terms are often used interchangeably. Society consists of people interacting with one another as citizens of the same country. But culture consists of (1) abstract entities—such as ideas—that influence people and (2) tangible, human-made objects that reflect those ideas. The tangible objects make up what is called the **material culture.** It includes all conceivable kinds of physical objects produced by humans, from spears and plows to cooking pots and houses. The objects reflect the nature of the society in which they were made. If archaeologists find that an ancient society made many elaborate, finely worked weapons, then they have reason to believe that warfare was important to that society. In their study of contemporary societies, however, sociologists are more interested in **nonmaterial culture,** which consists of *knowledge and beliefs* (its cognitive component), *norms and values* (normative component), and *signs and language* (symbolic component).

In this chapter, we will begin by examining those three components of culture. Then we will discuss why culture is essential to our survival and how and why culture varies from one society to another.

The Cognitive Component

Culture helps us develop certain knowledge and beliefs about what goes on around us. **Knowledge** is a collection of ideas and facts about our physical and social worlds that are relatively objective, reliable, or verifiable. Knowledge can be turned into technology, and as such it can be used for controlling the natural environment and for dealing with social problems. The high standard of living in modern societies may be attributed to their advanced knowledge and sophisticated technology. Knowledge is best exemplified by science, which we discuss more extensively in Chapter 13 (Education, Science, and Health). On the other hand, **beliefs** are ideas that are more subjective, unreliable, or unverifiable. They may include, for example, the idea that God controls our lives. The best example of beliefs is religion, which we discuss in Chapter 11 (Religion).

The Normative Component

Each culture has its own idea about not only what is important in the world but also how people should act. This is the normative component of a culture, made up of its norms and values. **Values** are socially shared ideas about what is good, desirable, or important. These shared ideas are usually the basis of a society's **norms,** rules that specify how people should behave. While norms are specific rules dictating how people should act in a particular situation, values are the general ideas that support the norms. Thus the specific American norm against imprisoning people without a trial is based on the general American value of freedom. Parents are required by a norm to send their children to school because society places a high value on mass education. We are allowed to criticize our government because we value freedom of speech. Even a norm as mundane as that against pushing to the head of a line is derived from a general value, one that emphasizes fairness and equal treatment for all.

Values and norms also vary from culture to culture. Because they are subjective, a value and its norms that may be considered good in one society may appear bad in another. If someone says to us, "You have done an excellent job!" an American norm requires that we say "Thank you." This may be traced to the value our society places on fair exchange: you scratch my back and I'll scratch yours, so if you praise me I'll thank you for it. In China, however, the same praise will elicit a self-effacing response like "Oh, no, not at all" or "No, I've done poorly." The reason is that humility ranks high in the Chinese value system. Thus, Americans might consider the Chinese weird for being unappreciative, and the Chinese might regard the Americans as uncivilized for being immodest.

Values and norms also change together over time. Forty years ago, most Americans supported the norm of school segregation because they valued racial inequality. Today the norm has given way to school integration because the value has leaned toward racial equality. In China before the late 1970s, ideological purity ("We would rather have a poor country under socialism than a rich one under capitalism") was the country's reigning value. One of its resulting norms was to send professors, students, scientists, and other intellectuals to the farm to learn equality from the peasants. After the late 1970s, the new value of pragmatism ("It doesn't matter if the cat is white or black as long as it catches mice") took over, and one of its accompanying norms has been to send many intellectuals abroad to learn modernization from the West. In 1989, however, these values and norms became less popular with the Chinese government after its brutal crackdown on the prodemocracy movement.

NORMS

Day in and day out, we conform to norms. They affect all aspects of our lives. As a result, we are usually not aware of them. If someone asked why we say "Hi"

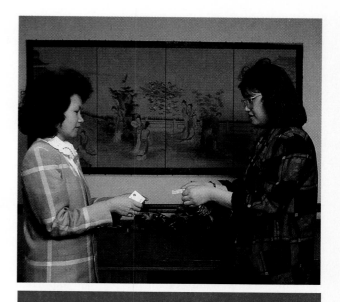

People in all societies conform to norms, which affect all aspects of our lives. The Chinese value humility, which requires that Chinese business people behave in certain ways toward one another, even in simple interactions, such as exchanging business cards.

when greeting a friend, we might be inclined to answer, "How else?" or "What a silly question!" We hardly recognize that we are following an American norm. This fact will dawn on us if we discover that people in other societies follow quite different customs. Tibetans and Bhutanese, for example, greet their friends by sticking out their tongues. They are simply following their own norms.

These norms are rather trivial; they reflect one type of norm called a **folkway.** They are relatively "weak," only expecting us to behave properly in our everyday lives. It's no big deal if we violate them; nobody would punish us severely. The worst we would get is that people might consider us uncouth, peculiar, or eccentric—not immoral, wicked, or criminal. Often society turns a blind eye to violations of folkways. Suppose we go to a wedding reception; we are expected to bring a gift, dress formally, remain silent and attentive during the ceremony, and so on. If we violate any of these folkways, people may raise their eyebrows, but they are not going to ship us off to jail.

Much stronger norms than folkways are **mores** (pronounced *mor-ayz*). Mores absolutely insist that we behave morally, and violations of such norms will be severely punished. Fighting with the bridegroom, beating some guests, burning down the house, and kidnapping the bride are violations of mores, and the offender will be dealt with harshly. Less shocking but still serious misbehaviors, such as car theft, shoplifting, vandalism, and prostitution, also represent violations of mores. In modern societies, most mores are formalized into **laws,** which are explicit, written codes of conduct designed and enforced by the state in order to control its citizens' behavior. Hence violations of these mores are also considered illegal or criminal acts, punishable by law. Some folkways—such as driving safely, mowing the lawn, or no liquor sale on Sundays—may also be turned into laws. Laws are usually effective in controlling our behavior if they are strongly backed by popular beliefs. If there is not enough normative support, the laws are hard to enforce, as in the case of legal prohibitions against prostitution, gambling, and teenage drinking.

In fact, all kinds of norms play an important role in controlling behavior, and society has various methods of enforcing them. These enforcement measures are called **sanctions.** They may be positive for rewarding conformity to norms, or negative for punishing violations. Positive sanctions range from a word of approval for helping a child across a street to public adulation for rescuing someone trapped in a burning building. Negative sanctions can be as mild as a dirty look for heckling a speaker or as severe as execution for murder. Some sanctions are applied by formal agents of social control such as the police, but most often sanctions are applied informally by parents, neighbors, strangers, and so on.

By regularly rewarding us for good actions and punishing us for bad ones, the agents of social control seek to condition us to obey society's norms. If they are successful, obedience becomes habitual and automatic. We obey the norms even when no one is around to reward or punish us, even when we are not thinking of possible rewards and punishments. But human beings are very complicated; we cannot be easily conditioned, as dogs are, by rewards and punishments alone. Thus, sanctions by themselves could not produce the widespread, day-to-day conformity to norms that occurs in societies all over the world. To obtain this conformity, something more is needed: the values of the culture.

VALUES

Because norms are derived from values, we are likely to abide by a society's norms if we believe in its underlying values. If we believe in the value our society places on freedom of religion, we are likely to follow the norm against religious intolerance. If we take to heart the American achievement values, we will accept the norm of studying and working hard. If employers still cling to the traditional belief that a woman's place is in the home, they will violate the norm against job discrimination by not hiring married women. In developing countries, parents often carry on the norm of producing many babies because they continue to subscribe to the traditional value of big, extended families. Why do values have such power over behavior? There are at least three reasons: (1) our parents, teachers, and other socializing agents (see Chapter 5: Socialization) teach us our society's values so that we feel it is right and natural to obey its norms; (2) values contain an element of moral persuasion: the achievement value, for example, in effect says, "It's good to be a winner; it's bad to be a loser"; (3) values carry implied sanctions against people who reject them (Spates, 1983).

People are not always conscious of the values instilled in them, nor do they always know why they obey norms. Sometimes norms persist even after the values from which they are derived have changed. Do you know, for example, why we shower a bride and groom with rice after a wedding? We may feel it is the proper thing to do, or a pleasant thing to do, or in a vague way a sign of wishing the newlyweds well. In fact, the norm is derived from the high value our ancestors placed on fertility, which was symbolized by rice. Thus, over time, a norm can become separated from the value that inspired it. It comes to be valued in itself, and we may follow the norm simply because it seems the right thing to do.

Values are not directly observable, but we can infer values from the way people carry out norms. When we see that the Japanese treat their old people with respect, we can safely infer that they put great value on old age. When we learn that the Comanche Indians were expected to save their mothers-in-law during a raid by an enemy before trying to save their own lives, then we conclude that the Comanche placed a high value on mothers-in-law. When we see that many American women are dieting, some to the point of becoming anorexic, we know that our culture places an enormous value on slenderness as the model for feminine beauty (Mazur, 1986).

According to Robin Williams (1970), there are 15 basic values that dominate American culture: success, hard work, efficiency, material comfort, morality, humanitarianism, progress, science, external conformity, individualism, in-group superiority, equality, freedom, patriotism, and democracy.

This list, however, points to some of the areas of conflict in American culture. When external conformity, freedom, and individualism are all highly valued, it is difficult to resolve clashes over whether flag burning, pornography, or abortion should be prohibited by law. Thus, the value of conformity has led some Americans to favor a constitutional ban on flag desecration, but concern with freedom has caused others to oppose it. Similarly, the conflict between those two values generated a controversy over whether 2 Live Crew's records, which contain violent and sexually explicit lyrics, should be available in stores. In the business world, the value given to efficiency and success often clashes with considerations of morality: Should companies, in pursuing efficiency and success, sell adulterated foods and other unsafe products, engage in deceptive advertising, or violate price-fixing laws? Or should they resist these immoralities and risk losing out to competitors? Cultures are basically integrated; they form coherent wholes. But as the inconsistencies among American values demonstrate, that integration is never perfect. This is not surprising because the cultures of large, modern industrial societies are generally less integrated than those of small, traditional ones (Archer, 1985; Salholz, 1990c).

Moreover, some of the values Williams identified have been changing. For one thing, contrary to some Japanese politicians' belief that Americans have become lazy, Americans work harder than ever before. In the past 15 years, the typical adult's leisure time has shrunk by 40 percent—down from 26.6 hours to 16.6 hours a week—and the work week has swelled by 15 percent—up from 40.6 hours to 46.8 hours (Lipset, 1990b). A more recent study also shows Americans working much harder than before, which has resulted from the greater demands of employers and the rise of addictive consumerism (Schor, 1991). However, although Americans work harder, they also try to enjoy themselves more—on the job and off. Interestingly, their work ethic has heavily influenced their pursuit of leisure, so that the harder they work on the job the harder they work at their leisure. In a content analysis of *Fortune* magazine from 1957 through 1979, sociologist Lionel Lewis found that business leaders, like many other Americans, strive to succeed in their leisure pursuits as well as in their work. As one avid jogger explains, "Running, like business, is full of drudgery. But inherent in our philosophy is the belief that physical fitness gives us a headstart over a less fit competitor" (Lewis, 1982).

Related to working harder is a greater interest in individual success. Concern with this personal value, however, has apparently caused a decline in community life and social responsibility. In relentlessly pursuing their personal ambitions, Americans have little or no time left for their families, friends, and communities. This leaves them "suspended in glorious, but terrifying, isolation" (Bellah et al., 1986). Moreover, increased concern with one's own welfare has developed a strong sense of individual

Values sometimes clash. Although most Americans probably conform to the rule of showing respect for the flag, and many would want to see a law prohibiting flag burning, American culture also values freedom and individualism.

rights but a weak sense of obligation to the community. Most Americans, for example, would demand their right to be tried by a jury of their peers, but if asked to serve on such juries they would strive to evade the call. Consequently, a group of social thinkers called "communitarians" have recently emerged to encourage social responsibility. Many individuals themselves have tried to move beyond the isolated self by spending more time with the family, seeking meaningful rather than casual relationships, and working to improve community life (Etzioni, 1993).

QUESTIONS FOR DISCUSSION AND REVIEW

1. Why is sociology's definition of "culture" different from popular uses of that word?
2. What are cultural values and norms, and how do they combine with sanctions to control people's behavior?
3. How do folkways differ from mores?
4. To what extent do your personal values agree with the list of cultural views identified by Williams?

The Symbolic Component

The components of culture that we have discussed so far—norms and values as well as knowledge and beliefs—cannot exist without symbols. A **symbol** is a word, gesture, sound, or anything that stands for some other thing. Symbols enable us to create, communicate and share, and transmit to the next generation the other components of culture. It is through symbols that we get immersed in culture and, in the process, become fully human. We can better appreciate the importance of symbols, and particularly language, from Helen Keller's (1954) account of her first step into the humanizing world of culture. Blind and deaf, she had been cut off from that world until, at the age of 7, she entered it through a word:

> Someone was drawing water and my teacher placed my hand under the spout. As the cool stream gushed over one hand she spelled into the other the word water, first slowly, then rapidly. I stood still, my whole attention fixed upon the motion of her fingers. Suddenly I felt a misty consciousness as of something forgotten—a thrill of returning thought; and somehow the mystery of language was revealed to me. I knew then that "w-a-t-e-r" meant the

wonderful cool something that was flowing over my hand. The living word awakened my soul, gave it light, hope, joy, set it free! There were barriers still, it is true, but barriers that could in time be swept away.

Once Helen Keller understood that her teacher's hand sign meant water, once she understood what a word was, she could share her world with others and enter into their world, because she could communicate through symbols. All words are symbols; they have meaning only when people agree on what they mean. Communication succeeds or fails depending on whether people agree or disagree on what their words or signs mean. Helen Keller's experience is a vivid example of the general truth that almost all human communication occurs through the use of symbols.

ANIMAL AND HUMAN COMMUNICATION

Animals, too, communicate. If you try to catch a seagull, it will call out "hahaha! hahaha!" to signal its friends to watch out for an intruder. A squirrel may cry out to warn other squirrels to flee from danger. But these signal systems differ in very fundamental ways from human communication.

First, symbols are *arbitrary*. If you do not speak Chinese, you would not know what a *gou* is. *Gou* is the Chinese word for dog. There is no inherent connection between the word and the thing itself. The Spaniards, after all, call the same animal *perro,* and the French call it *chien.* Even "dingdong" is an arbitrary symbol: a bell may sound like "dingdong" to us, but not to the Germans, to whom a bell sounds like "bimbam." Also, the crowing of a rooster may sound like "cock-a-doodle-do" to us, but it is "ki-ki-ri-ki" to the Mexicans. The meaning of a word is not determined by any inherent quality of the thing itself. It is instead arbitrary: a word may mean *whatever* a group of humans have agreed it is supposed to mean. The meaning of a word can also be said to be "socially constructed" because it is determined by a specific group or society. It is no wonder that there are a great many different symbols in human communication to represent the same thing (Plog and Bates, 1980). On the other hand, animals are not free to arbitrarily produce different symbols to indicate the same thing, because their behavior is to a large extent biologically determined. This is why, for example, all seagulls throughout the world make the same sound to indicate the presence of danger. Unlike humans, they cannot express a particular thought in more than one way (Cowley, 1988).

Second, animal communication is a *closed system,* whereas human language is an *open system.* Each animal species can communicate only a limited set of messages, and the meaning of these signals is fixed. Animals can use only one signal at a time—they cannot combine two or more to produce a new and more complex message. A bird can signal "worms" to other birds but not "worms" and "cats" together. Animal communication is also closed in the sense of being stimulus-bound; it is tied to what is immediately present in the environment. The bird can signal "worms" only because it sees them. It is impossible for an animal to use a symbol to represent some invisible, abstract, or imaginary thing. As philosopher Bertrand Russell said, "No matter how eloquently a dog can bark, he cannot tell you that his parents are poor but honest." In contrast, we can blend and combine symbols to express whatever ideas come into our heads. We can create new messages, and the potential number of messages that we can send is infinite. Thus, we can talk about abstractions such as good and evil, truth and beauty, for which there is no physical thing that is being signaled. It is this creative character of language that leads many people to believe that language is unique to humans.

NONVERBAL COMMUNICATION

Aside from using words, we also use signs to communicate. But our sign system is quite different from that of animals. Like our language, our nonverbal communication is socially constructed rather than biologically determined, open rather than closed. It consists of kinesics and proxemics.

Kinesics is "body language," the use of body movements as a means of communication. Kinesics plays an important role in our social life. To find a date in a singles bar, for example, a man typically uses body language. He looks around the room, and, if he spots a woman he likes, his gaze will rest on her. If the woman is interested, she will hold his gaze, then look away, and again look back at him. The man, getting the message, will move toward her. But the meaning of body language varies from one culture to another. In the United States, we nod our heads to mean yes and shake them to mean no. To the Bulgarians, however, the head nodding means no and the head shaking means yes. The Greeks nod their heads to indicate yes but jerk their heads back

Nonverbal communication may involve proxemics, the use of space as a means of communicating. The proxemics found in Arab cultures differs from that characteristic of North Americans. When conversing with people we do not know, we usually stand about three feet away, whereas Arabs tend to maintain a closer conversational distance.

with their eyes closed and eyebrows lifted to mean no. The Semang of Malaya thrust their heads forward to signal yes and cast their eyes down to signal no. The Ainu of northern Japan do not use their heads at all in saying yes and no; they use their hands.

We are usually less aware of **proxemics**—the use of space as a means of communication—unless someone violates what we consider our personal space. In North America, when talking to a person whom we do not know well, we ordinarily stand about three feet away. If one person moved in closer than that, the other would find it too close for comfort. But South Americans are inclined to stand much closer. We might find them too pushy for being too close to us, and they might find us too unfriendly for being too distant from them. If we converse with Arabs, they might even get closer and literally breathe on us. Their view of public space is also different from Westerners', as Edward Hall (1976) has observed:

In the Arab world you do not hold a lien on the ground underfoot. When standing on a street corner, an Arab may shove you aside if he wants to be where you are. This puts the average territorial American or German under great stress. Something basic has been violated. Behind this—to us—bizarre or even rude behavior lies an entirely different concept of property. Even the body is not sacred when a person is in public. Years ago, American women in Beirut had to give up using streetcars. Their bodies were the property of all men within reach. What was happening is even reflected in the language. The Arabs have no word for *trespass,* no word for *rape.*

Hall (1966) also noted that the interpersonal distance is small not only among Arabs and Latin Americans but also among Southern and Eastern Europeans, and that it is great among Asians, Northern Europeans, and North Americans. Many studies have supported Hall's observation in one way or another. Consider a typical investigation by two social psychologists. They recruited 35 Japanese, 31 Venezuelan, and 39 American students and asked each to have a five-minute conversation on his or her favorite sports or hobbies with a member of the same sex and nationality. The results showed that the Venezuelans sat closer together than did the Americans, who in turn sat closer than the Japanese, with the average conversational distance being, respectively, 32.3, 35.4, and 40.2 inches (Sussman and Rosenfeld, 1982). In practically all cultures, however, high-status people tend to invade the personal space of a lower-status person more frequently than the other way around. Professors may pat a student's back, but the student rarely reciprocates. Men in general let their hands rest on women's shoulders, but women seldom do the same to men. Doctors touch their nurses more often than nurses touch doctors. Bosses touch their employees more often than employees touch their bosses. Adults are more likely to touch children than vice versa (Gillespie and Leffler, 1983; Major et al., 1990).

The Influence of Language

In saying that the Arabs have no words for "trespass" and "rape," did Hall imply that they do not see these acts in the same way as we do? Apparently yes. Many

social scientists assume that language influences the way we perceive the world around us. Edward Sapir (1929) was the first to hold this view. Human beings, he said, live "at the mercy of the particular language which has become the medium of expression for their society." Sapir also wrote that language has "a tyrannical hold upon our orientation to the world." When societies speak a different language, "the worlds in which societies live are distinct worlds, not merely the same world with different labels attached to it."

This view was developed by Sapir's student Benjamin Whorf (1956) and became known as the *Sapir-Whorf hypothesis.* It holds that language predisposes us to see the world in a certain way. Sometimes, the hypothesis is put even more strongly: language molds our minds, determining how we think about the world. Whorf found, for example, that the language of the Hopi Indians of the southwestern United States has neither verb tenses to distinguish the past and the present nor nouns for times, days, seasons, or years. Consequently, according to Whorf, Hopi- and English-speaking people perceive time differently. Although we see the difference between a person working *now* and the same person working *yesterday,* the Hopi do not because their language makes no distinction between past and present.

There are many other intriguing differences among languages. We use the English words "fear" and "shame," which shows our ability to perceive these two feelings as different. But a tribe of Australian aborigines cannot tell them apart because the people do not have separate words for them. Instead, they have only one word *(kunta)* to refer not only to fear and shame but also to shyness, embarrassment, and respect. It is therefore difficult for the aborigine to appreciate the differences among these five feelings (Wierzbicka, 1986). In his novel *1984,* George Orwell (1949) provided a dramatic presentation of the possibilities of the Sapir-Whorf hypothesis. In the dictatorship portrayed in the novel, a language called *Newspeak* has been created. Among other things, Newspeak has no word for freedom, so that people cannot even think about freedom, much less want it.

Many scholars, however, have criticized the Sapir-Whorf hypothesis for overemphasizing the power of language. According to the critics, language only influences—rather than determines—how we think. If language determined thought, people who spoke different languages would always think differently. If this were the case, it would be impossible for us to comprehend English translations of foreign languages. But the critics do admit that language does have some influence on cognition. This is why people who speak different languages sometimes think differently, so that they cannot see eye-to-eye on some issues. Therefore, some scholars today try to determine the amount of influence language has on thinking (Ferro-Luzzi, 1986).

On the other hand, the Sapir-Whorf hypothesis has stimulated studies of language with the aim of understanding culture. An important finding is that the Garo of northeast India, who live in an environment full of ants, have more than a dozen words for different kinds of ants but no general term for "ant" (Plog and Bates, 1980). The Garo apparently find it useful to distinguish one kind of ant from another. Ants play so small a role in our lives that our language makes no distinction between them. We lump them all together in one word, and to most of us one ant looks just like another. Similarly, the Chinese have at least eight words for rice. They include *fan* for the cooked product, *dao* for the rice still in the paddy, *xian* for the long-grained variety, *mi* for the husked kernels, and *gu* for unhusked kernels. All this reflects the importance of rice to Chinese life (Kristof, 1991).

AMERICAN POP CULTURE

Like language, popular culture also reflects the significant interests and concerns of a society. **Popular culture** consists of relatively unsophisticated artistic creations that appeal to the masses of a society. Examples are movies, TV shows, musical performances, and other entertainments that attract large audiences. In 1992 then Vice President Dan Quayle publicly criticized prime-time television for promoting single motherhood by showing the famous TV character Murphy Brown bearing a child out of wedlock. He obviously believes that there is moral decay in American pop culture. But analysis of the pop culture reveals otherwise.

Unwed mothers rarely appear on prime-time TV—Murphy Brown is an exception. Even so, she does not represent most of the real-life unwed mothers. She is a forty-something overachiever, while most unwed mothers are very young or poor. The virtual absence of poor unwed mothers as TV characters reflects the popular belief that they are immoral and thus a threat to traditional family values. The same belief about homosexual couples also keeps them almost entirely out of sight on prime-time television. Instead, what is routinely presented to the audience is the traditional family: a heterosexual, monogamous couple and their children with a lot of familial love.

Analysis of popular culture shows that television does not present a threat to our social values but often mirrors them. TV character Murphy Brown is depicted as a successful news broadcaster and loving mother. (© 1993 Warner Bros. All Rights Reserved)

"The Cosby Show," which debuted in 1984 and ended in 1992, portrays the traditional two-parent family. So do the overwhelming majority of today's TV shows, ranging from nostalgic ones like "The Wonder Years" and "Brooklyn Bridge," to contemporary ones like "Home Improvement" and "Major Dad," from hilariously expanded ones like "Step by Step" to affectionately close-knit ones like "Life Goes On." Even most of the main characters of such hip shows as "Beverly Hills 90210" and "The Fresh Prince of Bel-Air" have strong families. The very few single parents on TV frequently have other caring adults—the three fathers in "Full House" and the compassionate housekeeper in "I'll Fly Away"—to strengthen the pro-family message. What about "Married . . . with Children," "The Simpsons," and "Roseanne?" They seem to attack the family, but actually the target of their sniping is television's sentimentalized portrayal of the family. For all the Bundys' cutting sarcasm, the Simpsons' "eat my shorts" irreverence, and Roseanne's biting wisecracks, they come through clearly as loving, cohesive families (Zoglin, 1992).

Popular movies and music may also seem morally offensive, with all their violence, sex, and raw language. But generally they reaffirm old values. Consider these top films: *Pretty Woman, Ghost, Goodfellas, Home Alone,* and *Dances with Wolves.* They show, respectively, a Beverly Hills version of the old movie

My Fair Lady starring a spirited prostitute with the proverbial heart of gold, a fantasy romanticizing widowhood, a classic gangster story, a funny kid caper, and a lavish western with the cavalry and Indians. All these movies support the status quo, just as the old ones did before the rebellious 1960s. Even rap music, whose lyrics are often angry and randy, conveys a message that supports traditional values: "Life on the streets is meaner and more unforgiving than ever, but the way out is to stay off drugs, stay in school, and take responsibility for yourself." The blast of heavy metal may sound subversive, but its appeal is quite limited compared with pro-traditional soft rock, soul-jazz, and country music, which now dominate the radio airwaves. An example of the pro-traditional music is Lee Greenwood's mushy "I'm Proud to Be an American," a sharp contrast to Johnny Paycheck's earlier rebellious hit, "Take This Job and Shove It" (Huey, 1991). In short, today's popular movies, series TV, and music mirror the conservative, nonrebellious times in which we live.

From the feminist perspective we can also see how the popular culture reflects the patriarchy of our society. At the 1993 movie award ceremony, Hollywood ostentatiously paid a special tribute to women in movies, proclaiming "Oscar Celebrates Women and the Movies" as the theme of the widely watched ceremony. But the facts showed otherwise, prompting a female film critic to say, "That Oscar theme is a joke, because men are now playing *all* the best roles. They get the macho roles *and* the sweet-sensitive roles, and they play the sexual pinups too. The best woman's role of 1992 was in *The Crying Game,* and *that* was played by a man" (Corliss, 1993). Of course, women did play strong, exemplary idealists in *Passion Fish, Lorenzo's Oil, Howard's End, Indochine,* and *Love Field.* But such movies are rare, and, more importantly, fail to become boffos. The reason is that the audience, under the influence of patriarchy, prefer movies that put women in their place. That's why Hollywood tends to produce blockbuster movies (such as *Basic Instinct, Single White Female,* and *Indecent Proposal*) in which women play major roles as predators or sex kittens. Explaining the predator role, Jon Avnet, director of *Fried Green Tomatoes,* observes, "The general feeling is that if a woman is bright, aggressive and successful, she's got to be a bitch." Explaining the sex kitten role, Callie Khouri, screenwriter of the feminist buddy movie *Thelma & Louise,* says, "Hollywood is trying to resexualize its women back into submission . . . The women who do best in this society are the ones who are the most

complacent in the role of women as sexual commodity, be it Madonna, Julia Roberts or Sharon Stone. If Stone hadn't spread her legs, would *Basic Instinct* have done as well as it did?" (Corliss, 1993).

QUESTIONS FOR DISCUSSION AND REVIEW
1. In what ways do human and animal communication differ?
2. How do kinesics and proxemics function as forms of nonverbal communication?
3. How does the language you use influence the way you see the world?
4. What is the nature of American pop culture today?

Evolution and Culture

Having just gone over the various components of culture, we may appreciate the tremendous influence culture has over us. Culture not only surrounds us but gets into us to become an important part of our being human. We are so dependent on culture that we can hardly survive without it. Without culture we would not readily know how to prepare foods, work, raise children, live with other members of society, or do endless other things. Why is culture so important to us but not to animals? An answer can be found in our biological evolution.

Humans today are the product of a tremendously long process of evolution, which began with the first living organisms more than 3 billion years ago. By having these same ancestors in the remote past, humans and all other living creatures are related to one another as distant cousins. We therefore share with other animals certain physical and behavioral characteristics. Even what may seem uniquely human traits can be found in other members of the animal kingdom. We can walk on two feet; so can birds. We can use our hands; so can all apes and monkeys. We can use tools; so can chimps and baboons—even sea otters and some birds. We can live as members of a society; so can some insects. We are not even the only species capable of learning and transmitting behaviors to new generations. Adult chimps can teach their young how to catch ants and termites.

At the same time, however, humans are very different from the rest of the animal kingdom. We are the only species with the capacity for culture—complex language, constant learning, use of sophisticated tools, and a flexible form of social organization. Why are we so different from the other animals who, after all, are descended from the same ancestors? The reason, according to Charles Darwin, known for his theory of how evolution occurs, is geographical separation. When some members of a species move into a radically different environment, they will evolve into a new species.

Such was the case with the biological evolution of the early humans (Leakey and Lewin, 1977). About 14 million years ago, the rain forests where the apes' earliest ancestors had been living thinned out, creating a shortage of fruits and nuts. Some of the apes began to venture into the savanna (grasslands), where they could search for new food sources such as seeds, roots, and finally the meat of other animals. The apes that remained in the forest evolved into today's chimps, gorillas, and orangutans. The savanna-dwelling apes evolved into our ancestors because the environment of the savanna forced them to develop a new set of characteristics.

On the savanna, it is useful to be able to stand upright in order to see over the tall grass to spot oncoming predators and to carry food to a home base. Some of the savanna-dwelling apes failed to develop an erect posture and died out. Others became bipedal (standing on two legs), which freed their hands from walking, and began to make tools. At this time these apes began to evolve more quickly into humans. Toolmaking required intelligence and sensitive hands, and living together at a home base further required social interaction involving cooperation, sociability, and vocal communication (Rensberger, 1984). In other words, the erect-walking apes were forced by their new environment to develop those required physical and behavioral characteristics. Eventually, about 100,000 years ago, the apes that did not develop those characteristics became extinct, while the other apes that did survived as humans. At the same time, those very traits that made possible the emergence of humans also made possible the development of a complex culture.

The long evolutionary process has caused us to lose our **instincts**—biologically fixed traits that enable the carrier to perform complex tasks. Apparently our instincts, such as those for climbing trees like a monkey, gradually became extinct because they did not help our ancestors adapt to the radically new environment in the savanna—they were useful only for our other ancestors, left behind in the forests, to continue dealing in a fixed, automatic way with their relatively unchanging environment. Because we have no instincts, we need a culture to survive. This need is most clearly seen in human infants' long dependence

on adults. Unlike newly born animals, whose instincts enable them to be on their own in only a few hours or days, human infants must depend on adults for many years—until they have learned enough of the culture to fend for themselves.

We are, then, the only species that depends greatly on complex language, constant learning, sophisticated tools, and a flexible form of social organization—all of which are parts of culture—for survival. The loss of instincts has made us dependent on each other, and the resulting development of culture has also loosened our bondage to the natural environment. Thus we have adapted to vastly differing environments—from arid deserts and arctic wastelands to rugged mountains and dense rain forests—from which various forms of culture have emerged. In short, since evolution gave the human species the capacity for culture, we have moved farther and farther away from our evolutionary home. Today, we largely depend on culture rather than instincts to survive (Rindos, 1986).

QUESTIONS FOR DISCUSSION AND REVIEW
1. How did the emergence of the early humans occur?
2. To what extent has the process of evolution caused humans to depend on culture for survival?

Cultural Variations

Everywhere on the planet, humans are the product of the same evolutionary process, and all of us have the same set of needs that must be met if we are to survive. Some of these, such as the need for food and shelter, are rooted in biology. Others—such as the need for clothing, complex communication, social order, and esthetic and spiritual experiences—are basic necessities of human life. Different societies, however, have developed their own cultures as a way of meeting these needs. Within each of these societies there have also emerged different **subcultures,** which are cultures within a larger culture.

In a small nonindustrial society in which people have similar backgrounds, experiences, and occupations, there are few subcultures. People in these societies are primarily differentiated by gender, age, and status, so that they have only the male and female subcultures, adult and adolescent subcultures, and higher- and lower-status subcultures. In modern industrial societies, however, people are differentiated along many lines. There are not only differences in gender, age, and status but in religious, racial, regional, and occupational background, all of which may provide bases for subcultures. In the United States, for example, there are subcultures of college students, adolescents, Hispanic-Americans, Italian-Americans, African-Americans, and many others.

As for the variations in human cultures around the world, they have long fascinated people. In the seventeenth and eighteenth centuries, Europeans read with wonder the tales of American Indians and South Sea islanders provided by missionaries and explorers. But the ability to understand other cultures and how our own culture shapes our lives has been undermined by other, equally old reactions. Most important, people tend to use their own culture as a point of reference for judging other cultures. Overcoming this tendency is the first step toward understanding cultural variations.

ETHNOCENTRISM

Almost from the time we are born, we are taught that our way of life is good, moral, civilized, or natural. We feel in our bones that the way we live is right and that other people's ways of life are wrong, uncivilized, or unnatural. This attitude that our own culture is superior to other people's is called **ethnocentrism.** How do you react to the following practices in other societies?

Among the Trukese people on the Caroline Islands in the West Pacific, boys and girls are encouraged to have sex when they reach the age of ten. Every male among the Keraki of New Guinea customarily engages in homosexual activities during adolescence and in bisexual behavior after marriage. Yanomamo Indian women in Brazil often kill their baby girls by banging their heads against a tree. In some African countries, it is customary to cut a young woman's clitoris to discourage sexual intercourse before or outside marriage (Ford and Beach, 1951; Harris, 1974; Perlez, 1990).

As Americans, we are inclined to consider all these behaviors strange, uncivilized, or even disgusting. On the other hand, the Siriono Indians of Bolivia find our custom of kissing very disgusting. People of many other societies find it odd that in our preferred position for sexual intercourse the male is on top of the female, a position called the missionary position by Pacific Islanders ever since their women copulated with missionaries many years ago (Kluckhohn, 1948).

Ethnocentrism is so deeply instilled in our minds that we tend to condemn cultural practices radically different from our own. Ethnocentrism is also so deeply ingrained in our bodies that we can become physically ill if we eat something our culture defines as sickening. Try to eat toasted grasshoppers, which most Japanese like; or ants, which some tribes in Brazil enjoy; or mice, which the Dahomey of West Africa find delicious. Just the thought of eating any of these things might turn your stomach. Similarly, peoples in other cultures find many of our favorite foods nauseating. The Hindus in India abhor beef, and the Jews and Muslims in many countries spurn pork. The Chinese consider cow's milk fit only for young children. Many Europeans consider corn on the cob fit only for animals. Numerous Asians and Africans recoil from cheese because they find it too smelly (Harris, 1985).

Because ethnocentrism is so powerful, it is bound to make us extremely biased against other cultures and to distort our observation of what they are really like. Witness how distorted the following analysis of *our* behavior in the bathroom and hospital can be if the analysis is done from the perspective of a foreign, preliterate society that believes in witch doctors:

> The supplicant entering the temple is first stripped of all his or her clothes. In everyday life the Nacirema [*American* spelled backward] avoids exposure of his body and its natural functions. Bathing and excretory acts are performed only in the secrecy of the household shrine, where they are ritualized as part of the body rites. Psychological shock results from the fact that body secrecy is suddenly lost upon entry into the latipsoh [hospital]. A man, whose own wife has never seen him in an excretory act, suddenly finds himself naked and assisted by a vestal maiden while he performs his natural functions into a sacred vessel. This sort of ceremonial treatment is necessitated by the fact that the excreta are used by a diviner to ascertain the course and nature of the client's sickness. Female clients, on the other hand, find that their naked bodies are subjected to the scrutiny, manipulation, and prodding of the medicine men (Miner, 1956).

Ethnocentrism is so prevalent and runs so deep that even anthropologists find it difficult to over-

When he first met the Yanomamo Indians in Brazil, anthropologist Napoleon Chagnon experienced ethnocentrism, the attitude that one's own culture is superior and that other ways of life are uncivilized. Although such feelings are difficult to overcome, even for an anthropologist, it is possible to enter another culture and learn its ways. Here Chagnon, wearing the tail of a black monkey as a headband, as is traditional for visitors, is seen talking with Yanomamo friends.

come. When Napoleon Chagnon (1968) first met the Yanomamo Indians in Brazil, he found them horrifying. Being very warlike, the Yanomamo "welcomed" him by aiming their drawn arrows at his face. They had large wads of green tobacco jammed between their lower teeth and lips. Long streams of green mucus incessantly ran down from their noses, the result of having taken a psychedelic drug. They proudly showed off the long scars—which they had painted red—on their heads, the result of constant fighting. "I am not ashamed to admit," Chagnon later said about this encounter, "had there been a diplomatic way out, I would have ended my fieldwork there and then." Another anthropologist, Elenore Bowen, also failed to suppress her feelings of disgust and revulsion toward her subject, the Tiv people of northern Nigeria: "They were all savages. For the first time I applied the term to them in my own thinking. And it fit" (Plog and Bates, 1980).

Both Chagnon and Bowen suggested that they found it hard to be objective in their work because they had not had much experience studying "primitives." But "even with extensive fieldwork experience," observed Paul Turner (1982), "perceptive anthropologists in the 20th century realize the difficulty or impossibility of ridding themselves of all traces of ethnocentrism." This has much to do, according to Francis Hsu (1979), with Western technological superiority, which "still nurtures in many the illusion of Western racial and cultural superiority in general." As a result, some Western anthropologists

continue to present inaccurate views of foreign cultures and even to propose policies aimed at changing the cultures of "underdeveloped" countries to make them more like our own. But for others to become more like us can bring trouble. In a village in Papua New Guinea, where cottage industries have been developed with small-scale technologies, some people have become successful entrepreneurs, gaining personal wealth. But in 1983 the local witch doctor, at the urging of village elders, killed a few of those businesspeople. The elders saw the victims as individualists, believing that they no longer contributed to the common good. The elders' culture had been based on community and cooperation, contrary to the individualism and competition that fuel the newly introduced Western economic system (Ellis and Ellis, 1989).

CULTURAL RELATIVISM

Nevertheless, most social scientists do strive to adopt an attitude of **cultural relativism.** It involves judging a culture on its own terms, which is, in effect, the opposite of ethnocentrism. Because the terms of the culture—the participants' perceptions, feelings, or viewpoints—are either completely or largely unknown to outsiders, social scientists usually try to become insiders so as to understand the natives' point of view. To become insiders, they can use the participant observation technique or simply identify with

Cultural relativism, in effect, the opposite of ethnocentrism, involves judging a culture on its own terms. In fact, the cultural relativist, to avoid any kind of criticism of another culture, such as that of Nazi Germany, would end up seeing nothing wrong in dictatorship or the Nazi practice of exterminating Jews and other "undesirable races."

the subjects (see Chapter 1: The Essence of Sociology). Only through becoming insiders can social scientists leave behind the blinders of ethnocentrism and take on the stance of cultural relativism. By adopting cultural relativism, we can better understand the cultures of other peoples. From an outsider's ethnocentric perspective, it appears disgusting for Tibetans to cut up their relatives' corpses and then feed them to vultures. But from the Tibetans' own perspective, this practice is necessary to ensure a higher incarnation for their loved ones.

A serious problem, however, can arise with cultural relativism. If we evaluate a society's beliefs and practices by its own standard only, we could never be critical of them. Consider Nazi Germany's belief in its racial purity and practice of exterminating Jews. There is no way that the cultural relativist, by assuming the Nazi point of view, could condemn them. Similarly, as a cultural relativist, one could not see anything wrong with such horrors as infanticide, cannibalism, torture, dictatorship, and totalitarianism in other countries. To the relativist, "the difference between a vegetarian and a cannibal is just a matter of taste" (Werner, 1986). Relativism may appear on the face of it only a moral issue, irrelevant to the scientific quest for valid and reliable knowledge. But it is not, because it involves trading one kind of ethnocentrism (the researcher's) for another (the subject's).

Such is often the case when a Western anthropologist adopts the values of a third-world culture he or she studies, simply because the natives are just as ethnocentric as the Westerner is. The exchange of the anthropologist's ethnocentrism for the natives' can be seen in "accounts that romanticize non-Western cultures while criticizing the industrial societies from which anthropologists come" (Hippler, 1978). It would obviously retard scientific knowledge of culture.

This problem can be found in studies on a tribe in Australia. A number of anthropologists, relying on the aborigines' perspective, have painted a highly favorable picture of them: "Aboriginal infants and young children are extremely well treated and cared for—by any conventional Western standards—and parents are very genuinely concerned for and involved with their children" (Reser, 1981). But this description contrasts sharply with the finding by another anthropologist, who did not use the natives' point of view: "Children are abused by mother and others when they cry. They are shouted at, jerked roughly, slapped, or shaken. The care of children under six years of age can be described as hostile, aggressive, and careless; it is often routinely brutal" (Hippler, 1978).

Most of the time, however, anthropologists do not carry their cultural relativism too far. To get a more accurate analysis, they integrate what they call an *emic* perspective (the natives' viewpoint) with an *etic* analysis (derived from the observer's skills as an objective scientist). Let us see how this approach can help us understand what appears to outsiders as a very strange culture, that of the Yanomamo Indians. Viewed from their own perspective, the Yanomamos' terrible fierceness and female infanticide may not look too strange. According to them, they frequently go to war to capture wives because they have a shortage of women (this is an emic view). Yet, in order to have a constant supply of fierce warriors, they have to kill baby girls to devote more time to raising the future fighters (also an emic viewpoint). But the Yanomamo do not realize that the female infanticide will create a shortage of women when the boys grow up, so they, in turn, will have to go to war to capture wives (this is an etic analysis). At the same time, the infanticide, along with the constant warfare, helps control the Yanomamo population and ensure their survival in the face of chronic scarcity of food sources (also an etic analysis). In the final (etic) analysis, it is the lack of food sources in their environment that causes the Yanomamo to practice warfare and infanticide. Thus, the addition of the observer's etic analysis to the participants' emic view enhances our understanding of the Yanomamo culture.

ECOLOGICAL AND FUNCTIONAL PERSPECTIVES

The ability to see a culture through the eyes of its members, tempered by scientific objectivity, has allowed social scientists to go beyond the condemnation or fascination that in the past often dominated accounts of distant cultures. It has allowed them to develop scientific explanations for cultural variations. Many of these are based on either the ecological or the functional perspective.

The *ecological perspective* attributes cultural variations to differences in the natural environment. Humans must adapt to their environment to survive, and they adapt through their cultures. Thus, as environments vary, so too will cultures.

Let us compare the Eskimo with the Yanomamo. The Eskimo live in an arctic wasteland. It offers limitations and opportunities far different from those in a tropical rain forest, where the Yanomamo live. Consequently, the cultural practices of the two peoples differ sharply. While the Eskimo hunt seals as their major source of fresh food, the Yanomamo catch and eat whatever can be found in the forest, such as wild turkeys, wild pigs, monkeys, alligators, anteaters, caterpillars, and spiders. While the Eskimo do not eat vegetables, fruits, or any other plant, which cannot grow in the severe cold, the Yanomamo eat wild fruits, nuts, and seed pods, and they grow some plantains, bananas, and potatoes. Although the Eskimo have the advantage of using nature as a giant freezer to save food for future consumption, the Yanomamo do not. The Eskimo live in igloos built with blocks of ice; the Yanomamo live in huts made from branches and leaves. The Eskimo wear multilayered garments and boots to fight off the arctic cold; the Yanomamo wear almost nothing because of the tropical heat.

There is a limit, though, to the utility of the ecological approach. It is obviously true that the Eskimo's and the Yanomamo's natural environments differ greatly. One is extremely cold, and the other is hot. But they are also quite similar in one respect: both are equally deficient in game animals, which can be hunted only after many days on a hunting trip. The ecological perspective suggests that just as different environments bring about different cultures, similar environments bring about similar cultures. Hence, we would expect that because the Eskimo and Yanomamo face similar shortages of food, they should have developed similar social practices. But they are very different. Old Eskimo are inclined to commit suicide to avoid becoming a burden on the economic well-being of their village, but the Yanomamo regularly kill their daughters to reduce population pressure on the consumption of scarce foods. Eskimo men are so hospitable that they would offer their wives to other Eskimo men for the night; the Yanomamo men are so hostile that they would kill other Yanomamo men to kidnap their women. The ecological perspective cannot explain why the Eskimo help one another and the Yanomamo kill one another.

The explanation can be found in the *functional perspective,* which explains cultural practice by referring to its function for the society as a whole. Thus the Eskimo are hospitable because their hospitality serves the function of ensuring similar treatment for themselves at a later time when they, too, travel great distances to hunt in a harsh environment. Without this reciprocal hospitality, it would be impossible for the Eskimo men to be away from home for days and survive in the severe cold. For the Yanomamo, their constant fighting leads to many deaths and thus controls the population. The constant fighting also serves the function of capturing wives from another village to offset their own shortage of women. Without the constant warfare, the male population would become much larger and put more strain on the shortage of food, seriously threatening the survival of the Yanomamo.

The functional approach also helps explain seemingly puzzling cultural practices. In India, which has the largest number of cattle in the world, there are many poor and starving people; yet the slaughter of cows is forbidden. Moreover, their 180 million cows are treated like gods and goddesses. They are given right of way in the street. They are even affectionately retired to "old-age homes" when they begin to become infirm. Why doesn't India feed starving humans by killing these animals for food? The popular explanation is simply that the Hindus consider their cows sacred. But why do they consider their cows sacred? The reason suggested by the functional perspective is that the sacred cows serve several important, practical functions. First, they produce oxen, which Indian farmers desperately need to plow their fields and pull their carts. Second, when the cows die

naturally, their beef is eaten by the poor lower castes and their hides are used by non-Hindu Indians to maintain one of the world's largest leather industries. Third, the cows produce an enormous amount of manure, which is used as fertilizer and cooking fuel. Fourth, the cows are tireless scavengers, eating garbage, stubble, and grass between railroad tracks, in ditches, and on roadsides. Thus it costs nothing to raise the cows, while they provide many things of value. In fact, India's peasant economy depends heavily on the cows. If the Indians ate their cows, many more people would starve to death. The Hindu belief in the sacredness of cows therefore saves the lives of people as well as of cows (Harris, 1985).

QUESTIONS FOR DISCUSSION AND REVIEW
1. What is ethnocentrism, and why is its influence so powerful?
2. How do the basic assumptions of the ecological and functionalist approaches to human cultures differ?
3. What are some practices in other cultures that you would find odd or disgusting, and how would sociologists explain them?

CHAPTER REVIEW

1. *What is culture?* It is a design for living. It consists of material culture, which includes all the things produced by members of a society, and nonmaterial culture, which comprises knowledge, beliefs, norms, values, and symbols.

2. *What are norms and values?* Norms are social rules dictating how to behave. There are two types: folkways, which simply expect us to behave properly, and mores, which practically force us to behave morally. Both are derived from values, socially shared ideas about what is good, desirable, or important.

3. *How does human communication differ from animal communication?* Animal communication is largely governed by instincts. It is also a closed system, tied to the immediate present, enabling animals to communicate only a limited set of messages. In contrast, human communication is arbitrarily de-

termined by people. It is also an open system, where people are able to create an infinite number of messages.

4. *How do humans communicate?* Verbally and nonverbally. In nonverbal communication, we use kinesics (body movements) and proxemics (space manipulation). In verbal communication, we use words, which influence our thinking and perceptions as well as reflect our social life. Verbal communication may also involve the use of pop culture, which reflects the times in which we live.

5. *What is the relationship between evolution and culture?* Our evolution from animals to culture-using humans has caused us to lose our instincts. Consequently, we must depend on culture to survive, and through cultures we have been able to adapt to widely different environments all over the world.

6. *What should we do to understand other cultures?* We should get rid of ethnocentrism, the atti-

tude that our own culture is superior to that of others, and adopt cultural relativism, which means judging other cultures on their own terms. Cultural relativism, however, should be tempered with scientific objectivity.

7. Why do cultures vary? The ecological perspective attributes cultural variations to differences in natural environments. The functional perspective explains variations by the functions that different cultures perform.

KEY TERMS

Belief An idea that is relatively subjective, unreliable, or unverifiable (p. 32).

Cultural relativism Evaluating other cultures on their own terms, with the result of not passing judgment on them (p. 43).

Culture A complex whole consisting of objects, values, and other characteristics that people have acquired as members of society (p. 32).

Ethnocentrism The attitude that one's own culture is superior to that of others (p. 42).

Folkways "Weak" norms that specify expectations about proper behavior (p. 33).

Instincts Fixed traits that are biologically inherited and enable their carrier to perform complex tasks (p. 41).

Kinesics Use of body movements as a means of communication (p. 37).

Knowledge A collection of relatively objective ideas and facts about the physical and social worlds (p. 32).

Laws Norms that are specified formally in writing and backed by the power of the state (p. 34).

Material culture All the physical objects produced by humans as members of society (p. 32).

Mores "Strong" norms that specify normal behavior and constitute demands, not just expectations (p. 33).

Nonmaterial culture Norms, values, and all the other intangible components of culture (p. 32).

Norm A social rule that specifies how people should behave (p. 32).

Popular culture A collection of relatively unsophisticated artistic creations that appeal to the masses of a society (p. 39).

Proxemics Perception and use of space as a means of communication (p. 37).

Sanction Formal or informal rewards for conformity to norms, or punishments for violation of norms (p. 34).

Subculture A culture within a larger culture (p. 41)

Symbol A thing that stands for some other thing (p. 36).

Value A socially shared idea that something is good, desirable, or important (p. 32).

SUGGESTED READINGS

Bellah, Robert N., et al. 1986. *Habits of the Heart: Individualism and Commitment in American Life.* New York: Harper & Row. Shows how Americans are torn between a lonely quest for their own success and a desire for close relationships with others.

Etzioni, Amitai. 1993. *The Spirit of Community: Rights, Responsibilities, and the Communitarian Agenda.* New York: Crown. Showing how individualism has adversely affected American life and proposing how the society can benefit from a renewed spirit of mutuality.

Harris, Marvin. 1985. *Good to Eat: Riddles of Food and Culture.* New York: Simon & Schuster. A fun-to-read book by a leading anthropologist on why people in various cultures relish or reject such foods as cows, pigs, horses, dogs, cats, insects, and human beings.

Schor, Juliet B. 1991. *The Overworked American.* New York: Basic Books. Shows how the American work ethic is more powerful than ever, evidenced by longer working hours and less leisure time.

Weinstein, Deena. 1991. *Heavy Metal: A Cultural Sociology.* New York: Lexington. An insightful sociological study of a controversial specimen of American pop culture.

3

SOCIAL
STRUCTURE

MYTHS AND REALITIES

Myth: Beauty is only skin deep. People would not consider a person competent just because he or she is good looking.

Reality: Unfortunately, attractive persons are assumed to be more capable than unattractive ones at most tasks. Those blessed with good looks are considered to be very competent, even if they are known to have graduated from inferior colleges or to be holding low-paying jobs.

Myth: Most college students identify strongly with their role as students.

Reality: Most students are not deeply committed to their role because many other roles—as a friend, date, leader, or athlete—compete for their time.

Myth: Being primitive, hunter-gatherers must be suffering from poverty.

Reality: They enjoy so much leisure time that an anthropologist has called them the "original affluent society." They need to work only two or three hours a day because their needs are simple.

Myth: Though by no means perfect, the United States is the most egalitarian society in the world.

Reality: Hunting-gathering societies are the most egalitarian because they do not attempt to accumulate food surplus.

Myth: In the Middle East, the religions of Jews and Arabs are so different that they have hardly anything in common.

Reality: Since the Jews, who founded Judaism and Christianity, and the Arabs, who founded Islam, used to be pastoral people, we can find in each religion the image of a god who looks after his people, in the same way that a shepherd looks after his flock.

Myth: In view of their nation's success as an economic giant in the world, Japanese citizens understandably enjoy a very high standard of living.

Reality: In terms of purchasing power, the average Japanese earns only three-quarters of what the average American earns. In fact, the Japanese standard of living is far below that of not only Americans but also French and Italians, primarily because nearly everything costs much more in Japan.

Myth: Competition always brings out the best in us because it makes us work harder to achieve our goals.

Reality: Competition may stimulate a nation's economic growth or motivate certain professionals, such as athletes, politicians, and lawyers to succeed, but most experimental studies on schoolchildren show that cooperation promotes higher achievement than does competition.

Myth: We can get more help from our close friends than from mere acquaintances when we are looking for a job.

Reality: Acquaintances are more effective in helping us find a job because our network of acquaintances is larger, exposing us to more employment opportunities.

Several years ago Lois Duncan (1991) and her husband got a call at midnight from the police. They were told that their daughter Kaitlyn, age 18, had been seriously hurt in a "random shooting." When they arrived at the emergency room, they found Kaitlyn in a coma. She never regained consciousness, and she died the next evening. Today Lois Duncan has few memories of the 24 hours during which her daughter's life was fading away, but she does remember that she and her husband were not alone. One friend came to them with a sack of quarters so they could make calls from the pay phone. Others went to the airport to meet the Duncans' out-of-town children and brought them to the hospital. A neighbor took care of their dog and cat. Duncan also clearly remembers what her friends and neighbors did for her during the first few weeks after her daughter's death, such as buying groceries, cashing checks, and returning library books. She is now grateful that all those little things have helped her and her husband work through their grief. Obviously, the people they know have cared enough to help them bear the unbearable.

We can clearly see the importance of human relationships in those simple gestures of friendship that bring comfort to Duncan and her husband. Relationships of one type or another embrace us all. As John Donne wrote nearly four centuries ago, "No man is an island, entire of itself; every man is a piece of the continent, a part of the main." True enough. We are always involved with people in some way. We do something to them, we do certain things with them, and we react to what they do. Even when we are alone, we become involved with them by thinking of them. Without human relationships, we could hardly survive. As infants, we would have died without them. As children, we learned to grow into adults through relationships with others. As adults, we are constantly sustained by social relationships.

Almost like the air we breathe, social relationships are essential to us. And like breathing, these relationships follow recurring patterns, which sociologists call **social structures.** Listen to a parent and child and you are likely to hear some echoes of your own childhood. Walk into your old grade school and you might feel you have taken a trip in a time machine. In friendships and business dealings, in schools, offices, and homes, we find recurring patterns of relationships that constitute social structures. The most common social structure is a *group,* two or more people who interact with one another and share some sense of a common identity. A group

may be a clique of friends, a baseball team, a business firm, or a political party. Often groups such as the last three are formed to achieve specific goals, in which case they are called *organizations.* Organizations are supported by **social institutions,** which are stable sets of widely shared beliefs, norms, roles, and procedures that are organized to satisfy certain basic needs of society. Both education and the family, for example, are social institutions. Even beyond these structures, however, we find patterns of stable relationships: groups and institutions form parts of a large social structure called **society,** which is a collection of interacting individuals sharing the same culture and territory. Societies, in turn, make up an even larger structure—an international community.

We will discuss groups, organizations, and institutions in other chapters. Here, we examine societies, along with the dynamic and static aspects of social structure. The dynamic part is **social interaction,** the process by which individuals act toward and react to one another. Social interaction runs through all social structures; it is their lifeblood, making them come alive. In an educational institution, when you ask your instructors questions, they will respond with answers. In a family, when the mother smiles at her son, he will react by smiling back. In a business organization, employees may work hard and their boss may respond by giving them a raise. In the international community, if France imposes heavy taxes on certain imports from the United States, the United States will likely reciprocate doing the same to imports from France. Each of these is an example of social interaction, and each always takes place within a context. This context involves people who have a certain relationship with one another, perhaps characterized by mutual like or dislike or by one liking the other without being liked in return. In a loving family, we can see parents and children being connected by affection. In the relationship between two countries, we often observe mutual distrust. However individuals or groups are tied to one another, the web of their relationships makes up the static, fixed aspect of social structure called a **social network.**

Societies

As large-scale social structures, societies are highly complex. They have so many diverse characteristics—including their cultures, religions, politics, economies, families, schools, and so on—that we may despair of trying to make sense of what they are like. Nevertheless, sociologists have long been aware of certain patterns in the way societies operate. First, all societies can carry on in the face of differences and conflicts among their members because they have developed the foundations of social structure called statuses and roles. And, second, people in different societies have their own ways of making a living and relating to one another. Let us take a closer look at statuses and roles as well as at various types of societies.

STATUSES AND ROLES

Social relations follow certain patterns. To a large degree these patterns derive from statuses and roles. As Peter Blau (1977) puts it, "people's positions and corresponding roles influence their social relations." **Statuses** are the positions people occupy in a group or society. **Roles** are expectations of what individuals should do in accordance with their statuses. Thanks to statuses and roles, we usually have some idea of what to expect of other people, and of what other people expect of us. They bring a measure of predictability to our interactions, but statuses and roles also carry the seeds of conflict.

Statuses When you interact with a friend, you are likely to be relaxed, informal, uninhibited. But when you talk with a professor, you are more likely to be a bit stiff, to act in a formal, inhibited way. Being a friend is one status; being a student or professor is another. A status is therefore a definition, an identification, of a person in terms of his or her relationship with another person or group.

In a complex society such as the United States, we have so many statuses that it is impossible to name them all. We are born with some of them. We are born male or female; we are born into some racial group. These statuses of gender and race as well as age are called **ascribed statuses.** They are given to us independently of what we do. All other statuses result from our actions. We earn them in some way. You must do something to be a student or a college graduate or a married person or any one of countless other things. These are called **achieved statuses.** In modern societies such as the United States, achieved statuses have grown in influence at the expense of ascribed statuses. In place of a king or queen who holds the position through inheritance, for example, we have a president who must win the office.

Statuses are sometimes ranked within a social structure; that is, one is considered higher than the other. According to public opinion polls, for example, Americans rank the position of doctor higher

Ascribed statuses are given to us independently of what we do. Achieved statuses result from our actions. President Clinton's status as the highest elected official of the United States is achieved. Similarly, although Hillary Rodham Clinton's traditional title of First Lady is ascribed, her status as a lawyer breaking new ground in assisting the president in his duties is achieved.

than that of plumber. In a family, the father's status is higher than the son's. In contrast to these *vertical* social structures are *horizontal* structures. In these, the various statuses are merely different from each other, not higher or lower. A student's status as a sociology major, for example, is different from but essentially equal to another student's status as a history major.

Despite our many statuses, we are usually influenced by only one status at a time when we relate to another person. When a woman interacts with her husband at home, she will behave primarily as a wife, not as a banker, employer, PTA leader, or athlete. Because the status of wife dominates her relationship with her husband, it is called the **master status** in this interaction. All of her other statuses—as a banker, employer, and so on—are less relevant to the interaction; hence, they are called **subordinate statuses.**

The nature of a society may determine which status becomes the master status. In a racist society such as South Africa, race is the master status and all others are subordinate to it. A white person interacting with a black physician would therefore use race as the master status and profession as the subordinate status. As a result, the white person would not be likely to treat the black physician with the respect usually given doctors.

In our society the master statuses of race and gender also influence the way others treat us. Research has shown that blacks in interracial groups and women in mixed company, when compared with their white and male colleagues, are often given fewer opportunities to interact, are less likely to have their contributions accepted, and usually have less influence over group decisions. This "interaction disability," as imposed by the master statuses of race and gender, is difficult to overcome unless the minorities appear highly cooperative and agreeable to the majority (Ridgeway, 1982). The influence of race and gender also appears in many other areas of social life (see Chapter 8: Racial and Ethnic Minorities, and Chapter 9: Gender and Age).

Physical appearance can also function as a master status. Murray Webster and James Driskell (1983) found that, like race and gender, beauty has a profound impact on how individuals are perceived and treated by others. Webster and Driskell discovered, among other things, that attractive persons are expected by college students to be more capable than unattractive ones at most tasks—even piloting a plane—and that good-looking individuals are considered to be very competent, even if they are known to

have graduated from an inferior college and to be holding low-paying jobs. Similar findings are duplicated in many earlier studies: attractive schoolchildren are expected by their teachers to be smarter than unattractive ones; attractive adults are perceived by many as more likable, friendly, sensitive, and confident (Clifford and Walster, 1973; Landy and Sigall, 1974; Miller, 1970; Horai, Naccari, and Fatoullan, 1974; Dabbs and Stokes, 1975).

Roles   For every status, there are rights and obligations. Children enjoy the right of receiving food, shelter, and love from their parents, but they are expected to show respect, obedience, gratitude, and affection to their parents in return. In other words, every status carries with it a role. Because of your status as a student, you act in certain ways that are part of the student role. Thus, status and role seem like two sides of the same coin. But they are distinguishable. A status is basically static, like a label put on a bottle. A role is dynamic, shaped by specific situations and persons.

Consider the role of nurse. In an emergency, nurses must be cool and professional, but they are also expected to convey warmth and concern to their patients. With doctors, nurses are expected to be obedient; with patients' relatives, they may be authoritative. The behaviors demanded by the role change with the situation.

In addition, various people play the same role differently, just as various actors perform the same role on the stage in diverse ways, even though they are working from the same script. The script—the set of expectations or norms about how a person should behave—is the **prescribed role.** How a person actually carries out the role is the **role performance.** The prescribed role of a college student calls for attending classes, reading, thinking, and learning, but students differ in how and to what extent they fulfill these expectations. They may understand the prescribed role differently. They may be more or less successful in fulfilling those expectations. They may simply differ in their manner of carrying out the role. Thus, some students may expect to get straight A's while others would settle for C's and B's. The ambitious ones would study harder. Whether ambitious or not, some would end up getting better grades than others. No matter how each individual defines and performs the student role, however, commitment to it is not necessarily total. In fact, as Donald Reitzes (1981) found, only 35 percent of the college students he studied identified strongly with their role. In Re-

The prescribed role of a student calls for attending classes, reading, thinking, and learning. But the role performance of students varies, depending, for example, on how they understand the prescribed role or how they attempt to carry it out.

itzes' view, most students are not deeply committed to their role because it is "structured for limited or short-term occupancy." A more important reason may be that there are many other roles—such as being a friend, date, leader, and athlete—competing for a student's time.

Indeed, all of us play many roles every day, and some of these roles are bound to impose conflicting demands. The role of judge prescribes an emotionless, objective attitude; the role of father requires emotional involvement. Usually, the conflicting demands of these roles present no particular problem because a person plays one role at a time. But if a judge found his or her daughter in court as the defendant, there would be a conflict. Similarly, if you are a student athlete, you will find yourself in conflict when your professor gives an exam on the day your coach wants you to play a game away from your school. When we are expected to play two conflicting roles at the same time, we experience **role conflict.** Even a single role may involve conflicting expectations and thus produce what is called a **role strain.** Supervisors are expected to be friendly with their workers, to be one of them. But they are also

expected to be part of management and to enforce its rules. Professors, too, are torn between the expectation to teach classes and the expectation to do research. Role conflict or strain is usually stressful, causing anxiety and other psychological aches and pains (Coverman, 1989; Voydanoff and Donnelly, 1989).

In the final analysis, statuses and roles are the foundation of social structure; they shape the pattern of relationships among particular individuals. Thus, members of a group (say, a family) can be expected to interact differently from those of another group (say, the opposing teams of a football game). One type of social interaction may be characterized by exchange and cooperation, whereas the other may be marked by competition and conflict. These patterns of relationships, however, vary from one society to

Role conflict results when we must reconcile opposing claims. A growing number of women find themselves caught between the traditional role of a mother and the modern role of a career woman.

another. Among preindustrial societies, there is more cooperation among hunter-gatherers and more conflict among pastoralists and horticulturalists. But there is still more conflict in industrial than preindustrial societies. Let us explore these various types of societies further.

PREINDUSTRIAL SOCIETIES

Most societies throughout history have been preindustrial. They range from tribes that lived thousands of years before the Roman Empire to the !Kung[1] people, who live today in the Kalahari Desert of southern Africa. These preindustrial societies differ from one another in how they obtain their food. They can therefore be classified into four types: (1) **hunting-gathering societies,** which hunt animals and gather plants to survive; (2) **pastoral societies,** which domesticate and herd animals for food; (3) **horticultural societies,** which depend on growing plants in small gardens to survive; and (4) **agricultural societies,** which produce food by relying on plows and draft animals.

Hunting-Gathering Societies   Throughout 99 percent of humankind's presence on earth, or until about 10,000 years ago, all societies survived by hunt-

ing wild animals, fishing, and gathering wild roots, fruits, birds' eggs, wild bees' honey, and the like. Today, less than 0.1 percent of the world's people live this way. Among the few remaining hunting-gathering societies are the !Kung of South Africa, the Batek Negritos of Malaysia, and the Alyawara of central Australia.

Hunter-gatherers move about a great deal in search of food, but they cover only a small area. Because their food sources are thus very limited, hunting-gathering societies are very small, each having only 20 to 50 people. There is a division of labor based on gender: men usually do the hunting; women do the gathering. Contrary to popular belief, though, hunter-gatherers do not live in isolation, eating only wild foods. For thousands of years, they have also practiced some herding and farming or have traded with herders and farmers (Headland and Reid, 1989).

Their lives are not necessarily hard. In fact, because their needs are simple, they might work merely two or three hours a day. It has been estimated that a family could easily collect enough wild cereal grain in three weeks to feed itself for a year. Sometimes the food must be processed, as in the case of some nuts that require roasting and cracking. Hence, hunter-gatherers may spend more time feeding themselves than finding the foods (Hawkes and O'Connell, 1981). Nevertheless, they still have so much leisure time that Marshall Sahlins (1972) has called them the "original affluent societies."

[1] The ! represents a click, a speech sound not used in English.

Hunter-gatherers move about in search of food. Limited food sources limits the size of the population in these societies, and division of labor is largely based on gender. Here a San woman of Africa, with children, dips for water from a tree.

Even so, most hunter-gatherers do not attempt to accumulate food surpluses. They do not even store food for emergencies, and they tend to share their food with one another. Sharing, in fact, is a central norm and value in these societies. The more successful hunters are denied the opportunity to build prestige and wealth with their skills. They are expected to be self-deprecating about their hunting success, and boasting is met with scorn. Because no one hoards, no one acquires great wealth. And because they have few possessions to fight about, hunter-gatherers are unlikely to engage in warfare. If a strong and skilled hunter tries to dominate others, order them about, or take their wives, he can be secretly killed, because there is no effective means of protection (like the police in other societies) and also because everyone has easy access to poisoned arrows, spears, or other hunting weapons. As a result, hunting-gathering societies are generally the most egalitarian in the world. When anthropologist Richard Lee (1979) asked a !Kung hunter-gatherer whether the !Kung have headmen, the man replied, "Of course, we have headmen. . . . In fact, we are all headmen; each one of us is a headman over himself!" This egalitarian trait of a hunting-gathering society is reflected in their religion: they believe in many gods (gods of rain, sunshine, rabbits, sickness, and so on) and consider these gods equal to one another.

Not all of the hunting-gathering societies are egalitarian, though. According to James Woodburn (1982), they fall into two categories: one with "immediate-return systems" and the other with "delayed-return systems." In the first type, people go out hunting or gathering and eat the food on the same day it is obtained; they do not store it for later use. In the delayed-return system, food is elaborately processed and stored. Woodburn found that the !Kung and other hunting-gathering societies with immediate-return systems are profoundly egalitarian for reasons like those discussed already. On the other hand, those with delayed-return systems, such as the aborigines of Australia, are marked by inequality because stored food can be turned into durable and exchangeable goods—hence leading to accumulation of wealth and power. Both systems, however, are patriarchal. Men exclude women from hunting activities. They even impose strict and extensive menstrual taboos on women, prohibiting them, when they are having their period, from touching any man and from handling such "male" things as bows, arrows, and fishing gear. They believe that menstruating women are dangerous to men, that the women may cause sickness,

injury, or loss of magical power in the man they touch (Kitahara, 1982).

Pastoral Societies In deserts, mountains, and grasslands, plants are difficult to cultivate, but animals can easily be domesticated for use as a food source. About 10,000 years ago, some hunter-gatherers began to specialize in the domestication of animals. Today there are a number of pastoral societies, mostly in North and East Africa, the Middle East, and Mongolia. The Africans specialize in keeping cattle; the Arabs, camels and horses; and the Mongols, various combinations of horses, cattle, camels, goats, and sheep. These peoples are different racially and far apart geographically, yet they show a considerable degree of cultural uniformity.

Unlike hunter-gatherers, pastoralists accumulate a surplus of food. One result is that pastoral societies can be far larger than hunting-gathering bands. Another result is the emergence of marked social inequality, based on the size of an individual's herd and the number of a man's wives. Some anthropologists argue that animal holdings represent an unstable form of wealth because, as a herder puts it, "Owning animals is like the wind. Sometimes it comes and sometimes it doesn't." When a disaster such as an epidemic or a severe drought strikes, the wealthy herders are assumed to suffer such great losses that social inequality cannot be maintained. But in his study of the Komachi pastoralists in south-central Iran, sociologist Daniel Bradburd (1982) found that disasters cannot wipe out inequalities in animal wealth. "While disasters befall rich and poor alike, they do not befall each with quite the same effect," Bradburd explains. "A poor man who loses half his herd frequently finds it reduced to a size from which recovery is impossible; on the other hand, a wealthy man who loses half his herd will frequently be left with enough animals to rebuild the herd without great difficulty."

Usually, pastoral peoples are constantly on the move, looking for fresh grazing grounds for their herds. Consequently, they become fiercely independent and inclined to scorn land boundaries. They also become rather warlike, and some use horses to enhance their war-making capabilities. They are just as likely to raid settled villages as they are to attack each other. The aim of such aggression is to increase their livestock as well as to warn others against encroachment. Sometimes they take captives and use them as slaves. Their religion and attitude reflect the pastoral way of life. The Hebrews who founded Judaism and

In pastoral societies, animals are domesticated for use as a major source of food. Since pastoralists can accumulate a surplus of food, social inequality develops in their societies. Because they are on the move in search of fresh grazing grounds for their herds, pastoralists have also become fiercely independent and tend to disregard land boundaries.

Christianity and the Arabs who founded Islam used to be pastoral people, and in each religion we can find the image of a god who looks after people in the same way that a shepherd looks after the flock. The Mongols have a religious taboo against farming, believing that plowing and planting offend the earth spirit. The African cattle herders, very proud of their pastoralism, regard horticulture as degrading toil. The non-Islamic tribes of the Hindu Kush mountains, on the borders of Afghanistan and Pakistan, treat their goats as sacred animals, which are capable of appeasing the gods and mountain spirits (Parkes, 1987).

Horticultural Societies   While some hunter-gatherers became pastoralists, others became horticulturalists, growing plants in small gardens. Horticulturalists do their gardening by hand, with hoes and digging sticks. Because their soil cannot support continuous intensive farming, many horticulturalists rely on slash-and-burn cultivation. They clear an area in the jungle by slashing undergrowth and cutting trees, allowing them to dry, and then burning them off, leaving ashes that help fertilize the soil. This procedure also ensures that the plot will be free of weeds. After two or three years of growing crops, the soil becomes exhausted, so new fields are slashed and burned.

Unlike pastoralists, horticulturalists live in permanent settlements. Like that of pastoralists, their society is marked by a sexual division of labor: men clear the forest, and women do the cultivation. Because horticulturalists can produce a food surplus, their societies are usually larger than those of hunter-gatherers. The existence of a surplus also gives rise to inequality in many horticultural societies, where the men can enjoy great prestige by possessing many gardens, houses, and wives.

Warfare, too, becomes common. Many tribes in a forest often raid each other, torturing, killing, or occasionally eating their captives. Victorious warriors receive great honors. They preserve and display their defeated enemies' skulls and shrunken heads, much as athletes today show off their trophies. In advanced horticultural societies, warriors hold power as well as prestige. These societies are usually divided into a small, powerful warrior nobility and a large mass of powerless common people. This social inequality is reflected in religion. Horticultural societies generally believe in capricious gods who must be worshipped. And they perform religious rituals to appease not only the gods but also the spirits of their dead ancestors, perhaps because they live in permanent settlements where the living remain close to their dead. Today, there are still some horticulturalists in the tropical forests of Africa, Asia, Australia, and South America.

Agricultural Societies   About 5,000 years ago, the invention of the plow touched off the agricultural revolution that radically transformed life in the Middle East and eventually throughout the world. When a field is plowed, weeds are killed and buried efficiently, fertilizing the soil. At the same time, nutrients that have sunk too deep for the plants' roots to reach are brought closer to the surface. Thus, the coming of the plow allowed peasants to obtain crop yields many times larger than the horticulturalists obtain with their hoes. If farmers use animals to pull their plows, then their productivity is increased further. As a result, farmers, unlike horticulturalists, can cultivate a piece of land continuously and intensively.

The giant leap forward in food production enables large populations to emerge in agricultural societies. Because each farmer can produce more than enough food for one person, some people are able to give up farming and pursue other occupations. They become tailors, shoemakers, tanners, and weavers. These people help cities emerge for the first time.

The towns, cities, and farms in an agricultural society come under the control of a central government. It is usually headed by a monarch with the power to enslave or even exterminate large numbers of people. This centralization of political control, coupled with the possession of valuable property, provides a strong stimulus for warfare. The common people who fight for their monarch tend to believe that the monarch has divine power. They also believe in a family of gods in which one is the high god and the others are lesser gods. This hierarchy of gods seems to mirror the peasants' experience with various levels of government officials, from the tax collector at the bottom to the monarch at the top.

Agricultural societies are the most complex of all preindustrial societies. They still predominate today in Africa, Asia, and South America. But since the Industrial Revolution in England 200 years ago, many preindustrial societies have become industrialized and use machinery to till their lands. These industrial societies differ sharply from preindustrial ones.

INDUSTRIAL SOCIETIES

The Industrial Revolution brought many changes in its wake. When a nation industrializes, it supplements human and animal power with machines. With industrialization, cities grow; new occupations are created; social structures and cultures change too. Old ways of life are disrupted.

We may find it easy to understand industrial societies by comparing them with preindustrial societies. This could be the reason why sociologists have

long tried to find the basic differences between those two types of societies. As early as 1887, German sociologist Ferdinand Tönnies described the preindustrial society as a **Gemeinschaft,** or "community," meaning that people in such a society have a strong sense of community and relate to each other in a personal way. In contrast, he described industrial society as a **Gesellschaft,** or "society." In such a society, people think of themselves as individuals first and relate to each other in an impersonal way, on the basis of their social roles, therefore becoming alienated from one another. Then in 1893 Durkheim used the term "mechanical solidarity" to describe the cohesion underlying preindustrial societies and "organic solidarity" to characterize industrial societies. As we saw in Chapter 1 (The Essence of Sociology), mechanical solidarity is social unity that comes about because people perform the same tasks and have similar values. In contrast, organic solidarity arises when people are forced to depend on one another because their jobs are very specialized. More recently, in 1941, American anthropologist Robert Redfield said that preindus-

An industrial society differs in many ways from a preindustrial society. As suggested by this modern factory setting, industrial society, for example, creates an elaborate division of labor, and social life changes from one in which individuals have strong and enduring emotional ties to one another, to one in which individuals may know each other only from coming together in the work place.

trial societies are small, nonliterate, and homogeneous societies in which group solidarity is strong; he called them **folk societies.** On the other hand, he described industrial societies as large, literate, and heterogeneous, with very little group solidarity; he called them **urban societies.**

Today various sociologists have used still other terms to describe these two types of societies. James Coleman (1982), for example, describes modern industrial societies as *asymmetric,* characterized by the dominance of "corporate actors" (the state, business, labor, and other big organizations) over "natural persons" (the individuals). He contrasts these modern societies with traditional agricultural societies, where person-to-person relations predominate. We can summarize the differences between these two types of societies in reference to four contrasting sets of traits.

1. *Simplicity versus complexity.* The social structure of preindustrial societies is relatively simple. There is very little division of labor, and it is usually based only on age and gender. There tends to be only one clearly defined institution, the family. It is the center of educational, occupational, and religious activities. Technology, too, is simple. The society supports itself by a simple food-getting technique that involves human and animal power.

The social structure of industrial societies is more complex. There is an elaborate division of labor, with thousands of different jobs. There are many social institutions, each more complex than the family. They perform many of the functions of the preindustrial family, as well as new functions. Technology, too, is complex.

2. *Homogeneity versus heterogeneity.* The populations of preindustrial societies are relatively small and homogeneous. Cultural values are so widely shared that social tranquility generally prevails. In contrast, the populations of industrial societies are larger and more heterogeneous. They include numerous diverse groups that cling to their own subcultures and find themselves in conflict with each other.

3. *Intimacy versus impersonality.* Social life in preindustrial societies occurs mostly in **primary groups** such as the family. These are small groups in which individuals have strong emotional ties to one another—ties that are intimate and enduring. From these personal relationships comes informal social control, which reinforces social order.

In industrial societies, more social life occurs in **secondary groups,** which consist of people who do not know each other well and who relate to each other in a superficial way. Their relationship is temporary and impersonal. With the growing predominance of impersonal encounters, individuals are more likely to exploit each other, and informal social controls are likely to weaken. Thus, formal social control in the form of laws is instituted.

4. *Traditionalism versus modernism.* Preindustrial societies are to a large degree tied to their past and uninterested in social change. They value social stability and emphasize the group's needs rather than the individual's interests. In contrast, industrial societies are more likely to look to the future and to be enthusiastic about social change. They believe in social progress and tend to support the individual's interests above the group's needs.

The four characteristics of each type of society are related. Together they reflect the core nature of each society. Simplicity in social structure, homogeneity in people and values, intimacy in social relationships, and traditionalism in outlook reflect the tendency of preindustrial societies toward *social order.* Complexity in social structure, heterogeneity in people and values, impersonality in social relationships, and modernism in outlook reflect the tendency of industrial societies toward *social conflict.*

It is important not to exaggerate the differences between industrial and preindustrial societies, which exist only in degree rather than in kind. Many industrial societies, such as the United States and Japan, are not totally industrial—that is, not categorically different from preindustrial societies—because they have some of the characteristics of preindustrial societies. They are considered industrial only because their industrial features seem more prominent than their preindustrial traits. Nor should we exaggerate the similarities among industrial societies. Japan is just as highly industrialized as the United States, but Japan retains to a greater extent the characteristics of a preindustrial society. Let us take a closer look at these characteristics, which may explain Japan's economic ascendancy.

JAPANESE SOCIETY

First, Japan has a relatively homogeneous population. Among the world's industrial societies, the United States is the most heterogeneous, and Japan is the most homogeneous. So, whereas the United States is made up of numerous racial and ethnic groups, Japan has long remained a homogeneous society. It does have some minorities, such as the Burakumin, Ainu, Koreans, and Okinawans, but these groups make up less than 1 percent of the nation's entire population. Consequently, the society is overwhelmingly Japanese. This is why Japanese culture is far more uniform than that of any other industrial society. Everywhere in Japan, schools teach the same subjects during the same weeks every year. Even most of the swimming pools open and close for summer use on the same date throughout the country, regardless of whether they are on the subarctic island to the north or on the nearly subtropical island to the south. Because practically everyone shares the same values, it is easy for Japan to be managed as a nation. To some extent, the Japanese resemble the Mormons in Utah; they have about the same orthodox family patterns, the same virtues of work and thrift, and the same emphasis on social harmony. Just as relatively homogeneous Utah is easier to govern than California or New York, Japan is easier to manage than the United States. For the same reason, Japanese companies are easier to manage than American companies (Fallows, 1990).

Second, the influence of primary groups pervades Japanese society. Because they share the same values and interests, the Japanese find it more natural to develop strong social relationships than Americans do. This has a significant impact on Japanese business practices. In the United States, impersonal contacts and professional obligations tend to take precedence over friendship and sometimes even family ties. But in Japan, personal ties and family relationships are far more important. Thus, most Japanese spend an enormous amount of time and energy building and nurturing intensely personal relationships. "The long hours of the Japanese businessman are legendary," Clyde Prestowitz (1989) observes. "Many of those hours are spent not working but socializing with fellow employees or members of some other group. This activity is an important part of maintaining the close personal ties that provide the group's spiritual sustenance in the same way family ties do." Businesspeople or employees refer to their company figuratively as *uchi*—"my house"—which reflects the Japanese view of the company as a family. Actually, the tie to the company is stronger, as the Japanese often spend time with colleagues or business associates after office hours—sometimes until eleven o'clock at night. They see their families only between eleven at night and seven in the morning (Wolferen, 1990).

Third, Japan is more traditional than any other industrial society. While Americans value the individual's rights and interests, the Japanese emphasize the importance of the group's needs for social harmony and stability. Thus, the Japanese identify strongly with their schools, clubs, companies, and, ultimately, their nation. If asked what kind of work they do, they will not say "plumber," "sales representative," or whatever; they will mention only the name of the company that employs them. The Japanese work hard for their companies, and their companies in turn give them lifetime employment. Labor and management have a harmonious relationship, cooperating to ensure the success of their company. Government-industry relations are also mutually supportive. When the U.S. dollar began to fall in 1985, the Japanese government immediately offered low-interest loans to companies affected by the strong yen. If an industry falls on hard times, the government will offer help. Generally, the government supports various industries with a panoply of market-protection measures against foreign imports, coupled with financial incentives such as tax credits, low-interest loans, and reserves for export losses, retirement, and price fluctuations. In return, corporations contribute heavily to politicians' election campaigns, and some business leaders become high government officials. Ultimately, all the individuals and groups cooperate like members of a big family to turn Japan into an economic superpower.

The economic triumph, however, exacts a price from average Japanese. Japan may be a rich nation, but its people are poor. Owing to the yen's soaring value, Japan's per-capita income is now much higher than that of the United States. But when adjusted for local purchasing power, the average Japanese earns only three-quarters of what the average American earns. The Japanese standard of living is far below that of the American, German, and British (see Table 3.1). Japan's houses are small, cramped, and expensive; the average home is about one-third smaller than that in the United States and about twice the price. Compared with any other major industrial society, Japan has the worst roads, sewers, and parks. Nearly everything costs much more in Japan than in other industrialized countries. The Japanese pay up to three times more for their beef, rice, oranges, many alcoholic beverages, and imported goods from cars to tennis balls. Much of these exorbitant prices results from Japan's restriction on imports of inexpensive foreign foods and products. Nevertheless, most Japanese consumers do not complain. In fact, they are very supportive of their government's and corporations'

TABLE 3.1 *How Japan Compares with Others*

JAPAN IS AHEAD IN NATIONAL ECONOMIC POWER:

	AVERAGE GNP* PER PERSON
Japan	$27,300
Germany	$24,700
United States	$22,200
France	$21,300
Britain	$17,600

BUT THE JAPANESE INDIVIDUAL'S WELFARE FALLS BEHIND:

AMOUNT OF HOUSING SPACE PER PERSON, IN SQUARE METERS		AVERAGE WORKING HOURS PER YEAR	
United States	61.8	Germany	1,590
Germany	37.2	France	1,680
Britain	35.2	United States	1,940
France	30.7	Britain	1,950
Japan	25.0	Japan	2,210

*Gross National Product
Source: Japanese and German Government Reports, 1992.

protecting their market against low-priced imports from foreign countries. The Japanese are apparently more interested in ensuring the economic success of their nation than in buying for themselves many things at bargain prices (Prestowitz, 1989; Fallows, 1990). In short, the group takes precedence over the individual.

ARE WE PRISONERS OF SOCIETY?

Through its food-getting technology, institutions, formal organizations, social groups, statuses, and roles, society affects the individual. In fact, some sociologists paint a picture of society in which the individual is its prisoner. Other sociologists believe that the individual exercises a great deal of freedom in his or her daily activities. These two views reflect two of the four theoretical perspectives discussed in Chapter 1—functionalism and symbolic interactionism.

The Functionalist View The central idea of functionalism is that the various parts of society serve the function of contributing to social order. One of these functions is to ensure social order by controlling the individual members of society. Political institutions control us through laws, police, courts, and prisons. Less explicitly, the people we go to school with, work with, or meet in public places control us by

Although Japan may be a rich nation, the Japanese standard of living is far below that of the American. The Japanese home, as shown here where a mother and daughters set the table for a traditional meal of sushi, is small and cramped, and the average Japanese house is about twice the price of one in the United States.

being ready to embarrass, ridicule, scold, or hurt us if we do not behave properly. Families and friends control us by threatening to withdraw their love, affection, or friendship if we fail to meet their expectations. All these social pressures push us to conform, to give up our individual freedom. They do not only prevent us from misbehaving, though. They also "systematically constrain our choices to form and maintain relationships" (Feld, 1982). In making friends, for example, we usually associate with people like ourselves. This is because a college, a workplace, or any other social structure typically brings together a homogeneous set of people—with a particular characteristic, such as being relatively young, having a college education, or adhering to the same religion. It appears that we are not as free as we like to think in choosing our friends—or in choosing how to live our lives.

Moreover, we lose our freedom by agreeing and cooperating with the forces that constrain us. We often share in the task of jailer by joining social groups of our own accord because we want to be accepted by others. We even willingly obey the law because we feel like doing so. As functionalists would put it, society ensures order through social consensus—through our willingness to cooperate with the forces that imprison us. As Peter Berger (1963) said, our "imprisonment in society" is carried out largely "from within ourselves":

> Our bondage to society is not so much established by conquest as by collusion. Sometimes, indeed, we are crushed into submission. Much more frequently we are entrapped by our own social nature. The walls of our imprisonment were there before we appeared on the scene, but they are ever rebuilt by ourselves. We are betrayed into captivity with our own cooperation.

There is certainly truth in the functionalist picture. In fact, in much of this text we will be seeing many more of the ways that society confines individuals with their collusion. But the functionalist view may exaggerate the extent to which we are imprisoned. As a macroanalysis (analysis of whole groups or societies), it may focus so much on the forest that it misses the trees. By stressing the social order and the forces that exist before and beyond individuals, it misses the details of everyday life in which we can experience freedom. It is these details that the symbolic interactionist view—a microanalysis—highlights.

The Symbolic Interactionist View   The key idea of symbolic interactionism is that human beings interact with each other—not by passively and rigidly following the rules imposed by society but by actively and creatively interpreting each other's actions. In these interactions we exercise considerable freedom.

Erving Goffman (1959) has provided many analyses and descriptions of interactions that demonstrate how people freely manipulate interactions, influencing each other's interpretations. According to Goffman, we are like actors performing on a stage for an audience. More precisely, we always engage in what Goffman calls **impression management**—presenting our "self" in such a way as to make the other person form the desired impression of us. In other words, we try to make a good impression by presenting ourselves in the most favorable light. When out with a new date, we try to act as charming as possible. When interviewed for a job, we try to appear as bright as possible. Sometimes, in order to ensure a peaceful and orderly interaction, we try to be friendly or respectful to obnoxious individuals. This is our "on-stage" performance. Backstage—after the date or

job interview or workday—we may relax and drop the act. Backstage, we may criticize, ridicule, or curse those obnoxious people we have treated so politely.

On many occasions, we perform with one or two persons as a team. This is designed to give a third party a desired impression, such as our being knowledgeable, competent, or efficient. Thus, teachers take care not to contradict each other in front of students. Doctors who consider each other incompetent praise each other when they are with patients. Occasionally, when a president of the United States fires a troublesome cabinet member, both tell the public how they admire each other, how much they regret the parting, and how much they will miss each other.

Goffman's analysis, however, may mislead us into thinking that the only freedom we have is to deceive each other. Other symbolic interactionists have stressed a different form of freedom to "negotiate" for better social expectations and opportunities associated with certain statuses and roles. This is why bureaucracies often operate in very unbureaucratic ways, with officials of different ranks communicating informally and directly rather than formally and through channels. Even prisoners are able to negotiate the nature of their roles with their captors. Thus, many annoying formal rules of the prison are not enforced, and prisoners are allowed to exercise a lot of authority in conducting their own affairs—as long as they do not try to escape or hold the warden and guards hostage (House, 1981; Zurcher, 1983).

In sum, despite the social control imposed on us by society, we can exercise freedom in face-to-face interactions with others. We can turn a social interaction to our benefit by manipulating the other's behavior as well as our own and by negotiating for a better deal in performing our roles. All this implies that we can see personal freedom more clearly if we go beyond society to take a close look at social interaction. Let us examine the nature of social interaction further.

QUESTIONS FOR DISCUSSION AND REVIEW
1. What are statuses, and why are they the building blocks of social structure?
2. How do prescribed roles differ from role performance?
3. What types of statuses and groups differentiate preindustrial society from modern industrial society?
4. In what ways is Japanese society different from American society?

According to the functionalist view, our society forces us to wait in lines to ensure social order. Scolding and ridicule result if we do not patiently wait. But the symbolic interactionist view suggests that we can exercise freedom. If we want to move ahead in the line, we can politely ask those in front of us for a favor, offering them a credible reason why we need to move ahead.

5. Do the confinements of the many roles you play make you a "prisoner of society"?

Social Interaction

Interaction is the stuff of social behavior. Society cannot survive without it. That is why we are always engaged in social interaction whenever or wherever we meet someone. We talk, smile, laugh, frown, scowl, scream, or do some other thing to communicate with others, who, in turn, respond in some way. Of course, we do not say and do the same thing with all kinds of people or in all sorts of situations. When a young man is with his parents, he will not tell them a dirty joke that he might use to crack up his buddies. If, at a funeral, you see an attractive person who is weeping for the deceased, you will not approach her or him with a big, cheerful smile and try to make a date. We obviously behave differently with different people or under different circumstances. Given the enormous diversity of social interaction, sociologists have classified it into a few major types: exchange, cooperation, competition, and conflict. Each of these types of interaction can be found in all kinds of social structures—families, corporations, even nations. Exchange and cooperation usually stabilize the social structure. Competition and conflict are more likely to unsettle it and may lead to social change.

EXCHANGE

If you help a friend study for an exam and your friend, in turn, types a paper for you, you have engaged in an exchange. An **exchange** is a transaction between two individuals, groups, or societies in which one takes an action in order to obtain a reward in return. The reward may be material, such as a salary or a gift, or it may be nonmaterial, such as a word of praise or gratitude. We find exchanges in all types of situations. Nations trade votes at the United Nations, employees exchange their labor for a salary, friends exchange advice and gratitude, children trade toys, and so on.

Social exchanges are usually governed by the norm of reciprocity, which requires that people help those who have helped them. If a favor has been extended to a person, he or she will be motivated to return the favor. Conversely, if an individual has not been helpful to another, the latter will not be helpful to the former. Therefore, if social exchanges are fair, the social structure involved is likely to be solid. The exchange reinforces the relationships and provides each party in the exchange with some needed good. But if exchanges are seen as unfair, the social structure is likely to be shaky. A friendship in which one person constantly helps another, expecting but not getting gratitude in return, is likely to be short-lived.

There are, however, a few cases where the norm of reciprocity does not hold. In an *unequal* relationship, unfair exchanges can go on indefinitely, with the more powerful group receiving favors but not returning them. In Iran, for example, the socially advantaged urban Iranians often visit the nomadic Qashqai's encampments, where they will get food and a chance to relax from the hosts. But, as anthropologist Lois Beck (1982) found out, "the guests felt no debt, socially or economically, to their hosts; the moral expectation for repayment was absent." Such an unfair exchange simply follows the historical pattern of exploitation of rural populations by the urban dominant classes in Iran. On the other hand, in an *equal* relationship, the participants cannot be too fussy about the fairness of exchange, unless they want the relationship to be something less than friendship. If you give someone a dollar and two cents and expect to get exactly the same amount back from that person later, chances are that he or she is not your friend. Thus, in exchanges between classmates, co-workers, or business associates who are not friends, the participants give benefits with the expectation of receiving precisely comparable benefits in return. In friendships, however, members actively avoid the exactly equitable exchange because it seems too impersonal, businesslike, or unsentimental. Instead, they work out complicated exchanges of noncomparable benefits. Such an exchange would occur if you were to offer consolation to a friend who is ill and later receive $100 from that friend when you are broke (Clark, 1981).

COOPERATION

In an exchange, a task can be adequately performed by only one of the parties. In cooperation, an individual needs another person's help to do a job or to do it more effectively. **Cooperation** is an interaction in which two or more individuals work together to achieve a common goal. Within this very broad category of interactions, there are some interesting differences. Robert Nisbet (1970) has distinguished four types of cooperation.

The oldest type is *spontaneous cooperation.* When neighbors come together to help a family whose house has just burned down, that is spontaneous cooperation. Without this kind of cooperation, human societies would not have emerged.

But spontaneous cooperation is unpredictable. Over time, some forms of cooperation occur frequently enough for them to become customary in society. It was a custom in parts of the American frontier, for example, for neighbors to work together to

build a barn. This type of cooperation, *traditional cooperation,* brings added stability to the social structure.

Because modern societies such as the United States include people with diverse traditions, they are more likely to depend on a third type of cooperation, *directed cooperation.* It is based not on custom but on the directions of someone in authority. Thus, we are directed by government to abide by the law, pay taxes, and send children to school.

A fourth type of cooperation is equally useful in complex modern societies: *contractual cooperation.* It does not originate from tradition or authority but from voluntary action. Nor does it happen spontaneously; it involves, instead, some planning. In contractual cooperation, individuals freely and formally agree to cooperate in certain limited, specified ways. As we can often see, individuals freely decide whether to enter a business project, and they spell out the terms of the cooperation. Or neighbors may agree to work together on a specific community project.

COMPETITION

In **competition,** as in cooperation, two or more individuals or groups aim for the same goal. But in a competitive interaction, each tries to achieve that goal before the other does. Thus, in a competition, there can be only one winner.

Competition is not the exact opposite of cooperation, though. In fact, a competition involves some degree of cooperation because the competitors must cooperate with each other by "playing the game" according to the rules. In a boxing match, for example, the fighters must cooperate by not hitting each other on certain parts of the body—by not turning it into a free-for-all. In politics, candidates competing for the same office must cooperate by following certain rules, the major one being that all contenders, especially the losers, must accept the outcome (Boulding, 1981).

It is widely believed that competition brings out the best in us. The economic prosperity of Western capitalist nations, as opposed to the lower standard of living in communist countries, is often attributed to the high value placed on competition. Especially today, faced with serious challenges from Japan and other countries in world markets, American businesses are under great pressure to be more competitive. It is apparently true that competition can stimulate eco-

In a competition between two or more individuals or groups, each tries to achieve the same goal before the other does. But competition involves some cooperation, since competitors such as these football players must cooperate with each other by playing the game according to the rules.

nomic growth. Certain types of professionals, such as athletes, politicians, and lawyers, are well known to thrive on competition. In our everyday life, however, we usually perform less well—or more poorly—when we are trying to beat others than when we are working with them. Several scholars have reviewed over 100 studies conducted from 1924 to 1981 that dealt with competition and cooperation in classrooms. They found that in 65 of the studies, cooperation promoted higher achievement than competition. In only 8 studies did competition induce higher achievement, and 36 studies showed no statistically significant difference. Research on college students, scientists, and workers has produced further data challeng-

ing the popular belief in the benefits of competition (Kohn, 1986; Azmitia, 1988).

Competition seems to hamper achievement primarily because it is stressful. The anxiety that arises from the possibility of losing interferes with performance. Even if this anxiety can be suppressed, it is difficult to do two things at the same time: trying to do well and trying to beat others. Competition can easily distract attention from the task at hand. Consider a situation where a teacher asks his pupils a question. A little girl waves her arm wildly to attract his attention, crying, "Please! Please! Pick me!" When finally recognized, she has forgotten the answer. So she scratches her head, asking, "What was the question again?" The problem is that she has focused on beating her classmates, not on the subject matter (Kohn, 1986).

CONFLICT

In competition, the contestants try to achieve the same goal in accordance with commonly accepted rules. The most important of these rules is usually that competing parties should concentrate on winning the game, not on hurting each other. When competing parties no longer play by these rules, competition has become **conflict.** In conflict, defeating the opponent, by hook or by crook, has become the goal. To use an extreme contrast, we can see competition in sports and conflict in wars.

Conflict exists in all forms of social structure. It occurs between management and labor, whites and blacks, criminals and police, but also between friends, lovers, family members, and fellow workers. It can both harm and help a social structure. Wars between nations and violent confrontations between hostile groups clearly are harmful. Yet war may also unify members of a society. This is most likely to occur if various segments of society, such as leaders and the rank and file, agree that the enemy is a real menace to the entire country, that it warrants going to war and defending the nation, or that internal conflict, if any, can be resolved (Markides and Cohn, 1982). Thus, the Vietnam War divided the American people because many did not agree with their government that South Vietnam was worth defending, but the Second World War was a unifying force because virtually all Americans looked upon the threat of Nazi Germany and Japan in the same light. Conflict can also stimulate needed change. Consider the black-white conflict in the United States. Spearheaded by

Conflict exists in all forms of social structure. It occurs between management and labor, between races or members of the same race, and between friends, lovers, and family members. As the photo shows, it also occurs between criminals and police.

the civil rights movement in the 1960s, this conflict has led to greater equality between the races.

Whether social interaction involves exchange, cooperation, competition, or conflict, it always reflects some underlying relationship that has brought the participants together in the first place. As we can see from the previous discussion, exchange and cooperation reveal a positive, solid relationship between the interacting parties, whereas competition and conflict produce a more negative, shaky relationship. Relationships of one type or another usually converge to form a social network, with certain consequences for the lives of its members. Let us, then, find out more about social networks.

QUESTIONS FOR DISCUSSION AND REVIEW
1. What are the four forms of social interaction, and how can they stabilize or unsettle the social structure?
2. Why is conflict not always a negative form of social interaction?
3. In what forms of social interaction do Americans most widely participate?

Social Networks

To the general public, "social networks" refer mostly to small groups of friends, relatives, or co-workers. Sociologists, however, see networks as varying in size and complexity. They run the gamut from a small clique of friends to a huge community of nation-states. Also, the general public always assumes that if you belong to a network, you should expect your fellow members to be nice and helpful to you. We can get this assumption from such popular sayings as "You can get ahead through the old-boy network," "It's not *what* you know but *who* you know," and "Friends in need are friends indeed." To sociologists, however, a network does not necessarily include only members who are friendly to one another. In fact, all kinds of social relationships can be found in networks. There are networks in which individuals express their affection, admiration, deference, loathing, or hostility toward each other (Knoke and Kuklinski, 1982). Finally, the general public often talks about "networks" as if this were merely a fancy word for "groups." Indeed, the two words do appear to mean the same thing. But as sociological terms, they have different meanings. The word "group" refers to only the *people* it includes. The term "network," however, focuses on the *relationships* among the members. Let us take a closer look at how these relationships form a network and how this affects human behavior.

CHARACTERISTICS

We are all involved in numerous social networks— webs of social relationships that link individuals or groups to one another. Since birth, we have been constantly developing or expanding our social networks by forming social ties with various people who come into our lives. As soon as we were born, our parents drew us into their networks, which became our own. When we began to attend school, we started to develop social ties with children in our neighborhoods, with our schoolmates and teachers, and with children in our churches, synagogues, or other places of worship. As adults, we often get into all kinds of networks, such as those at the college we attend, the place where we work, and the social organizations we belong to. These networks, however, are quite different from the ones that we joined before we turned 17 or 18. Our current adult networks are more diffuse, more loosely organized, and made up of weaker social ties (Shrum and Cheek, 1987).

Individuals are not the only ones joining and developing social networks. Groups, organizations, and even whole nation-states also forge ties with each other. That is why there are numerous intergroup networks (such as the relationships among lawyers, judges, doctors, business executives, and other professional groups), intercommunity networks (such as the U.S. Conference of Mayors), and international networks (such as the United Nations).

To make it easier to see what networks look like, sociologists use such devices as points (technically called *nodes*) and lines (or *links*) to represent them. A point can be a person, group, or nation-state. A line can be any kind of social relationship connecting two points. The relationship can be a friendship; an exchange of visits; a business transaction; a romantic entanglement; the flow of information, resources, influence, or power; or an expression of such feelings as affection, sympathy, or hostility (Knoke and Kuklinski, 1982; Cook et al., 1983). Consider what your college network may look like. Let's make A in Figure 3.1 represent you and B, C, D, and E your friends. The lines show that all five of you are *directly* connected to one another. Your college network also comprises 12 other people, namely, F through Q. This is because four of you—A, B, C, and D—are *indirectly* tied, through E, to those individuals. Because of your (A's) friendship with E and E's friendship with F, you belong to the same network as F and all the other individuals, whom you may not know. Thus, a social network can consist of both directly and indirectly connected individuals. Because each of the numerous individuals to whom you are indirectly linked knows, directly and indirectly, numerous other people, you may ultimately belong to a network involving millions of people all over the world. This is especially true today, because easily accessible air travel has made it possible for people from many different countries to establish links with one another.

Given the massive network to which we belong, we should not be surprised to meet a total stranger in some faraway city, state, or foreign country and discover that the stranger happens to know somebody that we know. On such an occasion, that stranger and we are likely to exclaim, "What a small world!" Indeed, a series of classic experiments have demonstrated how really small our world is. In one of those studies, the wife of a divinity-school student who lived in Cambridge, Massachusetts, was selected as a "target person." Her name, address, occupation, and other facts about her were printed in a booklet. Copies of this booklet were randomly distributed to a

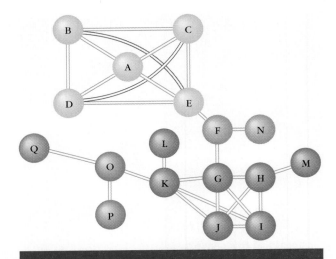

FIGURE 3.1 A Social Network
In this network, A, B, C, D, and E are directly linked to one another. This is a dense network because those five individuals know one another or often participate in the same activities. But through E's friendship with F, the other four members (A, B, C, and D) are indirectly connected to F, and all five (A, B, D, C, and E) are also indirectly linked to G, H, I, and so on. Thus the whole network of all the people shown here is less dense than the original network of five persons. Note the number of people involved in the less dense network. Would it be possible for an individual (say A) to get AIDS from a total stranger (say Q) through a series of sexual contacts within the network?

group of people in Wichita, Kansas. They were asked to send it directly to the target person only if they knew her personally. If she was a stranger to them, they were asked to send the booklet to their friends or acquaintances who they thought might know her. Interestingly, many (30 percent) of the booklets sent by strangers did finally reach the target, after passing through the hands of only about five intermediaries (Milgram, 1967; Travers and Milgram, 1969; Lin, 1982). Just as that woman in Massachusetts could receive booklets that had passed through the hands of unknown intermediaries, other people today could also get the AIDS virus indirectly from strangers. This is made possible by the huge network that connects us to millions of people all over the world. Of course, such a network is loose, lacking in "density." (A network is said to be "dense" if its members know each other well or often participate in the same activities.) But it can spread the deadly disease. How else can a loose network—or a dense one—affect our lives?

EFFECTS

A dense network usually acts as a support system for its members. It helps members maintain good physical and mental health or prevent physical and mental breakdown. It also reduces the risk of dying prematurely or of committing suicide. There are several reasons why this is the case. Our friends, relatives, and co-workers, as part of our dense network, can make us feel good by boosting our self-esteem despite our faults, weaknesses, and difficulties. Being more objective than we are about our own problems, they can open our eyes to solutions that we are too emotionally distressed to see. The companionship and camaraderie from our network, fortified by frequent participation in joint leisuretime and recreational activities, can bring us joys and pleasures while chasing away loneliness, worries, and trouble. Finally, our friends and relatives often give us "instrumental support"—money and service—to help us cope with our problems. All these social-psychological factors have a further physiological impact on our health. They keep our blood pressure and heart rate at low levels, presumably by lowering our brain's secretion of stress hormones (House et al., 1988; Pescosolido and Georgianna, 1989).

On the other hand, our intimates place many demands on our time and personal resources. They can further irritate us by criticizing us or invading our privacy. This is why in a study of the social networks of 120 widows, the women reported that more than two-thirds of the people who made their lives more difficult were their friends and relatives. In fact, these negative experiences seem to drag down people's sense of well-being more than the positive experiences of receiving social support can raise it up. Negative encounters usually have a stronger impact than positive ones, because an altercation sticks out like a sore thumb against a background of generally pleasant experiences. Thus, a pleasant exchange at a wedding that is already filled with strife between in-laws can restore only a little peacefulness, but a single heated exchange at an otherwise tranquil wedding can ruin the whole experience (Fischman, 1986).

The looser networks of mere acquaintances, however, can make our lives more pleasant. If we are unemployed, our loose network is more effective than friends and relatives in helping us find a job. Marked by weak ties among its members, a loose network is usually much larger than a dense one (see Figure 3.1). Hence, an acquaintance in that huge network is far more likely than a close friend in our tiny, dense network to know about the availability of a job (Granovetter, 1983; Lin, 1982; Bridges and Villemez, 1986). A large network, though, can also spread infectious diseases far and wide, as has been suggested.

In sum, social networks, whether they are dense or loose, can have both positive and negative consequences for people's lives.

QUESTIONS FOR DISCUSSION AND REVIEW
1. What are social networks, and what purposes do they serve?
2. How do loose social networks differ from dense social networks?
3. In what ways do social networks have positive or negative consequences for your life?

CHAPTER REVIEW

1. *What is social structure?* It is a recurrent pattern in the way people relate to each other. *What are the foundations of social structure?* Social structure is based on statuses and roles. Statuses are the social positions occupied by individuals in a group or society. Roles are the expectations of what people should do in accordance with their statuses. *How do we get our statuses?* They are either ascribed or achieved. *Are status and role equivalent?* No, although they are related. Whereas a status is a static label, a role is dynamic, varying with situations and persons. Different people may understand a prescribed role in various ways and perform the same role differently. *How can roles be a source of conflict?* Role conflict occurs when we are expected to play two conflicting roles at the same time. Role strain arises when a single role imposes conflicting demands on us.

2. *What are the two main types of societies?* Preindustrial and industrial. *How can preindustrial societies be classified?* On the basis of how they obtain food, there are four types of preindustrial soci-

eties: hunting-gathering, pastoral, horticultural, and agricultural. *How does an industrial society differ from a preindustrial one?* Whereas preindustrial society is simple, homogeneous, and intimate, industrial society is complex, heterogeneous, and impersonal. Preindustrial society is traditional; it emphasizes the past, social stability, and the interests of the group. Industrial society is modern, stressing the future, social change, and the interests of the individual. Japanese society, however, is more homogeneous, less impersonal, and more traditional than other industrial societies, which helps contribute to its economic success.

3. *Does society in effect imprison us?* Structural functionalists focus on social order and emphasize the power of its formal and informal sanctions over individuals. Symbolic interactionists concentrate on personal interactions and emphasize the extent to which individuals are free to manipulate and negotiate those interactions.

4. *In what forms can social interaction appear?* Social interaction can appear in the forms of exchange, cooperation, competition, or conflict. *How does cooperation differ from exchange?* In an exchange relationship, one of the parties can perform a task adequately, but in a cooperative relationship, an individual or group needs another's help in order to achieve a goal, or to achieve it more effectively. *How is competition like and unlike cooperation?* In both there is a common goal; but in competition, each party tries to achieve that goal before the other does. *What is the goal in a conflict relationship?* In a conflict relationship the objective is to defeat the other party, without regard to rules.

5. *How do social networks come about?* As soon as we are born, we are drawn into the network of our parents. As we grow up, we gradually develop social ties with our neighbors, schoolmates, co-workers, and many other people whom we come to know as friends or acquaintances. Because all these people have their own social ties to numerous other people, we become members of their networks as well, though we may not know most of these people. The ties that corral us into a network can be friendship, business transactions, sexual contacts, expressions of admiration or hostility, or some other kind of social relationship. *Can social networks affect our lives?* Yes. The smaller, denser networks of friends and relatives can help us maintain good health by giving us

social support. But they can also make our lives miserable by putting many demands on our time and personal resources, criticizing us, and invading our privacy. On the other hand, the larger, looser networks of mere acquaintances are more useful than the smaller, denser networks in helping us find a job. But large networks can also spread infectious diseases to numerous people.

KEY TERMS

Achieved status A status that is attained through an individual's own actions (p. 51).

Agricultural society A society that produces food by relying on plows and draft animals (p. 54).

Ascribed status A status that one has no control over, such as status based on race, gender, or age (p. 51).

Competition A relationship between two or more individuals or groups in which each strives to achieve the same goal before the other does (p. 63).

Conflict A relationship in which two individuals or groups struggle to achieve a goal by defeating each other without regard to rules (p. 64).

Cooperation A relationship in which two or more persons work together to achieve a common goal (p. 63).

Exchange A reciprocal transaction between individuals, groups, or societies (p. 62).

Folk society Redfield's term for a society that is small, nonliterate, and homogeneous, with a strong solidarity; used to distinguish preindustrial from industrial societies (p. 58).

Gemeinschaft Tönnies's term for a type of society marked by a strong sense of community and by personal interactions among its members (p. 57).

Gesellschaft Tönnies's term for a type of society characterized by individualism and by impersonal interactions (p. 57).

Horticultural society A society that depends on growing plants in small gardens for its survival (p. 54).

Hunting-gathering society A society that hunts animals and gathers plants to survive (p. 54).

Impression management The act of presenting one's "self" in such a way as to make others form the desired impression (p. 61).

Master status A status that dominates a relationship (p. 52).

Pastoral society A society that domesticates and herds animals for food (p. 54).

Prescribed role A set of expectations held by society regarding how an individual with a particular status should behave (p. 52).

Primary group A group whose members interact informally, relate to each other as whole persons, and enjoy their relationship for its own sake (p. 58).

Role A set of expectations of what individuals should do in accordance with a particular status of theirs (p. 51).

Role conflict Conflict between two roles being played simultaneously (p. 53).

Role performance Actual performance of a role (p. 52).

Role strain Stress caused by incompatible demands built into a role (p. 53).

Secondary group A group in which the individuals interact formally, relate to each other as players of particular roles, and expect to profit from each other (p. 58).

Social institution A set of widely shared beliefs, norms, or procedures necessary for meeting the needs of a society (p. 50).

Social interaction The process by which individuals act toward and react to one another (p. 50).

Social network A web of social relationships in which individuals or groups are tied to one another (p. 50).

Social structure A recurrent pattern in the ways people relate to one another (p. 50).

Society A collection of interacting individuals sharing the same culture and territory (p. 50).

Status A position in a group or society (p. 51).

Subordinate status A status that does not dominate a relationship; the opposite of master status (p. 52).

Urban society Redfield's term for societies that are large, literate, and heterogeneous, with little group solidarity (p. 58).

SUGGESTED READINGS

Bellah, Robert N., et al. 1991. *The Good Society.* New York: Alfred A. Knopf. Shows how American social structure is in danger of crumbling from individual citizens' neglect of its institutions (families, schools, corporations, government, churches, and the law) and how it can be improved through participatory democracy.

Drew, Paul, and Anthony Wootton (eds.). 1988. *Erving Goffman: Exploring the Interaction Order.* Boston: Northeastern University Press. A collection of clearly written analyses of Goffman's important works on social interaction.

Kohn, Alfie. 1986. *No Contest: The Case Against Competition.* Boston: Houghton Mifflin. Marshals an impressive array of data to challenge the popular assumption that competition enhances performance.

Lenski, Gerhard, Jean Lenski, and Patrick Nolan, 1991. *Human Societies,* 6th ed. New York: McGraw-Hill. The authors use the perspective of sociocultural evolution to analyze various types of societies, including those that have been briefly discussed in this chapter.

Little, Daniel. 1989. *Understanding Peasant China: Case Studies in the Philosophy of Social Science.* New Haven, Conn.: Yale University Press. A clearly written analysis of the conflicting views on changes in an agricultural society.

4

GROUPS AND ORGANIZATIONS

MYTHS AND REALITIES

Myth: Cooperation cannot end hostility because the hostile parties cannot be made to cooperate in the first place.

Reality: *Cooperation can end hostility, and hostile groups can be made to cooperate.*

Myth: In a group, you will never accept the view of others when you are certain it is wrong.

Reality: *The pressure to conform can make you accept that view if it is held by the majority.*

Myth: If you are a nice, compassionate person, you would help a victim whether other people are around or not.

Reality: *You would be less likely to help a victim when others are present than when you are alone with the victim.*

Myth: No organization can survive if it fails to realize its stated goal.

Reality: *When they fail to achieve their goals, most organizations break up, but not organizations such as antidrug agencies, which continue to exist because of their failure to eliminate drug trafficking.*

Myth: Bureaucracies in modern societies are so huge that they cannot be managed efficiently.

Reality: *Bureaucracies can be the most efficient form of administration because they are operated in accordance with impersonal rules and regulations rather than the whims of managers.*

Myth: It's always nice to be your own boss: in small businesses owned and managed by the workers themselves, the workers generally have an easy, pleasant life.

Reality: *While workers in such organizations are highly satisfied with their jobs, they tend to work too hard and often suffer stress and burnout as a result.*

Myth: Having long been run by executives and managers, American corporations would not adopt the Japanese practice of giving workers control over their jobs.

Reality: *The Japanese idea of worker control has been tried, albeit on a limited basis, in about 90 percent of the 500 largest American corporations.*

Several years ago, when Theresa Kump moved into Larchmont, a suburb of New York City, with her husband and baby, she did not know anybody and felt very lonely. Then she heard about a play group for preschoolers, organized by the local Newcomers Club, which she immediately joined. The play group changed her life. She first discovered that there were 13 other women her age having the same experiences: the frightening thrill of being a first-time mom and the unexpected loneliness of being home with an infant all day. These women soon became a cohesive group, held together by bonds of affection for their children and for one another. They enjoyed talking about their old and new experiences or whatever came to their minds as good friends do. But their hot rap sessions were often interrupted by the demands of their toddlers. So the young mothers decided to meet for a dinner at a restaurant once a month, without kids or husbands. At Moms' Night Out, which is what they call their "date," they share personal gripes and problems as well as give each other support. All had been gainfully employed before their children were born, but now half of the group work outside the home part-time and the other half at home full-time. These individual choices have been influenced by the group. Each member has compared notes and got feedback from others in the same situation (Kump, 1992).

These young mothers are only one of the numerous groups and organizations that have an impact on Kump's life. In fact, we are all like her because we live in an organized society. Groups and organizations are all around us. They touch virtually every aspect of our lives, from birth to death. We can hardly live without relatives, friends, neighbors, schoolmates, and other social groups. Our parents make it easier for us to grow up. Our friends, neighbors, and schoolmates make our lives easier with their concern, care, and assistance. Many formal organizations exert their influence on us. A hospital takes care of us when we are born, and a county bureau of records registers our birth. Schools educate us for 13 years; then a college or university takes over for a few more. A state agency gives us a driver's license, and city hall grants us a marriage license. Businesses sell us food, clothing, furniture, and other goods. With the aid of a law firm, a state court will grant us a divorce if we want it. When we die, at least two organizations—a funeral home and a law firm—will take care of us (Zucker, 1983). In this chapter we examine the characteristics of groups and organizations.

Social Groups

In a classic experiment, Muzafer Sherif (1956) took a group of white, middle-class, 12-year-old boys to a summer camp at Robbers' Cave State Park in Oklahoma. Sherif pretended to be a caretaker named Mr. Musee. For the first three days, the boys lived on one site at the camp and became acquainted. Then they were separated. Half of the boys were given one cabin and one set of activities, and the other half, another. Soon each group of boys had chosen a name, with one group calling themselves "Eagles" and the other, "Rattlers." Each had their own insignia on caps and T-shirts, their own jargon, and jokes and secrets.

Each band of boys, in short, had formed a **social group**—a collection of people who share some characteristics, interact with one another, and have some feeling of unity. A social group is more than either a social aggregate or a social category. A **social aggregate** is just a collection of people who happen to be in one place but do not interact with one another, such as the boys when they first arrived at the camp. A **social category** is a number of people who have something in common, but they neither interact with one another nor gather in one place. Men as a whole constitute a social category. So do women as a whole, college students as a whole, and so on. A social category becomes a social group when the people in the category interact with one another and identify themselves as members of the group. Thus, the boys at Robbers' Cave were members of a social category—12-year-old boys—but they became a social group only when they began to interact with one another and consider themselves members of the Eagles or the Rattlers. A closer look at Sherif's experiment can give us a clearer idea of the significance of groups.

IN-GROUPS, OUT-GROUPS, AND REFERENCE GROUPS

A few days after Sherif had put the boys in separate cabins, he arranged for the groups to compete against one another in baseball, tug of war, and other games. The winners of the games were awarded points toward a prize—camp knives. At first, the Eagles and Rattlers were very friendly with each other, but soon the games turned into fierce competitions. The two groups began to call each other stinkers, sneaks, and cheaters. They raided each other's cabins, and scuffles became common.

The boys' behavior showed that in forming each group, the youngsters set up a boundary between themselves as an **in-group** and the others as an **out-group.** Every social group defines a boundary between itself and everyone else to some extent, but a cohesive in-group has three characteristics. First, members of the in-group normally use symbols such as names, slogans, dress, or badges to identify themselves so that they will be distinguishable from the out-group. As we have seen, one group of boys in Sherif's experiment called themselves Eagles, and the other, Rattlers. Second, a characteristic of a cohesive in-group is that its members view themselves in terms of positive stereotypes and the out-group in negative stereotypes. Sherif's boys, for example, liked to say things like, "We are smart, and they are dumb!" Another study (Montgomery, 1980) also showed that college students tend to rate their own fraternities, sororities, or organizations higher in prestige than someone else's and to disparage others as "objectionable." Third, the in-group is inclined to compete or clash with the out-group.

Sherif's experiment showed how easily loyalty to an in-group can generate hostility toward an out-group and even aggression when there is competition for some resource (in this case, prizes). Competition with another group can also strengthen the unity within each group. But there was another phase in Sherif's experiment. He set up situations in which the groups had to work together to solve a common problem. When the camp's sole water tank broke down, he told the groups to work together to repair it. As they cooperated, friendships began to emerge between Eagles and Rattlers. In short, cooperation between groups eroded the hostility and divisions that competition had spurred. According to a more recent study, cooperation can even cause an in-group's higher-status members to shed their prejudice against and become friends with an out-group's lower-status members (Johnson and Johnson, 1984).

People often use a group as a frame of reference for evaluating their behavior or forming opinions: the group is then called a **reference group.** Members of a street gang, for example, may evaluate themselves by the standards of the gang and feel proud about a successful mugging. This positive self-evaluation reflects the *normative effect* of a reference group whose members share the same view of themselves. If other members of your reference group (say, your parents) have high self-esteem, you too are likely to have high self-esteem. However, reference groups can have "comparison effects" and "as-

"Of course you're going to be depressed if you keep comparing yourself with successful people."
Source: Drawing by Wm. Hamilton: © 1991 The New Yorker Magazine, Inc.

sociative effects" on self-appraisals. If most of your classmates shine in academic achievement, you are likely to compare yourself with them. As a result, you may have a negative self-evaluation, feeling that your academic performance is not up to par. Being associated with the brilliant group, though, you may feel proud of yourself, "basking in reflected glory" (Felson and Reed, 1986).

These reference groups are at the same time in-groups. But we do not have to be members of a group in order to use it as our reference group. As a student, you might have professional athletes as your reference group. If that is the case, you would probably judge your athletic skills to be inadequate—even if they are excellent compared with those of most amateurs—and perhaps you would work harder in an effort to meet professional standards.

Whether we are members of reference groups or not, they frequently exert a powerful influence on our behavior and attitudes, as has been suggested. In fact, their impact became well known long ago, after Theodore Newcomb (1958) published his study of the students at Bennington College, a very liberal college in Vermont. Newcomb found that most of the students came from conservative families and that most of the freshmen were conservative. A small minority remained conservative throughout their time at the school. But most became more liberal the longer they stayed at the college. These students, Newcomb concluded, used the liberal faculty or older students as their reference group, whereas the minority continued to look to their conservative families as their reference group.

PRIMARY AND SECONDARY GROUPS

It is not at all surprising that some students used their families as a reference group. After all, families are the best examples of the groups Charles Cooley (1909) called *primary* chiefly because they "are fundamental in forming the social nature and ideals of the individual." In a primary group the individuals have strong emotional ties. As discussed in Chapter 3 (Social Structure), it is one of the two main types of social groups. In the *secondary* group, relationships among the members are less personal.

Families, peer groups, fraternities, sororities, neighbors, and small communities are all examples of primary groups. They are marked by what are called *primary relationships.* Communication in these relationships is not limited by formalities. The people in a primary group interact in an informal way, and they relate to each other as unique, whole persons. Moreover, they enjoy the relationship for its own sake.

These characteristics become clearer when we compare them with those of secondary groups. A *secondary group* consists of individuals who do not know each other personally; they may have little face-to-face interaction. Members of a secondary group interact formally. They relate to each other only in terms of particular roles and for certain practical purposes.

Consider a salesperson and his clients or a supervisor and her staff. In both of these secondary groups, there are likely to be few if any emotional ties, and the people know little about each other. Their communications are bound by formalities. Sales clerks are not likely to kiss their customers or to cry with them over the death of a relative. The clerk will treat the customer as a customer only—not as a person who is also a mother of three, a jazz lover, a victim of an airplane hijacking, or a person who laughs easily but worries a lot. In contrast, we expect our families to treat us as whole persons, to be interested in our experiences, preferences, and feelings. The clerk is also likely to treat one customer much like another. We expect this attitude in a clerk, but the same attitude in our family or friends would hurt our feelings. Finally, the clerk and the customer have a relationship only because each has a specific task or purpose in mind: to buy or sell something. They use their relationship for this purpose. The relationship among family members, in contrast, is not oriented to a particular task but engaged in for its own sake. In fact, if we believe that a person in a primary group is interested in us only as a means to some end, we are likely to feel "used." Parents are hurt if they feel their children are interested only in the food, shelter, and money the parents provide.

Primary groups are very common in small, traditional societies. But in large, industrial societies, secondary relationships are pervasive. These do not provide the emotional satisfactions or intimacy of pri-

As members of a primary group, these high school students interact informally and relate to one another as unique persons. They also enjoy the relationship for its own sake.

mary groups. Indeed, they can make us feel isolated and lonely. In the prevalence of secondary relationships, some observers see the source of the interest in communes, encounter groups, singles clubs, computer dating services, and similar organizations. All these may be attempts to produce primary relationships. But because they often involve strangers who have no emotional commitment to each other, they are not genuine or durable primary groups.

The real primary relationships—with our friends, neighbors, or relatives—are very precious to us. As many studies have shown, they are particularly helpful when we are going through stressful life events. They help ease recovery from heart attacks, prevent childbirth complications, make child rearing easier, lighten the burden of household finances, cushion the impact of job loss by providing financial assistance and employment information (Albrecht et al., 1982; Brim et al., 1982; Hanlon, 1982). However, primary relationships are not always more beneficial than secondary relationships. As suggested earlier (Chapter 3: Social Structure), our close friends cannot help us get as good a job as our acquaintances can. The reason is that our friends move in the same social circle as we do, but our acquaintances, to whom we have only weak ties, move in different circles. Hence, we may already know the job openings that our friends know, but we may not be aware of the many job opportunities our acquaintances know about.

Although primary and secondary groups differ, they do sometimes overlap. In many families, teenagers may expect their parents to pay them for mowing the lawn or doing some other chore around the house. On the other hand, friendship may blossom among members of a secondary group at a school or workplace.

SMALL GROUPS

In discussing the various forms of social groups, whether they are primary, secondary, reference, ingroup or out-group, we have focused on the nature of interaction among the members. The very size of a group, however, may determine how its members interact. This is the most significant finding that has come out of small-group research.

A *small group* is one whose members are few enough to be able to interact directly with one another. We can see small groups everywhere. In fact, each of us belongs to at least five of them. These groups

may be our families, friends, small classes, discussion groups, weekend parties, fraternities, sororities, or athletic teams (Mills, 1967). Because there are more than 5 billion people on earth, the total number of small groups can be estimated to run as high as 25 billion. Our world indeed is crowded with small groups.

Leadership and Conformity In most small groups, there are two kinds of leaders. *Instrumental leaders* are concerned about achieving goals. They may say something like "Let's get to work!" or "Can't we get on with the job now?" or "I think we're getting off the track." Such tactics show the leaders as overseers, whose exchange with followers involves a "unidirectional downward influence" and a weak sense of common fate. Although this kind of leadership can get the group to move toward a goal, it can also rub people the wrong way (Mabry and Barnes, 1980; Duchon et al., 1986). It is no wonder that most people do not like their instrumental leaders. On the other hand, *expressive leaders* are more concerned with members' feelings, making sure that everybody is happy, so that harmony and cohesiveness can reign in the group. The exchange between such leaders and their followers reflects a partnership, characterized by reciprocal influence, a strong sense of common fate, and mutual trust, respect, and liking. A small group needs both types of leaders to function effectively.

Because they are seen as competently performing certain tasks for the group, leaders are usually given an "idiosyncrasy credit," which allows them to deviate from the group's norms. The rank and file, however, are expected to conform. In a small group, the pressure to conform is so powerful that individual members tend to knuckle under. They will go along with the majority even though they privately disagree with it. This point has been driven home by Solomon Asch's (1955) classic experiments. Asch brought together groups of eight or nine students each. He asked them to tell him which of the three lines on a card was as long as the line on another card. In each group only one was a real subject—the others were the experimenter's secret accomplices, who had been instructed to give the same obviously wrong answer. Asch found that nearly a third of the subjects changed their minds and accepted the majority's answer even though they were sure that their own answer was correct and the others' answer was wrong (Figure 4.1).

The small group to which Asch's subjects felt

Instrumental leaders are primarily concerned about achieving goals. Expressive leaders are more concerned with followers' feelings, making sure that harmony and cohesiveness can prevail in the group. A small group such as this basketball team needs both types of leadership from its coach to function effectively.

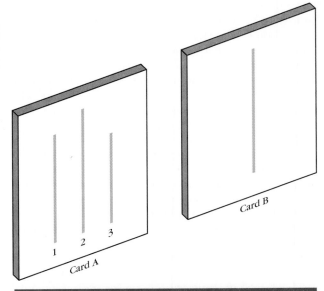

FIGURE 4.1 *Would You Conform?*
Asch's experiments suggest that if you are asked privately which line on card A is as long as the line on card B, there is a 99 percent chance that you would correctly pick line 2. But if you find yourself in a group where all the other members choose line 3—an obviously wrong number—there is about a 33 percent chance that you would yield to the group pressure to conform by choosing line 3.

compelled to conform were strangers. The pressure to conform is even greater among people we know. It usually gives rise to what Irving Janis (1982) calls **groupthink,** the tendency for members of a cohesive group to maintain consensus to the extent of ignoring the truth (Hensley and Griffin, 1986). Groupthink may lead to disastrous decisions, with tragic consequences. It caused President Kennedy and his top advisors to approve the CIA's unsound plan to invade Cuba. It caused President Johnson and his advisors to escalate the Vietnam War. It caused President Reagan and his advisors to get involved in the Iran-Contra affair. In each case a few members had serious doubts about the majority decision but did not speak out. It is even more difficult to voice dissent if the leader rules with an iron hand. About thirty years ago, when Nikita Khrushchev, ruler of what was then the Soviet Union, came to the United States, he met with reporters at the Washington Press Club. The first anonymous written question he received was: "Today you talked about the hideous rule of your predecessor, Stalin, who killed thousands of his political opponents. You were one of his closest aides and colleagues during those years. What were you doing all that time?" Khrushchev's face turned red. "Who asked that?" he shouted. No one answered. "Who

asked that?" he shouted again. Still no answer. "That's what I was doing: keeping my mouth shut" (Bennis, 1989). Leaders can obviously prevent groupthink by encouraging and rewarding dissent. Interestingly, the greater the disagreement among group members, the better their collective decision. This is because "with more disagreement, people are forced to look at a wider range of possibilities" (Bennis, 1989).

The Size Effect   Aside from pressuring people to conform, small groups also cause them to behave in other ways. This has a lot to do with the specific size of small groups. The smallest of these groups is a *dyad,* which contains two people. A dyad can easily become the most cohesive of all the groups because its members are inclined to be most personal and to interact most intensely with each other. This is why, as has been shown by the experiment of Ralph Taylor and his associates (1979), we are more willing to share our secrets in a dyad than in a larger group, secrets such as our parents getting divorced or father having been committed to a mental hospital. A dyad, however, is also the most likely to break up. If just one person leaves the group, it will vanish. Such a threat does not exist for a *triad,* a three-person group. If one member drops out, the group can still survive. A triad also makes it possible for two people to gang up on the third one or for one member to patch up a quarrel between the other two. But triads lose the quality of intimacy that is the hallmark of dyads, as described by the saying, "Two's company, three's a crowd."

If more people join a triad, the group will become even less personal, with each individual finding it extremely difficult to talk and relate to each of the other members. The upshot is the emergence of many different coalitions (made up of two against one, two against three, three against one, and so on) and many mediating roles for various conflicting subgroups. The reason is that even a small growth in the size of a group increases dramatically the number of relationships among its members. If a dyad, for example, grows into a seven-person group, the number of possible relationships will shoot up from 1 to 966 (Hare, 1962). Generally, as a group grows larger, it changes for the worse. Its members become less satisfied, participate less often in group activities, are less likely to cooperate with one another, and are more likely to misbehave. Even the Japanese, universally known for their politeness, may become rude on a crowded train. This is because increase in group size makes it difficult to maintain interpersonal relationships and individual recognition (Mullen et al., 1989; Levine and Moreland, 1990).

Research has also revealed other effects of group size. In a dyad or triad, the host usually has the edge over the visitor, with the host more likely to get his or her own way. Thus a businesswoman can strike a better deal if she invites the other person to her office. But such territorial dominance—the "home-court" advantage—may go out the window if the group is larger than a triad (Taylor and Lanni, 1981). In public places, a large group may also inhibit an individual from helping someone in distress. Over 50 studies have shown consistently that people are less likely to help a victim if others are around than if they are alone with the victim. A major reason is that the knowledge that others are present and available to respond allows the individual to shift some of the responsibility to them (Latané and Nida, 1981). The same factor operates in "social loafing": as the size of a group performing a certain task increases, each member tends not to work as hard. Social loafing, however, is less likely to occur in collectivist soci-

eties such as China and Japan than in individualistic societies such as the United States (Latané and Nida, 1981; Earley, 1989).

QUESTIONS FOR DISCUSSION AND REVIEW
1. What characteristics of social groups make them different from aggregates and categories?
2. What are some social functions of in-groups and reference groups?
3. Why do sociologists think that primary groups are fundamental for human existence?
4. How does the concept of groupthink help explain experiences you have had in small groups?

Formal Organizations

Some secondary groups are small and transitory, with their goals and rules unstated. A sales clerk interacts with a client on a temporary basis to achieve a generally known but unstated objective without following any explicitly described rules for carrying out the business transaction. Other secondary groups are large and more permanent, and they have explicit goals and working procedures. Government agencies, for instance, often last well beyond their members' lifetimes, and they are large and complex. Their goals and rules must be stated explicitly so that the work of their many members can be coordinated. These agencies are examples of the kind of social group called a formal organization.

Hospitals and colleges, business firms and political parties, the U.S. Army, and the Sierra Club—all these are formal organizations. A **formal organization** is a secondary group whose activities are rationally designed to achieve specific goals. Goals are the raison d'être of organizations. Without goals, organizations would not have come into being. Goals can help an organization determine what it should do. They can further be used as guidelines for measuring its performance—how successful it is in meeting its goals. Of course, most organizations will fall by the wayside if they fail to realize their goals. Some organizations, however, continue to exist and even thrive on their failure to achieve their goals. Government agencies for enforcing drug laws, for example, continue to exist because of their failure to put drug traffickers out of business.

Whether they achieve their goals or not, all organizations develop certain common means for

Although some secondary groups are small and transitory, others, such as a major political party, are larger and more permanent. Their goals and rules are explicitly stated so that the activities of their numerous members can be coordinated. Such groups are formal organizations.

achieving them. Generally, they engage in *rational planning.* They must decide what specific tasks are necessary for realizing the goals, who are best qualified to carry out the tasks, and how the various tasks are to be coordinated so that costly conflict is avoided and high efficiency is achieved.

More specifically, there is first a *division of labor,* whereby workers with different skills are assigned different tasks. This makes it easier for an organization to attain its goals than if all the workers perform the same task. But the division of labor may get out of hand, with each worker producing an item (say, a car door) that cannot be fitted into another item (a car body) made by the other worker. This makes it necessary for the organization to establish a *hierarchy of control.* Thus, a supervisor, a manager, and other administrators are responsible for supervising and directing the workers to ensure that various activities are properly coordinated. The administrators' actions are, however, governed by a set of *formalized rules.* They must deal with the workers in accordance with these rules, without showing any favoritism toward anyone. Their strict adherence to the rules may explain why formal organizations typically appear impersonal. The rules themselves may also explain why the organizations appear to have a life of their own, being able to outlive their members. The

departure of certain personnel cannot cause the organizations to collapse because the rules stipulate how replacements are to be found.

Organizational Models

We find formal organizations all around us. Much as we might try to stay in the warmer world of friends and family, we will encounter these organizations and feel their power. How the power is used affects the operation of the organizations as well as our ability to achieve goals we share with these organizations.

There have been many attempts to analyze just how organizations operate and what types of operation are most efficient. Under what circumstances, for example, can an organization do without moral persuasion? What is the most effective way to offer remunerative rewards, such as money and other similar incentives? How should managers and workers interact if the organization is to be effective? Answers to questions like these are contained in organizational models.

Some models describe what organizations are like, and others say what they should be like to achieve their goals. No one model yet devised portrays the nature of organizations with complete accuracy. Each tends to focus on certain aspects and obscure others. Taken together, however, organizational models can enhance our understanding.

SCIENTIFIC MANAGEMENT

Early in this century, American engineer Frederick Taylor (1911) published the first systematic presentation of what was soon called *scientific management.* Taylor assumed that the primary goal of an organization is to maximize efficiency. For a manufacturing company, this means getting maximum productivity, the highest possible output per worker per hour. He further assumed that workers are not too bright and can be manipulated. As a result, Taylor argued that the success of an organization depends on three elements: maximum division of labor, close supervision of workers, and an incentive system of piecework wages.

To obtain maximum division of labor, the production of a product must be broken down into numerous simple tasks that are extremely easy to perform. Each of these tasks is then defined down to the tiniest detail, so that it can be completed in the shortest time possible. One of Taylor's specific recommendations was that zigzag motions of the hands must be avoided; workers should begin and complete their motions with both hands simultaneously. To ensure that the task is properly carried out, the worker must be closely and continuously supervised. Taylor suggested that there be four types of supervisors—setting-up boss, speed boss, quality inspector, and repair boss—and that the supervisor in turn be controlled by a planning department. Finally, to be sure they work as hard as possible, workers should be paid by the piece: the more units each produces, the higher his or her pay.

Today, many companies still apply Taylor's basic principles. Productivity appears to decline if the basic points of this model are not applied to some degree. Scientific management works particularly well in the world of production, where the work is mostly routine. But the model ignores many aspects of organizations and human behavior. It looks only at the *official* organization, the formal relationships between workers and supervisors. Most sociologists have criticized the model for treating human beings as machines, arguing that this contributes to worker dissatisfaction and ultimately to lower productivity.

The scientific management model of industrial organization suggests that a company can achieve maximum productivity if its workers do a simple repetitive task under close supervision. Scientific management works best in manufacturing companies, where the work is mostly routine; but it has been criticized for treating workers as machines.

HUMAN RELATIONS

In the late 1920s, industrial psychologist Elton Mayo challenged practically all the assumptions of the scientific management model. He argued the following: (1) Workers' productivity is not determined by their physical capacity but by their "social capacity," their sensitivity to the work environment. No matter how fast they *can* do their job, they will not produce a lot if their fellow workers frown on the idea of working too fast. (2) Noneconomic rewards, such as friendship with co-workers and respect from management, play a central role in determining the motivation and happiness of workers. Thus, wages are less important than Taylor claimed. (3) The greatest specialization is not the most efficient division of labor. Extreme specialization creates problems for those coordinating the work. Supervisors are hard put to know all the details of very specialized tasks. (4) Workers do not react to management and its incentives as isolated individuals but as members of a group. They will reject management's offer of high pay for maximum productivity if their fellow workers are against working too hard (Roethlisberger and Dickson, 1939). These points make up the *human relations model.* In contrast to scientific management, it emphasizes the social forces affecting productivity, especially the informal relations among workers. These relations make up what is called the **informal organization,** in contrast to the official organization.

Empirical support for this model came from Mayo's studies at the Hawthorne plant in Chicago in the 1930s. As we discussed in Chapter 1 (The Essence of Sociology), one of these studies showed that workers increased their productivity regardless of changes in the physical environment. Productivity went up, for example, when the experimenter brightened the workplace, but it also went up when he dimmed the lights. Mayo concluded that the employees worked harder because the presence of the researcher made them feel important; management seemed to be treating them as people, not mere machines. Another study at the same plant examined whether output was determined by financial incentives. Surprisingly, it was shaped by an informal norm. The norm forbade working too hard as well as working too slowly. Anyone working too hard was ridiculed as a "rate buster," and anyone working too slowly was scorned as a "chiseler." As a result, each worker tried to produce as much as the other workers, rather than trying to meet management's goals (Roethlisberger and Dickson, 1939). These studies have clearly shown that informal relations can increase worker productivity. A more recent study has indicated that informal relations can also make the organization more effective in responding to crises (Krackhardt and Stern, 1988).

The human relations model covers parts of the organization ignored by scientific management, but it too has limitations. First, it exaggerates the importance of the informal group life at the workplace. Most workers will not wake up every morning feeling that they cannot wait to go to work in order to be with their co-workers. They are more interested in their families and friends outside the workplace. Second, informal social relations may create more pleas-

ant conditions in the plant, but they cannot significantly reduce the tediousness of the job itself. One may enjoy working with certain individuals, but this cannot turn an inherently boring job into an exciting one. Relations with co-workers, though, may be more significant to white-collar and professional workers than to blue-collar workers, because their jobs often involve a great deal of interaction with their co-workers.

IDEAL-TYPE BUREAUCRACY

Unlike the scientific management and human relations models, Max Weber's organizational model is neither an attempt to say how organizations should work nor a description of how specific, actual organizations do work. Instead, Weber tried to construct what he called an **ideal type.** It does not describe any actual organization, or an average organization, or an "ideal" to be sought. Rather, it describes what are theorized to be the essential characteristics of an organization. It can then be used to determine the extent to which actual organizations have these characteristics. Weber's analysis was so influential, and the type of organization he described is now so widespread, that parts of his model are also part of our definition of formal organizations.

According to Weber, modern Western society makes a specific form of organization necessary: bureaucracy. "In the place of the old-type ruler who is moved by sympathy, favor, grace, and gratitude," Weber said, "modern culture requires . . . the emotionally detached, and hence rigorously 'professional' expert" (Bendix, 1962). In every area of modern life there is a tendency toward **rationalization.** Traditional, spontaneous, informal, or diverse ways of doing things are replaced by a planned, unified method based on abstract rules. Applied to organizations, rationalization means the development of bureaucracies. They are, in Weber's view, the most efficient form of organization.

What is a **bureaucracy?** We sometimes use the word to refer to the administration of any organization. Sometimes it is used to mean a government agency. Here we are concerned with bureaucracy as a type of organization. A family farm is not a bureaucracy, but a farm managed by a large corporation is. According to Weber, the essential characteristics of a bureaucracy, which together distinguish it from other types of organization, are as follows:

1. There is a clear-cut division of labor among those in the bureaucracy, assigning to each po

sition certain limited duties and responsibilities.

2. There is a well-defined hierarchy. Those in a higher position have authority to give orders to those below them in the hierarchy, whose work they coordinate. Authority in the hierarchy is attached to the position, not the person. Orders are issued and obeyed regardless of who occupies the position. This ensures that the organization will not be disrupted by retirement, death, or similar events.

3. Employees are hired and hold authority on the basis of technical qualifications, which are often determined by examinations.

4. The activities of the bureaucrats and their relationships are governed by an elaborate system of explicit, formal, written rules and regulations. This is the most important characteristic of bureaucracies, marking a radical change from informal, more personal ways of organizing work. The reliance on rules in a bureaucracy maximizes efficiency in various ways. First, the rules tell officials what to do. Second, they compel bureaucrats to think and act, not on their own behalf, but as agents of the organization trying to achieve the organization's goal. As a result, bureaucrats become impersonal and objective in dealing with people. They hire, for example, the best-qualified person, not the boss's incompetent son or daughter.

This is the bureaucracy in theory. It is marked by specialization, impersonality, and rationalization. In practice, of course, even bureaucrats retain personal interests and feelings that may interfere with their obedience to rules and regulations. And even within a bureaucracy, informal groups almost certainly form. This informal organization exerts a powerful influence on how people work. If the informal groups are alienated from the formal organization, they will hinder its operation.

Real bureaucracies deviate from the bureaucratic model in yet another way. Weber held the bureaucracy to be the most efficient form of organization. Indeed, adherence to rules and regulations is likely to increase efficiency when tasks are stable and routine. But it can also produce inefficiency. Rules are based on what is known; they cannot tell people what to do about what cannot be anticipated. When changes occur frequently or when the unusual occurs, rules won't help. A lost I.D. card or birth certificate or other document can bring bureaucratic procedures

The chief source of the efficiency of bureaucracies is reliance on impersonal rules. Rules ensure that employees treat equally all the people they serve. Unfortunately, the consequences of bureaucratic efficiency may be rigidity on the part of personnel, such as being unable to help customers with unusual needs.

to a grinding halt. Extreme adherence to rules can be tantamount to inaction. When the Japanese bombed Pearl Harbor in 1941, U.S. military personnel rushed to the armories for weapons. But armory guards refused to issue the weapons unless a formal requisition was properly signed in accordance with regulations (Champion, 1975).

COLLECTIVIST ORGANIZATION

In Weber's view, bureaucracies emerge because they are an efficient form of organization. In contrast, Karl Marx argued that bureaucracies are the capitalists' tool for exploiting the working class. Eventually, Marx claimed, bureaucracies will be abolished in a classless, communist society. They will be replaced by collectivist organizations, in which managers and workers work together as equals and for equal pay. In the meantime, an approximation to this organizational model has been tried out in China. Other types of collectivist organizations can be found in Japan and the United States, but they have not been inspired by Marx. (See Table 4.1 for finer distinctions between bureaucratic and collectivist models.)

TABLE 4.1 *Bureaucratic versus Colletivist Model*

BUREAUCRATIC MODEL	COLLECTIVIST MODEL
1. Achieving organizational efficiency through technical competence.	1. Achieving organizational efficiency through worker commitment.
2. Using only technical competence in evaluating a member's worth.	2. Using both ideological dedication and technical competence.
3. Maximum division of labor.	3. Minimal division of labor.
4. Maximum specialization of jobs—monopolization of expertise.	4. Generalization of jobs—diffusion of expertise.
5. Emphasis of hierarchy of positions—justifying reward differentials.	5. Striving for egalitarianism—restricting reward differentials.
6. Authority in individual officeholders; hierarchical control; bureaucratic elitism.	6. Authority in collectivity as a whole; democratic control; subordinate participation.
7. Formalization of fixed and universalistic rules.	7. Primacy of ad hoc decisions.
8. Worker motivation through direct supervision.	8. Worker motivation through personal appeals.
9. Impersonality as ideal of social relations in organizations.	9. Comradeship as ideal of social relations in organizations.
10. Informal groups need not be co-opted.	10. Informal groups should be fully co-opted.

Source: Martin King Whyte, "Bureaucracy and Modernization in China: The Maoist Critique," *American Sociological Review*, 38, 1973, pp. 149–163; Joyce Rothschild-Whitt, "The Collectivist Organization: An Alternative to Bureaucratic Models," in Frank Lindenfeld and Joyce Rothschild-Whitt (eds.), *Workplace Democracy and Social Change*, Boston: Porter Sargent, 1982.

During the 1960s and 1970s, the Chinese government tried to implement the Marxist model throughout the country. To the Chinese, emphasis on technical competence promotes inequality between managers and workers and among workers as well. It particularly discourages average workers from meaningful participation in the organization. They will consider themselves incompetent and doubt that they can benefit from the organization. Hence, they will not work hard. Therefore, the government told workers to join administrators and technicians in making decisions, and it required the latter to join the former in working with their hands. All of them also had to attend regular meetings to raise their political consciousness, to heighten their enthusiasm for "serving the people" as opposed to pursuing self-interests (Whyte, 1973; Hearn, 1978).

As a result, all symbols of rank in the military were abolished, all workers received about the same pay, and other trappings of equality appeared everywhere. Meanwhile, China remained economically backward. Since the late 1970s, however, the new government has embarked on a vast modernization program. It seeks out skilled technicians, professionals, and experts to run organizations. It also uses pay incentives to motivate individual workers. In December 1984 it even pronounced that "Marxism is obsolete" and affirmed the role of such capitalist ideas as individual initiative and market competition in China's economic development. But this reform drive has suffered a setback since the Tiananmen Square massacre in 1989. If it resumes in full force, many Westerners suspect that it might produce a Western-style economy, which in turn would create a Western-style bureaucracy with emphasis on expertise and efficiency but with great inequality between management and labor. We could argue, however, that the Chinese organization would come closer to the Japanese organization than the Western bureaucracy. A basic reason is that China and Japan have about the same collectivist culture, which is more oriented to groups than individuals. But what is the Japanese organization like?

The heart of the Japanese organization is concern with group achievement. Employees begin each workday by singing their company song or reciting slogans of devotion to their company. They work in sections of eight to ten people, headed by the *kacho* (section chief). Each section, now well known as a "quality circle," does not await orders from the top but takes the initiative, and all its members work together as equals. Personnel of different sections often

Japanese companies are collectivist organizations. They are often run like families, encompassing every aspect of the worker's life, even providing low-cost housing and medical care. Employees may begin each day singing their company song or reciting slogans of devotion to the company. Here a group of factory employees eat lunch, consisting of fish, rice, vegetables, and tofu soup, together in the company cafeteria.

get together to discuss how best to achieve company objectives. Executives, then, merely rubber stamp most of the decisions made by employees at the section level. Workers, moreover, look upon their company as their family because they enjoy the security of permanent employment. Executives also feel secure and regard their company as their family. The security has "its roots in solid cultural ground and shared meanings" (Peters and Waterman, 1982). Thus, both workers and executives are highly committed to their company and work as hard as they can. In such a collectivist environment, the Japanese do not, however, scorn technical competence for fear of generating inequality as did the Chinese in the last three decades. Instead, the Japanese encourage potential innovators to "come forward, grow, and flourish—even to the extent of indulging a little madness" (Peters and Waterman, 1982). But they do so as part of their duty to contribute to the success of their company.

Whether Japanese or Chinese, the collectivist model of organization has a familiar ring to Americans in one sense: the call for participation by all members is a principle of democracy. This contrasts with the bureaucratic model, which is undemocratic because those on top of the organization dictate to those below, and those at the bottom may not choose who are above them or influence their decisions. In a collectivist organization, power flows from the bottom up, while in a bureaucracy, it flows from the top down. In the United States, this element of the collectivist model can be seen in some 5000 "alternative institutions" established during the 1970s. The free schools, free medical clinics, legal collectives, food cooperatives, communes, and cooperative businesses are a legacy of movements during the 1960s against authority and "the Establishment." These enterprises are collectively owned and managed, without any hierarchy of authority. They tend to be in craft production and other special niches of the economy that exempt them from directly competing with conventional companies. Most are quite small, averaging six employees per organization, but their small size helps preserve full worker participation. The workers are highly satisfied with their jobs and strongly identify with their firms. Because they are also owners, the workers tend to work too hard and often suffer stress and burnout as a result (Rothschild-Whitt, 1982; Rothschild and Russell, 1986).

The collectivist idea of giving workers control over their jobs has also been tried out on a limited basis in some 90 percent of the 500 largest American corporations as a way to combat worker alienation and low productivity. In these companies small groups of employees work together like the Japanese quality circles. They are encouraged with rewards and recognition—merit raises, cash bonuses, and bulletin-board praises—to contribute ideas on how to increase productivity and sales. They operate with the "open door" policy, whereby employees report directly to the top management, which further encourages them to work harder because it makes workers feel important and respected. Practically all these companies are in the manufacturing sector of the economy. Good examples are IBM and General Motors, which produce computers and automobiles, respectively. Recently, the quality-circle style of worker participation has begun to invade the service sector in such areas as the insurance business. All these collectivist practices can boost not only worker morale but also productivity, as has been demonstrated by the successful operation of the Honda auto plant and other Japanese businesses in the United States (Rothschild and Russell, 1986; Scott, 1986; Florida and Kenney, 1991).

QUESTIONS FOR DISCUSSION AND REVIEW

1. What are the special features of the scientific management, human relations, bureaucratic, and collectivist models?
2. Why does the ideal-type model of bureaucracy differ from the way bureaucracies operate in real life?
3. How can comparison of organizational models help managers improve the operations of business and government?

The Realities of Bureaucracy

Despite widespread dislike of bureaucracy, this form of organization is everywhere. Millions of Americans now work in bureaucracies, and even more must deal with bureaucratic organizations when they wish to enroll in school, to have a phone installed, to get a hospital bill paid, or to handle any number of other countless arrangements that are part of living in a modern society. The prevalence of bureaucratic organization affects both the small details of everyday life and the overall function of the government and economy. The vices and virtues of bureaucracy are thus worth a closer look.

BUREAUCRATIC VICES

In Weber's view, bureaucracy is inescapable but not very likable. "It is horrible," he once said, "to think that the world would one day be filled with nothing but those little cogs, little men clinging to little jobs and striving toward bigger ones" (Bendix, 1962). Finding an American to say a good word about bureaucracy is about as hard as finding a landlord who likes rent control. Why?

We have already noted some of the deficiencies of bureaucracies. The rules and regulations characteristic of bureaucracies are of little help when something unexpected happens. The blind adherence to rules may prevent necessary action. The hierarchies of authority characteristic of bureaucracies are undemocratic. Among a bureaucracy's best-known vices, however, is its tendency to produce a seemingly endless number of rules and regulations. Public bureaucracies, in particular, are well known for their mountains of rules. All these rules slow action by government employees and fall like an avalanche on private citizens and businesses that must comply with them. The nation's small businesses alone spend an immense amount of money every year in order to complete government forms.

Whenever there are a great many rules, it is virtually inevitable that some of them are irrational and contradictory. Not long ago, a millionaire was officially declared eligible for unemployment compensation. He was a 31-year-old supermarket employee who had won New York's millionaire lottery. After being laid off from his job, he applied for unemployment benefits. The application was approved because, according to official explanation, lottery winning is no bar to receiving such benefit. Another example is the federal government's spending millions of our tax dollars on an antismoking campaign while giving even more money to subsidize the tobacco industry. Sometimes the contradictory rules are so tangled up that they can entrap a person. Thus, the very compliance with one rule may mean violating another.

C. Northcote Parkinson (1957) popularized another criticism of bureaucracies. According to what is called **Parkinson's Law,** "Work expands to fill the time available for its completion." Parkinson believed that the natural tendency of bureaucracy is to grow and keep on growing, by at least 6 percent a year. Wanting to appear busy or important or both, officials increase their workload by writing a lot of memos, creating rules, filling out forms, and keeping files. Then, feeling overworked, they hire assistants. If the boss had just one assistant, that person might become a competitor for the boss's job. But if the boss hires two underlings, he or she will be the only person who understands both their jobs. Besides, the salaries that managers get are sometimes based on how many people they supervise. When two assistants are hired, however, the boss's work increases, because he or she must supervise and coordinate their activities. At the same time, there are powerful incentives for officials to increase their agency work forces, budgets, and missions. As Morris Fiorina (1983) points out, bureaucrats' rewards (such as salary, perquisites, status, and power) depend heavily on the size (employment and budget) of their agencies. The result is an ever-rising pyramid of bureaucracy. To functionalists, bureaucratic growth is necessary for accommodating to changing environments. Without growth, bureaucracies are assumed to be incapable of solving new problems efficiently. To conflict theorists, however, bureaucracies grow in order to serve the interests of those who run the organizations, enabling them to accumulate power, as Parkinson has implied (Meyer, 1985; Hasenfeld, 1987).

There is yet another popular cliché that challenges the functionalist view of bureaucracies as capable of doing a good job. It is known as the **Peter Principle:** "In every hierarchy every employee tends to rise to his [or her] level of incompetence" (Peter and Hull, 1969). Competent officials are promoted. If they prove to be competent in their new jobs, they are promoted again. The process continues until they are promoted to a position in which they are incompetent. And there they remain until they retire. The bureaucracy functions only because there are always employees still proving their competence before they are promoted beyond their abilities. Like Parkinson's Law, however, the Peter Principle, though an interesting idea, is based on impressionistic observation rather than rigorous scientific research.

BUREAUCRATIC VIRTUES

From Peking to Peoria, the vices of bureaucracy are well known. Why then do bureaucracies flourish? In part, it is because they are not all bad. Even red tape has its virtues: what is one person's "red tape," as Herbert Kaufman (1977) said, "may be another person's procedural safeguard." The process of getting a government permit to open a hazardous waste dump may seem an endless, expensive obstacle course of paperwork to the company that wants to operate the dump. But to people living near the proposed site, the rules and regulations that make up the red tape may seem the best guarantee that proper precautions to safeguard their health will be taken.

Similarly, the impersonality of bureaucracies, especially in government, is sometimes welcome. If you need a government-subsidized student loan, you are probably glad that impersonal rules—not political pull or personal friendships—determine whether you can obtain the loan. Bureaucracy encourages equality and discourages discrimination.

Even for employees, bureaucracies may bring some benefits. It is widely assumed that bureaucracies tend to stifle individual creativity and imagination, but this assumption is far from correct. Data collected by sociologist Melvin Kohn (1983) suggest that bureaucracies make their workers intellectually flexible, creative, and open-minded.

Kohn defined bureaucrats as people who work in large organizations with complicated hierarchies of authority, and nonbureaucrats as people who work in small organizations with only one level of supervision. Kohn found that, compared with nonbureaucrats, bureaucrats demonstrated a higher level of intellectual performance on tests administered by an interviewer. Bureaucrats also placed greater intellectual demands on themselves during their leisure time. They were more likely than nonbureaucrats to read books and magazines, attend plays and concerts, and go to museums. They also put greater value on self-direction, rather than conformity, and were more likely to take personal responsibility for whatever they did. Finally, they were more open-minded and more receptive to change than the nonbureaucrats.

Skeptics may argue that the bureaucrats' wonderful traits did not *result* from working in a bureaucracy. Perhaps the bureaucrats were better educated, more intellectually flexible, and more receptive to change in the first place. This argument assumes that bureaucracies hold some special attraction for people with these qualities. But because most people believe that bureaucracies suppress creativity, this assumption is far from convincing.

Kohn contended that bureaucracies themselves encourage the development of the positive traits he found in their employees. The more complex a job is, argued Kohn, the more intellectually flexible the worker becomes, and employees of bureaucracies tend to have more complex jobs than those with comparable education who work for an organization with just one or two levels of supervision. White-collar bureaucrats, such as factory managers, have very diverse responsibilities. They must constantly evaluate information, choose from among a multitude of alternatives, juggle competing interests, reconcile interpersonal conflicts, and move back and forth from meetings to solitary work. Similarly, blue-collar workers in bureaucracies typically perform a variety of tasks and deal with diverse situations. For blue-collar workers, however, Kohn argued that another characteristic of bureaucracies—job protection—is more important than complexity in encouraging the positive traits he found in these workers. In short, compared with a local auto body shop, General Motors is more likely to provide conditions that foster flexibility, creativity, and open-mindedness among employees.

THE CHANGING BUREAUCRACY

"We are witnessing," wrote Alvin Toffler in 1970, "not the triumph, but the breakdown of bureaucracy. We are in fact witnessing the arrival of a new organizational system that will increasingly challenge, and ultimately supplant bureaucracy." Toffler's declaration echoed an analysis presented by Warren Bennis and Philip Slater. In the future, they predicted in 1968, organizations

> will have some unique characteristics. The key word will be "temporary." There will be adaptive, rapidly changing *temporary* systems. These will be task forces organized around problems to be solved by groups of relative strangers with diverse professional skills (Bennis and Slater, 1968).

Toffler called this new type of organization an **adhocracy.** It was expected to be dissolved after completing its task. Moreover, according to Bennis, the temporary organization would be egalitarian, not hierarchical. In Bennis's view, "We should expect the [old] pyramid of bureaucracy to begin crumbling. . . . [New] organizational charts will consist of project groups rather than stratified functional groups."

Toffler and Bennis believed that these temporary, egalitarian organizations would emerge primarily because of two trends. First, the greatly increased rate of social and technological change creates numerous unexpected, nonroutine problems. Bureaucracies are ill equipped to cope with these because they are designed to deal with predictable, routine matters. To survive, organizations must become "adaptive, problem-solving, temporary systems of diverse specialists, linked together by coordinating and task-evaluating executive specialists" (Bennis and Slater, 1968). In other words, bureaucracies must give way to ad-hocracies.

More people working at home with computers will reinforce the trend toward the replacement of the bureaucratic, hierarchical structure by a more egalitarian organization. The workers will be the bosses, and the manager will take a supporting role as their planner and coordinator.

Toffler and Bennis also predicted that bureaucracies would be undermined by the increasing professionalization of employees, especially scientists and engineers. These people have a strong sense of independence, and they resent taking orders from managers who have less technical knowledge. The professionals would be more committed to their own standards of excellence and their professional societies than to their bosses. As a result, the hierarchy of bureaucracy, with power concentrated at the top, would collapse. In its place would emerge more egalitarian organizations, in which employees assumed greater responsibility for their own tasks.

The death-of-bureaucracy thesis soon came under fire for being based more on wish than on hard analysis. Critics argued that only a few experts would tackle the new, nonroutine problems (Shariff, 1979). Most employees would still carry on routine tasks, because everyday production, sales, and accounting tasks could not be turned over to a robot or a completely automated assembly line. In addition, the experts themselves would return to their original departments and ranks after they had resolved unexpected problems. The critics further contended that only a "microscopic minority" of scientists and engineers were prominent in professional circles and more committed to their profession than to their boss. The overwhelming majority of employees could not be expected to have this degree of professional loyalty. The critics concluded that there would be more, rather than less, bureaucratization, especially because both public and private bureaucracies are becoming increasingly large and complex.

Both views have proven to be partly correct. There is more bureaucratization today, particularly in the West, though not in Japan. In becoming larger, already large organizations are more impersonal, more subject to complex rules and regulations as well as managerial control. Most organizations in the United States are moving in this direction, as suggested by the recent growth of big government agencies, multinational corporations, multicampus universities, and agribusiness companies. Large organizational size usually leads to greater bureaucratic control, requiring numerous workers to follow standard rules and operating procedures so chaos can be avoided (Hsu, Marsh, and Mannari, 1983).

At the same time, there is less bureaucratization among higher-ranked technical experts and specialists within giant organizations. There is also less administrative control throughout the corporations that are on the frontiers of technology. In many successful corporations in the United States today, the highly trained specialists already enjoy a wide range of autonomy. According to Peter Drucker (1987), there has been a significant shift in the composition of the American work force from manual to knowledge work. Even in today's smokestack, manufacturing industries, only three out of ten employees fit the "labor" category—the rest are mostly in specialized, knowledge work. Given their increasing education, special skills, and desire for autonomy, these knowledge workers will increasingly press for the replacement of the bureaucratic, hierarchical structure of their companies by a much flatter, more egalitarian organization made up of numerous smaller units with six to ten employees each. In this new kind of organi-

zation, the manager will no longer be the "boss" and all others the "subordinates." Instead, the knowledge workers will be the "bosses," and the "manager" will act as planner and coordinator. In fact, there is some evidence in the early 1990s that the information revolution has forced many centralized bureaucracies—from education to business—to give way to the new model. In Dade County, Florida, experiments in shared decision making have created "school-basing autonomy," whereby the schools are managed by teams of teachers and parents rather than bureaucrats (Schlossstein, 1990). Many corporate employees have also freed themselves from bureaucratic control in order to focus on their personal development.

Interestingly, women are more likely to reject the hierarchical nature of traditional business organizations. Many female executives see being at the top as a lonely, disconnected position. They prefer to be in the center of things, connected to all the employees, like a spider's web. Unlike the hierarchical bureaucracy, which "values position, individual achievement won by competition, the web puts a premium on affiliation, on stay-close" (Helgesen, 1990). One advantage is that it permits flexibility without lowering morale. A person can serve on various teams, maximizing the use of his or her talents and skills. Another advantage is a greater flow of information. Employees feel free to communicate directly with anyone else in the company, without going through appropriate channels as required in a hierarchy. By emphasizing cooperation and collaboration rather than hierarchy and domination, the female style of management will become vital in dealing with America's increasingly heterogeneous workers (Helgesen, 1990; McWhirter, 1990; Eagly and Johnson, 1990).

QUESTIONS FOR DISCUSSION AND REVIEW
1. What vices of bureaucracy do Parkinson's Law and the Peter Principle illustrate?
2. Why does Alvin Toffler feel that bureaucracies will ultimately be replaced by ad-hocracy?
3. What personal experiences illustrate the virtues or vices of bureaucracy?

CHAPTER REVIEW

1. *What is a social group?* It is a collection of people who share some characteristics, interact with one another, and have some feeling of unity. *What are the two main types of social groups?* Primary

and secondary. A primary group is one whose members interact informally, relate to each other as whole persons, and enjoy their relationship for its own sake. In a secondary group, the individuals interact formally, relate to each other as players of particular roles, and expect to achieve some practical purpose through the relationship. *Does the size of a group matter?* Yes, it does. The pressure to conform is usually very great if a group is small enough for all its members to interact directly with one another. Moreover, the larger a group, the more impersonal it becomes, the more difficult it is for one member to influence another, or the less likely a member is to help someone in distress.

2. *What is a formal organization?* It is a group whose activities are rationally designed to achieve specific goals. In order to achieve their goals, organizations engage in rational planning. This includes a division of labor, a hierarchy of control, and a set of formalized rules.

3. *According to scientific management, what is the primary goal of an organization, and what must it do to achieve this goal?* Scientific management holds that organizations seek efficiency and that to obtain it they must have maximum division of labor, close supervision of workers, and a piecework system of wages. *How do the scientific management and human relations models differ?* Whereas scientific management focuses on the official organization and the effect of wages on efficiency, the human relations model emphasizes the influence of social forces—in particular the informal relations among workers—on job satisfaction and productivity.

4. *What are the principal characteristics of a bureaucracy?* A bureaucracy is characterized by a division of labor, a hierarchy of authority, the hiring of employees on the basis of impersonal procedures and technical qualifications, and a reliance on formal, written rules. As a result, a bureaucracy is marked by specialization, impersonality, and what Weber called "rationalization." In Weber's view, it is the most efficient form of organization. *How do collectivist organizations differ from bureaucratic ones?* In a bureaucratic organization, decisions are made by managers. In a collectivist organization, workers participate in the management of the organization.

5. *Why are bureaucracies so little loved?* Bureaucracies are undemocratic organizations that tend to produce an ever-growing number of rules—rules that may hinder effective action and may be contradictory. Moreover, popular stereotypes of bureaucracies hold that they are inefficient, overstaffed organizations that stifle creativity. *Do bureaucracies have any saving graces?* When tasks are stable and routine, they may be very efficient; their reliance on rules and their impersonality can protect people from the exercise of arbitrary power and favoritism. In addition, there is some evidence that bureaucracies foster among their workers intellectual flexibility, creativity, and openness to change. *Are bureaucracies here to stay?* Some writers have argued that bureaucracies will be replaced by a new type of organization in which *temporary* task forces will be formed to solve specific problems. The prediction of the late 1960s is coming true for many organizations, especially those in the forefront of technological advances. There may be more bureaucratization today because many already large organizations have grown even larger. But within the giant organizations, there is also more egalitarian sharing of information.

KEY TERMS

Ad-hocracy Toffler's term for an organization that assembles temporary groups of experts for solving specific problems (p. 86).

Bureaucracy An organization characterized by a division of labor, hierarchy of authority, the hiring of employees on the basis of impersonal procedures and technical qualifications, and reliance on formal rules (p. 80).

Formal organization A group whose activities are rationally designed to achieve specific goals (p. 77).

Groupthink The tendency for members of a group to maintain consensus to the extent of ignoring the truth (p. 76).

Ideal type Weber's term for a description of what are theorized to be the essential characteristics of a phenomenon, which can be compared with actual phenomena (p. 80).

Informal organization A group formed by the informal relations among members of an organization; based on personal interactions, not on any plan by the organization (p. 80).

In-group The group to which an individual is strongly tied as a member (p. 73).

Out-group The group of which an individual is not a member (p. 73).

Parkinson's Law Parkinson's observation—that "work expands to fill the time available for its completion"—for explaining why bureaucracy tends to keep growing (p. 84).

Peter Principle Peter's observation—that "in a hierarchy every employee tends to rise to his [or her] level of incompetence"—for explaining the prevalence of incompetence among bureaucrats (p. 85).

Rationalization Weber's term for the tendency to replace traditional, spontaneous, informal, and diverse ways of doing things with a planned, formally unified method based on abstract rules (p. 80).

Reference group A group that is used as the frame of reference for evaluating one's own behavior (p. 73).

Social aggregate A collection of people who happen to be in one place but who do not interact with one another (p. 72).

Social category A number of people who happen to share some characteristics but who do not interact with one another or gather in one place (p. 72).

Social group A collection of people who share some characteristics, interact with one another, and have some feeling of unity (p. 72).

SUGGESTED READINGS

Biggart, Nicole Woolsey. 1989. *Charismatic Capitalism: Direct Selling Organizations in America.* Chicago: University of Chicago Press. An interesting sociological study of Tupper, Amway, Mary Kay, and other direct-selling organizations.

Czarniawska-Joerges, Barbara. 1992. *Exploring Complex Organizations: A Cultural Perspective.* Newbury Park, Cal.: Sage. an interpretation of what goes on within an organization from the standpoint of the participants.

Hearn, Jeff, et al. (eds.). 1989. *The Sexuality of Organization.* Newbury Park, Calif.: Sage. An analysis of the relationships between gender relations and organizational life, focusing on such subjects as sexual harassment in the workplace and the self-image of women managers.

Waring, Stephen P. 1991. *Taylorism Transformed: Scientific Management Theory since 1945.* Chapel Hill: University of North Carolina Press. A historical analysis of the organizational model of scientific management.

Zeitlin, Maurice. 1989. *The Large Corporation and Contemporary Classes.* New Brunswick, N.J.: Rutgers University Press. An analysis of how managers have taken over the control of corporations from their owners.

5

SOCIALIZATION

MYTHS AND REALITIES

Myth: People are born with instincts to do many things.
Reality: *If instincts are biologically inherited capacities for performing complex tasks, only animals have them; humans do not.*

Myth: Infants will not die as long as they are well fed.
Reality: *Despite being well fed, infants can become retarded and even die if deprived of human contact.*

Myth: To be a genius, you must be born as such.
Reality: *Geniuses such as Mozart and Beethoven are not only born but made. Since childhood they have worked intensely to develop their potential abilities.*

Myth: By having many more toys and other material things, rich kids are likely to take them for granted and therefore become spoiled and unhappy, while poor kids tend more to appreciate the fewer toys they have and thus become happier.
Reality: *Children from higher social classes generally learn to feel happier and more satisfied than do children from lower classes.*

Myth: How you see yourself cannot affect your academic achievement; only brains and hard work can.
Reality: *Self-concept has a significant impact on academic achievement. Low self-esteem may lead to low achievement and high self-esteem, to greater creativity.*

Myth: Given the greater amount of delinquency among their children, lower-class parents must have been more permissive and lenient toward them as compared to middle-class parents.
Reality: *Lower-class parents are more authoritarian and strict, or less permissive and lenient, than middle-class parents.*

Myth: If working parents are more committed to career than parenting, they will fail to socialize their children adequately.
Reality: *While working parents cannot spend much time at home with their children, they are more likely than traditional parents to promote in their children understanding and mature behavior rather than unthinking obedience.*

Myth: It is difficult to change an adult's personality because it has mostly been formed in childhood.
Reality: *The specific nature of a job can easily shape adult personality: The more complex a job, the more likely the worker will value autonomy; the more simple and routine the work, the more likely the person will value conformity.*

Soon after 3-year-old Rebecca and her family moved to another town, her mother wanted to find a good pediatrician for her. She talked to many new neighbors and friends, and they all recommended the same doctor. After seeing Rebecca undergo a physical checkup for about five minutes, the mother was extremely pleased at how well her little girl was responding to the doctor. He was very friendly, talking gently to her and explaining everything he was doing. When it was time for him to test her reflexes, he said, "Rebecca, I'm going to hit your knee very lightly with a hammer." But immediately Rebecca let out a tremendous, blood-curdling scream. Shaken and puzzled, the doctor turned to her mother and asked, "What did I do wrong?" "Her father," said the mother, "is a carpenter" (Espinosa, 1992).

Actually Rebecca is just like all of us. She is to a significant degree a product of **socialization.** Socialization is the process by which a society transmits its cultural values through its agents, such as parents and teachers, to individuals so that they can function properly as its members. Without socialization, Rebecca could not have become a truly human being, a person who could take part in society and its culture like most children her age, as shown by her being an obedient daughter and cooperative patient most of the time. Simultaneously, though, Rebecca has developed through socialization a **personality**—a fairly stable configuration of feelings, attitudes, ideas, and behaviors that characterizes an individual—different from that of most of her peers. As we have seen, unlike other children, Rebecca reacts fearfully to the word "hammer." She obviously associates the physician's little, harmless hammer with the carpenter's big, powerful hammer, a result of having been socialized by her father.

Does this mean that children are like clay waiting to be shaped in one way or another? The roles of *nature* (what we inherit) and of *nurture* (what we learn) in making us what we are have long been argued. In this chapter, we will examine the roles of both nature and nurture and several theories of just how they influence our development. Then we will turn our attention to who it is that socializes us.

Nature and Nurture

To the seventeenth-century philosopher John Locke, the mind of a child was like a *tabula rasa* (blank slate). People became what they were taught to be.

By the second half of the nineteenth century, a quite different view was popular. Instead of looking to nurture—what people are taught—to explain human behavior, many social scientists looked to nature—what people inherit. The pendulum of opinion has swung back and forth ever since. In retrospect, the debate sometimes seems fruitless, but we have learned from it.

THE SIGNIFICANCE OF HEREDITY

Obviously, we do inherit something of what makes us who we are. But what? Race and sex are inherited, but their effect on human behavior and personality depends to a great extent on what society makes of them. (We discuss these effects in Chapter 8: Racial and Ethnic Minorities and Chapter 9: Gender and Age.) One important component of our inherited makeup is the absence of instinct within us. Instincts are biologically inherited capacities for performing relatively complex tasks. Only animals have instincts, which makes it unnecessary for them to learn how to live much of their lives. Instincts enable birds, for ex-

We inherit much of our physical makeup, including our eyes, hair, and skin color. But there is much dispute over whether we inherit nonphysical characteristics such as intelligence, aptitude, and personality. Sociologists maintain that although nature sets limits on what we can achieve, socialization plays a large role in determining what we do achieve.

ample, to catch worms, find mates, build nests, and raise their young. But humans, devoid of instincts, must be socialized to perform similarly complex tasks to survive.

People do appear to inherit temperament—an inclination to react in a certain way. Some people are inclined to be active, nervous, or irritable; others tend to be passive, calm, or placid. Psychologists have found that even infants show consistent temperaments. Some are active most of the time, whereas others move rather little. Some cry and fuss a lot, and others rarely do. Some react intensely to things like wet diapers, while others have only mild reactions. These differences may influence personality development. Very active infants, for example, are more likely than passive ones to become aggressive and competitive adults.

The role of heredity in determining intelligence and aptitude is more controversial. **Intelligence** is the capacity for mental achievement, such as the ability to think logically and solve problems. **Aptitude** is the capacity for developing physical or social skills, such as athletic prowess. The extent to which intelligence in particular is inherited has been the subject of some of the most bitter, emotional debates in all of social science. The debate is far from settled. For our purposes here, however, what is significant is that, although nature sets limits on what we may achieve, socialization plays a very large role in determining what we do achieve. Whatever potential is inherited may be developed or stunted through socialization.

THE SIGNIFICANCE OF SOCIALIZATION

The lack of instincts makes socialization both necessary and possible for human beings. As we saw in Chapter 2 (Culture), whatever temperament and potential abilities they are born with, human infants are also born helpless, dependent on others for survival. What may be more surprising, however, is the extent to which traits that seem very basic and essential to "human nature" also appear to depend on socialization. Evidence of the far-reaching significance of socialization comes both from case studies of children deprived of socialization and from instances in which children have been given very special, intensive training.

The Results of Deprivation Since the fourteenth century there have been more than 50 recorded cases of "feral children"—children supposedly raised by animals. One of the most famous is "the wild boy of Aveyron." In 1797 he was captured in the woods by hunters in southern France. He was about 11 years old and completely naked. The "wild boy" ran on all fours, had no speech, preferred uncooked food, and could not do most of the simple things done by younger children. A group of experts pronounced him hopelessly retarded. But Jean Itard, a physician, disagreed. He set out to train the boy, whom he later called Victor. After three months Victor seemed a little more human. He wore clothing. He got up at night to urinate in the toilet. He learned to sit at a table and eat with utensils. He started to show human emotions such as joy, gratitude, and remorse. But, although he lived to be more than 40 years old, he neither learned to speak nor ever became a normal person (Malson, 1972; Lane, 1976).

There is some doubt that Victor was raised by animals. He was probably old enough to scavenge for food himself when he was abandoned. Nevertheless, he was certainly deprived of normal socialization, and he bore the marks of this loss throughout his life. Less extreme cases also illustrate the significance of socialization. In the United States, there have been three well-known instances of such deprivation. They involved three children—Anna, Isabella, and Genie—who were kept secluded in their homes with their mothers.

Anna was born in Pennsylvania in 1932 as an illegitimate child, a fact that outraged her mother's father. After trying unsuccessfully to give Anna away, the mother hid her in the attic. Anna was fed just enough to keep her alive, was neither touched nor talked to, neither washed nor bathed. She simply lay still in her own filth. When she was found in 1938 at the age of 6, Anna looked like a skeleton. She could not talk or walk. She did nothing but lie quietly on the floor, her eyes vacant and her face expressionless. Efforts to socialize her were not very successful. Eventually she could do simple things such as walk, feed herself, brush her teeth, and follow simple directions. But she never learned to speak and was far from normal. She died at the age of 11 (Davis, 1947).

Isabella's story is a far happier one. Like Anna, she was an illegitimate child who was 6 years old when she was found in Ohio in 1938. Her grandfather had kept her and her deaf-mute mother secluded in a dark room. Isabella was more fortunate than Anna because she could interact with her mother. When she was discovered, Isabella showed great fear and hostility toward people and made a strange croaking sound. Specialists who examined her thought she was feebleminded and uneducable. Nevertheless, she was put on a systematic and skillful program of training. After a slow start, she began to talk. In only nine months she could read and write, and within two years she was attending school. She had become a very bright, cheerful, and energetic girl. Apparently, the intensive training by the specialists, coupled with the earlier interaction with her mother, made it possible for Isabella to develop into a normal person (Davis, 1947).

Intensive training, however, did not work out for Genie, who was found in California in 1970, primarily because she had been deprived of normal socialization for 12 years—twice as long as Isabella. From about 1 to 13 years of age, Genie had been isolated in a small, quiet room. During the day she was tied to her potty seat, able only to flutter her hands and feet. At night, if she was not forgotten, her father would straitjacket and cage her in a crib with an overhead cover. He would beat her if she made any noise. He never spoke to her except to occasionally bark or growl like a dog at her. Her terrified mother, forbidden to speak to Genie, fed her in silence and haste. When she was discovered, at age 13, Genie could not stand straight, was unable to speak (except whimper), and had the intelligence and social maturity of a 1-year-old. For the next eight years, psycholinguists, speech therapists, and special education teachers worked with her, but at the end, when she was 21, her language abilities could go no further than the 4-year-old level. She was finally placed in an institution (Pines, 1981).

These four cases are, to say the least, unusual. But even less severe forms of deprivation can be harmful. In 1945 psychologist René Spitz reported that children who received little attention in institutions suffered very noticeable effects. In one orphanage, Spitz found that infants who were about 18 months old were left lying on their backs in small cubicles most of the day without any human contact. Within a year, all had become physically, mentally, emotionally, and socially retarded. Two years later, more than a third of the children had died. Those who survived could not speak, walk, dress themselves, or use a spoon (Spitz, 1945).

Since Spitz's pioneering work, many other psychologists have documented the damage done to children who are placed in institutions in which they receive little human contact, attention, or stimulation. Normal human development seems to require, at the least, that infants have some continuing interaction, some bond of attachment, with another person.

Creating Geniuses The positive effects of specialized socialization are also instructive. According to

Both heredity and environment play a role in the development of personality. Japanese violinist Midori may have been born with some of her musical talent, but if as a child her interest in music had been discouraged, she might not have grown up to perform as she did here, with the New York Philharmonic.

Thomas Hoult (1974), a young woman named Edith finished grammar school in four years, skipped high school, and went straight to college. She graduated from college at the age of 15 and obtained her doctorate before she was 18. Was she born a genius? Not at all. Ever since she had stopped playing with dolls, her father had seen to it that her days were filled with reading, mathematics, classical music, intellectual discussions and debates, and whatever learning her father could derive from the world's literature. When she felt like playing, her father told her to play chess with someone like himself, who would be a challenge to her.

Like Edith, many geniuses have been deliberately subjected to a very stimulating environment. A well-known example is Norbert Wiener, a prime mover in the development of computers and cybernetics. He entered college at age 11 and received his Ph.D. from Harvard at 18. According to his father,

Norbert was "essentially an average boy who had had the advantage of superlative training." Another example is Adragon Eastwood DeMello, who graduated with a degree in mathematics from the University of California at age 11. When he was a few months old, his father gave up his career as a science writer to educate him. "The only way he could perform," said one of his teachers, "was when his father sat in the classroom next to him. From a very young age his father has trained him like a monkey" (Radford, 1990).

Nature draws the outline of our traits and potential abilities, but that outline is broad and vague. Nurture appears both to determine the actual boundaries and to fill in the details. Consider ace test pilot Chuck Yeager. He may have been born fearless. But, if his parents had been overprotective and kept him from jumping off barns, he might never have grown up to be the first flier to break the sound barrier (Wellborn, 1987). Obviously, both heredity and environment are involved in the development of personality. Even something that appears to be an inherited trait, like smiling, also has a social origin. Which has a greater influence? Sociologists would say environment, and sociobiologists, who emphasize the biological determinants of behavior, would claim heredity. The latest report from the Minnesota Center for Twin and Adoption Research suggests that both factors are about equally influential. The Minnesota researchers gave a battery of personality tests to 248 pairs of twins, including 44 pairs of identical twins who had been brought up in different homes. If twins were found to have the same personality traits, heredity was considered a key factor in personality development. But, if twins were found to have different traits, socialization was assumed to have played a larger role. The results showed that the subjects owed about half of their personality to nature and the other half to nurture (Leo, 1987). However, the California Adoption Project, a longitudinal study of adopted children, found that heredity accounts for only 15 to 25 percent of the subjects' intelligence. Similarly, a review of a vast number of studies on intelligence places the genetic contribution at around 30 to 40 percent. In other words, environmental factors contribute more than heredity to one's intelligence (Radford, 1990).

QUESTIONS FOR DISCUSSION AND REVIEW

1. How does the contribution of socialization to human personality differ from the contribution of heredity?
2. What do deprived and stimulating environments have in common?

Processes of Socialization

There are various processes of socialization through which children develop their personalities. The most important involve teaching children how to think, how to feel, and how to see themselves. Let us explore each of these socialization processes.

LEARNING HOW TO THINK

From close observation of children, Swiss psychologist Jean Piaget (1896–1980) concluded that they pass through certain stages of cognitive development. Today's sociologists find Piaget's studies useful for understanding how children learn new cognitive skills—perception, memory, calculation, reasoning, and other intellectual activities—as they grow up to become properly functioning members of society. Piaget has been criticized, though, for treating cognitive development as if it occurred in a social vacuum. Obviously, children cannot learn any cognitive skill by themselves—without some help from parents, teachers, and other important people in their lives. Piaget did not necessarily ignore the influence of those people on a child's cognitive development. He simply chose to focus on what new intellectual skills children develop at each stage of their lives. Let us take a close look at those skills while keeping in mind that they are influenced by some social forces such as family and education.

1. *Sensorimotor stage (birth to age 2):* Infants lack language, cannot think, and cannot make sense of their environment. They also lack a sense of self and are unable to see themselves as the cause of the events in their surroundings. If they shake a rattle, they do not realize that they cause the rattle to make a sound but act as if the rattle made the sound by itself. Unlike other people, who interact with the world by using their brains, infants use their senses and bodily movements to interact with the environment. Infants, for example, use their hands to touch, move, or pick up objects, and put things in their mouths or suck at some objects. This is why Piaget called this stage *sensorimotor*.

In using their sensorimotor capabilities, infants do not realize that an object, a human, or a cat has a relatively permanent existence. So, in the child's view, the mother exists only when she can be seen or touched, but she no longer exists when she leaves the child's field of vision.

2. *Preoperational stage (ages 2 to 7):* The term *preoperational* suggests that the child cannot

perform many simple intellectual operations. Suppose we take a boy, 2 to 4 years old, for a walk in a park; he may say "dog" every time he comes across one. If we ask him whether he sees the same dog or a succession of different dogs, he might get confused because he cannot distinguish "this particular dog" from dogs as a general category. Suppose we show slightly older children two glasses of the same size containing the same volume of water; they will correctly say that both glasses hold the same amount of water. But if we pour all the water from one of the glasses into a third glass that is taller and thinner, they will incorrectly conclude that the third glass holds more water than the other glass because its water level is higher.

These children are "precausal," unable to understand cause and effect. When Piaget asked 4-year-olds what makes a bicycle move, they replied that the street makes it go. When he asked 6-year-olds why the sun and moon move, the youngsters said that the heavenly bodies follow us in order to see us. These children are also animistic. They attribute humanlike thoughts and wishes to the sun and moon. They even attribute life to such inanimate objects as tables, chairs, and toys, which they believe can feel pain if we hit them. Moreover, they are egocentric, seeing things from their own perspective only. If we ask a young boy how many brothers he has, he may correctly say "One." But if we ask him, "How many brothers does your brother have?" he would say, "None." He has difficulty seeing himself from his brother's perspective.

3. *Concrete operational stage (ages 7 to 12):* In this stage, children can perform all the simple intellectual tasks just described. By 7 or 8 years of age, children are able, for example, to recognize that a given amount of water remains the same regardless of the shape of the glass that holds it. But their mental abilities are restricted to intellectual operations that involve manipulation of concrete objects only. If children between ages 8 and 10 are asked to line up a series of dolls from the tallest to the shortest, they can easily do so. But they cannot solve a similar problem put verbally—in abstract terms—such as "John is taller than Bill; Bill is taller than Harry; who is the tallest of the three?" The children can correctly answer this question only if they actually see John, Bill, and Harry in person.

4. *Formal operational stage (ages 12 to 15):* In this stage, adolescents can perform "formal operations"; they are capable of thinking and reasoning formally (abstractly). They can follow the form of an argument while ignoring its concrete content. They know, for example, that, if A is greater than B and B is greater than C, then A is greater than C—without having to know in advance whether the concrete contents of A, B, and C are vegetables, fruits, animals, or whatever can be seen and manipulated. Not everyone has the capability to progress into this stage of formal operations. In fact, it has been estimated that about half of the American population cannot understand abstract concepts well enough to be regarded as having passed into this stage. We should not, however, equate different stages of cognitive development with different levels of intelligence. In Piaget's view, young children are not necessarily less intelligent than older ones. They just think about things in a different way.

Of course, children do not always acquire the same cognitive abilities at the same age. Some are born smarter, so they may develop greater intellectual skills than others in their age group. But social forces are far more useful than innate intelligence for explaining why some 10-year-old children can think like a 13-year-old. An important reason is that they may have been *taught* to think that way. Sociologists have long known that children whose parents are highly educated professionals are more likely to be intellectually advanced beyond their age group, when compared with children whose parents are less educated. In fact, many other social forces, such as social class, racial discrimination, and family size, can influence the rate, amount, or speed of intellectual development. Consequently, the rate, amount, or speed, varies from one individual or group to another. Nevertheless, the order or sequence of mental development, as laid out by Piaget, does not. Among 10-year-olds, for example, some can think abstractly, like 13-year-olds, while others cannot. But whether or not they are able to think like older children, the 10-year-olds typically think concretely before—not after—learning to think abstractly (Oakes, 1985).

LEARNING HOW TO FEEL

While developing their cognitive abilities, children also learn to understand their own emotions and, by extension, others' emotions. This contributes significantly to how well they will function as adult members of society. Emotional socialization involves two tasks: how to identify feelings and how to manage them.

Children learn to understand their own emotions and, by extension, others' emotions. For example, through socialization, a child learns that a threat from his mother is expected to arouse fear.

There are a great variety of human emotions, ranging from such basic feelings as fear, anger, and happiness to more refined emotions, such as frustration, love, and jealousy. Children are taught how to identify these feelings because they cannot by themselves know what they are. Suppose a little boy at a day-care center engages in such expressive behaviors as fidgeting, sulking, biting, or kicking while waiting for his mother to pick him up. He may learn from an adult that what he feels is anger. Here is how such a scenario may occur (Pollak and Thoits, 1989):

> BOY *[restless]:* My mom is late.
> STAFF MEMBER: Does that make you *mad?*
> BOY: Yes.
> STAFF MEMBER: Sometimes kids get *mad* when their moms are late to pick them up.

The adult, then, teaches the child to identify an emotion by making a causal connection between a stimulus event (mother being late) and an emotional outcome (boy being angry). Through socialization—not only by parents and other caretakers but also by television, movies, and other mass media—children learn that a compliment is expected to give pleasure, a threat is expected to arouse fear, and uncertainty is expected to give rise to anxiety. While they learn that it is logical to feel resentful toward someone who has mistreated them, they also learn that it is not logical to feel affectionate toward that person. It is crucial for children to acquire this emotional logic. Failure to do so is popularly considered a symptom of mental disorder. If a 10-year-old tells you with a big smile that his or her mother has just died, you may suspect the child of being mentally ill (Rosenberg, 1990).

Children also learn how to manage their emotions in at least three ways. First, they learn how they *should* feel. They should have a feeling of love for their parents, or they should feel guilty if they displease their parents. They should feel proud of their country. They should feel grateful to someone who has been kind and helpful to them. These are some of the "feeling rules" that our society requires us to follow (Hochschild, 1983).

Second, children learn how to express or conceal emotions. They should *look* happy at a wedding, *look* sad at a funeral, *act* happy at a party, *appear* reverent at a religious service, or *display* excitement at a sports event. Failure to adhere to these and other "display rules" is likely to elicit scorn and condemnation from others. We should note, however, that, unlike the feeling rules, the display rules only require that we display sadness at a funeral, for example, without necessarily feeling sad. Of course, we may display sadness while genuinely feeling sad. But the display rules sometimes demand that we display an emotion that we do not have in us or that we conceal a feeling that we do have. If a friend gives you a present that you do not like, you should still show how much you like it. On the other hand, if you hate your boss, dislike certain customers, or feel bored with a lecturer, the display rules require that you conceal these negative feelings (Rosenberg, 1990).

Finally, while they learn to express or conceal certain emotions, children also learn how to produce or eliminate some feelings in themselves. It is more difficult to make oneself *feel* happy, for example, than to make oneself *look* happy. But there are ways of effectively manipulating one's emotions. If we are feeling blue, we can displace the unpleasant feeling with a pleasant one. We could do so by telephoning a delightful friend, reading an interesting novel, or going to see a movie. Indeed, when children feel bored or moody, their parents may tell them to call up some friends or to visit them. We can also eliminate unpleasant feelings through selective exposure. If we are talking to someone who angers us, we can cut short the conversation. If we are listening to news that depresses us, we can switch channels or turn off the television. Physical exertion can also be used to manipulate our emotions. Walking, jogging, aerobics, and other physical activities have proven capable of eliminating feelings of depression (Rosenberg, 1990).

Not all children learn to identify and manage emotions in the same way. Social forces, particularly gender roles and social classes, exert a strong influence on emotional socialization. Compared with boys, girls are taught to be more empathetic, more loving, less able to feel and express anger, but more able to feel and express fear and sadness. Higher-status children generally learn to feel happier and more satisfied than do lower-status children (Thoits, 1989). Traditional women of the middle and upper classes tend more to teach their daughters such emotional management as "expressing joy at the Christmas presents others open, creating the sense of surprise at birthdays, or displaying alarm at the mouse in the kitchen" (Hochschild, 1983). Because middle-class and upper-class people tend to work more with people than with things, they are more attuned to emotional management, such as smiling at customers even when they do not feel like smiling. Therefore, in teaching emotional management to their children, people in the middle and upper classes are more likely than the lower classes to show respect for the youngsters' feelings by using reasoning and persuasion. Suppose a child says, "I don't want to kiss Grandpa—why must I kiss him all the time?" Parents of the higher classes would respond, "I know you don't like kissing Grandpa, but he's unwell and he's very fond of you." By contrast, lower-class and working-class parents, who tend to be less sensitive to their offspring's feelings, would answer, "Children should kiss their Grandpa," or "He's not well—I don't want any of your nonsense." They, in effect, order the child to kiss his or her grandfather (Hochschild, 1983).

LEARNING HOW TO SEE ONESELF

Children are not born with a sense of who they are. Only through socialization can they develop their self-concept. Symbolic interactionists have long discovered how the self-concept emerges from interaction between children and their parents and other important people in their lives.

Cooley: The Looking-Glass Process American sociologist Charles Horton Cooley (1864–1929) was one of the founders of symbolic interactionism. He viewed society as a group of individuals helping each other to develop their personalities. According to Cooley, the core of personality is the concept of oneself, the self-image. And self-image, Cooley said, is developed through the "looking-glass process":

> Each to each a looking glass
> Reflects the other that doth pass.

We get our self-image from the way others treat us. Their treatment is like a mirror reflecting our personal qualities, and Cooley referred to that treatment as our **looking-glass self.** If we have a positive image, seeing ourselves as intelligent or respectable, it is because others have treated us as such. Just as we cannot see our own face unless we have a mirror in front of us, so we cannot have a certain self-image unless others react to our behavior.

The looking-glass process, however, works both ways. While others are judging us, we are judging them in return. The way we judge others affects how we interpret their impressions of us. Suppose certain individuals see us as stupid; we will reject such a view if we consider them stupid in the first place. In fact, as over 50 studies have consistently suggested, we tend to discredit others' negative views of us or to perceive ourselves more favorably than others see us (Shrauger and Schoeneman, 1979).

No matter what kind of self-concept emerges from the looking-glass process, it has a certain impact on our personality and behavior. If we have a favorable self-concept, we tend to be self-confident, outgoing, or happy. If we have a poor self-image, we are inclined to be timid, withdrawn, or unhappy. Research has also shown that low self-esteem has such undesirable outcomes as delinquent behavior and lower academic achievement, and that high self-esteem leads to such favorable consequences as better behavior and greater creativity (Gecas, 1982). The self-esteem, however, must be a genuine one, which has arisen from achievement-based praises rather than vacuous flattery from others (Adler, 1992).

Mead: The Role-taking Process The other founder of symbolic interactionism was George Herbert Mead (1863–1931). Like Cooley, Mead assumed

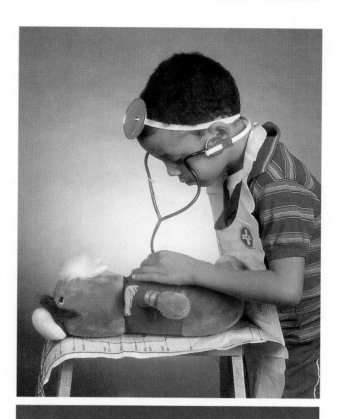

Mead emphasized role-taking, by which children internalize the values and attitudes of significant others, in socialization. Children first imitate their parents, without actually knowing the meanings of their actions; then, in play, they pretend to be their parents, thus internalizing their values. The boy in the picture is taking the role of a doctor, a generalized other, thus beginning to be a part of the larger society.

that the development of a self-concept is made possible by symbolic interaction—by interaction with others through symbols like language and gestures. But while Cooley stressed the importance of using others as our mirrors by observing their reactions to our behavior, Mead emphasized the significance of getting "under the skin" of others by taking their roles.

According to Mead, children develop their self-concept in three stages. First, during their initial two years, they simply imitate other people in their immediate environment. When they see their mother reading a newspaper, they will pretend to read it too. When they see their father talk on the phone, they may later pick up the phone and talk on it. In this imitation stage, however, they are not yet playing the role of father or mother, because they do not have

any idea of what they are doing. They simply learn to act like others without knowing the meanings of those actions. Then, at about age 3, children begin to go through the play stage. Now they take the roles of their parents, who are an example of what Mead called **significant others,** by pretending to be their mother and father while they play. In this world of make-believe, they learn to see themselves from their parents' perspective. In the process, they *internalize* their parents' values and attitudes, incorporating them into their own personalities. When they tell their baby dolls not to be naughty, they, in effect, tell themselves not to be naughty. As they grow older, they also come into contact with doctors, nurses, bus drivers, sales clerks, and so on. These people outside the family circle are not as significant as the parents, but they are representative of society as a whole. Mead called them **generalized others.** By this time, children pass through the game stage by playing the roles of the generalized others. In this third stage, they learn to internalize the values of society as a whole. Participation in organized games such as baseball and basketball also promotes this internalization. These games involve a complex interaction among the players that is governed by a set of rules. When they play such games, children are, in effect, playing the game of life. They are learning that life has rules too.

Internalized social values become only one part of our personality, which Mead called the *me.* Whenever we feel like obeying the law, following the crowd, and the like, we are sensing the presence of the *me.* It represents society within our personality. On the other hand, a portion of our personality cannot be easily "invaded" by society, no matter how often we have played childhood games. Mead referred to this part of our personality as the *I.* It is basically spontaneous, creative, or impulsive. Unlike the *me,* which makes all of us look alike in our behavior, the *I* makes each of us unique. People who live in a relatively free society or have been brought up in a permissive family are likely to have a stronger *I* than *me.* In contrast, those who live in a tightly controlled state or have been raised by overprotective parents tend to develop a more powerful *me* than *I.* But these two aspects of personality are complementary: without the *I,* there would be no individual creativity or social progress; without the *me,* there would be no social order or individual security. Both are inevitable and necessary.

Although Mead explained how the *me* emerges through role taking, he did not say where the *I* comes from. Norbert Wiley (1979) theorized that we get our *I* from both *me* and *we*. According to Wiley, babies first develop the *me* in the same way as Mead indicated, and through this *me* they identify with their parents so totally that they feel themselves an inseparable part of their parents. Then, through a tactile, giggly love experience between parents and infants, which Wiley calls a *we experience,* the adults are, in effect, saying to the youngsters, "You exist; you are a different person; and I love the person you are." The infant then learns to see itself as independent from its parents, at which point it develops the *I.*

QUESTIONS FOR DISCUSSION AND REVIEW

1. What mental abilities develop from birth through adolescence?
2. How do children learn to identify and manage their emotions?
3. How do children develop their self-concept?

Agents of Socialization

Every society tries to socialize its members. It slips the task into the hands of several groups and institutions, which are therefore called the *socializing agents* of society. Some of them, including the family and school, are in a sense appointed by society to transmit its cultural heritage to the young. Other agents, including the peer group and mass media, are not appointed by society. Their socialization of children is mostly unintentional (Koller and Ritchie, 1978; Elkin and Handel, 1988).

THE FAMILY

The family is the most important socializing agent, especially during the first few years of life. Many theorists, such as Piaget and Mead, have emphasized the significance of childhood experiences in the family. A review of various studies has concluded that warm, supportive, "reasonably constricting" family environments usually produce happy and well-behaving children; whereas cold, rigid, and "coercively restrictive" families cause youngsters to become rebellious, resentful, and insecure (Gecas, 1981). Research also established the family as the most influential socializing agent for adolescents (Davies and Kandel, 1981; Vandewiele, 1981). Various social forces, however, influence the way parents socialize their children.

A good example is social stratification, as can be seen in the differences between lower- and middle-class families. Research has long shown that lower-class families tend to be more adult-centered, more authoritarian than middle-class families. This

The cultural heritage is passed on directly from parents to children, which is why the family is the prime socializing agent of society. The family teaches the child to behave as the society expects. Since their parents follow Navajo traditions, these children are socialized to behave differently than if they were raised in a city where Navajo traditions had been set aside.

might be a vestige of the family pattern that prevailed in our past, when adults treated children as their property, slaves, or pets (DeMause, 1975; Lee, 1982). In these authoritarian families, parents tend to train children to respect and obey parental authority, to follow rules and orders. On the other hand, middle-class parents are more inclined to teach the value of independence. They are more permissive and child centered (Kohn, 1963, 1977). In one study, middle-class mothers spent twice as much time in mutual play with their 3-year-old children as did lower-class mothers (Farran and Haskins, 1980). Influenced by numerous child development experts, middle-class parents are also much more sensitive to their children's feelings. If a child while playing makes a baby doggy bite off the head of a daddy doggy, the parents would refrain from jumping in with the accusatory remark, "Oh, that's terrible!" They would instead show respect to the child's feeling by saying something like "Wow! It looks to me as if the baby doggy is really angry at the daddy doggy" (Crossen, 1991).

Family size, too, has been found to influence parenting style. In one study, high school students from large families were more likely to describe their parents as authoritarian. They reported that their parents seldom explained the rules imposed on children, were inclined to use physical punishment, and tried to control children longer. But large families are also more likely than small ones to give each child more independence and protection from parental supervision, despotism, and emotional absorption. The reason is that, in a large family, parental attention is spread over more children, which reduces parental influence on any one child (Gecas, 1981). Parental attention also declines when both father and mother work. Children in such families have been found to be less obedient to their parents and more aggressive toward their peers when compared with other children. Decreased obedience and greater aggressiveness, however, may reflect independence and assertiveness rather than social maladjustment (Collins and Gunnar, 1990). In fact, research has failed to support the popular belief that if parents are highly committed to work without also being highly committed to parenting, they will fail to socialize their children adequately. While working parents cannot spend much time at home with their children, they are more likely than traditional parents to promote in their children understanding and mature behavior rather than unthinking obedience (Greenberger and Goldberg, 1989).

Culture further influences how parents socialize their children. In a comparative analysis of over 100 societies, Godfrey Ellis and associates (1978) found that in societies where adults are closely supervised—as in the case of women being directed by mothers-in-law in child care, cooking, and other household chores—parents tend to socialize their children toward conformity. In cultures where adults are not closely supervised, self-reliance becomes the primary objective for socialization. In analyzing similar data, Larry Petersen and colleagues (1982) further discovered that in societies where conformity is emphasized in socialization, parents often resort to physical punishment as a way of teaching children to obey them. In societies such as the United States, where self-reliance is a primary goal for socialization, parents are more inclined to use psychological punishment, such as discontinuing allowances, prohibiting going out, or otherwise withholding love and making children feel guilty for having misbehaved.

THE SCHOOL

At home children are treated as unique persons. At school, however, they are more likely to be treated impersonally, as mere holders of a role. They would find that the school is mostly a system that treats all the children in the same way. They may learn to fit into that system by getting along with others. In fact, the schools often provide children with their first training in how they are expected to behave in impersonal groups.

Whereas socialization by families often contributes to the diversity of society, the schools are more likely to contribute to uniformity. Society, in effect, officially designates them as its socializing agents. They are expected both to help children develop their potential as individuals and to mold them into social conformity—two goals that may be contradictory. To meet the first goal, the school teaches its formal curriculum of academic knowledge and skills. The pursuit of this goal becomes increasingly important as students rise to progressively higher educational levels (Miller, Kohn, and Schooler, 1986). Thus, intellectual performance becomes more important to college students than it is to primary school pupils. By cultivating their intellectual capabilities, students are expected to turn into intelligent citizens capable of making a living while contributing to the prosperity of their society.

The pursuit of the second goal—social conformity—is more earnest at the lower grade levels. It involves teaching what has been called a "hidden curriculum," training students to be patriotic, to believe in the society's cultural values, and to obey its laws. This instruction is often made explicit in history and civics classes. But it is also implicit in classroom rituals (such as the Pledge of Allegiance), in demands that classroom rules be obeyed, in the choice of books to be assigned in English classes, and in a host of other activities (such as glorification of the competition and discipline of sports). The hidden curriculum, then, helps ensure social order and the continuity of a society's values from one generation to the next.

Some schools, of course, are more successful than others in meeting those goals. Generally, American schools do better with upper- and middle-class children than with lower-class children. There are at least three explanations (Elkin and Handel, 1988).

First, schools with mostly higher-income students tend to have more competent teachers and better resources than schools where poor children predominate. Second, higher- income parents are likely to have developed in their children a higher level of intellectual skills than have lower-income parents. Third, teachers, who usually hold middle-class values, tend to expect middle- and upper-class students to do better than lower-class students. Expectations can be self-fulfilling, as we saw in the Rosenthal and Jacobson experiment discussed in Chapter 1 (The Essence of Sociology).

THE PEER GROUP

As children grow older, they become increasingly involved with their peer group, which consists of children who are about the same age and have similar interests. As a socializing agent, the peer group is quite

"Can we go see 'Home Alone 2'? My friend Jeffrey says it's an important picture."

Drawing by Weber; copyright © 1992 by The New Yorker *Magazine, Inc.*

different from the family and school. While parents and teachers have more power than children and students, the peer group is made up of equals.

As a distinctive agent of socialization, the peer group teaches its members several important things. First, it teaches them to be independent from adult authorities, which may speed up their entry into adulthood. Second, it teaches social skills and group loyalties. Third, the peer group teaches its members the values of friendship and companionship among equals—values that are relatively absent in the socialization received from authority figures like parents and teachers. On the other hand, a peer group can socialize its members to thumb their noses at authorities and adults. If there is a rule against bringing toys from home to nursery school, some children will ignore it. Some may end up getting into trouble with the law one day. And many others may only innocently poke fun at adults behind their backs (Elkin and Handel, 1988; Corsaro and Eder, 1990).

Freeing themselves from the grip of parental and school authorities, peer groups often develop distinctive subcultures with their own values, symbols, jargon, music, dress, and heroes. Whereas parents and teachers tend to place great importance on scholastic achievement, adolescent peer groups are likely to put a higher premium on popularity, social leadership, and athletic attainment (Corsaro and Rizzo, 1988). The divergence between parental and peer values does not necessarily lead to a hostile confrontation between parents and teenagers. In fact, most youngsters are just as friendly with parents as with peers. They simply engage in different types of activities—work and task activities with parents but play and recreation with peers. Concerning financial, educational, career, and other serious matters, such as what to spend money on and what occupation to choose, they are inclined to seek advice from parents. When it comes to social activities, such as whom to date and what clubs to join, they are more likely to discuss them with peers (Sebald, 1986). This reflects the great importance placed by the peer group on "other-directed behavior"—looking to others for approval and support—as opposed to reliance on personal beliefs and traditional values. The peer groups, in effect, demand conformity at the expense of independence and individuality. Those in early adolescence are most willing to accept conformity; hence, they are most deeply involved with peer groups. As they grow into middle and late adolescence, their involvement with peers gradually de-

clines because of their growing predilection for independence. When they reach the final year of high school, they tend more to adopt adult values, such as wanting to get good grades and good jobs (Gelman, 1990a).

Gender and class have some influence on adolescent peer groups. Compared with boys, girls are more closely knit and egalitarian, more likely to share their problems, feelings, fears, and doubts with close friends. High school students from middle- and upper-class backgrounds are more likely to base their friendships on interests and activities, so they often switch friendships as their interests change. By contrast, students from working-class homes place greater emphasis on loyalty and stability, with friendships determining the choice of activities rather than the other way around. Middle-class girls are more concerned with developing social skills and being well liked. They are also more likely to strive for high status through friendship with popular girls and through such activities as cheerleading. Working-class girls, on the other hand, are more concerned with romance, sexual relationships, and marriage as a source of status, and also are more likely to see themselves as "nonconformists" and "troublemakers" at school. There is likewise some difference between middle-class and working-class boys. Middle-class boys are more concerned with athletic skills, dating, sexual prowess, and drinking stamina. Working-class boys are more likely to seek their status from peers by defying authority, rules, and academic work. They are also more likely to engage in fighting and insult exchanges, which they consider to be masculine (Corsaro and Eder, 1990).

THE MASS MEDIA

The mass media include popular books, magazines, newspapers, movies, television, and radio. They probably exert more influence on children than many other socializing agents. Among the mass media, television appears the most influential. It has been found to affect children in some ways.

First of all, children may come to expect their lives, their parents, and their teachers to be as exciting as those portrayed on television. Even the widely praised Sesame Street makes children expect their schools to be fast paced and entertaining. Thus, children are likely to be disappointed, finding their parents inadequate and their teachers boring. Second,

Television occupies a special place among the agents of socialization simply because children spend so much time watching it. It greatly influences the child's beliefs, values, and behavior. But the influence of television decreases as the child grows up.

there is some evidence that television tends to impoverish its young viewers' creative imagination. If they watch TV frequently, they may find it difficult to create pictures in their own minds or to understand stories without visual illustration. This is because watching television usually makes people feel passive. Third, through its frequent portrayal of violence, television tends to stimulate violence-prone children to actual violence, to make normal children less sensitive to violence in real life, and to instill the philosophy that might makes right. Television violence can further heighten children's senses of danger and vulnerability as well as their feelings of alienation and doom. Finally, television destroys the age-old notion of childhood as a discrete period of innocence. It reveals the "secrets" of adulthood that have been hidden from children for centuries. The spectacle of adults hitting each other, killing each other, and breaking down and crying teaches them that adults do not know any better than children (Zoglin, 1990).

On the other hand, television has the redeeming quality of enlarging children's vocabulary and knowledge of the world (Josephson, 1987). These effects, however, usually wear off as the younger viewer gets older. Although children who have watched television frequently begin school with a better vocabulary and greater knowledge than those who have not, this advantage disappears soon after schooling starts. By the time children are about 12 years old, they are likely to find commercials unreal and misleading. Older children may become so outraged at being lied to that they are ready to believe that, like advertising, business and other institutions are riddled with adult hypocrisy. With increased sophistication, older teenagers and adults also take TV violence for what it is—fake and for entertainment only (Freedman, 1986; Rice et al., 1990).

QUESTIONS FOR DISCUSSION AND REVIEW
1. Why is the family still the most important agent of socialization?
2. What is the hidden curriculum of the school, and how does it try to ensure social order?
3. Why are many adolescents more influenced by their peer groups than by their families?
4. In what ways do the positive features of television outweigh the negative?

Adult Socialization

The socialization process does not stop at the end of childhood. It continues with the emergence of adulthood and stops only when the person dies.

LEARNING NEW ROLES

Being socialized means, in effect, learning new roles. Like children, adults learn many new roles as they go through various stages of life. At the same time, adults' specific socialization experiences do differ from those of children. We can see this in the three types of socialization that all of us undergo.

One is **anticipatory socialization,** which involves learning a role that is to be assumed in the future. Many young children learn to be parents in the future by playing house. Young adults prepare themselves for their future professions by attending college. Generally, children tend to idealize their future roles, but adults are more practical about theirs. A child may wish to become the greatest lawyer on earth, but an adult is more likely to want to be one of the best lawyers in a city. Howard Becker and colleagues (1961) found that first-year medical students usually expect to acquire every bit of medical knowledge and then to serve humanity selflessly. Toward the end of their medical schooling, they become more realistic. They are likely to strive to learn just enough to pass exams and to look forward to a lucrative practice as a reward for their years of hard work. In short, as people get closer to the end of their anticipatory socialization, their earlier idealism gradually dies out, to be replaced by realism.

Like children, adults also go through **developmental socialization.** It involves learning roles that are already acquired, much like receiving on-the-job training. Children learn their currently acquired roles as sons or daughters, students, and members of their peer groups. Adults learn their newly assumed roles as full-time workers, husbands, wives, parents, and so on. If we compare these two sets of roles, we can see that adult socialization is more likely voluntary or self-initiated. Children cannot do away with their status of being sons or daughters, are required to go to school, and are largely restricted to hanging around with neighborhood kids. On the other hand, adults can *choose* to marry, become parents, get divorced, change jobs, move, and find friends from a wide area. Moreover, children are mostly socialized within the confines of primary groups, but adults are more likely to go beyond their families and friends and get involved in secondary relationships—with their bosses, co-workers, clients, and other members of formal organizations. There is, then, a great deal more self-determination and selectivity in adult socialization (Mortimer and Simmons, 1978).

The experiences that adults receive from their developmental socialization may depend on the nature of the socializing agents as well as the larger society. Business corporations, for instance, socialize their workers to achieve high productivity but at the same time encourage teamwork more than individual creativity, which may reflect the other-directed spirit of American society. The specific nature of a job can also mold adult personality. As demonstrated by Melvin Kohn's (1980) studies, the more complex a job, the more likely the worker will experience self-direction in the workplace and end up valuing autonomy in other aspects of life. On the other hand, the more simple and routine the work, the more likely it

is that the individual will be supervised by some higher-up and eventually will place a high value on conformity.

A third form of socialization is less common: **resocialization.** It forces the individual to abandon his or her old self and to develop a new self in its place. It happens to adults more often than to children. Resocialization can take place in prisons, mental institutions, POW camps, military training centers, and religious cults. Erving Goffman (1961) called such places "total institutions" because the inmates are not only totally cut off from the larger society but also totally controlled by the administrators. Resocialization in total institutions is usually dehumanizing. In a state mental institution, for example, the staff tends to treat new patients as if they were objects rather than humans. The staff may call them names, beat them, and prevent them from talking to the staff unless they are spoken to first. The staff may also enter the patients' rooms and examine their possessions at any time. The staff may even monitor the patients' personal hygiene and waste evacuation in the toilet. Such dehumanization, which Goffman called "mortification of self," is intended to strip the patients of whatever self-concept they have brought into the institution from their prior social life. Then the staff uses rewards and punishments to mold them into docile conformists, who do whatever they are told. Such patients usually suffer from "institutionalism"—a deep sense of hopelessness, pervasive loss of initiative, deterioration of social skills, and an inability to function in larger society.

ERIKSON: ADULT LIFE CYCLE

As we saw earlier, Piaget charted the various stages of personality development that children must pass through until they reach adulthood. Erik Erikson (1963, 1975) has applied the same concept of developmental stages not only to children but also to adults. Erikson views each stage as a crisis that stems from two opposite human desires. Individuals must resolve the crisis if they expect to lead a normal, happy life.

Erikson found three stages in adult life: early adulthood, middle adulthood, and late adulthood. In early adulthood, which lasts from ages 20 to 40, people face the crisis of having to resolve the conflicting demands for love and work. They usually meet the demand for love by falling in love, getting married, and raising a family. If they are too attached to their families, they risk losing the chance of realizing their youthful ambitions. At the same time, they may be eager to work extremely hard to establish themselves in their careers, but in doing so they risk losing intimacy with and incurring isolation from their families. In this stage, the young adult is confronted with the conflict between enjoying intimacy and suffering isolation.

In middle adulthood, which lasts from ages 40 to 60, people become acutely aware that their death will come, that their time is running out, and that they must give up their youthful dreams to start being more concerned with others rather than themselves. Usually, they choose to be what Erikson calls *generative*—by nurturing, guiding, teaching, and serving the younger generation. This would give them an elevating sense of productivity and creativity, of having made a significant contribution to others. On the other hand, they are also inclined to continue hanging on to their youthful dreams, to try to be active and feel young again. Because this is difficult to fulfill at this stage, the individuals risk getting weighed down with a depressing sense of disappointment, stagnation, and boredom. In short, the middle-aged adult is faced with the conflict between generativity and stagnation.

In late adulthood, from age 60 until death, people find themselves in the conflict between achieving integrity (holding oneself together) and sinking in despair (emotionally falling apart). Those who are able to maintain the integrity of the self are likely to have accepted whatever they have attained so far. But those who sink in despair do so because they regret that their lives have been full of missed opportunities and that the time is just too short for them to start another life. Therefore, death loses its sting for those who have learned to hold themselves together and to accept death as the ultimate outcome of life. But those who fall apart emotionally cannot accept death and are gripped with fear of it.

Research has established that most people do experience the two conflicting forces in each stage (Varghese, 1981; Ochse and Plug, 1986). We should also note that the word "crisis" does not have the negative connotation in Erikson's theory that it does in our culture. To Erikson, a crisis can be positive. It is basically the same as what the two characters in the Chinese word for crisis (*weiji*) represent: danger and opportunity. When faced with one of Erikson's crises, we need not succumb to the danger of isolation, stagnation, or despair—we could also seize the opportunity for intimacy, generativity, or integrity. According to Erikson (1975), sometimes we have to choose between two opposites, as in the case of integrity versus despair. Sometimes we have to incorporate them and put them in some manageable balance, as in the case of intimacy and isolation, so that we can have, say, both a successful marriage and a high-flying career at the same time. Indeed, many studies have shown that life-cycle changes—new parenthood, the "empty nest" (all children having grown and left home), and retirement—can be positive experiences (Bush and Simmons, 1981). There is also evidence that most adults succeed in attaining generativity and integrity as they get older (Darling-Fisher and Leidy, 1988). But Erikson has ignored the influence of social forces on those life-cycle experiences (Dannefer, 1984). As the following section suggests, whether the elderly fear death or not depends largely on the nature of society.

AGING AND DYING

Unlike traditional societies, modern societies do not adequately socialize their members for old age and death. In traditional societies, old people are highly valued and respected. It is quite an accomplishment to survive into old age in a traditional society, where most people die relatively young. Further, the experiences that the elderly have accumulated over the years are invaluable to younger generations, because their societies change so little and so slowly that old knowledge and values do not seem to lose their relevance. Because the aged live with their children and grandchildren, are given an honored role, and are often observed to dispense wisdom and advice, young people are easily socialized to know how to behave as wise old persons if they themselves become old.

In modern societies, old people typically live alone. By not living with their old parents and grandparents, younger people have little chance of learning how to grow old gracefully. Although they may visit their old relatives often, they do not relish the prospect of growing old themselves, because they believe that the aged live an unrewarding, lonely, or even degrading life.

Modern societies also have come up short in socialization for death. In traditional societies, people see their loved ones die at home, handle their

Our culture has traditionally not taught us to accept death as natural and unavoidable. The old have consequently felt afraid to die. But in recent years many have learned to face death calmly.

corpses, and personally bury them. But in modern societies, we seldom witness a dying scene at home because most deaths occur in hospitals. We may even be afraid to touch our relatives' corpses, as we always hire morticians to prepare them for burial. We may never have seen what death looks like because by the time the mortician has finished making up a dead body, it looks more like a live person sleeping. Although we are often bombarded with television and movie images of death as a result of war, famine, murder, and other violent acts, we do not weep and grieve over them but instead pull ourselves further away from the reality of death. If we were terminally ill, we would deny our impending death in order to forestall the social stigma associated with dying and to preserve our normal relations with families and friends (Beilin, 1982). Our culture, then, has not taught us to accept death as natural and unavoidable.

This is why, as Elisabeth Kübler-Ross (1969) has discovered, terminally ill patients usually go through five stages, from the time when they discover they are dying to the final moment of their death. Kübler-Ross refers to the first stage as "initial denial" because upon being told that they are dying, patients usually express disbelief: "No, not me; it just can't be me." At the second stage—anger—they believe they are dying but get angry with family, doctor, and God, protesting, "Why me?" When they move into the third stage—bargaining—they are no longer angry and ask God to let them live just a little longer in return for good behavior. In the fourth stage—depression—they can no longer postpone their death, so they sink into deep depression. Finally, in the fifth stage—acceptance—they feel calm and ready to die. Most patients, though, do not make it to the final stage.

Since the 1960s, however, the findings of Kübler-Ross have become less valid. Today many people die calmly and even happily. Our fear of death has diminished, thanks to a great outpouring of attention to the subject in books, television, and other media. This change in attitude began as early as the mid-1970s. In a 1977 survey of middle-aged and older people in Los Angeles, when asked "How afraid are you of death?" 63 percent responded "not afraid at all" and only 4 percent said "very afraid." According to a national survey conducted in the 1970s, most Americans of all ages did not find death terrifying. A majority agreed with such statements as "death is sometimes a blessing" and "death is not tragic for the person who dies, only for the survivors," whereas only one-tenth said that "to die is to suffer." There has also been a turnaround in doctors' attitudes toward death. One study of physicians who often treated terminal cancer patients indicated that in 1961 over 90 percent would *not* tell their patients they were dying. In 1979, however, 98 percent said it was their policy to tell their patients the truth (Riley, 1983; Retsinas, 1988).

QUESTIONS FOR DISCUSSION AND REVIEW
1. Why is socialization a lifelong process?
2. How do anticipatory and developmental socialization differ from resocialization?
3. What three development stages of adult life did Erikson discover, and what personal crisis does each stage contain?
4. Why is the fear of death relatively common in modern societies?

CHAPTER REVIEW

1. *What is socialization?* It is the process by which a society transmits its values to individuals so that they can function properly as its members.

2. *Can either nature or nurture alone explain human behavior?* No. Both heredity and environment make us what we are. The importance of heredity can be demonstrated by how our lack of instincts as well as our temperament, intelligence, and aptitude influence the development of our personality. The significance of socialization can be seen in the case studies of children who are feral, isolated, institutionalized, or gifted.

3. *How do children learn to think?* They develop increasingly advanced forms of mental abilities as they grow from birth through adolescence. *How do they learn to feel?* Through their parents and the mass media, they learn to identify and manage their emotions. *How do they develop their self-concept?* Through social interaction, they learn how to see themselves from the way others see them and from the roles of others.

4. *What is distinctive about each of the major socializing agents?* The family is the most important socializing agent for the child. It is, however, influenced by other social forces. The school is charged both with helping children develop their potential as individuals and with securing their conformity to social norms. The peer group socializes its members unintentionally. Made up of equals, the peer group often offers a set of values different from that presented by parents and teachers, which helps hasten the child's independence from adult authorities. The mass media, particularly in the form of television, exerts a powerful influence on the child's beliefs, values, and behavior. But this influence usually wears off as the child grows up.

5. *Does socialization stop with the end of childhood?* No. Adults continue to experience socialization as children do. They go through anticipatory socialization, developmental socialization, and resocialization. According to Erikson, adults go through various life stages, each a crisis that the individual must deal with. The most difficult crisis that con-

fronts members of modern society is aging and dying. Generally, the aged are not highly respected in modern societies, and death is not treated as a normal event of life to be accepted.

KEY TERMS

Anticipatory socialization Socialization that prepares a person to assume a role in the future (p. 104).

Aptitude The capacity for developing physical or social skills (p. 93).

Developmental socialization The kind of socialization that teaches a person to be more adequate in playing his or her currently assumed role (p. 105).

Generalized others Mead's term for people whose names are unknown to the child but who influence the child's internalization of the values of society (p. 99).

Intelligence The capacity for mental or intellectual achievement (p. 93).

Looking-glass self Cooley's term for the self-image that we develop from the way others treat us (p. 98).

Personality A fairly stable configuration of feelings, attitudes, ideas, and behaviors that characterizes an individual (p. 92).

Resocialization The kind of socialization that is aimed at replacing one's old self with a new self (p. 105).

Significant others Mead's term for specific persons, such as parents, who have a significant influence on the child because the child interacts mainly with them in his or her early years and plays at being these adults (p. 99).

Socialization The process by which a society transmits its cultural values to its members (p. 92).

SUGGESTED READINGS

Corsaro, William A. 1985. *Friendship and Peer Culture in the Early Years.* Norwood, N.J.: Ablex. An observational study of how nursery school children shape their own developmental experiences through interactions with peers, confirming the views of Piaget, Mead, and others.

Elkin, Frederick, and Gerald Handel. 1988. *The Child and Society,* 5th ed. New York: Random House. A useful basic text for studying childhood socialization.

Gilligan, Carol, et al. (eds.). 1990. *Making Connections.* Cambridge, Mass.: Harvard University Press. A series of research reports on how American society encourages adolescent girls to change from being confident about what they know and see to being uncertain and hesitant.

Raphael, Ray. 1988. *The Men from the Boys.* Lincoln: University of Nebraska Press. An analysis of how American boys grapple with the problems of becoming adults in a society that lacks a clear-cut rite of passage.

Whiting, Beatrice Blyth, and Carolyn Pope Edwards. 1988. *Children of Different Worlds.* Cambridge, Mass.: Harvard University Press. A comparative study of young children in the United States and six other countries, showing how parents and peers influence the formation of the children's social behavior.

6

DEVIANCE AND CONTROL

MYTHS AND REALITIES

Myth: "Guns don't kill, people do." Therefore, it is futile to outlaw the possession of guns.

Reality: *Of course, guns by themselves cannot kill, nor can their absence reduce the motivation to kill. But, were guns less available, potential murderers would use less lethal weapons, which would result in fewer deaths.*

Myth: Strangers don't care about us as much as our relatives, friends, and acquaintances do. It's no wonder that strangers are more likely to kill us.

Reality: *Strangers are less likely to kill us. Most murder victims were related to or knew their killers.*

Myth: Since sexually active men can easily get sex, they are unlikely to rape women, much less their dates.

Reality: *Sexually active men are more likely to rape their dates than men with little or no sexual experience.*

Myth: Mental illness is something that happens to someone else. Most of us have neither been nor will ever be mentally ill.

Reality: *Mental illness is virtually as common as physical illness. While 20 percent of American adults suffer from serious mental disorders that require psychiatric help or hospitalization, over 80 percent have some degree of impaired mental health.*

Myth: Deviance is always harmful to society.

Reality: *Deviance can bring benefits to society if it occurs within limits.*

Myth: The American criminal justice system is by any measure soft on criminals.

Reality: *Our country is softer on criminals if it is compared with communist countries such as China and Cuba but much tougher when it is compared with other democratic societies such as Sweden and Netherlands.*

Myth: Severe punishment, such as the death penalty or long prison terms, effectively deters crime.

Reality: *Severe punishment has not proven effective in reducing crime rates. Despite our harsher punishment, we still have more crime than other industrialized countries.*

I f you thumb through a newspaper or magazine, you may come across a story such as this: In 1988 Jeffrey Dahmer murdered three people. He first met 14-year-old James Doxtator at a bus stop and asked him to pose in the nude for photos. But soon after arriving at his apartment with the boy, Dahmer had sex with him, drugged him, strangled him, dismembered him, and smashed his bones with a sledgehammer. Several months later, Dahmer picked up 23-year-old Richard Guerrero at a gay bar, had oral sex with him, drugged him, and butchered him. Later in the same month, Dahmer strangled 24-year-old Anthony Sears and then kept his head after having boiled it to remove the skin and painted the skull. Dahmer later told the police that he only saved skulls of the most handsome victims so that he would not forget them. He also said that he ate the flesh of three young men "like filet mignon" by using salt, pepper, meat tenderizer, and A-1 steak sauce on them. By 1991, when he was arrested, the police found in his apartment at least 15 dismembered bodies, a head in the refrigerator and a heart in the freezer, and a blue barrel of acid for leftovers (Mathews, 1992a).

With crimes such as this popping up frequently in the news media, we may think of deviants as creatures who are foreign to us. But deviance is widespread, though most is far from as gruesome as Dahmer's. In the United States virtually everybody has committed one or more offenses, such as those listed in Table 6.1. Even in a society of saints, as Durkheim long ago suggested, its rules would be broken.

Despite the prevalence of deviance, many people's ideas about it are simplistic and erroneous. Virtually everyone thinks that armed robbery is more dangerous in every respect than unarmed robbery. In reality, it is unarmed robbery that is far more likely to result in sending the victim to the hospital. One study, for example, shows that 66 percent of unarmed robbery victims, compared with 17 percent of armed robbery victims, were seriously injured (Feeney and Weir, 1975). Many people also believe that mental illness runs in a family. This may be true for a few patients, but most have acquired the illness through socialization rather than genes. Many people assume, too, that traditional crimes, such as murder, assault, and robbery, are more harmful to society than corporate crimes, such as selling defective cars, industrial pollution, and tax fraud. Actually, the reverse is closer to the truth (Thio, 1988).

There are many more popular misconceptions about these deviant acts. We will take a closer look at four of them (murder, rape, corporate crime, and mental illness) in this chapter. But let us first discuss what deviance is. Then we examine each of those four examples of deviance, various sociological explanations for its occurrence, and society's attempts to control it.

TABLE 6.1 *Common Offenses Punishable by a Fine or Jail Term*

1. Taking office supplies or using office services for personal purposes.
2. Evading taxes (e.g. failing to report or exaggerating deductible expenses).
3. Gambling illegally (e.g., betting on a sport event or political election).
4. Committing computer crimes (e.g. copying software illegally).
5. Serving alcohol to minors.
6. Drinking in public, where prohibited.
7. Possessing marijuana in small quantities for personal use.
8. Committing adultery in states where illegal.
9. Engaging in prohibited sex acts such as sodomy.
10. Patronizing a prostitute.
11. Appearing nude in public (e.g., nude sunbathing, where prohibited).
12. Stealing TV signals, such as with a satellite dish.
13. Speeding or other moving-traffic violations.
14. Parking illegally.
15. Fishing illegally (without a license or keeping undersized fish).
16. Smoking in public, where ordinance prohibits it.
17. Failing to recycle where required.
18. Lying on application for government job or benefit.
19. Disregarding a jury summons.
20. Unauthorized sale of tickets to sports or music event.

SOURCE: Stephen J. Adler and Wade Lambert, "Common Criminals: Just About Everyone Violates Some Laws, Even Model Citizens," *Wall Street Journal,* March 12, 1993, p. A6.

Deviance in America

A man, recently fired, returns to the office where he has worked, rifle in hand, and begins firing. Executives from several companies conspire to keep prices for their products artificially high. In a dark alley, a mugger waits for a victim to pass by. In a nice home, a woman goes through the daily routine of drinking to the point of intoxication. In the pursuit of thinness, a young woman starves herself until she looks like a scarecrow. When two police officers try to arrest a man, he spits on them, thinking that he can transmit his AIDS virus to them in this way. These actions may appear to have little in common, but they are all examples of deviant behavior.

WHAT IS DEVIANCE?

Deviant behavior is generally defined as any act that violates a social norm. But the phenomenon is more complex than that. How do we know whether an act violates a social norm? Is homosexuality deviant—a violation of a social norm? Some people think so, but others do not. This suggests that deviance is not absolute, not real in and of itself. It is relative, a matter of definition. A deviant act must be defined as such by someone before it can be said to be deviant.

Because many people have different views, they are bound to define deviant behavior differently. It is no wonder that practically all human acts have the potential for being considered deviant. When sociologist Jerry Simmons (1973) asked people what they defined as deviant, he ended up with a list of 252 acts and persons, including homosexuals, prostitutes, alcoholics, murderers, communists, atheists, Democrats, Republicans, movie stars, smart-aleck students, and know-it-all professors. If you are surprised that some of these people are considered deviant, your surprise simply confirms that there are countless *different* definitions of deviance, including your own. Even among sociologists, there is disagreement on what deviance is. Most sociologists define deviance as something negative. To them, deviance is what the public considers negative, objectionable behavior. But a few sociologists argue that deviance can also be positive. To them, then, heroes, saints, geniuses, reformers, and revolutionaries are just as deviant as criminals because they all deviate from being average persons (Thio, 1988).

All definitions of deviance, however, do not carry the same weight. Rock stars may be regarded by

Deviant behavior is any act considered by public consensus or the powerful at a given time and place to be a violation of some social rule. This suggests that deviance is relative, a matter of definition. To many, the performances and lyrics of some rappers are deviant, whereas to others these works are merely forms of self-expression. In any case, rappers are not put in prison.

some people as deviant, but they are not put in prison. Murderers, on the other hand, are widely considered to be seriously deviant, so many are put on death row. What determines that being a murderer is more deviant than being a rock star? What determines which definitions of deviance have more serious consequences for the deviants? There are at least three determining factors: time, place, and public consensus or power.

First, what constitutes deviance varies from one historical period to another. Nearly 2000 years ago, the Roman Empress Messalina won a bet with a friend by publicly having a prolonged session of sexual intercourse with 25 different men. At the time, Romans were not particularly scandalized, though they were quite impressed by her stamina. Today, if a person with similar social standing engaged in such behavior, we would consider it extremely scandalous (King, 1985). In the last two centuries, opium was a legal and easily available common drug; today its use is a criminal offense. Nowadays cigarette smoking is legal in all countries, but in the seventeenth century it was illegal in most countries. In fact, in some countries at that time, smokers were punished harshly: their noses were cut off in Russia, and their lips sliced off in Hindustan (Goode, 1989).

Second, the definition of deviance varies from one place to another. A polygamist is a criminal in the United States but not in Saudi Arabia and other Muslim countries. Prostitution is illegal in the United States (except in some counties in Nevada), but it is legal in Denmark, Germany, France, and most other countries. In 1987 the Iran-Contra affair, like the Watergate scandal in the mid-1970s, was considered major news in the United States, especially by the American media and Congress, but people in Europe wondered what the fuss was all about.

Third, whether a given act is deviant depends on public consensus. Murder is unquestionably deviant because nearly all people agree that it is. In contrast, long hair on men is not deviant because hardly anybody considers it so. Public consensus, however, usually reflects the vested interests of the rich and powerful. As Marx would have said, the ideas of the ruling class tend to become the ruling ideas of society. Like the powerful, the general public tends to consider, for example, bank robbery to be a crime but not fraudulent advertising, which serves the interests of the powerful.

In view of those three determinants of deviant behavior, we may more precisely define **deviant behavior** as any act considered by public consensus or the powerful at a given time and place to be a violation of some social rule.

MURDER

Murder is a relatively rare crime. It occurs less often than any of the other major offenses, such as rape, robbery, and aggravated assault. We are less likely to be murdered by others than to get ourselves killed in a car accident. We are even less likely to be killed by others than to kill ourselves. But murder does not appear reassuringly rare if we see it from another angle.

According to the FBI (1990), one American is murdered every 26 minutes. The chance of becoming a murder victim for all Americans is 1 out of 157. The odds are especially high for African-American males, who have a 1 out of 29 probability of being murdered. Regardless of our race or gender, our chance of murder victimization peaks when we reach the age of 25. In recent years, the murder rate in this country has increased significantly, and it is expected to continue its upward trend in the 1990s. The forces that drive up the murder rate include the continuing wars among drug dealers, easy availability of more lethal weapons, greater social acceptance of violence, and increases in the number of people in their teens and twenties—the age group most likely to commit crime (Malcolm, 1989; Rosenthal, 1990).

Homicide occurs most frequently during weekend evenings, particularly on Saturday night. This holds true largely for lower-class murderers but not for middle- and upper-class offenders, who kill on any day of the week. One apparent reason is that higher-class murders are more likely than lower-class homicides to be premeditated—hence less likely to result from alcohol-induced quarrels during weekend sprees. Research has also frequently shown that most of the murderers in this country are poor. Marvin Wolfgang (1958) estimated that 90 to 95 percent of the offenders came from the lower end of the occupational scale. A more recent study showed that 92 percent of the murderers were semiskilled workers, unskilled laborers, or welfare recipients (Swigert and Farrell, 1976). The latest analysis by Robert Parker (1989) confirmed these and other similar findings. We should note, however, that the rich and powerful actually cause far more deaths than the poor. Every year, while fewer than 24,000 Americans are murdered mostly by the poor, over 100,000 U.S. workers die from occupational diseases alone, attributable to corporate disregard for safe working conditions (Simon and Eitzen, 1990).

Whatever their class, murderers most often use handguns to kill. Perhaps seeing a gun while embroiled in a heated argument may incite a person into murderous action. As Shakespeare said, "How oft the sight of means to do ill deeds, makes ill deeds done." Of course, firearms by themselves cannot cause homicide, nor can their absence reduce the motivation to kill. It is true that "Guns don't kill, people do." Still, were guns less available, many heated arguments would have resulted in aggravated assaults rather than murders, thereby reducing the number of fatalities. One study suggests that attacks with knives are five

The most personal crime, murder is mostly committed against relatives, friends, and acquaintances rather than strangers. It is also most often carried out with a gun. Here is a typical victim—he was shot after an argument at a stadium.

times *less* likely to result in death than are attacks with guns (Wright et al., 1983). In fact, the use of less dangerous weapons such as knives in attempted murders has been estimated to cause 80 percent fewer deaths (Newton and Zimring, 1969). Given the enormous number of guns in private hands (about 120 million), it is not surprising that far more deaths result from gun attacks in this country than in Canada, England, and Japan (Rodino, 1986; Rosenthal, 1990).

Ironically, murder is the most personal crime, largely committed against acquaintances, friends, and relatives. According to the latest national statistics, in cases where the relationship of the victim to the killer is known, 56 percent involve acquaintances, friends, and spouses, whereas only 23 percent involve strangers (Malcolm, 1989). Many of us may find it incredible that the people we know or even love are more likely to kill us than are total strangers. "This should really not be very surprising," Donald Mulvihill and Melvin Tumin (1969) have explained. "Everyone is within easy striking distance from intimates for a large part of the time. Although friends, lovers, spouses, and the like are a main source of pleasure in one's life, they are equally a main source of frustration and hurt. Few others can anger one so much." The act of murder requires a great deal of emotion. It is a crime of passion carried out under the overwhelming pressure of a volcanic emotion. It may be more difficult for us to kill a stranger for

whom we don't have any sympathetic or antagonistic feelings. Only psychotic or professional killers can do away with people in a cold-blooded, unemotional manner. But such impersonal killings are rare.

A cross-cultural study has shown that "nations with greater material deprivation, more cultural heterogeneity, more family dissolution, higher female labor force participation, and greater exposure to official violence generally have high homicide rates" (Gartner, 1990). Material deprivation is a major contributor to homicide because it brings poor people a lot of stress that often leads to interpersonal violence. Cultural heterogeneity in the form of ethnic, religious, and other social diversity tends to weaken social integration, which in turn lessens social control, thereby increasing the likelihood of homicide. Divorce is likely to reduce the control of the individual by society. By working away from home, women tend to become as vulnerable as men are to killing outside the home. Exposure to officially approved violence such as wars and executions encourages violent citizens to commit homicide. This is why murder rates are higher after a war or in countries where the death penalty is popular.

RAPE

Rape is a major and serious crime in the United States. It is also very common. The most conservative

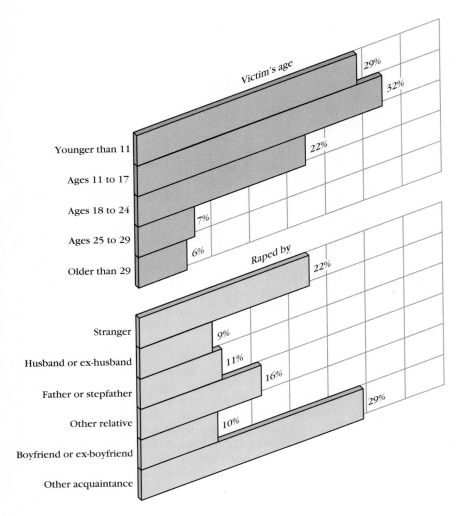

FIGURE 6.1 *Rapists and Their Victims*

Source: National Victim Center, 1992.

estimate has put an average woman's chance of being raped at "an appalling 1 in 10" (Dowd, 1983). Over the last decade, rape has increased four times as fast as the overall crime rate in the United States. We lead the industrial nations, with a rape rate 4 times that of Germany, 13 times as high as England, and 20 times as high as Japan (Gelman, 1990b). **Date rape**—in which a man commits sexual aggression against a woman he is out with—is especially common on American college campuses. In the mid-1980s, *Ms.* magazine conducted a nationwide survey of more than 700 college students on 35 campuses. It found that 13 percent of the women had been raped and that 52 percent had experienced some form of sexual assault (Sweet, 1985). According to the latest survey, 12.1 million or 13 percent of women have been raped at least once in their lives and 61 percent of

these women were raped as minors. In nearly 80 percent of the cases the victim knew her attacker (see Figure 6.1).

Why do we have so many rapes? Primarily because we live in a "rape-prone" culture. In a comparative study of 156 tribal societies, Peggy Sanday (1981) found that a few are "rape free," where women are treated with considerable respect and interpersonal violence is minimized. Most are "rape prone," like our society, characterized by male dominance and interpersonal violence. Indeed, we have a hidden culture of rape that encourages men to rape women. This culture shows itself through at least three prevailing attitudes toward women.

First, women are treated like men's property. If a woman is married, she is, in effect, her husband's property. Thus, in most of the states in our country, a man cannot be prosecuted for raping his wife (Finkelhor and Yllo, 1982; Barden, 1987). Many people seem to reason: How can any man steal what already belongs to him? The property logic may also explain the difficulty of getting a man convicted for raping a "cheap, loose woman" or a known prostitute. Such a female is considered as if she were every man's property, which she is assumed to have proven by having sex with many men. If a "good" woman is raped, we often say that she has been "ravaged," "ravished," "despoiled," or "ruined," as if she were a piece of property that has been damaged. The widespread availability of pornography further reinforces the popular image of women as men's sex objects. Because women are culturally defined as men's property, men may find it difficult to respect women. It is through this lack of respect that men are encouraged to rape women, as rape expresses the very essence of disrespect for a woman.

Second, women are treated as if they were objects of men's masculinity contests. In order for a man to prove his manhood, he is culturally pressured to "make out" with the largest number of women possible. The pressure to play this masculinity game often comes from friends who ask something like: "Did you score?" "Had any lately?" If the answer is no, they may say, "What's the matter? Are you gay or something?" Such social pressure tends to make many young men want to show off their "masculine" qualities, such as aggressiveness, forcefulness, and violence. Even if the peer pressure does not exist, the popular belief in sexual conquest as a badge of masculinity already encourages men to be aggressive toward women. If women say no, men are expected to ignore this response or even translate it into meaning yes. Such lessons in sexual conquest often come from the stereotype of the movie or television hero who forcefully, persistently embraces and kisses the heroine despite her strong resistance and is finally rewarded by her melting in his arms. In real life, such sexual aggression can easily lead to forcible rape. That's why many sociologists regard rape as an extension of the socially approved, conventional pattern of male sexual behavior. It is not surprising that some members of the Spur Posse, a group of high school boys in California who compete with one another by scoring points for sexual conquests, were jailed for a few days in 1993 on charges of molesting and raping girls as young as 10. It is also no wonder that other winners of the masculinity game, such as college men who have a lot of sexual experiences, are more likely to rape their dates than the so-called losers, who have

little or no sexual experiences (Kanin, 1983, 1985; Schur, 1984).

Third, there is a popular myth that, deep down, women want to be raped. One study shows that the majority (71 percent) of the people surveyed believe that women have an unconscious rape wish (Burt, 1980). This is why many people tend to hold the victim responsible for the rape. A key component of the myth is the assumption that the victim has "asked for it" by dressing sexily, hitchhiking, accepting a drink in a bar, or accepting a man's invitation to his house or apartment. As part of this myth, many college men assume that, if a woman enters their bedroom in a dorm or a fraternity house, it is an unspoken invitation for sex. Many college men also erroneously assume that kissing or heavy petting is an automatic prelude to intercourse (Celis, 1991). The general public further holds the related assumption that it is impossible to rape a woman if she resists, which is what the defense attorneys of some rapists like to argue. In the courtroom, the victim is often portrayed as a willing partner. In two recent cases, for example, one victim was accused of having a "kinky and aggressive" sex life and another was said to be "sexually voracious" and to have "preyed on men" (Lacayo, 1987). The willing-victim myth is a major motivating force behind many rapes. In one study of convicted rapists, 59 percent deny their guilt and blame their victims instead. They insist that their victims seduced them, meant yes while saying no to the sexual assault, and eventually relaxed and enjoyed the rape. Not surprisingly, men who believe this dangerous myth about women are likely to rape them (Scully and Marolla, 1984).

CORPORATE CRIME

Unlike murder and rape, corporate crimes are committed by company executives without the overt use of force, and their effect on the victims is not readily traceable to the culprit. If a miner dies from a lung disease, it is difficult to prove beyond reasonable doubt that the miner had died *because* his or her employer violated mine safety regulations. Corporate crimes may be perpetrated not only against employees but also against customers and the general public. Examples are disregard for safety in the workplace, consumer fraud, price fixing, production of unsafe products, and violations of environmental regulations. Compared to traditional "street crime," corporate crime is more rationally executed, more profitable, and less detectable by law enforcers. This is

Deliberately violating safety regulations or ignoring safety designs can cost society money, cause injuries, and claim lives. Knowingly building unsafe automobiles, such as those whose fuel tanks are placed so that collisions can lead to the kind of explosion shown here, may be regarded as a kind of corporate crime.

why in the savings-and-loan scandal most of the charges against those who have looted tens of billions of dollars will merely be narrow tax-evasion counts—instead of sweeping fraud charges. Finding enough solid evidence to support the far more serious fraud charges "could take the rest of our lives," says a federal investigator. "We've been through millions of pages of documents already" (Barrett, 1990). In addition, crime in the suite is distinguished from crime in the street by three characteristics, which may explain why corporate crime is common.

Three Distinct Characteristics First is the victim's unwitting cooperation with the corporate criminal, which results mostly from carelessness or ignorance. In a home-improvement scheme, the victims do not bother to check the work history of the fraudulent company that solicits them, and they sign a contract without examining its contents for such matters as the true price and the credit terms. Some victims purchase goods through the mail without checking the reputation of the firm. Doctors prescribe untested dangerous drugs after having relied on only the pharmaceutical company's salespeople and advertising. It may be difficult for the victims to know they are victimized, even if they want to find out the true nature of their victimization. Grocery

shoppers, for example, are hard put to detect such unlawful substances as residues of hormones, antibiotics, pesticides, and nitrites in the meat they buy.

A second characteristic is the society's indifference to corporate crimes. Generally, little effort is made to catch corporate criminals, and on the rare occasions when they are caught, they seldom go to jail. They plead for mercy and often get it after promising to repay their victims and to cooperate in prosecutions against others. They insist that a long prison term will do no good because their lives are already in ruins. Thus, in the more than a dozen convictions for Wall Street insider trading in recent years, most defendants were merely put on probation or sentenced to prison for less than six months. The convicted insider trader Ivan Boesky even managed to deduct from his taxes half of the $100 million he had paid as his penalty, in addition to keeping millions in ill-gotten gains. The government has vowed that in the 1990s the Justice Department will intensify its war against "Seven Deadly White-Collar Crimes"—antitrust violation, environmental violation, fraud in defense procurement, savings-and-loan fraud, insider trading, public corruption, and money laundering. The FBI has so far increased its staff for such cases by 14 percent over the last three years. But history suggests that it is difficult to turn this tough talk into a sustained, serious campaign. The basic pattern of wealthy crooks getting light punishment is likely to continue (Eichenwald, 1990; Gest, 1990).

These facts probably account for a third characteristic of corporate crime: the perpetrators often see themselves as respectable people rather than common criminals. Often they maintain their noncriminal self-image through rationalization. Violators of price-fixing laws, for example, may insist that they are helping the nation's economy by "stabilizing prices" and serving their companies by "recovering costs." There is no such crime as price fixing in their book.

Costs of Corporate Crime   The economic cost of corporate crime is high—about 27 to 42 times greater each year than the losses from traditional property crimes such as robbery and burglary. Estimates of the total cost of corporate crime range from $50 billion to $200 billion a year. Price fixing alone costs this nation about $45 billion annually. The fraud by B.C.C.I. (Bank of Credit & Commerce International) alone costs its depositors $12 billion. All this makes the annual estimated loss of $3 billion or $4 billion from traditional crimes look like small potatoes (Conklin, 1977; Pauly, 1979; Beaty and Gwynne, 1991).

Corporate crime also exacts a high physical cost. Bodily injury and even death may result from violations of health and safety laws, housing codes, and environmental regulations. The violence inflicted on the public by corporate criminals in their pursuit of profit far exceeds the violence by lower-class street criminals. According to the National Commission on Product Safety, 20 million Americans have suffered injuries from using consumer products, and among these victims 110,000 are permanently disabled and 30,000 are dead (Simon and Eitzen, 1990). It has been estimated that each year some 500,000 workers are needlessly exposed to such toxic substances as radioactive materials and poisonous chemicals because of corporate failures to obey safety laws (Anderson, 1981). Of the 4 million workers who have been exposed to asbestos in the United States, about 1.6 million are expected to die from lung cancer, a figure much higher than the total U.S. loss of 372,000 lives during World War II and subsequent wars (Balkan, Berger, and Schmidt, 1980).

There is also a high social cost imposed by corporate crime. Though unmeasurable, the social cost may be more far-reaching than the economic and physical toll. As a former U.S. attorney general wrote: "White-collar crime is the most corrosive of all crimes. The trusted prove untrustworthy; the advantaged, dishonest. . . . As no other crime, it questions our moral fiber" (Clark, 1971). Corporations sometimes weaken the democratic process by making illegal campaign contributions. In foreign countries, American corporations operating there often make political payoffs. Such bribes interfere with the political process of those nations by strengthening the existing power structure and reinforce their image of America as an imperialist nation (Jacoby et al., 1977; Simon and Eitzen, 1990).

MENTAL ILLNESS

Although corporate crime, rape, and murder are criminal acts, other forms of deviance are not. A clear example is mental illness. Contrary to popular belief, mental illness is extremely common. According to a nationwide survey, about 28 percent of the total adult population in the United States suffer from a mental disorder. The most common disorder is phobias (such as the fear of heights or enclosed spaces), followed by depression and alcoholism (Regier et al., 1993). In fact, all of us have been or will be mentally ill in one way or another. Of course, most of our mental disorders are not serious at all. We occasionally come down with only a brief anxiety or depression, "the common cold of mental ailments." But the types of mental illness that sociologists—and psychiatrists—study are rather serious. They include **psychosis,** typified by loss of touch with reality, and **neurosis,** characterized by a persistent fear, anxiety, or worry about trivial matters. A psychotic can be likened to a person who thinks incorrectly that 2 plus 2 is equal to 10 but strongly believes it to be correct. On the other hand, a neurotic can be compared to a person who thinks correctly that 2 plus 2 is equal to 4 but constantly worries that it may not be so (Thio, 1988).

Sociologists have long suspected that certain social forces are involved in the development of mental disorder. The one that has been most consistently demonstrated by many different studies to be a key factor in mental illness is social class: the lower the social class, the higher the rate of mental disorder.

This finding, however, has prompted two conflicting explanations. One, known as *social causation,* suggests that lower-class people are more prone

Mental illness is extremely common, although most of our mental disorders are not serious at all. Virtually all of us have experienced a brief anxiety or depression, as this mother in the picture. Sociologists have long discovered the role of social forces in the development of mental disorder.

to mental disorder because they are more likely to have the following experiences: being subjected to social stress, such as unemployment, family problems, or threat of criminal victimization; suffering from psychic frailty, infectious diseases, and neurological impairments; and lacking quality medical treatment, coping ability, and social support. The other explanation, called *social selection* or *drift,* suggests that the heavy concentration of mental disorder in the lower-class neighborhood results from the downward drift of mentally ill people into the neighborhood coupled with the upward movement of mentally healthy people out of it. This means that being a member of the lower class is a consequence rather than a cause of mental illness. Both explana-

tions have been found to have some basis in fact. In general, the evidence for the drift theory comes from studies of extremely serious mental illness such as schizophrenia. The early onset of such illness usually causes individuals to lose their jobs or suffer downward mobility. But the evidence for social causation comes from studies of less severe disorders such as depression and phobia. These problems are more likely to result from the social stresses of lower-class lives (Kessler, Price, and Wortman, 1985).

IS DEVIANCE ALWAYS HARMFUL?

We are accustomed to thinking of deviance as bad. But deviance is not always or completely harmful to society. It can bring benefits if it occurs within limits. Sociologists have noted at least five positive functions of deviance.

First, deviance may enhance conformity in the society as a whole by defining and clarifying norms. Norms are basically abstract and ambiguous, subject to conflicting interpretations. Even criminal laws, which are far more clear-cut than other norms, can be confusing. Through the crime a criminal commits and is punished for, other citizens obtain a concrete example of what constitutes a crime. During the Watergate scandal of the 1970s, for example, both politicians and the public clarified their opinions about which practices, though shady, were just "politics as usual" and which ones were unacceptable. From deviants we can learn the difference between conformity and deviance—we can see the boundary between right and wrong more clearly. Once aware of this boundary, we are more likely to stay on the side of righteousness (Erikson, 1966).

Second, deviance strengthens solidarity among law-abiding members of society. Differing values and interests may divide them, but collective outrage against deviants as their common enemy can unite them. Because it promotes social cohesion that decreases crime, Durkheim (1966) called deviance "a factor in public health, an integral part of all healthy societies." In large cities, however, crime may generate fear and cause people to stay home, which undermines social solidarity. Still, the ultimate result is less crime, because by staying home the urbanites limit the opportunities for crime (Liska and Warner, 1991).

The third function of deviance is the provision of a safety valve for discontented people. Through relatively minor forms of deviance, they can strike out against the social order without doing serious harm to themselves or others. Prostitution, for example, may serve as a safety valve for marriage in a male-dominated society, because the customer is unlikely to form an emotional attachment to the prostitute. In contrast, a sexual relationship with a friend is more likely to develop into a love affair, which would destroy a marriage (Cohen, 1966).

Fourth, deviance also provides jobs for many law-abiding people. The police, judges, lawyers, prison wardens, prison guards, and criminologists would be out of work if there were no criminals. Criminals also stimulate some useful developments. As Marx (1964) said, "Would locks ever have reached their present degree of excellence had there been no thieves? Would the making of bank notes have reached its present perfection had there been no forgers?"

Finally, deviant behavior sometimes induces social change. Martin Luther King, Jr., and other civil rights leaders were jeered and imprisoned for their opposition to segregation, but they moved the United States toward greater racial equality.

Despite these positive functions, widespread deviance obviously threatens the social order. First, it can destroy interpersonal relations. Alcoholism has torn many families apart. If a friend flies into a rage and tries to kill us, it will be difficult to maintain a harmonious relationship. Deviance can also undermine trust. If there were many killers, robbers, and rapists living in our neighborhood, we would find it impossible to welcome neighbors to our home as guests or babysitters. Finally, if deviance goes unpunished, it can weaken the will to conform throughout society. If we know that most people cheat on their taxes, for example, we may be tempted to do the same.

QUESTIONS FOR DISCUSSION AND REVIEW

1. Why do persons disagree about whether an act is deviant or not?
2. When do murders occur, and who usually commits them?
3. What are the social causes of rape?
4. What are the three distinct characteristics of corporate crime?
5. Why is mental illness seen as a form of deviance, and what are some of its causes?
6. What are some of the positive and negative consequences of deviance?

Sociological Theories

Obviously, society has a large stake in understanding why deviance occurs. At various times and places, deviance has been viewed as a sin or a sickness, as the result of possession by demons or living in a wicked world, as the product of choice or circumstance. Today some scholars attribute deviance to certain biological or psychological abnormality in the individual. But most deviants are physically or mentally normal. To understand why they commit deviant acts, we need to turn to sociological theories, which do not assume that there is something wrong with the deviant but instead seek out social environment as the source of deviance.

ANOMIE

More than 50 years ago, Robert Merton developed a theory of deviance that is still very influential today. He built on Durkheim's concept of **anomie,** which literally means "normlessness." More generally, anomie is a condition in which norms are weak or in conflict. Anomie may arise, said Merton, when there is an inconsistency between the culture and the social structure. In the United States, such an inconsistency surrounds the issue of success. American culture places great emphasis on success as a valued goal. From kindergarten to college, teachers encourage students to strive for good grades and to be ambitious. Parents and coaches even pressure Little League players not just to play well but to win. The media often glorify winning not only in sports but in business, politics, and other arenas of life. Meanwhile, the social structure does not provide all Americans with the legitimate means, such as good jobs and other opportunities, to achieve this goal of success.

How do people respond when they are taught, in effect, that "Winning isn't everything—it's the only thing"? They may either accept or reject the goal of winning, and they may either accept or reject the use of socially accepted means to that end. Merton analyzed five possible responses to this condition (see Table 6.2).

1. *Conformity* is the most popular mode of adaptation. It involves accepting both the cultural goal of success and the use of legitimate means for achieving that goal.

According to anomie theory, American society stresses success as a valued goal but does not provide everybody with the opportunity to achieve it. Those who find themselves caught in the gap between aspiration and opportunity are likely to engage in illegal activities, such as selling drugs.

2. *Innovation* is an adaptation that produces deviance, including crime. When people adopt this response, they accept the goal of success, but they reject the use of socially accepted means to achieve it, turning instead to unconventional methods. The thief and the pimp are, in this sense, "innovators."

3. *Ritualism* occurs when people follow social norms rigidly and compulsively, even though they no longer hope to achieve the goal set by their culture. Working hard by obeying the rules to the letter becomes more important than achieving success. A petty bureaucrat can be considered a ritualist.

4. *Retreatism* is withdrawal from society. Psychotics, alcoholics, drug addicts, and tramps are all retreatists. They care neither about success nor about working.

TABLE 6.2 *How Would You Respond to the Goals-Means Gap?*

In American Society, according to Merton, there is too much emphasis on success but lack of emphasis on the legitimate means for achieving success. Such inconsistency may cause deviant behavior, yet various people respond to it differently.

MODES OF ADAPTATION	CULTURAL GOALS	INSTITUTIONALIZED MEANS
1. Conformity	acceptance	acceptance
2. Innovation	acceptance	rejection
3. Ritualism	rejection	acceptance
4. Retreatism	rejection	rejection
5. Rebellion	rejection of old, introduction of new	rejection of old, introduction of new

Source: Adapted with permission of The Free Press, a Division of Macmillan, Inc., from *Social Theory and Structure* by Robert K. Merton. Copyright © 1957 by The Free Press; copyright renewed 1985 by Robert K. Merton.

5. *Rebellion* occurs when people reject and attempt to change both the goals and the means approved by society. The rebel tries to overthrow the existing system and establish a new system with different goals and means. This may involve replacing the current American system of pursuing fame and riches through competition with a new system of enhancing social relations through cooperation.

Anomie is not restricted to any one social group, but it has special implications for the poor. They receive the same message as other Americans: that success is a valued goal and that how one achieves that goal is less important than reaching it. But society does not provide them with equal opportunities to achieve success. For the poor, in particular, there is likely to be a gap between aspiration and opportunity, and this gap may pressure them toward deviance. According to Merton's theory, it fosters innovation, retreatism, and rebellion because each of these adaptations involves the rejection of socially accepted avenues of success. Each also produces deviant behavior.

Merton's analysis provides an explanation for high rates of property crime in the United States, particularly among its lower classes and disadvantaged minorities. But anomie theory cannot explain forms of deviance—such as murder, rape, and vandalism—that are unrelated to success. People who do these things are far from ambitious; they do not commit the crimes as a way of expressing their desire for success. The theory also fails to explain crimes such as embezzlement and tax fraud by those who are already successful. By not taking into account these white-collar crimes, Merton has been criticized for assuming that the poor are more prone to criminality in general than are the rich. Finally, Merton has drawn fire for his assumption of value consensus. As a structural functionalist (Chapter 1: The Essence of Sociology), he assumes that the same value—belief in success—governs various groups in our society. But this runs counter to the pluralistic and conflicting nature of American society, where many ethnic and religious groups do not share the same values. Thus, some may engage in deviant acts—such as gambling, cockfighting, violations of fish and game laws, and handling of poisonous snakes to prove one's faith in God—without having been influenced by the cultural goal of success (Thio, 1988).

DIFFERENTIAL ASSOCIATION

In the 1920s Clifford Shaw and Henry McKay (1929) discovered that high rates of crime and delinquency had persisted in the same Chicago neighborhoods for more than 20 years, although different ethnic groups had lived in those neighborhoods. This discovery led Shaw and McKay to develop the theory of **cultural transmission.** The traditions of crime and delinquency, they said, are transmitted from one group to another, much as language is passed from one generation to another. The key assumption is that deviant behavior, like language, is learned.

In the 1930s Edwin Sutherland explained how this cultural transmission might occur. Deviance, said Sutherland, is learned through interactions with other people. Individuals learn not only how to perform deviant acts such as burglary and marijuana smoking but also how to define these actions. Various social groups have different norms, and acts considered deviant by the dominant culture may be viewed positively by some groups. Each person is likely to be exposed to both positive and negative definitions of

these actions. But a person is likely to define them positively and become a criminal if he or she is exposed to **differential association**—the process of associating with criminal elements more than with noncriminal elements.

Note that Sutherland was not saying that "bad company" will turn us into criminals. If this were the case, we would expect lawyers, judges, and police officers to be criminals because they spend so much time with criminals. Rather, differential association theory holds that deviant behavior arises if interactions with those who view deviant behavior positively *outweigh* interactions with those who view it negatively. Which views are most influential depends not just on the frequency and duration of the interactions but also on the relationship between the people in the interaction.

Sutherland developed his theory to explain various forms of deviance, including white-collar crimes such as tax evasion, embezzlement, and price fixing. All these misdeeds were shown to result from some association with groups that considered the wrongdoings acceptable. But it is difficult, according to critics, to determine precisely what differential association is. Most people cannot identify the persons from whom they have learned a procriminal or anticriminal definition, much less know whether they have been exposed to one definition more frequently, longer, or more intensely than the other definition.

CONTROL

According to control theory, social control causes conformity, and, therefore, the lack of control causes deviance. This theory is based on the assumption that people are naturally inclined to commit deviant acts and will do so unless they are properly controlled by society. Those who lack social control, then, are likely to become deviants. There are, however, different sociological views on the specific nature of social control.

According to Travis Hirschi (1969), society controls us through our close bonds to others. If we do not have adequate social bonds, we are likely to engage in deviant activities. There are four ways in which we can bond ourselves to society. The first is by *attachment* to conventional people and institutions. In the case of teenagers, they may show this attachment by loving and respecting their parents, making friends with conventional peers, liking school, or working hard to develop intellectual skills. A *commitment* to conformity is the second way. Individuals invest their time and energy in conventional activities, such as getting an education, holding a job, developing an occupational skill, improving their professional status, building up a business, or acquiring a reputation for virtue. At the same time, people show a commitment to achievement through these activities. The third way is *involvement* in conventional activities. People keep themselves so busy doing conventional things that they do not have time to take part in deviant activities or even to think about deviance. A *belief* in the moral validity of social rules is the fourth way in which people bond themselves to society. Such belief involves the conviction that the rules of conventional society should be obeyed. People may show this moral belief by respecting the law. The lack of these four indicators of social bonding is likely to lead to crime and delinquency.

While Hirschi sees how society controls us through bonding, John Braithwaite (1989) looks at how society controls us through shaming. Shaming involves an expression of disapproval designed to invoke remorse in the wrongdoer. There are two types of shaming: disintegrative and reintegrative. In **disintegrative shaming**, the wrongdoer is punished in such a way as to be stigmatized, rejected, or ostracized—in effect, banished from conventional society. It is the same as stigmatization. **Reintegrative shaming** is more positive, which involves making wrongdoers feel guilty while showing them understanding, forgiveness, or even respect. It is the kind of shaming that affectionate parents administer to their misbehaving child. It involves "hating the sin but loving the sinner." Thus reintegrative shaming serves to reintegrate—or welcome back—the wrongdoer into conventional society. Reintegrative shaming is more common in communitarian societies (marked by strong social relationships or interdependence), such as Japan, whereas disintegrative shaming is more prevalent in less communitarian societies (characterized by weaker social relationships), such as the United States. At the same time, reintegrative shaming usually discourages further deviance, while disintegrative shaming or stigmatization encourages more deviance. This is why crime rates are higher in the United States than in Japan. Braithwaite concludes by arguing that the United States can significantly reduce its crime rates if it emphasizes reintegrative shaming rather than stigmatization in dealing with criminals as Japanese society does.

It is true that reintegrative shaming can reduce crime, especially if it is applied to first-time offenders who have committed relatively minor crimes. But it can hardly have the same positive impact on hardened criminals with little sense of shame for their crimes. Moreover, since reintegrative shaming is part and parcel of a communitarian society, it cannot be widely used as a crime-fighting strategy in a less communitarian society. In other words, the United States cannot treat its criminals in the same lenient, compassionate way as Japan unless it first becomes what it cannot be—as communitarian as the Asian society. As for Hirschi's social bond theory, it has received much support from studies on juvenile delinquency. But the theory is less applicable to white-collar crimes, which are typically committed by successful, respectable adults who do not lack any social bonds. A key reason is that when these people learn some conforming behavior, they simultaneously learn to perform a deviant act. If they learn to manage a bank, they also acquire the ability and opportunity to embezzle money from the bank. If they become government officials, they also acquire the ability and opportunity to accept bribes. Thus, contrary to the assumption of social bond theory, the acquirement of conformity does not necessarily mean a rejection of deviance (Thio, 1988).

LABELING

Anomie, differential association, control, and shaming theories focus on the causes of rule violation. In contrast, labeling theory, which emerged in the 1960s, concentrates on societal reaction to rule violation and the impact of this reaction on the rule violator.

According to labeling theorists, society tends to react to a rule-breaking act by labeling it deviant. Deviance, then, is not something that a person does but merely a label imposed on that behavior. As Howard Becker (1963) said, "Deviance is *not* a quality of the act the person commits, but rather a consequence of the application by others of rules and sanctions to an 'offender.' The deviant is one to whom that label has successfully been applied; deviant behavior is behavior that people so label." The label itself has serious and negative consequences—even beyond any immediate punishment—for the individual.

Once a person is labeled a thief or a delinquent or a drunk, he or she may be stuck with that label for life and be rejected and isolated as a result. Finding a

According to labeling theory, tagging a person as deviant can make the person deviant. A social drinker who gets labeled as "a man who can hold his liquor" can become an alcoholic because people begin to pressure him to live up to that image.

job and making friends may be extremely difficult. More important, the person may come to accept the label and commit more deviant acts. William Chambliss (1973) described what happened to the Roughnecks—a group of lower-class boys—when their community labeled them as delinquents:

> The community responded to the Roughnecks as boys in trouble, and the boys agreed with that perception. Their pattern of deviancy was reinforced, and breaking away from it became increasingly unlikely. Once the boys acquired an image of themselves as deviants, they selected new friends who affirmed that self-image. As that self-conception became more firmly entrenched, they also became willing to try new and more extreme deviances. With their growing alienation came freer expression of disrespect and hostility for representatives of the legitimate society.

Labeling people as deviants, in short, can push them toward further and greater deviance.

Much earlier, Frank Tannenbaum (1938) had noted this process of becoming deviant. According to him, children may break windows, annoy people, climb over a roof, steal apples, and play hooky—and innocently consider these activities just a way of having fun. Edwin Lemert (1951) gave the name **primary deviance** to such violations of norms that a person commits for the first time and without considering them deviant. Now suppose parents, teachers, and police consider a child's pranks to be a sign of delinquency or evil. They may "dramatize the evil" by admonishing or scolding the child. They may even go further, hauling the child into juvenile court and labeling the child as bad, a delinquent—a deviant. If the child accepts the definition, he or she may be on the same path as the Roughnecks. The child, then, may try to live up to his or her bad self-image by becoming increasingly involved in deviant behavior. Lemert gave the term **secondary deviance** to such repeated norm violations, which the violators themselves recognize as deviant. Secondary deviants are, in effect, confirmed or career deviants.

Labeling helps us understand how secondary deviance might develop, and it sensitizes us to the power of labels. The theory is actually a version of symbolic interactionism (Chapter 1: The Essence of Sociology). It is based on the assumption that deviance involves a symbolic interaction, with society acting toward certain people by labeling them deviant and these people reacting by becoming secondary deviants. But the theory has been subjected to many criticisms. First, it cannot explain why primary deviance occurs in the first place. Second, it assumes that individuals passively accept the label of deviant thrust on them by others. Hence, it cannot explain why some people, such as political leaders and corporate executives, are better able than others, such as juvenile delinquents, to resist accepting the "deviant" label. Third, labeling theory cannot deal with deviance that occurs in secret. Because secret deviance is not known by others, it cannot be labeled deviance. Therefore, without the deviant label, labeling theory logically cannot define it as deviance. Conflict theory, however, can deal with secret deviance, which it considers to be common among powerful people (Harris and Hill, 1982; Thio, 1988).

CONFLICT

Like labeling theory, conflict theory is concerned with the societal definition of deviance. But it also emphasizes power differentials as determinants of both deviant labeling *and* deviant behavior. Thus, it can explain what labeling theory cannot. According to conflict theory, the powerful are more likely than the powerless to commit profitable primary deviant acts (such as tax fraud and price fixing), to resist the label of deviant, and to engage in secret, undetectable deviant activities. There are, however, two versions of conflict theory: traditional and contemporary. One was introduced in the 1930s and the other in the 1970s.

Traditional Conflict Theory   Traditional conflict theorists focus mostly on *cultural* conflict as a source of deviant definition and behavior. Cultural conflict arises whenever what is considered right by one subculture is considered wrong by another, more powerful subculture—usually the dominant culture. A classic case of this conflict involved a Sicilian father in New Jersey in the 1930s: After killing his daughter's 16-year-old "seducer," he felt proud of having defended his family honor in a traditional way, but he was very surprised when the police came to arrest him (Sellin, 1938).

    The triumph and defeat of Prohibition—which outlawed the sale of alcoholic beverages between 1919 and 1933—has also been offered as another case of cultural conflict. The triumph of Prohibition in 1919 reflected the power and life-style of rural dwellers, Southerners, white Anglo-Saxon Protestants, and Americans of native-born parentage, all of whom considered drinking totally disreputable. By 1933 Prohibition was repealed because a new group that became more powerful saw nothing wrong with drinking. This group consisted of urban dwellers, northeasterners, non-Protestants (mostly Irish, Italians, and Jews), and sons and daughters of immigrants. The law, in essence, supports one subculture as worthy of respect and condemns another as deviant (Gusfield, 1967a). In other words, people become deviant because they are on the losing side of a cultural conflict.

Contemporary Conflict Theory   Most of the contemporary conflict theorists are Marxists, who focus mostly on class conflict in capitalist society as the mainspring of deviant labeling and behavior.

    Many people assume that the law is based on the consent of citizens, that it treats citizens equally, and that it serves the best interest of society. If we simply read the U.S. Constitution and statutes, this assumption may indeed seem justified. But study of the *law in the books,* as William Chambliss (1969, 1973)

Firms unable to compete with giant corporations, according to contemporary conflict theory, are likely to shore up their sagging profits by illegal means, such as hiring illegal immigrants from Mexico at wages below the legal minimum.

pointed out, may be misleading. The laws in the books do indeed say that the authorities ought to be fair and just. But are they? To understand crime, Chambliss argued, we need to look at the *law in action,* at how legal authorities actually discharge their duty. After studying the law in action, Chambliss concluded that legal authorities are actually unfair and unjust, favoring the rich and powerful over the poor and weak.

    Richard Quinney (1974) blamed the unjust law directly on the capitalist system. "Criminal law," said Quinney, "is used by the state and the ruling class to secure the survival of the capitalist system . . . criminal law will be increasingly used in the attempt to maintain domestic order." This involves the dominant class doing four things: First, it defines as criminal those behaviors (robbery, murder, and the like) that threaten its interests. Second, it hires law enforcers to apply those definitions and protect its interests. Third, it exploits the subordinate class by paying low wages so that the resulting oppressive life conditions force the powerless to commit what those in power have defined as crimes. Fourth, it uses these criminal actions to spread and reinforce the popular view that the subordinate class is dangerous, in order to justify its concerns with making and enforcing the law. The upshot is the production and maintenance of a high level of criminality by the powerless (Quinney, 1975).

Other Marxists argue that the capitalists' ceaseless drive to increase profit by cutting labor costs has created a large class of unemployed workers. These people become what Marxists call **marginal surplus population**—superfluous or useless to the economy. They are likely to commit property crimes to survive. The exploitative nature of capitalism also causes violent crimes (such as murder, assault, and rape) and noncriminal deviances (such as alcoholism, suicide, and mental illness). As Sheila Balkan and her colleagues (1980) explained, economic "marginality leads to a lack of self-esteem and a sense of powerlessness and alienation, which create intense pressures on individuals. Many people turn to violence in order to vent their frustrations and strike out against symbols of authority, and others turn this frustration inward and experience severe emotional difficulties."

Marxists further contend that the monopolistic and oligopolistic nature of capitalism encourages corporate crime, because "when only a few firms dominate a sector of the economy they can more easily collude to fix prices, divide up the market, and eliminate competitors" (Greenberg, 1981). Smaller firms, unable to compete with giant corporations and earn enough profits, are also motivated to shore up their sagging profits by illegal means. "One would thus expect," wrote David Greenberg (1981), "consumer fraud, labor law violations (such as hiring illegal immigrants at wages below the legal minimum), fencing operations, and tax evasions to occur more frequently when the economy is dominated by a few giant firms." The highly competitive nature of capitalism is also blamed for pressuring both big and small companies to cross the thin line from sharp to shady business practices (Gordon, 1973; Reiman and Headlee, 1981).

In evaluating conflict theory, we can see that it is useful for understanding why certain laws are made and enforced. The law of vagrancy, for example, originated in England as a capitalist attempt to force workers to accept employment at low wages—because a vagrant was, in the eye of the new law, one who does not work. Even laws that appear to protect the powerless may have resulted from the powerful's concern with their own interests. The law against

rape, for instance, can be traced to the old days when women were treated as men's property. Rape was in effect considered a property crime against a man—the victim's father if she was unmarried or husband if married.

Conflict theory is also useful for understanding how power differentials pressure the poor to commit less profitable crimes (such as murder, rape, and robbery) and tempt the rich to perpetrate more profitable crimes (such as tax fraud, price fixing, and false advertising). Some sociologists have criticized Marxists for condemning capitalism as the cause of all crimes and ignoring the existence of crime in socialist and communist nations. But Marxists actually assume that some forms of crime always exist in any society. They only argue that such crimes as corporate, employee, and street crimes are far more common under capitalism than under democratic socialism (Young, 1984). Moreover, Marxists are correct in assuming that there is generally more crime in capitalist societies. In capitalist West Berlin, for example, the crime rate is four times higher than in until recently communist East Berlin. But, since East Berliners turned capitalist in late 1989, their crime rate has soared (Stone, 1990).

FEMINIST THEORY

Virtually all the theories about deviance such as the ones presented above are meant to apply to both males and females. They assume that what holds true for men also holds true for women. Feminists, however, disagree. They argue that those theories are actually about men only. Consequently, they may be valid for male behavior but not necessarily so for female behavior. Consider Merton's anomie theory. First, this theory assumes that people are inclined to strive for material success. This may be true for men but not necessarily true for women. In fact, women are traditionally less interested in achieving material success, which often requires one-upmanship, and more given to attaining emotional fulfillment through close, personal relations with others. Second, the theory assumes that if some women have a strong desire for economic success but no access to opportunities for achieving the goal, they would be as likely as men in the same situation to commit a crime. Nowadays, given the greater availability of high positions for women in the economic world, the number of ambitious women in the "men's" world is on the rise. But when these women are faced with the lack of opportunities for greater economic success, they are not as likely as men to engage in deviant activities. And finally, Merton's theory explicitly states that Americans are likely to commit a crime because their society overemphasizes the importance of entertaining high success goals while failing to provide the necessary opportunities for all its citizens to realize those goals. This may be relevant to men but less so to women. In fact, despite their greater lack of success opportunities, women still have lower crime rates than men (Morris, 1987).

The lack of relevancy to women in anomie and other conventional theories stems from a male-biased failure to take women into account. In redressing this problem, feminist theory understandably focuses on women. First, the theory deals with women as victims, mostly of rape and sexual harassment. The crimes against women are said to reflect the patriarchal society's attempt to put women in their place so as to perpetuate men's dominance. Feminist theory also zeroes in on women as offenders. It argues that although the rate of female crime has increased in recent years the increase is not great enough to be significant. This is said to reflect the fact that gender equality is still far from being a social reality. Like employment opportunities, criminal opportunities are still much less available to women than men, hence women are still much less likely to engage in criminal activities. When women do commit a crime, they are also more likely to commit the types of crime that reflect their continuing subordinate position in society. They are minor property crimes, such as shoplifting, passing bad checks, welfare fraud, and petty credit-card fraud. In fact, most of the recent increases in female crime involve these minor crimes. The more profitable crimes, such as burglary, robbery, embezzlement, and business fraud, are still largely committed by men (Daly and Chesney-Lind, 1988). However, feminist theory has not been well-developed enough to explain the deviant behavior of both men and women.

QUESTIONS FOR DISCUSSION AND REVIEW

1. What did Merton mean by anomie, and how can this experience lead to deviant behavior?
2. Why do many sociologists criticize the assumptions of Edwin Sutherland's differential association theory?
3. How do bonding and shaming theories explain the occurrence of deviant behavior?
4. What factors might push persons from primary to secondary forms of deviance, according to labeling theory?
5. How does conflict theory explain why certain laws are made and enforced?
6. How does feminist theory differ from other theories?

Controlling Deviance

As we discussed in Chapter 5 (Socialization), society transmits its values to individuals through socialization. If families, schools, and other socializing agents do their jobs well, then individuals internalize the values of their society, accepting society's norms as their own. They become conformists and law-abiding citizens.

Internalization through socialization is the most efficient way of controlling deviant behavior. It produces unconscious, spontaneous self-control. As a result, most people find it natural to conform to most social norms most of the time. Violating the norms makes them feel guilty, ashamed, or at least uncomfortable. Most people act as their own police officers.

But, as we have seen, socialization is never completely successful. A few people commit serious crimes, and everyone deviates occasionally, at least from some trivial norms. Thus, control by others— **social control**—is also needed to limit deviance and maintain social order.

SOCIAL CONTROL

Social control may be either informal or formal. Teachers, preachers, peer groups, even strangers enforce informal controls through frowning, gossip, criticism, or ridicule. When deviant acts are serious, formal controls are usually imposed. These come from police, judges, prison guards, and similar agents. The formal controllers are specifically appointed by the state, and they can be expected to punish deviants severely.

In small, nonindustrialized societies, informal control is the primary or only means of handling deviance. It may involve such mild expressions of disapproval as a frown, scowl, scolding, or reprimand, as in modern industrialized societies. But it may also call for more serious punishment, such as beating, maiming, or killing. Such informal control is administered on a private basis, usually by the aggrieved party. This can be seen among the Mayan Indians of South Mexico, who believe that you should kill a person who has wronged you. The Eskimos of the American Arctic would also kill people for such offenses as adultery, insult, or being a nuisance. The Ifugao of the Philippines consider it necessary for any "self-respecting man" to kill an adulterer caught red-handed. Violence in these societies is nonetheless quite rare—so are adultery and other deviances—apparently a testament to the effectiveness of informal control. The deterrent effect of informal control in traditional societies is at least greater than that of formal control in modern societies. As Donald Black (1983) pointed out, in the 1950s the rape incidence among the Gusii of Kenya shot up after the British colonial government prohibited traditional violence against the rapist and started to use British law to deal with the criminal.

In our society, informal control can also be more effective than formal control in deterring deviance. In one study, Richard Hollinger and John Clark (1982) found that informal control in the form of fellow workers' expressions of disapproval constrained employee theft more than did formal control in the form of reprimand or dismissal by management. Earlier studies on shoplifting and marijuana use had also found informal sanctions by peers to be a stronger brake on deviant behavior when compared with the threat of formal—criminal or legal—sanc-

tions (Kraut, 1976; Anderson, Chiricos, and Waldo, 1977).

Nevertheless, our society is marked by an extensive system of formal control. Perhaps formal control has become more important in modern industrialized nations because, as discussed in Chapter 3 (Social Structure), they have become more heterogeneous and more impersonal than traditional societies. This societal change may have increased social conflicts and enhanced the need for formal control. Let us examine formal control as carried out by the criminal justice system.

CRIMINAL JUSTICE

The criminal justice system is a network of police, courts, and prisons. These law enforcers are supposed to protect society, but they are also a potential threat to an individual's freedom. If they wanted to ensure that not a single criminal could slip away, the police would have to deprive innocent citizens of their rights and liberties. They would restrict our freedom of movement and invade our privacy—by tapping phones, reading mail, searching homes, stopping pedestrians for questioning, and blockading roads. No matter how law-abiding we might be, we would always be treated like criminal suspects—and some of us would almost certainly fall into the dragnet.

American prisons are seriously overcrowded, a situation that is worsening because of the recent war on drugs. Sentencing criminals to community service is a desperate, futile attempt to deal with prison overcrowding.

To prevent such abuses, the American criminal justice system is restrained by the Constitution and laws. Americans have the right to be presumed innocent until proven guilty, the right not to incriminate themselves, and many other legal protections. The freedom of the police to search homes and question suspects is limited. Thus, Americans' freedom, especially freedom from being wrongly convicted and imprisoned, is protected. But these laws also make the U.S. criminal justice system less effective than its counterparts in more repressive societies such as China and Cuba or in less individualistic societies such as Japan and Canada.

Herein lies the dilemma of the criminal justice system: If it does not catch enough criminals, the streets will not be safe; if it tries to apprehend too many, our freedom will be in trouble. Striking a balance between effective protection from criminals and respect for individual freedom is far from easy. This may be why the criminal justice system is criticized from right and left. It is attacked both for coddling criminals and for being too harsh.

There is some merit in both criticisms. Most criminals in the United States are never punished. The FBI's annual *Uniform Crime Reports* shows that every year about 79 percent of those who commit such serious "street crimes" as robbery, rape, and auto theft are not arrested. An even higher percentage of white-collar criminals is left unpunished. Of those few street criminals who are unlucky enough to be caught, many (45 to 55 percent) manage to slip through the court system free, thanks to dropping and dismissal of charges by prosecutors and judges. Of those who are convicted, about 60 percent have taken advantage of **plea bargaining,** whereby the defendant agrees to plead guilty to a lesser charge and thus receive a less severe penalty. As a result, less than 8 percent of all the known perpetrators of serious crimes are eventually sent to prison. Finally, about 50 percent of the prisoners do not serve their full terms because they are released on parole (U.S. Justice Department, 1988).

Does this mean that the American criminal justice system is soft on criminals? Compared with China and Cuba, yes. Compared with other democratic societies, no. The United States treats convicted criminals more severely than any other democratic nation. In 1991, there were 426 people imprisoned for every 100,000 Americans—the highest imprisonment rate among Western industrialized nations. Most other countries had rates under 100. In Sweden, the rate was 32; in the Netherlands, 28. Since 1980,

"And if you want to talk to your attorney, you'll find him in the next cell."

owing to the introduction of pretrial detention and increased abolition of parole, we have been locking up more people and sentencing them to longer terms. In 1980, there were fewer than half a million prisoners. Since then, the number has soared to 1.1 million in 1991. Most prisons are therefore seriously overcrowded. Prison sentences in the United States are indeed the stiffest in the West. Again, Sweden provides a striking contrast. The length of imprisonment in the United States is measured in years; in Sweden it is only in months and weeks. A typical sentence for murder in the United States is life imprisonment; in Sweden, it is two years. The United States is also the only industrialized nation in the West that still executes convicted murderers (Morganthau, 1991).

Does the harsh treatment in the United States help to decrease crime rates? Apparently not. Although the number of Americans behind bars has more than doubled since 1980, the incidence of crime has declined only 3.5 percent, while violent crimes have not decreased at all (Wicker, 1991). Moreover, our rates of **recidivism**—repeated criminal offenses—are quite high. One study estimated that 74 percent of those released from American prisons are likely to be rearrested three years later (Coleman and Cressey, 1990). According to the U.S. Justice Department (1988), about 61 percent of all adult inmates have been in prison before. To some inmates,

American prisons are schools of crime, in which they learn to become more motivated and skillful criminals. These "crime schools" are expensive: it costs more to send a person to prison than to college. The annual cost for keeping a criminal in prison is about $25,000. The overcrowding in prisons has further made rehabilitation impossible. In fact, it has triggered riots by the inmates.

All these problems, however, have led to a few new solutions. A number of states have hired private companies to run some of their prisons at far lower costs than if the states were to do it themselves. Many judges throughout the nation have stopped sending people convicted of nonviolent crimes (such as mail fraud, car theft, and burglary) to prison. These criminals are sentenced to confinement at home or in dormitory halfway houses, with permission to go to work. In Lincoln County, Oregon, some burglars and thieves are given a choice between going to prison and publishing apologies for their crimes, with their photographs, in local newspapers. In Sarasota, Florida, and Midwest City, Oklahoma, motorists convicted of drunk driving are required to display on their cars bumper stickers announcing the fact (Lacayo, 1987; Malcolm, 1990). Criminals are also increasingly sentenced to community service. These measures, however, are merely a desperate, futile attempt to deal with the enormous problem of prison overcrowding. This problem has worsened further because of the recent war on drugs.

THE WAR ON DRUGS

According to the National Council on Crime and Delinquency, the war on drugs will continue to overwhelm the prison system. This is largely due to the drug war's greater emphasis on arresting drug traffickers and users than on treating drug users and providing drug-prevention educational programs. In other words, the war on drugs focuses on cutting off the *supplies* of drugs rather than reducing the *demand* for drugs. The federal budget for the drug war has quadrupled in the last five years and now approaches $13 billion a year. But over 70 percent of this budget is geared toward law enforcement—only 30 percent is spent on treatment and education (Falco, 1992). Drug arrests have gone up sharply, drug seizures by law-enforcement officials have also increased sharply, and several larger South American drug rings have been put out of business. Nevertheless, the government is still far from winning the

drug war. Drugs continue to pour into our streets. In fact, the abundance of drugs has caused the wholesale price of a kilo of cocaine to drop from $65,000 to about $16,000 since 1980 (Morganthau, 1989; Shenon, 1990). As long as there is a great demand for drugs in our society, there will always be some countries and smugglers to supply them. The recent crackdown on the drug traffickers in Colombia, the major source of cocaine for the United States, only forced these suppliers to move their operations to Peru, Bolivia, Venezuela, and Brazil. Even the invasion of Panama by the United States has failed to stop the cocaine smuggling that used to flourish under General Noriega's auspices (Uhlig, 1990).

Failure of the law-enforcement approach has led to calls for legalization of drugs. Advocates of legalization point out that, like Prohibition (of alcohol) in the 1920s, the current drug laws do more harm than good. For one thing, they generate many crimes, including murder. As Milton Friedman (1989a) says, "Addicts are driven to associate with criminals to get the drugs, become criminals themselves to finance the habit, and risk constant danger of death and disease." The drug laws also encourage official corruption. Because huge profits are reaped from drug sales, the criminals can bribe police to "look the other way." "From Brooklyn police precincts to Miami's police stations to rural Georgia courthouses," observes Hodding Carter (1989), "big drug money is purchasing major breakdowns in law enforcement." By legalizing drugs, the proponents argue, the government can take away obscene profits from drug traffickers, end police corruption, and reduce crime drastically. Those who oppose legalization respond that, if drugs are legalized, drug use and addiction will skyrocket. As William Bennett (1989), the former national drug-control policy director, says, "After the repeal of Prohibition, consumption of alcohol soared by 350%."

But legalizers disagree, arguing that drug use and abuse are not likely to rise much beyond their current levels. There is some evidence to support this argument. Consumption of alcohol and tobacco in the United States is declining. The percentage of high school students saying they have used illegal drugs continues to fall, even though the drugs are far more easily available and cheaper than before. The decriminalization of marijuana in some states has not increased its use for several years now. Heroin addiction has held steady at about 500,000 people for some time, despite the drug's much greater availability and lower price. Use of cocaine has plummeted in recent years, at least among middle and working classes, although the drug is abundantly available. The exception is crack, whose use has exploded among high school dropouts, the unemployed, and the inner-city criminal class. But because crack is already relatively cheap to buy, it will not be any more accessible under legalization than it is now under prohibition (Whitman, 1990; Treaster, 1991). Finally, legalizers believe that with legalization the huge amount of money currently spent on law enforcement can be used for drug treatment and education, which will dramatically reduce drug use and addiction.

In fact, most of the recent decline in drug use has come from educational programs, television commercials, and other similar efforts that focus on increasing public awareness of the harmfulness of drugs. In schools, for example, the youth are taught "social resistance skills," shown how to say no to peer pressure to use drugs; students are provided with scientific information that "not everybody is doing it," and they are accurately informed of the problems resulting from the use of various drugs. This is a far cry from the scare tactics of the failed antidrug campaign of the 1970s. At that time, the antidrug forces lost their credibility by wildly exaggerating how horrible the effects of drugs were.

If the history of drug use in the United States is any guide, the recently increased public awareness of the drug problem may soon reduce drug use drastically. According to medical historian David Musto (1986), societies typically pass through three stages in a cycle of drug use: an initial stage of *euphoria* as a small number of users report the harmless or even valuable and helpful effects of a drug; a middle period of *dispersion* as more and more people use the drug and more and more problems with the drug are reported; and, finally, a period of *powerful rejection* of the drug, when its popular image becomes as negative as it had once been positive. Musto found that the use of cocaine passed through those three stages from 1885, when cocaine started to become popular, to the 1920s, when widespread outrage discouraged cocaine use so much that the drug faded into obscurity. But the cycle of cocaine use started again in the mid-1970s. In the first stage of this second cycle, cocaine was widely reported as harmless. Dr. Peter Bourne, who was President Carter's drug advisor, said that "cocaine, once a component of many tonics and of Coca-Cola, is probably the most benign of illicit drugs currently in widespread use." As a consequence, the drug became increasingly popular toward the early 1980s. By that time, however, the extended use of cocaine began to cause a growing number of problems. During this second stage, cocaine deaths were multiplying. Since the early 1980s, as the wave of cocaine casualties continued to rise, public concern began to build up. Today we seem to be in the last stage of public rejection. As opinion polls show, Americans now consider drugs the most serious social problem in the United States (Shenon, 1990). We may eventually win the war on drugs, but largely through drug education rather than law enforcement.

QUESTIONS FOR DISCUSSION AND REVIEW

1. How does internalization of the norms of society deter deviance in a different way from social control?
2. In what ways can the criminal justice system balance the need to catch criminals with the need to respect individual freedom?
3. How does the United States treat convicted criminals more severely than any other democratic nation?
4. Can the war on drugs be won?

CHAPTER REVIEW

1. *What is deviant behavior?* It is an act considered by public consensus or the powerful at a given time and place to be a violation of some social rule.

2. *In what ways does murder occur?* Murder usually takes place on Saturday night, with the use of a gun. It often involves relatives, friends, or acquaintances. *What is the hidden culture of rape?* It encourages men to rape women by treating women as if they were men's property, as if they were the trophies of men's masculinity contests, and as if they wanted to be raped.

3. *How does corporate crime differ from street*

crime? Corporate crime is more rationally executed, more profitable, and less detectable. The victim often cooperates with corporate criminals unwittingly, society does little to punish them, and they do not see themselves as criminals. Corporate crime further exacts a higher economic, physical, and social cost.

4. *Are the poor more likely to be mentally ill than the rich?* Yes, according to many studies. But there are conflicting explanations about why this is so. One explanation is the stressful life of the poor. The other is that the mentally ill tend to move into lower-class neighborhoods and the healthy ones, out of them.

5. *Is deviance always harmful to society?* No. If it occurs within limits, it may help define and clarify norms, strengthen solidarity among law-abiding citizens, provide a safety valve, offer jobs, and stimulate social change.

6. *According to anomie theory, what is the cause of deviance?* American society overemphasizes success as an important goal for all individuals but underemphasizes—and fails to provide to all people—the socially approved means for achieving success. One possible response to this inconsistency is deviance.

7. *According to differential association theory, how does a person become a criminal?* Through learning in interactions with others: when a person's associations with those who view criminal behavior favorably outweigh his or her associations with those who view it unfavorably, criminal behavior results.

8. *How does control theory explain deviance?* Social control leads to conformity, and, therefore, the absence of control causes deviance. According to Hirschi, the absence of control arises from a lack of social bonds. To Braithwaite, the absence of control comes from a lack of reintegrative shaming.

9. *How is being labeled deviant likely to affect people?* The label may cause them to look upon themselves as deviant and to live up to this self-image by engaging in more deviant behavior.

10. *How does conflict theory explain deviance?* The traditional version of the theory emphasizes cultural conflict as the source of deviant definition and behavior. The contemporary version traces various crimes to class conflict under capitalism.

11. *What is the feminist theory of deviance?* Conventional theories may be relevant to men but not women. Women are likely to be victims of rape and sexual harassment, which reflects men's attempt to put women in their place. The recent increase in female crime is not significant. Besides, most of the increase involves minor property crimes with very little profit, which reflects the continuing subordinate position of women in a patriarchy.

12. *How does society control deviant behavior?* Through socialization, but it is never completely successful. It is supplemented by formal and informal social control. Informal control is more common in traditional societies, and formal control is more common in modern societies. Informal control, however, seems more effective in deterring deviance. *Is the American criminal justice system soft on criminals?* A low percentage of criminals is apprehended and punished, but compared with other Western countries, the United States imprisons proportionately more people and imposes longer prison terms. *How does the government wage the war on drugs?* It focuses its efforts on law enforcement against drugs rather than treatment and education. The resulting rise in drug-related crimes has led some to advocate legalizing drugs. The legalizers argue that treatment and education are more effective in reducing drug use and addiction.

KEY TERMS

Anomie A condition in which social norms are absent, weak, or in conflict (p. 121).

Cultural transmission The process by which the values of crime and delinquency are transmitted from one group to another (p. 123).

Date rape Rape committed by a man against a woman he is out with (p. 116).

Deviant behavior An act that is considered by public consensus or the powerful at a given place and time to be a violation of some social rule (p. 114).

Differential association The process by which potential deviants associate more with criminal elements than with noncriminal elements (p. 123).

Disintegrative shaming Punishing wrongdoers in such a way as to stigmatize, reject, or ostracize them (p. 124).

Internalization The process by which individuals incorporate the values of society into their personalities, accepting the norms of society as their own (p. 128).

Marginal surplus population Marxist term for unemployed workers who are useless to the capitalist economy (p. 127).

Neurosis Mental problem characterized by a persistent fear, anxiety, or worry about trivial matters (p. 119).

Plea bargaining A pretrial negotiation in which the defendant agrees to plead guilty to a lesser charge in exchange for a less severe penalty (p. 130).

Primary deviance An initial violation of a norm that is not considered deviant by the person committing the act (p. 125).

Psychosis Mental disorder typified by loss of touch with reality (p. 119).

Recidivism Repeated commission of crimes (p. 130).

Reintegrative shaming Making wrongdoers feel guilty while showing them understanding, forgiveness, or even respect (p. 124).

Secondary deviance Habitual norm violations that the person recognizes as deviant and commits in conformity with his or her self-image as a deviant (p. 125).

Social control Process by which individuals are pressured by others such as teachers, peers, and police to conform to social norms (p. 128).

SUGGESTED READINGS

Braithwaite, John. 1989. *Crime, Shame, and Reintegration.* Cambridge: Cambridge University Press. Explains how "reintegrative shaming" (social disapproval that invokes remorse in deviants, to be followed by efforts to reintegrate them into the community through gestures of forgiveness) prevents deviance, while "disintegrative shaming" (mere stigmatization) encourages deviance.

Cullen, Francis T. 1984. *Rethinking Crime and Deviance Theory: The Emergence of a Structuring Tradition.* Totowa, N.J.: Rowman & Allanheld. A theoretical statement of how certain social and social-psychological conditions can determine the transformation of a general deviant tendency into a specific form of deviant act.

Katz, Jack. 1988. *Seductions of Crime: Moral and Sensual Attractions of Doing Evil.* New York: Basic Books. An analysis of crime from the criminal's subjective perspective, focusing on how it feels to run afoul of the law.

Scully, Diana. 1990. *Understanding Sexual Violence: A Study of Convicted Rapists.* Boston: Unwin Hyman. Shows how a patriarchal society leads convicted rapists to rationalize away their guilt by blaming their own uncharacteristic behavior (such as drunkenness) or their victim for precipitating the rape.

Thio, Alex. 1988. *Deviant Behavior,* 3rd ed. New York: Harper & Row. A comprehensive and, according to a UCLA professor writing in the journal *Teaching Sociology,* "remarkably well-written text that takes the student two steps beyond most extant texts."

7

SOCIAL STRATIFICATION

MYTHS AND REALITIES

Myth: Given their great diversity, various groups of Americans are bound to disagree on whether a particular occupation is good or bad.

Reality: *Virtually all groups of Americans, rich or poor, rate occupations in the same way. Even people in other countries evaluate occupations in the same way as Americans do.*

Myth: Most welfare recipients become so dependent on welfare that they will never get off it.

Reality: *More than half of the welfare recipients leave the system within 1 to 5 years. Only 24 percent stay on welfare for 10 years or more.*

Myth: Welfare has become an incentive for producing out-of-wedlock births. That's why most single mothers on welfare have many children.

Reality: *Most welfare mothers have only one or two children, just like the average American families.*

Myth: As many rags-to-riches stories in the media show, it is not uncommon for a poor man's child to become a millionaire in this land of opportunity.

Reality: *It is uncommon for a poor American to become a millionaire. The success experienced by many Americans involves moving only a little way up the economic ladder.*

Myth: As the world's leading democratic society, the United States has the most equal distribution of income.

Reality: *While the U.S. income distribution is more equal than that of developing countries, it is less so than several other industrial nations, such as England, Sweden, and Germany.*

Myth: Because most immigrants are poor and need financial assistance, countries with unusually large numbers of them cannot become prosperous.

Reality: *The world's most prosperous societies, such as the United States, Canada, Israel, and Australia, have had unusually large numbers of immigrants.*

Myth: Compared to people with children, those without children have a better chance of succeeding in their careers because they can devote more time to their work.

Reality: *People with children are more upwardly mobile, probably because their family responsibilities tend to stimulate ambition and diligence.*

R obert Swanson was already relatively rich 10 years ago, but since then he has gotten richer. A decade ago, when he founded a semiconductor firm, he paid himself $125,000 in salary. Today, the 53-year-old California entrepreneur earns $360,000 a year, and his net worth has soared to $15 million. He revels in being a very rich man, often riding around in a 1992 Porsche. By contrast, Mary Huntley found the 1980s a time of stagnation rather than success. In 1982, the 41-year-old medical technologist from Fort Wayne, Indiana, took home $24,000 a year. Today, despite the inflation that has reduced the value of the dollar, she makes only $34,000. An avid moviegoer, she has to skip evening shows in favor of half-price matinees. "For me," says Huntley, "50 cents is 50 cents" (Hawkins, 1992).

"Those who have, get." This old saying suggests that in every society some people, like Robert Swanson, get more rewards than others, like Mary Huntley. The specific nature of the rewards may vary from one society to another. The rewards could be in the form of wealth, power, prestige, or whatever is highly valued by the society. All over the world, these rewards are distributed unequally. This patterned inequality is called **social stratification.** It is the division of society in such a way that some categories of people get more rewards than others.

In this chapter we will first see how these rewards are used as the bases for social stratification in the United States. Then we will examine what the social strata, or classes, are in this country, and whether people can move easily from one stratum to another. Finally, we will analyze the question of whether it is necessary for society to have this social stratification.

The Bases of Stratification

Social stratification is based on the unequal distribution of many different rewards. Sociologists have long identified three of these rewards as the most important bases of stratification in the United States: wealth, power, and prestige. These three usually go together. If we are rich, we are also likely to have a lot of political power and social prestige. But possession of one reward does not guarantee enjoyment of others. Compared with teachers, some garbage collectors may make more money but have less prestige and power.

WEALTH

In the last century Karl Marx divided industrial society into two major and one minor classes: the *bourgeoisie* (capitalists), the *proletariat* (workers), and the *petite bourgeoisie* (small capitalists). Marx differentiated them on the basis of two criteria: whether they own the "means of production"—tools, factories, offices, and stores—and whether they hire others to work for them. Capitalists are those who own the means of production and hire others. Workers neither own the means of production nor employ others. Hence they are forced to work for capitalists. As for small capitalists, they own the means of production but do not purchase the labor of others. Examples are shopkeepers, doctors, lawyers, and other self-employed persons. Marx considered these people a minor, transitional class because he believed that they would eventually be forced down into the working class.

Karl Marx believed that capitalists sought to maximize profit by exploiting workers. He had seen the appalling working conditions in factories in the mid-nineteenth century in England. Women and children were employed for long hours at low pay. Conditions in the United States were not much better, as shown here in a famous photograph of child laborers taken by Lewis Hine in the early twentieth century.

In Marx's view, exploitation characterizes the relationship between the two major classes: capitalists and workers. Capitalists, bent on maximizing profit, compel workers to work long hours for little pay. Such exploitation was indeed extreme in Marx's time. Consider his description of child laborers:

> Children of nine or ten years are dragged from their squalid beds at two, three, or four o'clock in the morning and compelled to work for a bare subsistence until ten, eleven, or twelve at night, their limbs wearing away, their frames dwindling, their faces whitening, and their humanity absolutely sinking into a stone-like torpor, utterly horrible to contemplate (Marx, 1866).

Marx believed that eventually workers would rise in revolt and establish a classless society of economic equals. But his prophecy of revolution has not materialized in any highly developed capitalist economy. Writing in the 1860s, Marx failed to foresee that the exploitation of workers would ease and that a large, prosperous class of white-collar workers would emerge. Even so, there are still significant economic inequalities in the United States.

According to the latest data available, the richest 20 percent of the population earn about 44 percent of the total national income. In contrast, the poorest 20 percent earn less than 5 percent of the national income. The distribution of wealth is even more unequal. Whereas *income* is the money people receive over a certain period of time, such as wages and salaries, *wealth* includes the income-producing things they own, such as stocks, bonds, savings accounts, and real estate. A large group of Americans own no assets, and most hold little wealth. The richest 20 percent of the population own 76 percent of the total national wealth, but the poorest 20 percent hold far less than 1 percent (see Figure 7.1).

POWER

Power—the ability to get people to do things they otherwise would not do—is associated with wealth. Most sociologists agree that people with more wealth tend to have more power. This is evident in the domination of top government positions by the wealthy. Higher-income Americans are also more likely to feel a strong sense of power. Thus they are more likely to be politically active, working to retain or increase their power. Meanwhile, lower-income Americans are more likely to feel powerless to influence major political decisions. They are therefore more indifferent to politics and less likely to participate in political activity—a reaction likely to reinforce their lack of power (Dahl, 1981; Kourvetaris and Dobratz, 1982).

It is clear that power is distributed unequally. But how unequal is that distribution? Does it match the distribution of wealth? Power cannot be identified and measured as easily as wealth can because people with power do not always express it. As a result, sociologists disagree about how it is distributed.

Both Marxist and elite theorists argue that a very small group of Americans holds the most power in the United States. According to *Marxist theorists,* that group consists of capitalists. Even if they do not hold office, say Marxists, capitalists set the limits of political debate and of the government's actions, protecting their own interests. This is why large corporations, through heavy political campaign contributions and congressional lobbying, are able to hold down their taxes. According to *elite theorists,* a lot of power is in the hands of a few hundred individuals who hold top positions in the executive branch of the federal government, in the military, and in corporations. Often, the same people hold power in all these three centers of power. In any event, they have similar backgrounds, values, and interests, and they form what elite theorists call the **power elite.**

In contrast to both Marxist and elite theorists, *pluralist theorists* argue that power is not tightly concentrated, but widely dispersed. It is more or less equally distributed among various competing groups. The power of big business, for example, is balanced by that of big labor, and government actions are ultimately determined by competition and compromise among such diverse groups. Even ordinary citizens have the power to vote anyone into office or out of it.

In short, while Marxists and elitists see a great deal of inequality in power distribution, pluralists see very little. Both views may be correct. Most of the power in American society is concentrated at the top, but the elite is not all-powerful. It is subject to challenge by voters from below. It is true that the general public is usually powerless—because it does not get organized. But occasionally, when it feels strongly enough about an issue to make its wishes known, as it did about its opposition to the Vietnam War in the 1960s, the government does change its policy to follow public opinion (Burstein, 1981). We examine the theories further in Chapter 12 (Politics and the Economy).

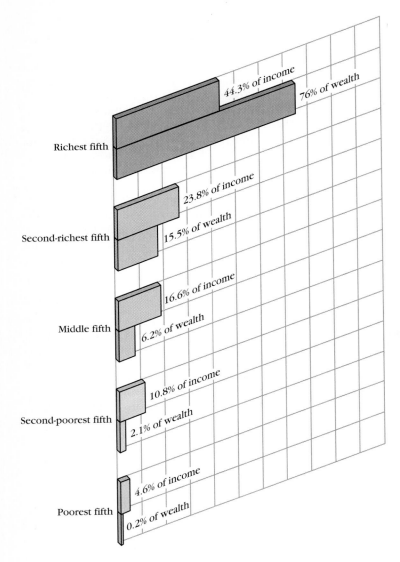

FIGURE 7.1 *Unequal Distribution of Income and Wealth*
Income in salaries and wages is unequally distributed among Americans. Wealth accruing from stocks, bonds, property, and the like is even more unequally distributed. The richest fifth of the population owns 76 percent of the national wealth, 380 times more than what the poorest fifth owns, which is a mere 0.2 percent of the nation's wealth.

Sources: Social Indicators, 1973 (Washington, D.C.: Government Printing Office), p. 182; Census Bureau, *Statistical Abstract of the United States,* 1992 (Washington, D.C.: Government Printing Office), p. 450.

PRESTIGE

A third basis of social stratification is the unequal distribution of prestige. Following Max Weber, sociologists call this kind of stratification a **status system.**

There is a difference between prestige, on the one hand, and wealth and power, on the other. Wealth and power are objective entities: a person can have them regardless of what other people think of him or her. But prestige is subjective, depending for its existence on how a person is perceived by others. If a person is rich and powerful but is seen by others as unworthy of respect, he or she has low prestige. The boss of an organized crime syndicate may make millions and exercise awesome power, but he might never acquire prestige because most people refuse to hold him in esteem—and they cannot be forced to do so. On the other hand, many college professors may not be rich and powerful, but they do enjoy more prestige than the crime boss.

Although prestige is not as concrete as money and power, most people do seek it. Consciousness of status, Gerhard Lenski (1966) has observed, "influences almost every kind of decision from the choice of a car to the choice of a spouse. Fear of the loss of status, or honor, is one of the few motives that can make men lay down their lives on the field of battle."

How do people obtain such an important social reward? Occupation seems the most important source of prestige. For many years, sociologists have found that people have very definite ideas about the prestige of various occupations. In 1947 a team of sociologists asked a large random sample of Americans to evaluate 90 occupations on a scale from "excellent" to "poor." Then in 1963 other sociologists repeated the study with other Americans. They found a nearly perfect correlation between the prestige scores given these 90 occupations in 1947 and in 1963. In those two years, physicians, for example, received one of the highest scores and garbage collectors one of the lowest. Almost all groups of Americans, rich or poor, rated the occupations in the same way (Hodge, Siegel, and Rossi, 1964). About the same finding appeared in the 1970s, 1980s, and 1990s (Table 7.1). Even people in many other countries— some industrialized and some not—have been found

TABLE 7.1 *How Americans Rank Occupations*

Occupation is probably the most important source of prestige. All kinds of Americans tend to give the same prestige rating to an occupation. The ranking of various occupations has largely remained the same for the last 45 years. How do people evaluate the occupations? The following table suggests that generally they give higher ratings to those jobs that require more education and offer higher incomes.

OCCUPATION	SCORE	OCCUPATION	SCORE	OCCUPATION	SCORE
Physician	82	Journalist	60	Childcare worker	36
Lawyer	75	Dietician	56	Hairdresser	36
College professor	74	Statistician	56	Baker	35
Architect	73	Radio/TV announcer	55	Upholsterer	35
Chemist	73	Librarian	54	Bulldozer operator	34
Physicist	73	Police officer	54	Meter reader	34
Aerospace engineer	72	Aircraft mechanic	53	Bus driver	32
Dentist	72	Firefighter	53	Hotel clerk	32
Geologist	70	Dental hygienist	52	Auto body repairman	31
Clergy	69	Social worker	52	Apparel salesperson	30
Psychologist	69	Draftsman	51	Truck driver	30
Pharmacist	68	Electrician	51	Cashier	29
Optometrist	67	Computer operator	50	Elevator operator	28
Registered nurse	66	Funeral director	49	Garbage collector	28
Secondary-school teacher	66	Real estate agent	49	Taxi driver	28
Accountant	65	Machinist	47	Waiter/waitress	28
Air traffic controller	65	Mail carrier	47	Bellhop	27
Athlete	65	Secretary	46	Freight handler	27
Electrical engineer	64	Insurance agent	45	Bartender	25
Elementary-school teacher	64	Photographer	45	Farm laborer	23
Mechanical engineer	64	Bank teller	43	Household servant	23
Economist	63	Welder	42	Midwife	23
Industrial engineer	62	Farmer	40	Door-to-door salesperson	22
Veterinarian	62	Telephone operator	40	Janitor	22
Airline pilot	61	Carpenter	39	Car washer	19
Computer specialist	61	TV repairman	38	Newspaper vendor	19
Office manager	60	Security guard	37	Shoe shiner	9

Source: General Social Survey Cumulative File, 1972–1992, Ann Arbor, Mich.: Inter-University Consortium for Political and Social Research, 1992.

to rank occupations in the same way (Hodge, Siegel, and Rossi, 1964; Treiman, 1977).

How do people evaluate occupations? A quick look at Table 7.1 suggests that the ranking has a lot to do with education and income. In general, the higher the education and income associated with an occupation, the greater its prestige, as is true of physicians and lawyers. This is not always the case, though. Compared with schoolteachers, truck drivers may make more money but rank lower in prestige.

Occupation, of course, is only one of a person's many statuses, such as those based on age, race, and gender. These statuses may have different social rankings, creating **status inconsistency.** An African-American lawyer and a female doctor have high occupational status, but they may have less prestige because of prejudice against their race or gender.

People plagued with status inconsistency usually experience considerable stress. They resent the source of their status inconsistency. They think of themselves in terms of their highest status and expect others to do the same. But others may treat them in reference to their lowest status. Consequently, compared with people who do not experience status inconsistency, those who do are more likely to support liberal and radical movements designed to change the status quo (Lenski, 1966). As research has shown, in the 1960s African-American bankers and physicians were more militant about changing racial conditions than African-American janitors and housekeepers (Marx, 1967).

QUESTIONS FOR DISCUSSION AND REVIEW

1. What is social stratification, and what bases are used to stratify American society?
2. How equally are income and wealth distributed in the United States?
3. In what ways is the power basis of stratification different from the system of prestige?
4. Why does status inconsistency create stress?

American Class Structure

Americans tend to believe that they live in a classless society. But inequality is entrenched in the United States. This inequality can be observed in the way American society is divided into different social classes, forming a distinctive class structure.

IDENTIFYING CLASSES

Sociologists have defined **social class** as a category of people who have about the same amount of income, power, and prestige. But how do we know who is in what class? There are three different methods for identifying what our class is. (1) The reputational method asks: What do others think of us? (2) The subjective method asks: What do we think of ourselves? (3) The objective method asks: What do we do, how much do we have, and how do we live?

Reputational Method Sociologists who use the **reputational method** select a group of people and ask them what classes they think others belong to. These selected individuals, or informants, can serve as "prestige judges" primarily because they have been living in the community for a long time and can tell the sociologists the standing of many other residents. Presumably, they rank others on the basis of their reputation in the town. If these "judges" are asked to

Status inconsistency is the condition in which the individual is given a different ranking in various social categories, such as a high ranking due to occupation but a low ranking because of prejudice against one's race. An African-American lawyer may experience status inconsistency.

rank a man whom they know to be a public drunk, they would put him in a lower-class category. If they are asked to rank a woman whom they know as a respectable banker, they would place her in an upper-class category. To the sociologists, then, whatever class in which the prestige judges place a person is his or her class.

The reputational method is useful for investigating the class structure of a small community, where everybody knows practically everybody else. But it suffers several disadvantages. First, the reputational method cannot be applied to large cities because it is impossible to find prestige judges who know thousands of other people. Second, it is impossible to generalize the findings from one community to another because the informants can judge only their own community. Third, it is impossible to find unanimity among the prestige judges in a community. There are always cases in which an individual is considered upper class by one judge but lower class by another.

Subjective Method   Instead of asking people what they think of others, sociologists may ask them what class they themselves belong to. This is called the **subjective method.**

In using the subjective method, sociologists have long discovered that, if asked whether they are upper, middle, or lower class, the overwhelming majority of Americans will identify themselves as middle class. Both "upper class" and "lower class" have connotations offensive to democratic values. To call oneself upper class is to appear snobbish. To call oneself lower class is demeaning because it implies that one is a loser in this supposed land of opportunity. As a result, many millionaires would call themselves middle rather than upper class; meanwhile, many low-income and lower-status Americans such as maids and laborers would also regard themselves as middle class. But, if given "working class" as a fourth choice, more Americans will identify themselves as working class than as middle class.

Thus, the weaknesses of the subjective method are clear. First, the results depend heavily on how the question is asked. Second, the answers are influenced by the respondents' attitude toward the class system. Despite these problems, the subjective method has at least two advantages. First, it can be used fairly easily to investigate large cities or even an entire society. Large numbers of strangers can simply be asked to respond—anonymously if they wish—to a question like, "If you were asked to use one of these names for

your social-class standing, which would you say you belong to: middle class, lower class, working class, or upper class?" Second, the subjective method is very useful for understanding and predicting behaviors that are strongly affected by attitudes. If self-employed auto mechanics, electricians, and plumbers identify themselves with the upper class, they can be expected to hold politically conservative views and to vote Republican, just as upper-class people tend to do (Form, 1982).

Objective Method   Both the subjective and the reputational methods depend on people's perception of class. The third method depends on objective criteria, such as amount of income.

To use the **objective method,** sociologists must decide what criteria are to be used to indicate individuals' class positions. Today, most sociologists use occupation, income, and education as the criteria, either singly or jointly. Some sociologists use occupation by itself to divide the population into classes. Others use income or education instead. Still others utilize all three criteria.

Like the subjective method, the objective method is useful for identifying the classes in large cities or an entire society. It has another advantage as well: sociologists can easily obtain the needed data on occupation, income, and education from the Bureau of the Census or by mailing questionnaires to the people themselves.

The objective method has some disadvantages, though. One is that the choice of the criteria for differentiating the classes is arbitrary. One sociologist, believing that education is the best indicator of class, may consequently place schoolteachers in a higher class than truck drivers, because teachers tend to have more education than truck drivers. But another sociologist may consider income the best criterion of class and, therefore, place the higher-paid truck drivers in a higher class than schoolteachers. A second disadvantage of the objective method is that the indicators of class are *continuous* measures, not discrete categories. When people answer "middle class" to a survey question, that is a discrete category, but their incomes and educational levels fall on a continuum of values. With these continuous measures, we can still distinguish clearly between the top and the bottom of the class ladder, but it is difficult to differentiate the people near the middle. This is a serious problem because the majority of Americans happen to cluster around the middle. Thus, sociologists are forced to establish an *arbitrary* boundary between classes—say, choosing 12 years of education rather than 11 or 13 as a boundary between the middle and working classes.

CLASS PROFILES

The three methods of identifying classes have been used in many studies with roughly the same result: in the United States, about 1 to 3 percent of the population are in the upper class, 40 to 55 percent in the middle class, 30 to 45 percent in the working class, and 15 to 20 percent in the poor, lower class. Sociologists disagree about the precise boundaries of these classes, but most accept these broad estimates of their sizes. Here is a brief profile of these classes that has emerged from various studies (Gross, Gursslin, and Roach, 1969; Rossides, 1976; Gilbert and Kahl, 1987; Kerbo, 1983).

The Upper Class   Though it is a mere 1 to 3 percent of the population, the upper class possesses at least 25 percent of the nation's wealth. This class has two segments: upper upper and lower upper. Basically, the upper upper class is the "old rich"—families that have been wealthy for several generations—an aristocracy of birth and wealth. Their names are in the *Social Register,* a listing of acceptable members of high society. A few are known across the nation, such as the Rockefellers, Roosevelts, and Vanderbilts. Most are not visible to the general public. They live in grand seclusion, drawing their income from the investment of their inherited wealth. In contrast, the lower upper class is the "new rich." Although they may be wealthier than some of the old rich, the new rich have hustled to make their money like everybody else beneath their class. Thus, their prestige is generally lower than that of the old rich. The old rich, who have not found it necessary to lift a finger to make their money, tend to thumb their noses at the new rich.

However its wealth is acquired, the upper class is very, very rich. They have enough money and leisure time to cultivate an interest in the arts and to collect rare books, paintings, and sculpture. They generally live in exclusive areas, belong to exclusive social clubs, rub elbows with each other, and marry their own kind—all of which keeps them so aloof from the masses that they have been called the *out-of-sight class* (Fussell, 1983). More than any other class, they tend to be conscious of being members of

a class. They also command an enormous amount of power and influence here and abroad, as they hold many top government positions, run the Council on Foreign Relations, and control multinational corporations. Their actions affect the lives of millions.

The Middle Class   The middle class is not as tightly knit as the upper class. Middle-class people are distinguished from those above them primarily by their lesser wealth and power, and from those below them by their white-collar, nonmanual jobs.

This class can be differentiated into two strata by occupational prestige, income, and education. The *upper middle class* consists mostly of professional and business people with high income and education, such as doctors, lawyers, and corporate executives. The *lower middle class* is far larger in size and much more diverse in occupation. It is made up of people in relatively low-level but still white-collar occupations, such as small-business owners, store and traveling salespersons, managers, technicians, teachers, and secretaries. Though they have less income and education than the upper middle class, the lower middle class has achieved the middle-class dream of owning a suburban home and living a comfortable life.

The Working Class   The working class consists primarily of those who have very little education and whose jobs are manual and carry very little prestige. Some working-class people, such as construction workers, carpenters, and plumbers, are skilled workers and may make more money than those in the lower reaches of the middle class, such as secretaries and teachers. But their jobs are more physically demanding and, especially in the case of factory workers, more dangerous. Other working-class people are unskilled, such as migrant workers, janitors, and dishwashers. There are also many women in this class working as domestics, cleaning ladies, and waitresses, and they are the sole breadwinners in their households. Because they are generally underpaid, they have been called the *working poor* (Gilbert and Kahl, 1987).

The Lower Class   This class is characterized by joblessness and poverty. It includes the chronically unemployed, the welfare recipients, and the impoverished aged. These people suffer the indignity of living in run-down houses, of wearing old clothes, of eating cheap food, and of lacking proper medical

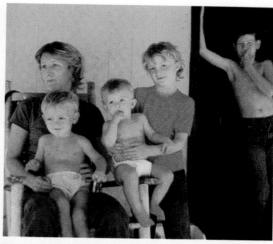

Left: In general, the middle class does not have inherited wealth and must earn the money for its life-style. Middle-class people can be wealthy if they own a successful business or rise to the top of their profession. They can also achieve a position that commands prestige. But others are rather poor, such as low-paid church ministers and school teachers.

Right: The lower class is made up of the working and nonworking poor. It consists of an increasing number of female-headed families.

care. Very few have finished high school. They may have started out in their youth with poorly paying jobs that required little or no skill, but their earning power began to drop when they reached their late twenties. A new lower class has emerged in recent years: skilled workers in mechanized industry who have become unskilled workers in electronically run factories. They have first become helpers, then occasional workers, and finally the hard-core unemployed. (Dahrendorf, 1984; Goldberg and Kremen, 1987). Most of these people are merely poor. Unfortunately, the media and conservatives often stigmatize them as "the underclass." They conjure up images of poor people as violent criminals, drug abusers, welfare mothers who cannot stop having babies, or able-bodied men on welfare who are too lazy to work. Let us, therefore, take a closer look at the poor—and the homeless, whom the public also often stigmatizes as "trash" (Feagin and Feagin, 1990).

POVERTY, WELFARE, AND HOMELESSNESS

Consider the case of Caroline Carter, a 30-year-old Milwaukee widow with two teenage children. She earns about $13,800 a year. Is she poor? The government says no, because her income is above the official poverty line of $10,560 for a family of three. But critics would say that Ms. Carter is definitely poor (DeParle, 1990). Who is right? The answer depends on the definition you choose to accept. We will see how the government and its critics define poverty. Then we will discuss who the poor and the homeless are, and why they are poor and homeless.

What Is Poverty? To determine the number of poor people, the government uses an absolute definition of poverty. It defines poverty as the lack of minimum food and shelter necessary for maintaining life, which sociologists call **absolute poverty.** It then decides what income is needed to sustain that minimum standard of living and sees how many people fall below it. This method of determining poverty originates from the research that Mollie Orshanksy did for the Social Security Administration in the early 1960s. Because she found that the average family then spent a third of its income on food, she determined the poverty line by multiplying the cost of the Agriculture Department's cheapest recommended

Absolute poverty is the lack of minimum food and shelter necessary for maintaining life. But poverty can also be relative: a state of deprivation resulting from having less than what the majority of the people have. Poor Americans find their poverty all the more disheartening when they see the vivid contrast between their lives and the lives of the wealthy. The conditions of the poor worsen when properous Americans, who tend to blame the poor for their poverty, are reluctant to support social programs. Which of the individuals in the photos look as though they might be living in a state of absolute poverty?

food plan by three. Her resulting figures, which varied with family size, were officially adopted in 1969. Since then, those original figures have been simply raised every year to take inflation into account. Thus, for 1991, the "poverty line" for a nonfarm family of four was $13,924, and 14.2 percent of the population—over 35 million Americans—fell below the poverty line (Pear, 1992).

Such figures have stirred up a controversy, however. Conservative critics argue that they overestimate the extent of poverty because they do not count as income many *noncash* benefits, such as food stamps, housing subsidies, and medical assistance, which the poor receive from the government. These noncash benefits account for two-thirds of government programs for the poor. If these benefits were added to cash incomes, many "poor" Americans would rise above the poverty line—and hence no longer be poor. In other words, the 1991 poverty rate would have come down to 10 percent from its official rate of 14.2 percent. Liberal critics, on the other hand, contend that the official rate *underestimates* the extent of poverty because it is based on the outdated assumption that the average American family today spends a third of its income on food, as it did

30 years ago. Actually, it now spends only a fifth of its income on food, largely because of increases in the cost of housing and child care. Therefore, in order to stay above the poverty line to meet basic needs, the family of 30 years ago needed an income only three times its food budget, but the family of today needs an income five times its current food budget. This formula should raise the 1991 official poverty rate of 14.2 percent to 21 percent. Most Americans would agree that there are more poor people than government statistics suggest. In a poll taken several years ago, a national sample of Americans were asked how much a family of four needed to avoid being poor. The average given was $15,017, higher than the official standard of $12,092 for that year. This translated into 18 percent of the population being poor, much higher than the official rate (DeParle, 1990).

Many social scientists suggest that a *relative,* not an absolute, definition of poverty be used, because how poor or rich we feel depends on how people around us live. Just because we are not starving to death or live far better than, say, the poor in Central America does not mean that we should consider ourselves well-off. According to a widely accepted relative definition of poverty, those who earn less than half of the nation's median income are poor because they lack what is needed by most Americans to live a decent life. By this definition, for more than 40 years, the percentage of the nation living in poverty has hovered around 20 percent. These people are said to suffer from **relative poverty,** a state of deprivation resulting from having less than what the majority of the people have. The psychological impact of relative poverty seems far greater in the United States than in other countries. In many developing countries, the poor may not find themselves too bad off because most people around them are just as poor. But it is tougher to be poor in a sea of affluence, such as the United States, where most Americans blame the poor for their poverty, stereotyping them as lazy, worthless, and immoral (Smith and Stone, 1989).

Feminist Perspective on Poverty Over the last several decades, there has been a **feminization of poverty,** a significant increase in the number of women bearing the burden of poverty alone, mostly as single mothers or heads of families. In the last 30 years the proportion of poor families maintained by women has grown from 23 to over 51 percent of all families. The feminization of poverty has affected African-Americans the most. While poor families maintained by white women have increased from 20 to 42 percent, those headed by black women have risen from 30 to 75 percent (Pearce, 1993). If we take into account all women, including those living as wives and daughters in male-headed households, the proportion of poor women is even higher—57 rather than 51 percent. This female share of the poverty population has, however, remained about the same over the last 25 years (Gimenez, 1990).

The feminization of poverty, which involves poor women maintaining a household, has been attributed to several changes in American society. Increases in divorce, separation, and out-of-wedlock birth have caused a growing number of women to become heads of poor households. The increase in divorced fathers not paying child support, along with the reduction in government support for welfare, has caused many more female-headed households to fall below the poverty line. Living longer than men has further contributed to a growing number of elderly women living in poverty alone. Finally, since men have suffered an increase in unemployment and a decline in wages as a result of the worsening economy over the last decade, increasing numbers of them have been unable to form a family or keep it from

falling apart, which in turn has increased the feminization of poverty. But most important, according to feminists, women as a group are more vulnerable than men to poverty because of the sexist and patriarchal nature of the society. Unlike men, who often can escape poverty by getting a job, women tend to remain poor even when being employed. This is because in the gender-segregated labor market, women are much more likely to work in low-paid, low-status jobs. By socializing women to become wives and mothers, the patriarchal society further discourages them from developing educational and occupational skills. This is likely to cause poverty among divorced women or widows, even those from relatively affluent families (Gimenez, 1990; Pearce, 1993). What about male poverty, or poverty in general? What causes it?

Causes of Poverty An old explanation blames the poor for their poverty. It is based on the assumption that there are plenty of opportunities for making it in America and that the poor have failed to grab any opportunity by not working hard. Attempts have long been made to find the source of this self-defeating behavior. Political scientist Edward Banfield (1974) claimed to have found it in the present-oriented outlook among the poor. They were said to live for the moment, unconcerned for the future. Earlier, anthropologist Oscar Lewis (1961) had found about the same life-style among the poor families that he studied. He found that the poor were fatalists, resigning themselves to being poor and seeing no way out of their poverty. They were said to have developed a "culture of poverty," characterized by a series of debilitating values and attitudes, such as a sense of hopelessness and passivity, low aspirations, feelings of powerlessness and inferiority, and present-time orientation. According to Lewis, this culture of poverty is passed on from one generation to another. All this, then, was assumed to discourage the poor from working hard, which, in turn, continues to keep them poor.

To sociologists, however, there are holes in the blame-the-poor explanation. For one thing, the poor are not necessarily averse to working hard. They are likely to work hard if given the opportunity. But the problem is that, even if they have the opportunity, they are likely to remain poor because of low wages. In fact, the working poor account for nearly 60 percent of those who fall below the poverty line. Another flaw in the blame-the-poor explanation is that it confuses cause and effect. The self-defeating values that Banfield and Lewis found among the poor are the effect, not the cause, of poverty. More credible explanations can be found in the sociological perspective, which regards society as largely responsible for producing poverty. One such explanation comes from the functionalist perspective. It suggests that society creates and maintains poverty because it can benefit from poverty. Poverty is assumed to perform some positive functions for society, such as the following:

1. Poverty makes it possible for society's "dirty work" to be done. Most Americans would stay away from many boring, underpaid, or unpleasant jobs such as washing dishes, scrubbing floors, and hauling garbage. Poor people are compelled to take such jobs because they cannot find better ones.
2. By working as maids and servants, poor people make it easier for the affluent to pursue their business and professional careers.
3. Poverty creates jobs for social workers and other professionals who serve the poor. It also produces jobs for police and other law enforcers who protect others from the poor (Gans, 1971).

These and many other functions of poverty are important to society. Without the poor performing them, American society would not be as prosperous as it is. But this functionalist theory still cannot explain how society has created poverty in the first place. Such an explanation can be found in the conflict perspective. It suggests that the inegalitarian nature of society makes inevitable the unequal distribution of economic opportunities, with the poor getting the short end of the stick. Receiving little or no opportunities, the poor are bound to be poor and remain so.

In recent years, however, the poor have gotten *poorer,* particularly in big cities. Again, there are two contrasting explanations. One is structural, attributing the increase in poverty to forces beyond the control of the individual. Over the last thirty years much of the middle class has left the cities for the suburbs. Many well-paying, low-skilled jobs in manufacturing industries have also left the cities. As a result, the poor who are left behind jobless have become poorer. According to another explanation, a new version of the old "blame the victim" theory, poor people have gotten poorer because they do not want to work. There are still many jobs that match their skills, such as working in sweatshops, in fast-food restaurants, and as maids or servants, but poor Americans today consider these jobs demeaning and prefer to be on welfare instead. Such behavior is said to scorn the traditional view that almost any honest job, however unpleasant, confers independence and therefore dignity, better than taking something for nothing (Mead, 1992). Why, then, do the poor choose the indignity of relying on welfare? This question has led to a popular critique of the welfare system.

Reforming Welfare   Today many Americans, both liberals and conservatives, believe that welfare encourages dependency, which they assume explains why the poor refuse to work. This is why welfare has become a dirty word to much of the general public. In a recent survey, when Americans were asked about the level of spending for "assistance to the poor," two-thirds said it is "too little." But when the

FIGURE 7.2 *Public Attitudes Toward Welfare*

Source: "The Answer Depends on the Question," *New York Times,* July 5, 1992. Copyright © 1992 by the New York Times Company. Reprinted by permission.

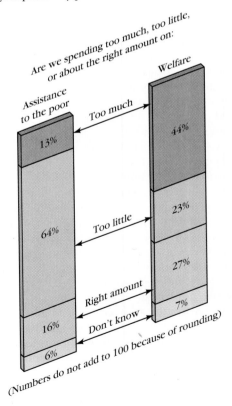

same question was re-asked, with the word "welfare" substituted for "assistance to the poor," only 23 percent said that our nation spends "too little" on welfare—and nearly twice as many said "too much" (see Figure 7.2). In another poll, 74 percent indicated their belief that most welfare recipients are so dependent on the system that they will never leave it. Majorities of the respondents also said that welfare encourages people to have many babies and that it discourages pregnant women from marrying (Toner, 1992). In each of these cases, however, the public perception may be true for some welfare recipients but not true for the majority—who are single mothers on the main welfare program, Aid to Families with Dependent Children (AFDC). The fact is that most do not stay on welfare permanently, that most leave welfare within less than ten years, often through marriage, and that most have only one or two children, just like most American families (see Figure 7.3).

Nevertheless, many critics believe that welfare recipients should not stay on the program for even one or two years. A number of proposals have been made in an effort to end welfare dependency. The latest welfare law, passed by Congress in 1988, requires every state to provide education and job-training programs so that able-bodied AFDC parents can join the work force. But this law is not expected to reduce welfare rolls significantly because, by exempting parents with preschool children, it requires only 10 percent of the AFDC parents to attend training classes or work part-time. President Clinton said during the 1992 presidential campaign that he would limit welfare payments to two years for all able-bodied recipients, after which he would require them to perform some form of community service. Similarly, welfare researcher David Ellwood would place a time limit on welfare for one to three years, enough time for divorced mothers to get back on their feet. He would also provide health care, day care, and enough tax credits to pull low-paid workers out of poverty. But journalist Mickey Kaus (1992) proposes to immediately cut off funds for all able-bodied recipients, including single mothers with young children. He would have the government provide them with jobs on useful public projects (such as sweeping streets, building roads and parks, or doing clerical work) while offering drug counseling, job training, and child care to those who need them. But this proposal is unlikely to be politically popular because it would cost up to $59 billion a year more than the $23 billion already spent annually by federal and state gov-

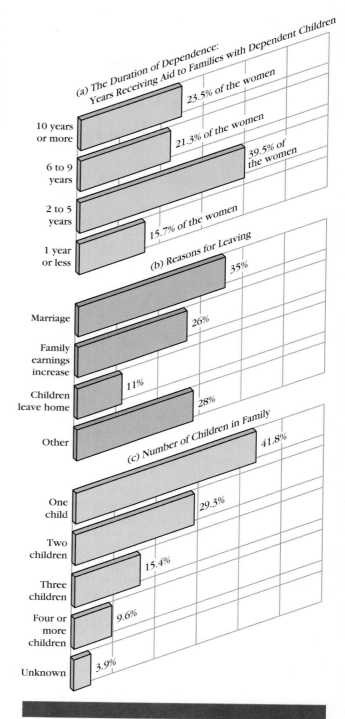

FIGURE 7.3 *Profile of Welfare Recipients*

Source: (a) David T. Ellwood, Harvard University; (b) House Ways and Means Committee; (c) Department of Health and Human Services, 1993.

ernments on welfare. At any rate, a growing number of states have attached some work or training requirement to welfare in a genuine attempt to reduce welfare dependency. But many economically hardpressed states have also used the pretext of reducing dependency to cut or stop welfare payments. This inevitably helps enlarge the ranks of the homeless.

Who Are the Homeless?   The homeless are among the extremely poor. They are by definition people who sleep in streets, parks, shelters, and places not intended as dwellings, such as bus stations, lobbies, or abandoned buildings. They are literally homeless, without a home to sleep in. Because there is no national survey on the homeless, it is impossible to know who exactly they are. But a study of the Chicago homeless population has shown that most of the homeless are black men in their middle thirties with an educational attainment largely similar to that of the general population. Most have never married; if they have, their marriage has failed. Most held their last steady job more than four years ago. Although a third of the homeless worked for some time in the previous month, the jobs were only temporary, involving low skills and paying low wages (Rossi, 1989). Studies in other cities have further indicated that many of the homeless suffer from one or more pathologies. Most studies have found about a third of the homeless to be mentally ill. But a few studies found rates of mental problems as high as 59 percent (Filer, 1990; Gory et al., 1990). It is, however, quite possible that the real proportion of the homeless who are mentally ill is lower than those studies indicate. The researchers may have missed many homeless who are normal and hence able to conceal themselves from the public (Snow et al., 1990).

Homelessness is not new. There have always been homeless people in the United States. But the homeless today are quite different from their counterparts of the 1950s and 1960s. More than thirty years ago, most of the homeless were old men, only a handful were women, and virtually no families were homeless. Today, the homeless are younger, and they include a much higher proportion of women and families with young children. Today's homeless are also more visible to the general public because they are much more likely to sleep on the streets or in other public places in great numbers. They also suffer greater deprivation. Although the past homeless men on Skid Row were undoubtedly poor, their average income from casual and intermittent work was three to four times more than what the current homeless receive. In addition, many of the elderly homeless men in the past had small but stable pensions, which today's homeless do not have (Rossi, 1989).

No one is sure about the number of homeless in the United States. There are only estimates, but they vary widely. On the one hand, the government estimates the number of homeless to be between 250,000 and 350,000, but advocates for the homeless, such as New York's Community Service Society, insist that there are well over 3 million homeless people (Filer, 1990). Sociologist Peter Rossi (1989) contends that most of the higher estimates are far off the mark because they are based on seriously flawed sampling methods. But sociologist David Snow and his colleagues (1990) argue that Rossi's own lower estimate of 300,000 to 500,000 is questionable. It fails to include large numbers of the "hidden homeless"— those who disavow their homeless status due to fear of being interviewed, the street homeless who avoid detection by getting out of harm's way at night, and those who escape being met by researchers by occasionally spending the night in a cheap hotel. Moreover, Rossi fails to take into account the growing number of rural homeless, who live in caves, under bridges, and in junk cars in many rural areas throughout the United States (Kilman and Johnson, 1991).

Why Are They Homeless?   The causes of homelessness can be categorized into two types: larger social forces and personal characteristics. One social force is the shortage of inexpensive housing for poor families and poor unattached persons. This shortage began in the 1970s and accelerated in the 1980s, as the Reagan administration cut government funding for subsidized housing programs from $33 billion in 1981 to only $8 billion in 1988. Another social force is the decreasing demand for unskilled labor in the 1980s, which resulted in extremely high unemployment among young men in general and blacks in particular. A third social force is the erosion of public welfare benefits over the last two decades. Today, none of the states that have income support programs for poor unattached persons provides enough to reach $4,000 a year, and many states have no such programs at all. These three social forces do not directly cause homelessness. They merely enlarge the ranks of the extremely poor, thereby increasing the chances of these people becoming homeless.

Certain personal characteristics may explain who among the extremely poor are more likely to become homeless. These characteristics have been found to include chronic mental illness, alcoholism, serious criminal behavior, and physical health problems. Most of the extremely poor do not become homeless because they live with their relatives or friends. But those who suffer from any of the personal disabilities just mentioned are more likely to wear out their welcome as dependents of their parents or as recipients of aid and money from their friends. After all, their relatives and friends are themselves extremely poor and already living in crowded housing (Rossi, 1989). We should be careful, however, not to exaggerate the impact of personal disabilities on homelessness. To some degree, personal disabilities may be the consequences rather than the causes of homelessness (Snow et al., 1990).

The Influence of Class

One of the most consistent findings in sociology is that social class is correlated with how people live. Of course, the correlation does not always indicate a causal relationship, but people in different classes do live differently. In fact, the influence of class is so great and pervasive that it is taken into account in nearly every sociological research study. That is why we have discussed, for example, the impact of class on childhood socialization, mental illness, and sexual behavior in previous chapters. We will also examine class differences in religion, politics, sports, and other human behaviors in later chapters. Here we focus on how social class affects life chances and life-styles.

Life Chances Obviously, the rich have better houses, food, and clothes than the middle class, who, in turn, live in more comfortable conditions than the poor. The upper classes can also devote more money, and often more time, to nonessentials like giving lavish parties; some rich people even spend more money on their pets than most people earn from their jobs. Their choices are often wider, their opportunities greater, than those of the lower classes. In other words, the upper classes have better **life chances**—a greater likelihood that they will obtain desirable resources and experiences, more opportunities for living a good, long, or successful life.

We can see the impact of class on life chances in the *Titanic* tragedy, which took 1500 lives. In 1912, on the night when the ship sank into the Atlantic Ocean, social class was a major determinant of who survived and who died. Among the females on

board, 3 percent of the first-class passengers drowned, compared with 16 percent of the second-class and 45 percent of the third-class passengers. All passengers in first class had been given the opportunity to abandon ship, but those in the third class had been ordered to stay below deck, some of them at the point of a gun (Lord, 1981; Hall, 1986).

Less dramatic but just as grim is the common finding in many studies that people in the lower classes generally live shorter and less healthy lives than those above them in the social hierarchy. An infant born into a poor family is much more likely to die during its first year than an infant born into a nonpoor family. For adults, too, mortality rates—the number of deaths per 1000 people—differ among the classes. Among whites between 25 and 64 years of age, lower-class men and women have a higher mortality rate than middle-class men and women. The lower classes are more likely to die from syphilis, tuberculosis, stomach ulcers, diabetes, influenza, and many other diseases. They are also more likely than higher-class people to obtain their medical care in emergency rooms or public clinics, rather than from a private doctor. Many other studies show the same influence of social class on these and other life chances (see Table 7.2).

Life-Styles Tastes, preferences, and ways of living—called **life-styles**—may appear trivial in comparison to life chances. But sociologists long ago discovered the importance of social class by studying life-style differences among people. In the following we will see how class shapes life-style.

Upper- and middle-class people are likely to be active outside their homes—in parent-teacher associations, charitable organizations, and various community activities. They are also likely to make friends with professional colleagues or business contacts, with their spouses helping to cultivate the friendship. In fact, they tend to combine their social and business lives so much that friendships are no longer a personal matter but are used to promote careers (Kanter, 1977). In contrast, working-class people tend to restrict their social life to families and relatives. Rarely do they entertain or visit their friends from work. Although male factory workers may "stop off for a beer with the guys" after work, the guys are seldom invited home. Many working-class men and women are also quite reluctant to form close ties with neighbors. Instead, they often visit their parents, siblings, and other relatives, which has prompted Lillian Rubin (1976) to describe the extended fam-

TABLE **7.2** *The Impact of Class on Life Chances*

People at the bottom of the American class structure are more likely to die at a given age, to suffer from chronic diseases, and to be victims of violent crime. Those at the top live longer, have more stable marriages, are less likely to be obese, and are more capable of sending their children to college. They are also more likely to feel very happy.

LIFE CHANCES	LOWER CLASS	MIDDLE CLASS	UPPER CLASS
Mortality rate			
White males 45–54 years old	2.12	1.01	.074
Victims of heart disease			
Number per 1000 persons	114	40	35
Obesity in native-born women	52%	43%	9%
Marital instability			
White males, age 25–34, never divorced	23%	10%	6%
Victims of violent crime per 1000 population	52	30	27
Children who attend college	26%	37%	58%
Describe selves as "very happy"	29%	38%	56%

Source: Dennis Gilbert and Joseph A. Kahl, *The American Class Structure.* 4th ed., Belmont, CA: Wadsworth, 1993.

ily as "the heart of working-class social life." Some observers believe that this kin-oriented sociability arises because working-class people feel less secure in social interactions, fearing or distrusting the outside world (Cohen and Hodges, 1963; Gilbert and Kahl, 1987).

People in different classes also tend to prefer different magazines, newspapers, books, television programs, and movies. Whereas the lower class is more likely to read the *National Enquirer* and watch soap operas or professional wrestling, the upper middle class is more likely to read *Time* and *Newsweek* and watch public television programs. The upper class does not go for TV viewing at all. When the richest 400 Americans were asked what they thought about TV's evening entertainment offerings, their typical responses were condescending: "very mediocre," "99 percent hogwash," "juvenile, boring and insulting" (Hacker, 1983). More generally, when compared with those of higher classes, working-class people read less; attend fewer concerts, lectures, and theaters; participate less in adult education; and spend less on recreation—they are more likely to watch television, work on their cars, take car rides, play cards, and visit taverns (Foner, 1979; Dardis et al., 1981).

There are speech differences between classes, too. The middle class seldom uses the double negative ("I can't get no satisfaction"), whereas the working class often uses it. The middle class rarely drops the letter "g" in present participles ("doin'" for "doing," "singin'" for "singing"), perhaps because they are conscious of being "correct." The working class often drops the "g," probably to show that they are not snobbish. They also tend to pronounce "fact" as "fack," "fewer" as "fure," or "only" as "oney." They like to say "lay" instead of "lie," as in "Let's lay on the beach," without necessarily suggesting a sexual performance. On the other hand, the middle class has a weakness for euphemism. To them, a toilet is a "bathroom," drunks are "people with alcohol problems," madness is "mental illness," an undertaker is a "funeral director," or a prison is a "correctional facility." They also tend to go for "fake" elegance. They would say "vocalist" instead of "singer," "as of this time" rather than "now," "subsequently" rather than "later," "make usage of" rather than "use," or "marketing" instead of "selling." The upper class distinguishes itself by its tendency to use such words as "tiresome" or "tedious" instead of "boring." Upperclass women are inclined to designate something seen in a store as "divine," "darling," or "adorable," whereas others simply say "nice" (Fussell, 1983). Although it is unfair to judge one speech superior to another, research has shown that people tend to find higher-class speakers more credible and likable (Kerbo, 1983).

QUESTIONS FOR DISCUSSION AND REVIEW

1. What methods do sociologists use to study social class, and what are the strengths and weaknesses of each?
2. What features make each American social class distinctive?
3. What are the feminization of poverty and its cause? Who are the poor and homeless, and what makes them so?
4. Why is the general public dissatisfied with the welfare program?
5. How does social class influence life chances and life-styles?

Global Stratification

We have so far discussed social stratification that exists within a society, but stratification also exists outside the society. In other words, stratification exists among various nations. In today's **world system,** which is a capitalist network of relationships among all the members of the world's community, nations can be divided into three classes (Wallerstein, 1987). The most industrialized nations, such as the United States, Western European countries, and Japan, make up the upper class called *core nations.* These nations have highly diversified economies, producing practically anything from corn to microchips. They also have a very high standard of living, stable governments, and a great deal of individual freedom. At the bottom of the world system is the lower class, called *peripheral nations.* These are the poor Third-World nations in Africa, Asia, and Latin America. Their economies are highly specialized, producing and exportating to core nations a few raw materials, such as oil, copper, or sugar. Their governments tend to be unstable or repressive.

In between those two types of nations is the middle class called *semiperipheral nations,* such as South Korea, Taiwan, and Thailand. These nations are richer than peripheral nations but less rich than core nations. Their economies are partly specialized and partly diversified. Their governments are less repressive than those of peripheral nations but more authoritarian than those of core nations. In short, fea-

tures of both core and peripheral nations can be found in semiperipheral nations. What about communist countries such as North Korea and China, which call themselves socialists? They, too, can be considered semiperipheral in the world system, although the system is basically a *capitalist* world-economy. A so-called socialist country is actually a collective capitalist society, (a capitalist system owned by the state), similar to a capitalist society, such as the United States (a system consisting of numerous privately owned corporations), or a corporation such as AT&T (owned by a group of individuals) in a capitalist society. All these are capitalist because they are in the business of selling for profit, which we should focus on rather than being misled by who the owners are.

According to standard Marxist analysis, core nations exploit peripheral nations in the world system in the about same way as the upper class exploits the lower class within a given society. More specifically, the cores buy raw materials from the peripherals at a low price and then use these raw materials to manufacture goods that are sold to the peripherals at a high price. The profits, however, are sent back home to the cores rather than invested in the peripherals. Consequently, the peripherals remain poor and economically underdeveloped, stuck on the treadmill of supplying raw materials to the cores. The semiperipherals also exploit the peripherals in about the same way, though they can at the same time sell manufactured goods to the cores. As a result, the global stratification can go on indefinitely, with the cores, peripherals, and semiperipherals each remaining as they are.

According to world-system analysis, however, it is impossible for the cores to persist in selling expensive goods to the peripherals. No matter how many more hours peripheral workers put in than do core workers in order to earn enough money to buy high-priced goods, there is a severe limit on how much the cores can sell to reap huge profit from a peripheral nation full of poor people. Thus the cores tend to sell considerably more goods to the more affluent semiperipherals. World-system analysts also suggest that the class structure of the world system is dynamic rather than static, or fluid and changing rather than rigid and fixed. Countries are said to be capable of changing from one class to another.

Peripheral countries can turn into semiperipherals under several conditions. First, they must already have a number of factories that manufacture goods rather than having only farms and mines that produce food and raw materials. Examples of such countries are Latin American states. When the price of their primary exports (raw materials) declines so as to cause high unemployment and other economic problems, the peripherals with adequate industrial bases already established are able to expand these bases to produce more goods and sell them to core and semiperipheral countries. Second, to turn into semiperipherals, peripherals must entice foreign investment with their abundance of cheap labor when the economies of core countries are booming. The foreign investment will broaden the peripheral's industrial base with the presence of many more manufacturing plants, as can be seen in the Ivory Coast of Africa. The third condition for peripherals to change into semiperipherals is a nationwide pursuit of economic development through self-reliance, as has been demonstrated by the African nation of Tanzania.

Semiperipheral countries can transform into cores if they meet at least two requirements. First, they must have developed and advanced technology that can turn out products at a lower cost than can their competitors. Second, they must have a large market to sell their products to. Japan, South Korea, Taiwan, and other newly emerging developed countries have achieved or are on the way to achieving the status of a core country.

Finally, core countries may lose their upper-class status in the world system. In recent decades the United States seems to have fallen a notch or two from its preemiment core status in the world system. One major source of the problem has been *deindustrialization,* the loss of jobs by numerous factory workers that results from relocating a massive number of manufacturing plants to poor, labor-cheap peripheral countries. Deindustrialization peaked in the midst of a deep economic recession in the early 1980s. After it began to slow down significantly by the mid-1980s, *reindustrialization,* the proliferation of unstable, low-skilled, low-paying jobs swept across the United States. While most of the victims of deindustrialization have been native-born white males, the beneficiaries of reindustrialization have been mostly poor women and illegal immigrants (So, 1990). If those problems had continued to wreak havoc, our country would have been in danger of losing the core status.

QUESTIONS FOR DISCUSSION AND REVIEW

1. How do core, peripheral, and semipheral nations differ from each other?
2. How can a nation change its class position in the world system?

Social Mobility

If nations can change their class positions in the global stratification system, can people within a society move from one position to another in that society's stratification system? The answer is yes. In all societies there is some **social mobility**—movement from one social standing to another. The amount of mobility, however, varies from one society to another.

In a relatively open society such as the United States, whose social stratification is called a **class system,** mobility is easier and more frequent. The positions in this stratification system are supposed to depend more on achieved characteristics, such as education or skill, than on ascribed status, such as race

In a caste system, a closed society, social mobility is difficult. The "untouchable" in this photo, one of the outcasts in the traditional caste system that developed in India, would likely never become a member of the sports club.

or gender. (For more discussion on achieved and ascribed status, see Chapter 4: Social Structure.)

On the other hand, in a closed society, whose stratification is called a **caste system,** mobility is more difficult. Positions in this hierarchy are determined by ascription more than achievement. People must marry within their caste, children are born into their parents' caste, and movement from one caste system to another almost never occurs. In India's traditional caste system, for example, the outcasts, or "untouchables"—people born into the lowest caste—could almost never become members of a higher caste. They were rigidly segregated from the rest of society. Members of other castes feared that they would suffer ritual pollution if they ever touched an outcast, passed through the shadow of an outcast, or were merely seen by an outcast. Although the caste system still dominates the lives of millions in India, it is breaking down. More important, it does not have the sanction of the government. South Africa's caste system, however, has until recently been backed by the government. Whereas India's caste system is associated with religion, South Africa's was based on color. Black, white, and "colored" groups were rigidly segregated by law as well as custom. Interracial marriage was prohibited. Schools, housing, hospitals, and other facilities were segregated.

In the following sections, we focus on social mobility in the United States, examining its patterns and its sources.

PATTERNS

Social mobility can take several forms. **Vertical mobility** involves moving up or down the status ladder. The upward movement is called *upward mobility* and downward movement, *downward mobility*. The promotion of a teacher to principal is an example of upward mobility, and demotion from principal to teacher is downward mobility. In contrast to vertical mobility, **horizontal mobility** is movement from one job to another within the same status category. If a teacher leaves one school for the same position at another, he or she is experiencing horizontal mobility.

Mobility may also be intragenerational or intergenerational. When an individual moves from a low position to a higher one, it is called **intragenerational mobility** (or *career mobility*)—a change in an individual's social standing. A foreman who becomes the vice-president of a company illustrates in-tragenerational mobility. When a person from a lower-class family gets a higher-status job, as in the case of a foreman's daughter becoming company vice-president, it is called **intergenerational mobility**—a change in social standing from one generation to the next.

Of those various forms of mobility, upward intergenerational mobility has attracted the most attention from sociologists. Their research has primarily focused on the question of how much such mobility exists in the United States. This is understandable because when the son of a poor farmer becomes president, politicians and journalists are likely to proclaim, "Only in America." It is an exaggeration, but it reflects the high place that social mobility holds in American values. Rags-to-riches tales make Americans feel good about their country, and they are interesting stories. By publicizing them, the media reinforce the vision of America as a land of opportunity, where through sheer hard work the son of a janitor can become a millionaire. This view of America is further reinforced by the experience of Americans who have achieved moderate, but real, upward mobility.

But is this picture accurate? Is upward mobility common? Until the early 1980s, the answer was yes and no: yes because numerous Americans climbed a little way up the social ladder; no because very few Americans rose from rags to riches. In recent years, however, the rich have gotten richer and the poor poorer. As Kevin Phillips (1990) points out, the share of national income in the hands of the wealthiest 1 percent jumped from 8.1 percent in 1981 to 14.7 percent in 1986. Between 1981 and 1989, the net worth of the 400 richest Americans nearly tripled. At the same time, the average blue-collar wage and after-tax income declined. Consequently, the gap between the rich and the rest of the population has widened enormously. In 1980, corporate chief executive officers (CEOs) made roughly 40 times the income of average factory workers. But by 1989, the CEOs made 93 times as much. The middle classes have been hurting, too. While corporate presidents and chairpersons have been riding high, as many as 1.5 million mid-level management jobs have been lost. Middle managers are said to have become insecure and to feel incredibly hurt—"they feel like slaves on an auction block." In recent years, most Americans have not experienced upward mobility. This is largely because the Reagan administration changed the tax laws to favor the rich (see Table 7.3) and reduced welfare spending, among other things. All this has made our nation's income distribution much more unequal

TABLE 7.3 *The Rich Get Richer*

The 1980s gave a windfall to the wealthy but laid a heavy burden on the poor and middle class.

	PERCENT CHANGE FROM 1977 TO 1990	
	REAL INCOME	FEDERAL TAX RATE
Poorest 20%	−9.0%	+2.6%
Middle 20%	+6.1%	+3.6%
Richest 20%	+34.4%	−4.6%
Richest 5%	+52.7%	−12.5%
Richest 1%	+91.2%	−23.2%

Source: Data from Congressional Budget Office, published in *U.S. News & World Report,* August 13, 1990, p. 49. Copyright, 8/13/90, U.S. News & World Report.

when compared with other industrialized countries, such as England, Sweden, and Germany (Phillips, 1990; DiPrete and Grusky, 1990; Nasar, 1992).

SOURCES

Why, in the pursuit of the American Dream, are some people upwardly mobile while others stay or fall behind? There are two major factors determining the chances for upward mobility: structural changes in the society and individual characteristics.

Structural Mobility Sometimes large changes in society enable many people to move up the social ladder at the same time. The mobility that results from these social changes is called **structural mobility.**

In the United States, there have been at least four sources of structural mobility in this century. First, there was a tremendous expansion of the industrial economy. In 1900, agricultural workers made up nearly 40 percent of the labor force, but massive industrialization reduced the proportion to only 4 percent today. At the same time, many unskilled jobs were gradually taken over by machines. As a result, numerous higher-status jobs—clerical, service, business, and professional jobs—sprang up. This created the opportunity for large numbers of people from farming and blue-collar families to get into those

higher-status occupations (Blau and Duncan, 1967; Kerckhoff et al., 1985). The stimulating effect of industrialization on upward mobility can also be seen in many other countries, as there is more mobility in industrialized countries than in less developed ones (Lipset, 1982). However, the enormous industrialization in the United States would have pushed the rate of upward mobility higher than it has if not for our great inequality in income. There is some evidence from cross-national studies to suggest that social inequality is an impediment to upward mobility in industrialized countries. Those studies indicate that the more inegalitarian a society is, the less mobility it has (Tyree et al., 1979; Grusky and Hauser, 1984).

A second source of structural mobility has been the dramatic increase in the educational attainment of the population. High school enrollment exploded

One source of structural mobility in the United States has been the influx of immigrants into this country willing to take lowly jobs as laborers on farms, in factories, and in mines. This influx has pushed up many native-born Americans into higher-status occupations.

from a mere 7 percent of the appropriate age group in 1900 to over 90 percent today. College enrollment jumped from only a quarter of a million in 1900 to 12 million today. Thus, more people achieved the knowledge and skills needed to fill higher-status jobs. We should be careful, though, not to exaggerate the impact of mass education on social mobility. The American system of education has indeed enabled many—at least a third—blue-collar children to go to college and achieve upward mobility. But the same system has simultaneously preserved the rigidity of the higher occupational structure, because most of its occupants, the wellborn, have gone much further in school (Featherman and Hauser, 1978; Davis, 1982).

A third source of structural mobility has been the lower birth rates in the higher classes than in the lower classes. In the early part of this century, professional and other white-collar workers had relatively few children, but manual workers, especially farmers, had many. It is estimated that whereas there were 870 sons for every 1000 professional men, there were 1520 sons for every 1000 farmers (Gilbert and Kahl, 1987). Obviously, the sons of professionals were too few to take over their fathers' jobs. In addition, as the economy expanded, there were many more new professional positions. Because there was a shortage of higher-status people to fill all those higher-status jobs, it provided the lower classes with an opportunity to take them. Today, young people who were born in 1965–75, the years when the nation's birth rate fell significantly, can also expect to experience upward mobility in their lifetimes. As their generation is relatively small—much smaller than the earlier baby-boom generation—they need not compete fiercely with one another for good jobs.

A fourth source of structural mobility has been the large influx of immigrants into this country. Immigrants usually took lowly jobs as laborers on the farm, in factories, and in mines, which pushed up many native-born Americans into higher-status occupations. When children of immigrants grew up, they too had the opportunity as native-born Americans to become upwardly mobile. Immigration had also helped open up many higher-status jobs for those people of native birth in at least two ways: by enlarging the population, which stimulated the economy with its greater demands for goods and services, and by directly increasing the productive capacity of the economy with the new arrivals' labor. It is, therefore, no accident that the world's most mobile societies—Israel, Canada, Australia, and the United States—have had unusually large numbers of immigrants (Tyree et al., 1979; Tyree and Semyonov, 1983).

In short, as a result of a rapidly industrializing economy, increasing education, lower birth rates in the higher classes, and considerable immigration, many Americans whose parents were factory or farm workers came to fill higher-status jobs. Nowadays, however, there is less structural mobility because there are fewer people with factory or farm origins (Hout, 1988).

Individual Mobility Even when structural mobility opens up higher-status positions, some people move up and some do not. Individual characteristics as well as structural changes influence whether a person experiences mobility. The mobility produced by these characteristics is called **individual mobility.**

Among the characteristics that influence individual mobility are racial or ethnic background, gender, education, occupation, fertility, number of siblings, place of residence, physical appearance, and sheer luck. More specifically, being African-American, Mexican-American, Puerto Rican, Indian, or female decreases an American's chances for upward mobility (in the next two chapters we will look at these racial and gender inequalities in detail). College graduates are six times more likely than the uneducated to be upwardly mobile. White-collar workers are four times more likely than blue-collar workers to experience upward career mobility. Men from families with fewer than four siblings tend to achieve much higher status than those with more than four siblings. People who live in urban areas have a greater chance of upward mobility than those who live in rural areas. The chances for success are also enhanced for women if they are beautiful and for men if they are tall. Finally, sheer luck often acts as the force pushing a person up the status ladder (Goodman and Marx, 1982; Kasarda and Billy, 1985).

Some of the personal characteristics are *achieved,* such as education, talent, motivation, and hard work. Others are *ascribed,* such as family background, race, gender, and physical appearance. The foregoing discussion suggests that both achieved and ascribed qualities have a hand in determining who gets ahead in American society. But the popular belief in equal opportunity would lead us to expect career success to be attained through achievement more than ascription. Is achievement, then, really the more powerful determining force in upward mobility? According to most sociological studies, achievement may appear on the surface to be the predomi-

Being white, male, and college educated increases one's chances for upward mobility. These characteristics are among those that influence individual mobility.

nant factor, but it is at bottom subject to the influence of ascription. Peter Blau and Otis Duncan (1967), for example, found that the more education people have, the more successful they are in their careers. But they also found that the amount of education people have is related to their family background. Thus, compared with children from blue-collar families, white-collar children can be expected to get more education and then have a better chance for career mobility.

QUESTIONS FOR DISCUSSION AND REVIEW

1. How does a caste system differ from a class system?
2. How do actual vertical and generational mobility patterns differ from the view that America is a land of opportunity?
3. What structural and individual characteristics influence a society's pattern of mobility?

Is Stratification Necessary?

Social stratification is in essence social inequality, contrary to the American belief in equality. But functionalists have argued that it is necessary. Conflict theorists disagree.

FUNCTIONALIST THEORY

More than 45 years ago, Kingsley Davis and Wilbert Moore (1945) made the most influential statement of the functionalist view that stratification is necessary. Davis and Moore were trying to explain why stratification exists in all societies. The reason, they said, is that stratification serves a useful, positive function—in fact, a function necessary for the survival of a society.

What is this function? According to Davis and Moore, stratification motivates people to work hard by promising them such rewards as money, power, and prestige. The amount of rewards depends on two things: how important a person's job is to society and how much training and skill are required to perform that job. A physician, for example, must receive more rewards than a garbage collector, not only because the physician's job is more important than the garbage collector's but also because it requires more training and skill. Without this system of unequal rewards, many jobs important to society would never be performed. If future physicians knew they would be paid and respected just as much as garbage collectors, they would not bother to spend years studying long hours at medical school. In short, stratification is necessary for society because it ensures that "the most important positions are conscientiously filled by the most qualified persons."

CONFLICT THEORY

The Davis-Moore theory has been subjected to many criticisms. Some critics argue that it is difficult to see why such large inequalities are necessary to fulfill the functions Davis and Moore described. Why is it functional to pay a corporate executive two or three times more than the president of the United States? The functionalist theory would suggest that the corporate executive's job is more important. But is it really? Many people may disagree. Even the physician's job is not necessarily more important than the garbage collector's, because uncollected refuse can present a serious problem to a society. The functionalist theory also fails to take into account the inherent interest of certain jobs. The intrinsic satisfaction of being a doctor far outweighs that of being a garbage collector. Why, then, should the doctor be given more rewards? More thorough criticisms of the Davis-Moore theory have come from conflict theorists.

Melvin Tumin (1953) criticized the functionalist theory for suggesting that stratification is functional. He argued that stratification is dysfunctional for several reasons. First, because it limits the opportunities of those who are not in the privileged class, stratification restricts the possibility of discovering and exploiting the full range of talent in society. When an intelligent teenager is too poor to stay in school and never develops his or her talents fully, society loses. Second, stratification helps to maintain the status quo even when it has become dysfunctional because the privileged class is able to impose on society the idea that existing inequalities are natural, logical, and morally right. Third, because the stratification system distributes rewards unjustly, it encourages the less privileged to become hostile, suspicious, and distrustful. The result may be social unrest and chaos.

COMPARING THE THEORIES

The central views of functionalist and conflict theories of stratification are summarized in Table 7.4. There are facts to support both views. Functionalist theory captures the fact that in open societies, such as the United States, achieved characteristics are an important basis for stratification. In these societies, poor people with talents and skills, as functionalist theory correctly suggests, should have a good chance of getting highly rewarding positions. Conflict theory, however, reflects the fact that in some societies ascribed status is the primary basis for stratification. In such societies, the privileged, as conflict theory correctly suggests, can continue to maintain their power and keep the poor down. Both theories also fit some facts about the same society. Functionalist theory is useful for explaining the mobility that exists in the United States within the middle stratum. Conflict theory is more useful for explaining the rigidity that characterizes the top and bottom strata, where people tend to inherit their positions of either power or powerlessness.

Finally, both theories assume, though for different reasons, that inequality is here to stay. Functionalists believe that stratification will persist because it is necessary. Conflict theorists also believe that inequality will continue, but because the powerful will not give up their privileged positions. Nevertheless, a new theory suggests that social equality can be achieved in American society.

TOWARD SOCIAL EQUALITY

Mickey Kaus (1992) argues that it is futile to pursue equality of money, income, or wealth in a capitalist society such as the United States, unless capitalism is

---

TABLE 7.4 A Comparison of Two Theories

Evidence can be found to support both views. They largely reflect two different kinds of social stratification. One is a fluid system with many mobility opportunities, and the other is a rigid system with few such opportunities.

FUNCTIONALIST THEORY	CONFLICT THEORY
1. Stratification is universal and necessary.	1. Stratification may be universal but not necessary.
2. Stratification is an expression of commonly shared social values.	2. Stratification is an expression of the values of powerful people.
3. Tasks and rewards are fairly allocated.	3. Tasks and rewards are unfairly allocated.
4. Stratification facilitates the optimal functioning of society and the individual.	4. Stratification impedes the optimal functioning of society and the individual.
5. Stratification can change gradually, as an evolutionary process.	5. Stratification can change drastically, as a revolutionary process.

Source: Jack L. Roach, Llewellyn Gross, and Orville R. Gursslin (eds.), *Social Stratification in the United States,* Englewood Cliffs, N.J.: Prentice-Hall, 1969, p. 55.

eliminated. But so long as we want to preserve capitalism, we are inevitably saddled with income inequality, selfishness, or even greed. These nasty parts of capitalism are the price for enjoying the prosperity that capitalism brings to the country. In fact, capitalism can generate prosperity only because it depends on money inequality as a spur to work—the more you work the more money you make. The success of capitalism also depends on *vast* inequality as a spur to risk-taking—people, especially greedy ones, will gamble their money on an economic venture because they will get rich if it succeeds. Finally, capitalism thrives on income inequality because most Americans do not resent the rich for they have their own dreams of getting rich themselves. It is, therefore, impossible to get rid of income inequality in order to achieve equality.

Although income equality cannot be achieved, *social* equality can. To Kaus, social equality is a social situation where people respect one another regardless of their wealth or lack of it. They have equal pride of being a citizen and treat one another as equals. There are no feelings of superiority among the rich, and there is no servile behavior among the nonrich. But "money talks," especially in a capitalist society, where wealth exerts a great influence on the other two aspects of inequality—prestige and power. That is why wealthy Americans generally enjoy greater prestige and power than other less fortunate

citizens. Recognizing this problem, Kaus calls for government action "to *restrict the sphere of life in which money matters,* and enlarge the sphere in which money *doesn't* matter." The aim is to restrain the influence of wealth, to prevent money inequality from translating into social inequality. The primary way to do this is through social institutions, where the capitalist principle of the marketplace ("rich beat poor") is replaced by the principle of equality of citizenship. Thus Kaus would create, or reinforce, essentially egalitarian institutions, such as military draft; mandatory national service (caring for the infirm elderly, tutoring the illiterate, maintaining or patrolling public spaces); more public financing of political campaigns; a national health care system; expanded day care (so that the toddlers of ordinary workers mix with the toddlers of company executives); revived schools, parks, museums, post offices, libraries, and mass transit. In these spheres of life the rich and nonrich interact, so that they can rediscover "the esthetics of democracy"—the joy of mingling with people of all classes while feeling equal as simply citizens.

QUESTIONS FOR DISCUSSION AND REVIEW
1. How does the functionalist theory of stratification differ from the conflict approach?
2. According to Kaus, what is social equality and how can it be achieved?

CHAPTER REVIEW

1. *What are the key social inequalities?* Inequalities in economic rewards, power, and prestige. The unequal distributions of these social rewards form the basis of social stratification

2. *How equal is the distribution of wealth and income in the United States?* The distribution is very unequal. The richest 20 percent of the population earn about 44 percent of the total national income, and the poorest 20 percent earn less than 5 percent of the total. The distribution of wealth is even more unequal.

3. *How is power distributed in the United States?* Very unequally, according to Marxist and elite theorists. They argue that power is concentrated in

the hands of a very few people. In contrast, pluralist theorists contend that power is widely dispersed among competing groups.

4. *What is the most important source of prestige in the United States?* Occupation, although one's occupational status may be in conflict with one's other statuses, resulting in status inconsistency.

5. *How do sociologists determine who is in what social class?* They may use the reputational method, asking a selected group of people to rank others; the subjective method, asking people how they rank themselves; or the objective method, ranking people according to such criteria as income, educational attainment, and occupation.

6. *How is the U.S. population distributed into social classes?* About 1 to 3 percent are in the upper class, 40 to 55 percent in the middle class, 30 to 45 percent in the working class, and 15 to 20 percent in the lower class. *What causes the feminization of poverty?* The cause is sexism and patriarchy, which forces women to become low-paid workers in the labor force and unpaid laborers in the home. *What causes poverty and homelessness?* To some social scientists, personal weaknesses cause people to be poor. To sociologists, however, society's need for "dirty work" to be done and its inegalitarian nature cause poverty. As for homelessness, it originates from a combination of social forces, such as housing shortage, and personal disabilities, such as mental illness. *What is the nature of the various proposals to reform welfare?* They basically attempt to reduce welfare dependency by requiring able-bodied recipients to work or get job-training while providing them with child care, health care, and other aid.

7. *How does social class affect our lives?* People in the higher classes have better life chances than those in the classes below them. They live more comfortably, with a better chance of obtaining desirable resources and experiences, and live longer and healthier lives. Higher-class people also have a different life-style, are more likely to participate in extrafamilial activities, engage in intellectual pastimes, and use "correct" speech.

8. *What is the nature of global stratification?* It is a world system in which nations can be divided into three classes. The most industrialized and wealthy nations make up the upper class, the poor Third-World countries constitute the lower class, and nations that are in between those two are the middle class.

9. *Is upward mobility common in the United States?* Yes; most of the mobility occurs within the middle segment. And no; few go from rags to riches. In recent years, most Americans have not experienced upward mobility. *What factors influence the opportunity for social mobility?* There are structural factors, including an expanding economy, increasing education, low fertility among higher classes, and massive immigration. There are also individual characteristics, such as social and ethnic background, gender, education, occupation, and luck.

10. *According to Davis and Moore, why is social stratification necessary?* They argue that it offers great rewards for those jobs that are relatively important to society and that require considerable training and skill, thus ensuring that these tasks are performed by competent people. *How do conflict theorists view stratification?* It arises from exploitation by the powerful. It is harmful to society—limiting opportunities for those not in the privileged class, deterring useful social change, and producing social unrest. *Is it possible to achieve social equality?* Yes, according to Kaus. It involves the government encouraging citizens of all classes to mingle in public spheres of life.

KEY TERMS

Absolute poverty The lack of minimum food and shelter necessary for maintaining life (p. 145).

Caste system A relatively rigid stratification system in which one's position is ascribed and there is almost no mobility (p. 155).

Class system A stratification system in which achieved characteristics play a large role in determining one's position and in which there is considerable social mobility (p. 154).

Feminization of poverty A significant increase in the number of women bearing the burden of poverty alone, mostly as single mothers or heads of families. (p. 147).

Horizontal mobility The movement of a person from one job to another within the same status category (p. 155).

Individual mobility Social mobility related to an individual's personal achievement and characteristics (p. 157).

Intergenerational mobility A change in social standing from one generation to the next (p. 155).

Intragenerational mobility A change in an individual's social standing, also called career mobility (p. 155).

Life chances The number of opportunities for living a good, long, or successful life in a society (p. 151).

Life-styles Tastes, preferences, and ways of living (p. 151).

Objective method The method of identifying social classes by using occupation, income, and education to rank people (p. 143).

Power elite A small group of individuals who hold top positions in the federal government, military, and corporations and who have similar backgrounds, values, and interests (p. 139).

Relative poverty A state of deprivation that results

from having less than what the majority of the people have (p. 147).

Reputational method The method of identifying social classes by selecting a group of people and then asking them to rank others (p. 142).

Social class A category of people who have about the same amount of income, power, and prestige (p. 142).

Social mobility The movement from one social standing to another (p. 154).

Social stratification A system in which people are ranked into categories, with some getting more rewards than others (p. 138).

Status inconsistency The condition in which the individual is given a different ranking in various social categories, such as being high in occupation but low in income (p. 142).

Status system System in which people are stratified according to their social prestige (p. 140).

Structural mobility A change in social standing that affects many people at the same time and results from changes in the structure of society (p. 156).

Subjective method The method of identifying social classes by asking people to rank themselves (p. 143).

Vertical mobility The movement of people up or down the status ladder (p. 155).

World System A capitalist network of relationships among all the members of world community (p. 153).

SUGGESTED READINGS

Allen, Michael Patrick, 1987. *The Founding Fortunes: A New Anatomy of the Super-Rich Families.* New York: E. P. Dutton. A data-supported investigation into the various strategies used by the rich to preserve their wealth from generation to generation.

Jencks, Christopher. 1992. *Rethinking Social Policy: Race, Poverty, and the Underclass.* Cambridge, Mass.: Harvard University Press. A collection of data-based articles dealing with, among other things, the welfare program and the American underclass.

Kaus, Mickey. 1992. *The End of Equality.* New York: Basic Books. Details a proposal on how to reform welfare and achieve social equality in the United States.

Mead, Lawrence M. 1992. *The New Politics of Poverty: The Nonworking Poor in America.* Argues that the failure of many poor Americans to work stems from defeatism, low self-confidence, and fatalistic dependency rather than a shortage of jobs that match their inadequate skills and schooling.

Rossi, Peter H. 1989. *Down and Out in America: The Origins of Homelessness.* Chicago: University of Chicago Press. An empirically based analysis of the plight of the homeless.

8

RACIAL AND ETHNIC MINORITIES

MYTHS AND REALITIES

Myth: People's racial characteristics, such as skin color and facial features, do not change when they move from one country to another. Therefore, if African-Americans go to another country, they will be considered blacks there, as in the United States.

Reality: *It is true that people's physical features do not change when they move to another country. But their racial identification as blacks or whites may change. Most African-Americans in the United States, for example, would be considered whites in some Latin American countries.*

Myth: If a white person discriminates against blacks, he or she must be prejudiced.

Reality: *Not necessarily. Many whites discriminate without being prejudiced, primarily because of social pressure. Unprejudiced white men, for example, might not date black women for fear of being ostracized.*

Myth: If all of the white people stopped discriminating, discrimination would immediately vanish.

Reality: *Even if not a single white person was discriminating, discrimination would still exist for some time because it has been built into various institutions and hence called "institutionalized discrimination."*

Myth: Since prejudice and discrimination are awful, they are bound to make minorities less successful than the dominant group.

Reality: *Prejudice and discrimination are indeed awful, or even evil. But the victims do not necessarily become poor. In the United States, for example, West Indian blacks have achieved greater educational, economic, and political success than whites.*

Myth: Unlike racist South Africa, our country has virtually eliminated racial segregation in the past 20 years.

Reality: *Segregation is most evident in housing. Most African-Americans still reside in segregated neighborhoods. They are also more likely than whites with similar incomes to live in overcrowded and substandard housing.*

Myth: It is reasonable for whites to fear blacks because most black people are violent.

Reality: *The vast majority (over two-thirds) of blacks are law-abiding and hard-working middle-class people. The remaining minority (about 32 percent) fall below the poverty line, but most (such as single mothers and their young children) are far from being violent criminals. Only a small minority commit violence, but they rarely target whites—most of the victims are blacks.*

Myth: Only Anglo-Americans would accuse "undocumented workers" (illegal immigrants) from Mexico of taking jobs away from American citizens.

Reality: *Many Mexican-Americans resent the illegal aliens. According to a survey, 66 percent of them accuse the illegal immigrants of taking jobs away from them.*

Myth: Since Jewish Americans as a whole are

prosperous, they tend to be conservative or to vote Republican, like other prosperous Americans.
Reality: *On the contrary, they tend more to* *be liberal, supporting welfare, civil rights, women's rights, and the like. They are also more likely to vote Democratic.*

I n the summer of 1992 a deluge of horror stories about human cruelties shocked the world. They poured out of newly independent Bosnia and Herzegovina, the most ethnically diverse republic of what used to be Yugoslavia. The Serbs were reported to engage in an "ethnic cleansing" campaign by "driving Muslims and Croats from their homes, torturing and killing some of them, and abusing and terrorizing the rest." In a northern Bosnian town, armed Serbs, after rounding up 100 prisoners for a move from one detention camp to another, pulled out about 30 of them and shot them. At a camp, the family of one starving prisoner tried to bring him some food, but the guards took it away and then beat the prisoner in front of his relatives. In a town called Doboj, the Serbs sprayed insecticide on loaves of bread, which they fed to Muslim boys, making them violently ill. Near Tuzla in eastern Bosnia, three Muslim girls were stripped and chained to a fence "for all to use." After being raped for three days, they were doused with gasoline and set on fire. Other Muslim and Croatian girls had been used as sex slaves for months, and if they became pregnant they were set free to "have Serbian babies." While most reports focused on Serbian cruelties, some Muslims and Croats struck back with atrocities of their own in areas where they predominate (Watson, 1992).

Mistreatment of minorities does not, however, take place in Bosnia alone. In other parts of Eastern Europe, minorities—such as the Slovaks in Czechoslovakia, ethnic Albanians in Yugoslavia, ethnic Hungarians in Romania, and ethnic Turks in Bulgaria—also suffer. In Western Europe, too, Pakistanis, Turks, Algerians, and other non-European minorities are often subjected to random insults and hostile stares, which sometimes escalate into gang attacks or firebombs thrown from the streets. In Japan, the Koreans, Burakumin (sometimes called *Eta,* meaning "much filth"), and Konketsuji (American-Japanese mixed bloods) are also targets of considerable prejudice and discrimination. In the United States, African-Americans, who suffer more than other minorities, are stereotyped as criminals, as unclean, or as disrep-

utable poor. As a consequence, they often encounter discrimination, including being given a wide berth (such as by a white couple crossing the street when seeing a black man approach); being given poor service in stores, restaurants, and other public accommodations; having racial epithets hurled at them; being harassed by white police; and being attacked by white supremacists (Feagin, 1991). These are only a few of the countless cases of mistreatment suffered by minorities in various countries.

In this chapter, we will examine the criteria for identifying minorities and the nature of prejudice and discrimination against them. Then we will analyze the alternative ways in which a society may reject or accept a minority group. Finally, we will find out how various racial and ethnic groups have fared in the United States.

Identifying Minorities

Americans are accustomed to thinking of a minority as a category of people who are physically different and who make up a small percentage of the population. But the popular identification of minorities is often misleading. The Jews in China do not "look Jewish"—they look like other Chinese. Similarly, the Jews in the United States look like other white Americans. Jews cannot be differentiated from the dominant group on the basis of their physical characteristics, but they are considered a minority. In South Africa, blacks are a minority group, even though they make up a majority of the population. Neither physical traits nor numbers alone determine whether people constitute a minority group. To get a clearer idea of what a minority is, we need first to see what races and ethnic groups are.

RACE

As a biological concept, race refers to a large category of people who share certain inherited physical characteristics. These characteristics may include

A minority is characterized by its experiences of prejudice and discrimination at the hands of the dominant group. Oppressed blacks in South Africa have been considered a minority even though they greatly outnumber whites in the country.

particular skin color, head shape, hair type, nasal shape, lip form, or blood type. One common classification of human races recognizes three groups: Caucasoid, Mongoloid, and Negroid. Caucasoids have light skin, Mongoloids yellowish skin, and Negroids dark skin—and other physical differences exist among the three groups.

There are, however, at least two important problems with such a classification of races. First, some groups fit into none of these categories. Natives of India and Pakistan have Caucasoid facial features but dark skin. The Ainu of Japan have Mongoloid faces but white skin. The Vogul of Siberia have Caucasoid faces but yellowish skin. Some aboriginal groups in Australia have dark skin and other Negroid features but blond hair (Jacquard, 1983). The Polynesians of Pacific Islands have a mixture of Caucasoid, Mongoloid, and Negroid characteristics.

Another problem with the biological classification of races is that there are no "pure" races. People in these groups have been interbreeding for centuries. In the United States, for example, about 70 percent of blacks have some white ancestry and approximately 20 percent of whites have at least one black ancestor (Sowell, 1983). Biologists have also determined that all current populations originate from one common genetic pool—one single group of humans that evolved about 30,000 years ago, most likely in Africa. As humans migrated all over the planet, different populations developed different physical char-

acteristics in adapting to particular physical environments. Thus, the Eskimos' relatively thick layer of fat under the skin of their eyes, faces, and other parts of the body provides good insulation against the icy cold of Arctic regions. The Africans' dark skin offers protection from the burning sun of tropical regions. Yet there has not developed a significant genetic difference among the "races." As genetic research has indicated, about 95 percent of the DNA molecules (which make up the gene) are the same for all humans, and only the remaining 5 percent are responsible for all the differences in appearance (Vora, 1981). Even these outward differences are meaningless because the differences among members of the same "race" are greater than the average differences between two racial groups. Some American blacks, for example, have lighter skins than many whites, and some whites are darker than many blacks.

Since there are no clear-cut biological distinctions—in physical characteristics or genetic make-up—between racial groups, sociologists prefer to define race as a social rather than biological phenomenon. Defined sociologically, a **race** is a group of people who are *perceived* by a given society as biologically different from others. People are assigned to one race or another, not necessarily on the basis of logic or fact but by public opinion, which, in turn, is molded by society's dominant group. Consider an American boy whose father has 100 percent white ancestry and whose mother is the daughter of a white man and black woman. This youngster is considered "black" in our society, although he is actually more white than black because of his 75 percent white and 25 percent black ancestry. In many Latin American countries, however, this same child would be considered "white." In fact, according to Brazil's popular perception of a black as "a person of African descent who has no white ancestry at all," about three-fourths of all American blacks would *not* be considered blacks. They would be considered white because they have some white ancestry (Denton and Massey, 1989). By sharp contrast, in South Africa some people with fair skin, blond hair, and blue eyes could until recently be classified as "colored" if one of their ancestors was not white. Several years ago, Cynthia Freeman, a South African woman who has those typically Nordic features, had to go to court to prove that she was white in order to continue living in a white neighborhood. But the judge ruled that she was colored because he found her flat nose and high cheekbones not typical of whites (Thurow, 1987). The definition of race, then, varies from one society to another in about the same way as the definition of deviance (see Chapter 6: Deviance and Control). Sociologists use this societal definition to identify "races" because it is the racial status to which people are assigned by their society—rather than their real biological characteristics—that has profound significance for their social lives.

ETHNICITY

Jews have often been called a race. But they have the same racial origins as Arabs—both being Semites—and through the centuries Jews and non-Jews have interbred extensively. As a result, as we noted earlier, Jews are often physically indistinguishable from non-Jews. Besides, a person can become a Jew by choice—by conversion to Judaism. Jews do not constitute a race. Instead, they are a religious group or, more broadly, an ethnic group.

Whereas race is based on popularly perceived physical traits, ethnicity is based on cultural characteristics. An **ethnic group** is a collection of people who share a distinctive cultural heritage and a consciousness of their common bond. Members of an ethnic group may share a language, accent, religion, history, philosophy, national origin, or life-style. They always share a feeling that they are a distinct people. In the United States, members of an ethnic group typically have the same national origin. As a result, they are named after the countries from which

they or their ancestors came. Thus, they are Polish-Americans, Italian-Americans, Irish-Americans, and so on.

For the most part, ethnicity is culturally learned. People learn the life-styles, cooking, language, values, and other characteristics of their ethnic group. Yet members of an ethnic group are usually born into it. The cultural traits of the group are passed from one generation to another, and ethnicity is not always a matter of choice. A person may be classified by others as a member of some ethnic group, for example, on the basis of appearance or accent. In fact, racial and ethnic groups sometimes overlap, as in the case of African- or Asian-Americans. Like race, ethnicity can be an ascribed status.

MINORITY

A **minority** is a racial or ethnic group that is subjected to prejudice and discrimination. The essence of a minority group is its experience of prejudice and discrimination. **Prejudice** is a negative attitude toward members of a minority. It includes ideas and beliefs, feelings, and predispositions to act in a certain way. For example, whites prejudiced against blacks might fear meeting a black man on the street at night. They might resent blacks who are successful. They might plan to sell their houses if a black family moves into the neighborhood.

Whereas prejudice is an attitude, **discrimination** is an act. More specifically, it is unequal treatment of people because they are members of some group. When a landlord will not rent an apartment to a family because they are African-American or Hispanic, that is discrimination.

A minority is not necessarily a small percentage of the population. Blacks are considered a minority in South Africa, even though they make up 68 percent of the population, because they are the subordinate group. Similarly, the dominant group need not make up a large part of the population. The whites in South Africa are the dominant group, although they make up only 18 percent of the population. In the United States, Americans of English descent today constitute only 22 percent of the population. But because of their continuing social and cultural influence, they are still considered the dominant group—as they were 200 years ago when they constituted more than 90 percent of the population. In the African state of Burundi, the Tutsi make up only 15 percent of the population, but they dominate the Hutu, who comprise the remaining 85 percent. As the dominant group, the Tutsi control the nation's economy and government. In 1972 they asserted their dominance by methodically slaughtering about 150,000 Hutus when the latter tried to take over the government (Sowell, 1981; Hotz, 1984; Brooke, 1987).

QUESTIONS FOR DISCUSSION AND REVIEW

1. Why do sociologists define race as a social rather than a physical phenomenon?
2. What is ethnicity, and why do sociologists prefer to use this concept to explain the diverse behavior of minorities?
3. When does a racial or ethnic group become a minority group?

Prejudice and Discrimination

We have seen that prejudice and discrimination are not the same. But do they always go together, as many people assume? Do prejudiced people always try to discriminate? Are discriminators necessarily prejudiced? In this section, we analyze how prejudice and discrimination are related. We also study their sources and consequences.

INDIVIDUAL REACTIONS TO MINORITIES

Dr. Martin Luther King, Jr., illustrated the difference between prejudice and discrimination when he said, "The law may not make a man love me, but it can restrain him from lynching me, and I think that's pretty important" (*New York Times*, 1966). Prejudice is an attitude; discrimination is an act. Robert Merton (1976) has found that the two do not necessarily go hand in hand. In analyzing the possible combinations of prejudice and discrimination, Merton has come up with a description of four possible reactions of dominant group members to minorities (see Table 8.1).

First are the *unprejudiced nondiscriminators*. These people believe in the American creed of equality and put their belief into action—their attitude and behavior are consistent. They are also called *all-weather liberals* because they are likely to abide by their belief regardless of where they are—even if their friends and neighbors are bigots. Theoretically, they could help the cause of racial equality by spreading their belief and practice. But often this potential is not fulfilled because, according to Merton, they tend to commit three related fallacies. First, they

Prejudice is a preconceived negative attitude toward members of a group. These attitudes are seldom critically examined. As a result, they are easily passed to children from parents, as well as from teachers and peers.

are likely to commit the "fallacy of group soliloquy": seeking out each other for moral support rather than persuading others to get rid of prejudice and discrimination. This would lead to the "fallacy of unanimity": as like-minded liberals, they would reach the consensus that it is awful to be prejudiced and discriminating but that they themselves are not. As a result, they feel that there must be many people who are not either. This, in turn, would lead to the "fallacy of privatized solution": they would conclude that if they can free themselves from prejudice and discrimination, the few others who are prejudiced can also do the same. Hence, prejudice and discrimination should be treated as a private matter, and people should be left alone to deal with them by themselves. Such a personal approach is a fallacy because racism

TABLE 8.1 *Individual Responses to Minorities*

Dominant group members differ in the way they respond to minorities. Some are prejudiced and others are not. Some discriminate and other do not. But do prejudice and discrimination always go togethr? The answer is no. It is possible for people to be prejudiced without discriminating against minorities, as shown by type 3 below. It is also possible to discriminate without being prejudiced, as exemplified by type 2. Of course, attitude and behavior can go togther, as demonstrated by types 1 and 4.

	NONDISCRIMINATOR	DISCRIMINATOR
Unprejudiced	1. Unprejudiced nondiscriminator (all-weather liberal)—is not prejudiced and does not discriminate, whatever the social pressure might be.	2. Unprejudiced discriminator (fair-weather liberal)—is not prejudiced but, because of social pressure, does discriminate.
Prejudiced	3. Prejudiced nondiscriminator (fair-weather illiberal)—is prejudiced but, because of social pressure, does not discriminate.	4. Prejudiced discriminator (all-weather illiberal)—is prejudiced and does discriminate, whatever the social pressure might be.

Source: From Robert K. Merton, "Discrimination and the American Creed," in Robert M. MacIver (ed.), *Discrimination and National Welfare* (Harper & Row, 1949), p. 103.

is not only an individual problem. It is also a social problem involving numerous people and, as such, can be more effectively tackled through collective actions, such as supporting a civil rights movement or antidiscrimination legislation.

The second type of dominant-group member in Merton's analysis is the *unprejudiced discriminator.* These people's discriminatory behavior is inconsistent with their unprejudicial attitude. Although free from prejudice themselves, they practice discrimination because of social pressure. Hence, they are also called *fair-weather liberals.* Unprejudiced homeowners are fair-weather liberals if they refuse to sell their house to a minority family for fear of offending the neighbors. An unprejudiced executive may also hesitate to promote minority employees to managers lest other employees be resentful. An unprejudiced person might not date another of a different race for fear of being ostracized. Presumably, if they lived in a social climate more favorable to minorities, unprejudiced discriminators would not practice discrimination.

Merton's third category is the *prejudiced nondiscriminator,* the prejudiced person who is afraid to express his or her prejudice through discrimination. Like the fair-weather liberals, these people do not practice what they believe in. They allow social pressure to keep them from doing what they want to do. But, since they are prejudiced despite their nondiscriminatory behavior, they are called *fair-weather illiberals* rather than liberals. Under the pressure of antidiscrimination laws, for example, prejudiced people will hire or work with minorities.

Finally, there is the *prejudiced discriminator,* who is deeply prejudiced against minorities and practices discrimination. Like all-weather liberals, these *all-weather illiberals* are consistent: their actions match their beliefs. Members of the Ku Klux Klan provide an example. Strict enforcement of antidiscrimination laws, however, could force them to stop their discriminatory practices. In the late 1950s and 1960s, for example, no-nonsense enforcement of federal laws and court orders, sometimes with the help of federal marshals and troops, forced many state officials in the South to desegregate their schools.

If legislation can compel people to give up discrimination, what about their prejudice? It is true, as many lawmakers believe, that we cannot legislate against prejudice because such legislation is practically unenforceable. That is probably why we do not have any antiprejudice law. But by legislating against discrimination, we can gradually eliminate prejudice. Ample research has long established that people tend to change their attitude if it has been inconsistent for some time with their behavior (Festinger, 1957). This usually involves changing their attitude so that it becomes consistent with their behavior. Thus, people can be expected to gradually change their prejudicial attitude into an unprejudicial one after they have been legally forced to develop the habit of behaving nondiscriminatorily. Indeed, since 1954 a series of civil rights laws and court rulings have caused many whites to stop their discriminatory practices and to reevaluate their attitude toward blacks. Today fewer whites are prejudiced. Most whites are still prejudiced, though. They do not express their prejudice in the traditional stereotypical "redneck" way but in a more indirect, subtle manner. According to a 1988–89 survey, 65 percent of whites agreed that "most blacks have less in-born ability to learn" or that "most blacks just don't have the motivation or will power to pull themselves out of poverty" (Kluegel, 1990).

INSTITUTIONALIZED DISCRIMINATION

Even if every single white were no longer prejudiced and discriminating, discrimination would still exist for some time. Over the years it has been built into various American institutions, so that discrimination can occur even when no one is aware of it. When blacks and whites have long lived in separate neighborhoods, neighborhood schools will remain segregated, even though no one tries to discriminate against blacks. If employers prefer to hire people who graduated from their own universities that have long denied entrance to blacks, then blacks will not have much chance of being hired. When law and medical schools prefer to recruit children of their wealthy and influential alumni, nearly all of whom are white, then the students are not likely to be black. When fire and police departments continue to use the height requirements in hiring that were originally intended for evaluating white applicants, then many otherwise qualified Mexican- and Asian-Americans— who are generally shorter than whites—will not get the job (Kimmel, 1986).

These are all cases of **institutionalized discrimination**, the persistence of discrimination in social institutions, not necessarily known to everybody as discrimination. They are traceable to the long history of discrimination by educational, economic, and other social institutions. They are not the products of individual prejudice. African-Americans suffer the most from institutionalized discrimination. Since they have long been victimized by racial oppression, many African-Americans lack adequate education and job skills. Many colleges and companies, then, have unintentionally practiced discrimination by denying

African-Americans college admission and professional or managerial positions, because of their inadequate scholastic and occupational performance, without recognizing that these are the effects of the long history of slavery and discrimination. To stop institutionalized discrimination, the federal government began in the 1960s to institute *affirmative action* policies, which require employers and colleges to make special efforts to recruit blacks for jobs, promotions, and educational opportunities. President Lyndon Johnson explained in 1965 why blacks should be given these special opportunities: "You do not take a person who for years has been hobbled by chains, and liberate him, bring him up to the starting line, and then say, 'You are free to compete with all the others'" (Hacker, 1992).

AFFIRMATIVE ACTION AND ITS CRITICS

Affirmative action has been effective mainly in reducing institutionalized discrimination. It has enabled many African-Americans to enter higher education and gain professional and managerial positions. But along the way it has turned into "goals" or "quotas"— the requirement that a certain percentage of personnel or students be minority members. This has provoked criticisms that it amounts to "reverse discrimination" against whites. Critics demand that only the best-qualified persons be hired or admitted to college, without regard to race or ethnicity. Most whites are now opposed to the idea that the government, because of past discrimination, should give special help to minorities (Langer, 1989).

A growing number of African-American scholars are also opposed to racial preference. Sociologist William Julius Wilson (1990) sees it as contrary to the long-term goal of the civil rights movement—namely, a society without racial preference. He points out that affirmative action has largely benefited middle-class African-Americans, who now can more easily obtain college admissions, higher-paying jobs, and promotions. But it has failed to help the masses of poor African-Americans, who in fact have become poorer over the last 10 years. Wilson also observes that many whites are now opposed to affirmative action because they feel it is unfair for them to pay for the long eras of racial injustice committed by their ancestors, with which they personally had nothing to do.

Historian Shelby Steele (1990), another African-American scholar, argues that affirmative action has

Discrimination is protested on a college campus. Many colleges have unintentionally practiced institutionalized discrimination, such as denying Africa-Americans college admission because of their inadequate scholastic performance, without recognizing that this is the effect of the long history of discrimination.

unexpectedly produced harmful consequences for African-Americans. He observes that "after 20 years of racial preferences the gap between median incomes of black and white families is greater than it was in the 1970s." He also points out that, on predominantly white campuses, African-Americans, who are mostly from middle-class families, are five times more likely than whites to drop out and have the lowest grades of any group. Steele explains how affirmative action has brought African-Americans "a kind of demoralization." Getting admitted to college or getting a job through affirmative action implies that the minority person is inferior to whites. This implied inferiority brings on racial as well as personal self-doubt, which in turn undermines the ability to perform, especially in integrated situations. In addition, as it is justified by African-Americans' past victimiza-

tion, affirmative action reinforces self-doubt by suggesting that they can acquire power from their past sufferings rather than from their present achievements. Affirmative action also subtly perpetuates white racism. It implies to whites that African-Americans are incapable of competing with them for college or jobs unless they are given racial preference. This revives the old racial myth that whites are superior to blacks.

As alternatives to affirmation action, these African-American social scientists have proposed some social policies. Steele favors the use of close monitoring and severe sanctions to eradicate racial, ethnic, and gender discrimination, such as reflected in the 1991 civil rights law, which allows victims to collect up to $300,000 in punitive damages for discrimination. He also wants the government to improve the educational and economic conditions of disadvantaged people, regardless of race. Disadvantaged children, for example, should have better schools, job training, safer neighborhoods, and better financial assistance for college. Wilson also favors similar race-neutral programs: full employment, job skills training, comprehensive health care, educational reforms in public schools, child care, and crime and drug abuse prevention programs. All these programs are, in effect, based on need rather than on race but can significantly help poor minorities. Since they are meant for all groups in the United States, they will be more acceptable to most Americans than racial preference, as public opinion polls have shown. They are also more likely to get approved by Congress, which has increasingly turned thumbs-down on racial preference policies.

For several years now, the Supreme Court has also been moving away from racial preferences. It has rejected preferences unless discrimination can be identified. It has further rejected the precedent that statistical racial imbalances are by themselves evidence of discrimination. It has even granted white males the right to challenge the use of preference for achieving racial balances in the workplace. But such Supreme Court decisions have horrified many civil rights leaders who believe that those decisions have worsened the plight of African-Americans. To Steele, though, the decisions merely protect the constitutional rights of everyone, rather than take rights away from blacks. Those decisions, Steele argues further, serve to take away from African-Americans only the crutch of racial victimization, which he believes can encourage African-Americans to focus more exclusively on their own efforts to enter the American mainstream.

However, Steele apparently exaggerates the negative impact of racial preference on African-Americans. He attributes the growing black-white gap in median income and educational achievement over the last 20 years to affirmative action only. But many other social forces, some more powerful than affirmative action, have been found to hit African-Americans especially hard. Among these forces are the continuing white resistance to improvement in race relations and the post-1973 slowdown in the nation's economic growth (Jaynes and Williams, 1989).

Moreover, there is no evidence to support Steele's argument that the black beneficiaries of affirmative action suffer from self-doubt, feeling incompetent in comparison to their white competitors. Most of these blacks are middle class, well educated, and competent. Compared with poor blacks, they are more capable of withstanding the racist notion about their being inferior and therefore less likely to suffer a loss of self-esteem. Given their experience of being black in the white-dominated society, they know that they are often not given a fair chance. They are therefore likely to feel entitled to the opportunities that make up for the inequities in their lives. After all, there is no loss of self-esteem among whites who have benefited from more traditional forms of preferential treatment. At Harvard, Yale, and other so-called selective universities, there are less demanding standards for admitting children of rich alumni. Yet these privileged offspring do not slouch around the campus with their heads bowing in shame (Hacker, 1992). Instead of having the feeling of self-doubt, those middle-class blacks tend more to **resent** the white perception of their being inferior (Carter, 1991).

Ironically, however, this perception, which reinforces racism, can be attributed to affirmative action, as Steele and others have pointed out. The critics are also correct in observing that affirmative action tends to aggravate racial tensions and benefits mostly middle-class blacks (Jencks, 1992).

SOURCES AND CONSEQUENCES

For more than 200 years, the United States has confronted the "American dilemma," proclaiming equality yet practicing discrimination. Since the Supreme Court banned racial segregation in public schools in 1954, however, prejudice and discrimination in our society have by and large lost steam. Although violent racist attacks continue to occur every now and then, they are not as devastating as in many other parts of the world. In India, for example, the assassination of Prime Minister Indira Gandhi by her Sikh bodyguards in 1984 triggered anti-Sikh riots that took nearly 1300 lives and left more than 50,000 people without shelter or livelihood. Earlier in the same year, a clash between Hindus and Muslims resulted in 216 dead, 756 injured, and 13,000 homeless. Many of the victims were mutilated with crowbars, swords, and scythes and then doused with kerosene and set afire. A year earlier, a similar conflict took more than 3000 lives (Johnson, 1984). What are the sources of such intergroup hostilities?

One source is social-psychological. Through prejudice and discrimination, members of the dominant group make themselves feel superior to minorities and so build up their self-image. Hostility against

Prejudice and discrimination can have extremely negative consequences for the victims, as in the former Yogoslavia, where Serbians have waged war against Bosnian Muslims. Shown here are Muslims being evacuated in a United Nations truck from the city of Srebrenica.

minorities is likely to mount when many dominant-group members are beset with unemployment and other problems, which threatens to deflate their self-image. They are, in effect, likely to treat minorities as **scapegoats,** blaming them for causing the problems. Thus, during the economic crisis of recent years, illegal aliens in the United States and non-European minorities in Western Europe have been blamed for taking away jobs from dominant-group members. In the last century, economic problems in the Deep South of the United States, such as depression, inflation, and decline in cotton price, were associated with increased mob violence against African-Americans. During the Middle Ages, when thousands of Europeans died in the plague, "rioters stormed Jewish ghettos and burned them down, believing that Jews were somehow responsible for the epidemic. Six centuries later, when Hitler and the Nazis set up extermination camps, Jews were still blamed for the troubles in Europe" (Coleman and Cressey, 1990; Beck and Tolnay, 1990).

A second source of prejudice and discrimination is socialization. If our parents, teachers, and peers are prejudiced, we are likely to follow their lead. They need not teach prejudice deliberately. In fact, they are more likely to do it unintentionally, by telling ethnic jokes (about, for example, Jewish mothers and Chinese laundrymen) and talking about minorities in terms of racist stereotypes ("lazy blacks"

and "happy-go-lucky Mexicans"). The jokes are especially effective in reinforcing prejudice because, in evoking the listeners' laughter, they make the stereotypes appear completely harmless. Many whites help perpetuate prejudice by bragging "Some of my best friends are blacks," which, in effect, patronizes the minority. Even parents opposed to racism may unknowingly plant seeds of racist thought when they select for their children such popular books as *Mary Poppins* and *The Story of Little Black Sambo,* which contain disparaging images of African-Americans (Madsen, 1982).

A third source of prejudice and discrimination is the dominant group's drive for economic and political power. According to Marxists, racism can enhance profits for the capitalists. It can ensure a huge supply of cheap labor from among oppressed minorities. It can further force down white employees' wages and break their strikes, as low-paid black workers can be recruited to replace them. The dominant group's affluent members also rely on racism to kill business competition from economically successful minorities. In 1913, for example, after the Japanese immigrants in California became successful farmers, legislation was enacted to prohibit them from owning or leasing land so that they could not compete with white farmers. The dominant group's working class also seeks economic benefits from its racism. Thus, white labor unions used to withhold memberships from blacks in order to protect their higher-paying jobs. Today, white workers who are in greater competition with blacks for employment also tend to be more intolerant (Cummings, 1980; Giles and Evans, 1986). For the dominant group as a whole, the greater the economic threat from minorities, the more hostile it is likely to be. This may explain why many of the great mass murders have been of minorities, such as the Armenians in Turkey and the Jews in Nazi Germany, that were economically better off than their murderers.

The dominant group may also be politically motivated, relying on widespread prejudice and discrimination to maintain their power. In South Africa, for example, the white regime has long denied its black citizens the right to vote. In the past in America, many state and local governments tried various means to keep minorities out of the political process. They passed laws to forbid blacks from voting. When these laws were overturned by the federal government, they attempted to discourage minorities from political participation by charging a poll tax, by requiring a literacy test, or by printing ballots only in English in areas where many minority people did not know the language. Just as minorities' economic threat can increase the dominant group's hostility, so can their political threat. When southern whites felt threatened by the emerging black power in their counties between 1889 and 1931, they lynched more blacks. Today, in both the South and the North, when perception of threat from blacks increases as a result of their growing populations, whites may not show outright hostility, but they do withdraw their support from racial integration. Growing political interest on the part of Armenians earlier in this century also provoked confiscations by the Russians and deportation and massacres by the Turks (Creech et al., 1989; Tolnay et al., 1989; Fossett and Kiecolt, 1989).

Obviously, prejudice and discrimination can have extremely negative consequences for the victims, such as wholesale enslavement, mass internment, massacre, and other atrocities suffered by minorities. Most such horrors no longer happen in the United States today. But the more common types of prejudice and discrimination do have some costly consequences for minorities. Blacks, Hispanics, and Native Americans, for example, still have higher rates of unemployment and poverty as well as fewer years of schooling and lower life expectancy than whites.

However, severe prejudice and discrimination do not always reduce minorities to poverty. West Indian blacks—immigrants or descendants of immigrants from the Caribbean—have suffered discrimina-

tion, but as a group they have achieved greater educational, economic, and political success than whites. The early Chinese and Japanese immigrants in the United States were subjected to segregation, discrimination, and mob violence, but their descendants today are more economically successful and proportionately better represented in medicine, engineering, and other lucrative professions than whites. The Jews in Europe have occasionally had their wealth confiscated by governments, but just as often they produced that wealth again later. Discrimination against the northern Italians in Argentina has not prevented them from climbing the ladder of economic success higher than native Argentines. The ability of these groups to transcend the pauperizing effects of prejudice and discrimination has been attributed to their exceptional cultural emphasis on hard work. This often translates into working longer hours than other groups. In New York City, for example, Korean storeowners, who are more successful than their white counterparts, work longer hours each day and are more likely to keep their shops open on Sundays (Sowell, 1983; Beer, 1987; Waldinger, 1989). There may be another reason for the economic success of those minority groups: discrimination spurs them to greater effort, their reasoning being that because of discrimination they have to be twice as good as their oppressors in order to do equally well. If they let discrimination convince them that effort is never rewarded or if they let discrimination make them so angry that they cannot work with their oppressors, they would have failed economically (Jencks, 1992).

QUESTIONS FOR DISCUSSION AND REVIEW
1. How does prejudice differ from discrimination?
2. What are the four possible combinations of prejudice and discrimination?
3. Are the criticisms of affirmative-action programs justified?
4. What factors can lead to the growth of prejudice and discrimination?
5. How have some minority groups overcome the pauperizing effects of prejudice and discrimination?

Racial and Ethnic Relations

We have seen that prejudice and discrimination are an integral part of the relations between the dominant group and minorities. But the amount of prejudice and discrimination obviously varies from one society to another. Thus the racial and ethnic relations may appear in different forms, ranging from violent conflict to peaceful coexistence. In the following sections, we analyze the various ways in which a society's dominant group rejects or accepts its minorities.

FORMS OF REJECTION

When a dominant group rejects racial and ethnic groups, those groups are restricted to the status of minorities. They are discriminated against to some degree. The three major forms of rejection, in order of severity, are segregation, expulsion, and extermination.

Segregation   **Segregation** means more than spatial and social separation of the dominant and minority groups. It means that minority groups, because they are believed inferior, are compelled to live separately, and in inferior conditions. The neighborhoods, schools, and other public facilities for the dominant group are both separate from and superior to those of the minorities.

The compulsion that underlies segregation is not necessarily official, or acknowledged. In the United States, for example, segregation is officially outlawed, yet it persists. In other words, **de jure segregation**—segregation sanctioned by law—is gone, but **de facto segregation**—segregation resulting from tradition and custom—remains. This is particularly the case with regard to housing for African-Americans. Like the United States, most nations no longer practice de jure segregation. Even South Africa finally ended its official policy of ***apartheid***—racial separation in housing, jobs, and political opportunities—in 1992. But the system of apartheid that has long been maintained by that official policy has become so entrenched that it will continue in the form of de facto segregation for many years to come.

Expulsion   Societies have also used more drastic means of rejecting minorities, such as expulsion. In some cases, the dominant group has expelled a minority from certain areas. In other cases, it has pushed the minority out of the country entirely. During the nineteenth century, Czarist Russia drove out millions of Jews, and the American government forced the Cherokee to travel from their homes in Georgia and the Carolinas to reservations in Okla-

Gypsies in Eastern Europe were among those whom Nazis systematically murdered during World War II. Wholesale killing of a racial or ethnic groups is called genocide.

homa. About 4000 Cherokee died on this "Trail of Tears." During the 1970s, Uganda expelled more than 40,000 Asians—many of them Ugandan citizens—and Vietnam forced 700,000 Chinese to leave the country (Schaefer, 1988).

Extermination   Finally, the most drastic action against minorities is to kill them. Wholesale killing of a racial or ethnic group, called **genocide,** has been attempted in various countries. During the nineteenth century, Dutch settlers in South Africa exterminated the Khoikhoin, or "Hottentots." Native Americans in the United States were slaughtered by white settlers. On the island of Tasmania, near Australia, British settlers killed the entire native population, whom they hunted like wild animals. Between 1933 and 1945, the Nazis systematically murdered 6 million Jews. In the early 1970s, thousands of Ibos and Hutus were massacred in the African states of Nigeria and Burundi. Also in the early 1970s, machine guns and gifts of poisoned food and germ-infected clothing were used against Indians in Brazil—

20 tribes were exterminated (Bodard, 1972). More recently, in 1992, the Serbs in Bosnia killed and tortured numerous Muslims and Croats as part of their campaign of "ethnic cleansing."

FORMS OF ACCEPTANCE

If a society treats its racial and ethnic groups in a positive way, it will grant them rights of citizenship. Still, its acceptance of these groups is not necessarily total and unconditional. The dominant group may expect other groups to give up their distinct identities and accept the dominant subculture. Acceptance of a racial or ethnic group may take three forms: assimilation, amalgamation, and cultural pluralism.

Assimilation   Frequently, a minority group accepts the culture of the dominant group, fading into the larger society. This process, called **assimilation,** has at least two aspects. The first is **behavioral assimilation,** which means that the minority group adopts the dominant culture—its language, values, norms, and so on—giving up its own distinctive characteristics. Behavioral assimilation, however, does not guarantee **structural assimilation**—in which the minority group ceases to be a minority *and* is accepted on equal terms with the rest of society. German-Americans, for example, have achieved structural assimilation, but African-Americans have not. Taken as a whole, assimilation can be expressed as A + B + C = A, where minorities (B and C) lose their subcultural traits and become indistinguishable from the dominant group (A) (Newman, 1973).

When the dominant group is ethnocentric, believing that its subculture is superior to others', then minority groups face considerable pressure to achieve behavioral assimilation. How easily they make this transition depends on both their attitude toward their own subculture and the degree of similarity between themselves and the dominant group. Minority groups that take pride in their own subculture are likely to resist behavioral assimilation. This may explain why Jews and various Asian groups in the United States display a lot of ethnic solidarity. Groups that are very different from the dominant group may find that even behavioral assimilation does not lead to structural assimilation. Skin color is the most striking case of a dissimilarity that hinders structural assimilation. A black, middle-class American, for example, may find structural assimilation more difficult than would a Russian immigrant who

speaks halting English. Nevertheless, most members of the disadvantaged minorities look upon assimilation as a promise of their right to get ahead—economically and socially—in the United States (Hirschman, 1983).

Amalgamation   A society that believes groups should go through the process of behavioral assimilation in order to be accepted as equals obviously has little respect for the distinctive traits of these groups. In contrast, a society that seeks amalgamation as an ideal has some appreciation for the equal worth of various subcultures. **Amalgamation** produces a "melting pot," in which many subcultures are blended together to produce a new culture, one that differs from any of its components. Like assimilation, amalgamation requires groups to give up their distinct racial and ethnic identities. But unlike assimilation, amalgamation demands respect for the original subcultures. Various groups are expected to contribute their own subcultures to the development of a new culture, without pushing any one subculture at the expense of another. Usually, this blending of diverse subcultures results from intermarriage. It can be described as A + B + C = D, where A, B, and C represent different groups jointly producing a new culture (D) unlike any of its original components (Newman, 1973).

More than 80 years ago, a British-Jewish dramatist portrayed the United States as an amalgamation of subcultures. "There she lies," he wrote, "the great melting pot—listen! . . . Ah, what a stirring and seething—Celt and Latin, Slav and Teuton, Greek and Syrian, Black and Yellow—Jew and Gentile" (Zangwill, 1909). Indeed, to some extent America is a melting pot. In popular music and slang you can find elements of many subcultures. And there has been considerable intermarriage among some groups—in particular, among Americans of English, German, Irish, Italian, and other European backgrounds. For the most part, however, the amalgamation is made up of these Western European peoples and their subcultures. Brazil, where interracial marriage is common, comes much closer than the United States to being a true melting pot of peoples.

Cultural Pluralism   Switzerland provides an example of yet a third way in which ethnic groups may live together. In Switzerland, three major groups—Germans, French, and Italians—retain their own languages while living together in peace. They are neither assimilated nor amalgamated. Instead, these diverse groups retain their distinctive subcultures while coexisting peacefully. This situation is called **cultural pluralism.** It is the opposite of assimilation and requires yet greater mutual respect for other groups' traditions and customs than does amalgamation. And unlike either assimilation or amalgamation, cultural pluralism encourages each group to take pride in its distinctiveness, to be conscious of its heritage, and to retain its identity. Such pluralism can be shown as A + B + C = A + B + C, where various groups continue to keep their subcultures while living together in the same society (Newman, 1973).

To some extent, the United States has long been marked by cultural pluralism. This can be seen in the Chinatowns, Little Italies, and Polish neighborhoods of many American cities. But these ethnic enclaves owe their existence more to discrimination than to the respectful encouragement of diversity that characterizes true pluralism.

For many groups in America, cultural pluralism has become a goal. This became evident during the 1960s and 1970s, when blacks and white ethnics alike denounced assimilation and proclaimed pride in their own identities. Today the ethnic pride has fueled a social movement calling for a multicultural curriculum in American schools, which, however, has run into some opposition.

Toward Multiculturalism? **Multiculturalism** is the belief that all racial and ethnic cultures in the United States should be equally respected and cultivated. But according to its advocates, the United States has failed to practice multiculturalism, even though we are the most racially and ethnically diverse country in the world. Multiculturalists urge that American students study African, Asian, and Latin American civilizations as much as Western civilization. Only thus can they understand the true meaning of being American, as captured by Herman Melville's observation that "We are not a narrow tribe, no. . . . We are not a nation, so much as the world." But the school curriculum has long failed to reflect the multicultural nature of American society. It has instead emphasized—and continues to emphasize—Western civilization as the representative of American culture, thereby downgrading the contribution of non-Western civilizations. In fact, as some black scholars assert, Western civilization was derived from Africa, because much of the culture and technology associated with ancient Greece came from Egypt. Besides, West-

ern civilization can hardly be considered superior to other civilizations, because it has supported slavery, imperialism, war, and exclusion of women and nonwhites from its rights and privileges (Gates, 1991).

Nevertheless, opponents of multiculturalism insist that it is necessary to give Western civilization the privileged place in our curriculum. Whatever its flaws, they are common to practically all the civilizations at any time in history. They should not be allowed to detract from the remarkable, unique contribution of Western civilization to the American heritage as a democratic society. The major contribution has involved asserting "the claims of the individual against those of the state, limiting its power and creating a realm of privacy into which it cannot penetrate." This has in turn brought about freedom and prosperity for ever-increasing numbers of people in the United States (Kagan, 1991). In short, the character of American society is said to derive largely from Western civilization. The unity of the United States as a nation, then, requires that Americans of all races or ethnicities accept the Western culture as their heritage. But the multiculturalists' emphasis on cultivating and reinforcing other cultures will promote cultural separatism and heighten ethnic tensions, which will further weaken the bonds of national cohesion in the republic that is already sufficiently fragile (Schlesinger, 1991).

Actually, the two opposing arguments reflect to a significant extent, though not totally, the pluralistic nature of American society. Because of the significantly growing numbers of nonwhites in the U.S. population, our nation has become more multicultural in being more able to absorb non-Western traditions into the American culture. At the same time, most Americans, including nonwhites, continue to accept Western civilization (such as the English language, Western legal system, and Western history and literature) as the dominant feature of American culture, though with less enthusiasm than before. Therefore, despite the inevitable increase in ethnic conflict, the United States still remains the most successful, stable large multiethnic nation in the world. This may be traced to the core of American culture, namely, the unique tolerance for diversity and conflict, which apparently is the product of a long history of being a plural nation.

QUESTIONS FOR DISCUSSION AND REVIEW
1. What can happen when a dominant group decides to reject a racial or ethnic minority?

2. In what different ways can the majority group accept members of a minority group?
3. How would you argue for or against multiculturalism?

Minority Groups in America

The United States is a nation of immigrants. The earliest immigrants were the American Indians, who arrived from Asia more than 20,000 years ago. Long after the Indians had settled down as Native Americans, other immigrants began to pour in from Europe and later from Africa, Asia, and Latin America. They came as explorers, adventurers, slaves, or refugees—most of them hoping to fulfill a dream of success and happiness. The British were the earliest of these immigrants and, on the whole, the most successful in fulfilling that dream. They became the dominant group. Eventually, they founded a government dedicated to the democratic ideal of equality, but they kept African-Americans as slaves and discriminated against other racial and ethnic groups. This "American dilemma"—the discrepancy between the ideal of equality and the reality of discrimination—still exists, though to a lesser degree than in the past. Let us look at how the major minority groups have fared under the burden of the American dilemma.

NATIVE AMERICANS

Native Americans have long been called Indians—one result of Columbus's mistaken belief that he had landed in India. The explorer's successors passed down many other distorted descriptions of the Native Americans. They were described as savages, although it was whites who slaughtered hundreds of thousands of them. They were portrayed as scalp hunters, although it was the white government that offered large sums to whites for the scalps of Indians. They were stereotyped as lazy, although it was whites who forced them to give up their traditional occupations. These false conceptions of Native Americans were reinforced by the contrasting pictures whites painted of themselves. The white settlers were known as pioneers rather than invaders and marauders; their taking of the Native Americans' land was called homesteading, not robbery.

When Columbus "discovered" America, there were more than 300 Native American tribes, with a

After more than two hundred years of subjugation, Native Americans today find themselves at the bottom of the socioeconomic ladder in the United States. Many live without electricity, heat, or plumbing.

total population exceeding a million. Of those he encountered around the Caribbean, Columbus wrote: "Of anything they have, if it be asked for, they never say no, but do rather invite the person to accept it, and show as much lovingness as though they would give their hearts" (Hraba, 1979). In North America, too, the earliest white settlers were often aided by friendly Native Americans.

As the white settlers increased in numbers and moved westward, however, Native Americans resisted them. But the native population was decimated by outright killing, by destruction of their food sources, and by diseases brought by whites, such as smallpox and influenza. With their greater numbers and superior military technology, the whites prevailed. Sometimes they took land by treaty rather than by outright force—and then they often violated the treaty.

During the last half of the nineteenth century, the U.S. government tried a new policy. It made the tribes its wards and drove them onto reservations.

The land they were given was mostly useless for farming, and it made up only 2.9 percent of the United States. Even on the reservations, Native Americans were not free to live their own lives. The federal government was intent on assimilating them, replacing tribal culture with the white settlers' way of life. Native Americans were forced to become small farmers, though they had for centuries been hunting and herding. Some of the tribal rituals and languages were banned. Children were sent away to boarding schools and encouraged to leave the reservations to seek jobs in cities. In 1887 those Native Americans who lived away from the tribe and "adopted the habits of civilized life" were granted citizenship. The government also disrupted the tradition of tribal ownership by granting land to the heads of families (Franklin, 1981).

By 1890 the Native American population had been reduced to less than a quarter of a million. Changes in the government's policy toward them came slowly. In 1924 Congress conferred citizenship on all Native Americans. In 1934 the federal government reversed course and supported tribal culture by granting self-government rights to tribes, restoring communal ownership, and giving financial aid. In 1940 the Native American population, which had been reduced to 0.3 million, began to grow.

By 1990, there were nearly 2 million Native Americans. Slightly more than half lived on 278 reservations, mostly in the Southwest. The rest lived in urban areas. After more than two centuries of colonial subjugation, Native Americans today find themselves at the bottom of the ladder—the poorest minority in the United States. Their unemployment rates usually stay at a devastating 40 to 50 percent, compared with less than 10 percent among the general population. On some reservations, the unemployment rates are even higher. On Pine Ridge, in South Dakota, 87 percent of Sioux Indians do not have jobs (Valente, 1991). Many are so poor that they live without electricity, heat, or plumbing. As a result, they have serious health problems. Compared with the general population, Native Americans suffer from much higher rates of pneumonia, influenza, diabetes, tuberculosis, suicide, alcoholism, and car accidents (Huntley, 1983; Mills, 1989; Rogers, 1989).

Since the early 1960s, Native Americans have begun to assert their "red power." In 1963 they started a vigorous campaign to have their fishing rights recognized in northwest Washington; these were eventually granted by the Supreme Court in 1968. In late 1960, they publicized their grievances by occu-

pying Alcatraz, the abandoned island prison in San Francisco Bay, for 19 months. In 1972 they marched into Washington to dramatize the "trail of broken treaties" and presented the government with a series of demands for improving their lives. In 1973 they took over Wounded Knee, South Dakota, for 72 days, during which they were engaged in a shooting war with government troops. These dramatic actions were mostly symbolic, designed to foster Indian identity and unity. Since the early 1980s, however, Native Americans have been seeking more substantive goals. Thus, an increasing number of tribes have been filing lawsuits to win back lands taken from their ancestors. They have been fighting through federal courts to protect their water and mineral resources as well as hunting and fishing rights. They have also been demanding more government assistance with health, educational, and social programs.

To some extent, the U.S. government has heeded those demands. In 1988 a federal Indian policy was instituted "to promote tribal economic development, tribal self-sufficiency, and strong tribal government." Today, on some reservations Native Americans are exempted from paying taxes and further allowed to sell gasoline, cigarettes, and other items tax-free to non-Indians. About 59 percent of the reservations are also permitted to run highly profitable gambling operations that cater to non-Indians. New York's governor even treats Native Americans' lands within his state as if they were sovereign nations. In fact, the U.S. government has recently allowed seven tribes to govern themselves virtually as sovereign nations. The tribes now can set their own budgets, run their own programs, and negotiate directly with the federal government for services—functions that have long been performed by the U.S. Bureau of Indian Affairs. If this experiment in self-government succeeds at the end of 1993, the U.S. government may extend it to all the other tribes (Gartner, 1990; Verhovek, 1990; Egan, 1991).

All this has sparked a national movement to recapture traditions, to make Native Americans feel proud of their cultural heritage. Virtually every tribe places a heavy emphasis on teaching the younger generation its native language, crafts, tribal history, and religious ceremonies. There used to be a lack of unity among the 300 tribes, but today intertribal visiting and marriage are common occurrences. Moreover, in the last 15 years, more than 500 Indian men and women have become lawyers—and more have successfully established themselves in the business and professional worlds. Of course, the majority of

Native Americans still have a long way to go. Without a viable economic base to draw on, they still find themselves "powerless in the face of rising unemployment, deteriorating health care, and a falling standard of living." The last 15 years have not been long enough to overcome two centuries of government oppression. In addition, Native Americans have to continue struggling with the federal government, which has cut funds for their programs despite its attempt to encourage tribal self-determination and attract private investment to develop reservation economies (Deloria, 1981; Huntley, 1983; Cornell, 1986).

AFRICAN-AMERICANS

There are more than 31 million African-Americans, constituting about 12.5 percent of the U.S. population. Blacks are the largest minority in the nation. In fact, there are more blacks in the United States than in any single African nation except Nigeria.

Their ancestors first came from Africa to North America as indentured servants in 1619. Soon after that they were brought here as slaves. During their two-month voyage across the ocean, they were chained and packed like sardines, often lying immobile for weeks in their own sweat and excrement. It was not unusual for half the slaves to die from disease, starvation, and suicide before reaching their destination.

From 1619 to 1820, about half a million slaves were taken to U.S. shores. Most lived in the southern states and worked on cotton, tobacco, or sugar-cane plantations. "Slave codes" that restricted their movement and conduct were enshrined in laws. These varied from state to state, but generally slaves could not leave a plantation without a pass noting where they would go and when they would return. Teaching slaves to read and write was forbidden. In seventeenth-century South Carolina, a slave who struck a white person could be punished by being castrated, branded, or burned alive (Unger, 1982). Whipping later became a popular punishment. Even obedient slaves were often abused, and the women were often raped with impunity. The institution of slavery reinforced the prevailing belief that slaves were subhuman and should be treated as such. Even those few African-Americans who were free faced severe discrimination.

By the time the Civil War broke out in 1861, the number of enslaved African-Americans had reached 5 million. The end of the Civil War in 1865 brought not only the end of slavery but also other new opportunities for southern African-Americans. For the first time, they could go to public schools and state universities with whites. The greatest black advance came in politics, but little was done to improve the economic position of African-Americans.

Then, in 1877, federal troops were withdrawn from the South. White supremacy reigned, and whatever gains African-Americans had made during Reconstruction were wiped out. Many so-called **Jim Crow** laws were enacted, segregating blacks from whites in all kinds of public and private facilities—from restrooms to schools. These laws were supplemented by terror. If an African-American man was suspected of killing a white or of raping a white woman, he might be lynched, beaten to death, or burned at the stake. Sometimes African-Americans were lynched if they married whites.

Lynchings occurred in the North, too. Still, the North offered more opportunities to African-Americans than the South did. As southern farms were mechanized and as the demand for workers in northern industrial centers rose during World Wars I and II, many southern African-Americans migrated north. When the wars ended and the demand for workers decreased, however, they were often the first to be fired. Even in the North, where there were no Jim Crow laws, African-Americans faced discrimination and segregation.

The federal government itself sanctioned segregation. In 1896 the Supreme Court declared segregation legal. In 1913 President Wilson ordered the restaurants and cafeterias in federal buildings segregated. Even the armed forces were segregated until President Truman ordered them desegregated in 1948.

A turning point in American race relations came in 1954. In that year, the Supreme Court ordered that public schools be desegregated. The decision gave momentum to the long-standing movement against racial discrimination. In the late 1950s and 1960s, the civil rights movement launched marches, sit-ins, and boycotts. The price was high: many civil rights workers were beaten and jailed, and some were killed. But eventually Congress passed the landmark Civil Rights Act in 1964, prohibiting segregation and discrimination in virtually all areas of social life, such as restaurants, hotels, schools, housing, and employment (Schaefer, 1988).

In the last 30 years, the Civil Rights Act has ended many forms of segregation and paved the way

In 1992, Carol Moseley Braun, of Illinois, became the first African-American woman to be elected to the United States Senate. Although representation of African Americans and women in the Senate falls behind that of white men, Braun's election is a sign of prejudice and discrimination declining as a result of strict laws and changing attitudes.

for some improvements in the position of African-Americans. Various studies have shown a significant decline in white opposition to such issues as school integration, integrated housing, interracial marriage, and voting for an African-American president. The proportion of African-American children attending white majority schools in the South rose from less than 2 percent in 1964 to 43 percent in 1980 and 75 percent in 1990. From 1961 to 1981, the number of African-Americans going to college soared by 500 percent, though their enrollment has declined steadily since the early 1980s. The number of African-Americans elected to various public offices more than quadrupled to over 7000 today. We can also see African-Americans holding positions of prominence in television and films and at major universities and colleges. Most impressive was Jesse Jackson's presidential candidacy in 1988, which would have been unthinkable a generation ago. The dramatic increase in social recognition for blacks can also be seen in the crowning of black women as Miss America, the sending of black astronauts into space, and the congressional proclamation of a national holiday to honor Dr. Martin Luther King, Jr. (Farley, 1985; Schuman et al., 1985; Marriott, 1990).

Full equality, however, is still far from achieved. Most evident is the continuing large economic gap between blacks and whites. The latest figures on median family income are $19,758 for blacks and

$31,435 for whites—with blacks earning only about 63 percent of the amount made by whites, compared with 62 percent in 1979 (see Figure 8.1). The unemployment rate for blacks is more than twice that for whites (11.3 versus 4.1 percent). Nearly 32 percent of blacks live in poverty, compared with fewer than 9 percent of whites. Another glaring racial inequality shows up in housing. Most blacks not only reside in segregated neighborhoods but are more likely than whites with similar incomes to live in overcrowded and substandard housing. In fact, residential segregation remains as high today as it was in the 1960s. Related to all these problems are the much higher rates of infant mortality, murder victimization, and incarceration for blacks than for whites (Hacker, 1992).

Less obvious is the fact that prejudice has become more subtle and complex than before. Many whites today no longer hold the blatantly racist idea that "blacks are inferior to whites." They do not see themselves as racists in any way. But they continue to stereotype blacks as disreputable or dangerous. This can be illustrated by a story that a white man told about his white wife:

> My wife was driving down the street in a black neighborhood. The people at the corners are all gesticulating at her. She was very frightened, turned up the windows, and drove determinedly. She discov-

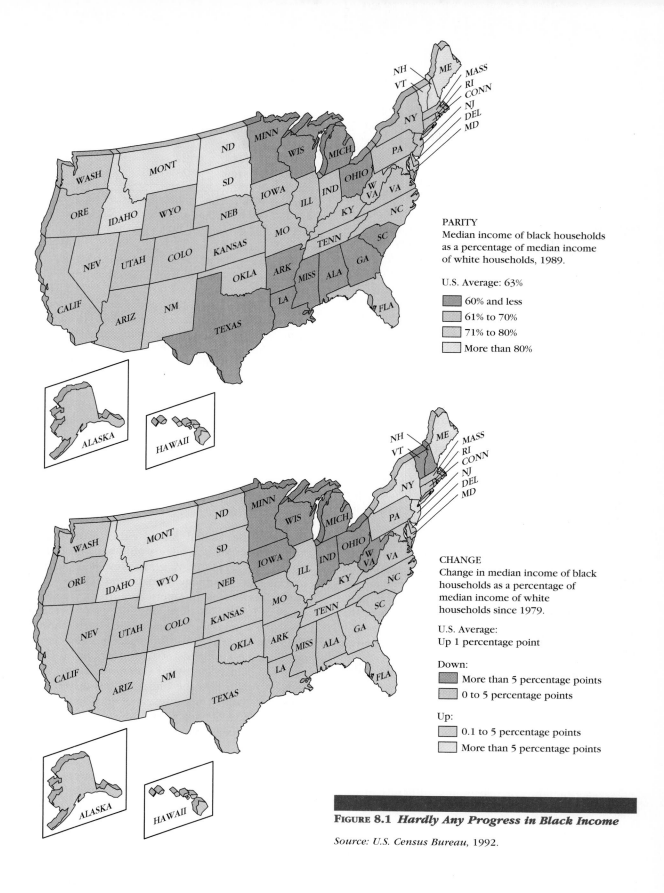

PARITY

Median income of black households as a percentage of median income of white households, 1989.

U.S. Average: 63%

- 60% and less
- 61% to 70%
- 71% to 80%
- More than 80%

CHANGE

Change in median income of black households as a percentage of median income of white households since 1979.

U.S. Average:
Up 1 percentage point

Down:
- More than 5 percentage points
- 0 to 5 percentage points

Up:
- 0.1 to 5 percentage points
- More than 5 percentage points

FIGURE 8.1 *Hardly Any Progress in Black Income*

Source: U.S. Census Bureau, 1992.

ered, after several blocks, she was going the wrong way on a one-way street and they were trying to help her. Her assumption was they were blacks and were out to get her. Mind you, she's a very enlightened person. You'd never associate her with racism, yet her first reaction was that they were dangerous (Terkel, 1992).

The stereotype that blacks are prone to criminal violence has added a new element to racism: many whites are now fearful of blacks. The reality does not seem to justify the fear. The vast majority (over two-thirds) of blacks are law-abiding and hard-working middle-class people. The remaining minority (about 32 percent) fall below the poverty line, but most (such as single mothers and their young children) are far from being violent criminals. Only a small minority commit violence, but they rarely target whites; most of the victims are blacks.

The stereotype of blacks as dangerous often causes African-Americans to suffer legal harassment in the hands of white police officers. In 1992 and 1993 most Americans came to know the police brutality suffered by Rodney King in Los Angeles. Although King was a convicted felon, his experience with the police symbolizes what many law-abiding blacks have encountered in their lives. Consider the experience of Cedric Holloway, a young black man in Florida. He wanted to invest $1000 of his savings in a certificate of deposit. Wearing baggy jeans, a shirt, and a cap, he went to a bank to investigate rates. Later he returned to the bank with more questions. When he was sitting in his car outside the bank going over the information, sheriff's deputies suddenly appeared with their guns pointed at him. They handcuffed him. Bank employees had told the police that they thought he might be planning a robbery. Only after 45 minutes of questioning did the police believe his explanation that he had tried to put his money into the bank. To avoid such incidents, some middle-class blacks have taken to wearing or carrying obvious symbols of class, such as suits, fancy pens, and briefcases. Nevertheless, police officers are still more likely to stop and question black men than white men as crime suspects (Feagin, 1991). The related stereotype about blacks being disreputable also brings African-Americans such disturbing experiences as bad service in shops or restaurants, difficulty in flagging down a taxi, and public humiliation from being falsely charged with shoplifting at shopping malls (Feagin, 1991). Not surprisingly, a recent survey

TABLE 8.2 *How African-Americans See Their Lives*

Over the last 10 years has the quality of life for blacks:	
Gotten worse	51%
Gotten better	24%
Stayed the same	23%

Source: Newsweek Poll of March 25–27, 1992, *Newsweek,* April 6, 1992, p. 21. Copyright © 1992 Newsweek Inc. All rights reserved. Reprinted by permission.

found that a large percentage of African-Americans see the quality of their lives deteriorating (see Table 8.2).

In sum, prejudice against African-Americans still exists. They still fall far behind whites in economics and housing, though they have shown significant gains in education and politics. It is true that, taking into account the long history of black oppression in America, the overall social status of African-Americans has improved dramatically, especially from 1939 to 1970, as a result of the civil rights movement and the nation's unprecedented economic growth. But since the early 1970s, though, black progress has slowed significantly (Jaynes and Williams, 1989; Hacker, 1992).

HISPANIC-AMERICANS

In 1848 the United States either won in war or bought from Mexico what would become Texas, California, Nevada, Utah, Arizona, New Mexico, and Colorado. Thus, many Mexicans found themselves living in U.S. territories as American citizens. The vast majority of today's Mexican-Americans, however, are the result of immigration from Mexico since the turn of the century. The early immigrants came largely to work in the farmlands of California and to build the railroads of the Southwest. Then numerous Mexicans began to pour into the United States, driven by Mexico's population pressures and economic problems and attracted by American industry's need for low-paid, unskilled labor.

The United States also added Puerto Rico to its territory in 1898, by defeating the Spaniards in the Spanish-American War. In 1917 Congress conferred citizenship on all Puerto Ricans, but they may not vote in presidential elections and have no representation in Congress. Over the years, especially since the early 1950s, many Puerto Ricans have migrated to the

U.S. mainland, lured by job opportunities and cheap plane service between New York City and San Juan. In the last two decades, though, more have returned to Puerto Rico than have come here.

Thus, a new minority group emerged in the United States—Hispanic-Americans, also called Latinos. The category actually includes several groups today. Besides the Mexican-Americans and Puerto Ricans, there are immigrants from Cuba, who began to flock to the Miami area since their country became communist in 1959. There are also the "other Hispanics"—immigrants from other Central and South American countries, who have come here as political refugees and job seekers. By 1990, the members of all these groups totaled about 22 million, constituting over 9 percent of the U.S. population. This made them our second largest minority. Because of their high birth rates and the continuing influx of immigrants, Hispanic-Americans could outnumber African-Americans in the next decade (Kenna, 1983; Davis, Haub, and Willette, 1983; Barringer, 1991a).

The Spanish language is the unifying factor among Hispanic-Americans. Another source of common identity is religion: at least 85 percent of them are Roman Catholic. There is an increasing friction, though, between Mexican-Americans and the newly arrived immigrants from Mexico. Many Mexican-Americans blame illegal aliens for lower salaries, loss of jobs, overcrowding of schools and health clinics, and deterioration of neighborhoods. According to one survey, for example, 66 percent of Mexican-Americans accused illegal immigrants of taking jobs from American citizens. On the other hand, the immigrants consider the Mexican-Americans "lazy" workers and also call them *pochos* (people who ignore their origins) or *Mexicanos falsos*. Whether they are immigrants or not, Hispanics share the distinction of being highly urban. At least 84 percent live in large metropolitan areas, compared with 66 percent of the general population (Kenna, 1983; Montana, 1986).

There are, however, significant differences within the Hispanic community. Mexican-Americans are by far the largest group, accounting for 61 percent of the Hispanics. They are heavily concentrated in the Southwest and West. Puerto Ricans make up 15 percent and live mostly in the Northeast, especially in New York City. As a group, they are the poorest among the Hispanics (Table 8.3), which may explain why many have gone back to Puerto Rico. Those born in the United States, however, are more successful economically than their parents from Puerto Rico. The Cubans, who constitute 7 percent of the Hispanic population, are the most affluent. They therefore show the greatest tendency toward integration with "Anglos"—white Americans. The remaining Hispanics are a diverse group, ranging from uneducated, unskilled laborers to highly trained professionals (Fitzpatrick and Parker, 1981; Nelson and Tienda, 1985; McHugh, 1989).

As a whole, Hispanics are younger than the general population. The median age is 23 for Hispanics, compared with 30 for other Americans. The youthfulness of the Hispanic population is due to relatively high fertility and heavy immigration of young adults. This is particularly the case with Mexican-Americans, who have the most children and are the youngest of all Hispanic groups. At the other extreme are Cubans, who have even fewer children and are older than non-Hispanic Americans, with a median age of 41.

Hispanics in general also lag behind both whites and blacks in educational attainment. Hispanic students are three times more likely to drop out of school than either their white or black peers. Among Hispanics aged 25 or older, only 10 percent have completed college, compared with 22 percent of other Americans (Kantrowitz, 1991). But some Hispanic groups are more educated than others. Cubans are the best educated, primarily because most of the early refugees fleeing communist Cuba were middle-class and professional people. Mexican-Americans and Puerto Ricans are less educated because they consist of many recent immigrants with much less schooling. The young, American-born Hispanics usually have more education. Lack of proficiency in English has retarded the recent Hispanic immigrants' educational progress. As many as 25 percent of Hispanics in public schools speak little or no English, which has resulted in their having higher dropout rates than non-Hispanic students (Bernstein, 1990). Nonetheless, most Hispanics believe that people who live in the United States should learn to speak English

TABLE 8.3 *How Hispanics Differ from One Another*

	POVERTY RATE (%)
Puerto Ricans	41
Mexicans	28
Central and South Americans	25
Cubans	17
U.S. as a whole	14

Source: U.S. Census Bureau, 1992.

TABLE 8.4 *Hispanic Attitude Toward Learning English*

RESPONDING TO THE STATEMENT THAT CITIZENS AND RESIDENTS OF THE UNITED STATES SHOULD LEARN ENGLISH, THE PERCENTAGE WHO:

	AGREE OR STRONGLY AGREE	DISAGREE OR STRONGLY DISAGREE
U.S. Citizens		
Mexican-Americans	93	7
Cuban-Americans	92	8
Puerto Ricans	91	9
Non-U.S. Citizens		
Mexicans	93	7
Cubans	92	8

Source: Latino National Political Survey, 1992.

(see Table 8.4). This apparently reflects a desire for assimilation into mainstream American society.

Hispanics are primarily clustered in lower-paying jobs. They earn about 70 percent of the amount made by Anglos. They also have a higher rate of unemployment than the general population. The proportion of Hispanic families falling below the poverty line is much larger than that of all white families. Hispanics are much less likely than Anglos of the same socioeconomic status to own homes. Again, Cubans fare better than Mexican-Americans and Puerto Ricans. Cubans are better represented in white-collar jobs and have lower jobless and poverty rates than the other Hispanic groups. This may explain why Cubans tend to vote Republican, whereas Mexican-Americans and Puerto Ricans are more likely to vote Democratic (Alter, 1983; Krivo, 1986).

In short, Hispanics as a group are still trailing behind the general population in social and economic well-being. However, the higher educational achievement of young Hispanics provides hope that more Hispanics—not just Cubans—will be joining the higher paid white-collar work force in the future. As shown by recent research, if Hispanics speak English fluently and have at least graduated from high school, their occupational achievement is close to that of non-Hispanics with similar English fluency and schooling (Stolzenberg, 1990). According to another study, the huge Latino population in Los Ange-

Henry Cisneros, a Hispanic, was appointed head of Housing/Urban Development under President Clinton. Hispanics make up the second largest minority group in the United States.

les is thriving, thanks to its traditionally stable families and community spirit (Table 8.5). Nationwide, Hispanics are also already a growing force in American politics. They now have more members of Congress, more state governors, and more mayors of large cities than before. Most important, the states with the largest concentration of Hispanics—California, Texas, New York, and Florida—are highly significant for both state and national elections. It is no wonder that Hispanics were eagerly courted by both parties in the last two presidential elections. Interestingly, though, while most Hispanics leaders describe themselves as primarily liberal, the majority of ordinary Hispanics consider themselves moderate to conservative (Suro, 1992).

ASIAN-AMERICANS

Since 1980, Asian-Americans have been the fastest growing minority. Their population has increased by 108 percent, far higher than the next highest increase rate of 53 percent among Hispanics. (For even sharper contrast, the U.S. population as a whole has grown only 10 percent.) Nevertheless, Asian-Americans remain a much smaller minority—3 percent of the U.S. population—than Hispanics and African-Americans. There is tremendous diversity among Asian-Americans, whose ancestry can be traced to over 20 different countries. Filipinos are the most numerous, followed by Chinese, Vietnamese, Koreans, and Japanese (Butterfield, 1991). But it is the second and fifth largest groups—Chinese and Japanese—that are the best-known in the United States because before 1980 they had for a long time been the largest Asian-American groups.

The Chinese first came during the gold rush on the West Coast in 1849, pulled by better economic conditions in America and pushed by economic problems and local rebellions in China. Soon huge numbers of Chinese were imported to work for low wages, digging mines and building railroads. After these projects were completed, jobs became scarce, and white workers feared competition from the Chinese. As a result, special taxes were imposed on the Chinese, and they were prohibited from attending school, seeking employment, owning property, and bearing witness in court. In 1882 the Chinese Exclusion Act restricted Chinese immigration to the United States, and it stopped all Chinese immigration from 1904 to 1943. Many returned to their homeland (Kitano, 1981; Henry, 1990).

Immigrants from Japan met similar hostility. They began to come to the West Coast somewhat later than the Chinese, also in search of better economic opportunities. At first they were welcomed as a source of cheap labor. But soon they began to operate small shops, and anti-Japanese activity grew. In 1906 San Francisco forbade Asian children to attend white schools. In response, the Japanese government negotiated an agreement whereby the Japanese agreed to stop emigration to the United States, and President Theodore Roosevelt agreed to end harassment of the Japanese who were already here. But when the Japanese began to buy their own farms, they met new opposition. In 1913 California prohibited foreign-born Japanese from owning or leasing lands; other Western states followed suit. In 1922 the U.S. Supreme Court ruled that foreign-born Japanese could not become American citizens.

Worse events occurred during World War II. All the Japanese, aliens and citizens, were rounded up

TABLE 8.5 *How Latinos Compare with Blacks and Whites in Los Angeles*

	LATINO	BLACK	WHITE
Population in L.A. County	38%	11%	41%
Traditional households (two parents with children)	43%	14%	16%
On welfare	6%	35%	12%
Males in labor force	81%	67%	76%
Life expectancy (in years)	79	69	75

Source: U.S. Census Bureau and UCLA Center for the Study of Latino Health, 1992.

188

SOCIOLOGY: A BRIEF INTRODUCTION

from the West Coast and confined in concentration camps set up in isolated areas. They were forced to sell their homes and properties; the average family lost $10,000. The action was condoned even by the Supreme Court as a legitimate way of ensuring that the Japanese-Americans would not help Japan defeat the United States. Racism, however, was the real source of such treatment. After all, there was no evidence of any espionage or sabotage by a Japanese-American. Besides, German-Americans were not sent to concentration camps, although Germany was at war with the United States and there *were* instances of subversion by German-Americans. In 1976, though, President Ford proclaimed that the wartime detention of Japanese-Americans had been a mistake, calling it "a sad day in American history." In 1983 a congressional commission recommended that each surviving evacuee be paid $20,000. In 1987, when the survivors sued the government for billions of dollars in compensation, the solicitor general acknowledged that the detention was "frankly racist" and "deplorable." And in 1988 the Senate voted overwhelmingly to give $20,000 and an apology to each of the surviving internees (Molotsky, 1988).

Despite this history of discrimination, Chinese- and Japanese-Americans are educationally and professionally among the most successful minorities in the United States today. They have higher percentages of high school and college graduates than whites. Al-

though Asians are only 3 percent of the U.S. population, they make up 8 percent of the student body at Harvard and 21 percent of the student body at the University of California at Berkeley. Among academics, scientists, and engineers, a higher proportion of Asians than whites have Ph.D.s. Asian professors also publish more than their white colleagues. Moreover, Asian-Americans as a whole have a higher percentage of white-collar jobs and a higher median family income than whites (Schwartz, 1987).

Nevertheless, Asian-Americans continue to suffer prejudice and discrimination. In 1986 the Commission on Civil Rights reported that "anti-Asian activity in the form of violence, vandalism, harassment, and intimidation continues to occur across the nation." In that year, Asians were attacked in 50 percent of the racial incidents in Los Angeles County and victimized in 29 percent of the racial crimes in Boston, where Asian-Americans make up less than 1 percent of the population. These attacks come mostly from the bottom of American society—working-class whites and ghetto blacks.

Anti-Asian treatment also emanates from the top of society—big corporations and elite universities (U.S. Commission on Civil Rights, 1992). In the United States as a whole, Asians make up 4.3 percent of professionals and technicians but only 1.4 percent of officials and managers. White bosses frequently cite language deficiencies as an excuse for denying pro-

Many Asian-Americans have become successful in education, business, and the professions. However, Korean storeowners in America's large cities, shown here, as well as other Asian-Americans, can attest to continuing prejudice and discrimination against Asian-Americans in the United States.

motions. Privately, they stereotype the Asians as weak and incapable of handling people, although Japanese-managed companies are well known for outperforming American companies. This reflects what is known as the *glass ceiling,* the racist belief that Asian talents can flourish in the classroom or laboratory but not in senior management. Thus, many Asian professionals bump their heads on the glass ceiling, through which they can see the top ranks in corporate America but are prevented from joining them.

The stereotype of Asians as a "model minority" also hurts. It implies that *all* Asians do well, which of course is not true because there is still much poverty among, for example, Filipinos and Chinatown residents. By suggesting that Asian-Americans are not victims of discrimination, the model-minority stereotype further shuts Asians out of affirmative-action programs. It is also used for the same purpose against Hispanics and African-Americans. They are told directly or indirectly that they do not need racial preferences because "the Asians have made it, so why can't you?" This serves to provoke resentment and even hostility against Asians, as shown by blacks against Korean stores in many cities. Finally, the model-minority stereotype puts undue pressure on young Asian-Americans to succeed in school, particularly in mathematics and science classes, which may lead to mental health problems and even teen suicide (U.S. Commission on Civil Rights, 1992).

Officials at Berkeley, Stanford, Harvard, MIT, and other elite universities have also been charged with discriminating against Asian-Americans. At those universities, admission of Asian-Americans has stabilized or gone down, even though the number of qualified Asian applicants has risen substantially. Today, the proportion of admissions among Asian applicants is one-third lower than that among whites, despite comparable or higher academic qualifications. The university officials are apparently fearful of being "swamped" by Asian-American students, often pointing out that there are already numerous Asian-Americans on their campuses. It is true that Asian-Americans are "overrepresented," composing about 8 percent of the freshman classes, although they constitute less than 3 percent of the U.S. college-age population. But 8 percent is hardly high in comparison to the proportion of Jewish-Americans, who make up 25 to 30 percent of the typical Ivy League student body. Yet they, too, constitute less than 3 percent of U.S. youth (Zinsmeister, 1987). The prejudice-driven fear of being swamped by Asian-American students recalls the past fear about Jews dominating elite universities and about blacks taking over professional sports.

Now that they are being increasingly assimilated into the white culture, however, Asian-Americans have begun to assume a more confrontational stance on the issue of racism. They have complained to the U.S. Justice Department and to the press about discrimination at the universities. They have also sued companies for job discrimination. On the other hand, some corporations have begun to correct past wrongs. Aware that the Asian nations are becoming ever more powerful in the global economy, they realize that they can get the competitive edge by making use of Asian-Americans' cultural backgrounds and language skills (Schwartz, 1987). Perhaps elite-university officials would follow suit by actively recruiting Asian-American students with excellent math and science skills, which the United States urgently needs today to retain its technological preeminence in the world. But those universities still prejudicially consider such students "too narrowly focused." They continue to use the "academic plus factor" (demonstration of interest in sports, music, and other extracurricular activities) to discriminate against Asian-Americans in admissions (U.S. Commission on Civil Rights, 1992).

JEWISH-AMERICANS

The first Jews came here from Brazil in 1654—their ancestors had been expelled from Spain and Portugal. Then other Jews arrived directly from Europe. Their numbers were very small, however, until the 1880s, when large numbers of Jewish immigrants began to arrive, first from Germany, then from Russia and other Eastern European countries. Here they were safe from the *pogroms* (massacres) they had faced in Europe, but they did confront prejudice and discrimination.

During the 1870s, many American colleges refused to admit Jews. At the turn of the century, Jews often encountered discrimination when they applied for white-collar jobs. During the 1920s and 1930s, they were accused of being part of an international conspiracy to take over U.S. business and government, and **anti-Semitism**—prejudice or discrimination against Jews—became more widespread and overt. The president of Harvard University called for quotas against Jews. Large real estate companies in New Jersey, New York, Georgia, and Florida refused to sell property to Jews. The Chamber of Commerce

Physicist Albert Einstein was one of the large number of Jewish immigrants who left Germany with the rise of fascism in that country in the 1930s. Today many Jews have become successfully integrated into American society.

of St. Petersburg, Florida, announced its intention to make St. Petersburg "a 100 percent American gentile city" (McWilliams, 1948). Many country clubs and other social and business organizations barred Jews from membership—and some still do.

The Jewish population in the United States rose as European Jews fled the Nazis' attempt to exterminate them. During and after World War II, anti-Jewish activities (such as bombings or bomb threats against Jewish property) subsided, but they increased again during the 1960s (Marden and Meyer, 1978). From 1964 to the present, however, anti-Semitism has declined sharply. Today a sizable minority (about one-third) of Americans still have some negative feelings toward Jews. They believe that Jews stick together too much, that Jewish employers hire other Jews only, and that Jews have too much power in business. But these negative images held by a minority of Americans pale in significance when compared with

a substantial majority's favorable attitudes toward Jews: 81 percent consider Jews hard-working, 79 percent see them as family-oriented, 71 percent believe Jews to be religious, 64 percent regard them as warm and friendly, and 54 percent feel that Jews have contributed much to our cultural life. The sharp decline in anti-Semitism can further be seen in a number of behavioral changes. There are fewer overt episodes of vandalism and violence against Jews; the membership of anti-Semitic hate groups is extremely small; economic and social discrimination against Jews has practically disappeared; and non-Jews have elected a growing number of identifiable and avowed Jews to high public office (Lipset, 1987).

Despite the past discrimination against them, Jewish-Americans as a group have become the most successful. They attain higher levels of education, occupation, and income than any other group. Fifty-eight percent of them have college degrees, compared with 29 percent of the total population. Fifty-three percent hold high-paying white-collar jobs, compared with 25 percent of all Americans. The median income of Jewish-Americans is 1.7 times higher than the median for the U.S. population as a whole (Waxman, 1981; Rose, 1983; Lipset, 1990a). Their success may stem from the emphasis Jewish culture gives to education, from a self-image as God's chosen people, and from parental pressure to succeed. Not all Jews are successful, though. They still have a significant amount of poverty in their midst—over 15 percent of New York City's Jewish population is poor. This poverty is largely due to the recency of their arrival in America, as can be seen in the experiences of three types of Jews. Most of the poor Jews are Orthodox, the most recent immigrants in the United States. Conservative Jews, who are more successful, have been in this country longer. Reform Jews, the wealthiest of the group, have been here the longest (Waxman, 1981; Schaefer, 1988).

Although Jews as a whole are prosperous, they are not conservative or inclined to vote Republican, as other prosperous Americans are. Instead, they tend more to be liberal—supporting welfare, civil rights, women's rights, civil liberties, and the like—and to vote Democratic. Perhaps this reflects their ability to identify with the dispossessed and oppressed, people like themselves when they came here to escape hunger and persecution in Europe. It also reflects the impact of Jewish norms underlying *tzedekah,* which requires the fortunate and the well-to-do to help individuals and communities in difficulty (Lipset, 1990a).

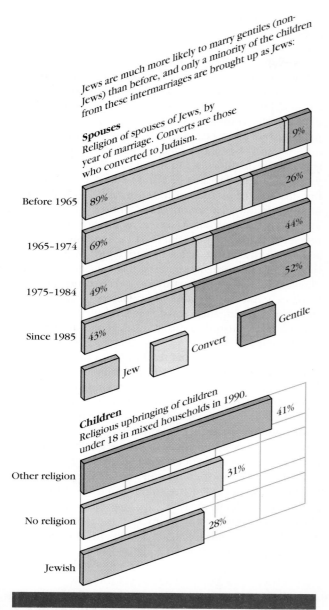

Jews are much more likely to marry gentiles (non-Jews) than before, and only a minority of the children from these intermarriages are brought up as Jews:

Spouses
Religion of spouses of Jews, by year of marriage. Converts are those who converted to Judaism.

	Jew	Convert	Gentile
Before 1965	89%		9%
1965–1974	69%	26%	
1975–1984	49%	44%	
Since 1985	43%	52%	

Children
Religious upbringing of children under 18 in mixed households in 1990.

Other religion	41%
No religion	31%
Jewish	28%

FIGURE 8.2 *Changes for American Jews*

Source: Report from the Council of Jewish Federations, 1991.

There is an irony about Jews being the most successful minority—and hence most successfully assimilated into American society. They are in danger of losing their traditional Jewish identity. There has been a substantial decline in affiliation with synagogues and in ritual observance. Today, about half of all Jews are not affiliated with a synagogue, and only 20 percent attend synagogue regularly. Marriage with

non-Jews has increased greatly, with over half of all Jewish marriages involving a non-Jew and most children from such marriages being brought up as non-Jews (see Figure 8.2). The Jewish birth rate has also declined. All this has caused consternation among some rabbis and Jewish communal workers. But Jewish sociologists point out that, despite all those changes in their lives, American Jews "have been able to maintain a stronger sense of group identity than most other ethnic groups" in the United States (Waxman, 1990). But the Jewish cohesion does not derive from traditional Jewish values. It comes from the situational forces of both occupational and residential concentration: Jews living together in urban areas and working in occupations with large numbers of Jews. By sharing similar residences, schools, occupations, organizations, and friends, Jews have been and continue to be able to maintain the highest level of cohesion (Zenner, 1985; Waxman, 1990).

WHITE ETHNICS

Jews were not the only European immigrants to face discrimination. From about 1830 to 1860, European immigration surged, and conflict grew between the immigrants—especially Catholic immigrants—and native-born Americans, the majority of whom were Protestants. The Irish immigrants, who tended to be both poor and Catholic, faced especially strong hostility. The notice "No Irish Need Apply" was commonplace in newspaper want ads.

Toward the end of the nineteenth century, there was a new wave of immigrants. These people came not from northern and western Europe, as most of the earlier immigrants had, but from southern and eastern Europe. They were Poles, Greeks, Italians. Many native-born Americans proclaimed these new immigrants to be inferior people and treated them as such. This belief was reflected in the National Origins Act of 1924. It enacted quotas that greatly restricted immigration from southern and eastern Europe—a policy that was not altered until 1965.

Today, the Italians, Poles, Greeks, and others from eastern or southern Europe are called **white ethnics.** Even in the 1950s and 1960s, they faced jokes and stereotypes about "dumb Poles" or "criminal Italians"; the Ku Klux Klan included Catholics on its list of hated enemies; and there were countless instances of discrimination against white ethnics who sought high-status jobs. But they are not popularly considered a minority group. If they choose to give up their ethnic identity, most can pass fairly easily as members of the dominant group.

It was politics that brought white ethnics to national attention as a group. During the conflicts in the early 1970s over racial policies and the Vietnam War, liberals sometimes stereotyped white ethnics as racists and unthinking supporters of the war. President Nixon and other conservatives applauded them as hard-working patriots and sought their support as the "silent majority." Some spokespersons for white ethnics began to argue that policies designed to aid blacks were discriminating against white ethnics, because they, more than British Protestants, were expected to share their jobs, share their neighborhoods, and pay their taxes (Novak, 1973). Some argued, too, that the media, academics, and many politicians were prejudiced against white ethnics, ridiculing them and their cultures. In response, some white ethnics called on their fellows to assert their power and be proud of their heritage (Mikulski, 1970; Gambino, 1974).

Prejudice against white ethnics has been called "respectable bigotry." Liberal journalists often describe them as ultraconservative and prejudiced against African-Americans. The stereotype overlaps with the image of uneducated blue-collar workers. In fact, a rising number of white ethnics are middle class, and about half have attended college, the same proportion as many Anglo-Saxon Americans (Alba, 1981, 1985). Several surveys have further shown that white ethnics largely favor "liberal" policies such as welfare programs, antipollution laws, and guaranteed wages. They are also relatively free of racial prejudice, perhaps because they can easily identify with blacks since, like blacks, many have held low-paying manual jobs and been subjected to discrimination (Greeley and McCready, 1974). More significant, white ethnics by and large can no longer speak their immigrant parents' language, do not live in ethnic neighborhoods any more, and routinely marry into the dominant group. In short, they have become such an integral part of mainstream American society that it is difficult to tell them apart (Steinberg, 1981). Traces of prejudice toward some white ethnics still exist, though. Most Americans, for example, continue to associate Italian-Americans with organized crime, although people of Italian background make up less than 1 percent of the 500,000 individuals involved in such activities. In general, the young and highly educated white ethnics are particularly sensitive to ethnic stereotypes, because they identify themselves more strongly with their ethnicity than others do (Giordano, 1987; Alba, 1990).

In conclusion, the status of all the minorities is generally better today than before. Getting closest to the American dream of success are Jews, Asians, and white ethnics, followed by blacks and Hispanics. Ironically, the original owners of this land—Native Americans—have experienced the least improvement in their lives. Of course, we still have a lot of prejudice and discrimination. But it is less than before, especially less than in South Africa, where racism has until recently been an official policy. It is also less serious than in Bosnia, India, and other countries, where a single incident of ethnic conflict often takes hundreds or thousands of lives. In fact, as black sociologist Orlando Patterson (1991) notes, "The sociological truths are that America, while still flawed in its race relations, is now the least racist white-majority society in the world; has a better record of legal protection of minorities than any other society, white or black; offers more opportunities to a greater number of black persons than any other society, including all those of Africa; and has gone through a dramatic change in its attitude toward miscegenation over the last 25 years."

However, Americans tend to focus on their own current racial problem, without comparing it with how things were in the past or with similar problems in other societies. Interestingly, although the lack of historical and cross-cultural concern may limit our understanding of race relations, it can intensify our impatience with our own racial inequality. This is good for American society because it compels us—especially the minorities among us—to keep pushing for racial equality. On the other hand, the historical and cross-societal analysis in this chapter, which shows some improvement in our race relations, is also useful. It counsels against despair, encouraging us to be hopeful that racial equality can be achieved.

QUESTIONS FOR DISCUSSION AND REVIEW

1. What different policies has the government adopted toward Native Americans, and why have these policies often been resisted?
2. Why are large numbers of African-Americans still not fully equal?
3. Who are the different groups of Hispanic-Americans, and what factors unify all of them?
4. Why have Asian-Americans gained more educational and professional success than most other minority groups?
5. How have the experiences of Jewish-Americans differed from those of other white ethnic groups?
6. Does the "American dilemma" still exist, or have American intergroup relations improved?

CHAPTER REVIEW

1. *Do racial classifications mean anything?* Biologically, they have little significance. They do not correspond to genetically distinct groups. Socially, however, racial classifications have had profound meaning, because people often think of themselves and respond to others in terms of race. *How does an ethnic group differ from a race?* People are categorized into races on the basis of their popularly perceived physical characteristics, but ethnic groups are based on shared cultural characteristics.

2. *Can a person be prejudiced without being discriminatory or be discriminatory without being prejudiced?* Yes, because prejudice and discrimination are not the same—one is an attitude and the other an act. Although the two are related, they do not always go together. *What is institutionalized discrimination, and how has the government dealt with it?* It is the practice of discrimination in social institutions that is not necessarily known to everybody as discrimination. The government has used affirmative-action policies to combat discrimination by giving minorities more opportunities. But critics argue that such racial preferences have harmed more than helped the minorities.

3. *What are the sources and consequences of prejudice and discrimination?* Prejudice and discrimination may bring psychological rewards by allowing individuals to feel superior to minorities or to use them as a scapegoat. They can also be perpetuated by socializing agents. They may bring economic and political advantages to the dominant group as well. The consequences for the victims may range from atrocities to poverty to self-hatred, but prejudice and discrimination have not always been effective in pauperizing their victims.

4. *What are the ways in which a society can reject a minority?* Through segregation, expulsion, and extermination. *What are the ways in which a society can accept a minority?* There are three patterns of acceptance: assimilation, amalgamation, and cultural pluralism. *What are the opposing positions on multiculturalism?* Advocates argue that the increasing number of nonwhites in the United States necessitates the cultivation of non-Western civilizations. Opponents insist that Western civilization

should continue as the main source of American culture, while criticizing the cultivation of other civilizations as a threat to national cohesion.

5. *Are there indications that Native Americans still experience discrimination?* Their income, employment, housing, and health all fall below the national average. But they have been struggling to protect their land, water, and mineral resources. They have also been recapturing their proud traditions.

6. *Have the civil rights laws of the 1960s made a difference?* Yes, but they did not end inequality. Their positive effects can be seen in the increased educational achievement of African-Americans and the enlarged number of African-American elected officials. Remaining inequalities are most obvious in segregated, substandard housing and in high rates of unemployment and poverty among African-Americans.

7. *What are the origins of Hispanic-Americans?* The category lumps many people together—from the descendants of Mexicans and Puerto Ricans who became Americans because the United States took their lands in wars, to recent immigrants from Cuba and other Central and South American countries. Mexican-Americans are the largest group.

8. *How have Chinese- and Japanese-Americans fared in recent years?* Despite a history of discrimination against them, they, along with Jewish-Americans, are the most successful minorities in education, profession, and income.

9. *What is the position of Jewish-Americans today?* Their educational, occupational, and economic status is very high. Their affluence, however, has not weakened their traditionally liberal stand on social and political issues.

10. *How did white ethnics come to be looked on as a minority?* As a result of political conflict, liberals stereotyped white ethnics as racists, whereas conservatives praised them as patriots. This drew national attention to them as a minority.

KEY TERMS

Amalgamation The process by which the subcultures of various groups are blended together, forming a new culture (p.177).

Anti-Semitism Prejudice or discrimination against Jews (p.189).

Assimilation The process by which a minority adopts the dominant group's culture, blending into the larger society (p.177).

Behavioral assimilation A minority's adoption of the dominant group's language, values, and behavioral patterns (p.177).

Cultural pluralism The peaceful coexistence of various racial and ethnic groups, with each retaining its own subculture (p.178).

De facto segregation Segregation sanctioned by tradition and custom (p.176).

De jure segregation Segregation sanctioned by law (p.176).

Discrimination An unfavorable action against individuals that is taken because they are members of some category (p.168).

Ethnic group People who share a distinctive cultural heritage (p.168).

Genocide Wholesale killing of a racial or ethnic group (p.176).

Institutionalized discrimination The persistence of discrimination in social institutions, not necessarily known to everybody as discrimination (p.171).

Jim Crow The system of laws made in the late nineteenth century in the South of the United States for segregating blacks from whites in all kinds of public and private facilities (p.181).

Minority A racial or ethnic group that is subjected to prejudice and discrimination (p.168).

Multiculturalism The belief that all racial and ethnic cultures in the United States should be equally respected and cultivated (p.178).

Prejudice A negative attitude toward some category of people (p.168).

Race A group of people who are perceived by a given society as biologically different from others (p.167).

Scapegoat The minority that the dominant group's frustrated members blame for their own failures (p.174).

Segregation The spatial and social separation of a minority group from the dominant group, forcing the minority to live in inferior conditions (p.176).

Structural assimilation Social condition in which minority groups cease to be minorities and are accepted on equal terms with the rest of society (p.177).

White ethnics Americans of eastern and southern European origins (p.191).

SUGGESTED READINGS

Hacker, Andrew. 1992. *Two Nations: Black and White, Separate, Hostile, Unequal.* New York: Scribner's. Shows with an analysis of statistical data the continuing presence of racial inequality.

Kotkin, Joel. 1993. *Tribes: How Race, Religion and Identity Determine Success in the New Global Economy.* New York: Random House. An interesting story of how Jews, Britons, Japanese, Chinese, and Indians have prospered in countries far away from their ancestral homes.

Lipset, Seymour Martin (ed.). 1990. *American Pluralism and the Jewish Community.* New Brunswick, N.J.: Transaction Publishers. A collection of insightful essays about American Jews.

Nabokov, Peter (ed.). 1992. *Native American Testimony: A Chronicle of Indian-White Relations from Prophecy to the Present, 1492–1992.* Includes hundreds of stories about the relations between Native and white Americans told by the Indians themselves.

Waters, Mary C. 1990. *Ethnic Options: Choosing Identities in America.* Berkeley: University of California Press. An analysis of the nature of ethnic identity from the perspective of white ethnics, such as Irish, Polish, and Italian Catholics.

9

GENDER AND
AGE

MYTHS AND REALITIES

Myth: As a group, women are more emotional than men in every way.

Reality: Women are more likely than men to express such emotions as sympathy, sadness, and distress, but they are more inhibited when it comes to anger and sexual desire.

Myth: Women receive lower pay than men simply because their jobs typically require few skills and less training.

Reality: Sexism is also a factor, because, even when women hold the same jobs as men, they earn less.

Myth: Physicians are among the highest paid professionals solely because of the importance of their work to society.

Reality: There is an additional reason: Most doctors in the United States are men. In the former Soviet Union, where medicine was considered a "feminine" occupation because most physicians were women, they were paid less than skilled blue-collar workers.

Myth: Nowadays, with the sexual revolution influencing every aspect of American life, parents can easily persuade their young daughters to play with traditionally "boy" toys or their young sons to play with "girl" toys.

Reality: Parents still cannot buck the influ-ence from toy advertisements on Saturday morning television or the pressure from their children's peers. As a result, children continue to prefer playing with gender-stereotyped toys.

Myth: It is natural for old people to be senile—experiencing serious memory loss, confusion, and loss of reasoning ability.

Reality: Old age does not inevitably lead to senility. Senility is an abnormal condition, not a natural result of aging. That is why a large majority of old people are not senile.

Myth: Since the elderly see doctors more often than healthy young people, the healing profession tends to show more understanding toward them.

Reality: On the contrary, elderly patients tend to be less successful than younger ones in getting doctors to answer their questions and address their concerns.

Myth: Elder abuse is similar to child abuse. That's why physical abuse is the most common when the elderly are victimized by their younger relatives.

Reality: While child abuse usually takes the form of physical assault, elder abuse often involves financial exploitation.

I n 1991 a plane jammed with businesspeople and tourists took off from a southern city in India to the country's capital, New Delhi. On that flight a 10-year-old Indian girl named Ameena sat sobbing, her hands covering her tears. Beside her was a 60-year-old Arab man staring blankly out of the window. A flight attendant came over and asked her what was wrong. Appearing afraid of the man, she did not answer and kept on weeping. After the attendant and several passengers ushered her away from him, she said, "This man came to our house. He found my elder sister dark and ugly. My father, who drives an auto-rickshaw, made me marry this man. He is taking me to Saudi Arabia. I don't want to go with him." When the plane landed in New Delhi, the police arrested the man and took the girl into protective custody. It turned out that the man had been bride shopping in southern India, buying the girl from her poor father for 6000 rupees ($240). Selling young daughters into marriage is quite common among lower-class Indians (Gargan, 1991).

In the same year, a shocking event of a different kind involved an old woman in the United States. When 70-year-old Margaret Embrey was brought into the emergency room of a hospital in Houston, her condition appalled the doctors and nurses. She was covered with bedsores, some as large as a hand. Maggots were gnawing at her wounds, which had cut into her bones. She also suffered from dehydration and malnutrition. Five-foot-seven tall, she weighed only 95 pounds, having lost 40 pounds over the previous six months. The old woman's 19-year-old granddaughter and her husband, aged 22, were later charged with criminal abuse. Such abuse is not uncommon. It happens to as many as 1.5 million elderly Americans—about 5 percent of the elderly population (Rosado, 1991).

These two cases of human abuse are part of the larger, common problem of prejudice and discrimination against females and older people. In this chapter, we will first discuss the gender roles and inequalities as well as their roots. Then we will examine how aging affects people, how it changes their role in society, and how elder abuse comes about.

Gender Roles and Inequalities

There are basic differences in what societies expect of men and women. These differences constitute **gender roles:** patterns of attitude and behavior that a society expects of its members because of their being male or female. Even when men and women hold the same jobs with the same status, they may face different expectations. In 1982 Svetlana Y. Savit-skaya, a Soviet parachutist and pilot, became the second woman in space. But after her space vehicle docked with the orbiting Soviet space station, one male cosmonaut greeted her by saying, "We've got an apron ready for you. . . . Of course, we have a kitchen for you; that'll be where you work" (Burns, 1982). Such traditional gender-role attitudes have declined in the United States, but many Americans still expect men to be "masculine" and women to be "feminine." What is the nature of these gender roles?

MASCULINE AND FEMININE IN AMERICA

For many years, American society assigned to men the role of breadwinner and to women the role of homemaker. The American man was expected to work out in the world, competing with other men in order to provide for his family. The "man's world" outside the home was viewed as a harsh and heartless jungle in which men needed strength, ambition, and aggression. "Woman's world" was the home, and her job was to comfort and care for husband and children, maintain harmony, and teach her children to conform to society's norms.

This basic division of labor has been accompanied by many popular stereotypes—oversimplified mental images—of what men and women are supposed to be, and to some extent these stereotypes persist. Men are supposed to be ambitious and aggressive; women, shy, easily intimidated, and passive. Men should be strong and athletic; women, weak and dainty. It is bad form for men, but not for women, to worry about their appearance and aging. Men should hold back their emotions and must not cry, but women are expected to be emotional, even to cry easily. Men are expected to be sexually aggressive and experienced; women, sexually passive and inexperienced. Men are supposed to be independent, fit to be leaders; women are believed to be dependent, in need of male protection. Men are expected to be logical, rational, and objective; women, inconsistent and intuitive.

These are the traits that most Americans have long associated with each gender. They represent both *stereotypes* about how men and women behave and *expectations* about how they should behave. Today, some Americans are more likely than others to hold or reject them. Among women, those who are relatively young, unmarried, well educated, gainfully

Americans have long assigned to men the role of being strong and aggressive. According to this expectation, men are not to worry about their appearance and aging. The man in this photo, being given a facial, obviously rejects this stereotype.

employed, or who have strong feelings of personal competence tend to reject the traditional gender-role attitudes (Morgan and Walker, 1983). Among men, lower-class whites are more traditional in gender-role outlook than middle- and upper-class whites. There is also a racial difference: black men are more traditional than white men (Ransford and Miller, 1983).

Although people may consciously reject the traditional gender roles, they tend to behave otherwise. Research has shown that women are more likely to be passive and men aggressive in a number of ways. Women tend to talk in terms of connection and intimacy, while men usually speak the language of status and independence. In interactions between the sexes, the male is more likely to initiate interactions and the female to respond. During a conversation, men tend more to touch women than vice versa. When a man opens the door for women, they tend to say "thank you" or smile their appreciation. But men

tend to look confused if a woman opens the door for them, because they are not accustomed to being women's passive beneficiaries. When attacked, women are more inclined than men to withdraw instead of launching a counterattack. Women are also more "social," more likely to seek security and intimacy in the company of others. There are more women than men calling up a same-sex friend just to talk. Women are also more likely than men to hug, kiss, or soothe an infant. Women are more people-oriented, more likely to help others, to be virtuous, to maintain faith, and to conform to customs. Finally, women are more concerned than men about their physical appearance. Women tend to think of their selves as residing in their bodies; men, in their heads. A recent analysis of personal ads in a major newspaper finds that men are more likely to seek women whom they view as "sex objects"—physically and sexually attractive— while women are more interested in men as "success objects"—financially secure and well educated (Rossi, 1984; Goleman, 1988; Joubert, 1989; S. Davis, 1990; Tanner, 1991; Williams, 1992). All this reflects the powerful influence of traditional gender roles, which make men and women behave differently.

SEXISM

At one time or another, laws have denied women "the right to hold property, to vote, to go to school, to travel, to borrow money, and to enter certain occupations" (Epstein, 1976). In recent years, there has been significant movement toward gender equality, but large inequalities remain, even in the United States. They are evident in education, in the workplace, in politics, and in religion. Underlying these inequalities is **sexism**—prejudice and discrimination based on the victim's gender.

A fundamental characteristic of sexism is the belief that women are inferior to men. Even when a man and a woman have the same personalities or are equally competent in performing the same task, she is still likely to be considered inferior to him. We can see this sexist attitude even in psychiatry, a profession that is supposed to be scientific and objective in analyzing human traits. According to a survey of mental health professionals, the respondents apply different definitions of mental health to men and women. A healthy, mature woman is characterized as submissive, dependent, unadventurous, easily influenced, excitable in minor crises, susceptible to hurt feelings, and conceited about her appearance. A man with these characteristics would be considered unhealthy and immature (Jaggar and Struhl, 1978). In general,

Prejudice and discrimination against women springs from the traditional notion that somehow women are inferior to men. This prejudice has forced many working women to work in low-status jobs. Even when women hold jobs comparable to those of men, they are frequently paid less than men.

men are described positively—as independent, courageous, and the like—but women are described negatively, as having "sexual timidity" and "social anxiety." Yet, if they get rid of sexual timidity and become sexually active, which is typically considered normal for men, women are likely to be diagnosed as abnormal (Goleman, 1990a).

Such a "damned if you do, damned if you don't" attitude toward women comes across in a recent study of introductory psychology students who were asked to evaluate men and women with various characteristics. Women with "feminine" traits, such as compassion and sensitivity to others' needs, were rated more poorly than men with "masculine" characteristics, such as assertiveness. But women with the "masculine" traits were also rated less favorably than

men with the "feminine" traits (Gerber, 1989). Similarly, successful women are less appreciated for their achievement than are their male counterparts. This sexist attitude is particularly hard on single women. Our society in effect says that no matter how much success a woman achieves, she hasn't really made it until she is married. As a married woman likes to say, "I graduated Phi Beta Kappa from college, and I got taken out to dinner. I made law review and my mother sent me a sweater. But I found a man to marry, and I was deluged with congratulations in the form of place settings, crystal, matching luggage, microwaves, and VCRs" (Myers, 1990). Successful men are not treated in the same way at all.

Sexism has long exerted a negative impact on women, making them feel as if they were inferior to men. In a classic study by Phillip Goldberg (1968), female college students were asked to rate scholarly articles for usefulness, competence, practicality, writing style, and the like. All the students read the same articles. But some were told that the author was "John T. McKay"; others, that the author was "Joan T. McKay." The women who were told the articles were written by "John" gave them high marks; those who believed they were written by "Joan" gave the articles low marks—although the articles were identical. Other researchers found that female university administrators, like their male counterparts, gave different responses to the same résumés, depending on whether the author was identified as male or female. Not surprisingly, they judged the fictitious male professors more qualified than the female ones—although the résumés cited the same education and job experience (Fidell, 1970). In a recent study, however, men were rated only slightly higher than women. The difference appeared so small as to be considered negligible. The subjects in this study—psychology students—may have rejected gender stereotypes because Goldberg's findings have been widely discussed in introductory psychology texts, while sex discrimination has often been presented in the media as a social problem. Because of the increasing number of successful women in society, the biased negative evaluation of women can be expected to happen less often today (Swim et al., 1989; Eagly and Mladinic, 1989).

Sexism has also made many women afraid to pursue successful careers (Horner, 1969). It is true that fewer women suffer from this fear today than in the 1960s—perhaps because gender-role stereotypes were vigorously attacked during the 1970s and 1980s (Tresemer, 1974; Hyland, 1989). Nevertheless, sexism is still powerful enough to make many women reluctant to pursue "masculine" careers. According to a recent study, college women, like college men, believe that men regard women who seek "masculine" occupations as least preferable as friends or romantic partners (Pfost and Fiore, 1990). In another study, female high school students in Great Britain agree with their male classmates that successful career women are likely to have marital problems, so they will give up their careers to protect their marriage and family and husbands' career (Janman, 1989). In yet another study, 93 male and female managers were asked to listen to a recording of a mild dispute between a male and a female manager. Like their male peers, the female subjects described the woman as aggressive, "pushy," or unfeminine, which they consider to be negative characteristics in women (Mathison, 1986). In fact, in recent years, women have become less willing to work and more willing to stay home to care for the family. In 1985, 51 percent of women preferred to work, but by 1991 that number fell to 43 percent—while 53 percent would rather stay home (Blackman, 1992). A major reason, according to Susan Faludi (1991), is the negative portrayal of career women in the mass media: suffering depression and burnout from the rat race, being confronted with fewer opportunities for marriage, and running up against infertility from postponing childbearing.

Sexism can also subtly influence the interaction between the sexes. Studies of nonverbal interaction have revealed that men often unconsciously exhibit their superiority to women—and women their inferiority. When talking to a man, women typically give such low-status signals as smiling, nodding, holding their arms to their bodies, or keeping their legs together. Men are more likely to use high-status gestures by smiling only occasionally, holding their heads still, and assuming asymmetrical, relaxed body postures. Added to this sexism-influenced pattern of body language is women's tendency to speak more politely than men, being more careful to say "please" and "thank you" as they are expected to. When men participate in a small-group discussion with women, men tend to have their arguments and decisions accepted more often (Cory, 1979; Inwald and Bryant, 1981).

Sexism may produce inequality between the sexes in two ways. When sexism takes the active form of discrimination against women, it obviously creates inequality. At each level of occupational skill, for example, men receive higher pay than women. Sexism may also foster inequality in a less direct way. If women have been socialized to feel inferior, they may lower their expectations, aiming to achieve less

than they otherwise might. Whether through overt discrimination or traditional gender-role socialization, sexism has brought gender inequalities in education, occupation, politics, religion, and sports.

EDUCATION

For a long time, women were deprived of the opportunities for higher education. They were barred from many colleges and universities, especially graduate and professional schools, far into the 1960s. In general, the more prestigious the institutions, the more strongly they discriminated against women. Harvard, for example, was one of the last to give up sex discrimination. It began to admit women to its graduate business program only as recently as 1963.

The women's movement made some headway in getting the government to pass laws against sex discrimination in the 1970s. Collectively known as Title IX, the laws require that schools (1) eliminate sex-segregated classes such as all-girl home economics or all-boy shop classes, (2) avoid sex discrimination in admissions and financial aid, (3) end sexist hiring and promotion practices, and (4) provide more opportunities for women's sports. But there is still significant inequality.

In public schools from preschool through high school, teachers tend to pay more attention to boys than girls: calling on boys more often, offering boys more detailed and constructive criticism, and allowing boys to shout out answers but reprimanding girls for doing so, especially in math and science classes. This may explain why girls have less interest in and do less well in math and sciences than boys (Chira, 1992). Receiving less attention from teachers, girls further suffer a drop in self-esteem when reaching high school. As revealed by a recent nationwide study of 3000 children, at age 9 a majority of girls are confident, assertive, and feel positive about themselves, but by age 14 less than one-third feel that way (Daley, 1991). In high school, though, girls still get better grades than boys and are more likely to graduate. In recent years, women have also become a little more likely than men to attend college and earn bachelor's or master's degrees. But they are less likely to receive degrees from graduate or professional schools. Although starting out with superior academic records, women fall further behind at higher levels of education. In addition, most women undergraduates continue to major in the liberal arts while more men study science, engineering, business administration, and other subjects that will lead to high-paying occupations (Coleman and Cressey, 1993; Census Bureau, 1993).

Inequalities persist, too, on the faculties and in the administration of the nation's colleges and universities. In the early 1980s, the proportion of women on the faculty in most disciplines had not exceeded the level achieved during the 1920s, which was less than 30 percent. Various studies have consistently shown that, compared with their male colleagues, female academics are less likely to be hired, more concentrated in the lower ranks of institutions, and less likely to be promoted. They are also paid substantially less. At the same time, there is evidence that women with Ph.D.s are just as productive as men in generating research, that female Ph.D. recipients have slightly greater ability than men, and that there is no significant difference in the teaching effectiveness of men and women (Bienen, Ostriker, and Ostriker, 1977; Grant and Snyder, 1984).

JOBS AND MONEY

For years inequality in education has contributed to inequality in the job market. Economic inequality between the sexes also increased because many people considered housekeeping and child care the only real career for a woman. Women who did work often had less experience, as well as less education, than men. Consequently, women lagged far behind men in employment and earnings.

These sexual differences have decreased over the years. Forty years ago, only 30 percent of women were employed outside the home. Today, more than half of all women are employed, including about 57 percent of those married and with children under 6 years old. For women in their thirties and forties, the rate of labor-force participation now stands at 78 per-

cent (Crispell, 1990). But the place of women in the work force is still very far from equal.

Women typically hold lower-status, lower-paying jobs than men. In 1988, men made up 75 percent of managers in companies with 100 or more employees, but women accounted for only 25 percent. In 1990 there were only three women CEOs (chief executive officers) in the nation's largest 1000 industrial and service companies (Marsh, 1991). In these companies as many as half the professional employees are women, but they hold fewer than 5 percent of the senior management positions. Even these senior jobs are mostly in less important areas, such as human resources, finance, and public relations (as opposed to core areas such as marketing, production, and sales), which typically do not offer the critical experience necessary for advancing to higher levels in the corporations (Lopez, 1992). Women are also underrepresented in such high-status professions as medicine, law, engineering, and college teaching. On the other hand, women are overrepresented in such low-paying jobs as nursing, public-school teaching, and secretarial work (see Table 9.1). These traditionally female occupations, known in sociology as **women's ghettos,** are subordinate to positions usually held by men. Thus, nurses are subordinate to doctors, schoolteachers to principals, and secretaries to executives.

Even when women hold the same jobs as men or have comparable skills, training, and education, they tend to earn less. Among college graduates, for example, women earn only about 52 percent of what men earn. As a whole, American women earn about 57 percent of what men make (see Table 9.2). The standard explanations for this disparity are that more women than men hold lower-level jobs and that many women have less seniority than men because they interrupt their careers to have children. An additional explanation is that because men are their families'

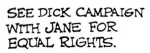

SEE DICK CAMPAIGN WITH JANE FOR EQUAL RIGHTS.

LOOK, LOOK, SEE DICK AND JANE GET A JOB AT THE MINES.

SEE DICK GET AN OFFICE JOB.

SEE JANE GET THE SHAFT.

TABLE 9.1 *The Women's Ghettos*

Despite their increased entrance into the labor force, women are still concentrated in low-status, low-paying positions. Among such jobs are these percentages held by women:

Secretaries	99%
Receptionists	97
Child-care workers	97
Cleaners and servants	95
Registered nurses	94
Billing Clerks	92
Bank tellers	90
Librarians	88
Elementary-school teachers	85
Health technicians	82
Waiters, waitresses	80

Source: Bureau of Labor Statistics, Employment and Earnings, 1993.

principal wage earners, they should be paid more. But these explanations invite discrimination against women. Several years ago the state of Washington began to fight discrimination by instituting the comparable-worth program, which pays women the same as men for doing different but equally demanding

work, such as office cleaning as compared to truck driving. Some other states have followed Washington's lead by developing similar programs (Kilborn, 1990a). But a significant gender gap remains in earnings.

POLITICS

Theoretically, women can easily acquire more political power than men. After all, women voters outnumber men—with 54 percent of the voting population being women. In addition, most of the volunteer workers in political campaigns are women. Yet, until recently, many women felt that politics was a male activity, that women should not plunge into the dirty world of politics. Sexism also tended to entrap women in a Catch-22 situation to squash their political ambition. If a woman campaigned vigorously, she was likely to be regarded as a neglectful wife and mother. If she claimed to be an attentive wife and mother, she was apt to be judged incapable of devoting energy to public office. But a man in a comparable situation—as a vigorous campaigner or a devoted husband and father—was considered to have a great political asset.

Not surprisingly, women have often helped men get elected, with the result that men have dominated the political process—and women as well. In

TABLE 9.2 *Gender Inequality in Income*

EDUCATION	GENDER	MONTHLY INCOME	PERCENTAGE OF MEN'S
Doctorate	Men	$4,915	
Doctorate	Women	$3,162	64%
Master	Men	$3,748	
Master	Women	$2,614	70%
Bachelor	Men	$3,235	
Bachelor	Women	$1,698	52%
Some college	Men	$2,002	
Some college	Women	$1,115	56%
High school	Men	$1,853	
High school	Women	$ 943	51%
Some high school	Men	$1,116	
Some high school	Women	$ 579	50%
	On average women earn 57% of what men make		

Source: U.S. Census Bureau, 1993.

Until recently, many women regarded politics as a male activity, and sexism against women has created a barrier to their entry into politics. In recent years, however, a few women, such as Roberta Achtenberg, appointed to the number two position in the Housing/Urban Development Department, have climbed to near the top of the ladder in government.

recent years, however, a growing number of women have assumed political leadership. Since 1980, the percentage of women who vote has surpassed that of men. Differences in the voting patterns of men and women have emerged, with women being more liberal and more likely to favor candidates who care deeply about the economy and social programs rather than foreign affairs.

Women have been developing into an important political force, but they still have a long way to go before reaching equality with men. Women make up over 50 percent of the voting population, but they capture no more than 5 percent of all public offices. Women seem likely to occupy more positions of political leadership in the future, though. Since 1990 a record number of women have been running for governor and other high offices. By May 1992 at least 189 women—a higher than usual number—were running for the Senate, House, and governorships. Today many are likely to win because they have greater credibility with the public than men do on questions of honesty and integrity. With the ending of the Cold War, women also hold the high ground on such quality-of-life issues as the environment, child care, and abortion. The decision of usually large numbers of male incumbents in Congress (more than 50 in 1992) to quit politics further ensures more women getting elected. Indeed, the 1992 election increased the number of women by 200 percent in the Senate and 68 percent in the House. Women continue to be a distinct minority, though. They hold only 6 out of 100 seats in the Senate and 48 out of 435 seats in the House (DiVall, 1992; Dowd, 1993).

RELIGION

The sexist notion of female inferiority, which has long been used to justify and to defend male dominance and female oppression, can be found in the sacred texts of all the world's major religions. Buddhism and Confucianism instruct wives to obey their husbands. The Muslim Koran states, "Men are superior to women on account of the qualities in which God has given them preeminence." The Bible says that after Eve ate the forbidden fruit and gave it to Adam, God told her: "In pain you shall bring forth children, yet your desire shall be for your husband, and he shall rule over you" (Genesis 3:16). And St. Paul wrote, "Man . . . is the image and reflection of God, but woman from man. Neither was man created for the sake of woman, but woman for the sake of man" (1 Corinthians 11:7–9). The daily Orthodox Jewish prayer for men includes this sentence: "I thank Thee, O Lord, that Thou has not made me a woman." Of course, all this should not be taken to suggest that religion always puts women down. In fact, as Mary Van Leeuwen (1990) observes, "Over the course of the four Gospels, there is a total of 633 verses in which Jesus refers to women, and almost none of these is negative in tone." But, on the whole, sexist ideas predominate. Even the most important concept of religion—God—is spoken and thought of as belonging to the male sex. Undoubtedly, to some feminists, the notion of the Supreme Being as male is the quintessence of sexism. Because of this, some liberal church leaders have begun purging hymnals and liturgies of references to God as male (such as "God the Father") and preaching about a genderless deity (called the Creator or Great Spirit). But many bishops, pastors, and laypeople have been protesting the changes (Niebuhr, 1992).

Sexism is not confined to sacred texts. It also shapes contemporary religious organizations and practices. In the United States, for the past 20 years, under the increasing influence of the women's movement, there have been more women enrolling in theological seminaries and becoming ordained ministers. But they still remain a small minority. Compared with their male counterparts, women clergy are more likely to be underemployed, more likely to be paid low salaries, less likely to be promoted to better positions, more often serving merely as assistant or associate pastors, and more frequently relegated to small congregations. Moreover, Conservative and Orthodox Judaism and the Missouri-Synod-Lutherans are still opposed to ordaining women. The Roman Catholic and Eastern Orthodox churches, which represent over half of all Christians, also continue to prohibit ordination for women (Anderson, 1988; Richardson, 1988; Ostling, 1992). These church hierarchies are at odds with the rank-and-file, though. Two-thirds of lay Catholics, for example, favor opening the priesthood to women (Goldman, 1992).

In sum, gender inequalities in religion involve both the sacred texts and the contemporary practices of the world's major religions. Both of these areas will continue to be a focus of debate as the world's religions confront gender-related issues.

SPORTS

The recent increase in female sports participation is extraordinary. Since the early 1970s, female involvement in collegiate sports has jumped by over 100 percent, and female participation in high school athletic programs has zoomed more than 600 percent. Although similar statistics for professional sports are not available, it is clear from reading the sports pages and watching sports on television that there are now many more women in sports than before. The trend

Because of the 1972 law, Title IX of the Educational Amendment Act, which prohibits sex discrimination in school sports, training and facilities for women's teams have improved since the 1970s. Ironically, however, Title IX has brought about a drop in the number of female coaches and administrators.

is apparently a spin-off from the women's liberation movement and the 1972 law (Title IX of the Educational Amendment Act) that prohibits sex discrimination in school sports.

Nevertheless, Title IX has not been fully enforced because unequal expenditures for male and female athletics are still legally acceptable. This means, among other things, that more funds may continue to be spent on men's sports, such as football and basketball, than on women's athletic programs (Flygare, 1979; Snyder and Spreitzer, 1989; Moran, 1992). Ironically, Title IX has brought about a drop in the number of female coaches and administrators. Because of the law, the equipment, training, and facilities for women's teams have improved significantly, and management salaries have also gone up substantially. Consequently, many men have sought top management and coaching jobs in women's athletic programs. And because of gender bias, men usually succeed in getting hired and taking the jobs away from women. Thus, women now account for only 16 percent of the administrators of women's programs, as opposed to 90 percent in 1972. The proportion of women coaching women's teams has also fallen, from 58 percent in 1972 to 47 percent in 1990 (Diesenhouse, 1990).

Gender bias also appears in the larger society. Most people still differentiate between male and female sports. Generally, the so-called male sports involve bodily contact during competition, the handling of a heavy object, the propelling of the body through space over long distances, and the employment of physical force to overpower an opponent. Examples are football, basketball, baseball, wrestling, boxing, weightlifting, and long-distance running. Women are expected to stay away from these supposedly men's sports. If they do not, they are popularly believed to be losing their feminine qualities. To maintain or enhance their femininity, women are expected to stick to the so-called women's sports, such as aerobic dancing, swimming, diving, gymnastics, tennis, and figure skating, all of which emphasize grace and beauty in the body's movement (Snyder and Spreitzer, 1989).

These sexist attitudes have caused women to participate primarily in "feminine" sports (Fishwick and Hayes, 1989). Sexism has also affected women who participate in "masculine" sports. They tend to feel that they are less feminine than other women. According to one study, 70 percent of female gymnasts perceived themselves as being "very feminine," but only 44 percent of women basketball players saw themselves in the same way (Snyder and Spreitzer, 1989). Moreover, most girls under 15 seem to lack the confidence to participate in traditionally male contact sports. Research has suggested that if young girls are asked to take physical tests that they perceive to be masculine, they tend to have less expectation of success than their abilities merit. Thus, very few girls take up "boy" sports. Girls join less than 1 percent of the Amateur Hockey Association of America's 11,104 teams. Pop Warner Football found that there were only 24 girls among its approximately 200,000 young competitors. Little League Baseball has been able to attract only one girl for every two or three hardball leagues of 100 or more boys. Instead, the girls overwhelmingly choose to play on all-female Little League softball teams (Monagan, 1983).

However, whatever sports women choose, gender bias discounts their athletic abilities. The media often describe female athletes as "pretty," "slim," "attractive," "gracious," and "lovely," as opposed to male athletes being "great," "tough," "brilliant," "cool," and "courageous." In the women's final of the 1988 U.S. Open tennis tournament, the male television announcers mentioned Gabriela Sabatini's good looks numerous times. But in the men's final, which pitted Mats Wilander against Ivan Lendl, Wilander's rugged good looks were not mentioned at all (Sidel, 1990). In 1992, the American figure skater Kristi Yamaguchi, who won an Olympic gold medal in that year, was described as having "a Betty Boop mouth and two beauty marks wonderfully positioned under the left eye and the lips" (Deford, 1992).

QUESTIONS FOR DISCUSSION AND REVIEW

1. What are gender roles, and what traits do most Americans associate with them?
2. What are the characteristics and consequences of sexism?
3. What is the current status of women in educational institutions?
4. Why have jobs traditionally reserved for women led to the creation of women's employment ghettos?
5. How have women fared in politics in recent years?
6. What impact does sexism have on religion?
7. What is the nature of sexism in sports and how does it influence women?

Sources of Gender Roles and Inequalities

What are the sources of gender roles and inequalities? The variations in the gender roles established by human societies suggest that these roles are learned, not inherited. But how are the roles learned? Also, why are women everywhere unequal? What sexual differences are inherited? How are gender roles and inequalities related to these differences?

BIOLOGICAL CONSTRAINTS

There are genetic differences between males and females: males have two different sex chromosomes, XY, and females have two similar chromosomes, XX. **Chromosomes** are the materials in a cell that transmits hereditary traits to the carrier from his or her parents. Males inherit the X chromosome from their mothers and the Y from their fathers, and females get one X chromosome from each of their parents. Although a particular composition of sex chromosomes determines a person's sex as a male or female, there is no guarantee that a genetically male person (with XY chromosomes) will look like a man or a genetically female person (with XX) will look like a woman.

Whether a person will develop the appropriate sex characteristics—say, facial hair or breasts—depends on the proportion of male and female sex **hormones,** chemical substances that stimulate or inhibit vital biological processes. If a man has more female than male hormones, he will end up with breasts rather than facial hair. If a woman has more male than female hormones, she will have facial hair instead. This is why people who have undergone sex-change operations are injected with a lot of hormones appropriate to their new sex. But in most men the proportion of male hormones is greater, and in most females the proportion of female hormones is greater. It is clear that men and women differ chromosomally and hormonally.

The chromosomal and hormonal differences lie behind other biological differences between the sexes. Stimulated by the greater amount of male sex hormones, men are on the average bigger and stronger—more able to lift heavy objects—than women. Yet due to their lack of a second X chromosome, men are less healthy. Men are susceptible to more than 30 types of genetic defects, such as hemophilia and color blindness, which are very rare in women. At birth, males are more likely to die. During the first month after birth, males are much more likely to have one of over 187 physical abnormalities, such as day blindness and progressive deafness. Throughout life, males tend to mature more slowly. They are more physiologically vulnerable to stress. They are stricken with heart disease at a younger age. And they die sooner (Stoll, 1978; Gorman, 1992).

There are also sex differences in brain structure. Neuroscience research has established that the left hemisphere, or half, of the brain controls speech, and the right hemisphere directs spatial tasks such as object manipulation. There is more specialization in the male's brain, so that he tends to use just one hemisphere for a given task, whereas the female tends to use both at the same time. For example, men are more likely to listen with the right ear while women with both ears. Moreover, the male experiences greater cell growth in his spatial perception-dominated hemisphere, while the female does so in her language-dominated hemisphere (Restak, 1979; Goy and McEwen, 1980; Gorman, 1992).

The differences in brain structure and hormonal production may have contributed to some behavioral differences between the sexes. Thus, female babies are more sensitive than males to certain sounds, particularly their mother's voices, and are more easily startled by loud noises. Female infants are also more quiet, but males are more vigorous and inclined to explore, run, and bang in their play. Female infants talk sooner, have larger vocabularies, and are less likely to develop speech problems—stuttering, for example, is several times more prevalent among males. Girls are superior not only in verbal abilities but also in overall intelligence, while boys excel in spatial performances such as mental manipulation of objects and map reading. When asked how they have mentally folded an object, boys tend to say simply "I folded it in my mind," but girls are more likely to produce elaborate verbal descriptions. Women are more sensitive to touch, odor, and sound. They show greater skill in picking up peripheral information as well as nuances of facial expression and voice. They are six times more likely than men to sing in tune (Rossi, 1984; Trotter, 1987).

In short, nature makes men and women different, but these differences do not add up to female inferiority. On some measures—such as physical health and early verbal ability—females as a group seem superior to males, and by other measures—especially size and strength—males as a group are superior. Males' dominance over females may appear partly rooted in their larger size and strength. As Penn Handwerker and Paul Crosbie (1982) found in their experimental study of social interaction in small groups, taller people tend to be dominant over shorter ones. But such physical factors seem significant only because they are culturally defined as such. Moreover, the sexual differences found in early childhood, such as boys' being superior in mathematics and girls' being better in verbal ability, will finally disappear if both are subjected to similar experiences in the home, school, and workplace. There is already some evidence that those sexual differences in mathematical or verbal ability have been narrowing over the last 20 years (Linn and Hyde, 1989). All this underscores the influence of socialization and culture.

THE ROLE OF CULTURE

The biological differences between males and females seem logically related to the division of labor between the sexes. If men are bigger and stronger,

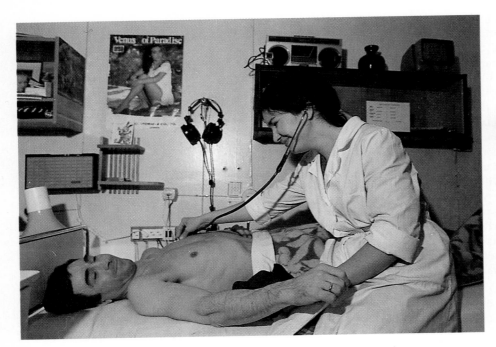

Gender roles vary from one culture to another. What is considered "men's work" in one culture may be regarded as "women's work" in another. In the United States, medicine is considered a man's profession and is a high-status profession with high pay. By contrast, in Russia medicine is a woman's profession and is accorded relatively low status and low pay.

then it makes sense for them to do the work that requires strength. And assigning women the care of the home and children may be a logical extension of their biological ability to bear and nurse children.

However, there are limitations to biological constraints on gender roles and inequalities. Since women generally have smaller hands and greater finger agility than men, they are logically more fit to be dentists and neurosurgeons. Yet men dominate these high-paying professions because our culture has long defined them as "men's work." Indeed, as we have seen, there are many variations from culture to culture in the details of sex roles. In breadth and depth, social inequalities between men and women far exceed their biological differences. Especially in modern industrial societies, biology sets few real constraints, because machines have taken over much of the work demanding physical strength. The cultural definition of gender roles, in fact, exercises awesome power. Because American culture has defined being a physician as men's work, for example, the majority of our doctors are males, and they are among the highest paid professionals. By contrast, in the former Soviet Union, where medicine was a "feminine" profession, most of the doctors were women, and they were generally paid "women's wages"—less than what skilled blue-collar workers made. Thus, biology

may promote the broad outlines of a sexual division of labor, but cultures draw the actual boundaries.

Furthermore, most of the biological differences between males and females (except for those involving reproduction) do not refer to absolute differences between individuals but to where the average male or female is likely to fall on some continuum. There are, after all, many boys who are smaller and weaker than the average girl. Nonetheless, they may conform to a culturally defined gender role, showing a typically "masculine" interest in sports and mechanical toys.

The complicated relationship between the biological characteristics of the sexes and their eventual gender roles is perhaps best illustrated by cases in which a person's sex was ambiguous or mislabeled at birth. In one such case, 38 boys in the Dominican Republic had been raised as girls because they had had an enzyme deficiency that made their external genitals look female when they were born. But at puberty, when they developed the normal male characteristics, they changed their sexual identity, taking on the male role (Kolata, 1979). In other cases, however, adults happily maintained the sex role they had been assigned at birth, even after they had developed characteristics of the opposite sex during puberty (Money and Ehrhardt, 1972). In these cases, culture, not biology, seemed to have the last word.

Obviously, biology sets males and females apart. But it cannot make us behave in any specific way. It can only predispose us to behave in certain ways, because society does much to accentuate gender differences. As Alice Rossi (1984) points out, women may have the natural tendency to handle an infant with tactile gentleness and soothing voice and men may have the natural tendency to play with an older child in a rough-and-tumble way, but these tendencies are often exaggerated through socialization. Also, boys may have been born with a slightly greater spatial ability than girls, but as adults, males perform much better on spatial tasks. This is largely the result of socialization: "most boys, but few girls, grow up throwing baseballs, passing footballs, building models, breaking down engines—activities that teach about space" (Benderly, 1989). Thus, we are born male or female, but we learn to become men or women.

SOCIALIZATION

The learning of gender roles is part of socialization. In whatever way a society defines gender roles, its socializing agents pass that definition from generation to generation. In the United States the family, schools, peer groups, and mass media all teach important lessons about these roles.

The Family Newborn babies do not even know their gender, much less how to behave like boys or girls. Influenced by their parents, children very quickly develop their sexual identity and learn their gender roles. Right from birth, babies are usually treated according to their gender. At birth, boys tend to be wrapped in blue blankets and girls in pink. When they are a little older, baby boys are handled more roughly than girls; boys are bounced around and lifted high in the air, but girls are cuddled and cooed over. Boys are often left alone to explore their environment, but girls are protected against any possible accident. Boys are given toy trains, play trucks, and building sets, whereas girls are given dolls, toy vacuum cleaners, and miniature kitchen appliances. Boys build houses, and girls play house. Mothers fuss about how pretty their little girls should look, but they generally care less about their little boys' appearance (Richardson, 1988).

When learning to talk, children become more aware of the gender difference. They are taught to

differentiate "he" and "his" from "she" and "hers." When they are older, they sense that males are more important than females, as the word "man" is used to refer to the entire human race, as if women did not exist (e.g., "the future of man" rather than "the future of humanity"). In learning to talk, children also pick up gender cues. Both parents use more words about feelings and emotions with girls than with boys, so that by age 2, girls use more emotion words

According to social learning theory, children learn gender roles by imitating older people of the same sex. Attending a hockey game, a boy may develop a gender identity: "I do boy things. Therefore I must be a boy," But according to cognitive development theory, gender identity is the cause of gender-role learning. First the boy learns that he is a male, then he seeks to act and feel like one: "I am a boy. Therefore I want to do boy things."

than boys do. Fathers tend to use more commanding or threatening language with sons than with daughters ("Turn off the TV"), while mothers talk more politely ("Could you turn off the TV, please?"). By age 4, boys and girls have learned to imitate those conversational styles of their fathers and mothers: when talking among themselves, boys use more threatening, commanding, dominating language, and girls emphasize agreement and mutuality (Shapiro, 1990).

Boys are taught to behave "like men," to avoid being "sissies." They are told that boys don't cry, only girls do. If, even in play, they try on makeup and wear dresses, their parents are horrified. Boys tend to grow up with a fear of being feminine, which forces them to maintain a macho image as well as an exploitative attitude toward women. Boys are also encouraged to be self-reliant and assertive, to avoid being "mama's boys." They are more likely than girls to receive physical punishment, such as spanking, so that they develop a sort of reactive independence. On the other hand, girls are taught to be "ladylike," to be polite, to be gentle, and to rely on others—especially males—for help. They are allowed to express their emotions freely. Seeing their mothers spend time and money on fashion and cosmetics, they learn the importance of being pretty—and feel that they must rely more on their beauty than on intelligence to attract men (Johnson, 1982; Brownmiller, 1984; Elkin and Handel, 1988; Power and Shanks, 1989).

Parents may deny that they treat their sons and daughters differently, but studies have suggested otherwise. When parents are asked, "In what ways do you think boys and girls are different?" many would say that boys are more active, stronger, more competitive, noisier, and messier and that girls are more gentle, neater, quieter, more helpful, and more courteous. Such gender typing has been found to cause parents to treat their children differently, even when they are not conscious of doing so. If they consider boys stronger, for example, they are likely to handle them more roughly than girls and to protect girls more than boys (Richardson, 1988). In recent years, however, there has been a definite trend toward more egalitarian gender-role socialization. Young parents, working mothers, and well-educated parents are particularly inclined to socialize their children into egalitarian gender roles, but parents with regular church attendance and fundamentalist religious identification tend to preserve traditional gender roles (Thornton, Alwin, and Camburn, 1983). At any rate, even if well-educated parents try to socialize their sons and daughters in the same way, their children are still subjected to traditional gender-role socialization outside the home. Under pressure from their peers and influence from toy advertisements on television, most children continue to enjoy playing with gender-stereotyped toys. Girls go for the Barbie doll, Dolly Surprise, Li'l Miss Makeup, and other frilly dolls with pretty hair and gorgeous wardrobes. Such toys teach girls the importance of dressing and grooming, dating, getting married, and other "feminine" activities. By contrast, boys prefer Nintendo, G.I. Joe, Hot Wheels, the Real Ghostbusters, and other action figures that stand ready to do battle with bad guys. These toys encourage boys to be "masculine" by being brave and tough (Lawson, 1989).

Schools and Peer Groups   The socialization of boys and girls into their gender roles gets a boost from schools. Until recently, schools usually segregated courses and sports on the basis of gender. Business and mechanics courses were for boys; secretarial courses and home economics, for girls. Boys played hardball; girls, softball. High school counselors were not very likely to encourage girls to go on to college, because they were expected to get married and stay home to raise children. If a girl was going to college, counselors were likely to encourage her to enter traditionally feminine careers, such as teaching, nursing, and social work.

School textbooks, too, have promoted sexual stereotypes. They have long conveyed the impression that males are smarter and more important than females. There are more stories about boys than girls and more biographies of men than of women. Clever boys are presented more often than clever girls. Moreover, girls are led to believe that they are not as proficient in mathematics as boys. Sometimes girls are directly discouraged from taking advanced math or pursuing math as a career. If a gifted female student has built a robot, her achievement may be trivialized with questions like "Did you build it to do housework?" More subtly, when they find young men engaging in more social, joking, and nonacademic conversations in the high school mathematics classroom, young women get the hint that this is the environment where only men belong. Since math is stereotyped as a male domain, boys benefit more than girls from math classes. They are spoken to more, are called on more, and receive more corrective feedback, social interaction, individual instruction, praise, and encouragement. They learn more than what is in the textbook. In contrast, girls are mostly consigned to learning by rote the math in the text, with very little exposure to extracurricular math and science. It is no surprise that girls end up scoring lower on standardized math tests, though they may receive better grades on classroom exams—which largely require memorization of course material (Kimball, 1989).

The structure of the school has also helped to reinforce traditional stereotypes of male superiority. In virtually all the elementary and secondary schools, men hold positions of authority (as coordinators, principals, and superintendents), and women are in positions of subservience (as teachers and aides). In such a male-dominant atmosphere, children are led to believe that women are subordinate and need the leadership of men. As Laurel Richardson (1988) observes, "Children learn that although their teacher, usually a female, is in charge of the room, the school is run by a male without whose strength she could not cope; the principal's office is where the incorrigibles are sent."

This notion about males being strong and females being weak also exists among boys' peer groups. Before adolescence, boys like to play ball together, excluding girls. Girls learn about male exclusivity and contempt when they are told by boys that "ball games are for boys only because 'girls aren't hardly made' for ball games" (Bernard, 1981). During adolescence, the peer group tends to pressure boys to prove their manhood and sexual prowess with girls and girls to prove their popularity with boys. As a result, young men may take advantage of women, sometimes to the extent of committing date rape without seeing it as rape.

The Mass Media Of all the sources of sexual stereotypes, the mass media—television, newspapers, magazines, radio—are the most pervasive. In such traditional magazines as *Good Housekeeping* and *Family Circle,* there has, until recently, been the tendency to talk down to women as if they were children needing endless reiterations of basics. Today, they are more sophisticated, but they still tend to define the female role in terms of homemaking and motherhood, and to offer numerous beauty tips to help attract men or please husbands. In less traditional magazines, such as *New Woman* and *Working Woman,* we still can see the perpetuation of sexual stereotypes. Although women are portrayed working outside the home, they are nonetheless presented as responsible for housework and children—no protest being raised that women, much more often than men, are expected to perform two jobs simultaneous-

ly. If such magazines go all out to demolish the sexual stereotypes, they may lose many of their readers to the more traditional women's magazines. Today, the traditional "seven sisters"—*Better Homes and Gardens, Family Circle, Woman's Day, McCall's, Ladies' Home Journal, Good Housekeeping,* and *Redbook*—continue to surpass considerably in readership the new women's magazines, such as *Working Woman, Savvy,* and *Working Mother.* The traditional magazines have a combined circulation of 37 million, compared with only 3 million for the new magazines (Conant, 1987; Carmody, 1990; Peirce, 1990).

These women's magazines are not alone in perpetuating sexual stereotypes. In popular Sunday comics, too, women are presented as more passive and less important than men. In children's picture

The mass media have been a pervasive source of sexual stereotypes. How does Madonna fit into the stereotypes that the media present of women in our society?

books, females, whether as humans, ducks, or frogs, are likely to be portrayed as performing the "feminine" role of pleasing and serving males (Brabant and Mooney, 1986; Williams et al., 1987).

Television commercials also present women as sex objects and dedicated housewives. Until recently, young sexy women were shown admiring an old cigar smoker who used an air freshener. Housewives were shown in ecstasy over their shiny waxed floors or the sparkling cleanliness of their dishes. Women were shown stricken with guilt for not using the right detergent to get rid of their husbands' "ring around the collar." Prime-time television programs also reinforce traditional gender roles and inequalities. Over the past 15 years before 1982, TV researcher George Gerbner analyzed 1600 prime-time programs, including more than 15,000 characters. He concluded that women were generally typecast as either lovers or mothers. They were mostly portrayed as weak, passive sidekicks to powerful, effective men (Waters, 1982). A content analysis of the television portrayals of nurses and doctors for a period of 30 years shows that 99 percent of the nurses are females and 95 percent of the doctors are males. Most of these TV nurses are presented not only as subservient to male physicians but also as sex objects. By contrast, the male doctors are mostly portrayed as highly competent professionals (Kalisch and Kalisch, 1984).

Today, the mass. media are more likely to present women as successful, being able to support themselves and their families, but the traditional stereotypes of women still come across. On television and in movies, women are still too often depicted as sex objects, even when they are shown as successful professionals. In 1990 the National Commission on Working Women analyzed 80 TV series and 555 characters, and found a preponderance of women working as secretaries and homemakers and a world of young, beautiful, and scantily dressed women. In men's as well as general-interest magazines, women are told that they can be successful in the workplace, but they are also reminded that they should be provocative, sexy, and dependent. They are told that they can "have it all, do it all, and be it all," but that they should wear the right clothes and the right makeup because "looks are crucial." In advertisements, women are portrayed as being in charge of their own lives, but they are shown "literally being carried by men, leaning on men, being helped down from a height of two feet, or figuratively being carried away by emotion" (Sidel, 1990).

The Learning Process   We may know much about what a socializing agent teaches, but we still have to know how the child learns the gender role in the first place. As we saw in Chapter 5 (Socialization), there are various explanations of how such learning occurs. According to the psychoanalytic theory, the child turns from unacceptable sexual love of the opposite-sex parent to identification with the same-sex parent—thus taking on an appropriate gender role. While psychoanalysts see the source of gender-role development—libido, or sexual love—as biologically determined, social learning theorists point to such environmental factors as conditioning and imitation. Children are rewarded for behaving in ways that parents and others consider appropriate for their gender—and punished for not doing so, so they eventually conform to their society's gender roles. A little boy, for example, learns to hide his fears or pain because he has been praised for being brave and scolded for crying. Children also learn by imitation. They tend to imitate their same-sex parent and other adult models because these adults are powerful, nurturant, and able to reward or punish them. Through reinforcement and imitation, children engage in certain gender-typed activities, which lead to the development of a stable gender identity—"I do girl things. Therefore I must be a girl."

According to cognitive development theory, however, gender identity is the cause rather than the product of gender-role learning. As Lawrence Kohlberg (1966) explains, children first learn to identify themselves as a male or female from what they observe and what they are told. Then they seek to act and feel like one: "I am a boy, therefore I want to do boy things." Thus, children are not passive objects in the acquisition of gender roles. They are active actors developing their gender identities and performing their gender roles. How clear their identities are and how well they perform their gender roles depend significantly on their cognitive skills or the levels of their cognitive development.

Apparently, all the processes discussed here—identification, conditioning, imitation, and cognition—play a part in the learning of gender roles. They are also related to each other. Children cannot rely on their cognition alone to distinguish what is masculine from what is feminine. They have to depend on their parents to serve as models of masculinity and femininity. In serving as such models, the parents are likely to reinforce specific gender-typed behavior ("Boys don't play with dolls" or "See how nicely Janie plays"). Identification with the same-sex parent may also result from, as well as influence, the parents' tendency to reinforce certain gender-typed behavior (Basow, 1986).

FUNCTIONAL NECESSITY OR EXPLOITATION?

According to the functionalist perspective, it is functional for society to assign different tasks to men and women. This division of labor was originally based on the physical differences between the sexes. In primitive hunting-gathering societies, men were more likely to roam far from home to hunt animals because men were larger and stronger, and women were more likely to stay near home base to gather plant foods, cook, and take care of children because only women could become pregnant, bear and nurse babies. Today, muscle power is not as important as brain and machine power. Contraceptives, baby formula, child-care centers, and convenience foods further weaken the constraints that the childbearing role places on women. Yet traditional gender roles persist.

The reason for this persistence, functionalists assume, is that these roles continue to be functional to modern societies. How? Talcott Parsons and Robert Bales (1953) argued that two basic roles must be fulfilled in a group: the **instrumental role** of getting things done and the **expressive role** of holding the group together, taking care of the personal relationships. In the modern family, the instrumental role is fulfilled by making money; playing this role well requires competence, assertiveness, dominance. The expressive role requires offering love and affection, and it is best filled by someone warm, emotional, nonassertive. When men are socialized to have the traits appropriate for the instrumental role and women are socialized to have the traits suitable for the expressive role, then the family is likely to function smoothly. Each person fits into a part, and the parts fit together.

The role differentiation may have worked well for many traditional families, and especially for those in traditional third-world societies, as suggested by their lower rates of divorce. But functionalists may have exaggerated the role differentiation because women do perform the instrumental role to a large degree. Every day American housewives spend many hours on cooking, dishwashing, housecleaning, laundering, shopping, and other instrumental tasks. Even in many highly sex-segregated preliterate societies,

women perform a significant instrumental role. As Joel Aronoff and William Crano's (1975) research shows, in nearly half the preindustrial societies women contributed at least 40 percent of their societies' food supply. In practically all gathering-hunting societies, only women carry out the instrumental task of gathering food, without which the family would risk starvation because male hunters often come home empty-handed (Tanner, 1983). If women's contributions are so important to the family and society, why does gender inequality exist?

Conflict theory suggests that gender inequality arose not because it was functional, but because men were able to exploit women. According to the classic Marxist view, gender inequality is part of the larger economic stratification. By restricting women to childbearing and household chores, men ensured their freedom to go out to acquire property and amass wealth. They also used their power over women to obtain heirs and thus guarantee their continued hold on their economic power. Moreover, men have directly exploited women by getting them to do much work with little or no pay. Thus, housewives are not paid for doing housework and child care, which would cost about half of most husbands' income if those services were purchased from others. Gainfully employed wives also do most of the housework and child care, although they work as much as their husbands outside the home. In addition, as we have seen, they are usually paid less than men for their work outside the home (Hochschild 1989; Shellenbarger, 1991).

Some conflict theorists give greater weight to sexual, rather than economic, exploitation as the source of gender inequality. Randall Collins (1975) argues that "the fundamental motive is the desire for sexual gratification, rather than for labor per se; men have appropriated women primarily for their beds rather than their kitchens and fields, although they could certainly be pressed into service in the daytime too." More recently, according to some feminists, so-called surrogate motherhood has emerged as the ultimate exploitation of women by men because it turns women into mere breeding machines. Although other feminists defend the rights of women to sell their services as surrogate mothers, they do see the men and women who *arrange* surrogacies (for fees of at least $10,000 each) as "the pimps" of the surrogacy movement (Peterson, 1987). Conflict theorists would view surrogate motherhood as a modern way of shoring up gender inequality.

According to some feminists, so called surrogate moth-erhood has emerged as the ultimate exploitation of women by men because it turns women into mere breeding machines. In the photo, a man claims "Baby M" after the 1987 surrogate mother trial that awarded him and his wife custody of the baby they had paid the surrogate mother $10,000 to have with his sperm.

QUESTIONS FOR DISCUSSION AND REVIEW

1. How do females differ biologically from males?
2. Can biological differences alone explain the differ-ent and unequal statuses of women?
3. What contributions do the family, schools, peer groups, and the mass media make to sexual stereo-types?
4. How do girls and boys learn gender roles through the processes of identification, conditioning, imita-tion, and cognition?
5. According to functionalist and conflict theories, what is the source of gender inequality?

Age and Ageism

Recently, sociologist Pat Moore described an unusual and dramatic experiment. For three years, she repeat-edly put on elaborate makeup, gray wig, and dark wardrobe to make herself look like a woman in her eighties. In that disguise, she wandered city streets all over the United States and Canada. She was rou-tinely treated rudely, disrespectfully called "sweetie," "honey," or "dearie," shortchanged by cashiers, bumped into on the street by fast-moving pedestri-ans, and cut ahead of in lines by people who appar-ently assumed she wasn't paying attention. Later, she removed her disguise and, as an attractive young woman, returned to the places she had been. At stores where she had been treated rudely, short-changed, or ignored as a "little old lady," she was treated much better as a young woman, even though she encountered the same salespeople and made the same requests (Dychtwald, 1989).

Prejudice and discrimination against older peo-ple are common in our society. They do not come from ordinary people only, as suggested in the social experiment just described. They also come from the well-educated and sophisticated. When an 82-year-old man went to visit a doctor with the complaint that his left knee was stiff and painful, the physician ex-amined it. Then he said, "Well, what do you expect? After all, it's an 82-year-old knee." The patient retort-ed, "Sure it is. But my right knee is also 82, and it's not bothering me a bit" (Dychtwald, 1989). In fact, age prejudice with its underlying stereotype of the el-derly as frail or weak, as illustrated by the doctor, has become so ingrained in many people that they are unaware of its existence. Consider the popular AT&T commercial in which the elderly woman's son calls "just to say I love you, Ma." It has won the hearts of many television viewers because they were apparent-ly touched by how sweet the son was to his mother. But they did not realize that it also implied that older people waste their time doing nothing. As one older person says about the commercial, "What do you think we do—just sit around waiting for someone to call?" (Beck, 1990a).

An awareness of how older people are treated has increased significantly in recent years. This is due to the "graying of America": the number of old peo-ple has risen sharply, and they now make up a signifi-cant part of the population. In 1900 the average num-ber of years an American infant could expect to live was only 47. Today it is 74—a dramatic increase of 27 years. From 3000 B.C. to the beginning of this centu-ry, there was a gain of about 29 years of life ex-pectancy. We have achieved in less than 90 years what was gained in the preceding 5000 years (Butler, 1984). Today, the elderly make up over 11 percent of the U.S. population, compared with only 4 percent in

1900, and the size of the elderly population is expected to continue growing. Here we will examine how aging affects people and how it changes their role in society. We will also look at the position of the elderly as targets of prejudice, discrimination, and abuse.

BIOLOGICAL EFFECTS

Sooner or later, all of us gradually lose our energies and our ability to fight off diseases. This physical process of aging is called **senescence.** Biologists have been trying to crack the mystery of why it occurs, but without much success. Some believe that we are genetically programmed to age; others point to the breakdown of the body's immunological system, cells, or endocrine and nervous systems. In any event, it is clear that senescence involves a decline in the body's functioning, increasing the vulnerability to death. It is a gradual process in which the changes come from within the individual, not from the environment. It is also both natural and universal, occurring in all older people.

Old age has many biological effects. The skin becomes wrinkled, rough, dry, and vulnerable to malignancies, bruises, and loss of hair. Because aging also causes the spinal disks to compress, most elderly people lose one to three inches in height. Another result of aging is a loss of muscular strength. More important, blood vessels harden as we age, creating circulatory problems in the brain and heart, problems that raise the incidence of stroke and heart disease among the elderly. Functioning of the kidneys shows the greatest decline with advancing age (Atchley, 1988; Levin and Levin, 1980).

Although aging has all those deteriorative effects, they do not cause disability in most of the elderly. Moreover, the speed of aging varies greatly from one individual to another. Thus, some people at age 85 look like 65 and others who are 65 look like 85. A number of factors may determine the disparities. The older look, characterized by the sagging and wrinkling of the skin, may stem from too much sun exposure in earlier years. Lack of exercise may speed up the aging process, so that those who sit in a rocking chair waiting for the Grim Reaper usually look and feel older than those who are physically active. Social isolation, powerlessness, and poor health further enhance aging. These largely social, environmental factors suggest that, if aging can be accelerated, it can also be retarded (Gelman, 1986; Begley, 1990).

PSYCHOLOGICAL EFFECTS

Aging also affects such psychological processes as sensory perceptions, psychomotor responses, memory, and personality. By the time they are 65, more than 50 percent of American men and 30 percent of American women suffer hearing losses severe enough to hinder social interaction. Visual acuity also declines with age: 87 percent of those over age 45 wear glasses, compared with only 30 percent of those under 45. Older people further tend to have slower but more accurate psychomotor responses—such as being able to type at lower speeds but with fewer errors—than young people. Moreover, short-term memory—recall of recent events for a brief time—seems to decline with age, although memory of remote events does not. Old age, however, does not inevitably lead to **senility,** which involves serious

Aging does not cause disability in most of the elderly. It also varies from one person to another. Some look younger than their age, whereas others look older. Being physically and socially active can slow down the aging process, making the elderly look younger.

memory loss, confusion, and loss of the ability to reason. Senility is an abnormal condition, not a natural result of aging (Butler, 1984). Aging does not necessarily lead to a decline in intellectual performance, either. In fact, **crystalline intelligence**—wisdom and insight into the human condition, as shown by one's skills in language, philosophy, music, or painting—continues to grow with age. Only **fluid intelligence**—ability to grasp abstract relationships as in mathematics, physics, or some other science—tends to stabilize or decline with age (Butler, 1984). With advancing age, people also tend to change from an active to a passive orientation to their environment, becoming less inclined to bend the world to their own wishes and more likely to conform and accommodate to it.

The severity and rate of these changes vary greatly, reflecting the influence of social factors. Elderly people who are well educated, and thus presumably accustomed to flexing their minds, do not experience the same loss of short-term memory as those who are not mentally active. Many people who have long had the habit of paying close attention to speech patterns retain much of their hearing ability in old age. Also, for most people, hearing and visual problems are generally inconveniences, not disabilities. Much of the decline in psychomotor and intellectual performance amounts to only a slowing down of work, not a falling off of quality. The elderly may lose some mental speed, but their accumulated experience more than compensates for the loss of quickness. Therefore, contrary to the stereotyped assumption about the aged automatically experiencing mental deterioration, many studies have shown job performance to improve with age (Atchley, 1988; Meer, 1986).

SOCIAL DEFINITIONS

Physical and psychological aging doubtless have social effects. People confined to wheelchairs may feel isolated. People with impaired hearing may find it difficult to interact with others, so that they withdraw into their private worlds. To a great extent, however, the social effects of aging are society's doing, not nature's. Although the effects of age vary greatly from individual to individual, societies tend to lump all people of a particular age together and to assign them statuses and roles according to their chronological age. The way the elderly are treated, however, varies from one society to another.

In preindustrial societies, the elderly often hold high status. They are esteemed, and they assume positions of power. By merely living to be old at a time when few survive past middle age, they earn a certain respect. Because societies change slowly, the knowledge and skills of the aged remain useful. In fact, their experience is greatly valued. They are the community's "experts." Thus, throughout Africa, growing old results in rising status and increased respect. Among the Igbo, old people are widely regarded as wise, consulted for their wisdom, and accorded great respect. The male Bantu elder is known as "the Father of His People" and revered as such. In Samoa, too, old age is considered "the best time of life," and the elderly are highly respected. Similar respect for older people has also been observed in various other countries, from Thailand to rural Mexico (Cowgill, 1974).

In many societies, however, the norm changed when industrialization came. The elderly lost their previous role and status. No longer were they the storehouses of a community's knowledge or the guardians of its traditions, because the knowledge important to the community was changing and traditions were losing their hold. According to modernization theorists, the elderly lose status in modern societies because their skills become obsolete. In fact, the elderly's loss of status can be found not only in most of the industrialized countries but also in rural areas that have been touched by modernization. In a remote community in the Nepal Himalayas, for example, the elderly are unhappy with their lot, wishing that they were dead, complaining that their children have abandoned them, and trying to drown their sorrows in home-brewed liquor every day. The reason is that many of their young men have gone to India to work on construction projects and brought back ideas and attitudes that have no room for the traditional value of filial devotion (Goldstein and Beall, 1982; Gilleard and Gurkan, 1987).

Modernization does not always have such adverse effects on the elderly, though. Faced with an extremely high level of industrialization, Japan nonetheless continues to embrace its long-standing tradition of respect for old people. This tradition is derived from the Confucian principle of filial duty, which requires children to repay their parents a debt of gratitude for bringing them up. It is further supported by a sharply inegalitarian social structure, which requires inferiors, like servants, students, and children, to respect superiors, like masters, teachers, and parents (Palmore and Maeda, 1985). Nevertheless, the case of Japan is only an exception to the rule that modernization reduces the elderly's status.

In contrast to Japan, the United States is founded on the ideology of equality and individualism. With egalitarianism opposing the traditional inequality between old and young, elderly Americans began to lose their privileged status when independence was declared in 1776. Individualism also helped loosen the obligations between young and old (Fischer, 1977). Assisted by this ideological background, extreme industrialization has decisively brought down the status of elderly Americans. Today, it sometimes seems as if we expected the elderly to do nothing but wait to die. There is no prestige attached to being old; it is generally seen as a handicap. This is why older people tend to lie about their age. As census takers often find, 55-year-old women suddenly become 45, or 75-year-old men are 65 again (Levin and Levin, 1980). The elderly are frequently imprisoned in a **roleless role**—assigned no role in society's division of labor. In fact, mandatory retirement laws have traditionally forced them out of the job market after age 65—now, after 70. It is also very difficult for them to get new jobs again. Little if any value is placed on the elderly's experience. It is often considered irrelevant to the present world.

In short, contemporary American society has not aided the elderly to deal with the biological and psychological effects of aging. Instead it has augmented these effects by defining the aged as people on the fringes of life, as less capable than others of contributing to the work of society. In our future postindustrial society, though, older people will probably receive a higher status, because there will be a wider range of highly valued roles, especially volunteer and leisure roles, that they can occupy (H. Cox, 1990).

Prejudice and Discrimination

Some sociologists believe that it is more accurate to talk of the aged as a minority. Like minority groups, they face prejudice and discrimination, which, by analogy to racism and sexism, is called **ageism.** Like race and gender, age is an ascribed status, over which the individual has no control. And, like race and gender, age may be used as the basis for judging and reacting to people, whatever their individual characteristics.

Prejudice against the elderly is evident in the popular beliefs that old people are set in their ways, old-fashioned, forgetful, or likely to doze in a rocking chair. Some of these ageist beliefs are expressed in jokes such as "Old college presidents never die; they just lose their faculties." Prejudice can further be found in mass communication: in prime-time television shows, the aged tend to be depicted as evil, unsuccessful, and unhappy. Stereotypes about the aged being accident prone, rigid, dogmatic, and unproductive are often used to justify firing older workers, pressuring them to retire, or refusing to hire them. This is ironic because, as has been suggested, many studies have shown job performance to improve with age (Levin and Levin, 1980; Meer, 1986).

Discrimination against the aged can be seen in mandatory retirement laws, substandard nursing homes, and domestic neglect and abuse of elders. Even well-intentioned people may unconsciously practice discrimination by patronizing the elderly, treating them like children. This often comes across in the "baby talk" directed to the elderly. As the famous psychologist B. F. Skinner (1983) observed from his experience as a 79 year old: "Beware of those who are trying to be helpful and too readily flatter you. Second childishness brings you back within range of those kindergarten teachers who exclaim, 'But *that* is very *good!*' Except that now, instead of saying, 'My, you are really growing up!' they will say, 'You are not really getting old!'" In fact, doctors often remark that "when they get old, we have to treat them like children." In a recent study, five physicians were audiotaped when interviewing eight patients each. Half the patients were 45 or younger and the other half 65 or older. In analyzing the tapes, the researchers found that the physicians were less egalitarian, patient, engaged, and respectful with their older patients. These elderly patients were much less successful than the younger ones in getting the doctors to answer their questions and address their own concerns (Schanback, 1987).

Elder Abuse

Although most older people are capable of taking care of themselves, a significant minority of them have difficulty doing so. Today, about 20 percent (6 million) of the elderly require long-term care. Some of these live in nursing homes, but the vast majority live at home, most often being cared for by their daughters.

Helping aging parents is for the most part a highly stressful job. It is particularly hard on 40 to 50 percent of the daughters who work outside the home and are still raising children of their own. Consider the case of Sandy Berman, a 47-year-old school-teacher. One day she discovered that her parents, ages 83 and 74, had been living with trash in their home for almost a year. She convinced them to move closer to where she lived. Her father had become for-getful, and her mother could not find her way from the bedroom to the bathroom. For months, Berman called them every morning before going to work, and stopped by to see them every afternoon. She worried that she was neglecting her husband and son. Conse-quently, she lost 30 pounds and had fantasies of run-ning away. Finally, her father died, and she put her mother in a board-and-care home and enrolled her in an adult day-care center. Today, she visits her twice a month, and calls once a week, but she still worries that she might not be doing the right thing for her mother (Beck, 1990). Many other women find that the trap between child care and elder care prevents them from working outside the home. Though hav-ing been on the "mommy track," they have assumed that they could get back to their careers, but now they find themselves on an even longer "daughter track." Because the elderly population continues to get larger and older, chronic and disabling conditions will become more common, so that many more daughters will care for aged parents. A government study has estimated that the average American woman will spend 17 years raising children and 18 years caring for aged parents (Beck, 1990b).

Is the stress that comes from elder care likely to cause elder abuse? The answer is no. Most of the stressed caregivers do not abuse their elders, and most abusers do not suffer from stress because they do not spend long hours caring for their aged rela-tives. Elder abusers tend to be severely troubled indi-viduals with histories of problems, such as alco-holism, drug addiction, antisocial behavior, and emo-tional instability. Contrary to popular belief, however, elder abuse is not the same as child abuse. It rarely takes the form of physical abuse. Instead, it often involves financial exploitation because the abusers—who tend to be economically dependent on their aged relatives—are chronically beset with money problems (Pillemer and Finkelhor, 1989). Most caregivers are free from those personal and fi-nancial problems. Why, then, don't they resort to elder abuse when they are overburdened with the stress of taking care of their parents? A clue can be found in the fact that three-fourths of the caregivers are daughters. Women seem to have been socialized to feel closer to their parents and to take family re-sponsibilities more seriously than men. As caregivers, they "see their efforts as a chance to repay the time and care their parents gave them—a chance to say, again, *I love you*, before it's too late" (Beck, 1990b).

QUESTIONS FOR DISCUSSION AND REVIEW
1. Why does crystalline intelligence grow with age while fluid intelligence stabilizes or declines?
2. How does the biological process of aging differ from changes caused by age norms and stratifica-tion?
3. Why do many sociologists observe that the elderly are trapped in a "roleless role"?
4. What beliefs make up the ideology of ageism, and why do they support the view that the elderly are members of a minority group?
5. What causes elder abuse?

CHAPTER REVIEW
1. *What are the traditional gender roles of American men and women?* Men are expected to be breadwinners, aggressive, and ambitious. Women are expected to be homemakers, passive, and dependent. Consequently, the sexes tend to behave differently. *What is sexism?* It involves prejudice and discrimina-tion against women, based on the belief that women are inferior to men.

2. *Do women today match men in educational attainment?* No. Men still outnumber women in more lucrative majors and in graduate and profession-al schools, though the educational gap has narrowed. *Have women in the workplace achieved equality with men?* No. Although more than half the women are in the work force, they tend to hold lower-status jobs and to be paid less than men. *How have Ameri-can women fared in politics?* Better than before. But

they are still far from achieving political parity with men. *What is the impact of sexism on women in religion?* Women are accorded low status even though they are ideal for running religious organizations. *How does sexism in sports influence women and girls?* Women tend to lose to men top management and coaching jobs in women's athletic programs. Women tend to feel unfeminine if they participate in so-called men's sports. Young girls also avoid "boy" sports. No matter what sport women choose, sex bias discounts their athletic abilities.

3. *Do biological differences make women inferior to men?* No. In some ways women seem biologically superior and in other ways inferior. Men do tend to be bigger and stronger, which may give them an edge in establishing dominance over women. *What kind of influence does culture have over gender-role differences and inequalities?* It defines what the gender differences should be, so that the specifics of gender roles vary from society to society. *How do we learn our gender roles?* Through socialization by families, schools, peer groups, and the mass media. *What is the process by which children learn gender roles?* Identification, conditioning, imitation, and cognition have each been proposed as the key process by which this learning occurs.

4. *According to functionalists, why are gender roles still functional in industrial societies?* With men playing the instrumental role and women the expressive role, the family's smooth functioning can be ensured. *How do conflict theorists explain gender inequality?* It stems from economic or sexual exploitation of women.

5. *What are the biological and psychological effects of aging?* With age, we become more vulnerable to disease and stress. There are many more specific changes that typically accompany old age—from wrinkled skin to declining visual acuity and slowing of psychomotor responses. These changes are usually inconveniences, not disabilities, and the rate of change varies from person to person.

6. *How does society influence aging?* It tends to magnify the biological and psychological effects of aging and underestimate individual differences in rates of aging. Society defines norms for people according to their chronological age groups. The elder-

ly are usually accorded high status in preindustrial societies but lower status in industrial societies.

7. *What is ageism?* It is prejudice and discrimination against the elderly. *Does caregiver stress often lead to elder abuse?* No. Elder abuse is likely to result from the caregiver's financial dependence and emotional problems rather than a stressful situation.

KEY TERMS

Ageism Prejudice and discrimination against people because of their age (p. 217).

Chromosomes The materials in a cell that transmit hereditary traits to the carrier from his or her parents (p. 206).

Crystalline intelligence Wisdom and insight into the human condition, as shown by one's skills in philosophy, language, music, or painting (p. 216).

Expressive role Role that requires taking care of personal relationships (p. 213).

Fluid intelligence Ability to comprehend abstract relationships, as in mathematics, physics, or some other science (p. 216).

Gender role The pattern of attitudes and behaviors that a society expects of its members because of their being male or female (p. 198).

Hormones Chemical substances that stimulate or inhibit vital biological processes (p. 207).

Instrumental role Role that requires performing a task (p. 213).

Roleless role Being assigned no role in society's division of labor, a predicament of the elderly in industrial society (p. 207).

Senescence The natural physical process of aging (p. 215).

Senility An abnormal condition characterized by serious memory loss, confusion, and loss of the ability to reason; not a natural result of aging (p. 215).

Sexism Prejudice and discrimination based on the victim's gender (p. 199).

Women's ghettos Traditionally female low-paying occupations that are subordinate to positions held by men (p. 202).

SUGGESTED READINGS

Dychtwald, Ken. 1989. *Age Wave: The Challenges and Opportunities of an Aging America.* Los Angeles: Jeremy Tarcher, Inc. An upbeat view of aging in the United States, with numerous interesting examples and research data.

Faludi, Susan. 1991. *Backlash: The Undeclared War Against American Women.* New York: Crown. Showing how the movies, television, journalists, and politicians blame the feminist movement for "every woe besetting women, from mental depression to meager savings accounts, from teenage suicides to eating disorders to bad complexions."

French, Marilyn. 1992. *The War Against Women.* New York: Summit Books. A hard-hitting analysis of how patriarchal institutions, culture, and men are involved in dominating, exploiting, or abusing women.

Hochschild, Arlie. 1989. *Second Shift: Working Parents and the Revolution at Home.* New York: Viking. A well-written, compassionate account of how working mothers do most of the housework.

Sidel, Ruth. 1990. *On Her Own: Growing Up in the Shadow of the American Dream.* New York: Viking. An insightful analysis of how young women deal with the opportunities opened up by the women's movement.

10

THE FAMILY

MYTHS AND REALITIES

Myth: Thanks to the sexual revolution, husbands and wives in most of the two-career families do about the same amount of housework.

Reality: *In an average two-career family, the husband contributes only 11 hours per week to housework, but the wife puts in 51 hours.*

Myth: The traditional American family, which consists of a breadwinner father and a homemaker mother, has been around for hundreds of years. Its existence can be traced all the way to the colonial period.

Reality: *On the farms of colonial America, the family was, in effect, a two-career family, with the wife working side by side with her husband. Only toward the end of the last century, when industrialization was in full swing, did the wife lose her status as her husband's economic partner and acquire the subordinate position as homemaker.*

Myth: Male homosexual experience is quite rare. No more than 10 percent of American men have had some sexual experience with another male during their teens or adult years.

Reality: *The most conservative estimate from a Kinsey Institute review of various studies is that at least 25 percent of American men have had a homosexual experience. The majority of these men, however, think of themselves as heterosexual and mostly or even entirely engage in heterosexuality throughout the rest of their lives.*

Myth: The popularity of romantic love in the United States causes young people to choose their mates irrationally.

Reality: *American youth do not irrationally fall in love with undesirable characters. Most make sound choices, using their heads more than their hearts in choosing whom to love.*

Myth: There is no difference between dating and marriage in the choice of mates. In both cases people are equally likely to choose someone close to their own level of attractiveness.

Reality: *The similarity in attractiveness is greater among married couples than dates. In marriage people usually choose someone whose looks match theirs, but this is less true in dating.*

Myth: Given the high divorce rate in the United States, it is no wonder that many Americans are unhappy with their marriages.

Reality: *The overwhelming majority of Americans say they are "very happy" or "pretty happy" with their marriages. Married couples are even much more likely than single people to say that they are happy about love, sense of recognition, personal growth, or job satisfaction.*

Myth: High divorce rates in the United States means that fewer people want to get married.

Reality: *Despite high divorce rates, marriage remains popular. The United State has higher marriage rates than do Japan, the Philippines, and other countries that have lower divorce rates.*

Myth: Most of the single mothers in the United States are either never-married teenagers who

223

go on welfare or older single-career women like the television character Murphy Brown deciding to have babies before it is too late.
Reality: *The majority of single mothers are women who have been divorced, separated, widowed, or abandoned by their husbands.*
Myth: The absence of a father in many female-headed homes causes the children to have a larger share of such problems as poor school work, truancy, and delinquency.
Reality: *The problems that the children from female-headed homes have do not result directly from the absence of the father, but from factors that can also exist in two-parent homes, such as low income, poor living conditions, and lack of parental supervision.*

riving home from work, Janice Edwards, a 27-year-old single mother, tells the journalist who interviews her how she felt when her husband left her five years ago, just after their second child was born: "I thought we'd fall apart with no man there. There was a time I had no money for formula, no gas, no water, no electricity, and I didn't know what in the world we would do." But she has managed for all those years to work at least two jobs at a time to keep her family going. She has mostly had an office job during the day and another job at Kmart in the evening. At one point, she has even delivered newspapers from 2 to 5 in the morning. She says proudly, "I'm going to work 17 jobs if I have to, but I'm going to take care of my children. I'm not going to listen to people who tell me single mothers are bad. I'm not single by choice; I'm single by force, and I'm not going to listen to those negative things." Like many single mothers, Ms. Edwards is indeed doing reasonably well for her family (Lewin, 1992a).

The traditional image of the average American family shows Mom tending her two kids and a house in the suburb while Dad drives off to work. In fact, such a family is relatively rare today. Meanwhile, new forms of the family unit, such as single-parent families like the one just described, have become increasingly common. In this chapter, we will discuss various forms of family. But first we will analyze the relationship between the family and society, sex and abortion, and marriage and divorce.

The Family and Society

The family is an essential and universal institution. However, throughout time and around the world, as societies have varied, so too has the relative impor-

tance of the family's various functions. In this section, we look at these functions and how the American ideal of the family has emerged.

FUNCTIONS OF THE FAMILY

We can see from the functionalist perspective that the family in virtually all societies serves the same basic functions. Although the importance of each function varies from one society to another, the family provides for sexual regulation, reproduction, socialization, economic cooperation, and emotional security.

Sexual Regulation   No society advocates total sexual freedom. Although societies have very different sexual norms, all impose some control on who may have sex with whom. Even societies that encourage premarital and extramarital sex restrict and channel these activities so that they reinforce the social order. The Trobrianders of the South Pacific, for example, use premarital sex to determine whether a girl is fertile and to prepare adolescents for marriage. Traditional Eskimo society condones extramarital sex, but under conditions that do not disrupt family stability: as a gesture of hospitality, husbands offer their wives to overnight guests.

Traditionally, Western sexual norms have been relatively restrictive, demanding that people engage in sex only with their spouses. Tying sex to marriage seems to serve several functions. First, it helps minimize sexual competition, thereby contributing to social stability. Second, it gives young people an incentive to marry. Even today, most young adults eventually feel dissatisfied with unstable, temporary sexual liaisons and find a regular, secure sexual relationship in marriage an attractive prospect. Even most of the divorced, who usually find their postmarital sex lives very pleasurable, eventually remarry because they are more interested in sex with commitment, as available in marriage. Finally, encouraging people to marry and confining sexual intercourse to those who are married tends to ensure that children will be well cared for.

Reproduction   In order to survive, a society must produce children to replace the adults and elderly who die, and practically all societies depend on the family to produce these new members. In some traditional societies, such as the Baganda of Uganda, children are considered so important that a marriage must be dissolved if the wife turns out to be barren. In many industrialized nations like the United States, families with children are rewarded with tax exemptions, and sexual acts that cannot produce pregnancy, such as homosexuality and anal intercourse, are condemned as perversions.

Socialization   To replace its dead members, a society needs not just biological reproduction but also "sociological reproduction." It needs, in other words, to transmit its values to the new generation, to socialize them. As we saw in Chapter 5 (Socialization), the family is the most important agent of socialization. Because parents are likely to be deeply interested in their own children, they are generally more effective socializing agents than other adults.

Economic Cooperation   Besides socialization, children also need physical care—food, clothing, and shelter. Fulfilling these needs is the core of the family's economic function, and it can facilitate effective socialization. Generally, however, the family's economic role goes beyond care for children and embraces the whole family. Family members cooperate as an economic unit. Each person's economic fate rises and falls with that of the family as a whole.

Emotional Security   Finally, the family is the center of emotional life. As we saw in Chapter 5 (Socialization), the relationships we form in our families as children may shape our personalities and create hard-to-break patterns for all our relationships. Throughout life, the family is the most important source of primary relationships, the most likely place for us to turn to when we need comfort or reassurance.

Variations   At various times and places, some of these functions have been more important than others. In some societies in the past, the family was the center of educational, religious, political, economic, and recreational activities. Children received all their education from their parents. Religious practices were an integral part of family life. The head of the family assumed authority for allocating chores and settling disputes. The whole family pitched in to work on their farm or to make tools and other prod-

In preindustrial societies, families usually operate as the center of diverse activities. Children receive their education and religious training from parents, and family members work together to earn a living and entertain one another.

ucts in their home. Leisure activities were typically a family affair, with members entertaining one another.

Today, such all-embracing families still exist, especially in more traditional societies, but they are not typical of industrialized societies. Instead, specialized institutions have taken on a big share of the family's functions—a process called **institutional differentiation.** The schools educate children, and the media entertain us all. Whereas once the whole family usually worked together to secure a livelihood, people now go outside the home to earn wages to support other family members. The family has ceased to be an economic unit that produces goods and services. At most it is a unit of consumption. Even its role in producing economic security has been reduced, as the government's role in aiding the poor and providing help in time of crisis has increased.

Although business, schools, churches, and government have taken over a large share of many of the family's functions, these impersonal organizations cannot provide intimate emotional support. This function still falls almost entirely on the family. A large extended family provides diffuse emotional security, in which the married couple expects companionship not only from each other but also from many other relatives. In the nuclear family, relations between husband and wife become more intense and exclusive. Their emotional importance is accentuated in societies such as the United States, which emphasizes individualism and privacy. Often, we view the world outside as a mass of strangers. We feel lonely, isolated, and alienated from that world, and see the family as a refuge. The emotional satisfactions of the family have become its main bond, its main reason for being.

THE CONFLICT PERSPECTIVE

We have just looked at the family from the functionalist perspective. Since it assumes that the family ensures the survival of society, it emphasizes only the positive functions of the family. But family life also has a dark side, which we can see through the conflict perspective.

First of all, the family, because of the strong feelings it generates, can be a powerful source of not just love and care but also pain and conflict. As a major study concludes, the family is "the most violent institution in American society except the military,

and only then in time of war" (Straus et al., 1988). The single most frequent type of murder involves family members—we are more likely to die at the hands of a relative than a stranger (see Chapter 6: Deviance and Control). In most families, there can be found instances of conflict and violence, such as anger, bitter feelings, hatred, physical punishment of children, or pokes and slaps of husbands and wives. In fact, the family is one of the few groups in society empowered by law and tradition to hit its members. It is, for example, legal for parents to spank their children as a form of punishment. Moreover, many husbands who strike their wives to keep them in line are not arrested, prosecuted, or imprisoned (Skolnick, 1987). Domestic violence is indeed a serious problem.

From the conflict perspective, we can also see the family as a tool for men's exploitation of women. Homemakers and mothers have greatly contributed to the rise and maintenance of capitalism with such forms of labor as reproduction and care of children, food preparation, daily health care, and emotional support. Without this "household production," men would not have been free to go out working. Yet, while men are paid for their jobs outside the home, women do not get any wages for their work in the home. Ironically, women's household work is on the average worth more than men's paid employment. If a woman were paid for services as mother and homemaker according to the wage scale for chauffeurs, baby-sitters, cooks, and therapists, she would earn over $40,000—more than most men make in a year (Strong and DeVault, 1989). By demeaning women's housework, however, the family serves the interests of male domination. A century ago, Karl Marx's collaborator, Friedrich Engels (1884), observed that the family is an arena of class conflict where "the well-being and development of one group are attained by the misery and repression of the other." That observation is still relevant today. In the United States, although more than half of the married women are now gainfully employed, they still do most of the housework. Marriage benefits men more than women in another way. According to a recent study, married men from ages 45 to 64 are half as likely to die within 10 years as men who live alone or with somebody other than a wife. But this lifesaving advantage of marriage does not accrue to married women, whose likelihood of death is about the same as that of their unmarried sisters (Angier, 1990b).

In colonial America, the wife was typically an essential economic partner with her husband. If they had a craft, she would work with her husband as a skilled craftsperson. In the case of the husband being a weaver, the wife would shear the sheep and spin and dye the yarn.

THE AMERICAN EXPERIENCE

Both functionalist and conflict analyses have raised some questions about the American family: Is our nuclear family a new phenomenon, brought to us by industrialization? Has the American woman's domestic work always been downgraded? How has the provision of emotional support become the single most important function of the family? What other changes have occurred in the American family? The answers can be found in research on the history of the American family.

Before our country became industrialized, our nuclear family had in the preindustrial seventeenth and eighteenth centuries contained a nuclear family of husband, wife, and children, with no other relatives. One reason is that few people lived long enough to form an extended, three-generation family. Another reason is that impartible inheritance practices—which allow for only one heir to inherit all the property—forced sons who did not inherit the farm to leave and set up their own households (Cherlin, 1983).

On the farms of colonial America, men, women, and children helped produce the family's livelihood.

The wife was typically an essential economic partner to the husband. If her husband was a farmer, she would run the household; make the clothes; raise cows, pigs, and poultry; tend a garden; and sell milk, vegetables, chickens, and eggs. If the husband was a skilled craftsman, she would work with him. Thus, weavers' wives spun yarn, cutlers' wives polished metal, tailors' wives sewed buttonholes, and shoemakers' wives waxed shoes (Tilly and Scott, 1978). During the nineteenth century, the American "household ceased to be a center of production and devoted itself to child rearing instead" (Lasch, 1979). Industrialization took production out of the home. Initially husbands, wives, and children worked for wages in factories and workshops to contribute to the common family budget. But, due to the difficulty of combining paid employment with the domestic tasks imposed on them, married women tended to work for wages irregularly. As wages rose, increasing numbers of families could earn enough without the wife's paid work. Then, increasingly, the home was seen as the emotional center of life and a private refuge from the competitive public world. The woman's role became emotional and moral rather than economic. Women were expected to rear their children and comfort their husbands. This became the stereotype of a typical and ideal American family. Thus, after industrialization had been in full swing, women lost their status as their husbands' economic partners and acquired a subordinate status as housewives (Cherlin, 1983).

By the end of the last century, a decline in marriage and fertility rates and an increase in divorce, as well as the women's suffrage movement, fueled fears that the family was falling apart. Some social commentators worried that children, especially those of immigrants, were not being reared properly, and that social decline and moral decay would be the result. New groups and institutions stepped in where the family seemed to be failing. The "helping professions"—made up of teachers, social workers, doctors, psychologists—grew. Public education expanded, and the schools were forced to assume responsibilities formerly laid upon the home. As two educators wrote at that time, "Once the school had mainly to teach the elements of knowledge, now it is charged with the physical, mental, and social training of the child as well" (Lasch, 1979). Social workers and the juvenile courts took over in cases where even the schools failed. Eventually, "almost every other traditional function of the family passed out of the home and into the hands of institutions and professional providers, from the care of the sick to support of the poor, from the preparation of food to instruction in leisure activities" (Woodward, 1978).

From the functionalist point of view, these changes represent a natural, functional evolution in response to the surge of marital conflict, juvenile delinquency, and other problems faced by the family. Schools, social workers, psychologists, and government moved to help individuals when family could no longer cope.

Christopher Lasch (1979) presents a less benign conflict view of the transformation of the American family. Rather than being the result of inevitable social and economic forces, the changes reflect the outcome of capitalist exploitation:

During the first stage of the industrial revolution, capitalists took production out of the household and [into] the factory. Then they proceeded to bring the workers' skills and technical knowledge [under managerial control]. Finally, they extended their control over the worker's private life as well, as doctors, psychiatrists, teachers, child guidance experts, officers of the juvenile courts, and other specialists began to supervise child-rearing, formerly the business of the family. . . . They have made people more and more dependent on the managerial and professional classes—on the great business corporations and the state—and have thus eroded the capacity for self-help and social invention.

Throughout all the turmoil of this century, Americans by and large maintained the view that the typical and ideal family consisted of a breadwinning father and homemaking mother living with their children. Today, such a family is far from typical—only about 26 percent of American households fit this stereotype. About half of the mothers with young children are now working outside the home, while the proportions of such nontraditional households as single-parent families, unmarried couples living together, and individuals living alone have increased dramatically in the last 20 years (Busacca and Ryan, 1982; Census Bureau, 1990).

QUESTIONS FOR DISCUSSION AND REVIEW
1. What are the major social functions still performed by the institution of the family?
2. How does the conflict view of the family differ from the functionalist view, and what questions does each raise about the modern American family?
3. How have changes in the economy since colonial times led to several transformations of the family in the United States?

Sex and Abortion

Few social issues affect the American family today more powerfully than sex and abortion. As has been suggested, sex is a crucial part of virtually all marriages, and the regulation of sex contributes to the preservation and stability of the family. Abortion can also prevent the deterioration of family life for married couples and especially poor single mothers and their children. In fact, the availability of abortion results in healthier and better-adjusted children because parents can invest more in their children (Posner, 1992). But abortion can also threaten marriage by creating stress, guilt, and conflict (Strong and DeVault, 1989). Either way, abortion is obviously an important issue that we need to discuss along with sex.

COMMON SEX MYTHS

We are constantly bombarded by the mass media with movies, TV talk shows, books, and magazine articles about sex. We can even find graphic presentations of every aspect of adult sexuality in comic strips (Rubin, 1990). Nevertheless, according to a recent survey by the Kinsey Institute, most of us still do not know the birds from the bees. In the survey, a national representative sample of Americans were asked 18 questions about sex, and the majority—55 percent—could not answer 10 questions correctly (Reinisch, 1990). Their answers suggest that they believe in certain myths about sexuality. Let us discuss the most common ones.

Myth 1: Today, most Americans start having sexual intercourse for the first time at a very young age—about 13 or 14. Most studies report that most Americans have their first intercourse between the ages of 16 and 17.

Myth 2: A majority of married American men have been sexually unfaithful to their wives at least once. From a comprehensive review of many studies, the Kinsey Institute concludes that only about 37 percent of all married men have had at least one extramarital affair.

Both myths 1 and 2 seem to have originated from the mass media. Over the last decade, the media have often resorted to sensationalism by exaggerating the young age of first-timers and the prevalence of extramarital sex. It is true that young people today have their first sexual experience at a younger age than their parents did, but most are not as young as popularly believed. Similarly, more men today are sexually unfaithful to their wives than before, but most men are not.

Myth 3: Male homosexual experience is quite rare; no more than 10 percent of American men have had some sexual experience with another male during their teens or adult years. Based on a Kinsey Institute review of various studies, the most conservative estimate is that at least 25 percent of men have had a homosexual experience. Having had a same-sex experience is not unusual for men, although the majority of these men think of themselves as heterosexual and mostly or even entirely engage in heterosexuality throughout the rest of their lives. Most people fail to recognize the relative prevalence of homosexuality because they believe that their society still considers it a taboo.

Myth 4: It is usually easy to tell whether people are homosexual by their appearance or gestures. In fact, it is difficult to tell, because homosexual men can appear extremely masculine, average, or effeminate and can be football players, political leaders, truck drivers, or in any other type of occupation—just like heterosexual men. Similarly, homosexual women can be extremely feminine, average, or masculine and can have any kind of job—just like heterosexual women.

Myth 5: A woman cannot get pregnant when menstruating. It is true that the chances of pregnancy during menstruation are not as high as at other times, but pregnancy can and does happen. Sperm can live for up to 8 days in a woman's reproductive tract and may fertilize an egg if ovulation occurs about a week after her period.

Myth 6: A woman or teenage girl cannot get pregnant if the man pulls out before he comes. Withdrawal has been found *not* to be a very effective method of contraception. Even a drop of the clear fluid that sometimes forms at the tip of an aroused penis may hold enough sperm to fertilize an egg.

These last three myths are likely to come from friends, the most popular source of sex information that Americans receive when growing up.

CHANGES IN SEXUAL ATTITUDE

Today, sex is no longer the hush-hush matter it used to be. Nudity can be seen in theaters, in movies, and on television. Pornographic magazines and films are easily available. Premarital sex is widespread. Abortion is easily available. Homosexuality is becoming more open. These are the obvious consequences of the sexual revolution that swept the United States during the last two decades. The revolution has also brought about some basic changes in our sexual attitude and behavior.

First, there is more tolerance for various forms of sexual behavior. An example is the tolerance for homosexuality. As much as 47 percent of the general public believes that homosexual acts between consenting adults should be legal, although only 25 percent have had some homoerotic experience and only 2 to 4 percent are exclusively homosexual (Reinisch, 1990; Salholz, 1990a). This suggests that it is all right for others to do what we may not want to do ourselves. The same tolerance extends to premarital sex. Those who want to postpone sexual relations until they are married do not mind if their friends engage in premarital sex. As Mary Meyer, founder of the National Chastity Association for singles who, like her-

Homosexuality is no longer the hush-hush matter it used to be. It is becoming more open today. Such openness, along with the general public's greater tolerance for it, is one of the consequences of the sexual revolution that has swept our country in the last twenty years.

self, desire to preserve sex for marriage, says, "Recreational sex might work for other people. That's fine with me. I only know what works for me" (D. Johnson, 1990a). This tolerance extends to most sexual acts. As a female teenager says, "There are things I won't do, like anal sex. My last boyfriend started to do it, and it hurt. It's terrible; I made him stop. But my best friend says she likes it, and if that's what she wants, that's okay. I don't think anyone has a right to judge what people do. It's nobody's business as long as the couple both agree" (Rubin, 1990).

Second, the **double standard** that allows men to have premarital sex but condemns women for doing so is not as pervasive as it has been in the past. One indication has been the dramatic increase in women's premarital experience. Between 1965 and 1980, the percentage of college males having had premarital sex climbed from 65 to 77, a difference of only 12 percent; the percentage of college women with similar experience soared from 29 to 64—a difference of 35 percent (Robinson and Jedlicka, 1982). Moreover, more women than before expect to enjoy sex and reach orgasm. This means that there are now more women who enjoy the sexual freedom that has traditionally been "for men only." But the double standard has not disappeared completely. While women may no longer be condemned for losing their virginity before marriage, they may be condemned

for having many different sex partners. They are likely to be called "sluts." Men with the same experience, however, are called "studs," a term that connotes far more approbation than opprobrium. This obviously reflects the continuing influence of gender inequality. Teenage girls, though, have increasingly used the word "stud" sarcastically, in order to warn other girls to beware. Only among boys does the word still evoke images of masculinity and feelings of envy (Rubin, 1990).

Third, there is a fundamental change in the perceived purpose of sex. In the past, the primary motive for sex was reproduction. Today, most Americans want more than procreation from sex. They also want recreation from it. Thus, couples are now much more inclined to engage in a variety of sex acts that are aimed more at giving pleasure than at reproduction. For example, many engage in prolonged foreplay and oral sex. Others may use mechanical sex aids, attempt multiple orgasms, or engage in anal intercourse. The most remarkable is the surge in anal sex, which was nearly unheard of among heterosexuals 20 years ago. Today, 30 to 40 percent of women have tried anal intercourse at least once (Reinisch, 1990). To many unmarried Americans, however, recreational sex has become too impersonal to be satisfying. Even men who have had numerous "one-night stands" tend to speak of being left empty and wasted. Women are particularly likely to feel this way because they are less able to separate emotion from sex. As a 30-year-old woman says, "For sex to really work for me, I need to feel an emotional something. Without that, it's just another athletic activity, only not as satisfying, because when I swim or run, I feel good afterward" (Rubin, 1990).

Fourth, a new sexual morality has largely replaced the old. In the past, people were more concerned with the "location" of sex, whereas today they emphasize the quality of the partners' relationship. According to the old ethic, a sex act that occurs within marriage is moral, and a sex act that takes place outside marriage is immoral. But, according to the new ethic, regardless of whether a sex act is marital or nonmarital, it is moral if the couple care for each other and immoral if they sexually exploit each other. Consequently, what is considered right by one ethic may be regarded as wrong by the other, and vice versa. If a man and woman engage in premarital sex for love, they are immoral to the old moralist but not to the new. On the other hand, if a man forces his wife to have sex with him, he is considered a rapist by the new moralist but not by the old. There is also an increase in cohabitation—a man and woman living together outside marriage—but the cohabitors are similar to married couples in terms of sexual exclusivity. Premarital sex, too, is on the rise—more so between couples who have some kind of emotional connection with each other than between strangers. There are, of course, a few who are interested only in casual sex, rejecting emotional involvement as the prerequisite for sex. But the threat of AIDS has led many of these people to stop pursuing one-night stands (Rubin, 1990).

In changing our sexual attitude and behavior, the sexual revolution has also raised our consciousness about the larger issue of gender equality. Most people believe that women should have the same right as men to choose how to live their lives and that this includes, among other things, their right to have an abortion. Supporters of this view, however, have been encountering serious opposition. Let us then take a closer look at the continuing battle over abortion.

THE BATTLE OVER ABORTION

In 1973, the U.S. Supreme Court made its landmark decision to legalize abortion. The *Roe* v. *Wade* decision overturned a Texas state law that prohibited

abortion. More specifically, it allows women to have an abortion before the fetus is viable—able to survive outside the womb, which is about 6 months after conception, or 3 months before birth. The Supreme Court based its decision mainly on the grounds that the constitutional protection of individual rights to privacy should extend to women as well as men.

The desire for gender equality is what drives the pro-choice (for abortion rights) forces. As Kate Michelman, president of the National Abortion Rights Action League, says, "Reproductive choice is the cornerstone of women's equality—if the right to have an abortion is eroded in any way, so are all other rights—the right to work, the right to have a family, the right to dignity, the right to economic security, the right to good health" (Steinmetz et al., 1990). Pro-choice groups believe that women should be equal to men in rights and responsibilities, but they see women's reproductive and mother roles as potential barriers to full equality. They blame traditional society for having made motherhood a low-status role, subordinate to the man's traditional role of breadwinner. They also value sex as an end in itself rather than as a means to reproduction. To them, the primary purpose of sex is to give pleasure to men and women alike. Not surprisingly, they tend to use relatively effective contraceptives and have few children. If pregnancy occurs unexpectedly, they are likely to see it as a disaster—a serious threat to their individualistic aspiration or career achievement—and therefore seek an abortion.

In contrast, those who are pro-life (against abortion rights) are more traditional in regard to sexuality and gender roles. Procreation is viewed as the primary purpose of sex. Consequently, they are opposed to the use of most contraceptives, and they tend to have many children. They are also opposed to premarital sex. They consider teenagers to be financially and emotionally unprepared to become parents and believe that the availability of contraceptives encourages teen sex. To pro-life forces, men are best suited to the public world of work and women to the private world of managing homes, rearing children, and taking care of husbands (Scanzoni and Scanzoni, 1988; Strong and DeVault, 1989). By subscribing to this traditional view of gender inequality, which relegates women to an inferior status, those who are pro-life see nothing wrong in equating pregnant women with unviable fetuses—even to pre-embryos or fertilized eggs. As Congressman Henry Hyde, a leading opponent of abortion, says, "The pro-life argument assumes that fertilization creates a new member of the human family. . . . From the moment of conception forward, the principle of the sanctity of human life ought to apply. Under our Constitution, equal protection applies to every person" (Steinmetz et al., 1990). Those who are pro-life, then, consider even a fertilized egg as a person, although most—about two out of three—fertilized eggs cannot survive in the womb (Grobstein, 1988). This is why they are fiercely opposed to the Supreme Court's *Roe* v. *Wade* decision, which does not regard an unviable fetus as having the same value as a pregnant woman.

Most Americans support the legalization of abortion. But, ever since the Supreme Court legalized abortion in 1973, pro-life forces have repeatedly managed to chip away at abortion rights through various laws, federal regulations, and other judicial decisions. Today, women on welfare cannot receive Medicaid for abortions, women in the armed forces cannot get medical benefits for abortions, and many public hospitals refuse to perform abortions for fear of losing federal funds. In some states teenage girls are discouraged from seeking abortions because of laws that require them to notify their parents, even if their parents have terrorized them through physical or sexual abuses. After visiting a clinic women must wait 24 hours to have an abortion, which imposes an undue burden on many poor women who cannot afford an overnight stay in a hotel. Certain states do not allow public employees to perform abortions, nor can abortions be performed in public buildings. And, until 1993, federally funded health clinics have not even been allowed to discuss abortion. Consequently, abortion is not available to many poor, minority, and young unmarried women (Steinmetz et al., 1990). In the meantime, the abortion battle continues on both federal and state levels.

Even if illegal, abortions will continue to be performed. If women are determined to terminate a pregnancy, a law against abortion cannot stop them from having one. In Romania, for example, although abortion was banned in 1989, massive poverty led to 1.2 million abortions, as opposed to only 30,000 births (Binder, 1990). However, legal abortions are far safer than illegal ones. Most of the legal abortions in the United States (about 91 percent) are performed during the first 3 months of pregnancy, and these first-trimester abortions are statistically six times safer than childbirth (Strong and DeVault, 1989). By contrast, illegal abortions are much more dangerous because they are often performed by the pregnant woman herself, by unscrupulous doctors, or in unsanitary conditions. While abortion was banned in Romania, many women resorted to self-abortion,

which resulted in numerous maternal deaths. Such deaths are rare in the United States today, largely because abortion is legal.

Every year there are about 6 million pregnancies in the United States. Slightly more than half are unintended, and about half of these—1.5 million—are terminated by induced abortions. Even though it is legal, abortion does not necessarily leave a woman with a sense of relief. She may feel a sense of loss. And although a woman's husband or boyfriend is often either forgotten in abortion or blamed for it, he may also feel guilty, anxious, and powerless. It is fairly common for couples to split up as a result of the stress, guilt, and conflict that result from abortion (Strong and DeVault, 1989). In fact, guilt about abortion is quite common. A large majority of Americans (over 70 percent) regard abortion as a form of killing, although they also feel that every woman should decide for herself whether or not to have an abortion (Scott, 1989; Rosenblatt, 1992). Compared with men, women are far more likely to feel that abortion is morally wrong. All this suggests that most women do not choose abortion casually. Instead, they reluctantly choose abortion because of such overwhelming reasons as being too poor or too young to raise the child (Steinmetz et al., 1990). Perhaps, given the ambivalence felt by most Americans (supporting legal abortion but considering it morally wrong), both pro-choicers and pro-lifers should call off their battle over abortion and work together toward eliminating the need for abortion, namely, the causes of unwanted pregnancy. This may involve providing sex education, encouraging contraception, improving our schools, reducing poverty, and offering other programs to better the lives of the young and the poor—the casualties of the current battle over abortion (Rosenblatt, 1992)

QUESTIONS FOR DISCUSSION AND REVIEW
1. How do sex myths develop, and what can be their consequences?
2. How does the new sexual morality compare with the old?
3. How do pro-life and pro-choice supporters differ in their views?

American Marriages

The American family is by and large nuclear and monogamous. It has become increasingly egalitarian. Its cornerstone is the relationship between husband and wife. In this section we discuss how Americans prepare for marriage, how they choose their spouse, how most American couples achieve marital success, and how others fail.

PREPARING FOR MARRIAGE

Most Americans do not consciously prepare themselves for marriage or diligently seek a person to marry. Instead, they engage in activities that gradually build up a momentum that launches them into marriage. They date, they fall in love, they choose a mate, and in each of these steps they usually follow patterns set by society.

The Dating Ritual Developed largely after World War I, the American custom of dating has spread to many industrialized countries. It has also changed in the United States in the last two decades. Before the 1970s, dating was more formal. Males had to ask for a date at least several days in advance. It was usually the male who decided where to go, paid for the date, opened doors, and acted chivalrous. The couple often went to an event, such as a movie, dance, concert, or ball game.

Today, dating has become more casual. In fact, the word "date" now sounds a bit old-fashioned to many young people. Usually you do not have to call somebody and ask for a date. "Getting together" or "hanging around" is more like it. Spontaneity is the name of the game. A young man may meet a young woman at a snack bar and strike up a brief conversation with her. If he bumps into her a day or two later, he may ask if she wants to go along to the beach, to the library, or to have a hamburger. Males and females are also more likely today than in the past to hang around—get involved in a group activity—rather than pair off for some seclusive intimacy. Neither has the responsibility to ask the other out, which spares them much of the anxiety of formal dating. Getting together has also become less dominated by males. Females are more likely than before to ask a male out, to suggest activities, pay the expenses, or initiate sexual intimacies. Premarital sex has also increased, but it tends to reflect true feelings and desires rather than the need for the male to prove himself or for the female to show gratitude (Strong and DeVault, 1989; F. Cox, 1990).

The functions of dating, however, have remained pretty constant. Obviously, it is a form of entertainment. It is also a way of achieving status. By going out with a person of high prestige, an individual's own status may rise. More important, dating

For most people, dating provides opportunities for learning to get along with members of the opposite sex. It also offers opportunities for falling in love with one's future spouse.

provides people with opportunities for learning to get along with people of the opposite sex—to develop companionship, friendship, and intimacy. Finally, it offers opportunities for courting, for falling in love with one's future spouse (Winch, 1974; Laner, 1989). "Playing the field" does not lead to a higher probability of marital success, though. Those who have married their first and only sweetheart are just as likely to have an enduring and satisfying marriage as those who have married only after dating many people (Whyte, 1992).

Romantic Love If someone is asked why he or she wants to get married, the answer is usually "Because I am in love." In American and other industrialized societies, love between husband and wife is the foundation of the nuclear family. In contrast, people in many traditional societies have believed that love is too irrational to form the basis for a marriage and that intense love between husband and wife may even threaten the stability of the extended family. To them, it is more rational to marry for such pragmatic considerations as economic security and good character.

But does romantic love really cause people to choose their mates irrationally? Many studies have suggested that the irrationality of love has been greatly exaggerated. An analysis of these studies has led William Kephart and Davor Jedlicka (1988) to reach this conclusion: "Movies and television to the contrary, American youth do not habitually fall in love with unworthy or undesirable characters. In fact, [they] normally make rather sound choices." In one study, when people in love were asked, "Does your head rule your heart, or does your heart rule your head?" 60 percent answered, "The head rules." Apparently, romantic love is not the same as infatuation, which involves physical attraction to a person and a tendency to idealize him or her. Romantic love is not as emotionalized as infatuation, but it is expected to provide intrinsic satisfactions, such as happiness, closeness, personal growth, and sexual satisfaction. These differ from the extrinsic rewards offered by a pragmatic loveless marriage—rewards such as good earnings, a nice house, well-prepared meals, and overt respect.

In the United States over the last 20 years, the belief in romantic love as the basis for marriage has grown more fervent than before. In several studies in the 1960s, 1970s, and 1980s, college men and women were asked, "If a person had all the other qualities you desired, would you marry this person if you were not in love with him/her?" Today, as opposed to earlier decades, a greater proportion of young people say no (Simpson et al., 1986). Older people, however, are less romantic. They do not share the same concern for romantic love. This may explain the increasing number of prenuptial agreements, which spell out in cold detail what the couple will and will not do, share, or pay when married and if divorced. Most of the couples who negotiate such contracts in an unromantic, businesslike fashion are over age 30 or have been married before. Those who marry later than age 30 have usually acquired substantial assets, and those who remarry often have property that they want to protect for their children by prior marriages. Aside from trying to protect their money from their prospective spouses, they may hammer out such "life-style agreements" as how often they will have sex, who will take out the garbage, and who will do the dishes. The growing popularity of marriage as a business proposition may have partly resulted from the widely publicized prenuptial agreements among the rich and famous, such as Donald and Ivana Trump. But a more important reason is that nowadays many new marriages in-

volve older or divorced men and women. The over-30 couples account for about 37 percent of all new marriages, and couples with one or both partners having been previously divorced account for 45 percent (Dolan, 1990).

MARRIAGE CHOICES

While romantic love is far from blind, it also does not develop in a social vacuum. Its development depends heavily on the partners' support from others, particularly family and friends. Such support is usually available if the couple goes along with the norm of **homogamy**, which requires people to marry those with social characteristics similar to their own.

Most marriages occur within the same social class. In a classic study, 55 percent of the couples came from the same class, 40 percent were one class apart, and only 5 percent were more than one class apart (Roth and Peck, 1951). Social class is still a significant factor in mate selection today. "Most people marry within their own socioeconomic class," explain Bryan Strong and Christine DeVault (1989), "because of shared values, tastes, goals, occupations, and expectations."

Most marriages also involve members of the same race. Although there are now twice as many interracial marriages as in 1970, they constitute no more than 2 percent of all marriages (Census Bureau, 1990). Even these marriages may reflect the influence of homogamy. In most interracial marriages studied by Robert Merton (1941), the husband was an upper-class black and the wife a lower-status white. When severe racial prejudice entered into the calculation, the black husband's higher class position was balanced by the higher status of the wife's race. Thus, the couple came out socially even. A recent study also shows that blacks are generally more physically attractive than their white partners in a romantic relationship. Again, racial prejudice makes these couples socially even. The attractive blacks' status is brought down to the level of their white mates (Murstein et al., 1989).

Usually, people also choose mates of the same religious faith, although the frequency of intrafaith marriages varies from one group to another. The stronger the cohesion of the religious group and the lower the proportion of the group in a community, the more homogamous the group is. Jews are more likely to marry Jews than Catholics are to marry Catholics. Catholics, in turn, are more likely to marry

Catholics than Protestants are to marry Protestants. Among Catholics, the lower the socioeconomic status, the higher the probability of homogamy. There are now more interfaith marriages than ever before, accounting for at least one-third of all marriages (Strong and DeVault, 1989).

Americans also tend to marry people very close to their own ages. Most couples are only two years apart. If a man is 18 or younger when he marries, he is likely to marry a woman a few months older. But men older than 18 usually marry women slightly younger than they are. Most men who marry at 25 select a wife who is three years younger; at 37, most men marry a woman six years younger. A major reason why older men tend to marry much younger women is that men generally place greater importance on their mates' physical attractiveness than women do. But the age difference between husbands and wives increases only until the men reach age 50. After this, most men marry women close to their own age (Schulz, 1982; Mensch, 1986).

People of similar race, religion, and class are also likely to live close to one another, so it is not surprising that people tend to marry someone who lives nearby. This tendency may be weakening as cars and airplanes continue to increase Americans' mobility, yet most couples still come from the same city, town, or even neighborhood. According to many studies, there is more than a 50–50 chance that one's future spouse lives within walking distance (Kephart and Jedlicka, 1988). As James Bossard (1932) said, "Cupid may have wings, but apparently they are not adapted for long flights."

Homogamy applies to the *social* characteristics of couples. What about their individual characteristics, such as aggressive personalities and physical attractiveness? Do they also follow the same pattern? The answer is no, according to Robert Winch's (1971) famous theory of complementary needs. Winch argues that people with "different" personality traits are attracted to each other if these traits complement each other. This theory resembles the popular belief that "opposites attract." Thus, aggressive men tend to marry passive women; weak men like strong women; talkative women go for quiet men; rational men find emotional women attractive; and so on. Winch's own research has supported the complementarity theory, but more recent studies by other investigators have backed the social psychological version of homogamy—the theory that people with similar traits are attracted to each other, much as "birds of a feather flock together" (Wilson, 1989;

Morell et al., 1989). This is largely due to the impact of greater gender equality in recent years. Men are now more sensitive than before, while women are more assertive than before. The sexes have, in effect, become more alike: men are closer to being as sensitive as women, and women are closer to being as assertive as men. At the same time, more men today are attracted to women whom they consider to be assertive like themselves, and more women want men whom they consider to be sensitive like themselves.

However, because gender equality is far from complete, traditional sex roles continue to exert their influence. Thus, some women try futilely to find a Mr. Right who has the qualities of not only the ideal modern man but also the ideal traditional man. Similarly, some men insist on finding a Ms. Right who possesses the qualities of both the ideal modern and traditional woman. As Lillian Rubin (1990) observes, those men want women who are assertive and successful but who will also be happy to stay home and care for children, whereas those women want men who are tender, sensitive, and gentle but who are also president of a Fortune 500 company. Most people, however, are more pragmatic, so they tend to marry a person who has about the same amount of assertiveness or tenderness as they do.

Homogamy also reigns in regard to physical attractiveness. Everybody prefers a person of his or her dreams, but most people end up marrying someone close to their own level of attractiveness. Interestingly, the similarity in attractiveness is greater among deeply committed couples than among casual ones. When people are playing the field, their looks may not match their dates'. But they are more likely to get serious with the dates who have about the same level of attractiveness (Kalick and Hamilton, 1986; Steven et al., 1990).

MARITAL HAPPINESS

With time, both the physical attraction and the idealization of romantic love are likely to fade, so that marital love involves mostly commitment. Love may be less exciting after marriage, but as William Kephart and Devor Jedlicka (1988) observe, it "provides the individual with an emotional insight and a sense of self-sacrifice not otherwise attainable," qualities that may be keys to marital success.

How successful are American marriages? The answer obviously depends on how we define "successful." Gerald Leslie and Sheila Korman (1989) suggest that in a successful marriage the couple have few conflicts, basically agree on major issues, enjoy the same interests during their leisure time, and show confidence in and affection for each other. To others, this sounds like a static, spiritless relationship. Instead, some argue, a successful marriage is one that is zestful and provides opportunity for personal growth. Such disagreement among scholars suggests that a "successful marriage" is basically a value judgment, not an objective fact (Strong and DeVault, 1989).

It is, therefore, best simply to look at whether people themselves consider their marriages successful, however experts might judge them. By this standard, most American marriages are successful. Several studies have shown that the overwhelming majority of Americans say they are either "very happy" or "pretty happy" with their marriages (Bradburn, 1969; Freedman, 1978). In fact, married couples are much more likely than single people to say that they are happy, whether it is about love, sense of recognition, personal growth, or even job satisfaction. Marriage, however, rather than parenthood, is the focal point of marital happiness. As research has suggested, the presence of children often detracts from marital happiness because the couple see their relationship less as a romance and more as a working partnership. In fact, these working partners often find parenting so stressful that they feel relieved when their children have grown up and left home. This is why a recent study by Lynn White and John Edwards (1990) found that there are significant improvements in marital happiness after the children leave home and that the improvements are greatest immediately after the children leave.

What makes for marital happiness? By comparing happily married with unhappily married couples, researchers have come up with a long list of characteristics associated with happy marriages. Among these are having happily married parents; having known the prospective spouse for at least two years; having been engaged for at least two years; getting married at an age above the national average (about 25 for men and 23 for women); being religious or adhering to traditional values; having only little conflict with one's spouse before marriage; regarding one's spouse as a friend; being of the same religion and race; having the same level of education; and having good health, a happy childhood, emotional stability, parental approval of the marriage, and an adaptable personality (Kephart and Jedlicka, 1988; Hatch et al., 1986). Given the great complexity of marital happi-

ness, however, conflicting findings always exist. While most social researchers have found richer and better educated people to be more happily married than poorer and less educated people, other investigators have not found this to be the case (Brandt, 1982). For many years, researchers have also found that interaction between husband and wife causes marital happiness, but one study shows that spousal interaction is not the cause but instead the consequence of marital happiness (White, 1983). One study indicates that marital satisfaction declines if husbands have more education than their wives, which is consistent with the finding of other studies that educational similarity between spouses contributes to marital happiness. But the same study also reveals that marital satisfaction increases if wives are better educated than their husbands, which contradicts the findings of the other studies just mentioned (Tynes, 1990). Thus, we should regard the preceding list of characteristics as tentative and not the final word on marital happiness.

DIVORCE

The divorce rate in the United States is very high. It is about 50 percent among people who marry for the first time and 60 percent among those who remarry. Although it has begun to dip slightly since 1982, it is still twice as high as it was in 1960—the year when the rate began to rise annually. It is also the highest in the world (Census Bureau, 1992).

Although it provides an escape from an unhappy marriage, divorce often brings new problems. Divorced people are more likely than others to experience an increase in such personal difficulties as depression, insomnia, loneliness, decreased efficiency, excessive smoking and drinking, or anger toward both themselves and their ex-spouses (Goode, 1982).

Divorce creates an especially great economic hardship for women. Their standard of living in the year after divorce falls by an average of 73 percent, while their former husbands' standard rises 42 percent. The 73 percent drop in living standard consigns many divorced women to a hand-to-mouth existence. As one of them describes it, "[My children and I] ate macaroni and cheese five nights a week. There was a Safeway special for 39 cents a box. We could eat seven dinners for $3.00 a week. I think that's all we ate for months" (Weitzman, 1985).

Traditionally, divorce has been very hard on the children. It has become even harder nowadays, be

"Until irreconcilable differences do you part."

cause most divorced fathers never or rarely visit their children, nearly 90 percent of whom live with their mothers. It is not surprising that children tend to suffer emotionally. Although they make up one-third of all children, those from divorced families account for 60 to 80 percent of children in mental-health treatment, in special-education classes, or as referrals by teachers to school psychologists. The majority of children, though, do not suffer permanent emotional scars from divorce. But as married adults they have a higher chance of getting divorced themselves than those from intact families (Wallerstein, 1989; Kantrowitz, 1992).

Why do so many marriages end in divorce? Numerous studies have compared divorced couples with nondivorced couples and found a number of personal problems and social characteristics to be associated with divorce. They include infidelity, incompatibility, financial difficulties, lower socioeconomic status, and marrying too young. But these data cannot explain why industrialized Western societies have higher divorce rates than traditional Eastern societies, or why the U.S. divorce rate today is far higher than it was a century ago. A cross-cultural analysis may suggest at least five larger social forces behind the current high divorce rate in the United States.

1. *Decreased social disapproval of divorce.* In many traditional societies, unhappily married couples stay married because of the stigma attached to divorce. In the United States, there is virtually no stigma. Divorce has gained wide acceptance as a solution to marital unhappiness, and it has become easier to obtain from the courts. As one sociologist says, "We, as a society, have made it easy for people to divorce" (Kantrowitz, 1987).

2. *Greater availability of services and opportunities for the divorced.* In traditional societies, men depend heavily on marriage for sexual gratification, cooking, and housecleaning, and women look to it for sex and financial security. Such services and opportunities are more easily available to American men and women "without" being married. American men can get sexual gratification outside marriage, and American women can become financially independent without husbands. In recent years, fast-food restaurants have proliferated, and a growing number of businesses offer to clean homes, run errands, and provide other services for unmarried people. In addition, the higher divorce rate in the United States has expanded the pool of eligible new partners. All this makes divorce more attractive to unhappily married couples (Levitan and Belous, 1981; Udry, 1983).

3. *The increased specialization of the family in providing love and affection.* In societies with high divorce rates, such as the United States, the family has become specialized in offering love and affection, while the importance of its other functions has declined. When love and affection are gone, the modern couple are likely to break up their "empty shell" marriage. By contrast, in societies with low divorce rates, the family's other functions—such as providing economic security and socializing many children—remain important. Thus, even when little love remains between the parents, there are still many reasons for keeping the family together. Besides, since love is less reliable and less durable than the other, more mundane functions of marriage, the union based on love alone carries a higher risk of ending in divorce.

4. *Higher expectations about the quality of marital relationship.* Young people in traditional societies do not expect an exciting romantic experience with their spouses, especially if their marriages are arranged by their parents. But Americans expect a lot, such as an intense love relationship. These expectations are difficult to fulfill, and the chances of disillusionment with the partner are therefore great (Thornton and Freedman, 1983; Berger and Berger,

Western societies such as the United States have higher divorce rates than more traditional Eastern societies, such as Japan. One of the several reasons for this difference is the increased individualism in the United States; in more traditional societies, by contrast, people are more likely to subordinate their needs to those of the kinship group.

1983). Since young people have higher marital expectations than older ones, it is not surprising that most divorces occur within the first four years of marriage. Today, however, more brides and grooms are older when they first marry, and a growing number of couples want to improve their unhappy marriages rather than get out of them. The rising age at marriage and the increasing willingness to endure less-than-perfect marriages reflect a more realistic, less idealistic view. This has helped to slow down our ever-rising rate of divorce since the early 1980s (Glick and Lin, 1986; Kantrowitz, 1987; Scott, 1990).

5. *Increased individualism.* The rights of the individuals are considered far more important in high-divorce societies than in low-divorce societies. Individualism was so prominent in the United States during the late 1970s that it was called the "me decade." An individualistic society encourages people to put their own needs and privileges ahead of those of their spouses and to feel that if they want a divorce, they are entitled to get one. In more traditional societies with low divorce rates, people are more likely to subordinate their needs to those of the kinship group and thus to feel they have no right to seek a divorce.

The current high divorce rate in the United States does not necessarily mean that our marriages are more unhappy than those in other societies. Often, low divorce rates reflect social disapproval of divorce, not a large number of happy marriages. High divorce rates also do not mean that marriage is on the way to extinction. In fact, Americans remain among the most marrying peoples in the world. The marriage rates are higher in the United States than in countries with lower divorce rates, such as France, Hungary, Costa Rica, Panama, Japan, and the Philippines. While our divorce rates increased steadily over the last two decades, so did our marriage rates (Census Bureau, 1991). For Americans, divorce does not represent a rejection of marriage as an institution but only of a specific partner. That's why most divorced Americans eventually remarry—and close to half of all recent marriages are remarriages for one or both partners (Levine, 1990). In fact, high divorce rates may mean that the American institution of marriage is strong rather than weak. Since unhappy marriages are weeded out through divorce, there are proportionately more happy ones in the society as a whole. For example, between 1957 and 1976, while the divorce rate rose significantly, the proportion of Americans saying that their marriage was very happy also increased—from 68 to 80 percent (Veroff et al., 1981). These happy marriages reflect a tremendous achievement on the part of the couples because, as we have suggested, they expect much more from each other than their counterparts do in other countries with lower divorce rates. But the fact that divorce has become commonplace does indicate significant changes in the American family, which we discuss in the next section.

QUESTIONS FOR DISCUSSION AND REVIEW
1. What roles do dating, romantic love, and homogamy play in preparing Americans for marriage?

2. What social factors are associated with marital happiness?
3. What are the principal causes of marital breakups?

Changes in the American Family

The traditional family, which consists of two parents living with children, is no longer the typical American family. As far back as 1970, the proportion of traditional families had already declined to 40.3 percent. In 1991 it was only 25.9 percent (see Figure 10.1). Increasingly, Americans are choosing either new patterns of family life or life outside the family; some are experiencing violence in the family.

DUAL-CAREER MARRIAGES

In the last 50 years, there has been a tremendous surge of married women into the labor force. The proportion of gainfully employed wives shot up from only 14 percent in 1940 to about 57 percent in 1990. Their employment has increased family income significantly. In 1987 the median income of dual-career

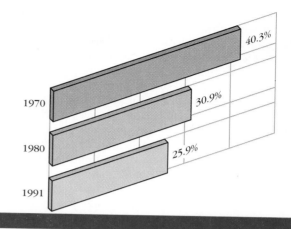

FIGURE 10.1 *Traditional Families: A Decreasing Minority*
Married couples with one or more children under age 18 have decreased as a percentage of all households.
Source: U.S. Census Bureau, 1992.

families ($37,300) was more than 37 percent higher than the median for one-career families ($27,000). At the low end of the income scale, the wife's contribution is so great that relatively few dual-earner families fall below the poverty line (Waldrop, 1988; Smolowe, 1990).

There may be more strain in two-career marriages. But in cases where the husbands fully support their wives' employment by doing their share of housecleaning and child care, the couples are able to avoid marital stress and achieve marital happiness.

Does this economic gain bring marital happiness? It apparently does for most dual-career couples. But when comparing them with one-career families, research has produced conflicting results. Some studies found that the wife's employment was good for her but not for her husband. In one such study, employed wives reported more marital happiness, more communication with husbands, fewer worries, and better health, while their husbands were less contented with their marriage and in poorer health (Burke and Weir, 1976). But other studies found more strain in dual-career marriages because the wife was still expected to be a homemaker rather than a career seeker (Skinner, 1980). The strain is much heavier for the employed wife than for her husband, because she does most of the housework, as we observed earlier. The effect of a wife's employment seems to depend on how much support she gets from her husband. Many husbands still find it difficult to render total support to their wives' careers, particularly if their wives earn more than they do. Consequently, in cases where the wife outperforms the husband, sex lives are more likely to suffer, feelings of love are more likely to diminish, and marriages are more likely to end in divorce. Lack of support for the wife's career may also explain why premature death from heart disease is 11 times more frequent among husbands whose wives outshine them professionally (Rubenstein, 1982). On the other hand, in cases where the husbands fully support their wives' employment by doing their share of house cleaning and child care, the couples do head off marital stress and achieve marital happiness (Cooper et al., 1986). Generally, supportive husbands have long been exposed to egalitarian ideologies and life-styles. They have accepted the value of gender equality. They have also seen their mothers as competent and influential individuals who shared equal status with their fathers (Rosin, 1990).

SINGLE-PARENT FAMILIES

With increased divorce, there has been a phenomenal rise in the number of children growing up in households with just one parent. From 1970 to 1991, the proportion of all families being single-parent families increased from 11 to 28 percent (see Figure 10.2). The overwhelming majority (90 percent) of such families are headed by women. About a quarter of the children today live for some time in these female-headed families. It has been estimated that more than

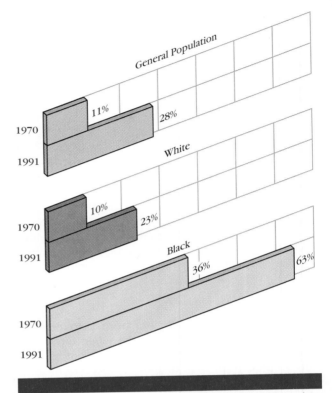

FIGURE 10.2 *Single-Parent Families: A Fast-Growing Group*

Source: U.S. Census Bureau, 1992.

half of the children born in 1980 will live with their mothers alone before they reach age 18.

To the general public, single mothers are either unwed teenagers on welfare or older, single career women who, like the television character Murphy Brown, decide to have babies before it is too late. In reality, while never-married mothers are growing fast, they are still a minority. Most (about 70 percent) single mothers today are women who have been divorced, separated, widowed, or abandoned by their husbands (Lewin, 1992a). Most of these families live below or near the poverty level. Even women of higher-income groups tend to suffer a sharp drop in household income as a result of marital breakup. Black mothers are more likely to reside with the children's grandmothers, who provide free child care. But they are far from well prepared to cope with the challenges of single parenthood (Hogan et al., 1990).

Compared with two-parent families, female-headed families are more likely to experience social and psychological stress, such as unemployment, job

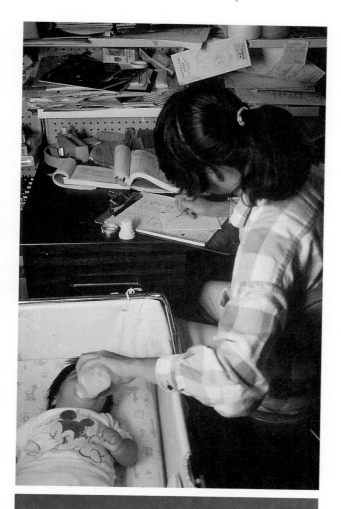

Compared with two-parent families, single mothers are more likely to experience social and psychological stress because they are more often severely limited in financial resources.

change, lack of social support (from friends and neighbors), negative self-image, and pessimism about the future (McLanahan, 1983). Children from single-parent families have also been found to have a larger share of such problems as juvenile delinquency, truancy, and poor school work. Whatever problems these children may have, however, they do not result directly from the absence of a father in a female-headed home, as popularly believed, but from factors that can also be found in a two-parent family, such as low income, poor living conditions, and lack of parental supervision. Because fewer than half of all divorced and separated women with children receive

child-support payments, most of which are extremely inadequate, "the most detrimental effect for the children is not the lack of a male presence but the lack of a male income" (Cherlin and Furstenberg, 1983). A cross-cultural analysis indicates that in many tribal societies children from single-parent families generally do not have problems because of sufficient material resources, concerned and helpful relatives, and a culture of friendliness toward the youngsters (Bilge and Kaufman, 1983). Since our single mothers are often severely limited in financial resources, it is not surprising that they report greater stress and strains in their lives than other people (Thornton and Freedman, 1983).

STEPFAMILIES

Given the high rates of divorce and remarriage, stepfamilies have become quite common. They number about 4.5 million and account for almost one-fifth of all married couples with children under the age of 18. Because women usually win custody of children in divorce cases, most stepfamilies—also called "blended families"—consist of mothers, their biological children, and stepfathers. Nine out of ten stepchildren live with their biological mothers and stepfathers (Otten, 1990).

The success of such families depends largely on how well the stepfather gets along with the children. It is extremely tough to be a stepfather. Society has not yet provided a script for performing the stepfather role as it does for the father role. Many men who remarry assume that they have learned much from their experiences as fathers of their biological children in previous marriages. But they quickly discover that those experiences do not necessarily make them effective stepfathers. Consider the case of a 40-year-old stepfather of a 12-year-old boy and a 15-year-old girl. He thought that his new marriage would be perfect because he considered himself smart enough to avoid the mistakes of his first. Soon after the second marriage, he wanted to spend time with his stepchildren and make a good start. So he told them, "Let's go camping this weekend, let's go to a movie, let's play Monopoly." But, according to him, "All I get in return are these drop-dead looks and they go running off to their father's house and tell him I pick my teeth after dinner or that my own kids who visit us on weekends are dorks" (Nordheimer, 1990).

Having long been accustomed to living with their biological fathers, children tend to regard their stepfathers as interlopers or as distant, unwanted relatives overstaying their visits. They may resent having to change their life-style, as a 15-year-old girl sobs to her mother, "I can't stand it. I have to put on my bathrobe at 10 o'clock at night in 'our' own house to go downstairs to get an apple from the refrigerator because 'he's' there in 'our' living room." Aside from running into such conflicts over territoriality, stepfathers are likely to have problems with discipline. If they tell their 13-year-old stepson that he should not watch an R-rated cable movie, he may fume: "My dad lets me watch them. Besides, it's Mom's television set" (Nordheimer, 1990).

Conflicts over territoriality and discipline are most likely to erupt with teenagers. Young children can quickly accept a stepfather's love and discipline because of their physical and emotional dependence on adults. But teenagers are striving to break free of adult authority, as they are preoccupied with their developing sexuality, schoolwork, friends, and sports. They accept parental discipline only out of love and respect, which the stepfather initially does not or may never have. During an argument, they are likely to shout at their stepfathers: "You're not my real father!" Not surprisingly, the presence of stepchildren has been found to be a major reason why second marriages fail at a higher rate than first marriages. It has also been found that couples with stepchildren are 70 percent more likely than remarried couples without stepchildren to divorce (Levine, 1990; Nordheimer, 1990).

The problem does not stem from stepchildren alone. The legal system and society in general also play an important role: stepfathers may give their new wives' children full financial support, but they have few legal rights unless they adopt them—yet adoption is impossible in most states without the natural father's consent. The natural father, then, has more legal rights to minors even if he has disappeared without providing any child support. The biological mother is, of course, expected to feel that, since her children belong to her more than to anybody else, their discipline should primarily be her responsibility. Many stepfathers, however, find it hard to play a secondary role. By coming down too hard on the children, they not only nettle their mothers but also embitter the children. One study shows that the more active a disciplinary role the stepfather plays, the more likely the children will have behavioral problems during the first two-and-a-half years of the marriage. Another study found that stepchildren are three to five times more likely than other children to receive psychological counseling and up to twice as likely to fail at school (Levine, 1990).

Most of the problems, however, are not permanent. Most stepfamilies do not break up, either. Stepchildren may contribute to parental divorce, but a combination of other factors is more important, including financial strain, impulsiveness, and the past experience of divorce itself. Remarried couples are more likely than couples in first marriages to suffer from financial strain because of less education and lower income. Impulsiveness is more common among remarrieds, because they are more likely to have been married first as teenagers, the age group that has the highest divorce rate. And the past experience of divorce itself makes it easier to call it quits again when things go badly in a second marriage. In view of these reasons, remarriages are more likely than first marriages to end in divorce. Nevertheless, most stepfamilies are relatively free of trouble and conflict (Strong and DeVault, 1989; Levine, 1990).

FAMILY VIOLENCE

As mentioned earlier, family violence is quite common in the United States. Its exact incidence is hard to pin down, because various researchers do not define family violence in the same way. There is, of course, little disagreement about extreme cases where a family member is killed or seriously injured by another. But there is disagreement as to what kinds of behavior are acceptable for disciplining children or dealing with spousal conflict. Some investigators consider spanking, for example, an act of violence, whereas others do not (Klaus and Rand, 1984). Thus, there have been different estimates of the extent of family violence in the United States. According to one study, about 3 million Americans experience violence in the home each year, whereas another study puts the number at 8 million. The estimated proportions of families where violence occurs range from 10 to 20 percent a year, and anywhere between 25 and 50 percent of all couples have been estimated to suffer serious family violence during the course of their marriage (Straus et al., 1988; Levitan and Belous, 1981; Long et al., 1983). All this should give us a sense of the enormity of the problem. After all, the family is supposed to be "home sweet home."

Why does violence occur in so many families? A major reason is stress. Research shows that the incidence of violence is highest among groups most likely to feel under stress, such as the urban poor, families with a jobless husband, and those with four to six children (Straus et al., 1988). The stress that triggers violence can also be social-psychological. Husbands who have been socialized to play the dominant role are likely to feel uneasy if their wives have more education or higher-status occupations. Such husbands are more likely than others to assault their wives (Rubenstein, 1982). Stress by itself, however, does not necessarily cause violence. People would not resort to violence as a way of relieving stress if they were not culturally encouraged to do so. There seems to be a "culturally recognized script for behavior under stress" in American society. The violence on television, corporal punishment in schools, and the death penalty, for example, convey the idea that violence is an acceptable solution to problems (Straus et al., 1988). Research further suggests that a lot of marital violence is transmitted from one generation to another. It has been found that most of the violent couples have, as children, seen their parents hit each other (Kalmuss, 1984).

Ironically, though, as many as half of the battered women do not leave their husbands who continue to abuse them. Why? Most do not have money and cannot earn enough to support themselves or their children. If they leave, their husbands will likely stalk them to inflict more serious violence. And the victims are afraid of losing their children if they leave, because their husbands, controlling the money, can hire good lawyers to gain custody of the children. These reasons, along with repeated abuse, cause the victims to feel helpless, which forces them to survive in the same way as hostages, prisoners of war, or concentration camp victims do: by accommodating their captors and living from hour to hour (Brody, 1992).

LIVING TOGETHER

In the past, very few couples lived together without a formal wedding ceremony or marriage license. These couples were said to be "living in sin." They were mostly the very rich, who could afford to ignore society's rules, and the very poor, who had little to lose by ignoring them. But today cohabitation has spread to other sectors of American society, including college students and young working adults. The result is a dramatic rise in cohabitation. In 1970, the number of unmarried couples living together was only slightly over half a million. But since then it has more than quadrupled to 2.8 million today. Young people—

under age 30—are nearly twice as likely as other adults to be currently cohabiting. The proportion of those living together before their first marriage has soared from only 11 percent in the early 1970s to more than 50 percent today. Social disapproval has vastly diminished, and courts have stepped in to protect couples' rights as if they were legally married (Bumpass and Sweet, 1989; Lewin, 1990a).

Since the incidence of cohabitation continues to rise, there is some fear that it may undermine the institution of marriage. In Sweden, where cohabitation is already four times as prevalent as in the United States, living together does not pose a threat to marriage at all. Most cohabitants live like married couples, and intend to marry eventually. About the same situation exists in the United States. Cohabitation as a permanent alternative to marriage, which is often called common-law marriage, is relatively rare today. It occurs mostly among the very poor. For most of the cohabitants, living together is a temporary arrangement, which usually lasts for fewer than two years. Although it does not imply a commitment to marry later, cohabitation often leads to marriage. It is a modern extension of the courtship process, comparable to the traditional custom of "going steady" (Spanier, 1983; Gwartney-Gibbs, 1986; Tanfer, 1987).

Does living together lead to more marital happiness than the traditional courtship? Couples who live together often argue that cohabitation works like a trial marriage, preparing them for marital success. A study in Canada has indeed suggested that premarital cohabitation contributes to marital stability (White, 1987). But research in the United States generally suggests otherwise. In one study of couples who had been married for four years, those who had lived together before marriage had about the same rate of divorce as those who had not cohabited. Among those still married, both groups reported about the same amount of marital satisfaction (Newcomb and Bentler, 1980). This suggests that premarital cohabitation does not lead to more marital happiness. Other studies even show higher divorce rates or "less" marital satisfaction among couples who have lived together than among those who have not (Barringer, 1989; Trussell and Rao, 1989; Whyte, 1992). But this does not necessarily mean that divorce or marital dissatisfaction is the result of premarital cohabitation. The type of people who cohabit are likely to be poorly suited for marriage in the first place, because they do not have as strong a commitment to marriage as other couples. As Alfred DeMaris and Gerald Leslie (1984) found, couples who have lived together before marriage are "less" likely to agree with the statement that "no matter how much trouble a husband and wife are having getting along, the best thing to do is to stay married and try to work out their problems." In short, premarital cohabitation by itself neither helps nor hurts married life (Watson and DeMeo, 1987).

STAYING SINGLE

Of the "alternatives" to marriage, staying single is by far the most common. In 1990 about 10 percent of Americans lived alone, accounting for 24 percent of all U.S. households. This represents an increase of more than 112 percent over the last 20 years, from only 10,850,000 singles in 1970 to 23 million today. Many of these people are in their thirties and forties. But most are younger adults, who postpone marriage into their late twenties. More significant, because of today's tough economic times, a growing number of

Most singles are not opposed to marriage; they expect to be married eventually. They remain single because they have not met the "right person." However, the longer they wait, the harder it is to find that person.

young adults—currently 32 percent of single men and 30 percent of single women—live with their parents and will also stay single for some time (Crispell, 1990; Nemy, 1991; Gross, 1991).

Most singles are not actually opposed to marriage and expect to be married sooner or later. In fact, they are likely to be married within five years. The reason for their current singleness is that they have not met the right person. However, the longer they wait, the harder it becomes to find that person. This is especially true for older, well-educated women. There are at least two reasons for the difficulty of finding Mr. Right. First, single women in their thirties and forties far outnumber marriageable men. This is partly because most women marry men several years their senior, and partly because the pool of these older men is smaller than that of the somewhat younger women. Second, since women tend to marry "up" not only in age but also in status and men tend to marry "down," the result is likely to be a surplus of well-educated, successful women. Many of these women will probably never marry. Seeing themselves as "the cream of the crop," they tend to regard the remaining single men as being "at the bottom of the barrel" (Salholz, 1986).

A growing number of women—and men—choose to stay single. Some studies have found them to be happier than their married counterparts (Harayda, 1986). They are also more likely to see themselves as very romantic (see Table 10.1). If asked why they are single, they are likely to say that "marriage entails too much commitment and responsibility" or "I prefer the life-style" (Simenauer and Carroll, 1982). There are several sociological reasons for the increase in committed singlehood. Basically, the social pressure to get married has decreased, and the opportunities for those who are single have grown. This is especially true for women. As educational and career opportunities open up for women, along with the freedom to choose to be a single mother, marriage stops being the only road to economic security, emotional support, social respectability, and meaningful work. The influence of social pressure and opportunity on the popularity of the single life can also be seen in the fact that the single life tends to thrive in big cities and in the upper class. City dwellers face far less social pressure to marry than people in small towns, and the upper classes have money, an important weapon in combating loneliness, which is the chief drawback to being single. Many social scientists see another factor behind the rising number of peo-

TABLE 10.1 *Romantic Self-Image*

Single men and women are more likely than their married counterparts to see themselves as very romantic.

I AM:	PERCENT SINGLE		PERCENT MARRIED	
	MEN	WOMEN	MEN	WOMEN
Very romantic	**28**	**41**	**17**	**33**
Romantic	54	36	55	46
Realistic	13	14	23	17
Cautious	4	7	4	3
Cynical	1	2	1	1

Source: Samuel S. Janus and Cynthia L. Janus, *The Janus Report on Sexual Behavior,* New York: John Wiley & Sons, 1993, p. 154.

ple who prefer the single life-style. They perceive a "new narcissism," a greatly increased preoccupation with oneself. Although singles are generally happy and respected, our society, like most others, still relegates them to a diminished status, treating their way of life as less desirable than that of married couples (Nemy, 1991).

DEATH OF THE FAMILY?

Do the changes in the family signal its end? The death of the family has been predicted for decades. Carle Zimmerman (1949) concluded from his study on the family that "We must look upon the present confusion of family values as the beginning of violent breaking up of a system." By the "confusion of family values," Zimmerman referred to the threat that individualism presented to the tradition of paternalistic authority and filial duty. He assumed that individualism would eventually do the family in. Today, many continue to predict the demise of the family, pointing out as evidence the increases in divorce, out-of-wedlock births, cohabitation, and staying single.

But the family is alive and well, as we have suggested. The problem with the gloomy forecast is that it confuses change with breakdown. Many of the traditional families—with husbands as breadwinners and wives as homemakers—have merely changed into two-career families, which still hang together as nuclear families rather than disintegrate. Despite the increased number of people staying single, an over-

whelming majority of those who now live alone will eventually marry. Even in view of the "marriage squeeze" resulting from the shortage of marriageable men, 80 percent of female college graduates will also marry. In 1988 only 5 percent of men and 4 percent of women had remained single when they reached an age between 55 and 64 (Census Bureau, 1990). Although divorce rates have doubled over the last two decades, three out of four divorced people remarry, most doing so within three years of their marital breakup. Most of the young adults who live together before marriage will also marry eventually. However, as we have discussed, single-parent families, especially those resulting from out-of-wedlock births, do pose problems for many mothers and their children. But the problems have to do with economic deprivation rather than single parenthood as a new form of family.

Evidence from public opinion polls also points to the basic health of the American family. In one national survey, 78 percent of all adults said that they get "a great deal" of satisfaction from their family lives; only 3 percent said "a little" or "none." In the same survey, 66 percent of married adults said they are "very happy" with marriage; only 3 percent said "not too happy." In another survey, a large majority of children (71 percent) agreed that their family life is "close and intimate" (Cherlin and Furstenberg, 1983). According to a more recent poll, 85 percent of married Americans said that if they were single they would marry their present spouses (Harris, 1987). Such a strong, enduring faith in marriage is indeed remarkable in view of our having the highest divorce rate in the world.

What will the American family be like in the next 20 years? It should be basically the same as it is today: continuing diversity without destroying the basic family values. As sociologists Andrew Cherlin and Frank Furstenberg (1983) sum it up, "'Diversity' is the word for the future of the American family. There will be more divorces, single-parent families, and mixed families from remarriages, but the ideal of marrying and having children is still very much a part of the American experience." The continuing acceptance of these traditional family values comes through clearly in two recent studies. One shows that, compared with Europeans, Americans are more likely to tie the knot, to marry at an earlier age, and to have slightly larger families, despite their higher incidence of divorce and single-parent families (Sorrentino, 1990). Another study is longitudinal, tracking changes in family attitudes and values from the

1960s to the 1980s. It indicates that most people today are more accepting of divorce, premarital and extramarital sex, and other alternative life-styles, but do not endorse them for themselves. The vast majority of Americans still value marriage, parenthood, and family life—still plan to marry and have children as well as expect to be successful in marriage (Thornton, 1989).

QUESTIONS FOR DISCUSSION AND REVIEW

1. How has the entry of large numbers of married women into the labor force changed the family?

2. What special problems do single mothers and step-fathers face in raising children?

3. Why do American families experience so much violence?

4. How do sociologists interpret the dramatic increase in the numbers of Americans who cohabit?

5. What are the reasons so many Americans choose to stay single, and what are some consequences of this trend?

6. How will dual-career marriages and staying single affect the future of the family?

CHAPTER REVIEW

1. *What are the basic functions performed by the family?* Sexual regulation, reproduction, socialization, economic cooperation, and emotional security. The family's functions are not equally important in all societies, though. Preindustrial families tend to be all-purpose, operating as the center of educational, political, economic, and recreational activities. Industrial societies have undergone institutional differentiation, so that providing emotional support is now the family's main function. *What does the family look like from the conflict perspective?* The family can be a source of pain and conflict and an opportunity for men to exploit women.

2. *How did industrialization change the American family in the nineteenth century?* In general, families were no longer centers of production. Family life and the world of work were increasingly separated. There emerged the stereotype of the ideal family that portrayed a wife as keeping house and caring for children while her husband went out to work.

3. *What are the common myths of sex?* They include the following: Americans start having sex at a very young age, and too many men are sexually unfaithful to their wives. Homosexuality is quite rare; it is easy to identify homosexuals by their appearance or gestures; menstruating women cannot get pregnant; and pregnancy cannot occur if the man withdraws before orgasm.

4. *How has the sexual revolution changed our attitude and behavior?* It has encouraged sexual tolerance, weakened the double standard, changed sexual purposes from procreation to recreation, and emphasized unexploitative sex as more important than whether or not the partners are married. *What is the controversy over abortion about?* Pro-choice forces want constitutional protection of a woman's right to choose abortion, but pro-life forces want protection of the unborn by denying the woman's reproductive choice.

5. *How do Americans prepare for marriage?* Usually, they do not prepare for marriage intentionally, but dating and falling in love are the traditional preparatory steps in the United States. *Is there any truth to the saying that opposites attract?* Winch believes so, but most studies support the contrary view, saying that birds of a feather flock together. The theory that people of similar personality traits are attracted to each other gains further support from the norm of homogamy—that a person is likely to marry someone of the same class, race, religion, and other social characteristics.

6. *Are most American marriages successful?* Most married couples consider themselves happily married, although the United States has the highest divorce rate in the world. *Why do we have such a high divorce rate?* Among the likely social causes are (1) decreased social disapproval of divorce, (2)

greater availability of services and opportunities for the divorced, (3) increased specialization of the family in providing love and affection, (4) higher expectations about the quality of marital relationships, and (5) increased individualism. Higher divorce rates, however, do not necessarily mean that marriages are more unhappy than those in other societies.

7. *What changes have taken place in the American family since 1970?* It has taken on diverse forms, such as dual-career marriages, single-parent families, stepfamilies, living together, and staying single, while producing a great deal of marital and parental violence. But these changes do not reflect the end of the American family. The basic family values, such as marrying and having children, are still very much alive.

KEY TERMS

Double standard The social norm that allows males, but not females, to engage in nonmarital sex (p. 230).

Homogamy Marriage that involves two people having similar characteristics, or norm that requires such a marriage (p. 234).

Institutional differentiation The process by which the functions of one institution are gradually taken over by other institutions (p. 226).

SUGGESTED READINGS

Benson, von der Ohe. 1987. *First and Second Marriages.* New York: Praeger. A research report on the differences between first and second marriages.

Billingsley, Andrew. 1993. *Climbing Jacob's Ladder: The Enduring Legacy of African-American Families.* New York: Simon & Schuster. A rare analysis of the resourcefulness and resilience of African-American families.

Janus, Samuel S., and Cynthia L. Janus. 1993. *The Janus Report* New York: John Wiley & Sons. A nationwide survey on the changes in sexual attitudes and practices that have taken place in the United States in the 1980s and 1990s.

Rosenblatt, Roger. 1992. *Life Itself: Abortion in the American Mind.* New York: Random House. An insightful analysis of how most Americans are torn between their support for abortion rights and their disapproval of abortion itself.

Sweet, James A., and Larry L. Bumpass. 1987. *American Families and Households.* New York: Russell Sage Foundation. A study of the changes in American families and households, dealing with such issues as divorce, cohabitation, and single-parent families.

11

RELIGION

MYTHS AND REALITIES

Myth: A belief in God is present in all religions.

Reality: *A belief in God is present in some religions, such as Christianity, but not in others, such as Buddhism.*

Myth: Religion is the opiate of the masses. It makes people become conservative, accepting the status quo.

Reality: *While religion can make some people conservative, it can also inspire others to become liberal or radical, rejecting the status quo by fighting for a better society.*

Myth: It is always beneficial for the faithful to identify as strongly as they can with their religion.

Reality: *History has shown that when people identify too strongly with their religion, they tend to end up believing that there is only one true religion, namely, their own. The consequence is that they become intolerant of others' religions, which they consider false.*

Myth: People who are affiliated with a successful, respectable, or popular religion must be very religious. Otherwise, their religion cannot be successful.

Reality: *The more successful a religion is, the less religious its members become.*

Myth: Virtually all Protestant churches are equally free of prejudice against Jews and other minorities, because such prejudice is contrary to their religious belief.

Reality: *More conservative Protestant churches are more prejudiced than liberal ones. This is because prejudiced people are more inclined to join conservative churches in the first place.*

Myth: Most people who have left the liberal churches join the conservative ones, which stimulates a fundamentalist revival in the United States.

Reality: *Most people who have left the liberal churches do not join the conservative ones; they simply stop going to church.*

Myth: Since most Americans believe in God and belong to some religious group, they must have a strong commitment to religion.

Reality: *Most Americans claim to believe in God and have a religion but without much commitment. Less than half attend religious services regularly.*

Myth: The young people who join such far-out cults as the Moonies and Hare Krishnas are mostly abnormal and come from unhappy or unconventional homes.

Reality: *These people are mostly normal and come from stable, religious families that embrace the traditional values of family life and morality.*

Myth: Most of the immigrants from predominantly Muslim Arab countries are Muslims, so that a majority of Arab-Americans are Muslims.

Reality: *Most Arab-Americans are Christians, because Christians from those Arab countries are more likely to emigrate to the United States.*

Myth: Those who often watch religious television do not attend church regularly or are dissatisfied with their experience of worshiping in church.

Reality: *They do attend church regularly and find worshiping in church highly satisfying.*

I n St. Anthony's Roman Catholic Church in the South Bronx of New York City, congregants sway back and forth, with their arms above their heads, to the rhythm of a Caribbean tune. Amid the sounds of an amplified guitar and tambourine that fills the crowded church, shouts of "Blessed be God. Alleluia, Alleluia!" can be heard. These are soon followed by voices offering thanks to God or beseeching God for help with loneliness, illness, and other problems. At the end of the mass, some worshipers are crying and others embracing (Newman, 1992).

The influence of religion reaches far beyond the walls of this church. In fact, religion is everywhere. Some form of religious belief exists all over the world. It ranges from belief in an invisible deity to worship of an animal. Some people may think that religion is a carryover from the superstitious past, hence highly important for "primitive" or "backward" societies only. Actually, religion is also very much a part of our modern social life. Although we are one of the world's most scientifically and technologically advanced societies, we are also one of the most religious. An overwhelming majority of Americans believe in God. Large numbers go to church on Sunday or attend other religious services regularly. Most (78 percent) Americans pray at least once a week, and more than half (57 percent) pray at least once a day. Even among the 13 percent of Americans who are atheists or agnostics, one in five prays daily, wagering that there is a God listening to them (Woodward, 1992).

What exactly do religious people believe? What can religion do to people? Why does religion continue to play a vital role in modern society? In trying to answer questions such as these, sociologists do not analyze religious beliefs for their truth or falsity. As a science, sociology can neither support nor undermine the validity of any religion. What sociologists do is study religion as a social institution—as an institution that, like the family or education, is created by human beings and fulfills human rather than divine needs. Thus, in this chapter, we will deal with the human dimensions of religion. First we will discuss

the varieties of religion. Then we will see what religion looks like through the eyes of three sociological perspectives and how it is related to society in general. Finally, we will discuss religion in the United States.

Varieties of Religion

According to some native religions of Africa, one god created the world, but he then withdrew. The spirits of ancestors and other gods now influence the world. These gods, as well as the creating god, are neither good nor evil, but they require animal sacrifices (Curtin et al., 1978). Christians hold that there is one all-powerful and all-good God and that one sacrifice—the death of Christ—was sufficient to redeem all people. Different as these religions are, they have several elements in common, elements characteristic of all religions.

These elements can be found in Emile Durkheim's (1915) classic definition of **religion** as a unified system of beliefs and practices regarding sacred things that unites its adherents into a single moral community. Thus, religion consists of (1) something that is considered **sacred,** which transcends the everyday world and inspires awe and reverence, (2) a set of beliefs about the sacred thing, (3) the affirmation of beliefs through **rituals**—behavioral expressions of the beliefs, and (4) an organization of believers who participate in the same rituals.

We can spot these four elements in theistic, god-related religions such as Christianity, Judaism, and Islam. But the same elements can be found in beliefs that do not involve a deity. Democracy, communism, Confucianism, and humanism are just as sacred to their adherents as God is to his believers. The political ideologies and secular philosophies also have their own beliefs, rituals, and communities. Thus, they can be considered religions in the same way as Christianity, Judaism, and Islam are. In fact, religion appears in many different forms, each with what it regards as sacred along with its own beliefs, rituals, and community. They can be classified into three major types: **theism, ethicalism,** and **animism.**

THEISM

Theistic religions define the sacred as one or more supernatural beings. These religions center on the worship of a god or gods. There are two subtypes of theism: **monotheism,** or belief in one god, and **polytheism,** belief in more than one god.

Christianity, Judaism, Islam, and Zoroastrianism are all monotheistic. With over a billion followers, Christianity is the world's largest religion (see Table 11.1). It is split into three principal groups—Roman Catholic, Protestant, and Eastern Orthodox—but these groups share a belief in God as the creator of the world and in Jesus as its savior. Judaism worships Yahweh, the God of the Old Testament, as the creator of the universe and teaches that he chose the people of Israel as witness to his presence. Islam, the world's second-largest religion, was established by the prophet Muhammad in the seventh century A.D. It

emphasizes that believers must surrender totally to the will of Allah (God), the creator, sustainer, and restorer of the world. Zoroastrianism is an ancient, pre-Christian religion, which still has a quarter of a million followers known as Parsees in India. They believe in one supreme God whose omnipotence is, however, temporarily limited by an ongoing battle with evil—although God is ensured of eventual victory. The faithful join forces with God by keeping themselves pure through ablution, penance, and prayers.

The best-known polytheistic faith is Hinduism. The great majority of Hindus live in India. In small villages throughout India, countless gods are worshipped. Each is believed to have a specific sphere of influence, such as childbirth, sickness, the harvest, or rain. These local deities are often looked on as manifestations of higher gods. Hinduism also teaches that we are *reincarnated*—born and reborn again and again—into new human or animal bodies. People may escape the cycle of reincarnation and achieve salvation by practicing mystical contemplation and stead-

TABLE 11.1 *Religions Around the World*

The great variety of religions around the world can be divided into three major types: theism, ethicalism, and animism. Theists believe in the existence of a god or gods. Christians, Muslims, Hindus, and Jews are all theists. Ethicalists ascribe sacredness to moral principles. Ethicalists include Buddhists, Confucians, and Shintoists. Animists believe that spirits capable of helping or harming people reside in animals, plants, or some other objects. Most of the animists are shamanists. The sizes of various religions are listed below in numbers of followers and in percentages of total world population.

Total Christians		1,833,022,000 (33.4%)
Roman Catholics	1,025,585,000 (18.7%)	
Protestants	373,698,000 (6.8%)	
Orthodox	170,422,000 (3.1%)	
Anglicans	74,883,400 (1.4%)	
Other Christians	188,433,600 (3.4%)	
Muslims		971,328,700 (17.7%)
Hindus		732,812,000 (13.4%)
Buddhists		314,939,000 (5.7%)
Jews		17,822,000 (0.3%)
Shamanists		10,493,000 (0.2%)
Confucians		6,028,000 (0.1%)
Shintoists		3,222,800 (0.1%)

Source: Adapted with permission from 1993 *Britannica Book of the Year.* Copyright © 1993 by Encyclopaedia Britannica, Inc.

Islam, like Judaism, Christianity, and Zoroastrianism, is a monotheistic religion. Shown here, Muslim worshipers in Mauritius, wearing hooks and needles as part of the ritual, form a procession to mark the anniversary of the battle that took the life of the prophet Muhammad's grandson in A.D. 680.

fast endurance and by following traditional rules of conduct for their castes, families, and occupations.

ETHICALISM

Some religions do not focus on supernatural beings. Instead, *ethicalist religions* ascribe sacredness to moral principles. The heart of these religions is a set of principles they offer as guides for living a righteous life. The best examples are Buddhism, Confucianism, Taoism, and Shintoism.

Buddhism was founded in India in the sixth century B.C. by Gautama, who is known as the Buddha ("enlightened one"). It is today the largest ethical religion. According to Buddhism, there is no independent, unchanging "self" and no physical world—both are illusions. Belief in their reality, attachment to them, and craving for human pleasures are, according to Buddhism, the source of human misery. To escape this misery is to attain Nirvana (salvation). It requires meditation—freeing one's mind from all worldly desires and ideas—and right thinking, right speech, right action, and the right mode of living.

Confucianism was founded by Confucius (551–479 B.C.) in China. For well over 2000 years, it was practically the state religion of China. Confucianism stresses personal cultivation through learning and self-examination, so that the individual becomes

imbued with confidence and serenity. It also urges harmony between individuals. Confucius described proper social conduct as "reciprocity," which means,

Shintoism is an ethicalist religion that is popular in Japan. It teaches the importance of striving for a bright and pure mind, which can be attained through physical and spiritual purification, and symbolized by this ceremony at a Shinto wedding.

in his words, "Do not do to others what you would not want others to do to you."

Like Confucianism, Taoism has shaped the Chinese character for more than 2000 years, but today it has a much smaller following. Whereas Confucianism compels its adherents to be austere and duty-conscious, Taoism encourages joyful, carefree quietism, nonintervention, or "not overdoing." According to Taoism, every deliberate intervention in the natural course of events sooner or later turns into the opposite of what was intended. In essence, in a mystical manner, Taoism tells people to yield totally to the Tao ("the Way"), accepting what is natural and spontaneous in people. Actually, Taoism and Confucianism pursue the same goal—the subordination of individuals to groups, such as families and society. They differ only in the means of achieving that goal. While Confucianism urges activism through performance of one's social duties, such as obeying one's parents and being polite to others, Taoism teaches passivity through avoidance of self-indulgence, power seeking, and self-aggrandizement.

Shintoism has always been a part of Japanese culture. It teaches that people should strive for *magokoro*—a "bright and pure mind" or "truthfulness, sincerity, or uprightness." This means that individuals must be sincerely interested in doing their best in whatever work they have chosen, and they must be truthful in their relationships with others. Purification, physical and spiritual, is the path to these goals. To remove the dust of humans' wickedness believed to cover their divine nature, purification rites are performed at Shinto shrines.

ANIMISM

Belief in spirits capable of helping or harming people is the basis of **animism.** The spirits may reside in humans, animals, plants, rivers, or winds. They are not gods to be worshipped, but supernatural forces that can be manipulated to serve human ends. Rituals such as feasting, dancing, fasting, and cleansing are often performed to appease the spirits so that crops can be harvested, fish caught, illness cured, or danger averted.

Among indigenous peoples in North and South America, a type of animism called **shamanism** is common. The shaman ("one who knows") is thought to communicate with the spirits, either by acting as their mouthpiece or by letting the soul leave the shaman's body and enter the spiritual world. The spirits, in effect, live in the shaman. By communicating with them, the shaman heals the sick, discovers lost animals, sees events in distant places, foresees those in the future, and forecasts prospects for farming, fishing, and hunting.

Another form of animism, **totemism,** is popular among native peoples of Australia and some Pacific islands. It is based on the belief that a kinship exists between humans and an animal (or, less commonly, a plant). This animal, called a *totem,* represents a human family, a clan, or a group of ancestors. It is thought of as a person—but a person with superhuman power—and it must be treated with respect, awe, and fear. Killing, eating, touching, and even seeing the animal are often prohibited. The totem is relied on as a helper and protector, but it also punishes those who breach a taboo.

QUESTIONS FOR DISCUSSION AND REVIEW
1. What are the four basic elements of religion?
2. How do theistic religions differ from ethical and animistic beliefs?
3. To which varieties of religion do Buddhism, Shintoism, totemism, and Christianity belong?

Religion and Society

Whatever the truth of any of its beliefs—and that is a matter of faith—a religion is of immense importance to the society as well as to its individual members. The nature of religion's relationship to society, as you probably suspect, has been much debated. Why do religions vary from one society to another? Does religion merely reflect the structure of a society, or can religion influence that structure? Durkheim, Marx, and Weber offered three very different sociological perspectives on religion.

DURKHEIM: SOCIETY AS GOD

Emile Durkheim presented his functionalist view of religion in *The Elementary Forms of Religious Life,* first published in 1912. It was Durkheim's aim to refute the popular view that God—or whatever is worshipped as sacred—is merely an illusion, a figment of human imagination. According to Durkheim, if religion were an illusion, it would have disappeared in rational modern societies. But it has not. "It is inadmissible," said Durkheim, "that systems of ideas like religion, which have held so considerable a place in history, and to which people have turned in all ages for the energy they need to live, should be mere tissues of illusion." If God were merely a product of the individual's imagination, Durkheim also argued, it would occupy the same status as any other idea—a part of the profane world incapable of inspiring reverence, awe, and worship. Instead, God must be sacred and far above humans, as demonstrated by the fact that the deity is widely worshiped.

If this revered entity is both real and superior to us, then what is God? Durkheim's answer: society. Society is more powerful than any of us and beyond our personal control. It is separate from us, yet we are part of it, and it is part of our consciousness. It outlives each of us, and even our children. We are dependent on it, and it demands our obedience to it. It is neither a person nor a thing, yet we feel and know its reality. These attributes of society are also characteristics of the sacred—in Western religions, of God. In short, the sacred, according to Durkheim, is the symbolic representation of society. By worshiping God, we in effect are worshiping society.

Such a view of religion led Durkheim to emphasize that religion functions to preserve social order. Every religion, he argued, possesses both rituals and moral norms. Through their religion's rituals, people sanctify and renew their bonds to one another. Their

belief in the sacred and their acceptance of common norms are strengthened. Thus, religion binds the society and helps maintain it.

There is empirical support for the functionalist theory that religion helps maintain social order, as we will see later. But there is something wrong with Durkheim's argument that society is God. It is simply not empirically testable. The analogy that Durkheim drew between the characteristics of society and God may be interesting, but it cannot be used as scientific evidence to support his argument. The analogy only shows that society is in some ways *similar to* God, not that society *is* God.

MARX: RELIGION AS PEOPLE'S OPIUM

Unlike Durkheim, Karl Marx considered religion an illusion. Writing before Durkheim, Marx presented the conflict theory that if a society is divided into classes, its dominant religion represents the interests of the ruling class. The religion disguises and justifies the power of that class, though. The deception is not deliberate. The ruling class is not conscious of the true state of things. Yet religion, argued Marx, is nonetheless a real and an oppressive illusion, one that helps the ruling class perpetuate its domination of the

Marx assumed that oppression tends to make people embrace religion for consolation. Although many studies have supported this assumption, it is also true that religion can inspire social movements that change society. In support of "liberation theology," the Vatican in 1986 issued a document defending the right of the oppressed to revolt. Here a priest influenced by liberation theology says Mass in a warehouse occupied by striking Coca-Cola workers in Guatemala City.

masses. In medieval Europe, the Roman Catholic Church bolstered the feudal system by promoting the notion that kings ruled by divine right. In India the Hindu religion for thousands of years has provided religious justification for the caste system. Religion supports the ruling class by justifying existing inequalities.

If religion is merely an oppressive illusion, why would the masses support and even cling to it? The reason, according to Marx, is the prevailing social inequality and oppression, which drive the masses to seek solace somewhere. "Religion," Marx declared, "is the sigh of the oppressed creature, the heart of a heartless world, the soul of soulless circumstances. It is the opium of the people" (Acton, 1967). Opium offers relief and escape, and it drains one's will to find the source of problems. Similarly, religion brings relief to oppressed workers, dulls their sensitivity to suffering, and diverts them from attacking the root of their pain—their exploitation by the wealthy and powerful. Religion accomplishes all this by emphasizing the superiority of spiritual over earthly matters or promising eternal bliss in the afterlife with such doctrines as "Blessed are the poor." As a result, religion ends up "alienating" workers from themselves by acquiring a harmful power over them—causing them to develop a "false consciousness," an acceptance of the dominance of their oppressors.

Many studies have supported Marx's assumption that poverty or oppression tends to make people embrace religion for consolation (Wimberley, 1984). But religion is not always the opiate of the people that makes them accept the status quo. Religion can and does inspire social movements that change society. The black civil rights movement in the 1960s and 1970s owed much of its success to Dr. Martin Luther King, Jr., and other Christian ministers. Protestants, Catholics, and Jews have joined protests against South Africa's racist policies and U.S. ties with that country. Abroad, in the late 1970s, Muslim clergy spearheaded the revolution that has transformed Iran into a fanatically religious state. Many churches in Latin America today identify with guerrilla movements or revolutionary forces. Their "liberation theology" may sound ironically Marxist, but they argue that God always favors the poor and the oppressed and opposes the rich and powerful. In 1986 the Vatican issued a document defending the right of the oppressed to revolt—even to use armed struggle, though only as a last resort. Earlier that year, Catholics in the Philippines participated in the revolution that brought down the Marcos government. In

the late 1980s churches in Poland, Chile, and South Korea were also active against their repressive regimes, pressing for democratic reforms.

WEBER: THE ORIGIN OF CAPITALISM

Marx assumed that there are two types of social forces: material (such as economic conditions) and ideal (such as religious beliefs). He contended that the material forces largely determine the character of the ideal forces, that the economic structure shapes religious belief. Max Weber took a different position, arguing that in some cases an ideal force can influence a material force. Religion, therefore, can influence economic structure, changing society.

Weber provided his best-known discussion of the influence of religion on economic behavior in *The Protestant Ethic and the Spirit of Capitalism.* This "spirit" elevates hard work to the status of a moral duty and produces the disciplined and rational, not speculative, pursuit of economic gain. In contrast, traditional economic activity was marked by easygoing work habits and speculative acquisition. Some way of life, certain ideas and habits, Weber argued, must have produced this change in economic activity. Protestantism was a likely place to look for one source of the change. In Germany, the largely Protestant regions around the turn of this century were more industrialized than the predominantly Catholic regions, and there was also a higher percentage of wealthy Protestants than Catholics. Although religion and the pursuit of wealth are usually considered contradictory, the Baptists and Quakers of the seventeenth century were known for both their piety and their wealth.

But how could Protestantism encourage the development of capitalism? The early Protestants—especially those of the Calvinist sect—believed that long before they were born, God had predestined them to either salvation in heaven or damnation in hell. But they could not know their eternal destiny. This generated a great deal of anxiety. But such doubt, Calvin taught, was a temptation. To relieve anxiety and resist temptation, the Calvinists could turn only to constant self-control and work. They further believed that, whether saved or damned, the faithful must work hard for the glory of God so as to establish his kingdom on earth. Work came to be seen as a "calling" from God, and the worldly success that work brought came to be interpreted as a sign of election to heaven. And the Calvinists did work hard.

The purpose of hard work, however, was to glorify God, not to indulge in one's own pleasures. Early Protestants believed that they should not spend their wealth on worldly pleasures. Instead, they reinvested their profits to make their businesses grow. The constant accumulation of wealth—the continual reinvestment of profit—is another foundation of capitalism. To paraphrase what Marx said in *Das Kapital*, "Accumulate, accumulate, this is the law of capitalism." This law, according to Weber, happened to be compatible with the Protestant ethic.

Weber further argued that capitalism did not emerge in predominantly Catholic countries or China or India because the religions in those countries had world views that differed from the Protestant ethic. Catholicism does not teach predestination. It encourages people to seek their rewards in heaven, and it does not view earthly success as a sign of God's favor. Confucianism values social harmony, not individualistic strivings. Taoism teaches acceptance of the world as it is and withdrawal from it. Buddhism views worldly things as illusory and encourages escape from them through meditation. Hinduism requires its believers to endure the hardships of life and fulfill the obligations of their respective castes. These religions, Weber argued, did not offer ideas and habits favorable to the development of capitalist industrialism, but Calvinist Protestantism did.

You may have noticed that Weber's theory is compatible with the symbolic interaction perspective discussed in Chapter 1 (The Essence of Sociology). As symbolic interactionism would suggest, religion as an interpretation of one's world influences one's behavior toward that world. This is the essence of Weber's theory. But since its appearance in 1904, it has provoked many criticisms and countercriticisms to this day. Jere Cohen (1980), for example, claims to have found evidence that rational capitalism had originated under Catholicism in Italy—before the emergence of Protestantism. But R. J. Holton (1983) disagrees, arguing in defense of Weber that the capitalist development in Catholic Italy was actually insignificant. At any rate, we can be sure about one thing: it is difficult to recognize either today's Protestantism or today's capitalism in Weber's description. Both have changed.

Most Protestant denominations today do not stress that most of us are predestined to hell. The "spirit" of modern American capitalism is based as much on consumption as on work and production and as much on spending as on investing. Capitalists need markets or buyers. Advertising that lures its au-diences to indulge their desires and buy, to seek more leisure and buy, has become a major tool of American capitalism. These changes make it difficult to see how Weber's thesis can be valid today. In the late 1950s, Gerhard Lenski (1961) did find that Protestants were more likely than Catholics to achieve upward mobility. But by the 1960s the difference had diminished, especially among the younger generation (Glenn and Hyland, 1967), and by the 1980s there was a higher percentage of well-off Catholics than some Protestants such as Methodists and Baptists (Gallup and Castelli, 1989). Today Catholics who came from nearly every European country are better off in America than Protestants who came from the same country (Jencks, 1992). Moreover, capitalism is booming in such non-Protestant countries as Japan, South Korea, Taiwan, Hong Kong, and Singapore.

FUNCTIONS AND DYSFUNCTIONS

Durkheim, Marx, and Weber pointed to some of the ways in which religion satisfies the needs of individuals and of society. Some of these functions are positive, while others are negative (O'Dea and Aviad, 1983). Paradoxically, when a religion is too successful in carrying out its positive functions, it may become a negative force.

First, religion often performs a *supportive* function, by providing consolation, reconciliation, and relief from anxiety or fear. By praying, believers may become less fearful about losing their jobs or about old age and death. Faith may console those who have lost a loved one or are beset by loneliness, disappointment, frustration, or sorrow. Religion can reconcile people to the sinfulness of others, the hostility of enemies, the injustices of society, or other unpleasant aspects of this world. All this may explain why the more religious people are, the less likely they are to commit suicide (Stack, 1983a, 1983b). As Rodney Stark and his fellow researchers conclude, religion helps "cushion the despair and desperation that can drive people to take their own lives."

However, if it offers *too much* support and consolation, it can impede useful social change. In Marx's terms, as we have discussed, religion can be an opiate for the pains created by society. Many religions urge their believers to see all worldly things as trivial compared with the life of the spirit. Others perceive this world as a mere way station, or a "vale of tears" that is meant to be a test of love and faith, or even as an illusion. All these beliefs can encourage the faithful, not only to be consoled but also to endure their suffering docilely. Thus, religions can discourage people from confronting the sources of their suffering, from joining a social or revolutionary movement that may help to alleviate their suffering.

Second, religion may perform a *social control* function, strengthening conformity to society's norms. Religion may sacralize (make sacred) the norms and values of society with such commandments as "Thou shalt not kill" and "Thou shalt not steal." Then the laws of the state may be taken to be the laws of God, fulfilling divine purposes. If believers are taught to accept the authority of their church, they may be more likely to obey the authority of the state and society's other norms. Indeed, over 50 research studies since 1970 have shown that religious participation inhibits crime, delinquency, and deviant behavior in general (Ellis, 1985; Peek et al., 1985). More positively, religion encourages good, friendly, or cooperative behavior with the story of the Good Samaritan, the proverb "do unto others as you would have others do unto you," and other such teachings. Research does show that more religious people seem more friendly and cooperative—more likely to stop and comfort a crying child, to be good listeners, and even to get along with loud-mouthed, obnoxious people (Morgan, 1983, 1984). However, the *individual's* religiousness alone does not necessarily produce good behavior. One study by Rodney Stark and his colleagues (1982) suggests that religious individuals are more likely to refrain from deviant acts if they live in a community where the majority of the residents are also religious. Religious individuals are just as likely as others to engage in deviance if most of their friends are not religious. Thus, religion inhibits deviance largely by influencing large numbers of people rather than just a few.

However, religion's power to reinforce social control may set up yet another roadblock to useful change. If religion completely sacralizes the norms and values of a society, it may help preserve unjust laws and harmful values, such as those supporting racial and sexual inequality. The extremely faithful may consider them too sacred to question or change, perhaps saying, for example, "it is God's will that women should stay home and be wives and mothers only."

Third, religion may be a source of social change. This is known as the *prophetic* function—recalling the role of the ancient Jewish prophets, who dared to challenge the society and political authori-

When God is seen as supporting the established norms and values of society, then religion is not likely to welcome social change. But when a discrepancy is perceived between the way things are and the way God intends them to be, religion can favor change. The Reverend Martin Luther King, Jr., based his fight against racial discrimination on the ethical principles of the Judeo-Christian religion.

ties of their day in order to call their people to fulfill their covenant with Yahweh. Similarly, Dr. Martin Luther King, Jr., based his fight against racial discrimination on the ethical principles of Christianity. During the 1960s and 1970s, many religious leaders were in the forefront of the civil rights and anti-Vietnam War movements. During the 1980s, Anglican Archbishop Desmond Tutu and other church leaders played an important role in the blacks' struggle against the white racist government of South Africa. In Poland, the late Stefan Cardinal Wyszynski, leader of the Roman Catholic Church, resisted the Communist government's restrictions on religious freedom; his successor, Archbishop Jozef Glemp, continued to fight until the Communist regime was toppled. In the

Philippines, Jaime Cardinal Sin, the church's leader, helped bring down Marcos's repressive government. In the United States, some church leaders preach "green" theology to save the environment.

But prophetic calls for reform may produce violent fanaticism. During the seventeenth century, some 20,000 peasants in Russia were inspired to burn themselves as a way of protesting liturgical reforms in the Russian Orthodox Church. In 1835 the Reverend Jan Bockelson incited his Anabaptist followers in Germany to "kill all monks and priests and all rulers that there are in the world, for our king alone is the rightful ruler." In 1420 the Adamites, a religious cult of Bohemians in Europe, set about making holy war to kill the unholy. They believed that they must continue killing until they could make the blood fill the world to "the height of a horse's head" (Morrow, 1978). Today, the Muslim terrorists in Lebanon, including those who hold American and European hostages, welcome death as God's blessing for themselves while trying to kill their enemies. As a young Lebanese terrorist says, "I want to die before my friends. They want to die before me. We want to see God" (Galloway, 1987).

Fourth, religion may perform an *identity* function. By enabling individuals to consider themselves Baptist or Muslim, Catholic or Jewish, religion can tell believers who they are, what they are, and what the purpose of their lives is. In modern societies marked by impersonal relations and a confusing variety of values and norms, this function may be especially important to individuals. Without a religious identity, people may fall into an existential vacuum, finding life meaningless and merely muddling through.

However, if people identify too strongly with their own religion, social conflict may be intensified. In defining themselves by their religion, people tend to believe that there is only one true religion—their own—and become intolerant of all other, "false" religions. Loyalties to different religions may be yet one more factor dividing two groups and making compromise more difficult to achieve. In Africa's Sudan, since 1983, when the Muslim-led regime started a strict enforcement of Islamic law—which includes amputating the arms of robbers—animist and Christian rebels have reacted with shootings and terrorism (Maloney, 1984). Indeed, history is filled with persecutions and wars related to religious differences. Consider the medieval Christian Crusades against Muslim "heathens," the Thirty Years' War between Catholics and Protestants in seventeenth-century Europe, the persecution and slaughter of Mormons in the United States during the last century, the Hindu-Muslim conflicts that resulted in the creation of mostly Hindu India and a separate Islamic Republic of Pakistan in 1947, the strife between Protestants and Catholics in today's Northern Ireland, the violence between Christians and Muslims as well as between different Muslim sects that continues to tear Lebanon apart, and the clash between Buddhists and Hindus that plagues Sri Lanka today.

When people identify too strongly with their own religion, they find it difficult to make compromises with other faiths. History is filled with persecutions and wars related to religious differences, as shown by these victims of the violence between Catholics and Protestants in Northern Ireland.

CONFRONTATION AND COMPROMISE

A religion is concerned with the sacred, but it exists in this world, in an earthly rather than heavenly society. It must stand in some relation to that society—in harmony or confrontation, as an integral part of other institutions or withdrawn from them, or in some position in between these extremes. Even within Christianity, different groups have established different relations to society. We will examine these relationships, and then see the problems a religion faces as it becomes an accepted, established part of a society.

Church and Sect   Ernst Troeltsch (1931) has classified Christian religious bodies into two categories: the church and the sect. Speaking very generally, we can say that the church compromises with society; the sect confronts it. Many religious groups do not quite fit into either of these extreme categories, but we can think of mainline Protestant groups, such as the Episcopal and Presbyterian churches, as examples of what Troeltsch called a church, whereas Pentecostals and Jehovah's Witnesses are examples of sects.

A **church** tends to be a large, established religious group, with a formalized structure of belief, ritual, and authority. It is an inclusive organization, welcoming members from a wide spectrum of social backgrounds. Thus, members often have little but

their religion in common, and they may hardly know one another. Members tend to be born into the church, and the church sets up few if any requirements for membership. Its demands, on both its members and society, are not very exacting. Over the years, the church has learned to take a relatively tolerant attitude toward its members' failings. It has learned to reconcile itself one way or another with the institutions of the society, coexisting in relative peace with society's values.

The church's compromises do not satisfy the **sect,** a relatively small religious movement that has broken away from an established church. Time and again, groups have split off from Christian churches because some members believed the church had become too worldly. The sect that results holds itself separate from society, and it demands from its members a deep religious experience, strong loyalty to the group, and rejection of the larger society and its values. The sect is a tightly knit community, offering close personal relations among its members.

The Dilemmas of Institutionalization   Most pure sects do not last long. They either fail to maintain their membership and disappear, or they undergo change. Consider Methodism, which was founded in opposition to the Church of England. It was at first a sect that sought to correct social injustices and to aid the poor. Then Irish immigrants brought it to the

The more "successful" religions, such as the Roman Catholic Church, need a large organization to function smoothly. But such an organization has an elaborate hierarchy of authority, with some members occupying higher positions than others, that, in effect, is a form of social inequality. This becomes a dilemma for the church because of its belief that all people are equal before God. By contrast, sects such as the Jehovah Witnesses, which have fewer members and are less organized, do not have the same dilemma.

United States, where it was initially associated with the lower classes. But it has become a highly institutionalized religion today—successful, respectable, middle class, and less demanding of its members.

A paradoxical relation exists between religiousness and success. The more "successful" a religion is—in the sense of being more popular and more respectable in society as well as having more members—the less religious its members are. Established churches, such as the Episcopal, Methodist, and Catholic, are more successful than sects such as the Amish and Jehovah's Witnesses. But members of sects tend to be more religious, devoting more of their time to such religious matters as reading the Bible, praying, and door-to-door evangelizing. They may even show greater willingness to suffer or even die for their beliefs, as their ancient counterparts such as Jesus, his disciples, and early Christians did.

There are at least five dilemmas that accompany the success and institutionalization of a religion (O'Dea and Aviad, 1983).

1. *The dilemma of mixed motivation.* The success of a church offers its leaders new, self-centered motives for their careers—motives such as power and prestige. A similar change may occur among the rank and file. Once a religion is institutionalized, its members may be born into the church rather than converted to it. The security, friendship, or prestige that the church offers may become a motive for membership greater in importance than religious conviction. These motives may be useful for ensuring the success of a church, but they are basically secular, opposed to the religious doctrines that stress single-minded devotion to God and that emphasize God-centered rather than human-centered needs.

2. *The dilemma of administrative order.* The organization that emerges with institutionalization brings another problem as well: bureaucracy. The Roman Catholic Church, for example, has a vast and complicated bureaucracy, with an elaborate hierarchy of authority including the pope, cardinals, archbishops, bishops, monsignors, priests—plus many other ranks and lines of authority. Such an administrative order is necessary for maintaining the success of the church. But its hierarchy of positions—which is essentially a practice of social inequality—is contrary to the religious idea that all people are equal before God and should be treated as such.

3. *The symbolic dilemma.* At the heart of religions are symbolic expressions of the sacred. They are necessary for ensuring the success of a church, because they can make profound, complex religious concepts comprehensible and help people relate to God better. But people may end up misusing the symbols and missing the message behind them. The cross, for example, is a Christian symbol of God's love for humanity, which should cause us to accept and worship Christ with fervor. But illiterate Christians in traditional societies may be so awed by the cross that they worship it as an idol or use it as a talisman to ward off evil spirits. Better-educated Christians in traditional and industrial countries may find the cross so beautiful that they use it as a mere ornament. In short, the sacred symbols of a popular religion can lead to such irreligious behaviors as idolatry and vulgarization of God.

4. *The dilemma of oversimplification.* The oversimplification dilemma is similar to the symbolic

dilemma. In order to ensure the success of its religion, the institutionalized church oversimplifies its teachings so that people can easily comprehend them. To make people understand how much God still loves us even though we are so wicked, worthless, or lost, Christian preachers may tell the story about the prodigal son or about the lost sheep. They would say that God is like the prodigal son's father, who still loves us despite our sins like those of the prodigal son, or that God is like the shepherd who is still looking everywhere for his one lost sheep, though he has many sheep left. To show how much God supports the institution of marriage, the preachers may tell the story about Jesus turning water into wine at a wedding party. Just as symbols may be transformed into idols, however, the stories, parables, fables, and other preaching techniques of oversimplification may become mere objects of admiration and awe, so that the faithful miss the message behind the stories. Thus, some Christians may say "Oh, how moving the prodigal son story is!" but they continue to sin. Some married Christians may insist that Jesus actually turned water into wine, but instead of treating their marriages as sacred they opt for divorce.

5. *The dilemma of power.* To survive, the church makes accommodations with society. If it is successful, its values and society's may be increasingly similar. It may join forces with the secular authority, using the state to enforce religious conformity and lending its authority to sanctify what the state does. Coercion may replace faith. In many places in the past, heresy was punished by torture and even death. All this may ensure the success of the church but is basically irreligious, because the church is supposed to show compassion, love, and forgiveness instead.

A more subtle form of power—radio and television—is employed today to capture the souls of prospective followers. Those religious leaders who have easy access to this power of the mass media are more successful than those who do not. But the success is bought at the price of irreligiosity. Televangelists must induce audiences to send in money. Thus, their religious programs are, in effect, commercials. They may not look like commercials because they are much longer than most other advertisements. Nonetheless, these preachers expect people to buy their product (God) with money ("donation"), just as other advertisers do. In selling God like soap or pantyhose, though, they turn the holy into the profane. Here's how televangelist Richard Roberts does it: he urges his viewers to "sow a seed on your Mas-terCard, your Visa, or your American Express, and then when you do, expect God to open the windows of heaven and pour you out a blessing" (Woodward, 1987). As a group, TV evangelists use from 12 to 42.6 percent of their air time to appeal explicitly for funds. They do so by offering souvenirs and memen-tos, personal help or service, healing, and success (Marty, 1988).

QUESTIONS FOR DISCUSSION AND REVIEW

1. Why did Emile Durkheim assert that the supreme objects of religious belief are really manifestations of society?
2. What arguments did Marx provide to support his view that religion is "the opium of the people"?
3. According to Weber, how did the Protestant ethic lead to the origin of capitalism?
4. What are the functions and dysfunctions of reli-gion, and when does religion change from a posi-tive to a negative force?
5. Why does the evolution of sects into churches cre-ate dilemmas of institutionalization for religions?

Religion in the United States

As early as 1835, Alexis de Tocqueville observed that "there is no country in the world in which the Chris-tian religion retains a greater influence over the souls of men than in America." Still today, religion is perva-sive in the United States. According to a recent sur-vey, 94 percent of Americans believe in God, 90 per-cent pray, and 88 percent believe that God loves them. Some 56 percent of Americans also consider religion "very important" in their lives. By contrast, far smaller proportions of Italians, Spaniards, Bel-gians, Germans, Britons, and other Europeans believe in God or regard religion as very important in their lives (Gallup and Castelli, 1989).

Just what is it all these Americans believe? There is an amazing diversity of religions in the Unit-ed States. The tolerance for this diversity is one strik-ing characteristic of American religion. Another is the paradoxical coexistence of a high level of reli-giousness and a very high degree of secularization. Let us, then, discuss these characteristics as well as the relationships between religion and other aspects of American society.

RELIGIOUS AFFILIATION

There are more than 280 religious denominations in the country, but a few large churches have the alle-giance of most Americans. Protestants constitute the largest group, although Catholics outnumber the largest Protestant denomination—the Baptists. Ac-cording to the latest surveys, 92 percent of Ameri-cans have a specific religious preference, with 53 per-cent saying they are Protestants, 26 percent Catholics, and 2 percent Jews. The Baptists constitute 15 percent of all Americans (see Figure 11.1).

The correlation between affiliation with an or-ganized religion and religious belief and practice is far from perfect. Although 92 percent of Americans claim to have a religious preference, only 58 percent believe in life after death and 40 percent attend reli-

FIGURE 11.1 *Most Americans Belong to a Few Major Churches.*
We are a "denominational society," having numerous religious denominations. Only a few, though, attract the majority of Amerians into their fold. Protestants make up by far the largest group. But if Protestant are divided into different denominations, Catholics out-number even the largest Protestant group—the Bap-tists.

Source: Encyclopedia Britanica, 1993, p. 741; The Universal Almanac, 1993, p. 227.

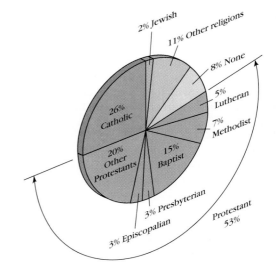

TABLE 11.2 *How Religions Rank Socioeconomically*

Religion and social stratification are connected. Despite their belief in equality before God, various religious groups are unequal socioeconomically.

RANK	RELIGION	COLLEGE GRADUATES	RANK	RELIGION	INCOME OF $40,000 OR MORE
1	Episcopalian	44%	1	Episcopalian	39%
2	Jewish	44	2	Jewish	36
3	Presbyterian	29	3	Presbyterian	30
4	Lutheran	24	4	Lutheran	25
5	Methodist	21	5	Catholic	23
6	Catholic	17	6	Methodist	22
7	Mormon	15	7	Mormon	18
8	Baptist	10	8	Baptist	14

Source: George Gallup, Jr., and Jim Castelli, *The People's Religion: American Faith in the 90's.* New York: Macmillan, 1989, pp. 101–117.

gious services regularly. Most Americans believe that you do not have to go to church or synagogue in order to be a good Christian or Jew (Gallup and Castelli, 1989). Among those who go to church, very few do so for strictly religious reasons. As a survey of Minnesota Christians shows, less than 10 percent cited worship as the primary reason they attend church (Bilheimer, 1983). Obviously, religious affiliation reflects something besides religious belief and practice. Belonging to a church can also afford a way of conforming to social norms or a way of obtaining fellowship. Various religions meet these and other needs in different ways. Some are more "respectable" than others, and some are more likely than others to offer friendship. Not surprisingly, the churches differ, too, in the typical social characteristics of their members.

Social Characteristics Catholics and Jews tend to be urban residents; Protestants tend to live in small towns and rural areas. Catholics, Jews, Episcopalians, and Presbyterians can be found mostly in the Northeast. Baptists, Methodists, and Lutherans predominate in the South and West. The largest proportion of other religions, such as the Mormons and Disciples of Christ, are in the Midwest. How religious Americans are varies also with the region in which they live. Southerners seem to be the most religious, and Westerners the least, with Midwesterners ranking second and Easterners third. (Gallup and Castelli, 1989)

Most religious groups favor the Democratic party over the Republican, just as the majority of Americans do. But Protestants are not as overwhelmingly Democratic as Catholics and Jews. In fact, Episcopalians and Presbyterians are more Republican than Democratic. In general, Protestants are more socially conservative and less supportive of civil liberties than Catholics and Jews. Among Protestants, the most heavily Republican groups—Presbyterians and Episcopalians—are most likely to be socially liberal and pro-civil liberties, whereas the most staunchly Democratic—the Baptists—are most likely to be socially conservative and least supportive of civil liberties. The more conservative Protestant churches are also more prejudiced against Jews and other minorities. Most likely, prejudiced people are inclined to join more conservative churches in the first place (Lipset and Raab, 1978).

Social class may lie behind many of these associations. Although they may consider themselves equal before God, various religious groups are unequal socioeconomically. They have different statuses, and they tend to attract people from different educational and income levels. Usually, Episcopalians, Jews, and Presbyterians top the status hierarchy. They are followed by Lutherans, Methodists, and Catholics, and trailed by Mormons and Baptists (see Table 11.2).

Social class also influences religious participation. In general, the higher a person's class, the more likely he or she is to attend church regularly, join Bible study groups, and provide his or her children with religious education. Moreover, people of higher classes hold most of the church's leadership positions, such as membership on a church's board of trustees. But these facts do not mean that higher-status people are more religious. In fact, belief in God is more widespread among the poor than among the rich. Moreover, the lower classes are more likely to believe in the literal interpretation of the Bible, to believe in a personal God, and to be emotionally involved in religion. The high rate of participation by upper-status people seems to reflect the fact that they are more inclined than the lower classes to participate in *all* kinds of voluntary organizations. For many higher-status people, religious participation appears to be a public activity required for social respectability.

For about the same reason, adults above age 24 are more active in their church than younger people. Religious involvement normally begins to escalate by age 25, first with marriage and then with parenthood. Adults are also more involved in a variety of social, political, and charitable activities—more likely, for example, to be registered to vote. Church involvement, then, reflects a broader pattern of social in-

volvement (Wilson, 1978; Gallup and Castelli, 1989). But differences in church involvement can be found among baby boomers, who are now in their thirties and forties. During their teens or early twenties, two-thirds dropped out of their churches and synagogues and one-third did not. Now, in the 1990s, 33 percent remain loyalists, who have never strayed from formal religion; 25 percent have returned to religious practice; and 42 percent continue to be dropouts. The loyalists are the least likely to lose confidence in the country and the most likely to have traditional lifestyles, values, and attitudes (see Table 11.3). Although the dropouts are no longer involved in traditional religion, they continue to have a strong belief in God. What about the returnees? Why do they return to organized religion? One reason is their feeling that religion is important for bringing up children. Another reason is their personal quest for meaning, triggered by feelings of emptiness and loneliness. A third reason is their need for belonging to a community—being with others, sharing faith, and doing things together. Despite their differences, though, the baby boomers have something in common. They distrust institutions and leaders, seek personal fulfillment, and are not totally committed to any faith (Wade, 1993).

TABLE 11.3 *How the Three Groups of Baby Boomers Differ*

	LOYALISTS (N = 174)	RETURNEES (N = 141)	DROPOUTS (N = 204)
Growing Up in the '60s and '70s			
Opposed to American involvement in Vietnam War	40%	43%	51%
Little or no confidence in country	7	16	20
Smoked marijuana	32	48	67
Current Attitudes, in the '90s			
Little or no confidence in country	21	26	31
Life better than expected	66	49	47
Feel need for more excitement	17	35	34
Opposed to legal abortion	54	48	24
Opposed to legalization of marijuana	86	75	62
Not wrong for unmarried couples to live together	17	27	52

Source: Wade Clark Roof, *A Generation of Seekers* (New York: HarperCollins, 1993), p. 189.

TABLE 11.4 *Winners and Losers Among Churches*

	1970	LATEST	CHANGE
Over The Last Decade, Fundamentalist Churches Have Gained Members:			
Southern Baptist Convention	11,628,032	14,907,826	Up 28%
Church of Jesus Christ of Latter-Day Saints (Mormons)	2,073,146	4,370,690	Up 111%
Assemblies of God	625,027	2,137,890	Up 242%
Seventh-Day Adventists	420,419	701,781	Up 67%
Church of the Nazarene	383,284	561,253	Up 46%
In That Same Period, Many Mainline Churches Have Declined:			
United Methodist Church	10,509,198	8,979,139	Down 15%
Presbyterian Church (U.S.A)	4,045,408	2,886,482	Down 29%
Episcopal Church	3,285,826	2,433,413	Down 26%
Lutheran Church in America	2,788,536	2,609,025	Down 6%
Christian Church (Disciples of Christ)	1,424,479	1,052,271	Down 26%

Source: The Universal Almanac, 1993, p. 227.

The Fundamentalist Revival Although religious membership among Americans remains high, the growth in church membership has not kept pace with the growth of the general population. Since the early 1970s, the American population has grown by over 12 percent, but religious institutions have expanded by only 4 percent. Some churches have actually lost members. Others, however, have gained many members (Naisbitt and Aburdene, 1990).

Generally, the large mainline churches—Episcopal, Methodist, Presbyterian, and Congregational—have lost many members. Those churches that have registered large gains tend to be smaller, less established religious groups. They are also the more conservative groups. Among them are fundamentalists, evangelicals, and pentecostals (see Table 11.4). In contrast to mainline Protestants, fundamentalists emphasize a literal interpretation of everything in the Bible. Evangelical, "born again" Christians also stress emotional demonstrativeness rather than quiet devotion at church services. Through the experience of being "born again," they believe that their lives have been dramatically changed. Some of these groups, known as charismatics or pentecostals, also speak in tongues, utter prophecies, and heal the sick.

Southern Baptists, Jehovah's Witnesses, Mormons, members of the Church of God, and Catholic Pentecostals are among the groups participating in this revival. In the past, fundamentalist and evangelical Christianity was associated with the poor and uneducated. Today, however, its appeal has spread, and business executives and prominent politicians are among its advocates. It has also spawned most of the new forty-three superchurches, each of which accommodates 5000 or more worshipers every Sunday. The growing strength of fundamentalism has further helped many African-American churches to hold their own in the midst of various social ills, such as rising drug use, unemployment, crime, and family disintegration. Like white fundamentalism and evangelicalism, black Christianity preaches the reality of flesh-and-blood Jesus and the urgency of spiritual rebirth. But it also includes social and economic liberation in its gospel (Lincoln and Mamiya, 1990; Ostling, 1991).

The fundamentalist revival is a reflection of the conservative trend in society. It is also a culmination of a number of factors. One is the aggressive, skillful use of television, as illustrated by the popularity of such fundamentalist preachers as Jerry Falwell and Pat Robertson. Another is the social changes of the last two decades that have driven many conservative Americans into fundamentalist churches. These social changes have involved the women's movement, homosexuals, unmarried mothers, legalization of abortion, and court decisions against school prayer. Moreover, the fundamentalist churches, because of their highly personal style of worship, tend to attract the casualties of this fast-changing, high-tech age—"people who are socially isolated, mentally depressed, alienated, and dehumanized by modern society" (Moberg, 1984). Finally, there is an organizational difference between mainline and fundamentalist churches. Mainline churches tend to be "religious audiences." Their members gather periodically to participate in worship services but often hardly know one another. But fundamentalist churches are closer to being "religious communities." Their members are more often likely to find their best friends within the congregation and to be deeply involved in the church's activities (Stark and Glock, 1968; Hammond, 1985; Marty and Appleby, 1992). Thus, for those who seek fellowship from a church, the fundamentalist groups are more attractive than mainline churches.

Many mainliners have begun to fight back, though. To increase its membership, one Episcopal church uses newspaper and direct-mail ads. One lampoons the fundamentalist competition by showing a man with his mouth taped. The accompanying caption says: "There's only one problem with religions that have all the answers. They don't allow questions" (Woodward, 1986). But it is doubtful that such efforts can stop most of the mainliners from drifting into the sidelines. Contrary to popular belief, most people who leave the liberal churches do not join the conservative churches. They simply stop going to any church because these individuals lack religious commitment in the first place. Ridiculing fundamentalist churches will not bring these religious dropouts to rejoin the liberal churches. Moreover, the "demographic weakness" of aging membership and declining birth rates in the liberal churches makes it doubly difficult to regain former clout and prosperity. Ironically, though, given their rising number of aging members, who are generally conservative, and their declining number of young members, who are generally liberal, the mainline churches may eventually become as conservative as the fundamentalists (Roof and McKinney, 1988).

Cults Although some evangelical and charismatic groups represent a rebuke of mainline churches, they are not new religions. They remain Christian. In contrast, cults reject established religions. They usually claim to offer a new belief system. Like evangelical groups, American cults have been growing. Today, there are about 2500 cults. They run the gamut from The Farm, which condemns all forms of violence, to the Bible of the Church of Satan, which teaches that "if a man smites you on the cheek, smash him on the

other." Most are very small, and the total number of cultists is only about 3 million (Beck, 1978; Levine, 1984).

A **cult** is usually united by total rejection of society and extreme devotion to the cult's leader. A dramatic example is the Branch Davidians in Waco, Texas. Led by David Koresh in the late 1980s and early 1990s, members gave up all their bank accounts and personal possessions. They also let Koresh take their wives and daughters as his concubines. Koresh claimed that he was Jesus Christ but, as a sinful Messiah, he understood sinful humanity better than the earlier, more virtuous Christ. He also convinced his followers that he was destined to lead them in bringing about the end of the world. In 1993 nearly all the Branch Davidians died when the compound where they lived was torched in response to an attempt by government agents to force them out with tear gas. Another example of a cult is the People's Temple, founded by Jim Jones in San Francisco in the 1970s. Jones later moved his cult from San Francisco to Jonestown, Guyana, because, he said, evil people in the United States would try to destroy the Temple. He told his flock that to build a just society required a living God—namely, himself. To prove his divinity, he "healed" parishioners by appearing to draw forth "cancers" (which actually were bloody chicken gizzards). He claimed that he had extraordinary sexual gifts, required Temple members to turn over all their possessions to him, and insisted that they call him "Dad" or "Father." Then the People's Temple shocked the world. In November 1978 more than 900 members committed mass suicide at the order of their leader when a U.S. congressman and other officials went there to investigate the cult's activities.

The Unification Church has been more successful. Its founder, Sun Myung Moon, a South Korean businessman, declares himself the New Messiah. According to him, Jesus has appeared to him, telling him that he has been chosen by God to complete the mission that Jesus could not finish because of the crucifixion. Moon's mission is to combine all the world's religions and nations into one, to be headed by Moon himself. He teaches that sex is evil, demands that sexual feelings be totally repressed, and arranges all marriages within the cult. Members of the cult, most of whom are young, must break all ties with their families, work 18 hours a day soliciting donations, and give all their possessions to the church. The result is that Moon lives in splendor on a huge estate, owns several yachts, and controls an enormous business empire. He also uses his great wealth to influence

A cult is usually united by total rejection of society and extreme devotion to the cult's leader. Left: *David Koresh and his devoted followers formed a tight-knit religious community that saw themselves at odds with the outside world. They died in an FBI siege on their Waco compound in 1993.* Right: *Foreshadowing Koresh was Jim Jones, who led his flock to a mass suicide in Jonestown, Guyana, in 1978.*

conservative politicians, with the aim of achieving "the natural subjugation of the American government and population" (Judis, 1989).

A cultist's life is not easy at all. Why, then, would anyone want to join a cult? Primarily because it offers something that meets a specific need of the joiner, which cannot be found in traditional churches. The Synanon Church provides drug addicts with a home and rehabilitation program. The People's Temple emphasized egalitarianism and offered a communal home to the oppressed, especially poor blacks, prostitutes, and other outcasts. Most of the other cults, such as the Unification, Hare Krishnas, and Children of God, are more popular with middle-class youth. Contrary to popular belief, the young people who join a cult are mostly normal and come from stable, religious families that uphold "traditional values of family life, morality, and decency." Most have maintained good relationships with their parents and have done particularly well in school. Indeed, their warm, concerned parents have given them every material, social, and intellectual benefit (Barker, 1984;

Wright and Piper, 1986). What possible rewards can *they* find from joining a cult?

After studying at least 100 cults and interviewing more than 1000 individual members, Saul Levine (1984) concludes that the cults provide the youth with "desperate detours to growing up." Like most of their peers, the youthful joiners must grow up to be free and independent by leaving their parents. But they are more likely to lack the skill, confidence, or courage to strike out on their own in the harsh, cold world. They are more likely to find it too painful to leave their warm families for the cold world outside. For these youngsters, a cult provides separation without the accompanying pain, because the communal group typically operates as an exaggerated and idealized family that offers an enormous amount of love and care. It even gives careful attention to serving good, nutritious food, an emphasis that rivals a mother's care in ensuring a wholesome diet for her children.

Serving as a halfway house between the parental home and the outside world, though not intentionally, the cult enables the young joiners to pick up skills for living an independent life. Once they have learned to take care of themselves, cult members usually leave the groups, resuming their previous lives and finding gratification in the middle-class world. In fact, more than 90 percent of the cult joiners return home within two years, and virtually all joiners eventually abandon their groups (Levine, 1984).

Nevertheless, many people, especially parents, are fearful of cults. Recently, they have begun to fear Satanism. Satanists, or devil worshipers, are believed to be promoting drug abuse and sexual orgies, snatching youngsters off the street, organizing child pornography rings, breeding babies for ritualistic sacrifice and cannibalism, mutilating cattle in the countryside, and influencing the lyrics of rock music. A Catholic cardinal has warned his congregation that heavy-metal rock music is "pornography in sound" that can lead teenagers to spiritual entrapment and suicide. Many anticult groups, such as the Cult Awareness Network, have fueled Satan-fear to hysterical proportions. However, it is difficult to find evidence of Satanists' nefarious activities. Most reports on Satanism have come from sensational newspaper articles, undocumented secondary sources, or unsubstantiated claims. Police have never, for example, found any evidence for the frequently reported claim that about 50,000 human lives are sacrificed to the devil every year in this country (Shupe, 1990; Bromley, 1991).

NEW AGE

A new religious group that has recently attracted the most attention is the New Age movement. In every major city, its devotees can be seen seeking insight or personal growth with spiritual teachers, at a metaphysical bookstore, or at an educational center. But surprisingly, according to a recent poll, only 28,000 Americans regard themselves as New Agers (Goldman, 1991). Despite their small number, they have been given far more attention than any other new group on the American religious landscape because they represent the most affluent, well-educated, and successful Americans. Ninety-five percent of the readers of *New Age Journal,* for example, are college educated, with average incomes of $47,500. New Agers are still unorganized (without an organization like the United Methodist Church or the Southern Baptist Convention). They do not have a coherent philoso-

phy or dogma, either. They may believe in various phenomena, such as reincarnation, telepathy, auras, out-of-body and near-death experiences, spirit channeling, candle meditation, and extraterrestrial revelation. Two of these beliefs have been widely publicized as the major characteristics of the New Age. One is the belief in reincarnation—a person's being reborn, after death, in a new body or life form. Another is channeling—using one's body and voice as a vehicle for some wise person from the great beyond.

Running through these beliefs is a strong sense that the divine resides in humanity. Thus, New Agers seek to realize the limitless potential of humanity for themselves. They are not interested in transforming the world, but themselves. Many New Agers used to be Christians who attended church regularly but who were left spiritually hungry. "They wanted God, not to hear God," as a Harvard theologian said. In the New Age movement, they find God within themselves. Some Christians say that the notion of a person being God is blasphemous. They believe that only through Christ can humanity be *united* with the divine—humanity alone cannot *be* divine. Actually, the New Age's concept of human divinity is similar to the Christian belief that people are made in the image and likeness of God, therefore possessing a divine spark. But New Agers prefer to seek God in their own way—such as through meditation—rather than with the help of an organized Western religion. They regard Jesus as merely an enlightened teacher like Buddha, Muhammad, or Gandhi, rather than as the only savior of humanity (Hoyt, 1987; Naisbitt and Aburdene, 1990; Bloom, 1992).

ISLAM

Compared to New Age, Islam in the United States has received far less attention but has considerably more adherents. About 1.4 million Americans identify themselves as Muslims. But they have been widely estimated to number between 3 million and 6 million. This is probably due to the popular assumption that virtually all immigrants from predominantly Muslim Arab countries are Muslims. Actually, Christians from those countries are more likely to emigrate to the United States, which explains why most Arab-Americans are Christians (Goldman, 1991). Nevertheless, American Muslims are still one of our fastest-growing religious groups.

Slightly over half of all Muslims are immigrants, whose entry into this country has doubled in the past two decades. However, a steadily increasing number of native-born Americans have been converted. Moreover, the Islamic community includes large numbers of African-Americans. Most of these Americans used to espouse a militant, antiwhite, and separatist philosophy, but they now embrace orthodox, mainstream Islam. They make up about 40 percent of the American Muslim population. Despite its significant growth in the United States, though, Islam is still widely misunderstood. In the minds of many Americans, the word "Muslim" conjures up an image of Arab terrorists, recently reinforced by Iraq's invasion of Kuwait and its holding of Western hostages. Of course, not all Arabs are terrorists, just as the high murder rate in the United States does not make all Americans murderers. Islam is popularly associated with Arab countries. Actually, Arabs make up only 20 percent of the world's Muslims—most live in Indonesia, Pakistan, India, and Africa. Many Americans also see Islam as somehow foreign, mysterious, and threatening to our Judeo-Christian heritage. In fact, as we have previously suggested, Islam is monotheist, like Christianity and Judaism. It also regards all people as the descendants of Adam and Eve, accepts the Old Testament, and reveres Jesus and the Virgin Mary (Sheler, 1990).

Nevertheless, Islam has its own distinctive features. Its faithful believe that their Koran—holy scriptures—was revealed in Arabic to the prophet Muhammad. The Koran tells all Muslims to perform five basic devotional duties: (1) declaring their belief that "there is no God but Allah (Arabic for "the God") and Muhammad is his Prophet," (2) praying five times a day while facing Mecca, (3) fasting from dawn to dusk during the month of Ramadan, (4) donating about 2.5 percent of one's income to charities, and (5) making a pilgrimage to Mecca at least once. In addition, Muslims must follow a strict code of ethics and diet. They must not consume alcohol, illicit drugs, or pork. They must refrain from premarital and extramarital sex and dating. They are forbidden to gamble or pay or accept interest on loans or savings accounts. These religious rules bring Muslims into conflict with the dominant American culture. American Muslims find it difficult to leave their jobs for afternoon prayers. Many are compelled to pay interest on bank loans needed for purchasing homes and cars. Devout Muslims find American society shockingly permissive, riddled with what they consider moral problems, such as sexual freedom, drug use, crime, and lack of respect for authority. Immigrant parents often argue with their teenage children about dating and drinking (Ostling, 1988; Sheler, 1990).

The clash between Islamic and Western cultures may ultimately produce a distinctively American brand of Islam. In many ways, some American mosques already function more like Christian churches than traditional mosques in Islamic countries. The Toledo center—the most impressive American mosque, located in Perrysburg, Ohio—has 22 nationality groups among its members. Weddings and funerals are held in the mosque. There are Sunday classes for children and teenagers as well as "lectures" for adults. After the afternoon prayer service, the faithful get together for a meal in a lower-level dining room. The problem is that there is still a lack of Western-trained imams (Muslim prayer leaders, comparable to Christians' pastors or Jews' rabbis) and Islam scholars. Nearly all imams come from the Middle East with little firsthand experience in Western culture. There are also no Islamic "divinity schools" in North America (Sheler, 1990).

SECULARIZED RELIGION

Common sense suggests that the more secular a society is, the less likely religion is to thrive. But the United States, as Will Herberg (1983) said, is "at once the most religious and the most secular of nations." The churches have retained large memberships despite the secularization of society. One reason may be the nature of most Americans' religion: it is, to a great extent, "secularized religion"—in effect, nonreligious religion. The religious elements are easy to see. But what are the nonreligious elements?

First, the high rate of religious affiliation does not reflect a strong commitment to religion. Close to half of Christian church members reject such traditional articles of faith as Christ's miracles, the resurrection, life after death, the virgin birth, and the second coming of Christ. An overwhelming majority do not believe that the devil exists. Neither do they consider divorce "always wrong or sinful." Many Christians take little part in their church's rituals and do not seem to take seriously the Christian doctrine that the faithful should not be of this world. Most Catholics disagree with the Pope on many issues. They ignore the church's ban on birth control and on the use of condoms to prevent AIDS. They reject the teaching that abortion should be totally illegal. They also favor permitting women to be priests and allowing priests to marry, which the church opposes (see

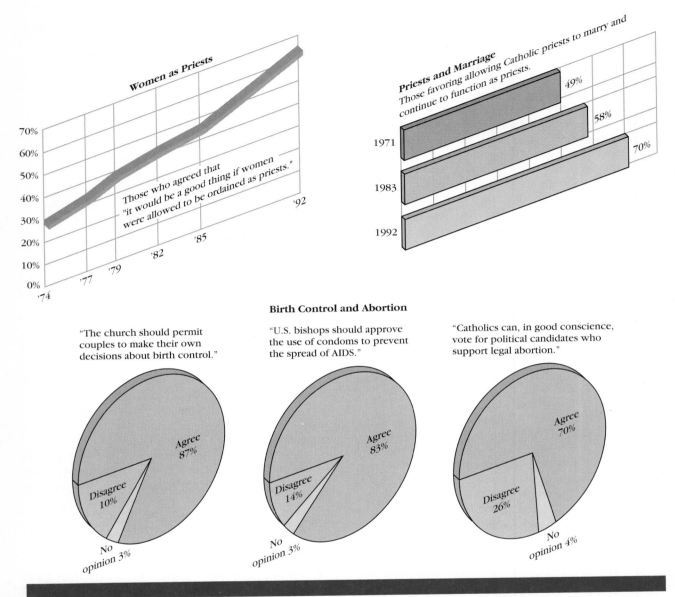

FIGURE 11.2 *Catholics Speak Out*
Many people of faith reject particular elements of their faith. Catholics disagree with the Pope on many issues, including permitting women to be priests, allowing priests to marry, and abortion and birth control.

Source: New York Times, June 19, 1992, p. A8. Copyright © 1992 by the New York Times Company. Reprinted by permission.

Figure 11.2). In other words, many religious people hold the same beliefs as secular, nonreligious people. Yet they still consider themselves to be religious. As one poll shows, an overwhelming 93 percent of Catholics believe that "it is possible to disagree with the Pope and still be a good Catholic" (Bilheimer, 1983; Ostling, 1987).

Even the attitudes of the clergy reflect this retreat from traditional religious belief. Hellfire-and-brimstone sermons are rare in most churches. The clergy refrain from emphasizing the uncompromising stands of Jesus, Isaiah, Amos, and other prophets in opposition to the "wicked" ways of this world. Some clerics, said Peter Berger (1967), even "proclaim the senselessness of prayer." In fact, the clergy are also more critical of the Bible than the laity are (Bilheimer, 1983). In 1991 an official committee of the Presbyterian Church urged the church to follow social currents by condoning sex outside marriage, which violates the Biblical commandment that "Thou shalt not commit adultery."

If traditional prayer and conviction are vanishing, what is left in the churches? In Herberg's (1983) words, there is "religiousness without religion. . . a way of sociability or belonging rather than a way of reorienting life to God." Without their traditional beliefs, some churches begin to look like social clubs, offering exercise classes, day-care programs, and singles' nights. In addition, some religions have turned to emphasizing ethics and social action, sometimes nonreligious in nature. They urge their congregations to strive not for personal holiness but for love of neighbors, social justice, international peace, the creation of a humane society, and the realization of the kingdom of God on earth. These could be the seeds of a shift from a theistic religion to an ethical one.

Secularism has not hit all religious bodies in the same way. In particular, most conservative groups have retained traditional beliefs. As we have noted, it is the conservative religious groups that have experienced growth during the last decade. However, their televangelists have secularized their religion to some degree. To have an authentic religious experience, we must have a special place for the performance of a religious service. A church, synagogue, temple, or mosque usually suffuses anything that happens there with a religious aura. But any other place will do if it is first decontaminated—divested of its secular, profane uses. Thus, a gymnasium, dining hall, or hotel room can be sacralized with a cross on a wall, candles on a table, or a sacred document in public view. Moreover, our behavior must befit the otherworldliness of the place. This can be attained by sitting quietly, meditating, kneeling down at appropriate moments, wearing a skullcap, or some other religious conduct. But most people who watch a religious television program can hardly derive a real religious experience. They do not separate the sacred from the profane. They eat and drink and talk and occasionally walk to the refrigerator for more refreshments or to the bathroom for bodily relief—all these right in the middle of a religious service. Sometimes they even watch in the kitchen or bedroom—hardly a sacred place for worship. What they get from the TV religious program is, in effect, secularized religion—the experience being similar to watching a secular program such as "Cheers" or "L.A. Law" (Postman, 1985).

RELIGIOUS TELEVISION

According to a Gallup survey, 49 percent of the U.S. population (about 120 million) have watched a religious program on television at some time in their lives, 39 percent (96 million) have watched within the past 30 days, and 25 percent (61 million) have done so within the past seven days (Gallup and Castelli, 1989).

Who are these people, particularly those who watch a religious program at least once a week? According to this survey, they are more likely than nonviewers to be relatively old (over age 50), female, low-income, and poorly educated. They are also more religiously active and conservative. They are more likely to attend church regularly, to consider religion very important in their lives, to have tried to encourage nonbelievers to accept Jesus Christ as their savior, and to believe the Bible to be the literal word of God. They are highly satisfied with their experience of worshiping in church. Why, then, do they turn to religious television? One reason is that most TV evangelists are conservative, and their messages are compatible with those of the audience. Another reason is that religious television serves as a supplement to, rather than a replacement for, church life. Feeling deeply religious, the regular viewers of religious television apparently hunger for more than what they get from their church. But because their church remains the main source of their religious experience, they do not expect as much from television. They only expect a little extra benefit from it. Hence, they do not feel put off by the fact that religious television is less effective than church service in satisfying the needs of the faithful.

Support for religious television has declined sharply over the last several years. This has largely resulted from the sexual and financial scandals involving the famous TV evangelists Jim Bakker and Jimmy Swaggart. In the early 1980s, about one-third of religious-television viewers contributed money to a TV evangelist, but by 1990 only one-tenth did so. Public confidence in televangelists also suffered a significant decline. The proportion of Americans seeing television ministers as "trustworthy" fell from 41 to 23 percent (Gallup and Castelli, 1989; Shipp, 1991).

Nevertheless, large numbers of people still watch religious television, with at least 61 million doing so once a week. For these Christians, religious television continues to be a part of their spiritual life. They can choose between two kinds of TV evangelists. Some evangelists, such as Robert Schuller and Oral Roberts, focus their messages on achieving personal needs like success and miracles. Other evangelists, such as Jerry Falwell and Pat Robertson, are more socially oriented and political—condemning the sinful ways of life in today's society (Frankl, 1987). Given their unique styles and messages, individual evangelists appeal to different audiences. Billy Graham has the largest percentage of viewers who are women, white, and older than 50. Jimmy Swaggart's viewers include the highest percentage of men, rural dwellers, and southerners. Oral Roberts' followers are especially likely to be divorced, widowed, or single. Pat Robertson has the highest percentage of viewers who are relatively young and married and who attend church most frequently (Gallup and Castelli, 1989).

CIVIL RELIGION

Groups such as the Moral Majority are calling for the moral reform of the nation, but they do not condemn the country itself. Indeed, according to the Reverend Jerry Falwell (1981), the United States is "the only logical launching pad for the world evangelization" because it is a "great nation . . . founded by godly men upon godly principles to be a Christian nation"—but it has been corrupted. What the Moral Majority and similar groups appear to be seeking is a renewal of America's old civil religion.

Every nation has its own **civil religion,** a collection of beliefs, symbols, and rituals that sanctify the dominant values of the society. The civil religion is a hybrid of religion and politics. The state takes up certain religious ideas and symbols, and religion sacralizes certain political principles, backing up the government's claim to a right to rule with its own moral authority. Falwell, for example, has argued that the free-enterprise system is outlined in the Bible's Book of Proverbs. Thus, aspects of political institutions take on religious overtones. The civil religion links religion and politics, harmonizing them (Bellah and Hammond, 1980). Whatever its content, a civil religion can unify the citizens of a country by heightening their sense of patriotism.

What American civil religion is depends on who is defining it. For conservatives, such as the Reverend Jerry Falwell, civil religion in America includes the belief that America is chosen by God to spread Christianity, traditional family values, and free-enterprise capitalism. By contrast, liberals believe that America is obligated as a Judeo-Christian nation to show compassion by using its vast resources to solve such world problems as poverty, hunger, and social injustice.

What is the content of this civil religion in the United States? It includes, first of all, faith in the American way of life, with freedom, democracy, equality, individualism, efficiency, and other typically American values as its creeds. The "American way of life," said Herberg (1983), is the common religion of American society by which Americans define themselves and establish their unity. Protestantism, Catholicism, and Judaism are its "subfaiths."

God plays an important role in this civil religion. He is cited on our coins ("In God We Trust") and in national hymns ("God Bless America"). References to God are made in all oaths of office, in courtroom procedures, at political conventions, in the inaugural address of every president, and on practically all formal public occasions.

But the God of American civil religion is not the god of any particular church. Adherence to American civil religion requires only our belief in God, however we choose to define the deity—as a personal God, an impersonal force, a supreme power, an ideal, or whatever. We do not have to believe in Moses, Jesus, the Bible, heaven and hell, or any other doctrine of a particular religion. We are instead exhorted to "go to the church of your choice." "Our government makes no sense," President Eisenhower is reported to have said, "unless it is founded on a deeply felt religious faith—*and I don't care what it is.*" The civil religion does not favor one particular church but religion in general. Everyone is expected at least to pay lip service to religious principles, if not to join a church or synagogue. It is considered un-American to be godless or, worse, to attack religion.

Like a genuine religion, American civil religion contains symbols, rituals, and scriptures. Its sacred writings are the Declaration of Independence and the Constitution. George Washington is seen as the Moses who led his people out of the hands of tyranny. Abraham Lincoln, our martyred president, is seen as the crucified Jesus; his Gettysburg Address is a New Testament. The civil religion's holy days are the Fourth of July, Thanksgiving, Memorial Day, and Veterans Day, when we sing sacred hymns such as "The Star-Spangled Banner" and "America the Beautiful," invoke the name of God, listen to sermonlike speeches, and watch ritualistic parades. The American flag, like the Christian cross, is supposed to inspire devotion. Since the 1960s, however, the American civil religion has divided into two groups. The conservatives believe that America is chosen by God to spread Christianity, traditional family values, and free-enterprise capitalism all over the world. The liberals believe that America is obligated as a Christian nation to show compassion by using its vast resources to solve such world problems as poverty, hunger, and social injustice (Wuthnow, 1988).

It is popularly believed that religion is less relevant to our lives as we become more scientifically and technologically sophisticated. This turns out to be a myth. As we have seen, the United States, despite its being the world's leader in science and technology, is more religious than many other nations. Americans are also more religious today than they were some 60 years ago. There are now proportionately more churches, more people attending religious services, and more money donated to churches (Caplow et al., 1983; Greeley, 1989). Since 1975 there has also been no decline in church attendance among Catholics, despite their growing opposition to the Pope's teachings. "In their hearts," conclude Michael Hout and Andrew Greeley (1987), "they are as Catholic as the Pope, whether he thinks so or not." Why is religion so popular in the United States? The answer could be found in the unique nature of American religion. As has been discussed, we have a tremendous diversity of religious beliefs, a high level of religious tolerance, a secularized religion, and a civil religion. All this makes it easy for all kinds of individuals to be religious *in their own way*. That's probably why, as we have noted, most Americans can claim to believe in God or have a religion, but without much commitment.

QUESTIONS FOR DISCUSSION AND REVIEW

1. What are the traditional religious affiliations of Americans?
2. What does the current fundamentalist religious revival have in common with the upsurge in cults, and how do these two types of religious movements differ?
3. Who are the New Agers and Muslims in America? What is the nature of their religions?
4. What contributes to the development of secularized religion in American society?
5. Why is religious television relatively popular in the United States?
6. What is civil religion, and what beliefs are included in the American version of this religion?

CHAPTER REVIEW

1. *What is religion?* A religion is a unified system of beliefs and practices regarding sacred things that unites its adherents into a single community. *Must a religion focus on the worship of a god?* No, only theistic religions do so. Ethical and animistic religions define the sacred in a different way.

2. *According to Durkheim, what is God?* Durkheim argued that God is a symbolic representation of society. By their worship, members of society strengthen their bonds to each other and their acceptance of the society's norms. Thus, religion helps preserve social order. *How did Marx view religion?* To him, religion is an oppressive illusion, which helps

the rich and powerful to perpetuate their domination of the masses. He argued that religion justifies society's inequalities and gives solace to the masses, diverting their attention from the source of their oppression. *Can religion influence economic structure, or do material forces always determine ideal forces?* Unlike Marx, Weber argued that in some cases religion can influence economic structure, changing society, and he contended that Protestantism was one force that encouraged the development of capitalism.

3. *What functions does religion serve, for individuals and for society as a whole?* It can support and console people, provide social control, stimulate social change, and provide individuals with a sense of identity. If these functions are carried too far, however, religion can become dysfunctional. By offering too much solace and maximizing social control, religion can impede social change. Crusades for social reform can develop into violent fanaticism. Too strong an identification with a religion can lead to conflict with other groups. *How can "success" sap a religion of its vitality?* As a religious group grows and becomes institutionalized, it faces dilemmas involving mixed motivation, administrative order, symbols, oversimplification, and power.

4. *What are some distinguishing characteristics of religion in the United States?* A high percentage of Americans belong to some church, even though ours is a very secular society. Many religions have themselves been secularized. And there is great diversity of religions and religious tolerance. *Are American religious groups growing?* Overall, their membership is not increasing as fast as the population. More liberal, mainline churches have suffered a decline, but the less established, more conservative religious groups have recently experienced considerable growth. The New Age movement and Islam have also surged in size.

5. *In what ways have many Christians and their churches become secularized?* Many Christians reject the traditional doctrines of their faith and seem to turn to their churches for the sake of fellowship, not commitment to God. Many churches now stress social reform rather than worship—an emphasis that might indicate evolution from a theistic to an ethical religion. Secularism even influences fundamentalists, who in large numbers watch religious television despite its failure to provide a genuine religious experience. *What is the American civil religion?* It

includes belief in God, support for religion in general—but not for any particular religion—and celebration of the "American way of life."

KEY TERMS

Animism The belief in spirits capable of helping or harming people (p. 253).

Church A relatively large, well-established religious organization that is integrated into the society and does not make strict demands on its members (p. 259).

Civil religion A collection of beliefs, symbols, and rituals that sanctify the dominant values of society (p. 272).

Cult A religious group that professes new religious beliefs, rejects society, and demands extreme loyalty from its members (p. 266).

Ethicalism The type of religion that emphasizes moral principles as guides for living a righteous life (p. 252).

Monotheism The belief in one god (p. 251).

Polytheism The belief in more than one god (p.251).

Religion A unified system of beliefs and practices regarding sacred things that unites its adherents into a single moral community (p. 250).

Ritual Behavioral expression of a religious belief (p. 250).

Sacred Whatever transcends the everyday world and inspires awe and reverence (p. 250).

Sect A relatively small religious group that sets itself apart from society and makes heavy demands on its members (p. 259).

Shamanism The belief that a spiritual leader can communicate with the spirits, by acting as their mouthpiece or letting the soul leave his or her body and enter the spiritual world (p. 253).

Theism The type of religion that centers on the worship of a god or gods (p. 251).

Totemism The belief that a kinship exists between humans and an animal or a plant (p. 253).

SUGGESTED READINGS

Bloom, Harold. 1992. *The American Religion: The Emergence of the Post-Christian Nation* New York: Simon & Schuster. An analysis of how the Mormons, the Southern Baptists, and other made-in-America religions reflect the American preoccupation with the self.

Gallanter, Marc. 1989. *Cults: Faith, Healing, and Coercion.* New York: Oxford University Press. Shows how cults effectively use rewards and benefits rather than coercion to gain loyalty from members.

Greeley, Andrew M. 1989. *Religious Change in America*. Cambridge, Mass.: Harvard University Press. A data-packed analysis of how Americans continue to be as religious as ever despite all the social changes around them.

Marty, Martin E., and R. Scott Appleby (eds.) 1992. *Fundamentalism Observed*. Chicago: University of Chicago Press. A collection of articles by scholars from various disciplines dealing with a wide range of fundamentalists.

Roof, Wade Clark 1993. *A Generation of Seekers: The Spiritual Journeys of the Baby Boon Generation*. New York: HarperCollins An analysis of how the baby boomers, who are now in their thirties and forties, feel about religion.

12

POLITICS AND THE ECONOMY

MYTHS AND REALITIES

Myth: The president of the United States, being the commander in chief, has the constitutional authority to declare war on a foreign country.

***Reality:** The president may believe that he does, but members of Congress disagree, insisting that only they have the legal power to authorize war.*

Myth: War is unavoidable because it is part of human nature.

***Reality:** War can be stopped because it is a product of society, not biology, as proven by great societal variations in being warlike or peaceful.*

Myth: The fact that blacks have lower voting rates than whites means that race plays a significant role in voting.

***Reality:** Class, not race, is a primary factor. Blacks and whites of similar education and income have about the same voting rates.*

Myth: In the United States, violence does not pay. Nonviolent protests against the government are more likely to achieve their objectives.

***Reality:** A study of 50 U.S. protest movements shows that 75 percent of the violent groups got what they fought for, compared with 53 percent of the nonviolent groups.*

Myth: Poverty is the breeding ground for revolution and terrorism. Revolutionary leaders and terrorists are therefore mostly poor.

***Reality:** Most of the revolutionary leaders and terrorists come from relatively affluent families.*

Myth: Industrialization can be a boon to the world by helping all nations to prosper, so that international peace can be achieved.

***Reality:** According to a 50-nation study, industrialization creates global inequality, with highly industrialized nations enjoying higher status and more power than the less industrialized ones, which threatens world peace.*

Myth: In the United States and Japan, the world's most capitalist societies, the government pursues a strict laissez-faire, free-enterprise policy by eschewing interference in economic affairs.

***Reality:** Governments in even the most capitalist societies do not follow a strict laissez-faire policy. They often step in to regulate business.*

Myth: Most adult Americans work for huge companies, such as GM and IBM, which have more than 1000 employees each.

***Reality:** Most adult Americans work in relatively small firms, which have fewer than 100 employees.*

Myth: Most Americans would rather pursue leisure than work.

***Reality:** Most Americans are satisfied with their jobs. Even if they inherited enough money to live comfortably without having to lift a finger, they would still want to work.*

277

T wo weeks before the 1992 election, presidential candidates George Bush and Bill Clinton continued to hammer each other on the issues that had dominated their final televised debate the night before. Campaigning by passenger train in several small towns in Georgia and South Carolina, Bush attacked Clinton's record as Arkansas governor, assailed his "tax and spend" economic proposals, warned repeatedly that he "flip flops" on difficult issues, and emphasized his inability to tell the truth about his avoiding the Vietnam war draft. Meanwhile, Clinton, campaigning in Illinois and Wisconsin, assured voters that he would not raise taxes on the middle class, which he insisted had been seriously hurt by Republican "trickle down" economic policies. He also counterattacked Bush on the issue of character and trust, saying that Bush was the one who said "read my lips," in reference to Bush's 1988 later-broken promise not to raise taxes. While Clinton and Bush were out on the hustings, the third candidate, Ross Perot, returned to his home base in Dallas to launch a series of advertising offensives that would later appear on the three major television networks (Harwood and Noah, 1992).

Like those three presidential candidates and the millions of Americans who supported them, people everywhere are "political animals." This is because the scarcity of valued resources, such as jobs and money, compels people to play politics, to determine who gets what, when, and how. **Politics** is the type of human interaction that involves some people acquiring and exercising power over others. In most societies, however, the state steps in to dictate how politics should be played. The **state** is a political institution that regulates conflict and allocates resources among the citizens of a country. We often equate the state with the government, but the two words have somewhat different meanings. The state is an *abstract entity,* such as the U.S. presidency, Congress, and Supreme Court combined. The government consists of *specific individuals* who run the affairs of the state, such as the president, Supreme Court justices, and so on. Government officials come and go, but the state remains.

In this chapter, we will see how the state has the power to carry out its task and how it varies from one society to another. We will further examine various views on who controls the American government and how the citizens respond to it. Since the government has a significant influence on our **economic institution,** a system of producing goods and services and distributing them, we will also analyze the industrial revolution, modern economic systems, and the nature of work in the United States.

Power and the State

The state can do its job of regulating conflict and allocating resources only because it has a tremendous amount of power. In some societies, the government has the power to tell citizens what work they will do and what god, if any, they can worship. Governments take their citizens' money and spend it to educate their children or to overthrow a foreign government or to do many other things. Max Weber argued that the modern state is distinguished from other institutions by its power to monopolize the use of physical force. To understand the state, we therefore begin by taking a closer look at what power is and, more specifically, what kinds of power governments may wield.

THE NATURE OF POWER

Weber (1954) defined **power** as "the possibility of imposing one's will upon the behavior of other persons." If a robber forces you to hand over your wallet, that is an example of power. If your friends convince you to cancel a dinner and help them move, that is power. Power is at work when you pay taxes and when you write a term paper. It is an aspect of all kinds of social interaction, but obviously there are important differences in the types of power people can exercise.

The most basic difference is between illegitimate and legitimate power. *Illegitimate power* is control that is exercised over people who do not recognize the right of those exercising the power to do so. Thus, illegitimate power requires the use or the threat of physical force in order to compel obedience. Weber called it **coercion.** In contrast, *legitimate power* is control that is exercised over people with their consent; they believe that those exercising power have the right to do so.

Exercising power through coercion requires constant vigilance. If it is the only source of power leaders possess, they are not likely to be able to sustain their power for long. In contrast, legitimate power can often be exercised with little effort, and it can be very stable. Employers, for example, often need do little more than circulate a memo in order to control their employees' behavior. A memo goes out telling workers to stop making personal telephone calls or to request vacations in writing a month in advance, and, at least for a while, workers are likely to obey.

There are at least two kinds of legitimate power. One is **influence,** which is based on persuasion. Frequently, those who wield other types of power also exercise influence. They may acquire influence because of wealth, fame, charm, knowledge, persuasiveness, or any other admired quality. Business executives may use their wealth to achieve influence over politicians through campaign contributions. Television reporters may acquire the ability to influence public opinion because of their personal attractiveness and journalistic skill. In general, influence is less formal and direct, and more subtle, than other forms of power. Moreover, there is **authority,** the type of legitimate power institutionalized in organizations. When authority exists, people grant others the right to power because they believe that those in power have the right to command and that they themselves have a duty to obey. Authority is essential to the state.

TYPES OF AUTHORITY

What is the source of the state's authority? For an answer, we turn again to Weber (1957). He described three possible sources of the right to command, which produce what he called traditional authority, charismatic authority, and legal authority.

Traditional Authority In many societies, people have obeyed those in power because, in essence, "that is the way it has always been." Thus, kings, queens, feudal lords, and tribal chiefs did not need written rules in order to govern. Their authority was based on tradition, on long-standing customs, and it was handed down from parent to child, maintaining traditional authority from one generation to the next. Often, traditional authority has been justified by religious tradition. For example, medieval European kings were said to rule by divine right, and Japanese emperors were considered the embodiment of heaven.

Charismatic Authority People may also submit to authority, not because of tradition, but because

There are three types of authority. Traditional authority, as held by Queen Elizabeth, is based on long-standing custom. Charistmatic authority, represented by Mahatma Gandhi, derives from some exceptional personal quality attributed to an individual. President John. F. Kennedy represents legal authority, which comes from explicit rules and procedures that spell out the leader's rights and duties, although Kennedy is often said to have possessed charisma as well.

of the extraordinary attraction of an individual. Napoleon, Gandhi, Mao Zedong, and Ayatollah Khomeini all illustrate authority that derives its legitimacy from **charisma**—an exceptional personal quality popularly attributed to certain individuals. Their followers perceive charismatic leaders as persons of destiny endowed with remarkable vision, the power of a savior, or God's grace. Charismatic authority is inherently unstable. It cannot be transferred to another person. If a political system is based on charismatic authority, it will collapse when the leader dies. Otherwise, it will go through a process of "routinization," in which the followers switch from "personal attachment" to "organizational commitment," with their personal devotion to a leader being replaced by formal commitment to a political system (Madsen and Snow, 1983). In essence, charismatic authority is transformed into legal authority.

Legal Authority   The political systems of industrial states are based largely on a third type of authority: legal authority, which Weber also called *rational authority*. These systems derive legitimacy from a set of explicit rules and procedures that spell out the ruler's rights and duties. Typically, the rules and procedures are put in writing. The people grant their obedience to "the law." It specifies procedures by which certain individuals hold offices of power, such as governor or president or prime minister. But the authority is vested in those offices, not in the individuals who temporarily hold the offices. Thus, a political system based on legal authority is often called a "government of laws, not of men." Individuals come and go, as American presidents have come and gone, but the office, "the presidency," remains. If individual officeholders overstep their authority, they may be forced out of office and replaced.

In practice, these three types of authority occur in combinations. The American presidency, for example, is based on legal authority, but the office also has considerable traditional authority. Executive privilege, whereby a president can keep certain documents secret, even from Congress, acquired its force from tradition, not through the Constitution or laws. Some presidents, like Abraham Lincoln, Franklin Roosevelt, or John F. Kennedy, have also possessed charismatic authority. Still, the primary basis of the power of the president is legal authority. In general, when societies industrialize, traditional and charismatic authority tends to give way and legal authority becomes dominant. It is not always clear, however, how much legal authority the president has.

THE POWER TO DECLARE WAR

It is not always clear how much power the president has, because the Constitution from which he derives his power is subject to different interpretations. This problem came to a head when former President Bush was contemplating initiating military action against Iraq in late 1990. The president believed that he had the power to declare war. As his Secretary of State, James Baker, told the Senate Foreign Relations Committee, "We should not have a constitutional argument about whether or not the president, as commander in chief, has the constitutional authority to commit forces. It's been done going all the way back, I think, to World War II." Many members of Congress disagreed. They believed that only Congress has the power to authorize war. Hence, according to them, President Bush could not plunge us into offensive war in the Persian Gulf without congressional approval.

Historian Arthur Schlesinger (1990) agrees, arguing that the Constitution of 1789 quite clearly granted the war-making power to Congress only. But for many years, various presidents have ordered military action without congressional authorization. In the last century, there were numerous military interventions ordered unilaterally by presidents. These actions, though, were not directed against sovereign states such as Iraq, Korea, or Vietnam. They were, instead, directed against stateless and lawless groups, such as revolutionaries, angry mobs, and pirates. During the Second World War in the 1940s, Franklin Roosevelt did wage war on sovereign states without congressional authorization. But he felt that he had to act quickly on his own because of overwhelming national emergency. He did not actually claim that he had the constitutional right to declare war. However, the right to go to war was claimed as an inherent and routine presidential power when President Truman involved the country in the Korean War in 1952 and Presidents Kennedy and Johnson got Americans into the Vietnam War in the 1960s—without seeking congressional authorization. President Reagan did not get congressional authorization, either, before he sent U.S. troops to liberate Grenada or before he ordered the U.S. Air Force to bomb Libya. Even if Congress had not voted, as it eventually did, to authorize him to wage war against Iraq, President Bush would have gone ahead and ordered U.S. troops into battle.

Thus, presidents usually believe that, as commander in chief, they have the power to make war—and they have often carried out that power. They also think that they know foreign policy better than anybody else because of their direct contact with foreign leaders. They therefore resent what they consider to be congressional interference. But Congress may insist on exercising what it believes is its constitutional prerogative to deny the president the power to make war. Congress may choose to use its constitutional power of the purse to cut off funds to stop the president from waging war, as it did eventually during the Vietnam War. In effect, both the president and Congress have the power to declare war in their own ways (Crovitz, 1991).

WAR AND PEACE

The scope of presidential authority is limited, because this is a democratic country that grants its people a lot of freedom. But a totalitarian state exercises nearly total control over the politics, economics, and other aspects of its citizens' lives. Does this totalitarian policy encourage domination over other countries? If it does, the totalitarian state is likely to resort to war because it would find that other countries are not willing to hand themselves over to it. Moreover, totalitarian states have a history of killing large numbers of their own citizens. From 1918 to 1953, for example, "the Soviet government executed, slaughtered, starved, beat or tortured to death, or otherwise killed some 39.5 million of its own people" (Rummel, 1986). If the Soviet government killed that many of its own people in order to ensure complete control over its citizens, would it have used similar violence—war—to apply its totalitarian policy to other countries? The answer would have been yes if the Soviet Union had continued to be a totalitarian state. As the nineteenth-century military strategist Karl von Clausewitz said, "War is simply the continuation of state policy by other means."

But war is a complex phenomenon. It cannot be attributed to totalitarianism alone. After all, as a democratic society, the United States has engaged in so many wars that it is said to have a "warrior culture." What, then, are other reasons for nations going to war?

The general public assumes that war is part of "human nature," that humans are naturally warlike (Zur, 1987). Similarly, sociobiologists believe that warfare arises from people struggling for reproductive success. Ethologists, who specialize in the study of animal behavior, observe that the human species is the most warlike in the animal kingdom. Tigers, lions, and other beasts rarely kill members of their own species. By contrast, humans often kill one another because they have failed to evolve the ability to neutralize the killer instinct they share with the lower animals. To support these biological theories, advocates emphasize the prevalence of war or the rarity of peace in world history. One points out that in the last 5600 years there have been only 292 years when peace reigned in the world (Farley, 1987). In other words, for an astounding 95 percent of that long history, war has occurred somewhere in the world. Sociologists, however, discount the biological theories because all societies are not equally war-like. As we observed in Chapter 2 (Culture), the Yanomamo are warlike, but the Eskimos are peaceful.

Sociologists maintain that the prevalence of war can be explained sociologically. Using the functionalist perspective, we can argue that war occurs because it serves some useful functions for society. Most notably, it enhances social solidarity by focusing people's attention on fighting a common enemy. Another function of war that is often mentioned is the stimulation of scientific and technological development. War has made possible, for example, "the improvement of airplanes, the invention of new surgical techniques, and the harnessing of nuclear energy" (Coleman and Cressey, 1993). But the loss of lives and property may outweigh the benefits of war for the society as a whole. If this is the case, another sociological perspective may be a better guide to understanding war. The conflict perspective suggests that war reflects an exploitation of the masses by the ruling elite. Political leaders have been known to whip up a war frenzy against some foreign enemy as a way of regaining popular support or diverting people's attention from domestic problems. Other members of the power elite also benefit, with military brass becoming heroes and business tycoons reaping profits from sales of military hardware. More important, members of the ruling elite do not have to suffer the heart-rending familial consequences of war. During the Gulf crisis, no one in President Bush's cabinet had a son or daughter serving in Saudi Arabia. Of the 535 members of Congress, only two had sons involved in the war against Iraq (Lacayo, 1990). It is usually poor, working-class, and minority families whose children do the fighting and dying.

Although these sociological perspectives suggest the general forces that may lead to war, they cannot predict precisely when a nation will start a war. This is because many other factors may be involved.

To functionalists, war occurs because it serves useful functions, such as enhancing national unity or stimulating technological progress. But to conflict theorists, the loss of lives and property may outweigh any possible benefits of war for the society as a whole. Conflict theorists also argue that war primarily serves the interests of the ruling class.

If two countries are traditional, long-standing enemies, as in the case of Israel and its Arab neighbors, they are likely to attack each other every now and then. If nations have become polarized into two hostile camps, a single incident may trigger a world war. Given the polarization between Germany, Austria, and Hungary on one side and Great Britain, France, and Russia on the other, World War I broke out when an Austrian duke was assassinated. A combination of an inflammatory ideology and a charismatic leader can also be a powerful recipe for war. Nazi Germany started World War II by invading its neighbors because the Germans, under Hitler's strong, mesmeric leadership, came to believe that they were the "master race," destined to rule the world. Finally, if nations are militarily prepared to defend themselves or their allies, they are likely to engage in war. Fortified with huge armies and enormous stockpiles of weapons, the United States and the former Soviet Union have until recently stood ready to "defend" themselves against each other. The United States did so by sending troops to Vietnam in the 1960s and, more recently, by supporting Israel in its conflicts with Syria and aiding the Contra rebels in their attempt to overthrow the pro-Soviet Sandinista government of Nicaragua. Similarly, the former Soviet Union dispatched troops to Afghanistan, supported Syria and Nicaragua, and aided the rebels in El Salvador in their effort to topple pro-American governments.

In such warfare, the two superpowers scrupulously avoided a direct confrontation. When the former Soviet Union invaded Afghanistan, the United States protested loudly but did not send troops there to confront the Soviets. When the United States invaded South Vietnam, the former Soviet Union protested loudly but did not send troops there to fight the Americans. Apparently, the two superpowers were afraid that, if they fought each other directly, they might have started a nuclear war that would destroy them both and much of the rest of the world as well.

Today, the threat of nuclear war has diminished considerably, because the United States and the former Soviet Union agreed to eliminate their missiles in Europe and to withdraw their troops. In fact, the two superpowers recently became superpartners in their joint attempt to get Iraq to withdraw from Kuwait. The former Soviet Union's foreign policy is no longer decided by the elite of the once all-powerful Communist Party, but rather with much wider participation by many noncommunist parties. Because of the crumbling of communism in Russia and Eastern Europe, the United States has lost any justification for fighting communism. But now as the only superpower left in the world the U.S. remains tempted to go to war somewhere, such as in Bosnia, in defense of American self-interest or international law and democratic values.

QUESTIONS FOR DISCUSSION AND REVIEW
1. How do sociologists define *politics* and *power*?
2. How does legitimate power differ from illegitimate power, and what is the difference between influence and authority?

3. In the United States, who has the power to declare war?

4. What factors help explain why war is more prevalent in some societies than in others?

Who Really Governs?

The emergence of political parties and interest groups in the United States has brought us a long way from the government envisioned by James Madison. It was his hope to exclude "interests" and "factions" from the government. Legislators were to represent and vote for the public good, not one interest or the other. Where has this evolution brought us? Are the interest groups and parties mechanisms through which the people gain more effective control of government, or have the people lost control? Who in fact has **political power,** the capacity to use the government to make decisions that affect the whole society?

THE PLURALIST VIEW

A pluralist looking at American government sees many centers of power and many competing interest groups. Government reflects the outcome of their conflict. In this view, the interest groups are central to American democracy. Together they create a mutually restraining influence. No one group can always prevail. Thus, through their competition the interests of the public are reflected in government policy.

We have seen in Chapter 7 (Social Stratification), however, that there are large inequalities of wealth, power, and prestige in the United States. How, in the face of such inequality, can pluralism be maintained? Cannot one group marshal its resources to dominate others? Why doesn't one group or one coalition of groups gradually achieve a concentration of power?

The reason, according to Robert Dahl (1981), is that inequalities are *dispersed,* not cumulative. Inequalities would be cumulative if a group rich in one resource (wealth, for example) were also better off than other groups in almost every other resource—political power, social standing, prestige, legitimacy, knowledge, and control over religious, educational, and other institutions. In the United States, however, one group may hold most of one of these resources, but other groups may have the lion's share of others. What the upper middle class lacks in wealth, for ex-

ample, it makes up for in knowledge and legitimacy. Power over economic institutions may be concentrated in the hands of corporations, but U.S. religious institutions elude their grasp.

This dispersal of power in society is reflected in a dispersal of political clout. The country's many competing groups vie for control over government policy and end up dominating different spheres. Corporations may dominate the government's decisions on taxes but not on crime. Even tax policy is not dictated solely by corporations, because labor unions and other groups fight with the corporations for influence on politicians and voters. The structure of the government, with its separation of powers, promotes this pluralism. What civil rights groups could not win in Congress in the 1950s, they sometimes won in the courts. Corporations that have lost a battle in Congress may win the war by influencing regulations issued by the executive branch. In the end, in Dahl's view, competing groups usually compromise and share power. Thus, there is no ruling group in the United States. It is instead a pluralist democracy dominated by many different sets of leaders.

David Riesman (1950) and Arnold Rose (1967) have developed a somewhat different analysis. In their view, America has become so pluralistic that various interest groups constitute *veto groups.* They are powerful enough to block each other's actions. To get anything done, the veto groups must seek support from the unorganized public. The masses, then, have the ultimate power to ensure that their interests and concerns are protected. The bottom line is that the overall leadership is weak, stalemate is frequent, and no one elite can emerge to dominate the others.

THE ELITIST VIEW

It is obvious that there are many competing groups in the United States. But does their competition actually determine policy? Is the government merely the neutral arbitrator among these conflicting interests? According to elitist theorists, the answer is no.

Many years ago, Italian sociologists Vilfredo Pareto (1848–1923) and Gaetano Mosca (1858–1941) argued that a small elite has governed the masses in all societies. Why should this be so? If a nation is set up along truly democratic lines, isn't control by an elite avoidable? According to German sociologist Robert Michels (1915), there is an "iron law of oligarchy" by which even a democracy inevitably degenerates into an oligarchy, which is rule by a few. A democracy is an organization, and according to Michels, "who says organization says oligarchy."

In Michels's view, three characteristics of organizations eventually produce rule by the elite. First, to work efficiently, even a democratic organization must allow a few leaders to make the decisions. Second, through their positions of leadership, the leaders accumulate skills and knowledge that make them indispensable to the rank-and-file. Third, the rank-and-file lack the time, inclination, or knowledge to master the complex tasks of government, and they become politically apathetic. Thus, in time, even a democracy yields to rule by an elite.

How does this view apply to the United States? According to C. Wright Mills (1916–1962), there are three levels of power in this country. At the bottom are ordinary people—powerless, unorganized, fragmented, and manipulated by the mass media into believing in democracy. In the middle are Congress, the political parties, interest groups, and most political leaders. At this level, pluralism reigns. The middle groups form "a drifting set of stalemated, balancing forces" (Mills, 1959a). Above them, however, ignored by pluralist theorists, is an elite—what Mills called the *power elite*—that makes the most important decisions.

The base of the elite's power lies in three institutions: the federal government, the military, and the large corporations. According to Mills, power in the United States is increasingly concentrated in these three institutions, and those who lead them control the nation. Further, those leaders now form a cohesive, unified group. They are unified first because they share many social and psychological characteristics. They are mostly WASPs (white Anglo-Saxon Protestants) who attended Ivy League universities, belong to the same exclusive clubs, have similar values and attitudes, and know each other personally. They are unified, too, in that they form an "interlocking directorate" over the three key institutions. The three key institutions are increasingly interdependent: the government, the economy, and the military are tightly linked. Decisions by one affect the others, and the leaders of these institutions increasingly coordinate their decisions. Moreover, the *same* people move back and forth between leadership positions in the military, corporations, and the federal government. Corporate executives head the Department of Defense; high government officials routinely become corporate lawyers or executives; and generals easily exchange their uniforms for civilian clothes to head federal commissions or join the boards of directors of huge corporations. Thus, the country is ruled by "a handful of men" who head the federal government, military, and large corporations and form a cohesive, united group—the power elite.

If Mills is correct, all the hoopla of campaigns and debates, all the fund-raising by interest groups and earnest debate in the media, are but so much sound and fury. The power elite is free to do as it chooses. The government can allocate billions to defense to strengthen the military and enrich the cor-

According to sociologist C. Wright Mills, one of the institutions that form the base of the power elite in the United States is the military. In this view, leaders such as General Colin L. Powell, former Chairman, Joint Chiefs of Staff, are among the "handful of men," often WASPs (Powell is an exception), who form a cohesive, united group who make the most important decisions in the country.

porations from which the weapons are purchased. Big business can support political leaders with campaign money. The politicians can aid business with favorable legislation. Where is the evidence to support Mills's view?

There is indeed evidence that the three institutions Mills singled out have accumulated increasing power. There is also evidence for Mills's view that a cohesive elite exists. Time and again researchers have found that top officials in both Democratic and Republican administrations previously held high positions in corporations, that they return to corporations after leaving the government, and that leaders come disproportionately from upper-class backgrounds. After collecting data to show that a power elite exists within the upper class, William Domhoff (1978, 1983) argued that no more than 0.5 percent of the population owns about 25 percent of all privately held wealth, controls major banks and corporations, runs the executive and judiciary branches of federal government, heavily influences the federal legislature and most state governments, and dominates the formulation of national economic and political policies (Barlett and Steele, 1992).

THE MARXIST VIEW

Power-elite theory has been criticized by pluralists and Marxists. Pluralists argue that an elite does not enact policies only in its own interests. It may hold liberal values, trying to eliminate racism, abolish poverty, educate the masses, and generally do good. Even if an elite is quite conservative, it may also keep the public interest in mind when formulating policies. The framers of the U.S. Constitution, for example, were quite "pro-rich." Nevertheless, they believed that "a strong national government, protection of private property, and opening of national markets would benefit everyone," not just themselves as wealthy landowners and capitalists (Page, 1983). According to the Marxists, Mills's analysis confuses the issue. They argue that his political and military elites are not free to act in their own interests—they are merely agents of the corporate elite. What we have are not three elites that come together but one ruling class.

American sociologist Albert Szymanski (1978) provides an example of this approach. According to Szymanski, there are four classes in the United States. The first is the capitalist class, which owns and controls the major means of production and is commonly known as big business. The second is the petty bour-

geoisie, which includes professionals, small-business people, and independent farmers. Some of these people own the "means of production," but they must work with it themselves. The third class is the working class, including industrial, white-collar, and rural workers; they must sell their physical or mental labor to live. The fourth is the lumpenproletariat, which consists of the unemployed, welfare recipients, criminals, and down-and-outs. Szymanski argues that the capitalist class uses the state as an instrument for exploiting the other three economically subordinate classes. Unlike Mills, Szymanski does not argue that the masses are hopelessly passive and manipulated. Instead, in his view, there is a constant "class struggle" in which the capitalists try to dominate the masses, who, in turn, continually resist the domination. But the capitalist class more often wins than loses because it has the state do its bidding.

To control the state, capitalists may use the same methods employed by interest groups, such as lobbying and supporting sympathetic candidates. In using these tools, however, the capitalist class has a big advantage over the run-of-the-mill interest group: they have more money. The capitalist class also has indirect methods that give it a position far superior to that of any interest group. First, its values—such as free enterprise, economic growth, and competition—permeate society. They are propagated by the media, schools, churches, and other institutions. Violations of the values that further the interests of the capitalist class are often taken to be un-American, giving capitalist interests a potent weapon against unsympathetic politicians. Few American politicians want to be branded as antigrowth and antibusiness—or as socialists. Second, if the government acts against the interests of capitalists, they can, in effect, go on strike: they can refuse to put their capital to work. They might close plants or stop investing or send their money abroad (Greider, 1992). As a result, "business can extort favors, virtually without limit, from the political authorities. For . . . governments have a deep interest in continued and increasing productivity, but they have very little power over the owners of capital. In order to get businessmen to do their job, they must provide extensive protection, not only against violence but also against economic risk" (Walzer, 1978).

Thus, politicians of all stripes have often talked about molding an economic policy that would "send a message" to "reassure Wall Street." In state after state in recent years, gubernatorial and mayoral campaigns have been fought over the issue of whether a particular candidate would create a good or bad "business climate," over which candidate had the best plan of subsidies and tax breaks to lure business into the city or state. The public interest is identified with business interests, and political choices thus become hostages to the decisions of capitalists. Marxist theorists do not claim that capitalists dictate government policy or have their way on every issue, but they do argue that the capitalist class sets the limits to change and controls the "big" issues.

The issue of who really governs in American society boils down to three questions: Which group holds the most power? Where does it get the power? And what role do the masses play in the government? The three views that we have discussed are different in some respects and similar in others. Both elitists and Marxists see power concentrated in the hands of a small group and hardly any influence by the masses on the government. These theorists differ, however, in regard to the key source of power. To elitists, the ruling elite's power comes from its leadership in business, government, and the military, whereas to Marxists, the ruling class gets its power from controlling the economy. On the other hand, pluralists disagree with both. They argue that political leaders ultimately derive their power from the citizenry, and they must compete among themselves to stay at the top (see Table 12.1).

Which view, then, most accurately represents the reality of American government? It is difficult, if not impossible, to answer the question because relevant data are unavailable. But it seems obvious that each of the three views captures only a small portion, rather than the complex whole, of the political reality. Pluralists are most likely to hit the bull's eye in regard to most domestic issues, such as jobs and inflation, about which the public feels strongly. In these cases the government tries to do what the people want. Elitists and Marxists are more likely to be correct on most foreign and military policy matters, about which the masses are less concerned and knowledgeable. This explains why defense contractors are able to sell the U.S. government far more arms than are needed (Page, 1983). The three views may be oversimplistic and one-sided, but they are basically complementary, helping to enlarge our understanding of the complex, shifting nature of political power.

QUESTIONS FOR DISCUSSION AND REVIEW

1. What is political power, and what are the different theories about who exercises power in the United States?
2. How does the elitist view of who exercises political power differ from the pluralist view?
3. According to the Marxist view, which elite makes the most important decisions, and how does this elite exercise power?

The People's Response

Each of the three theories we have discussed focuses on the decision makers. Here we turn to those who are governed. What influences their attitudes toward government, and what are those attitudes? Are most

TABLE 12.1 **Who Really Governs?**

VIEW	KEY RULING GROUP	CHIEF SOURCE OF POWER	ROLE OF THE MASSES
Pluralist	Elected officials; interest groups and their leaders	Various political resources, including wealth, authority, and votes	Indirectly control leaders through competitive elections and interest group pressures
Elitist	Cohesive power elite, made up of top corporate, government, and military leaders	Control of key institutions, primarily the corporation and the executive branch of government	Manipulated and exploited by the power elite
Marxist	Capitalists, owners and controllers of the corporate world	Wealth and control of society's productive resources	Manipulated and exploited by the capitalist class

Source: Adapted from Martin N. Marger, *Elites and Masses,* 2nd ed. Copyright © 1987 Wadsworth Inc. Reprinted by permission.

Americans as powerless and passive as elitists and Marxists suggest, or are they potentially powerful and capable of taking an active part in government?

POLITICAL PARTICIPATION

Americans can participate in government and politics in numerous ways. They can attend a rally or run for office, form an interest group or send money to a candidate, write to their representatives or work for their opponents. But it seems that few Americans choose to take an active role in their government. Compared with people elsewhere, though, we are more interested in public affairs, more politically active, prouder of our governmental institutions, more satisfied with the way our political system works, and less suspicious of our politicians (Wolfinger, 1986).

The most popular form of political participation is probably the easiest: voting. According to many election specialists, the percentage of people who bother to vote is lower in the United States than in nearly all other Western nations. Usually, only 50 to 55 percent of the voting age population in the United States go to the polls, compared with over 80 percent in Belgium, Sweden, Italy, Germany, and other European countries except Switzerland. As a consequence, our officials are usually put into office by a minority of Americans eligible to vote. In the 1992 presidential election, which was widely reported to attract enormous voter interest, only 24 percent of the eligible electorate voted for Clinton (Clymer, 1992). In the earlier, 1980 election, Reagan's victory was often called a landslide because he beat Carter by a wide margin. But most Americans either voted for someone else or did not bother to vote at all. Only about 20 percent of eligible voters chose to vote for Reagan (Ranney, 1983). Why the lower turnout of American voters?

One reason is that, although it is easy to vote, it is not as easy in the United States as in most other Western countries. Voting laws vary from one state to another, but Americans must meet residency requirements and must register to vote some time before an election. The biggest obstacle to voting is the requirement that every time you change residence you must sign up all over again. The nuisance of reregistration reduces voting turnout, because a great many Americans move. In contrast, voter registration in other democracies is automatic—otherwise, public officials go out to register citizens at their homes. This may partly explain why those countries have higher voter-participation rates than we do. Recognizing this fact,

Of the various ways Americans can participate in government, the most popular, and probably the easiest, is voting. Still the percentage of people who bother to vote is lower in the United States than in nearly all other Western nations.

the U.S. Senate recently passed legislation to ease voter registration. Specifically, applications for a driver's license or disability benefits would double as voter-registration forms, and states would be required to allow registration by mail (Wines, 1993).

These measures, however, may not increase voter turnout substantially, because there are other reasons why people do not vote. First, many Americans simply get tired of voting because there are many more elections here than in other countries. Second, many Americans regard political campaigns as mean-spirited, lacking in substance. The profusion of negative political advertising launched by two candidates against each other makes *both* look like liars and crooks. Third, even in regard to substantive issues such as jobs and taxes, voters see little or no difference between candidates, who are equally inclined to promise the same things that voters like to hear. Fourth, the long-standing political stability of this country makes it seem unnecessary to vote, so we can usually forget about politics and focus on the serious business of living—our education, jobs, families, and the like.

Those reasons, however, cannot explain the significant differences in the voting turnout of various groups of Americans. In general, those who are poorer, younger, or less educated are less likely to vote. Blacks also have lower voting rates than whites, but class, not race, seems to be the primary factor. When blacks and whites of similar education and income are compared, there is hardly any gap between the turnout of blacks and whites (Kourvetaris and Dobratz, 1982; Glass et al., 1984). Traditionally, lower-status Americans' lack of political participation is blamed on their feelings of apathy, alienation, and distrust. But research has suggested that the fault lies more with political parties and candidates, who are less likely to write or speak personally to the poor than to the rich. Voter contact by a political party or candidate does encourage voter participation (Zipp, Landerman, and Luebke, 1982).

Does the low voting turnout pose a threat to democracy? Most political scientists say yes. They assume that a true democracy requires citizens' full participation because the people are supposed to rule. Without adequate support from its citizens, the government lacks legitimacy and therefore tends to be unstable. The government is also likely to ride roughshod over the people. But there is a contrary view: the low voting turnout means people are relatively contented with their lives. They "see politics as quite marginal to their lives, as neither salvation nor ruin" (Krauthammer, 1990). Nonvoting, then, reflects a preference against politics, which is assumed to be healthy because it reminds politicians that our country was founded on the belief that the government is best when it governs least. Nonvoters apparently accept the status quo—they are, at least, not too displeased with the existing government. Even if they decided to vote, their vote would hardly make a difference. According to an analysis of many national election studies, nonvoters are really no different from voters. Nonvoters are not as well informed about public affairs, but they are also not more egalitarian, not more hostile to business, and not more in favor of government ownership and control of key industries (Bennett and Resnick, 1990). If they voted, nonvoters would vote in about the same way as current voters do.

POLITICAL VIOLENCE

There is yet another form of political participation: political violence. In 1786 armed mobs of American farmers, angry about foreclosures on their farms, forcibly prevented county courts from convening. In 1877 railroad workers, incensed over wage cuts and increased working hours, seized railroad facilities in several cities and confronted armed militias of local governments. In the 1960s, after years of nonviolent protest, some civil rights and antiwar protesters turned to violence. Throughout American history, various groups have resorted to one form of violence or another, generally because they believed the government would not respond to their needs. After analyzing 53 U.S. protest movements, William Gamson (1975) found that 75 percent of those groups that used violence got what they wanted, compared with only 53 percent of those that were nonviolent. Violence, it seems, can pay off.

Much of the violence in American history has taken the form of riots or brief, violent seizures of property for limited aims, inspired by specific grievances. Violent as our history is, we have seen rather little of the two forms of political violence—revolution and terrorism—that have the broader aim of overthrowing the government.

Causes of Revolution　If a protest movement turns to violence, it may produce a **revolution**—the violent overthrow of the existing government and drastic change in the social and political order. There have been numerous studies on revolutions in many different societies. They differ in explaining the causes of revolution, but they all suggest in one way or another that a revolution is likely to occur if the following conditions are met (Goldstone, 1982).

1. *A group of rather well-off and well-educated individuals feel extremely dissatisfied with the society.* They may be intellectuals or opinion leaders such as journalists, poets, playwrights, teachers, clergy, and lawyers. These people would withdraw support from the government, criticize it, and demand reforms. Discontent may also exist within such elites as wealthy landowners, industrialists, leading bureaucrats, and military officials. It is from among all these people that revolutionary leaders emerge.

2. *Revolutionary leaders rely on the masses' rising expectation to convince them that they can end their oppression by bringing down the existing government.* By itself, poverty does not produce revolution. Most of the world, after all, is poor. When people have long lived with misery, they may become fatalists, resigned to their suffering. They may starve without raising a fist or even uttering a whimper against the government. But, if their living conditions improve, then fatalism may give way to hope. They may expect a better life. It is in times of such a *rising expectation* that revolutionary leaders may succeed in attracting mass support.

3. *A deepening economic crisis triggers peasant revolts and urban uprisings.* In a social climate of rising expectation, large masses of peasants and

workers tend to respond explosively to serious economic problems. When the state raises taxes too high and landlords, in turn, jack up the dues of tenant farmers or take over their lands, the peasants are likely to revolt. When the cost of food and the rate of unemployment soar, food riots and large-scale antigovernment protests would erupt in the cities.

4. *The existing government is weak.* Usually, before a government is overthrown, it has failed to resolve one problem after another and has gradually lost legitimacy. As the crisis mounts, the government often tries to initiate reforms. But the effort tends to be too little or too late. It only reinforces people's conviction that the regime is flawed, and encourages demands for even bigger reforms. All this can quicken the government's downfall. As Machiavelli (1469–1527) said in his warning to rulers, "If the necessity for [reforms] comes in troubled times, you are too late for harsh measures. Mild ones will not help you, for they will be considered as forced from you, and no one will be under obligation to you" (Goldstone, 1982).

Revolution in Eastern Europe and the Soviet Union   Those four conditions can be found in the revolution that brought down the communist governments, one after another, in Eastern Europe in late 1989 (Echikson, 1990).

1. *Most of the revolutionary leaders were well educated.* They included writers, professors, journalists, and college students. The most famous was playwright Václav Havel, who later became president of Czechoslovakia. An exception was electrician Lech Walesa, who organized his fellow workers into a politically powerful force in Poland. This was extraordinary because "everywhere else the initial pressure for revolution came from intellectuals, with workers providing back-up support." Nevertheless, Walesa felt it necessary to have intellectuals as his advisors. As he told them, "We are only workers. These government negotiators are educated men; we need someone to help us." Walesa started the revolution because he and other workers felt exploited by the communist bureaucracy. Havel and other intellectuals were primarily angry over the lack of civil and human rights.

2. *Expectation for freedom rose significantly after 1985.* Before Mikhail Gorbachev became the Soviet leader in 1985, Eastern Europeans had long lived in fear under communism. They knew that if they spoke out against the communist rule, they could lose their jobs, cars, homes, and even face prison or death. The examples of the 1956 Soviet invasion of

Hungary, the 1968 invasion of Czechoslovakia, and the 1981 suppression of Solidarity in Poland further showed how dangerous it was to question the status quo. Soon after 1985, however, Gorbachev removed this fear. He conceded the failure of the Soviet system of government, refused to interfere with the internal affairs of Eastern European nations, and decided to thin out Soviet forces in those countries. Consequently, the masses of Eastern Europe were no longer afraid. Their expectation for freedom rose, and they took to the streets to demonstrate against their repressive governments.

3. *Economic crisis added impetus to the revolution.* After Eastern Europe turned communist in 1945, its traditionally impoverished, rural societies enjoyed a certain amount of modernization. By the mid-1960s, their officially reported economic growth rates were among the highest in the world. A whole generation of workers, who were mostly peasants' children, could live in apartments with running water and toilets. But after the transformation from peasant to industrial societies, the communist system proved incapable of continuing the economic growth. It could not upgrade outdated technology, improve labor productivity, or use energy efficiently. As a result, beginning in the early 1980s, incomes and living standards plummeted, inflation and foreign debt accelerated, and economic growth and innovation went downhill. Even worse, after 1985, Eastern Europe began to lose the subsidy of raw materials such as oil and gas that it had long received from the former Soviet Union. Beset by his own country's economic problems, Gorbachev refused to supply the precious raw materials to Eastern Europe in exchange for its low-quality and obsolete products that could not be sold on the world market. The worsening economic crisis provoked many antigovernment strikes and protests, especially among the workers in Poland.

4. *The communist governments in Eastern Europe became weak.* For a long time, those governments had largely been imposed by the Soviet Union. They had been able to rule with an iron hand because of the tremendous military force that the Soviet Union had used to prop them up. But after 1985 the Soviet Union, under Gorbachev, decided that it would no longer use its troops to squash any uprising in Eastern Europe. Without the Soviet support, the Eastern European regimes became weak, which encouraged a fast-growing number of people to join the revolution.

Interestingly, the forces that had caused the revolution in Eastern Europe finally toppled the Soviet government itself in late August 1991: (1) Boris Yeltsin and other revolutionary leaders are all well-educated people who chafed at the slowness of the liberal reforms started by Gorbachev; (2) under Gorbachev's liberal leadership, the expectation for freedom had soared throughout the Soviet Union; (3) like the Eastern Europeans, the Soviets were hit with a worsening economic crisis; and (4) the Soviet government, which had long derived its power from the Communist Party, had become increasingly weak. Not surprisingly, when the Party's hard-liners staged a coup to take over the government, they failed quickly after only two days of resistance by the people. With the collapse of the Communist Party, the Soviet Union disintegrated, and all of its 15 republics declared independence one after another.

According to most of the U.S. media, the collapse of communism in Eastern Europe and the Soviet Union proves the failures of socialism. But the socialism that has been practiced in those countries was not real socialism—not the same as the socialism expounded in Marxist theory. According to Marx, a socialist state is supposed to reduce social inequality by freeing the poor masses from exploitation by the rich. But the communist regimes have merely turned this Marxist idea into slogans such as "All power to the people," while creating a privileged elite to exercise absolute power over the masses. It is true that the capitalist practices of private ownership and enterprise were eliminated to end the exploitation of the poor by the rich. But the communist rulers took over the exploitation themselves, causing even more misery to the masses than in capitalist countries. In fact, there is arguably more socialism in the United States today than there ever was in the Soviet Union, as there is more power for ordinary people, who have more opportunity to influence American government and economy.

Terrorism What if the masses do not support the opposition to the government and the government is not weak? In that case, a violent protest is likely to produce not revolution but terrorism. The would-be leaders of a revolution become terrorists, trying on their own to destabilize, if not to topple, the government through violence. Their methods include bombing, kidnapping, airplane hijacking, and armed assault. Terrorist groups include the anti-Israeli Palestinians, anti-British Irish, and anti-Turkish Armenians. Most terrorists are in their early twenties and have attended college. They almost always come from the middle or upper classes. In short, their back-

Some terrorists may be powerless individuals who are fighting a government while others carry out their government's policies. Shown here are Irish terrorists on the 297th anniversary of the siege of Londonderry by Protestants.

ground resembles that of leaders of revolutions—but the terrorists are self-styled leaders without followers.

These terrorists are basically powerless individuals futilely fighting a government. There is, however, another kind of terrorist—individuals carrying out their governments' policies. There are, in effect, terrorist governments. They represent a wide spectrum of international politics, from the radical right to the far left. Militant regimes in Libya, Syria, and Iran—known as the "League of Terror" to the U.S. State Department—have sent terrorists to assassinate their opponents in foreign countries. Syria and Iran may have encouraged the 1983 bombing of the U.S. Marine barracks in Beirut that took 241 lives. Iran is also known to support the terrorists holding American and European hostages in Lebanon. More recently, Iraq held for a while the largest number of foreign hostages, using them as human shields against possible attacks by the United States and other nations that demanded Iraq's withdrawal from Kuwait. In Peru, Guatemala, El Salvador, and other rightist-regime countries in Latin America, death squads, with varying degrees of implicit or explicit government support, have kidnapped, tortured, and killed hundreds of people in these countries every year. The victims include students, teachers, unionists, religious workers, and peasants (Gruson, 1990; Mendez, 1990).

American and European governments have generally adopted hard-line, "no ransom, no concessions" policies on terrorism. Since 1986, they have also stepped up their cooperative efforts against terrorism. They have imposed arms embargoes, improved extradition procedures, reduced the size of diplomatic missions of terrorism-supporting countries, and refused to admit any person expelled from another country because of suspected involvement in terrorist activities.

Nevertheless, "get tough" policies have not always translated into practice in a democratic society like ours. Under the pressure of public opinion, the Reagan administration for several years took a posture of strength, proclaiming a no-concessions all-out war against terrorists. But in 1986 the plight of the hostages and the appeals of their families finally compelled Reagan to secretly swap arms with Iran for the hostages. The Iranians got the weapons, but the hostages were not released. The failed ransom attempt brought the president tremendous political embarrassment here and abroad. Humanitarian concerns have also compromised the Israeli government's tough, no-concessions stance against terrorists. In 1984, pressured by appeals from hostages' families, Israeli officials secretly negotiated with the Palestinian organizations. This resulted in the freeing of nearly 1200 Palestinian prisoners—including terrorists convicted of killing Israeli citizens—in exchange for three Israeli soldiers held by the Palestinians. In early 1986, the prime minister of France also compromised his strong public position against concessions to terrorists. He got the release of French hostages by agreeing to return to Iran the late Shah's billion-dollar investment in France (Oakley, 1987). Finally, toward the end of 1991, all American hostages were released. A major reason was the conciliatory stance expressed by President Bush telling the terrorist governments that "good will begets good will." A more important reason is those governments' increased need for trade and investment from the West (Dowell, 1991).

But terrorism will always occur somewhere, even in the United States, as recently brought home to us by the bombing of the World Trade Center in New York, which killed six people and injured about 1,000. The reason is that no country can eliminate the causes of terrorism—deep feelings of anger or in-

justice, such as the resentment that the World Trade Center terrorists held against the U.S. for supporting Israel.

QUESTIONS FOR DISCUSSION AND REVIEW

1. Why do so many Americans fail to participate in politics and government?
2. Do low voting turnouts threaten democracy?
3. What social conditions usually exist before a revolution occurs?
4. When does terrorism emerge as a form of political participation, and why has it become such a problem today?

Contemporary Economic Systems

To understand the economic world today, we need to look back at least to the eighteenth century, when the **Industrial Revolution** took hold in England. That revolution was a dramatic economic change brought about by the introduction of machines into the work process. The revolution transformed not only the world's economies but also its societies.

THE INDUSTRIAL REVOLUTION

For 98 percent of the last 10,000 years, the pattern of economic life changed rather little: practically all our ancestors eked out a mere subsistence living from relatively primitive economies such as hunting and gathering or agriculture (see Chapter 3: Social Structure). During all those years, as sociologists Raymond Mack and Calvin Bradford (1979) pointed out, "the whole economic process was wrapped up in the individual." This was especially true for craftsworkers: they owned their own tools, secured their own raw materials, worked in their own homes, set their own working hours, and found their own markets for finished products.

But gradually, as the population grew and the demand for goods increased, individual craftsworkers became more and more dependent on intermediaries to find raw materials and to sell their finished products. Some of these intermediaries took over the economic process, telling craftsworkers what to produce and how much. In essence, these intermediaries became capitalists, and the formerly independent craftsworkers became employees. Craftsworkers, however, still worked separately in their own homes, forming what is called a *cottage industry.*

As the Industrial Revolution was about to dawn in England, cottage industry began to give way to a *factory system.* Capitalists found it more economical to hire people to work together in one building than to collect goods from many scattered cottages. They began to own every part of the manufacturing process: the factory, the tools, the raw materials, and the finished products. In effect, they even owned the landless workers, who had only their labor to sell in order to survive. To make the process more efficient, capitalists increased the division of labor. Some individuals were hired to spin thread, others to weave cloth, and one person to oversee all the workers as their supervisor.

Then, with the invention of steam engines, spinning jennies, and other machines, mass production became possible, and the Industrial Revolution was underway. It began in England around 1760, and during the following century it profoundly changed the economic structure of Western Europe and North America. The Industrial Revolution brought the substitution of machines for human labor to perform many tasks, the great improvement in the getting and working of raw materials, the widespread development of railroad and steamship to transport huge

quantities of raw materials and manufactured goods, and the movement of labor and resources from agriculture to industry. All this created tremendous wealth in the West. At the same time, the small machines were replaced by big ones, the little mills became giant factories, and the modest partnerships changed into large corporations.

Consequences   The results of industrialization are far-reaching. First, it changes the nature of work. The mechanization of agriculture calls for few operators, causing most people to leave farming for industrial work. Bigger and better machines in the factory, in the mines, and at construction sites further require fewer workers, which reduces the number of blue-collar jobs. But, because technology is highly productive, it brings prosperity, which increases the demand for all kinds of services, from education and health to entertainment and money management. Thus, white-collar occupations proliferate. Even in manufacturing companies, white-collar workers outnumber blue collars. The General Electric Company, for example, produces numerous different items from turbines to light bulbs, but the majority of its employees are engaged in services from accounting to marketing—less than 40 percent work in production. Of the factory workers in the United States today, no

Sparked by the invention of spinning jennies and other machines, which made mass production possible, the Industrial Revolution began in England around 1760. It later brought tremendous wealth to the West, while changing work patterns, the distribution of population, human relations, and social values. But it has also brought about global inequality.

more than 7 percent are subjected to the physical and psychological strain of working on the assembly line. Better-educated white-collar workers tend to be self-directed, demanding the freedom to decide what work to do, how to do it, and even when to do it. Increasingly, their bosses let them have considerable autonomy in their work—and address requests rather than give orders to them (Ginzberg, 1982).

Industrialization also brings about demographic changes—changes in the characteristics of a population. In general, as a society industrializes, cities grow, and fewer people live on farms. The population as a whole further increases when a society industrializes. But once a society has developed an industrialized economy, population growth tends to slow, and the percentage of elderly people in the population rises.

Industrialization also changes human relations. In industrial societies, people usually spend much of their time in huge, bureaucratic organizations. They interact with a broad range of people, but their relationships with these people tend to be formal, fragmentary, and superficial. Ties to primary groups loosen (see Chapter 3: Social Structure). Industrialization alters other institutions as well. Formal schooling tends to become more important, and functions once served by the family are taken over by other institutions, such as business and government (see Chapter 10: The Family). According to a study of 50 countries, industrialization also creates international inequality, with highly industrialized nations enjoying higher status and more power than the less industrialized (Rau and Roncek, 1987).

Finally, industrialization changes the values of a society. Traditional values and ways of living are discredited. People learn to view change as natural and to hope for a better future. Thus, industrialization brings a dynamism into society. It produces greater energy and open-mindedness but also restlessness and discontent. Social and political conflict often follows. So, too, does the "social notion of gain." In Robert Heilbroner's (1972) words, "The idea of gain, the idea that each man not only may, but should, constantly strive to better his material lot . . . [as] an ubiquitous characteristic of society, is as modern an invention as printing."

A Postindustrial World   Many countries have been trying to achieve in a few years the industrialization that developed over two centuries in the West. Social instability has been one result. In Iran, for example, the clash between the new values encouraged by in-

dustrialization and the values of traditional Islam helped bring on a revolution in the late 1970s. Many developing countries are plagued by widespread poverty, high rates of unemployment, military coups, and wars. A basic cause is "the partial character of their modernization." They have imported Western technology to lower death rates but not birth rates, so that population growth has eaten up or outstripped their gains in income. They have instituted Western-style education, enough to let people dream of a better life but not enough to create and operate a modern economy. They have seen the rewards of an industrial technology—and developed a craving for what they believe to be a material paradise—but they do not have the means to satisfy their appetite.

Meanwhile, the advanced countries continue to industrialize and have taken the process a step further. During industrialization, machines take over tasks that humans have performed, and people control the machines. Now the task of controlling the machines is increasingly given over to computers. A growing number of factory workers will sit at computer terminals in clean, quiet offices. They will monitor tireless, precise robots doing the kind of work that assembly-line workers do with dirty, noisy machines. Along with computers, other related technological breakthroughs, such as electronics, microchips, and integrated circuits, are ushering in an information economy. In this new "postindustrial" age, the predominant activities are collecting, processing, and communicating information. This has brought postindustrial societies such as the United States a high degree of affluence and leisure. It has also made it possible for everyone on the globe to be in instant communication with everyone else. Consequently, the spread of technology throughout the world will mean greater output per worker and hence a higher standard of living in other societies. Instant communication will further undermine authoritarian controls, as it has done in Eastern Europe, and keep democratic governments on their toes with a new degree of scrutiny. In short, we will see more economic wealth and political freedom in the postindustrial world (Bartley, 1991).

CAPITALISM AND SOCIALISM

No factory exists on its own. It must buy raw materials and sell its products. It is enmeshed in a complicated network of exchanges. This network must be organized in some way, but how? There are two basic alternatives. The economy may be organized through markets. A market economy is driven by the countless decisions made by individuals to buy and sell. This is **capitalism.** Alternatively, the economy may be controlled by the authority of the government. This is **socialism.** In fact, all economies in the world represent some mixture of these basic alternatives. But to understand them better, we look first at how two great theorists interpreted the essence of capitalism.

Adam Smith and Capitalism   At the core of capitalism lies a belief about the psychology of human beings: we are inherently selfish and act to serve our own interests. Capitalism works by allowing this pursuit of self-interest to flourish. It does so through two key characteristics: (1) private ownership of property and (2) free competition in buying and selling goods and services. Without these, capitalism does not exist.

Private ownership is considered important for the health of the economy because it motivates people to be efficient and productive. This is often taken to explain why Federal Express and other private companies in the United States are generally more successful than the U.S. Postal Service and other government-owned enterprises. Private ownership is also used to explain why the small, privately owned lands in the former Soviet Union and China are far more productive than the large state-owned farms. Although private plots make up less than 3 percent of Russia's arable land, they produce about 50 percent of the country's meat, milk, and green vegetables and about 80 percent of its eggs and potatoes. In China the private plots constitute only 4 percent of all cultivated land but produce some 33 percent of the country's meat and dairy products and 50 percent of its potatoes (Naisbitt and Aburdene, 1990).

Free competition is also believed to be beneficial to the economy because it compels businesses to make the most efficient use of resources, to produce the best possible goods and services, and to sell them at the lowest price possible. Only by doing so can they expect to beat their competitors. Competition, then, acts as an "invisible hand," bringing profits to the efficient producers and putting the inefficient ones out of business.

Doesn't the pursuit of self-interest reduce society to a jungle and harm the public good? Adam Smith claimed that the answer is a resounding no. In 1776, in *The Wealth of Nations,* he argued that when there is free competition, the self-serving decisions of individuals to buy and sell end up promoting the public good. How does this work? Because there is competition, people must take account of others' interests in order to serve their own. If Apple Computer does not meet your needs, you can buy a product from Texas Instruments or IBM—and Apple knows it. It is in their interest to serve your interests. Since many businesses strive to serve their own interests by serving those of the public, the whole society will benefit. There will be an abundance of high-quality, low-priced goods and services, which will entice many people to buy. Businesses will then produce more to meet consumers' increased demand, which will create more jobs and raise wages. The result is a prosperous economy for the society as a whole. As the editors of the *Wall Street Journal* (1986) say, "By doing well for themselves, capitalists as risk-taking entrepreneurs create jobs and new opportunities for others. A rising tide does lift all boats." In his recent study of 10 nations, Michael Porter (1990) also found that the more competition there is in a country, the more prosperous that country is.

The government, in Smith's view, should therefore adopt a *laissez-faire,* or hands-off, policy toward markets. Left to themselves, the markets will provide a self-regulating mechanism that serves society's interests. If government interferes by, say, imposing price controls, businesses will lose their incentive to produce. The energy shortage in the 1970s, for example, has been blamed on government control of oil and gas prices.

Karl Marx and Socialism   While Smith saw how private ownership of property and private hiring of labor would produce a prosperous economy, Karl Marx saw the inevitability of private property owners exploiting their laborers by paying them as little as possible. There are also other basic differences between the two men's views. When Smith looked at specialized division of labor in industrial capitalism, he saw a key unlocking economic well-being to masses of ordinary people. To Smith, specialization enhances *efficiency* in the generation of wealth. When Marx looked at specialization, he saw a source of **alienation of labor.** Because workers own neither their tools nor the products they make and because they cannot exercise all their capacities as they choose but are forced to perform an isolated, specific task, their work is no longer their own. Instead, it becomes a separate, alien thing.

Other aspects of industrial capitalism also looked starkly different to Marx than they did to Smith. Where Smith saw a self-regulating system internally propelled on an upward spiral of prosperity, Marx saw a system that had within it severe contradictions and would create "its own gravediggers." One contradiction grows from capitalism's devotion to individualism. As Heilbroner (1972) said, "Factories necessitated social planning, and private property abhorred it; *capitalism* had become so complex that it needed direction, but *capitalists* insisted on a ruinous freedom." Marx saw another contradiction as well. Capitalists depend on profit, but according to Marx, their profit comes from the fact that workers put more value into products than they are given in the form of wages. To increase their profits, capitalists often hold down wages, and, whenever possible, substitute machines for human labor as well. As a result, the poor get poorer from lower wages or job loss. This, in turn, reduces the demand for the capitalists' products, thereby decreasing their profits. The economy can work itself out of this crisis, but such crises will recur, with each one getting worse until the workers revolt.

Ultimately, Marx believed, the contradictions of capitalism would lead to communism, to a classless society, that would operate on the principle of "from each according to his ability, to each according to his needs." In this society, the state would wither away. First, however, the destruction of capitalism would be followed by a temporary era of socialism.

No state, including the so-called communist countries, such as the former Soviet Union and China, has ever reached communism, but many have tried socialism. In a socialist economy, the state owns and operates the means of production and distribution, such as land, factories, railroads, airlines, banks, and stores. It determines what the nation's economic needs are and develops plans to meet those goals. It sets wages and prices. Individual interests are subordinate to those of society.

ECONOMIES IN THE REAL WORLD

No state has a purely socialist or purely capitalist economy. In all socialist economies, there is still some buying and selling outside of government control and some individual ownership of property. In pre-1990 communist Poland, independent-minded farmers produced much of the country's food supplies on private plots. Similarly, in the cities of Hungary, taxi drivers, artisans, shopkeepers, and restaurants operated almost as freely as their counterparts in the capitalist West. Even in the former Soviet Union, perhaps the most anticapitalist before 1992, some service industries kept the profits they earned, rather than turning them over to the government. This "second economy"—a free market operating within and parallel to the state-controlled, command economy—continues to exist in countries that remain communist, such as Cuba, Vietnam, and Angola (Los, 1990). Nevertheless, in all the communist countries, the state still owns and controls key industries, such as steel and oil, and bans large, privately owned companies.

On the other hand, no government in capitalist societies has followed a strictly laissez-faire policy. In the United States, for example, government policies provided the canals, roads, railroads, cheap land, and education that laid the foundation for America's economic growth. When the American public became disgusted with outrageous railroad freight fares, contaminated meat, and similar problems around the turn of the century, the government stepped in with new laws to regulate business. When capitalism failed in the Great Depression of the 1930s, the government established an array of programs to regulate business practices and to provide people with a cushion against the impact of hard times. When people realized that Smith's "invisible hand" did not prevent business from producing dangerous levels of pollution and wasted resources, environmental regulations were passed. To protect workers against gross exploitation, the government passed laws governing wages, hours, and working conditions. Most of these socialist elements of government ownership and control still exist in the United States today (Friedman, 1989b).

Classifying Economies Although all economic systems are **mixed economies,** containing elements of both capitalism and socialism, the "mix" between these elements varies considerably. Thus, we can arrange economies along a continuum from most capitalist to most socialist.

The United States and Japan are among the most capitalist. Yet, as we have seen, the United States does not follow a laissez-faire policy, and competition is limited in many ways. In Japan the government takes a leading role in planning investment for the future, in turning corporations toward industries that are likely to grow.

Ranging along the middle of the continuum are the European democracies. From time to time, several of these democracies have had socialist governments. In general, these nations have combined capitalist enterprise with wide-ranging government control—and high taxes. They tend to establish stricter controls on business and more extensive social services than the United States. All these states, for example, provide a national system of health insurance. Over the years, their governments have owned and managed many industries. Great Britain, for example, has had the coal, steel, automobile, and television industries under government control at various times. Even before France elected a socialist government in 1981, its government had created subway and aerospace industries. Nevertheless, these European democracies are so much more capitalist than socialist that they are usually considered capitalist.

At the socialist end of the continuum we find countries such as China, North Korea, Cuba, and Vietnam. Their governments largely control their economy. But some have recently tried to introduce a new economic arrangement in which centralized direction of the economy by the government is reduced. China has adopted some free-enterprise practices. It has abolished most rural communes, restored family farms, established a free market for agricultural and consumer goods, granted state-owned enterprises wide autonomy in running their businesses, and opened up its coastal regions to foreign investors. This free enterprise, however, is still very limited. The economies of China and other Communist countries are still very much in the hands of the state.

Economic Performance   The socialist economies have a decidedly mixed record. Their total wealth is generally far below that of capitalist countries. True, under socialism, nations such as Cuba and China have improved the standard of living for vast numbers of people who had been destitute. In general, socialist nations have reduced the extremes of poverty, inflation, or unemployment that occasionally hit capitalist states. But significant economic inequalities still remain. Managers make much more money than ordinary workers. They also have special privileges and access to luxury goods that ordinary citizens cannot get. Furthermore, the central planning of socialist states often creates inefficiencies and bottlenecks. Perhaps their greatest problem is production. Severe shortages often plague socialist states. The absence of adequate incentives comparable to private-property ownership is the major cause of the low productivity of the state-run farms in socialist countries (Benjamin et al., 1992).

In the meantime, capitalist economies in the West have little trouble producing ample quantities of goods, although they have faced periodic bouts of extreme inflation and unemployment, as in the late 1970s and early 1980s. Moreover, their social peace to a great extent has depended on economic growth, which gives even the poor some hope of improving their standard of living. Their ability to sustain this growth may not be certain all the time. Around 1980, the U.S. economy, for example, seemed to get stuck, unable to continue up the spiral that Adam Smith predicted would generate more productivity and more wealth. In fact, its productivity went down, increasing unemployment as well as inflation. But in 1983 the U.S. economy began to make a dramatic comeback, showing a substantial growth in productivity and a decline in unemployment and inflation. The economies in Canada, Western Europe, and Japan also rebounded. In 1991 another worldwide economic recession hit these capitalist countries, and again there have been some signs of recovery in late 1992. Despite the ups and downs of their economic conditions, the capitalist countries always remain considerably more productive than their socialist counterparts. According to a study by the WorldWatch Institute, Western European countries' labor productivity rates were often twice as high as those of formerly socialist Eastern Europe, and the United States was nearly 20 times more productive than the former Soviet Union. The capitalist system's higher efficiency can be attributed to the freedom for pursuing personal gain or the absence of socialist-style government control (Rheem, 1986).

THE AMERICAN ECONOMY TODAY

There are both bright and dark spots in the U.S. economic picture. For about 10 years now, the American economy has been producing an abundance of jobs. Massive numbers of women and immigrants have joined the baby-boom generation in entering the labor force without causing a bulge in unemployment. Inflation has also gone down to a level that generates only little discomfort. But our standard of living is now lower than 10 years ago. Although some people have become fabulously rich, the majority of American workers earn little, if any, more in real take-home pay than they did before 1980. Low-income Americans have suffered more, with real incomes falling, more people dropping below the poverty line, and homelessness rising. Let us examine more closely these and other aspects of the American economy.

Throughout most of the 1980s, only about 5 percent of our work force was unemployed. This was a remarkable achievement. The American economy has managed to create jobs for huge numbers of baby-boomers, women, and immigrants. By contrast, in Europe, few new jobs have been generated, so that unemployment there has increased sharply. During the 1992 recession our jobless rate went up to 7.6 percent, causing profound distress and fear among millions of unemployed and employed workers. But that rate was still far lower than the 10.8 percent of a decade before, and it will come down soon when the recession ends. Another success story is that the inflation rate came down from 12 percent in 1980 to about 5 percent today. Most economists consider this rate moderate and acceptable (Krugman, 1990; Gwynne, 1992).

Despite lower unemployment and lower inflation over the last 10 years, our living standard has mostly failed to improve. Income has remained relatively stagnant for most Americans. Significantly more Americans have to moonlight to meet regular household expenses or to pay off debts. A key reason is that since 1970 we have suffered a slowdown in productivity growth. Although the U.S. economy has grown significantly since 1983, its growth is still much smaller today than 30 and 40 years ago. Since 1970 American output per worker has risen an average of only 1.2 percent a year, compared with 2.8 percent in the 1950s and 1960s. This has made it impossible for most Americans to improve their living standard. If the productivity growth continues to remain low, today's young families will live no better than their parents (Krugman, 1990).

Related to our slowdown in productivity growth is our large trade deficit. Before 1984 there was a trade surplus—we sold more goods and services to foreign countries than we bought from them. But since 1984 we have annually spent about $130 billion (2.3 percent of our national income) more on foreign imports than we earned from our exports abroad. As a result, foreign companies have been using their profits to buy a steady stream of American assets, such as stocks, bonds, real estate, and whole corporations. This further causes a drain on our national income, because the United States has to pay interest to foreign bondholders, dividends to foreign stockholders, and rents to foreign landowners. All this is no cause for panic, as long as the foreigners continue to keep their American investments and profits here. But we are running the risk that foreigners will precipitate an economic crisis here by liqui-

dating their American assets and taking their profits home. This is likely to occur if their confidence in the American economy wavers or their own economies worsen considerably. Fortunately, largely because of the recent fall in the foreign exchange value of the dollar, American exporters have been able to sell their products more cheaply abroad and also make foreign products more expensive in the United States. But the trade deficit remains. To eliminate it requires improving the quality of American products and increasing productivity growth, so that more Americans here and more foreigners abroad will buy American goods. If this does not happen, we will continue to live with the trade deficit (Krugman, 1990).

Another economic problem is the huge federal budget deficit. Every year the government spends much more than it takes in. Many fear that the government may someday be unable to pay the debt and become as bankrupt as many Latin American countries are today. We have already changed from a creditor to a debtor nation. Before the 1980s, the United States invested more abroad than foreigners invested here. But since 1980, we have become a massive net importer of capital by inducing foreigners to buy American businesses. There is always a threat that foreigners will stop financing our federal budget deficit by withdrawing investments and profits from the United States. Most Democrats want to reduce the budget deficit by raising taxes but do not take the lead for fear of alienating voters. Republicans tell Americans that they want to eliminate the deficit by cutting government spending but fear alienating voters by cutting popular social insurance programs (primarily Social Security), which account for 40 percent of the federal expenditure. Instead they would cut less popular programs such as foreign aid and antipoverty programs. Thus the great budget deficit continues (Krugman, 1990). In fact, it had risen to $290 billion in 1992, and is expected to go up to $346 in 1997. But the new Clinton administration has proposed to reduced the deficit to $206 billion over the next four years by stimulating the economy, raising taxes, and cutting spending. Whether this goal can be achieved remains to be seen.

QUESTIONS FOR DISCUSSION AND REVIEW

1. How did the Industrial Revolution change the economic institutions of societies?
2. How does capitalism differ from socialism?
3. Why do economies in the real world incorporate both socialist and capitalist principles?

4. How do sociologists classify economies, and how well has each type performed in recent history?
5. What is the condition of the U.S. economy today?

Work in America

When Americans meet strangers, one of their first questions is likely to be, "What do you do?" We answer, "I am a salesperson" or "I am a cabdriver" or a doctor or lawyer, or whatever. Work is not just a way to make enough money to pay the bills. For many of us, work helps define our identity and our sense of self-worth. Just what it is we are able to do, however, depends to a great extent on the economic institutions we have described. As we will see in the following sections, the kinds of workers needed by our complex economy further affect job satisfaction and the workplace.

THE LABOR FORCE

The labor force includes all those over 16 years of age who are gainfully employed as well as those who are jobless but are actively seeking paid employment. It excludes full-time homemakers, students, and retired people—anyone who is not paid for his or her work and is not seeking a paying job. In 1988 about 66 percent of Americans over the age of 16 were in the work force—this figure is expected to grow to 69 percent in 2000—compared with about 55 percent in 1940 (Crispell, 1990). This increase has been accompanied by dramatic shifts in what American workers do and who makes up the work force.

Occupations   The stage was set for the appearance of today's labor force by the industrialization of the farm—a process that accelerated greatly after World War II. Thanks to technological innovations ranging from new machinery to new fertilizers to new breeding techniques, agricultural productivity has soared during this century. In 1900 one American farmer on average produced enough food to support seven other people. Today, one farmer produces enough for more than 60 people.

This increasing agricultural productivity pushed many workers off the farm. In just five years, from 1950 to 1955, a million workers migrated out of agriculture. As a result, about 1 percent of the American labor force works on the farm today, compared with nearly 60 percent in 1870 and 30.2 percent in 1920.

The continuing farm exodus also reflects the increasing failure of small family farms to survive. Government subsidies and other "save the family farm" programs, such as crop insurance, production control, food stamps, school lunches, and distribution of surplus butter and cheese to low-income families, have largely come to naught. What remains is the increasingly smaller number of highly efficient farms that need only a few workers to produce enough food for the whole nation. In fact, they are capable of producing so much food that the federal government has to pay them about $10 billion a year *not* to produce more than necessary (Robbins, 1990).

Many of those who left the farm in earlier decades went to work in manufacturing industries, producing clothes, furniture, cars. But major changes were under way in manufacturing as well. As in agriculture, new machines decreased the number of people needed to produce one item or another. Since World War II, the share of jobs in manufacturing held by white-collar workers—managers, professionals, clerical workers, salespersons—rather than blue-collar workers has increased greatly. Before 1945, blue-collar workers had long outnumbered white-collar workers, but then white collars began to grow so fast in numbers that today they are three times as numerous as blue collars. At General Motors Corporation, 77.5 percent of the work force is white collar, compared with 22.5 percent blue-collar workers. At IBM, 91.5 percent of the staff is white collar, and, at General Electric, it is 60 percent (Rosecrance, 1990).

Meanwhile, the growth in jobs in manufacturing and other goods-producing industries has slowed, but jobs in service industries—education, health care, banking, real estate, insurance—have increased. In 1900 about 75 percent of the labor force was employed in production and fewer than 25 percent in service. But by 1982 the situation was reversed—74 percent in service and 26 percent in production. In the 1990s, the largest job growth in service industries will be among retail salespeople, janitors and maids, waiters and waitresses, and registered nurses, along with doctors, lawyers, teachers, accountants, and other professionals (Crispell, 1990). The rapid growth in the service sector as a whole results largely from an increased demand for health care, entertainment, and business and financial services.

The Workers   The composition of the American labor force has changed, too. The most publicized change has occurred in its gender. In 1984 the U.S. Department of Labor announced that since 1960 the number of women in the labor force had nearly doubled. Today, about 53 percent of women are in the labor force, compared with just 33 percent in 1960. The number of women workers will continue to rise, which is projected to account for about two-thirds of the entire labor force growth between 1982 and 1995. The feminist movement—through its publicizing and legitimizing of the rights and needs of women to earn enough money to support themselves and contribute to total family income—has largely aided the increase (see Chapter 9: Gender and Age).

Important changes have also occurred in the age and racial composition of the work force. In the last two decades, the employment rate for men older than 65 declined significantly. Age discrimination and retirement programs, such as Social Security and private pension plans, have probably played a part in this decline. But in recent years, a growing industrial demand for cheaper labor has fueled a dramatic increase in labor-force participation among Americans of African, Hispanic, or Asian descent, as well as among immigrants. These minorities will account for 88 percent of work-force growth between 1989 and 1999. Meanwhile, there will be proportionately fewer white men in the labor force (Solomon, 1989).

These breakdowns by gender, race, and age do not tell us much about what is actually going on in the American economy. We have a *dual* economy, with a *core* of giant corporations dominating the market and a *periphery* of small firms competing for the remaining, smaller shares of business. In addition, there is a third sector, consisting of various government agencies. About 30 percent of the American labor force work in the third, state sector, and the rest are employed in the private core and peripheral sector. Contrary to popular belief, most of the privately employed Americans do not work in the core's huge companies (with more than 1000 employees each). Only 30 to 40 percent do so. Most work in the peripheral sector, especially in small firms with fewer than 100 employees (Granovetter, 1984). Whatever sector they work in, American workers are now better educated than before. In 1940 most workers had just slightly more than a grade school education. Today, more than half have some college and three out of four are high school graduates (Census Bureau, 1993). Unfortunately, they are faced with problems that did not exist before.

In today's fiercely competitive global economy, many American companies have begun to minimize production costs by paying their employees low wages, comparable to those received by skilled but low-paid workers in the fast developing economies of Asia and Eastern Europe. A popular way to keep payroll costs low involves hiring temporary, contingent, part-time, or contract workers. In fact, since 1982 temporary employment has soared by nearly 250 percent, compared with less than 20 percent increase in all employment. Now most of the jobs created by U.S. companies are temporary positions. Such jobs obviously pay much less than regular, full-time employment. Moreover, temporary workers are given no health insurance, no pensions, no vacations, no promotions or raises, and no job security. They do not even have the right to sue their employers for wrongful dismissal. They are, in effect, treated as second-class citizens in the workaday world. A few of these workers are highly skilled, such as doctors, engineers, accountants, and financial planners, who prosper. But the majority are far less skilled and have to struggle to survive. Temporary workers now compose one-third of the American labor force, and their ranks are growing so fast that they are expected to outnumber permanent full-time workers by the end of this decade (Castro, 1993).

JOB SATISFACTION

Although it is unpleasant to be a temporary worker, does permanent full-time employment bring happiness? Are Americans really happy with their jobs? In many studies during the last two decades, representative samples of workers have been asked whether they would continue to work if they inherited enough money to live comfortably without working. More than 70 percent replied that they would. When asked how satisfied they were with their jobs, even more—from 80 to 90 percent—replied that they were very or moderately satisfied. But when asked whether they would choose the same line of work if they could begin all over again, most said no. Only 43 percent of white-collar workers and 24 percent of blue collars said yes. And when asked, "Do you enjoy your work so much that you have a hard time putting it aside?" only 34 percent of men and 32 percent of women answered affirmatively (Glenn and Weaver, 1982; Burtless, 1990; Lipset, 1990b). In short, most Americans seem to like their jobs but are not too excited about them.

Studies have also shown that job satisfaction varies from one group to another. Generally, older workers are more satisfied than younger ones. One reason is that older workers, being more advanced in

Job satisfaction does not depend solely on economic rewards. Workers such as the men on the oil rig, who do strenu-ous physical labor or boring repetitive tasks, may find the job worthwhile if it pays an adequate wage. But white collar workers, such as the woman shown here, generally like their jobs because they can enjoy a great deal of au-tonomy or self-management.

their careers, have better jobs. Another reason is that younger workers are more likely to expect their jobs to be highly interesting and stimulating, hence are more likely to be disillusioned because of the difficul-ty in realizing their high aspirations. White-collar workers, especially professionals and businesspeople, are also more likely than blue collars to feel genuine-ly satisfied with their jobs. Among blue-collar work-ers, union members report significantly *less* job satis-faction than nonmembers, which reflects job dissatisfaction as the primary reason for joining unions in the first place (Schwochau, 1987). Women, however, are equally or more satisfied with their jobs than men are with theirs. Isn't this puzzling? After all, women are generally paid less and have less pres-tigious jobs than men, as we have seen in Chapter 9 (Gender and Age). Why, then, are women not less happy with their jobs? A major reason is that they ex-pect less than men from the job market and so can more easily fulfill their lower expectations. If they get jobs that are as good as men have, which goes be-yond their expectation, they are likely to express more satisfaction than men. Another reason is that, in evaluating their jobs, working women tend to use tra-ditional homemakers rather than male co-workers as their reference groups. In comparing themselves to those engaged in household work, working women feel more satisfied with their jobs. In addition, the more aware they are of the unsatisfactory nature of

domestic work, the more satisfied working women are with their jobs. This is why working women whose mothers have never worked outside the home like their jobs better than their female counterparts whose mothers have been gainfully employed (Hod-son, 1989; Weaver and Matthews, 1990).

People with satisfying jobs have better mental health than those with less satisfying work. Thus, white-collar workers are less likely than blue collars to suffer from psychosomatic illnesses, low self-esteem, worry, anxiety, and impaired interpersonal relationships. People who are happy with their jobs also tend to have better physical health and to live longer. Although diet, exercise, medical care, and ge-netics are all related to the incidence of heart dis-ease, job dissatisfaction is more closely linked to the cause of death (O'Toole, 1973).

A fundamental cause of dissatisfaction could be the increasing specialization of work. For doctors and lawyers and other professionals, specialization may stimulate the mind while it fattens the checkbook. But for less-educated manual workers, specialization can be numbing. It can produce monotonous, repeti-tive tasks. A person working in the slaughter and meatpacking industry, for example, can be a large stock scalper, belly shaver, crotch buster, gut snatch-er, gut sorter, snout puller, ear cutter, eyelid remov-er, stomach washer, hindleg-toenail puller, frontleg-toenail puller, or oxtail washer. Sorting the guts of hogs eight hours a day is far from an interesting job. Neither is identification of oneself as a gut sorter likely to boost one's ego.

Specialization of work, if carried too far, leaves little room for responsibility or initiative by the worker. It can mean that some people are assigned the job of controlling those who actually produce goods or deliver services. When Studs Terkel (1974) interviewed workers, he found "the most profound complaint is 'being spied on.' There's the foreman at the plant, the supervisor listening in at Ma Bell's, the checker who gives the bus driver a hard time." Moreover, by tying the worker to an isolated task, to a small part of some large task, specialization can empty jobs of their meaning. The result can be dehumanizing for some workers, as Terkel (1974) found when he interviewed people across the country: "'I'm a machine,' says the spotwelder. 'I'm caged,' says the bank teller. 'I'm a mule,' says the steelworker. 'A monkey can do what I do,' says the receptionist." Today, many workers who use computers also feel dehumanized. Their employers sometimes program high performance goals into their computers to push employees to work faster and meet them. If employees stand up now and then to get some relief from long stretches of sitting at a computer terminal, their supervisors may tell them to sit down and continue working. As a result, most of these workers show symptoms of depression (Kilborn, 1990b).

What, then, can generate job satisfaction? In one study, researchers asked 64 workers to define what constitutes a good working life (Levine et al., 1984). They came up with 34 items. Then the investigators presented these items to 450 other employees, asking them to choose the ones that they thought reflect a high quality of work life. Only seven conditions were found to be significant. They are, in the order of importance:

1. My superiors treat me with respect and have confidence in my abilities (similar to work autonomy).
2. There is variety in my daily work routine (the opposite of specialization).
3. There is challenge in my work.
4. My work at present leads to good future work opportunities.
5. My work gives me self-esteem.
6. My work can be enhanced by my nonwork life.
7. The work I do contributes to society.

Note that the list does not include a big paycheck. In the past, most jobholders regarded work as a business transaction for pay only. They would be satisfied even if their work was disagreeable, unpleasant, or degrading, as long as they were adequately paid. Today, most Americans expect more. They want their work to be pleasant and interesting. Indeed, in the last 20 years there have been significant changes in worker attitudes, aspirations, and values.

THE CHANGING WORKPLACE

In a survey, only 26 percent of American workers still held the traditional view of work. Some of these workers said that "the more I get paid, the more I do." Others agreed that "work is one of life's unpleasant necessities. I wouldn't work if I didn't have to." A bumper sticker says it all: "Work sucks, but I need the bucks." In contrast, a large majority (73 percent) of the respondents expressed more positive attitudes toward work. Many agreed with the statement: "I have an inner need to do the very best I can, regardless of pay." They most frequently rated as "very important" certain nonmonetary, inherent qualities of work, such as interesting jobs, developing their own skills, and seeing how good the results of their work are (Yankelovich and Immerwahr, 1984). The American work ethic has taken on a new quality.

As we noted in Chapter 11 (Religion), the Protestant ethic elevated hard work to the status of a moral duty. Working hard was seen as a way of serving God. This work ethic motivated the early Protestants. But as the power of religion declined, so did the influence of ideas about moral duty. As a result, as Max Weber (1930) wrote, "the idea of duty in one's calling prowls about in our lives like the ghost of dead religious beliefs." Although work lost its religious idea of serving God, the Protestant ethic of self-denial—the notion of sacrificing for others—continued to hold sway. Thus, more Americans have until recently worked hard to support their families, disregarding how unpleasant and boring their work might be. They believed that "a man with a family has a responsibility to choose the job that pays the most, rather than one that is more satisfying but pays less." Today, however, a majority of Americans reject that view. As a national survey shows, only 9 percent of employed adults regard salary as what they like most about their jobs (Cramer, 1989). Most Americans are more interested in jobs that allow for personal growth, self-fulfillment, and other post-materialist values. There is, then, a shift in the work ethic, from an emphasis on self-sacrifice to a stress on self-development as the primary motive for hard work (Schor, 1991).

How has this new ethic come about? As we have observed, the number of white-collar workers and the amount of average workers' education have increased substantially over the last several decades. It is these white-collar and better-educated workers who value autonomy and personal growth in the workplace. Hasn't this new focus on the self led to the death of the American work ethic? No. According to a Gallup study, an overwhelming 88 percent of all working Americans feel that it is important for them "to work hard and to do their best on the job." The work ethic is particularly strong among college graduates. In one survey, 63 percent of college-educated jobholders feel a sense of dedication to their work, compared with only 47 percent for those who never went to college. The better-educated are more likely to have a strong commitment to work because they have more satisfying, challenging, or interesting jobs (Yankelovich and Immerwahr, 1984).

Unfortunately, many U.S. industrial companies still follow the precepts of "scientific management" as practiced in the 1920s (see Chapter 4: Groups and Organizations). In those days, managers were paid to think, while workers—largely illiterate or barely educated—were paid to follow orders as unthinking extensions of a machine. Such management is obviously unsuited to the workers of today, who are better-educated and independent-minded. Moreover, in the recent recession, increasing numbers of workers have felt pressured to stay on the jobs they disliked, have worried about losing their jobs, have been pushed to do more with less, and have seen their wages barely keep pace with inflation. All this has caused a lot of alienation, with many workers feeling abused by their employers. As one worker said, "Gee, if the company doesn't care about me, why should I care about them?" The result has been a loss of desire to work hard (Davis and Milbank, 1992). However, attempts have been made to reorganize the workplace. They usually include offering workers more interesting jobs, more autonomy, and increased participation in decision making. A growing number of companies give workers some freedom to set their own working hours within specified limits. Some have introduced mechanisms that allow workers to take part in decisions about production methods, promotions, hiring, and firing. Some companies have even raised wages by sharing profits with workers. These efforts have boosted productivity by 5 to 40 percent. In short, workers are more productive when management treats them as equal partners and provides them with a sense of ownership (Yankelovich and Immerwahr, 1984; Gwynne, 1990; Wartzman, 1992).

QUESTIONS FOR DISCUSSION AND REVIEW
1. What occupations make up the American labor force, and what kinds of Americans fill these positions?
2. Why does specialization lessen the satisfaction of workers with their jobs?
3. What factors have contributed to the changes in the American work ethic?

CHAPTER REVIEW

1. *What are states?* They are political institutions that regulate conflict and allocate resources among citizens. They dictate how the game of politics—the process of determining who gets what, when, how—is to be played. *How is legitimate power different from illegitimate power?* When power is exercised over people with their consent, the power is called legitimate. The legitimate power institutionalized in the state is called authority. It may be derived from tradition, from the charisma of a leader, or from a set of legal rules. *Does the U.S. Constitution grant the president the authority to declare war?* American presidents usually think so, but others believe that the authority belongs to Congress.

2. *Is war "the continuation of state policy by other means"?* Probably yes, because a state's use of mass killings as a way to impose its will on its own citizens is akin to a country's use of war to impose its will on a foreign nation. This may explain the research finding that totalitarian states have been more likely than their democratic counterparts to wage war. In addition to totalitarianism, the causes of war include the society's attempt to seek solidarity and

other benefits from war, the power elite's exploitation of the masses, a long-standing hostility between two nations, a combination of a fiery ideology and a strong leader, and a high level of military preparedness.

3. *According to pluralist theory, who governs America?* Diverse interest groups share power. *Who controls the government according to Mills?* A power elite made up of those who hold top positions in the federal government, the military, and corporations. Mills believed that pluralism reigns in the middle levels of power, but that, above the competing interest groups, there is an elite that makes the important decisions. *According to Marxists, what is wrong with Mills's power-elite theory?* It does not recognize that the power elite serves as the agent for the capitalist class. In Marxists' view, capitalists use the state to maintain their dominance over the other classes.

4. *Are Americans active participants in their government?* No. Most limit their participation to voting, and the percentage of those who bother to vote has been low. In general, those who are poor, young, or have little education vote less than other Americans. The low voting turnout, though, does not threaten democracy. Were nonvoters to vote, they would not change the status quo because they would vote in the same way as current voters.

5. *What conditions make revolution likely?* There are four: (1) some disgruntled, well-off, and well-educated individuals; (2) the masses' rising expectation; (3) a sudden economic crisis; and (4) weak government. These four conditions can be found in the 1989 revolution in Eastern Europe and the former Soviet Union. *What about terrorism?* It is likely to occur if the would-be leader of a revolution does not have the support of the masses and if the government is strong.

6. *How did the Industrial Revolution change the economic process?* Machines replaced much human labor, mass production in factories displaced cottage industry, and agriculture lost ground to industry. *What are some effects of industrialization?* Industrialization speeds up production, shrinking blue-collar employment and enlarging white-collar work. It further changes demographic features, human relations, and the values of society.

7. *What are two basic types of economic organization?* Capitalism and socialism. Capitalism is based on private ownership of property and on competition in the buying and selling of goods and services. Its driving force is the self-interest of individuals. In contrast, socialism subordinates the individual's interests to those of society and puts the ownership and control of the economy in the hands of the state. *How do real economies differ from the models offered by capitalist and socialist theories?* No economy is purely capitalist or purely socialist. All economies have capitalist and socialist elements. They differ only in degree, ranging on a continuum from the most capitalist to the most socialist. Generally, capitalist economies are more productive than socialist ones. *What is the condition of the American economy?* The rates of unemployment and inflation are relatively low, but the productivity growth and living standard are largely at a standstill, while the trade and budget deficits remain high.

8. *How has the American labor force changed in recent years?* The number of jobs in agriculture has dropped sharply, the number in service industries has risen, and the population of white-collar workers has expanded. Meanwhile, the employment rate for women, blacks, and other minorities has increased, while the rate for older men has declined significantly. At the same time, temporary employment has increased sharply. *Who are more likely to be satisfied with their work?* Older and white-collar workers. Given the same kinds of jobs, women are happier than men. *What is the basic cause of job dissatisfaction?* Extreme specialization of work. *How has the American workplace changed?* Workers are less willing to accept unpleasant jobs and more likely to expect meaningful ones. They continue to want to work hard, but management has failed to give them enough recognition for hard work. However, efforts have been made to give employees more interesting jobs, more freedom, and more power in the workplace.

KEY TERMS

Alienation of labor Marx's term for laborers' loss of control over their work process (p. 294).

Authority Legitimate power that derives from traditions, a leader's charisma, or laws (p. 279).

Capitalism An economic system based on private

ownership of property and competition in producing and selling goods and services (p. 294).

Charisma An exceptional personal quality popularly attributed to certain individuals (p. 280).

Coercion Illegitimate use of force or threat of force to compel obedience (p. 278).

Economic institution A system for producing and distributing goods and services (p. 278).

Industrial Revolution The dramatic economic change brought about by the introduction of machines into the work process about 200 years ago (p. 291).

Influence The ability to control others' behavior through persuasion rather than coercion or authority (p. 279).

Mixed economy An economic system that includes both capitalist and socialist elements (p. 295).

Political power The capacity to use the government to make decisions that affect the whole society (p. 283).

Politics Process in which people acquire and exercise power, determining who gets what, when, and how (p. 278).

Power The ability to control the behavior of others, even against their will (p. 278).

Revolution The violent overthrow of an existing government and drastic change in the social and political order (p. 288).

Socialism An economic system based on public ownership and government control of the economy (p. 294).

State A political institution that regulates conflict and allocates resources among the citizens of a country (p. 278).

SUGGESTED READINGS

Echikson, William. 1990. *Lighting the Night: Revolution in Eastern Europe.* New York: Morrow. A personal account of the facts and faces behind the series of events that culminated in the collapse of the communist regimes throughout Eastern Europe.

Erikson, Kai, and Steven P. Vallas (eds.). 1990. *The Nature of Work: Sociological Perspectives.* New Haven, Conn.: Yale University Press. A collection of insightful articles by well-known researchers on the subject.

Etzioni, Amitai. 1988. *The Moral Dimensions: Toward a New Economics.* New York: Free Press. Discusses how, contrary to traditional economic assumptions, people do not maximize their self-interests only, often make irrational rather than rational decisions, and are an integral part of social groups rather than isolated individuals.

Krugman, Paul. 1990. *The Age of Diminished Expectations: U.S. Economic Policy in the 1990s.* Cambridge, Mass.: MIT Press. An evenhanded presentation of the arguments and facts about the major problems facing the American economy today.

Osborne, David, and Ted Gaebler. 1992. *Reinventing Government: How the Entrepreneurial Spirit Is Transforming the Public Sector.* Reading, Mass.: Addison-Wesley. Shows how government can serve its citizens better by decentralizing authority, reducing bureaucracy, and promoting competition.

13

Education,
Science, and
Health

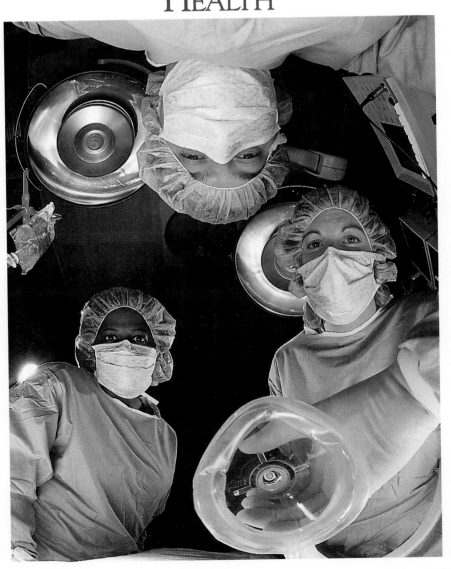

MYTHS AND REALITIES

Myth: Since skilled workers are needed for industrial growth, industrialization must have caused schools to proliferate in the first place.

Reality: *Industrialization does not cause schools to proliferate. In both developing and developed countries, educational expansion has often preceded rather than followed industrialization.*

Myth: A major function of schools is to teach children nothing but the truth about their country.

Reality: *A major function of schools is to foster national unity. Therefore, the nation's glorious achievements are played up, but its shameful acts are watered down or left out.*

Myth: The fact that American students have lower test scores than their counterparts in other countries proves the failure of our educational system.

Reality: *It does not, because our educational system is far more democratic or less elitist than others'. Given the larger number of socially disadvantaged students in the United States, the average test scores of American students as a whole are bound to be lower.*

Myth: Japanese schools are so much better than ours that American society will benefit if our educators emulate the Japanese.

Reality: *Japanese schools are not necessarily better. They can be worse. By emphasizing extreme conformity, they tend to stifle individuality and creativity, qualities that American school cultivate.*

Myth: Because they reject the use of faith to accept ideas, scientists often repeat each other's experiments before they will accept their colleagues' findings as valid.

Reality: *Most scientists rarely replicate others' experiments. They often make certain assumptions, taking certain things on faith, just like everybody else.*

Myth: The theory of evolution was developed only by Charles Darwin.

Reality: *The theory of evolution was also developed independently by Alfred Russel Wallace. Science is full of multiple discoveries— the same discoveries made independently by different scientists.*

Myth: Scientists are single-mindedly objective. They would reject scientific ideas for objective reasons only.

Reality: *Scientists are just as human and emotional as the rest of us. Strict objectivity is more a scientific ideal than a reality. Scientists are far from objective and are much more intent on confirming their own ideas than those of others.*

Myth: Being frail, old people are more likely than younger ones to fall victim to virtually all kinds of illness.

Reality: *While they are more likely to suffer from such chronic illnesses as arthritis, heart disease, and cancer, old people are less susceptible to acute and infectious illnesses, such as measles and pneumonia.*

Myth: Compassionate and sensitive, most doc-

307

tors listen to their patients' complaints with great attentiveness and understanding.
Reality: Most doctors tend to interact poorly with patients. *Consequently, about 60 percent of their patients fail to understand adequately the instructions about their medication.*

S everal years ago, Francine Vogler went to see a neurosurgeon when she suffered a neck injury. After a quick examination, the doctor was cruelly blunt as he prescribed immediate surgery: "You have a 5% chance of dying or becoming a quadriplegic." Immediately the patient began to cry, but the surgeon walked briskly out of the room. "I was totally shocked," she says today. As a physician herself, she now teaches medicine at the University of Southern California, and she makes sure that her students learn how to treat patients more humanely (Nazario, 1992). This real-life story suggests what research has found, namely, that health, science, and education are related to one another. Highly specialized physicians such as neurosurgeons have largely been trained to be rigorously scientific, objective, and dispassionate toward medical problems. It is little wonder that they tend to lack warmth and sensitivity in dealing with patients, treating them as if they were mere diseases. In this chapter we will discuss this and other issues relating to health, science, and education.

Social Aspects of Education

According to the functionalist perspective, education performs many functions for us as individuals and for society as a whole. Here we discuss only the most important functions: teaching knowledge and skills, enhancing social mobility, promoting national unity, and providing custodial care.

KNOWLEDGE AND SKILLS

The most obvious function of education is to provide a new generation with the knowledge and skills necessary to maintain the society. Thanks to our schools, we have "a democratic system of government, a dynamic free enterprise economy, and an enduring social system, all of which are the envy of the world" (Warner, 1983).

But, oddly enough, over the last 20 years, there has been a lot of controversy over whether schools can help students develop cognitive skills. Since the late 1960s, there have been many observers who believe that schools make little difference in how much we learn. They have found that raising the quality of high schools could improve academic performance by only 1 percent or less. They have also found that school variables such as the quality of teachers and curricula accounted for a mere 2 to 3 percent of the variance in scholastic attainment, a figure way below the estimated 50 percent attributed to family background. All this was taken to mean that how much we learn depends far more on what kind of home we come from than on what kind of school we go to. If we are from middle-class families, we would do much better academically than our classmates from lower-class homes. The quality of the school has very little impact on our academic achievement. Such findings and interpretations have led to the conclusion that "additional school expenditures are unlikely to increase achievements, and redistributing resources will not reduce test score inequality" (Jencks et al., 1972).

Such a conclusion has recently been called into question. Many studies have shown real and substantial effects of schooling on student achievement. Of course, they do not discount completely the importance of family background. Given the greater learning resources—such as a daily newspaper, dictionary, and encyclopedia in their homes—upper- and middle-class students do have higher educational attainment than their lower-class peers (Teachman, 1987). But when researchers take family background into account, they still find that schools do make a difference in how much their students learn. Students from lower-income families attending "good" high schools, for example, have been found to learn more and have a better chance of going to college than other lower-income students attending "bad" schools. Moreover, studies conducted during summer months and teacher strikes have shown that inner-city and minority youngsters are most likely to suffer sharp drops in learning skills and knowledge when not in school. Other studies have found that 45 or 50 percent of student learning can be attributed to the quality of schools. Studies in developing countries, where schooling is not available to all children, have also shown that whether or not children attend school has a significant influence on their cognitive development. In fact, an extensive review of relevant studies concludes that schools can and do make a big difference in transmitting knowledge and skills to students (Rutter, 1983; Heyneman and Loxley, 1983; Mortimore, 1988; Griffith et al., 1989).

SOCIAL MOBILITY

As individuals, Americans tend to value the knowledge and skills transmitted by the schools not for their own sake but because they hope to translate those skills into good jobs and money. Many students are attracted to college because of job and career considerations. Does education really enhance the individual's opportunity for social mobility? (Figure 13.1)

The answer is no, according to the conflict perspective. Conflict theorists argue that formal education is often irrelevant to occupational achievement. Whatever training is needed comes more from work experience than from formal education. Even highly technical skills can be learned on the job. For the most part, education seems to provide credentials rather than skills. In effect, a diploma or degree certifies to employers that the holder is employable. It gives them a place to start in screening potential employees, and those who have the right educational credentials are likely to make the "first cut" in competing for a job.

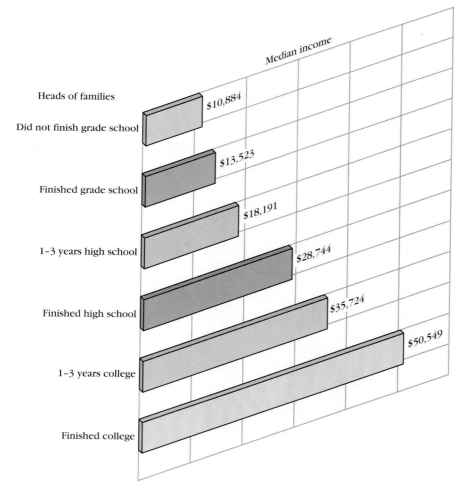

FIGURE 13.1 *How Education Raises Our Income*
A major function of education is to enhance the individual's opportunity for social mobility. The more education people have, the bigger their earnings.

Source: Census Bureau, *Statistical Abstract of the United States,* 1992, p. 446.

Median income

Heads of families
Did not finish grade school — $10,884

Finished grade school — $13,523

1–3 years high school — $18,191

Finished high school — $28,744

1–3 years college — $35,724

Finished college — $50,549

More positively, functionalist theory suggests that education serves a useful function by upgrading prospective workers' skills—human capital—which in turn boosts earnings for individuals and promotes economic growth for society. There is evidence to support this view. As Figure 13.1 shows, education and income are strongly related. In 1991 the average college graduate, for example, made $50,549, whereas the high school graduate earned $28,744. In analyzing the relationship between education and income from 1950 to 1970, sociologists Richard Wanner and Lionel Lewis (1982) concluded that "the overall trend is toward a stronger relationship." In fact, recent labor-market data have confirmed that, due to the increasing reliance of modern industries on highly skilled workers, the value of a college education is high and has risen dramatically. In 1980 college graduates earned about 32 percent more than high school graduates, but today the earnings difference has gone up to 61 percent (Kosters, 1990).

NATIONAL UNITY

To foster national unity, schools—mostly primary and secondary schools rather than colleges and universities—play an important role in transmitting the culture to a new generation. Students are taught to become good citizens, to love their country, to cherish their cultural values, and to be proud of their nationality—American, Mexican, Nigerian, Russian, or whatever it may be. The teaching of good citizenship may involve the performance of rituals. In the United States, schoolchildren are taught to recite the Pledge of Allegiance to the flag and to stand at attention to the playing of "The Star-Spangled Banner" before a ball game. Schools also plant seeds of patriotism in their young charges by teaching civics, history, and other social studies. In these courses, the glorious national achievements are played up. But the shameful acts, which can hardly inspire love and respect for one's own country, are watered down or left out. Thus, American children are taught that their European ancestors came to this country as heroic pioneers, even though they slaughtered numerous Indians and stole their lands. In Japan, school textbooks do not contain information or pictures showing Japanese wartime atrocities in China, such as massacring 200,000 Chinese civilians in the city of Nanjing, bayoneting Chinese civilians for practice, or burying Chinese civilians alive (Sayle, 1982; Kim, 1983).

Like Japan and other countries, the United States has long recognized the importance of using

To functionalists, schools play an important role in the Americanization of young people, enabling the nation to enhance its unity and minorities to improve their life chances. But conflict theorists see the so-called Americanization as a threat to the cultural heritage of minorities.

education to unify its people by teaching history from its own viewpoint. Our Founding Fathers believed that the schools should teach the American idea of democracy, ensuring individual freedom and good government. With the influx of immigrants getting larger and larger since 1860, more and more states found it necessary to enact compulsory education laws so that their children could become "Americanized." Americanization involves thinking of oneself as an American, supporting the American democratic idea, and becoming assimilated into the mainstream of American culture. Today, the process of Americanization continues with the children of new immigrants, particularly those from Southeast Asia and Latin America. Americanization is also targeted to black, Hispanic, Native American, and other minority children.

Seen from the functionalist perspective, Americanization is not only necessary for the nation as a whole, but it is also useful to the immigrants and minorities. It enables the nation to enhance its unity and the minorities to improve their life chances. But conflict theorists argue that Americanization is cultural imperialism, forcibly imposing the WASP (White Anglo-Saxon Protestant) culture on Americans of other cultural backgrounds. The typical American history textbook is written from the white's point of view so that it presents more white heroes than black heroes. Hispanic schoolchildren are expected to give up their Spanish and to be taught in English only. Thus, the so-called Americanization not only threatens to destroy the minorities' cultural heritage but also encourages teachers to stereotype minority students as "culturally deprived."

Both functionalist and conflict views on Americanization may be correct, but they are less relevant today than in the past. Since 1970, primarily because of the civil rights movement, such minority-oriented programs as black studies and bilingual education have been instituted in a number of schools. This means that there is less destruction of minority heritage, contrary to what conflict theory suggests. However, schools seem less effective in teaching the political culture of the nation than functionalist theory suggests. Large numbers of Americans cannot recognize the Bill of Rights when it was read to them. Many teenagers also do not know how Congress or the president is selected.

CUSTODIAL CARE

Another major but latent function of schooling is to offer custodial care of children—providing a place to put them and someone to watch them. Schools keep children off the streets, presumably out of trouble. The importance of this function has increased, as there have been many more dual-career and single-parent households. Schools have traditionally done a good job in performing their custodial role. As research often showed, many schools were run almost like boot camps, where teachers diligently enforced rules and regulations and students obeyed them without question. But since 1970 a fast-growing number of schools seem to have turned into "blackboard jungles," where violence and drugs are rampant.

According to a 1989 Gallup poll, the public ranked "use of drugs" and "lack of discipline" as the top two problems in schools. The National School Safety Center also found that violence by young students is a trend throughout the country, with at least 5 percent of the children carrying a gun in the school (Morganthau, 1992). "The age at which youngsters are expressing their anger at teachers is getting younger and younger," said the Center's executive director, "and the things they're doing are more terrible. In the past, it might have been telling a teacher off; now it's using knives and guns" (Lee, 1990). We should not, however, blow school violence out of proportion. Although there is more violence than before, an orderly routine still prevails in most schools. Teachers play a crucial part in maintaining this order. But some teachers find this custodial function degrading to their profession. They resent being "treated like babysitters." As Martha Fiske, a distinguished teacher who quit her high-paid position in one of the nation's best high schools, said, "If you want me to be a professional and publish articles on 'King Lear,' don't ask me to pick up litter in the girl's room, or catch potato puffs on lunch duty. Why not hire minimum-wage people? Isn't it counterproductive to pay someone $36,000 to supervise a bathroom?" (Marquand, 1986).

The custodial function of schools is important for yet another reason: it keeps the young out of the job market. Adults may find this reason embarrassing, but it is quite real today. In the past, when unskilled labor was in great demand, children made up a large portion of the labor force. This is why for a long time farmers and manufacturers who needed child labor, as well as poor families who needed the money brought home by child labor, were opposed to mass compulsory education, which would take away the children from their jobs. Only when the need for unskilled labor began to diminish did they cooperate and send their children to school. Today there are so few unskilled jobs that if there were no compulsory school attendance to keep the youngsters from work-ing, the nation's unemployment rate would shoot up dangerously. The need for keeping young people out of the job market, however, requires that they spend a lot of time in school—more than necessary for ac-quiring basic knowledge and skills. Thus, most stu-dents take 12 years—from grades 1 through 12—to acquire basic reading and mathematical skills that could be achieved in about three years of intensive training between ages 15 and 18 (White, 1977). It is no wonder that students are given ample opportuni-ties for recreational, extracurricular, or nonacademic activities. Their curriculum is often filled with such nonacademic electives as public speaking, putting out a yearbook, leadership ("how to plan and con-duct meetings"), and "survival of singles" ("how to manage time and money while making wise choices in buying, preparing and selecting food, clothing, household furnishings, automobiles, and insurance"). In many schools, the time spent on learning to cook and drive even counts as much toward a high school diploma as the time spent on studying English, math-ematics, chemistry, American history, or biology (Na-tional Commission on Excellence in Education, 1983; Tharp, 1987). The schools apparently play their cus-todial role well, as most students consider games, sports, and friends—not books, classes, and teach-ers—the most important features of their school ex-perience (Goodlad, 1984).

In high school, youths from upper and middle classes are usually channeled into college preparatory courses, but lower-class students are more likely to end up in vocational courses, which lead to lower-status jobs.

THE CONFLICT PERSPECTIVE

If schools can serve all the functions that we have dis-cussed, can they also reduce social inequality in the larger society? Most Americans seem to believe so, because they think education can improve the life chances of the poor and minorities. But conflict theo-rists argue just the opposite—that schools reinforce the existing social structure of inequality.

To conflict theorists, American education sup-ports the capitalist system by producing an array of skills and attitudes appropriate for maintaining social inequality. This idea is based on the assumption that the educational system gives children from different social classes different educational experiences, so that they develop skills and attitudes appropriate for their status. In elementary and secondary schools, lower-class children are trained to respect authority and obey orders—characteristics that employers like in menial laborers. In high school, higher-income youths are usually channeled into college preparatory

courses, and thus eventually into higher-status jobs, while lower-income students are typically guided into vocational courses, which lead to lower-status jobs. After graduating from high school, higher-income students are more likely to attend college than lower-income students. Those in elite universities learn in-dependent thinking and decision-making skills, which are useful for leadership positions. Meanwhile, in average universities and colleges, middle-class youth are taught responsibility, dependability, and the ability to work without close supervision—quali-ties needed for middle-level professions and occupa-tions. In short, education teaches youth to know their place and fill it (Carnoy and Levin, 1985; Weis, 1988).

Conflict theorists do not, however, blame schools for producing inequality within themselves or in the larger society. As Samuel Bowles and Her-bert Gintis (1976) wrote, "education is relatively powerless to correct economic inequality. The class, sex, and race biases in schooling do not produce, but rather reflect, the structure of privilege in society at large." In order for schools to reduce inequality, conflict theorists conclude, the capitalist society would have to change into a socialist one.

There is evidence to support the conflict argument about the relationship between social class and educational experience. In his study of nearly 900 high school classes in various parts of the United States, John Goodlad (1984) consistently found that higher-track (higher-ability) and lower-track (lower-ability) classes were taught differently. There were disproportionately large numbers of higher-income students in higher-track classes and of lower-class and minority students in lower-track classes. Higher-track, higher-income students were taught "a more independent type of thinking—self-direction, creativity, critical thinking, pursuing individual assignments, and active involvement in the process of learning." Lower-track, lower-class students were taught "a more conforming type of classroom behavior—working quietly, punctuality, cooperation, improving study habits, conforming to rules and expectations, and getting along with others." A more recent study also shows that track assignment reinforces inequalities in achievement among students from different social classes (Gamoran and Mare, 1989). Lower-class students are, in effect, taught to become low-paid manual workers, whereas higher-income students are taught to be high-paid professionals. Similarly, many black and Hispanic students are segregated from their white peers in the same school. As a large-scale study shows, disproportionately large numbers of blacks and Hispanics are placed in low-ability mathematics and science classes, while few minorities get into high-ability classes. The same study further indicates that the low-ability classes are taught by less-qualified teachers and receive less laboratory equipment and other resources (Putka, 1990).

But the conflict assumption that only capitalism is responsible for the inequality in schools is less convincing. To the extent that all societies are stratified, educational inequality exists everywhere, even in socialist countries. In the former Soviet Union, for example, an overwhelming majority of children from higher-status families (whose parents are government officials, scientists, and other members of the Soviet intelligentsia) attended elite schools that would lead them into a profession or government service. They avoided vocational schools that lead to farm or factory work, despite the government's urging that more Soviet youth switch to such schools and "give their strong young arms and hot hearts where they are most needed" (Williams, 1984).

AMERICAN PROBLEMS IN PERSPECTIVE

For some time now, there have been many critiques of education in the United States. They all document a decline in educational standards and achievement when compared with our past and with other countries. Scores on Scholastic Aptitude Tests (SAT) taken by college-bound high school seniors fell continuously from 1963 to 1980, and in the early 1970s American students scored lower on 19 academic tests than their counterparts in Japan and other industrialized countries. In 1989 more than 60 percent of all American high school students could not understand what they read, including newspaper stories and subjects that they were studying in class. In view of such facts, the National Commission on Excellence in Education had earlier warned that the United States is "a nation at risk" because "the educational foundations of our society are presently being eroded by a rising tide of mediocrity that threatens our very future as a nation and a people." Many other national task forces on education have raised the same alarm (Davies and Slevin, 1984). The media have also fanned our fear with the warning that we are in danger of becoming a second-class economic power because of our students' poor showing on math and science tests (Lord and Horn, 1987).

Is American education really in a state of crisis? The answer is probably no if we put the discouraging data in proper perspective.

First, the decline of SAT scores may have partly resulted from the opening up of educational opportunities for larger numbers of the poor and minorities, who are encouraged to go to college. Because of inadequate academic preparation or the tests' cultural bias or both, the socially disadvantaged students did not do as well on the SAT as the socially advantaged, which helped bring down the average score for the entire group. But the investment in equal education may have begun to pay off. Since 1980 the national SAT averages have begun to level off or pick up, partly a result of the steady improvement in test scores among African-American, Hispanic, and other minority students. Moreover, the top 10 percent of students, who come largely from higher-income and better-educated families, have scored significantly *higher* than they did 10 years ago (Kolata, 1991; De Witt, 1992).

Second, the lower academic achievement in the United States than in other industrialized nations may also reflect the impact of educational democratization in our society. Compared with the schools in other countries, our public schools are far less selective, containing a larger proportion of lower-class, foreign-language-speaking, immigrant, and other culturally different children. In contrast to the continued elitism of foreign educational systems, we simply have many more students with widely diverse backgrounds. This inevitably lowers the average test score of American students as a whole (Kolata, 1991). But the lower achievement at the precollege level does not hurt the American educational system as a whole, because the standard and quality of education become increasingly higher as we go from high school to college to graduate or professional school. This may explain why the United States produces the largest number of Nobel laureates and attracts a larger number of foreign students than does any other country. As Professor Shibuya of Japan's Joetsu University says, "Consider the number of Nobel prizes won so far by Japanese—fewer than ten. The number in the U.S.? More than 100" (Bowen, 1986).

Third, the United States is not alone in having some educational problems. Japan, which is often touted as taking over America's preeminence in science and technology, has serious problems with its higher education. Although Japanese schoolchildren are under enormous pressure to study hard, university students are allowed to take it easy, as if in reward for having beaten their brains out before college. As Robert Christopher (1983) observes, "the great majority of Japanese universities are extraordinarily permissive: once you get into one, it takes real effort to get kicked out . . . Japanese university authorities do not regard a student's failure to attend classes or even to pass courses as a ground for dismissal." Moreover, many Japanese college students have little incentive to work hard, because employers are more interested in the college from which potential recruits graduate than in their grades. Japanese political and business leaders are now concerned about the lax atmosphere in their colleges. They also worry that their schools' emphasis on conformity, such as finding the "single right answer" to a problem, is depriving their society of much needed creativity, especially in the current age of rapid change (Fiske, 1987).

Fourth, our schools are not to blame for the lower achievement of our students as compared with that of the Japanese. For one thing, our schools are expected to dilute their teaching resources by deal-

Japanese society offers a setting for schoolchildren that is different from that in the United States. Unlike American schools, Japanese schools do not spend time dealing with such problems as alcohol and drug abuse or teenage pregnancy. Japanese mothers make sure their children study three to four hours a night, and Japanese adolescent peer culture pressures teenagers to study hard.

ing with such social problems as alcohol and drug abuse and teenage pregnancy, which Japanese schools do not have. In fact, American teachers often have to spend 40 percent of their time on nonteaching tasks. Given the high rates of divorce, single parenthood, and dual-career couples, American parents are too stressed, tired, or self-absorbed to do what Japanese mothers do—helping with their children's homework and making sure they study three or four hours a night. Two-thirds of American teenagers hold part-time jobs, which significantly reduces their ability to hit the books after school. By contrast, working during the school year is virtually unheard of in Japan. American teenagers are also under great pressure from their peers to look good, drink, socialize, date, and even have sex. This is the opposite of the Japanese adolescent peer culture, which pressures teenagers to study hard. Japanese students like to say, though a little facetiously, "Four you score; five you die," meaning "If you sleep five hours a night instead of four, you won't pass the exams" (Steinberg, 1987). In short, it is largely social problems, the lack of support from parents, and the adolescent subculture that make it hard for American schools to compete with their Japanese counterparts. Our schools, then, are hardly to blame for our students' lower academic achievement.

Finally, while many problems can be found in America's schools, there is a lot of good in them, particularly in their mission of providing quality with equality (Goodlad, 1984). Although education researcher and reformist Theodore Sizer (1984) criticizes the nation's high schools for being rigid and impersonal, he still finds that "they are, on the whole, happy places, settings that most adolescents find inviting, staffed by adults who genuinely care for youngsters." In contrast, most Japanese students do not enjoy their school experience, because they feel like robots or prisoners in a rigidly controlled environment. Moreover, some Japanese professors who have taught in the United States have observed that American students are more creative than their Japanese counterparts. As a math professor in Japan says, "Japanese kids at 18 know everything. But, in terms of logical thinking, American kids can think better" (Tharp, 1987). Japanese schools, like their society, stress extreme conformity, pressuring students to do what everybody else is doing while discouraging them from sticking out by taking risks. In contrast, American schools, like American society, place a high premium on individuality, prodding students to think for themselves. This is why there are proportionately more original thinkers in the United States, as shown by the numerous American scientists who have won the Nobel prize. The American education system may turn out to be the ace in the hole in our economic competition with Japan.

QUESTIONS FOR DISCUSSION AND REVIEW

1. What major functions does education perform for American society, and which of these are latent rather than manifest?
2. Why do critics charge that schools have failed to promote knowledge and skills?
3. What are some of the ways in which schools attempt to promote national unity, and why do some ethnic groups oppose this activity?
4. Why is the custodial care function of schools so important to American society?
5. How does the conflict perspective on education differ from the functionalist approach?
6. What is the nature of our educational problems?

Science and Society

The family, religion, economy, and other institutions have been around for thousands of years. But science began to emerge as a social institution only 300 years ago. Only then did it begin to become widely accepted as a necessary means of satisfying societal needs. This came about when scientific knowledge was used to improve technology, which led to improvements in daily life. Today, science and technology are so intertwined that we often use the words interchangeably, but they do refer to different things. **Science** is a body of knowledge developed through systematic methods. **Technology** can mean any kind of tool or practical know-how, but it has come to mean the practical application of scientific principles. If science did not have practical uses, it would probably have little influence or prestige. It has become an important social institution primarily through its marriage to technology. How did this come about?

THE EMERGENCE OF SCIENCE

Through trial and error, ancient peoples discovered how to light a fire, build huts, make bows and arrows, and so on. Some 3000 years ago they even learned to mix tin with copper in order to produce a stronger metal, bronze. All this and more they did without benefit of science. They created and used technologies without knowing the principles behind their inventions. Even the Industrial Revolution owed little if anything to science. The steam engine was invented and used before people understood how it worked. The rapid technological progress of modern societies, however, has depended on the rise of science.

The First Scientists Like technology, science has ancient roots. We can trace it back to Greeks such as Plato, who advocated mathematics as a means of disciplining the mind, and Aristotle, who classified animals and plants. But their science was not based on what is now called the scientific method. It was not until the seventeenth century that the seed of modern science began to grow in Western Europe, especially in England. Then "a growing habit of testing theories against careful measurement, observation, and upon occasion, experiment" spurred rapid progress in the natural sciences (McNeill, 1963; Lindberg, 1992).

A radical change in philosophical ideas about nature was a key factor stimulating scientific growth.

Earlier students of nature had seen it as a living cosmos, filled with spiritual or human qualities. The new scientists treated the universe as a dead thing. Natural phenomena were no longer believed to act randomly, on their own whim, or by the will of a supernatural power. Instead, scientists now regarded nature as an object that behaves predictably, like a machine. It could be studied through direct observation, measured, and controlled. Respect for nature gave way to the quest to dominate, control, and use it.

A second factor in the development of modern science was the emergence of cooperative scholarship among those who regarded themselves as scientists. Through cooperative communication, scientists can expand their knowledge more easily and quickly and avoid repeating the work and mistakes of others. The world's first example of cooperative scholarship among scientists came into being in 1662 when the Royal Society of London was organized. Its members, being gentlemen of wealth and leisure, could afford to spend long hours studying nature and discussing their findings with each other. But unlike their scholarly predecessors, they were not prejudiced against "dirtying their hands with anything but ink" (McNeill, 1963). They not only shared the new, mechanistic philosophy of nature but also believed that experiments provided the path to knowledge.

These early scientists were also for the most part deeply religious Protestants. We might expect that their dedication to science would clash with their religion. But two characteristics allowed them to maintain fidelity to both religion and science. First, the potential for conflict was eased by the fact that the early scientists "were content with striving to understand only a small segment of reality at a time, leaving the great questions of religion and philosophy to one side" (McNeill, 1963). A second characteristic reconciling their religion and their science, according to Robert Merton (1973, 1984), was the Protestant ethic. They believed that their scientific activity fulfilled the demands of this ethic, which, as we have seen, required them to work hard for the glory of God. They reasoned that "the scientific study of nature enables a fuller appreciation of His works and thus leads us to admire and praise the Power, Wisdom, and Goodness of God as manifested in His creation" (Merton, 1973). Furthermore, the scientists believed that their experiments would eventually lead to improvements in the human condition. Thus, through their scientific endeavors they were also heeding the Christian tenet to serve their neighbors. In Merton's view, the Protestant ethic helped make science a legitimate activity in the eyes of both the public and scientists themselves.

The Institutionalization of Science The members of the Royal Society had a committee devoted to improving "mechanical inventions," but for many years science did little to aid technology. In fact, it was technology that aided science. Galileo, for exam-

For many years, science did little to aid technology. It was technology that aided science. Galileo, shown here before the Court of the Holy Office, 1633, was able to make his astronomical observations because of the invention of the telescope.

ple, was able to make his astronomical observations because a Dutchman playing with lenses had invented the telescope.

Lewis Mumford (1963) has dated the beginning of the modern technological age at around 1832, when a huge water turbine was perfected as a result of scientific studies. This marked, in Mumford's view, the emergence of a new pattern, in which science drives technology onward. In the modern age, there is "deliberate and systematic invention" based on "the direct application of scientific knowledge to technics and the conduct of life." The Germans pioneered in giving this new approach institutional form. Their chemical and electrical companies created research laboratories, staffed them with chemists and physicists, and made invention a "deliberate, expected, normal affair." Science and technology, then, were not only wedded to each other but also embedded into the routines of economic life.

Today, science and technology depend on each other, as we depend on both of them. Modern technological developments such as computers and nuclear reactors could not have been invented through trial and error. Their invention required an understanding of scientific principles. Current technological advances in computer chips, tiny semiconductor lasers, the liquid crystals of computer displays, optic devices, composite materials of extraordinary strength, and so on would not have existed without scientific knowledge of condensed-matter physics, which studies such phenomena as proton and electron transport (Broad, 1990a).

To carry on their work, however, most scientists require extremely complicated technology. Biologists use electron microscopes, physicists use particle accelerators, and astronomers use NASA's satellites—all extremely sophisticated technology. Without having the advanced X-ray astrophysics laboratory satellite in outer space, which the United States plans to build at the projected cost of $1.6 billion, scientists will find it difficult to investigate black holes, dark matter, and the age of the universe. Similarly, without the planned construction of the $8 billion Superconducting Supercollider in Texas, it will be hard to unravel one of the deepest mysteries facing scientists—why elementary particles have the masses they do (Goldberger and Panofsky, 1990). Although it enables scientists to do their research, technology can also by itself suggest new scientific ideas. For example, the search to eliminate a technological problem—static in radiotelephony—led to the birth of the science of radio astronomy and hence to the

discovery of quasars and other astronomical phenomena. Thus, the flow of knowledge goes not only from science to technology but also from technology to science.

There would not have been much progress in both science and technology if they had been differentiated—with one being highly developed to the neglect of the other. Scientific ideas, especially mathematics and logical proof, reached great heights in ancient Greece, but science never flourished there for want of interest in technical problem-solving. The technology in ancient China was highly sophisticated, bringing forth papermaking, gunpowder, iron casting, and many other inventions long before they appeared in the West. But these technical innovations later fell far behind Western technology because the Chinese failed to pursue conceptual abstraction and theoretical generalization—the essence of science (Münch, 1983). In contrast, as we have seen, Westerners have shown much interest in both science and technology since the seventeenth century, which may explain why both are so highly advanced in the West today.

SCIENTIFIC PROGRESS

Science is so much a part of modern society that it is easy to take it for granted. Defining just what it is scientists do, and explaining how science advances, however, is not easy. We frequently say, for example, that science depends on not accepting facts or ideas on the basis of faith. Instead, scientists must subject everything to the test of observation and experiment. Taken literally, however, this would mean that scientists would be repeating each other's experiments endlessly. In fact, scientists often find replication an impractical undertaking. One reason is the incompleteness of many published descriptions of experiments. Just as cookbook recipes cannot include all the tiny details that every good cook knows, neither can scientists be exhaustive in describing their experiments. But these little technical points are often necessary for a successful replication. Many scientists would rather do original research. In science, the prizes go for originality, not for repeating someone else's experiment. Besides, replication may require just as much time, effort, and money as original research. Contrary to popular belief, then, most scientists seldom repeat each other's experiments (Broad and Wade, 1983).

If they do not constantly replicate experiments, scientists must make certain assumptions, taking certain things on faith, just like everyone else. Most biologists today accept as a basic assumption Darwin's theory of natural selection. Physicists use the theory of quantum mechanics as a working assumption. Each of these constitutes what Thomas Kuhn (1970) calls a **paradigm,** a model for defining, studying, and solving problems. For hundreds of years, for example, astronomers shared the Ptolemaic system of the heavens as their paradigm. They believed that the earth was the center of the universe and the sun revolved around it. Most scientists work within the paradigm of their discipline. They are not inclined to doubt its basic assumptions. How, then, does science advance? How do innovations—new facts and ideas—appear?

Kuhn divides innovation into two types: ordinary innovation and scientific revolution. Ordinary innovation is the product of everyday research, such as Foucault's discovery in 1850 that light travels faster in air than in water, or the invention of the transistor in 1949 by a team of scientists at Bell Labs. Journeymen scientists routinely conduct research that produces such innovations all the time, and Kuhn calls those scientists' routine research **normal science.** As normal science keeps producing new ideas and data, however, some of these create problems for the existing paradigm. They are **anomalies,** incompatible with or unexplainable by the paradigm. If these anomalies keep piling up, they generate a "crisis" that compels some very innovative scientists to develop a new paradigm. The scientists, in effect, initiate a **scientific revolution,** replacing an old paradigm with a new one, such as Newton's law of gravity or Einstein's theory of relativity (Kuhn, 1970).

All this suggests the importance of cultural accumulation. Normal science does not operate in an intellectual vacuum but through the guidance of a paradigm. The paradigm itself is a product of an earlier scientific revolution, which, in turn, resulted from the accumulation of anomalous theories and data, the fallout of routine research. At each stage of cultural accumulation, there is a storehouse of scientific ideas and facts that can be used to fashion an innovation. Even Isaac Newton acknowledged a debt to this cultural storehouse, claiming in great modesty, "If I have seen farther, it is by standing on the shoulders of giants." This cultural accumulation explains why science is full of multiple discoveries—the same discoveries made independently by different scientists. Calculus, for example, was discovered independently by Isaac Newton and Gottfried Leibniz. The theory of evolution was developed independently by Charles Darwin and Alfred Russel Wallace. The basic laws of genetics were discovered independently by Gregor Mendel and, later, by three other scientists. Of course, not all scientific discoveries are multiples. There are singletons—discoveries made by individual scientists alone (Patinkin, 1983). But multiples are numerous enough to suggest the importance of cultural accumulation for scientific progress.

MODERN SCIENCE

As science advanced over the years, its methods were applied to more and more areas of life, and it achieved great prestige in Western society. As recently as 40 years ago, however, scientists were poorly paid, worked alone on shoestring budgets, and were popularly viewed as eccentric characters. This era of "little science" ended in the United States with World War II and the development of the atomic bomb. In a sense, scientists had enabled the United States to end the war. The Cold War and the arms race with the Soviet Union that followed ensured that the government, like industry, would continue to have a large interest in fostering scientific development. When, in 1957, the Soviet Union surprised Americans by launching the first satellite into space, the government intensified its role in science. It poured new money into research and scientific education.

The billions of dollars that the government, industry, and private foundations spent on research after the war gave birth to the era of "big science." The number of scientists and the prestige and influence of science have soared. Increasingly, scientists work as narrow specialists within huge bureaucracies. In Jacques Ellul's (1964) words, "The research worker is no longer a solitary genius." For the most part, scientists work as members of teams. Only by joining the "team" of a bureaucracy can they gain access to the expensive, sophisticated equipment most scientists require. Since the 1920s, the percentage of papers written by one person has declined substantially. Now it is very common for two or more scientists to collaborate on a paper. It is also very common for several scientists to make the same discovery independently (Merton, 1976).

Big science will become even bigger in this decade. The U.S. government has already embarked on the most ambitious array of gigantic science projects ever. Some of these projects are the $1.15 billion Hubble Space Telescope now orbiting high above the earth, the $3 billion Human Genome Initiative designed to map out the entire human genetic

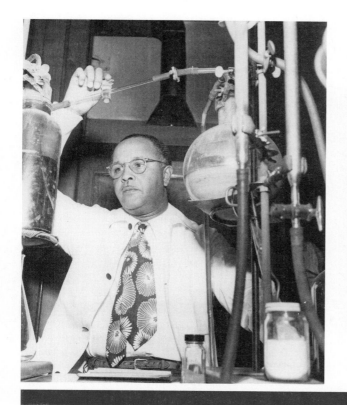

Left: *The era of "little science" is seen in the relatively simple working conditions of chemist Percy Julian shown working in his lab in the 1940s. This era ended in the Unites States with World War II, the development of the atomic bomb, and the beginning of the Cold War with the former Soviet Union.* Right: *In the photo, workers show how big the excavation is of a tunnel access shaft for the supercollider atom smasher in Texas.*

code, the $8 billion Superconducting Supercollider for studying elementary particles, and the $30 billion space station Freedom for conducting scientific experiments and possibly serving as the stepping stone to Mars. These and other similarly huge projects now planned for completion in the 1990s will cost more than $60 billion to build, and more than $100 billion will be needed to operate them over their lifetimes.

Critics, however, warn that this enormous cost could cripple vital parts of American scientific effort by reducing support for smaller projects. Smaller projects have contributed much more to scientific advances than have large projects, as shown by the greater number of Nobel prizes awarded to scientists working on smaller projects. The great contribution from small science can be found in the field of superconducting materials that promises to revolutionize electric devices. In 1987 Dr. Paul Chu, a University of Houston physicist, made a key breakthrough in superconductivity, and in that year his laboratory ran on

only $130,000, a pittance compared with the billions spent on big science projects. But more scientific discoveries can be expected to come out of the big science projects of the 1990s. The reason is that small science projects cannot produce information on big questions, such as the origin of our universe and its stars, galaxies, black holes, and quasars (Goldberger and Panofsky, 1990).

Whether their projects are big or small, American scientists have managed to keep their nation in the forefront of scientific research, which is evidenced by the fact that most of the Nobel prizes have been awarded to them every year (see Figure 13.2). The United States is not likely to lose its scientific preeminence to Japan, as is popularly believed. We will continue to make more scientific discoveries because our culture puts a high premium on creativity and innovativeness. The Japanese, though, seem to do a better job in turning our scientific discoveries into profitable products. This has to do with their

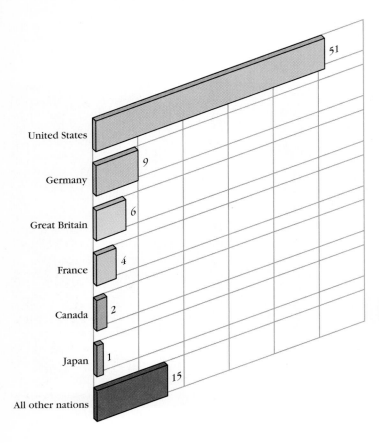

FIGURE 13.2 *U.S. Leads World in Science*
The United States continues to be in the forefront of scientific research. The latest data show that between 1981 and 1992, American scientists won far more Nobel prizes than their peers in any other country.

Source: The Universal Almanac, *1993, p. 616-626.*

emphasis on commercial research, carried out mostly within companies rather than universities (Broad, 1992).

SCIENTIFIC IDEALS

Unlike their seventeenth-century predecessors, modern scientists do not need to justify their work to themselves or others by saying that it glorifies God. From the outset of their training, scientists are socialized to consider science worthy of their dedication for its own sake and to keep it "pure": "Science must not suffer itself to become the handmaiden of theology or economy or state" (Merton, 1973). The self-confident insistence on autonomy attests to the power and influence of science today. Robert Merton argues that the autonomy and purity of science are maintained through four norms, which are "binding on the man of science" and "in varying degrees internalized by the scientist."

The first norm is **universalism,** which holds that scientific ideas should be evaluated by imperson-

al criteria. When they evaluate ideas or findings, scientists should not consider the author's personality, race, age, sex, or other personal characteristics. Instead, they should evaluate ideas by considering only their consistency with logic and observations. Scientists, as Alfred Maurice Taylor (1967) says, "must hold scientific theories in judicial detachment. Scientists must be passionless observers, unbiased by emotion, intellectually cold"—toward their own work as well as that of others.

A second norm, **organized skepticism,** sets science apart from other institutions. Whereas the church and the state often ask people to bow to their authority, and may see skepticism as a sign of disloyalty, science elevates skepticism to the status of a virtue. According to this norm, scientists should take nothing in science at face value and should carefully scrutinize all findings, even those by the most respected scientists, for faulty logic or factual error. They must be prepared "to drop a theory the moment an observation turns up to conflict with it" (Taylor, 1967).

A third norm, **communality,** requires scientists to share their knowledge and regard discoveries as public property, not as private property which they might keep secret or sell to the highest bidder. As a result, their discoveries can provide springboards for further knowledge, just as past discoveries made today's advances possible. The only "property right" scientists may claim is professional recognition and esteem.

A final norm, **disinterestedness,** governs motives for engaging in scientific work. Scientists should not expect to gain great wealth, fame, or power. Seeking these rewards may be appropriate for businesspeople, politicians, lawyers, and others—but not for scientists. They must seek the truth and only the truth, and they should consider the thrill of making a discovery sufficient reward for their work. So long as scientists follow this norm, it is unlikely that they will be tempted to falsify data.

SCIENTIFIC REALITIES

Contemplating his colleagues' denial of any interest in fame, one modern scientist wondered, "Why do even the greatest minds stoop to such falsehood? For, without being conscious lies, these denials are undoubtedly false" (Merton, 1973). The denials suggest that the norm of disinterestedness does influence scientists, but they are ambivalent toward it. Scientists do not totally reject this and the other norms Merton identified, but they do not enthusiastically support them either. In fact, they find these norms irrelevant to their everyday scientific activities and tend to break all of them.

Consider the norm of universality. Ian Mitroff (1974) found clear violations of this norm by the scientists who analyzed lunar rocks brought back by Apollo astronauts. Instead of being impersonal, objective, or emotionally neutral, the Apollo scientists, especially the best ones, "were emotionally involved with their ideas, were reluctant to part with them, and did everything in their power to confirm them." Every one of the scientists considered it naive and nonsensical to say that scientists are objective. Science is an intensely personal enterprise.

Scientists violate Merton's norms not only by preferring their own ideas but also by bowing to authority. Most scientists, we have said, work within the paradigm of their discipline. Furthermore, they frequently praise the work of the famous while ignoring the findings of unknown scientists. The tendency is called the **Matthew effect,** after Matthew 25:29—

"For to everyone who has, more shall be given, and he shall have plenty. But from him who has not, even that which he has shall be taken away from him." When two scientists independently make the same discovery, for example, the more famous one is likely to get most if not all the credit. If several scientists collaborate on a subject, the most prestigious one usually receives more of the glory, even if others have done the bulk of the work (Merton, 1973). Like most of us, scientists are more likely to accept ideas if they are proposed by people who are well known and well respected. For more than 30 years, psychologists accepted the renowned Cyril Burt's data on the heritability of IQ, until the data were revealed as fraudulent in 1972 (Weinstein, 1979). All this clearly violates the norms of skepticism and universalism, which require scientists to evaluate ideas and research without considering the personal characteristics of the author.

Personal characteristics and emotions may also play a part in the resistance with which scientists commonly greet revolutionary ideas and discoveries. Of course, they may resist a new idea because of justified skepticism, especially when that idea contradicts a paradigm that has long seemed accurate. But the emotional reaction that frequently greets new scientific ideas suggests that less objective factors are at work. Darwin's theory of evolution, for example, aroused considerable hostility. In a debate on the theory between Bishop Wilberforce, who had been carefully coached by a leading biologist, and T. H. Huxley, who supported Darwin's theory, the bishop attacked both Huxley and the theory contemptuously. The bishop asked Huxley, "Are you related to an ape on your father's or your mother's side?" Huxley replied that if he had to choose for a grandfather either an ape or a man who resorted to ridicule rather than reason in a scientific discussion, then "I unhesitatingly affirm my preference for the ape."

Such emotional behavior suggests that scientists are just as human as the rest of us. They may reject scientific ideas, not because of objective and scientific considerations, but because of their nonscientific beliefs. The fact that Darwin's evolutionary theory contradicted a literal reading of the Bible fueled opposition to his ideas. Professional specialization and jealousies may be another cause of resistance. Physicians used to reject Pasteur's germ theory because they regarded him as "a mere chemist poaching on their scientific preserves, not worthy of their attention" (Barber, 1961).

Violations of the norms Merton described do not bring science to a halt. In fact, they sometimes

promote scientific progress. Being emotionally involved with one's work, for example, may pay off. In
Mitroff's lunar rocks study, the three scientists perceived by their colleagues to be the most emotionally
committed to their own hypotheses were also judged
the most outstanding and creative of those in the program. "Without emotional commitment," one of the
scientists said, "one couldn't have the energy, the
drive to press forward, sometimes against extremely
difficult odds."

If we compare Merton's other norms with scientists' actual behavior, we find similar violations
and, sometimes, beneficial results. Perhaps most
striking are violations of the norm of disinterestedness. Far from being motivated only by an idealistic
quest for knowledge, most scientists take part in a
very competitive game.

QUESTIONS FOR DISCUSSION AND REVIEW

1. How does technology differ from science?
2. Who were the first scientists, and what happened
   when the activities of scientists became institutionalized?
3. How do scientific anomalies sometimes lead to scientific revolutions?
4. What are the characteristics of "big science"?
5. What four key norms make up the ideals of science, and why do scientists often fail to follow
   them?

The Social Realities of Health

As a social phenomenon, health varies from one society to another and from one group to another within
the same society. From these variations, we can see
how social factors affect health and what consequences an outbreak of illness has for society. We
can also track down the origin of a disease by examining all its victims for something that they have in
common as a social group.

AMERICAN HEALTH

As the Population Reference Bureau has shown,
Americans are much healthier than ever before. Since
1900 our life expectancy has increased by more than
50 percent, from about 49 years in 1900 to 75 today.
At birth we can expect to live 26 more years than did
our counterparts in 1900—more than one-and-a-half
times as long as they did then. Another indicator of

our health, the infant mortality rate, has shown even
more dramatic improvement. While about 15 percent
of all American babies died during the first year of
life at the turn of this century, only 1 percent die
today. All this can be chalked up to healthier living
conditions, better diet, immunization, and penicillin
and other antibiotics.

These breakthroughs have further vanquished
most of the major killer diseases around 1900—particularly pneumonia, influenza, and tuberculosis—
along with such infectious childhood diseases as
smallpox and measles. Most of these diseases are
acute. **Acute diseases,** usually caused by invading
viruses or bacteria, last for a short time, during
which the victims either recover or die. Such diseases
have been replaced by the major killers of today—
heart disease, cancer, and stroke. These **chronic diseases** last for a long time before the victims die.
They usually cannot be cured, but the pain and suffering that they bring can be reduced. To a certain
extent, the emergence of the chronic diseases as
today's big killers is, ironically, due to our increased
longevity and rising living standard. Because of our
high living standard, we tend to eat, smoke, and
drink too much. When these self-indulgent behaviors
are carried on for a long time, made possible by the
rising life expectancy, chronic illnesses such as heart
disease and cancer are likely to occur. It is no wonder
that older Americans—above age 55—are far more
likely than younger Americans to have high blood
cholesterol levels and to suffer from those chronic
diseases (Thompson, 1987).

Even our increased life expectancy by itself
loses its impressiveness in comparison with that of
other industrialized countries. Among 12 such nations, the United States ranks close to the bottom
rather than near the top. People in at least 9 industrialized countries live longer than do Americans. Our
standing in regard to infant mortality is the same.
Proportionately more babies die in the United States
than in 9 out of 11 industrialized nations, which puts
our health condition near the bottom of the ranking
system (see Table 13.1). This is ironic, because we
spend more money on health care than any of these
nations. As Joseph Califano pointed out, "Although
the U.S. spent $1,600 for the health care of each per-
son in 1984 and Singapore [a newly industrialized
country] spent only $200, residents of both nations
have the same life expectancy" (*Medical World News,*
1987). However, compared with the developing
countries in the third world, the United States has a
much higher life expectancy and a considerably
lower infant mortality rate.

BANX

"He's been falsifying research data for years."

SOCIAL FACTORS

Americans are not all equally likely to get sick. Instead, the incidence of sickness varies from one group to another. Old people are less likely than young people to suffer from acute and infectious illnesses such as measles and pneumonia. But they are more susceptible to chronic illnesses such as arthritis, heart disease, and cancer. Cancer deaths, in particular, have been climbing steeply and steadily among people aged 55 and older. Some illnesses have been attributed to exposure to workplace hazards

some 30 or 40 years ago, certain preservatives once used in food (including traces of mercury and arsenic), and a high-fat diet (Angier, 1990a; Census Bureau, 1993).

Health also varies with gender. Women have higher rates of both chronic and acute illnesses than men of the same age, yet women live longer than men. Why? One reason is biological superiority. Women are more able to endure sickness and survive. They also are less likely to develop hemophilia and other diseases linked to the X chromosome. Their sex hormones further protect them from cardiovascular

TABLE 13.1 *Life Expectancies and Infant Mortality Rates*

Our health record is far from impressive. Among industrialized nations in 1986, the United States ranked near the bottom in life expectancy and infant mortality.

COUNTRY	LIFE EXPECTANCY	COUNTRY	INFANT MORTALITY RATE
Japan	79.2	Japan	4.4
Italy	78.1	Sweden	5.9
Sweden	77.8	Italy	6.0
Netherlands	77.8	France	6.1
France	77.8	Netherlands	6.9
Canada	77.5	Germany	7.1
Australia	77.0	Canada	7.2
Great Britain	76.5	Great Britain	7.2
Germany	75.8	Australia	7.9
United States	75.7	United States	10.3
Russia	69.8	Russia	22.7

Source: Statistical Abstract of the United States, 1992, pp. 824–825.

morbidity up to the time of menopause. A second reason is that women maintain stronger emotional ties with others than men do. By offering social support and deterring loneliness, intimate human relationships can reduce the severity and duration of illness. A third reason is the greater tendency of men to smoke, drink, and drive. Such behaviors increase the risk of serious chronic diseases and physical injuries (Verbrugge, 1985). It is also possible that women are more attuned to their bodies and thus more likely to sense problems and seek medical help before an illness becomes serious.

Race and ethnicity are also correlated with health. Blacks, Hispanics, and Native Americans all have shorter life expectancies than do Anglo-Americans. Blacks are far more likely than whites to suffer from cirrhosis, influenza, pneumonia, heart disease, kidney disease, AIDS (acquired immunodeficiency syndrome), and hypertension (high blood pressure). Blacks are more than twice as likely as whites in the same age bracket to die from most of those diseases. Hispanics, too, are much more likely than Anglo-Americans to die from influenza, pneumonia, tuberculosis, and AIDS. Hispanics are also more likely to develop diabetes, kidney diseases, and stom-

ach cancer. Native Americans suffer the most from acute diseases. They are 10 times more likely than other Americans to get tuberculosis, 30 times more likely to get strep throat, and 66 times more likely to get dysentery. Both Hispanics and Native Americans, however, are less likely than Anglos to die from heart disease and cancer (Cockerham, 1989; Johnson et al, 1991).

These racial and ethnic differences may largely reflect another social factor that influences health: social class. The diseases that hit minority groups the hardest are those associated with poverty. In particular, acute and infectious diseases, such as tuberculosis and influenza, are more prevalent among the lower social classes. Researchers have attributed the higher rates of disease among the lower classes to several related factors: toxic, hazardous, and unhygienic environments; stress resulting from life changes, such as job loss and divorce; and inadequate medical care (Syme and Berkman, 1987). More recent research has found another problem: unhealthy eating habits. Poor people are much more likely than others to eat high-sugar, high-salt, and high-fat food. This may result from a lack of knowledge about nutrition, but the fear of looking thin may also be a factor.

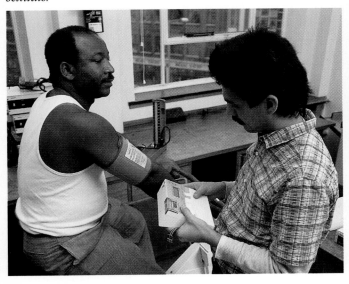

Social factors figure strongly in health. Left: *Poverty can aggravate the problem of hypertension suffered by minorities.* Right: *While the rate of AIDS infection among homosexual men has fallen sharply, that among intravenous drug users has shot up, largely among poor black and Hispanic heterosexuals.*

Thinness may carry the stigmas of hunger, being on welfare, AIDS, and drug addiction, which are more prevalent in lower-class neighborhoods (Freedman, 1990). Poverty can also aggravate the problem of hypertension suffered by minorities. Because they may be less able to deal with the sociopsychological stress induced by racism in the United States, poor African-Americans are significantly more likely to have high blood pressure (Klag et al., 1991).

There are many other instances in which social factors strongly influence health condition. Of course, we should not deny the crucial role of natural, biological factors in the development of disease. The point to be emphasized here is that social factors can aggravate, soften, or even neutralize the biological impact on health. One medical researcher identified four Mormon families who carry a gene for a dangerously high cholesterol level. Since 1900 the men in these families have died from heart disease, on average, by age 45. But the researcher discovered that, before 1880, the men had lived up to age 62 or even 81. They had lived longer because their life-style had included a more healthful diet and more physically active occupations (Carey and Silberner, 1987). This illustrates how social factors can sidetrack a gene from producing a disease. Social factors can also make the body susceptible to disease. However, tracking them down requires a kind of detective work called **epidemiology,** the study of the origin and spread of disease in a given population.

AIDS: AN EPIDEMIOLOGICAL ANALYSIS

AIDS is a deadly disease that destroys the body's immune system, leaving the victim defenseless against such conditions as pneumonia, meningitis, and a cancer called Kaposi's sarcoma. Common symptoms include a persistent cough, prolonged fever, chronic diarrhea, difficulty in breathing, and multiple purplish blotches and bumps on the skin. In Africa, AIDS is also known, as a "slim disease," for its victims' emaciated appearance, the result of a painful wasting away of body tissues and uncontrolled weight loss. The disease first came to the attention of American physicians in early 1981. Since then, it has spread rapidly.

The AIDS virus, referred to by medical investigators as the human immunodeficiency virus (HIV), has been shown to be the direct cause of the disease, and this discovery has made it possible to determine infection before the disease symptoms appear. The virus is so elusive, though, that there are as yet no

tests that can detect the virus directly in the infected person. The currently available tests are designed to identify antibodies specific to the virus; their presence can be safely taken to suggest that the individual has been infected with the virus. This is because when a foreign germ invades the blood, the body's immune system produces antibodies specific to that type of germ. The immune system of a child with measles, for example, produces antibodies that specifically fight measles.

In searching for the cause of AIDS, epidemiologists have found clues in the social characteristics and behaviors of the victims. So far most of the victims have been homosexual or bisexual men. The second largest group has been intravenous drug users. The rest are non-drug-using heterosexuals, people who have received blood transfusions, and children born to mothers with AIDS.

In recent years, however, the number of *new* victims among homosexual men has fallen sharply. This is largely because gay men have drastically changed their sexual behavior—by practicing monogamy and using condoms. In contrast, new infection among intravenous drug users has skyrocketed, so the majority of new AIDS cases now appear among drug users. Most of these are poor, African-American, and Hispanic heterosexuals in the inner city. They often share contaminated needles when shooting drugs and pass the virus on to one another. New infection has risen even more significantly among non-drug-using heterosexual men and women, mainly because of their failure to practice safer sex. New infection has also soared among babies whose mothers have acquired the virus from shooting drugs or having sex with infected male addicts. The total numbers of these heterosexuals and babies, though, still remain much smaller than for gay men and drug users, who have been infected with the AIDS virus longer (see Figure 13.3).

All these epidemiological facts clearly suggest that AIDS spreads mostly through sexual intercourse with an infected person and through the sharing of a hypodermic needle that has been contaminated with the virus. By examining the blood, semen, or vaginal secretions of AIDS victims, medical scientists have been able to discover HIV, the virus that causes AIDS. Studies in other societies can also be useful. For example, epidemiologists have discovered some similarities and differences between African AIDS victims and their American counterparts. Unlike the American victims, the African patients do not have histories of intravenous drug use, homosexuality, or blood

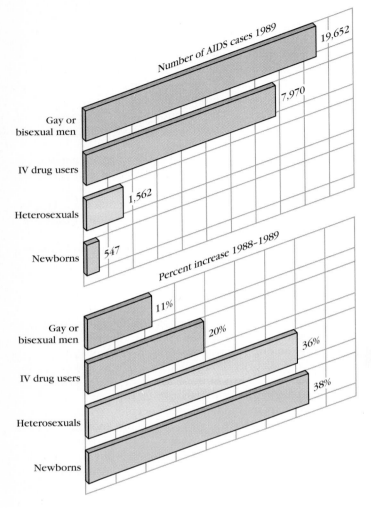

Number of AIDS cases 1989

Gay or bisexual men — 19,652

IV drug users — 7,970

Heterosexuals — 1,562

Newborns — 547

Percent increase 1988–1989

Gay or bisexual men — 11%

IV drug users — 20%

Heterosexuals — 36%

Newborns — 38%

FIGURE 13.3 *The Changing Profile of AIDS*
Most AIDS patients are still gay men and IV drug users. But the greater rate of increase among heterosexuals and newborns proves that the virus knows no boundaries.

Source: Newsweek, June 25, 1990. Chart by Whitney Vosburgh. Copyright © 1990. Newsweek, Inc. Data from Center for Disease Control. All rights reserved. Reprinted by permission.

transfusion. But like American homosexuals with AIDS, African heterosexuals with the disease are mostly upper-middle-class, live in large cities, and have had sex with many different partners. Thus, AIDS has spread among Africans in the same way as it has among homosexuals in the United States: through sex with multiple partners. By itself, though, promiscuity is not the source of the virus. It is largely due to the law of probability that the more sexual partners one has, the more likely one is to pick up the infection. In other words, becoming infected through promiscuity "is not due to the cumulative effect of sex with 'too many partners.' It is due to the increased possibility of having sex with the 'wrong partner'" (Slaff and Brubaker, 1985). The risk of in-

fection from a single act of sexual intercourse with an infected partner is 1 in 500, which is a million times as high as the risk from one sexual encounter with a partner who has been tested negative (Hearst and Hulley, 1988).

The epidemiology of AIDS, however, suggests that behavioral changes can slow the spread of the disease. As has been noted, the rate of new infection has plummeted among homosexual men because they have largely practiced monogamy and safer sex. But the soaring rate of new infection among intravenous drug addicts suggests that this high-risk group continues to use contaminated needles. If clean needles are used, infection can be reduced, not only for drug addicts themselves but for their sex partners and unborn babies as well. Similarly, non-drug-using heterosexuals can avoid infection by practicing safe sex.

THE CHANGING MEDICAL PROFESSION

Over the last 10 years, there have been significant changes in the medical profession. Today, doctors often find their autonomy eroded, their prestige reduced, and their competence challenged by everyone from insurance companies to patients.

Before 1980 most doctors practiced alone. But today more than half are salaried employees, working in group practices or health maintenance organizations (HMOs). This is partly because the cost of starting a private practice is very high—too high for most young doctors whose medical training has landed them deeply in debt. In the past, doctors could set fees that patients paid out of their own pockets. Now 79 percent of the payments come from the federal government and private health insurance companies, which limit what doctors can charge. To get paid, doctors must fill out forms to justify their fees. This paperwork often proves too burdensome for a private doctor to handle, or it may be too expensive to hire someone else to do it. So most doctors choose to work for a health organization (where the paperwork is done for them). The salaries are still very comfortable, ranging from $80,000 to $180,000 a year, with the average being $144,700. Nevertheless, employers, the government, and insurance companies continue to find ways to control costs. Medicine is no longer a gold mine for doctors (Altman, 1990).

Efforts to control costs have caused many doctors to complain that they are losing their professional autonomy. They must seek permission from outside regulators—government agencies or insurance companies—for major but nonemergency hospitalization and surgeries. If the regulators do not approve the case in advance, they will not pay. They occasionally refuse to authorize a treatment that they consider too costly or unnecessary (Kramon, 1991). While chafing at these outside regulators, doctors also complain of internal controls from their employers. HMOs routinely pass around lists ranking their physicians on the time spent with patients and the amount of medications prescribed. This is intended to give the doctors the subtle but clear message that those highest on the list cause a financial drain on the organization. But many doctors object to being urged to

spend as little time on their patients as possible, even though that is the way the organization can maximize its profit. As one doctor said, "I would be confronted by my bosses on how long it would take me to do a physical. Why wasn't I more like Doctor X, who does it faster? The system doesn't reward people for being competent or good or up to date. It rewards them for being superficial" (Belkin, 1990).

The general public also seems to hold less esteem for doctors than before. According to a Gallup poll, 57 percent of the people questioned agreed that "doctors don't care about people as much as they used to." Sixty-seven percent said that doctors are too interested in making money. Seventy-five percent complained that "doctors keep patients waiting too long." And 26 percent said that they have less respect for doctors than they did 10 years ago (Kolata, 1990). Many patients do not fully trust their doctors, and the better educated often feel obliged to make themselves as informed as possible about their illness so that they can get the best treatment. This has led many doctors to complain that some patients challenge their expertise after only learning about medical advances on television or in newspapers and magazines. According to the Gallup poll just mentioned, half of the doctors questioned said that patients are demanding more services, tests, and procedures than necessary. As a result of this deteriorating doctor-patient relationship, along with the other changes in the medical profession, a large number of doctors have become dissatisfied with their careers. According to another Gallup poll, nearly 40 percent of the doctors interviewed said they would definitely or probably not have entered medical school if they had known what they know now about medicine as a career. The social scientists who have studied the medical profession find that doctors have brought the changes in the profession on themselves. As an expert in health-care economics said, "Physicians have lived like kids in a candy store. We, the payers, want the key back" (Altman, 1990).

The growing discontent among doctors has apparently discouraged many college students from pursuing a medical career. The number of students applying to medical school dropped from 35,944 in 1985 to only 26,915 in 1990. This drop-off, though, has come only from white males, who have traditionally dominated the medical school and profession. As has been suggested, most white male students who choose to study medicine do so because they have been influenced by family doctors or family members

The recent dropoff in student applying to medical school comes from white males, who have traditionally dominated the medical profession. At about the same time there has been an increase in women and minority members among medical school applicants.

and friends who are doctors. Not surprisingly, given the recent increase in doctor complaints, the number of white male applicants to medical school has fallen about 50 percent since the mid-1970s. But there have been great increases in women and minority members among medical school applicants. In 1988–89, for the first time ever, there were more women and minorities than white men in the first-year class. These demographic changes will make the medical profession more representative of American society and, because of a more moderate income expectation, will probably more effectively meet the needs for health care in the future (Altman, 1990).

THE RIGHT TO DIE

Advanced medical technology can prolong life. But, ironically, the same technology can also prolong the agony of dying for the hopelessly ill—and the suffering of the families who have to live with their loved one's living death. Today, about 10,000 patients lie irreversibly comatose in hospital beds across the United States. They are kept alive by machines such as respirators and feeding tubes. Many have been living in the vegetative, semideath state for years. Most of their loved ones would like to let them die in dignity. But they cannot have the treatment halted unless

they first get authorization from a court. The problem is that the court may deny the patient's right to die.

Usually, a physician is required to obtain **informed consent** from the patient (or the patient's parent or guardian) before carrying out a surgery or some other important treatment. Informed consent is the approval that a patient gives to the doctor for a treatment after receiving adequate information on it. This clearly implies that the patient has the right to *refuse* treatment. Formally, courts have supported the notion of informed refusal. But the courts have been less enthusiastic in support of a patient's choice when there is disagreement between patient and doctor or prosecutor (Capron, 1990).

In 1983 Nancy Cruzan, age 25, was involved in an auto crash that severely damaged her brain. For the next 7 years she remained completely unconscious. Although her eyes sometimes opened, she showed no sign of recognizing her family. Her body was rigid, and her hands and feet were contracted and bent. From a month after the accident until 1990, she had been kept alive with a feeding tube implanted in her stomach. In 1987 Cruzan's parents went to court to ask that the tube be removed, so that she could die a dignified death. They said that before the accident their daughter had told them and her friends she would rather die than remain alive like a vegetable. They argued that they had a legal basis for their request, in both the constitutional right to privacy and the right to refuse unwanted medical treatment. A year later, the judge granted the request. But the Missouri Supreme Court disagreed, and the Cruzans took the case all the way to the U.S. Supreme Court. In 1990 the Supreme Court ruled that a person has a constitutional right to die but only if the wish to die is clearly known. This meant that Missouri could continue to reject the Cruzans' request because it found no "clear and convincing evidence" of their daughter's wish to die. Nancy Cruzan had only indicated in a general way to family and friends that she would never want to live like a vegetable, but this does not, according to Missouri, constitute "clear and convincing evidence" of her wish to die. Nevertheless, two months after the Supreme Court ruling, Missouri changed its mind and withdrew from the *Cruzan* case, which in effect allowed the feeding tube to be removed. Twelve days later, after the tube was removed, Nancy Cruzan died.

From this case it should be obvious that the Supreme Court decision supports as well as undermines the right to die. Today, in principle, any rational adult has the right to refuse any medical treatment, including the one that prolongs a vegetative life. But, in practice, it is unrealistic for comatose patients to have anticipated their living death. Because virtually all the currently comatose patients have failed to leave clear instructions that they prefer being dead to a state of vegetating, many may have a hard time having their lives ended. Normally, when patients are incapable of giving their informed consent regarding a medical treatment, loved ones such as their parents or spouses are allowed to make the decision for them. But this does not necessarily apply in cases of semidead patients. The Supreme Court allows any state to reject requests from families that respirators or feeding tubes be removed from their hopelessly ill relative. Most Americans, however, disagree with the Supreme Court: 80 percent of those surveyed in a nationwide poll recently said that decisions about ending the lives of terminally ill patients who cannot decide for themselves should be made by their families and doctors rather than lawmakers (Gibbs, 1990). Some states, though, do authorize parents to have their children's vegetative lives ended, without any written or clear instructions from the patients themselves.

Even in those states, however, many people never make it to court for the authorization. One reason is the high legal costs, which most Americans cannot afford. A standard lawyer's fee of $10,000 is hardly exorbitant, given the huge amount of time spent on such a case, but it may seem as prohibitive as $10 million for most Americans. Another reason is the fear of bad publicity, hate mail, and other harassment by right-to-life advocates. These individuals argue in favor of the sacredness of human life and thus condemn as "murderers" those who support terminating a hopelessly ill relative's life. Such a stance has further prodded pro-life forces to rally opposition to the notion of a right to die (Quindlen, 1990; Johnson, 1990b). Nevertheless, the Supreme Court ruling on the *Cruzan* case has stirred a great deal of interest in **living wills**—advance instructions on what people want their doctors to do in the event of a terminal illness. Still, only the rich and well educated are likely to draw up a living will. The poor will more likely have their fates determined by the states. Even among the small, highly educated group of Americans, young people are the least interested in living wills. They are unlikely to anticipate suffering major brain damage, although they are the most likely of all age groups to be involved in automobile accidents (B.

Davis, 1990). In view of these factors, many hopelessly ill patients can expect to be unable to exercise their right to die.

QUESTIONS FOR DISCUSSION AND REVIEW
1. Why have chronic diseases replaced acute diseases as the chief threat to Americans' health?
2. How do social factors like gender, race and ethnicity, and social class influence a person's health?
3. What are the sources of the AIDS virus?
4. What are the recent changes in the medical profession?
5. Is it easy for hopelessly ill patients to die? Why or why not?

Perspectives on Health

From the functionalist perspective, we can see the positive aspects of medical care and even the positive functions of sickness for society. By contrast, the conflict perspective directs our attention to the negative side of health and medical care. While these two perspectives deal with the larger issues of health, a third perspective—symbolic interactionism—focuses on the direct interaction between doctor and patient.

FUNCTIONALISM

According to functionalists, both physicians and patients play roles that contribute to social order. Patients must play the **sick role,** a pattern of expectation regarding how an ill person should behave. As discussed in Chapter 3 (Social Structure), role is associated with status, which in turn presents the person with a set of rights and obligations. In his classic definition of the sick role, Talcott Parsons (1975) essentially laid out what rights a sick person can claim and what obligations he or she should discharge. First, the sick should not be blamed for their illness because they do not choose to be sick. They are not responsible for their illness. Therefore, they have the right to be taken care of by others. Second, the sick have the right to be exempted from certain social duties. They should not be forced to go to work. In the case of students, they should be allowed to miss an exam and take it later. Third, the sick are obligated to want to get well. They should not expect to remain ill and use the illness to take advantage of others' love, concern, and care for them and to shirk their work and other social responsibilities. And fourth, the sick are obligated to seek technically competent help. In seeing a doctor, they must cooperate to help ensure their recovery.

On the other hand, doctors have their own rights and obligations in playing the **healing role,** which is necessary to the orderly functioning of society. Basically, doctors are obligated to help the sick get well, as required by the Hippocratic oath, which they take when embarking on their medical careers. At the same time, however, they have the right to receive appropriate compensation for their work. Because their work is widely regarded as highly important, they may expect to make a great deal of money and enjoy considerable prestige.

Seen from the functionalist perspective, both the sick and healing roles serve a social control function. They help to prevent illnesses from disrupting economic production, family relations, and social activities. Many sociologists, though, have criticized Parsons's theory of the sick role for a number of reasons. First, the theory may be relevant to Western societies but not necessarily to non-Western societies, where the sick are more likely to turn to folk medicine rather than seeking technically competent treatment. Second, even within a Western society, the sick role does not affect all social groups in the same way. Racial and ethnic minorities are less likely than whites to seek treatment from physicians. Third, the sick role may apply to serious illnesses but not to mild ailments, because the latter do not lead to exemption from normal activities (Twaddle and Hessler, 1987). Nevertheless, the critics do not question the basic point of Parsons's functionalist theory—namely, that the sick role serves a social control function for society, as previously indicated.

Moreover, the functionalist perspective suggests that the system of medical care helps maintain the health of society. Thus, functionalists tend to attribute an improvement in the nation's health to medicine, the physician, the medical profession, or some new technology of treatment. Such medical discoveries as the germ theory and such medical interventions as vaccines and drugs are credited for our great victory over infectious diseases. All this, however, is a myth to conflict theorists.

THE CONFLICT PERSPECTIVE

According to conflict theorists, improvements in the social environment contribute far more than do med-

ical interventions to the reduction of illness and mortality. As one study shows, only about 3.5 percent of the total decline in mortality from five infectious diseases (influenza, pneumonia, diphtheria, whooping cough, and poliomyelitis) since 1900 can be attributed to medical measures. In many instances, the new chemotherapeutic and prophylactic measures to combat those diseases were introduced several decades *after* a substantial decline in mortality from the diseases had set in (McKinlay and McKinlay, 1987). According to the conflict perspective, this decline in mortality has been brought about mostly by several social and environmental factors: (1) a rising standard of living, (2) better sanitation and hygiene, and (3) improved housing and nutrition (Conrad and Kern, 1986). Moreover, since 1950, the year when the nearly unrestrained, precipitous rise in medical expenditure began, the health of Americans has *not* improved significantly. Most of the marked increase in longevity or decline in mortality in this century occurred before 1950. Since that year, the death rates of middle-aged men have actually risen (Hollingsworth, 1986).

Conflict theorists, however, do not mean to suggest that modern clinical medicine does not alleviate pain or cure disease in some individuals. Their point

According to the conflict perspective, the profit motive has driven corporations to oversell many expensive technological advances, even though they have benefited only a limited number of patients and have not significantly improved the nation's health.

is that the medical institution fails to bring about significant improvements in the health of the population as a whole. Why, then, does our society continue to spend such vast sums of money on medical care? This, according to conflict theorists, has much to do with the pursuit of private profit in our capitalist society.

In his Marxist analysis of coronary-care technology, for example, Howard Waitzkin (1987) finds that, since its introduction in the 1960s, the expensive coronary-care units have become so popular that today they can be found in half of all the acute-care hospitals in the United States. But the intensive care provided by that medical technology has not been proven more effective than simple rest at home. Waitzkin argues that the proliferation of this expensive but relatively ineffective form of treatment can be traced to the profit motive. He finds that corporations such as Warner-Lambert Pharmaceutical Company and the Hewlett-Packard Company have participated in every phase of the research, development, promotion, and dissemination of today's coronary-care technology, which produces huge profits for them. Waitzkin also points out that the same profit motive has driven corporations to oversell many other expensive technological advances, such as computerized axial tomography and fetal monitoring, even though these devices have not significantly improved the nation's health; they have benefited only a limited number of patients.

It is also the profit motive that has led many doctors—and more recently big corporations—to turn medical care into a lucrative business more than a social service. This is why doctors tend to avoid treating the poor or those without any medical insurance. Physicians also tend to increase their already high incomes by performing more surgeries than necessary, as indicated by the fact that about half of all the expensive cardiac pacemaker and coronary by-pass operations have been estimated to be unnecessary.

The conflict perspective further suggests that the unequal distribution of health and medical care reflects the larger social inequality. We have discussed in some detail how health and medical care are unequally distributed. First, wealthy, industrialized countries have considerably lower infant mortality rates and higher life expectancies than do poor, developing countries. Second, in the United States, the lower classes suffer from higher rates of most diseases than do the middle and upper classes. Third, the poor are more likely to receive inadequate medical care or to die from being refused treatment by hospitals for an inability to pay the bills.

SYMBOLIC INTERACTIONISM

An important aspect of medical practice is the relationship between doctor and patient. Research has suggested that patients tend to evaluate warm, friendly doctors favorably even when these doctors have not provided successful treatment. By contrast, patients are most likely to sue for malpractice those physicians who are the most highly trained and who practice in the most sophisticated hospitals. Although these physicians are not intentionally negligent, they are most likely to be viewed by their patients—not just the ones that sue them—as cold and bureaucratic (Twaddle and Hessler, 1987). It is the friendly doctor's "affiliative style" of communication that enhances patient satisfaction, and it is the highly competent but bureaucratic doctor's "dominant style" that alienates patients. "Affiliative style" involves behaviors that communicate honesty, compassion, humor, and a nonjudgmental attitude. "Dominant style" involves the manifestation of power, authority, professional detachment, and status in the physician's interaction with the patient (Buller and Buller, 1987).

Why does the doctor's communication style affect patient satisfaction? Why are patients likely to be satisfied with the friendly doctor's treatment even if it has failed to cure the disease? Why do patients tend to sue highly competent but dominant doctors? From the perspective of symbolic interactionism (see Chapter 1: The Essence of Sociology), we can assume that, in interacting with patients, friendly doctors are more likely than dominant doctors to take into account the views, feelings, and expectations held by the patients about themselves, their illnesses, and their doctors. To the patients, the illness is unusual, as it does not happen to them every day. Moreover, their suffering is a highly intimate, emotional reality. Thus, they expect their doctors to show a great deal of concern. They obviously want a cure, but they also crave emotional support. If doctors attune themselves to these expectations, they can develop warm relationships with their patients. But this is no easy task because physicians have been trained to take an objective, dispassionate approach to disease. They have learned to view patients unemotionally, especially in cases where they must perform surgeries that cause considerable pain. After all, they have learned "to perform acts unpleasant to them personally—sticking your hands inside diseased strangers is not many people's idea of a good time—without flinching or losing their nerves" (Easterbrook, 1987).

Such emotional detachment often intrudes into the medical interview. According to the National Task Force on Medical Interviews, "In the typical doctor-patient encounter, all too often the doctor dominates with questions based on his technical understanding of the cause and treatment of the illness, while the patient, often in vain, tries to get the doctor to pay attention to his very personal sense of the illness" (Goleman, 1988). In one study, average patients were found to have three different problems on their minds when they went to see their doctors, but their efforts to tell their stories were cut off by the doctors within the first 18 seconds of the interview. In fact, most patients never got beyond the first question. Moreover, when the patients were allowed to talk, the physician often responded only with an "um hum." Such a response is noncommittal and indicates only minimal interest (Goleman, 1988). Detached professionalism may be effective for diagnosing and treating disease, but it tends to exact a price by alienating patients. They often feel that they are being treated as mere diseases rather than as people. Thus, such patients are likely to be dissatisfied with the medical care they receive. In fact, poor interaction between doctors and patients is a major cause of malpractice suits. There are also other consequences: about 60 percent of patients leave their doctors' offices confused about medication instructions, and more than half of new prescriptions are taken improperly or not at all (Winslow, 1989; Nazario, 1992).

QUESTIONS FOR DISCUSSION AND REVIEW
1. How do the roles played by patients and physicians contribute to the social order?
2. What facts about American health care do followers of conflict theory emphasize?
3. What is the nature of the doctor-patient relationship today?

CHAPTER REVIEW

1. *What are the functions of education?* The main functions today are teaching knowledge and skills, promoting social mobility, fostering national unity, and providing custodial care for children. *Do our public schools succeed in transmitting knowledge and skills?* Earlier studies showed that schools make little difference in how much the students learn, but recent analyses indicate otherwise. *Does our educational system promote social mobility?* In the 1970s, critics argued that education by itself has little to do with occupational achievement. In the 1980s, there was evidence to suggest that education not only raises the individual's income but stimulates the nation's economic growth. *How do our schools promote national unity?* By teaching the American idea of democracy and what it means to be an American. Conflict theorists, however, argue that the process of Americanization threatens minorities' cultural heritage. *What benefits does society gain from having the schools provide custodial care?* The schools keep children off the streets, presumably out of trouble. They also keep young people out of the labor market, which holds down the nation's jobless rates.

2. *What is the conflict perspective on education?* The American educational system, as a reflection of the capitalist system, reinforces inequality by channeling students of different socioeconomic backgrounds into different classes, colleges, and universities. But the assumption that this can happen only in capitalist societies is not convincing, because educational inequality can be found in communist countries as well. *Does the decline in educational standards and achievement mean that there is a crisis in American education?* Not necessarily. The drop in SAT scores may have reflected the opening up of educational opportunities for the poor and minorities. Lower achievement scores in the United States compared to other industrialized countries may have also reflected the impact of democratization. The United States is not the only country having some problems with its schools. All in all, American education is in good shape, though some people do not think so.

3. *When did modern science begin to develop?* In seventeenth-century Europe. Its development was nurtured by the emergence of a mechanistic philosophy of nature, cooperation among the new scientists,

and the achievement of social legitimacy by scientists. Science became established as a social institution, however, only as scientists began to achieve success in applying their knowledge to improve technology. *How are science and technology related today?* They are virtually inseparable, and technology has come to mean the application of scientific knowledge to practical purposes. Science is routinely applied to technological problems today, and most current technological advances could not occur without science. But to carry on their work, most scientists today require complicated technology, and the flow of knowledge goes from technology to science as well as from science to technology.

4. *How is scientific knowledge advanced?* Cultural accumulation is fundamental. Most scientists work within the reigning paradigm of their discipline. The paradigm is a cultural product, a heritage scientists share as a result of the work of earlier scientists. Normal research produces an accumulation of scientific ideas and findings. Some of these will be anomalies, from which a new paradigm is eventually fashioned, and thus a scientific revolution occurs. *When did the era of "big science" begin?* After World War II. Billions of dollars were poured into scientific research, and the number and prestige of scientists soared. Increasingly, scientists worked as narrow specialists with huge bureaucracies. Collaboration and multiple, independent discoveries have become common. Big science has become even bigger in the present decade.

5. *What norms help preserve the integrity of science?* Robert Merton identified four: universalism, organized skepticism, communality, and disinterestedness. *Do scientists follow the norms Merton identified?* They frequently violate them. Scientists are often emotional about their work, more enthusiastic about their own discoveries than those of others, strongly motivated to seek recognition, and ready to accept or reject new ideas for nonscientific reasons.

6. *How healthy are Americans?* Americans are much healthier than before. Our life expectancy has increased substantially. But while acute diseases were more common in the past, chronic illnesses are more prevalent today. Compared with most other industrialized countries, the United States has a higher infant mortality rate. *What social factors influence our health?* One is gender: women are more likely than men to experience chronic and acute illnesses, though they do live longer. Blacks, Hispanics, and Native Americans also have lower life expectancies and higher illness rates than whites. Poor people, too, are more likely than higher-income groups to become ill.

7. *What causes AIDS, and how has the disease spread?* The cause of AIDS is the human immunodeficiency virus (HIV), popularly known as the AIDS virus, which can be found in the blood, semen, or vaginal secretions of those who are infected. In the early 1980s, the disease spread rapidly in homosexual communities. It then arose among intravenous drug addicts, their sex partners, and their unborn children, as well as among heterosexuals who had received blood transfusions. Today, new infection has dropped sharply among homosexuals but has increased dramatically among drug addicts and their sex partners and unborn children. The AIDS virus is transmitted largely through sexual intercourse and needle sharing. *How has the medical profession changed over the last decade?* Doctors find it difficult to charge as much as they did before. Also, their autonomy has eroded, their prestige has declined, and their competence is more open to challenge by laypersons. *Do terminally ill patients have the right to die?* In principle, they do. But in reality, it is difficult to exercise that right, because the courts may prevent it while high legal expenses and pro-life advocates discourage it.

8. *How do functionalists and conflict theorists view health and medical care?* To functionalists, the sick role and the healing role contribute to social order, and the system of medical care significantly maintains health or reduces illness. But to conflict theorists, change in the social environment reduces mortality from diseases much more than medicine does. In this view, medical care and technology serve mostly the interests of doctors and corporations, and there is considerable social inequality in health and medical care. *How can symbolic interactionism shed light on the doctor-patient relationship?* If doctors take into account the patients' own views about themselves, their illnesses, and their doctors, patients are likely to be happy with the medical treatment they receive.

KEY TERMS

Acute disease A disease that lasts for a short time, during which the victim either recovers or dies (p. 322).

Anomaly Kuhn's term for a research finding that cannot be fitted into the existing paradigm and thus cannot be explained by it (p. 318).

Chronic disease A disease that lasts for a long time before the victim dies (p. 322).

Communality The norm that requires scientists to share their knowledge freely with each other (p. 321).

Disinterestedness The norm that requires scientists to pursue truth rather than self-interest (p. 321).

Epidemiology The study of the origin and spread of disease within a population (p. 325).

Healing role A set of social expectations that defines the doctor's rights and obligations (p. 330).

Informed consent The approval that a patient gives to a doctor for a treatment after receiving adequate information on it (p. 328).

Living will Advance instructions on what people want their doctors to do in the event of a terminal illness (p. 329).

Matthew effect The tendency to praise famous scientists and to ignore the contributions of those who are not well known (p. 321).

Normal science Kuhn's term for routine research (p. 318).

Organized skepticism The norm that requires scientists to be critical of any scientific idea or finding (p. 320).

Paradigm A model for defining, studying, and solving problems in accordance with certain basic assumptions (p. 318).

Science A body of knowledge about natural phenomena that is acquired through the systematic use of objective methods (p. 315).

Scientific revolution Kuhn's term for the replacement of an old paradigm by a new one (p. 318).

Sick role A pattern of expectations regarding how a sick person should behave (p. 329).

Technology The application of scientific knowledge for practical purposes (p. 315).

Universalism The norm that requires scientists to evaluate ideas in accordance with impersonal criteria (p. 320).

SUGGESTED READINGS

Barber, Bernard. 1990. *Social Studies of Science.* New Brunswick, N.J.: Transaction. A collection of articles about various social aspects of science written over the last 35 years by a founder of the sociology of science.

Chubb, John E., and Terry M. Moe. 1990. *Politics, Markets, and America's Schools.* Washington, D.C.: Brookings Institution. Shows how excessive bureaucracy has ruined public education, and proposes that schools be run entirely by teachers and that parents be allowed to choose schools for their children.

Cozzens, Susan E., and Thomas F. Gieryn (eds.). 1990. *Theories of Science in Society.* Bloomington: Indiana University Press. A collection of articles discussing, with interesting case studies, various theories about the relationship between science and society.

Polednak, Anthony P. 1989. *Racial and Ethnic Differences in Disease.* New York: Oxford University Press. An extensive review of the data on the influences of race and ethnicity on various diseases, such as cancer, heart disease, infectious diseases, and chronic disorders.

Ratcliff, Kathryn Strother (ed.). 1989. *Healing Technology: Feminist Perspectives.* Ann Arbor: University of Michigan. A collection of articles about how health-care, environmental, and occupational technologies affect women's health.

14

POPULATION, ECOLOGY, AND URBANIZATION

MYTHS AND REALITIES

Myth: Since they have a far larger population than rich countries, poor countries inevitably contribute more to the world's environmental pollution.

Reality: Despite their smaller population, rich countries consume more resources than poor countries and thereby contribute more to environmental pollution. By burning far more fuel than the average Brazilian, the average American contributes five times as much to the greenhouse effect.

Myth: The world's total population has become very large today, because it has taken many thousands of years to grow.

Reality: Most of the world's population growth has occurred only in relatively recent years. Before the modern era began in 1600, the global population had taken more than 500,000 years to reach only about half a million. But since then it has taken less than 400 years to skyrocket to more than 5.06 billion today.

Myth: The poor countries' high birth rates are virtually the only reason for their tremendous population growth.

Reality: The introduction of modern medicine, along with better hygiene and sanitation, also contributes significantly to population growth by sharply reducing death rates.

Myth: Sterilization is a drastic birth-control method. It has often been recommended to the peasants in poor countries. It is not likely to become popular with Americans.

Reality: Of all the birth-control methods used in the United States, the most popular is sterilization.

Myth: The 1986 American law that prohibits hiring of undocumented workers can effectively discourage poor foreigners from coming here illegally, as it was intended to.

Reality: The sanctions against employers for hiring illegals have failed to be an effective deterrent. Besides, they have produced widespread discrimination against Hispanic and Asian Americans.

Myth: Living in the impersonal world of strangers, city dwellers are more lonely than rural and small-town people.

Reality: Those who live in the city are no more lonely than those who live in small towns and rural areas. Urbanites visit friends and relatives as often as do rural people.

Myth: All suburbs are basically alike. If you have seen one, you have seen them all.

Reality: There is a diversity of suburbs. There are predominantly upper-class suburbs, middle-class suburbs, blue-collar suburbs, poverty-ridden suburbs, and various ethnic suburbs, much like the different neighborhoods within a large city.

I t was a hot day in Bardera, a small town in southern Somalia in Africa. A crowd of starving, emaciated people gathered at a United Nations feeding center. They were waiting for a meal of brown gruel. A 5-year-old boy passed out. Two relief workers rushed over, picked him up, and put him down under a shade tree. The child was suffering from severe dehydration. A nurse quickly inserted an intravenous tube, hooking the bottle to a branch. But it was too late. The boy's eyes rolled back beneath quivering eyelids, which an older woman gently shut with her fingers. The boy had come from a village 34 miles away, where both his parents and eight brothers and sisters

African countries such as Somalia have experienced, and continue to face, massive starvation. Although such starvation is triggered by marauding armies or drought, it can be traced to population explosion.

had also died from starvation the past six months. Weak and hungry, he had walked for four days to this town with his last relative, an elder brother. Now his sibling was rocking and weeping quietly by his lifeless body (Purvis, 1992).

The mass starvation in Somalia and other African countries, though triggered by marauding armies or drought, can be traced to population explosion. Even hard-won advances in food production cannot catch up with the continuing enormous growth in population. In fact, population explosion has turned Africa from an exporter of food to the world's leading importer of food. Because of increased population pressure, many of Africa's farms and fields have become barren through overuse. In addition, demands for heating and cooking fuel have run so high that woodlands—firewood is Africa's chief source of energy—have virtually disappeared outside many cities. The resulting deforestation has damaged flood control, sped up erosion, and increased the hardship of simply staying alive. Population explosion has further taken a toll on cities, stretching education, health care, and housing beyond limits.

Significant population increases can also be found in Asia and Latin America, though to a lesser degree, and with less severe consequences for human life, the environment, and cities. Although the affluent, developed countries in the West are not saddled with serious population growth, they do contribute to the world's ecological problems by polluting the environment. This is because rich countries consume much more resources than poor ones. Although inhabitants of the United States make up only about 6 percent of the world's population, we consume more than 30 percent of the world's energy and raw material. By burning far more fossil fuel in our power plants, factories, and family cars, each American contributes to the greenhouse effect five times as much as does the average Brazilian (Easterbrook, 1989). The high level of industrialization in affluent societies also has a big impact on urban development and city life. In this chapter, we examine the conditions of population, ecology, and urbanization.

Population

The scientific study of population is called **demography**. More than any other area of sociology, demography is based on a large body of reasonably accurate data. Most of these data come from censuses and vital statistics. **Vital statistics** consists of information about births, marriages, deaths, and migrations into and out of a country. Since 1933, the U.S. government has required all states to record these data. The other source of population information, the **census,** is a periodic head count of the entire population of a country. It includes a wealth of data, such as age, sex, education, occupation, and residence. Most early censuses were incomplete and unreliable, but the quality of modern census data is considerably better. We may know why by taking a look at the way the latest U.S. census was conducted.

THE LATEST U.S. CENSUS

Census taking has been around for a long time. As early as 3000 B.C., China conducted a census in some parts of the country for tax purposes. In biblical times, after escaping from Egypt, the Israelites listed all men aged 20 and older to assess their military strength. These and other ancient censuses were intended to control particular individuals—to identify who should be taxed, drafted into military service, or forced to work on certain government projects, such as building the Great Wall in China. Early censuses did not seek to count the entire population—only people in particular categories, such as family heads or males of military age.

By contrast, the modern census, which started to evolve in the seventeenth century, is designed to count all people within a country for governmental, scientific, and commercial purposes. A good example is the U.S. census, which has been taken every 10 years since 1790. It is used for determining the number of congressional seats for each state and allocating federal and state funds to local governments. It is also used for scientific analyses of the nation's demographic traits and trends, economic development, and business cycles. As for its commercial use, an orthodontist, for example, would find the census data worthwhile, because they can show where there are a lot of teenagers in high-income households. But how does one take a census of the United States, which is a large, complex society?

Taking the 1990 U.S. census was indeed a massive task. It required the orchestration of some 500,000 workers and the delivery of 106 million forms to people throughout the United States, Puerto Rico, Guam, the American Virgin Islands, Samoa, and other American-held Pacific locales. Using a decentralized approach, the U.S. Bureau of the Census, which is part of the Department of Commerce, set up about 484 computer-equipped district offices, hiring mainly local people from a wide variety of backgrounds. Most of the census takers worked part-time only. But they all had received special training as office managers, data-entry people, payroll clerks, regular enumerators, and Special Place enumerators (who went to such places as bus depots and abandoned buildings to count the homeless). They compiled and checked address lists, marked census questionnaires, followed up on nonrespondents, conducted local reviews (if there were complaints about undercounting people), and reported results.

Problems appeared in all these operations, but in most cases the Census Bureau had anticipated them and had developed solutions from having spent the previous 6 years planning the project. The most common problem was the public's fear that their personal data would fall into the hands of the Internal Revenue Service, Immigration, and other government agencies. Thus, the Census Bureau waged massive national and local public relations campaigns via television, radio, newspapers, fliers, and posters to convey repeatedly the message that strict confidentiality had been ensured by law for 72 years, with census workers being sworn to secrecy. But some 10 percent of the potential respondents remained skeptical. They were typically minorities—the poor and nonwhites—ironically, the very people who stand to benefit the most from government funds if they are counted. The Census Bureau tried to solve this nonresponse problem by door-to-door canvassing, with enumerators making three or more personal visits. As Barbara Bryant, the Census Bureau's director, said, "Eighty or 90 percent of our effort is targeted at the 10 percent we're most likely to miss" (Little, 1991).

The 1990 census made the first-ever attempt to count the homeless. Special Place enumerators fanned out to where the homeless were known or suspected to stay. In addition to established shelters, the places included rail, bus, and air depots; hidden spots under viaducts; abandoned buildings; laundromats; heating grates; and shanties. Many indigents were found only between midnight and 6 A.M. Critics charged that the enumerators could not possibly give an accurate tally and that the undercount would result in too few dollars being allocated to agencies aiding the homeless. But no critic put forth a viable alternative method. More important, it was the first time the Census Bureau acknowledged the social significance of the homeless. As a resident of a shelter

The latest, 1990 census made the first-ever attempts to count the homeless. Census takers fanned out to such places as heating grates, where the homeless were known or suspected to stay.

for the homeless said, "It shows that they're starting to recognize us as humans and not the scum of the earth" (Roberts, 1990; Little, 1991).

The census put the 1990 U.S. population at 249,632,692—an increase of more than 23 million people, or 10.2 percent, over the 1980 total. Is this number, and the numbers for various subgroups, accurate? Probably not; the census could not be perfect. Some African-American leaders have already accused the Census Bureau of undercounting minorities. Cities that were shown to have suffered population decline have also complained of an undercount. But, given the extraordinary efforts to enumerate the population accurately, the 1990 census must be more accurate than any of the past decennial censuses. It is a far cry from the 1890 census, which asked families if they had any "idiots" and whether their heads were larger or smaller than average; from the 1910 census, which missed most of the numerous immigrants in Chicago who hid from the counters for fear of being deported; from the 1910, 1920, and 1930 censuses, which classified female homemakers as "idlers" despite protests by women who asked that "housewife" be included as an occupation; and from the 1960 and 1970 censuses, which seriously undercounted people in many cities despite the great migration from rural to urban areas that had begun 20 and 30 years earlier (Roberts, 1990).

From current censuses such as the 1990 U.S. census, along with vital statistics, demographers can tell us a great deal about population characteristics and changes. These variables are greatly influenced by social factors, and they vary from one society to another.

DEMOGRAPHIC PROCESSES

The world's population is increasing about 1.73 percent a year. This means that there are about 17 new members a year for every 1000 people in the world. This growth rate may appear small, but it represents an enormous addition of people—some 93 million, about 37 percent of the U.S. population, being added in 1990 alone (Haub, 1991). Moreover, given the same growth rate every year, population does not increase linearly, with the *same* number of people added annually. Instead, it grows exponentially, with an *increasingly larger* number of new people appearing in each succeeding year. (It works like your savings account, which earns an increasingly larger rather than the same interest in each succeeding year.) Thus, the world's current growth rate of 1.73 percent a year means that there will be about 86 million more next year, 88 million more the following year, 90 million more the year after that, and so on. This is why, given the same annual growth rate of 1.73 percent, global population will double in only about 40 years—instead of 60 years if it grew linearly.

Increases in population are therefore far more dramatic in modern times of big populations than in

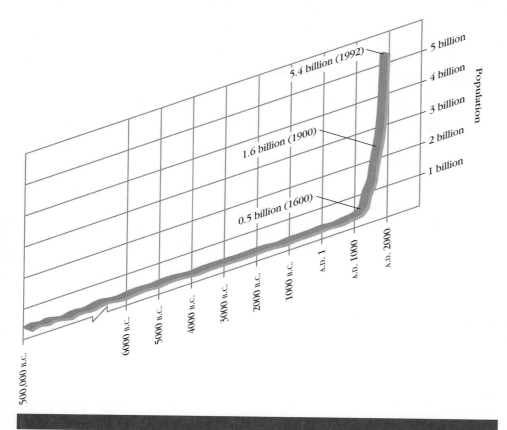

FIGURE 14.1 *How the World's Population Grows*
In recent history, the world's population has experienced an exponential growth. Before the modern era began in A.D. 1600, it had taken more than 500,000 years for global population to reach only about half a billion. But since then it has taken less than 400 years for the population to skyrocket to more than 5.4 billion today.

Source: Population Reference Bureau, "How Many People Have Ever Lived on Earth?" *Population Bulletin,* Feb. 1962, p. 5. *The Universal Almanac,* 1993, p. 326.

ancient times of small populations. Before the year 1600, it took more than 500,000 years for the human population to reach about 500 million. Thereafter, the population skyrocketed to 5.4 *billion* in less than 400 years. Today it takes only 5 or 6 years, as opposed to the 500,000 years before 1600, for the world to produce 500 million people. (See Figure 14.1 for the remarkable population growth in the modern era.)

In general, populations are growing much faster in poor, developing countries than in rich, developed ones. Rich nations generally have an annual growth rate of 1 percent or less. In contrast, poor nations typically grow at a rate far above 2 percent.

The growth of a nation's population is determined by the number of births minus the number of deaths plus the net immigration rate—the excess of people moving into a country (immigrants) over those leaving it (emigrants). Thus, the growth rate of a nation's population equals the birth rate plus the net immigration rate minus the death rate (see Figure 14.2). Because births, deaths, and migrations are population changes that take place continually, demographers call them **demographic processes.**

Birth Rates The **birth rate** is the number of babies born every year for every 1000 members of a given population:

$$\frac{\text{Births}}{\text{Total population}} \times 1000$$

For many years the birth rates of most industrialized nations have been far lower than 20 per 1000 population, whereas those of most agricultural countries have far exceeded 30 per 1000.

Indeed, people in poor countries do tend to have larger families—an average of four or more children—than people in rich countries, who have an average of about two children per family. Because of high birth rates in past years, poor countries also have a very large number of women entering their childbearing years. As a result, even if these women average fewer children than their mothers did, their nations' birth rates will remain high. Meanwhile, developed countries are close to or already experienc-

ing *zero population growth,* a situation in which the population stops growing. Consequently, well over 90 percent of the world's population increase in coming decades will occur in the poorest nations. By the year 2000, the United States will probably account for only about 4 percent of the total population (Census Bureau, 1991).

Death Rates The **death rate** is the number of deaths in a year for every 1000 members of a population. Rich nations have an average of 10 deaths per 1000 population, and the poor nations have 13. The difference is surprisingly small. In fact, death rates obscure the large gap between rich and poor nations in health and living conditions. Because the percentage of young people is much higher in developing countries than in developed ones and the percentage

FIGURE 14.2 *How to Calculate Population Growth*
The growth rate of a population is determined by the birth rate minus the death rate plus the net immigration rate. In 1992, for example, the U.S. growth rate was 16.2 (birth rate) − 8.5 (death rate) + 2.4 (net immigration rate) = 10.1 (growth rate). The 10.1 means there were 10.1 more people in 1992 than in 1991 for every 1000 population, so the growth rate can be said to be 1.01 percent.

Source: Encyclopedia Britannica, 1993, p. 741.

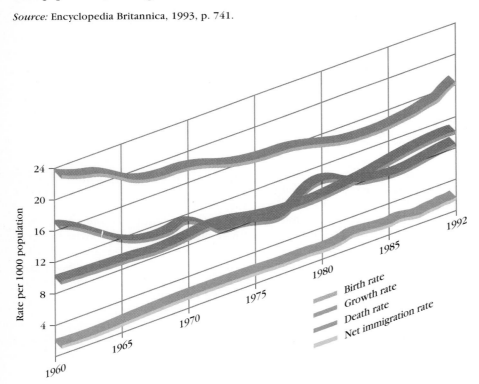

"You figure it. Everything we eat is 100 percent natural yet our life expectancy is only 31 years."

of old people much lower, the death rates in these two kinds of nations are more similar than we might expect.

To compare the health and living conditions of nations, demographers therefore use refined rates, especially the **infant mortality rate,** which shows the number of deaths among infants less than 1 year old for every 1000 live births. In many developed countries, the infant mortality rate is far lower than 20. In many developing countries, it is far higher than 30 (Census Bureau, 1993).

Another indicator of health conditions is **life expectancy,** which is the average number of years that a group of people can expect to live. If the group being considered is a nation's newborn infants, then life expectancy rates reflect infant mortality rates. In developing nations, the average life expectancy is 56 years. In the United States, the life expectancy has soared from 49 years at the turn of the century to 75 years today. All over the world, however, females tend to live longer than males (see Chapter 13: Education, Science, and Health).

Migration International migration—movement of people from one country to another—obviously does not increase or decrease the world's population, but it may greatly alter the population of a specific country. Israel is a case in point. For several years after it was established in 1948, Israel experienced a tremendous annual population growth of 24 percent. Ninety percent of this growth was a result of immigration by European Jews. Another notable example is the United States. Between 1880 and 1910, more than 28 million European immigrants settled in the United States. During the 1970s, many European countries attracted millions of immigrants from the Middle East, North Africa, Asia, and the Caribbean region (Wrong, 1990).

The effect of immigration goes beyond the immediate addition to the population. Most immigrants are young adults from lower-class families—categories with relatively high fertility rates. As a result, through their children and grandchildren the immigrants multiply population growth, producing an effect that echoes through the years.

Unlike international migration, internal migration—movement within a country—does not affect the size of a country's population. But it obviously changes the populations of regions and communities. Through internal migrations, cities have been created and frontiers conquered. The United States is probably the most mobile country in the world. Since the nation was founded, people have migrated westward. For many years after the Civil War, there was also significant migration out of the rural South to the industrial North and from rural areas to the cities and then to the suburbs. Recently, while westward migration continues, other migration patterns have changed. Since the 1970s, many people have moved to the South and Southwest, the so-called Sunbelt. This may explain the Census Bureau's recent finding that most of the 10 percent population increase since 1980 has taken place in the South and Southwest—in particular, Florida, Texas, and California. Meanwhile, migration to large industrial centers of the North and Northeast has essentially stopped, and rural areas and small towns have grown at a faster rate than cities (Census Bureau, 1993).

QUESTIONS FOR DISCUSSION AND REVIEW
1. What is demography, and how are its data collected?
2. How do birth rates, death rates, and migration influence the demographic characteristics of a society?

Combating Population Growth

For thousands of years, there have been individuals who practiced birth control, but many nations at various times in their histories have sought to *increase* their population because they associated big population with great military power and national security. Religious, medical, and political authorities often argued against birth control. For more than a century, the United States even had laws that prohibited the mailing of birth control information and devices. During the 1950s and 1960s, however, many governments began to see population growth as a social problem. By 1984 most countries, representing about 95 percent of the world's population, had formulated official policies to combat population growth (Davis, 1976; Russell, 1984). These policies can be classified into two types: encouragement of voluntary family planning and compulsory population control.

FAMILY PLANNING

A number of governments make contraceptives available to anyone who wants them. They encourage birth control, but they do not try to impose a limit on how many children a couple may have. For this voluntary family planning to work, however, people must prefer small families to large ones—otherwise they will not use birth control.

This is the heart of the problem with family planning. Family planning programs have reduced birth rates significantly in advanced developing countries such as Taiwan and South Korea, because these societies value small families. Family planning is even more successful in the more industrialized nations of the West, where the preference for small families is strong. However, many less advanced developing countries retain the preference for large families that is typical of agricultural societies. As a result, voluntary planning programs in these nations have failed to reduce birth rates as significantly as they have in developed countries (Ainsworth, 1984).

During the last decade, for example, there has been no fertility decline in Africa. There have been substantial fertility declines, though, in the developing countries in Asia, the Pacific, Latin America, the Caribbean, and the Middle East. Still, among these countries, virtually none has reached a birth rate of under 20 births per 1000 population—the level of all developed countries—and a third of them still have birth rates above 40. Obviously, their family planning programs have not worked well enough. Their preferred family size is simply too high, ranging from an average of 4.0 children per family in Asia to 7.1 in Africa—far above the average of 2 in developed countries (Lightbourne and Singh, 1982). Especially in

Africa, having many children is a status enhancer, particularly for the less educated. Moreover, the extended family that is common in third-world countries reverses some of the direct economic penalty of a large family. In fact, children are considered a form of old-age pension because there are no social welfare systems like the ones we have in the United States. Because many children die early, parents are even more anxious to have a large family to increase their chances of being looked after in their senior years (Francis, 1987). As a result of the relative ineffectiveness of family planning in the developing countries, several have tried compulsory programs.

POPULATION CONTROL

In the early 1970s, India forced government employees who had more than two children to undergo sterilization. With the encouragement of the central government, some states in India also forced men to be

India has failed to control its relentless population growth because of low literacy and a dearth of sustained family-planning information and services. Shown here is an attempt to promote family planning on a placard on the back of a bus in India.

sterilized after their second child was born. If the men refused, they could be fined $250 and imprisoned for up to a year. In some villages, overzealous government officials rounded up and sterilized all the men, without checking how many children they had. The program stirred up widespread opposition. Demographer Frank Notestein had predicted in 1971 that if a developing country tried to force its people to practice birth control, it "would be more likely to bring down the government than the birth rate." Indeed, the sterilization program apparently contributed to the fall of Prime Minister Indira Gandhi's government in 1977. Since then, India has returned to a voluntary program, which, however, has failed to control the relentless population growth because of low literacy and a dearth of sustained family planning information and services. India now has a fertility rate of 4.3 children per woman (compared with 1.9 in the United States), and it will become the world's most populous nation by about 2045 (Russell, 1984; Crossette, 1990).

China has had more success with its program of combining rewards and punishments. For a couple with only one child, rewards are substantial. The parents get a salary bonus, and the child receives free schooling, priority in medical care, admission to the best schools and universities, and preference in employment. In contrast, multichild parents are severely penalized. They must pay all costs for each additional child, are taxed about 10 percent of their income, and are often denied promotion for two years. Since it started this "one-child family" campaign in 1979, China has halved its birth rate, a record unmatched by any other developing nation.

Beginning in 1986, though, the birth rate began to rise again because the government relaxed its one-child policy—by allowing rural couples to have a second baby if their firstborn was a girl. One reason for the relaxation has been the increasing prosperity among the Chinese, many of whom are willing to pay the fines for having more than one child. Another reason is the international criticism that China has received for pressuring women to abort fetuses even late in pregnancy. A third reason is that the one-child policy has encouraged, albeit unintentionally, the killing of female infants by parents who hope to have sons. Nevertheless, China continues to exhort couples to have only one child, though it now focuses on persuasion, education, and publicity campaigns rather than coercion and penalties. All this has been quite successful with urban couples, though it tends to fall on deaf ears in the countryside. Recently, in 1990, more than half of all births in China were of first children, and an additional 25 to 30 percent were of second children. Only 15 percent were of third children (Kristof, 1990).

U.S. POPULATION POLICY

During the 1960s, the U.S. government began to recognize global population growth as a potential problem, and by 1968 it had spent several hundred million dollars to help developing nations control their population growth. However, in the early 1970s, a number of leftist governments in the third world dismissed population control as an imperialist ploy by rich countries to keep poor nations' populations down in order to perpetuate Western dominance over the globe. They argued that poor nations should be more concerned with economic development because "development is the best contraceptive," that is, elimination of poverty will lead to lower birth rates. Later, those leftist governments reversed themselves and pursued population control—with a vengeance in China's communist regime.

Ironically, in the 1980s, the conservative Reagan administration also saw economic growth as the answer to world overpopulation. But it held that only a free-market economy can guarantee economic growth as well as low birth rates. It cited as supporting evidence the experiences of Western European nations, Canada, the United States, Japan, Singapore, Hong Kong, South Korea, Taiwan, and New Zealand. All these countries have free-market economies, are highly prosperous, and have very low birth rates (Abraham, 1984). The Reagan administration also favored the cutting of family planning aid to organizations or countries if they continued to include abortion in their population-control programs. This is because the administration found abortion morally offensive, seeing it as a form of infanticide (Russell, 1984). Thus, the administration ended its $15-million-a-year support for the London-based International Parenthood Federation in 1985 and suspended $25 million in aid to the United Nations Family Planning Agency in 1986 because these two international organizations advocated abortion as a family planning option. The conservative Bush administration was also opposed to abortion. Some pro-life groups in the United States are even opposed to the use of such contraceptives as the pill and the IUD, because they are believed to promote promiscuity. Thus, pro-life groups have mounted campaigns to defeat politicians

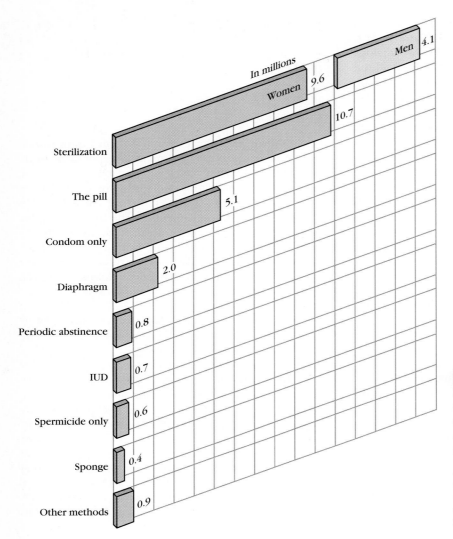

FIGURE 14.3 *Contraceptive Choices Of America's 58 million women of childbearing age, 60 percent practice some form of contraception. These are what they use.*

Source: Newsweek, December 24, 1990. Chart by Sotoodeh/Newsweek. Copyright © 1990, Newsweek, Inc. Data from National Center for Health. All rights reserved. Reprinted by permission.

who support family planning and to urge the public to undercut support for the nation's 5000 government-aided family planning clinics (Nazario, 1990).

Our government has been spending over $100 million a year to assist family planning centers. But our population growth has slowed, primarily because of social and economic factors, not government action. In fact, family planning has become the norm rather than the exception. Even the majority of American Catholics practice forms of birth control forbidden by their church. Today, sterilization is the most popular type of birth control in the United States, followed by the pill and the condom (see Figure 14.3). The use of sterilization and the condom has increased faster than most other methods, because of

concern and controversy over the side effects of the pill and the IUD. But all these devices are antiquated; the pill and the IUD, for example, were introduced 30 years ago. They are also less convenient and less effective than the contraceptives coming out in Western Europe. Only as late as December 1990 was the innovative Norplant device—introduced in Europe 20 years ago—approved for use in the United States. Norplant, when properly implanted in a woman's upper arm, can protect against pregnancy for 5 years. Yet it is likely to elude the poor (who have the highest incidence of unwanted pregnancy), because it costs $350 in the United States, though it is priced as low as $23 in 17 other countries (Nazario, 1991). Because of the lack of modern and inexpensive contraceptives in the

United States, more than half of all American pregnancies every year are accidents or unwanted—more than in Western Europe. This may explain why our rate of abortion as a form of birth control is among the highest in the developed world, despite restrictions by the federal government and many state governments on the use of Medicaid funds for abortions (Elmer-DeWitt, 1991).

Nevertheless, the use of contraception is prevalent enough. And given the added prevalence of abortion, the Census Bureau believes that in the coming decades American women in their childbearing years will average just 1.8 births—less than the replacement rate of 2.1. (Demographers determine the replacement rate at 2.1 rather than 2.0 to take into account young people who die before reaching their reproductive age.) It seems inevitable that if the "birth dearth" continues, our society will rely increasingly on immigration to stop the population from declining. Today, immigration—both legal and illegal—accounts for about 26 percent of the nation's population growth. But that proportion will rise to 50 percent early in the next century, and then immigration will provide the bulk of the nation's population growth in the second half of the twenty-first century. History has shown the great contribution of immigrants to the prosperity of this country. Hoping to benefit the U.S. economy more quickly, Congress has passed a bill that will admit larger numbers of highly educated and skilled immigrants, such as scientists, engineers, and medical technicians, as Canada and Australia have done for years. But since most immigrants come from nonwhite countries rather than Europe, they are resented by some Americans. According to a Gallup poll, about half of the American public thinks the United States has too many Hispanics and Asians. Although immigration does not increase unemployment, large numbers of Americans believe that immigrants take jobs from American workers. But a large majority of Americans believe that immigrants improve the country with their different cultures and talents (see Table 14.1).

Every year more people enter this country illegally than legally, and the growth in the number of illegal aliens has accelerated in recent years. In late 1986, the U.S. Congress passed a law that offers amnesty—in effect, legal residency status—to aliens who have been living in this country since January 1, 1982. But at the same time the United States will beef up its efforts to stop foreigners from entering the country illegally. Because the small number of agents from the U.S. Immigration and Naturalization Service

TABLE 14.1 *American Attitudes Toward Immigrants* *
Percentages of Americans answering the following:
Are the numbers of immigrants now entering the United States from each of the following areas too many, too few, or about the right amount?

	TOO MANY	TOO FEW	RIGHT AMOUNT
Africa	36%	13%	35%
Asia	49%	7%	31%
Europe	31%	10%	47%
Latin America	54%	7%	28%

DO IMMIGRANTS TAKE THE JOBS OF U.S. WORKERS?

Yes 53%　　No 43%

DO IMMIGRANTS HELP IMPROVE OUR COUNTRY WITH THEIR DIFFERENT CULTURES AND TALENTS?

Yes 69%　　No 28%

*For this *Newsweek* Poll, The Gallup Organization interviewed a national sample of 767 adults by phone Aug. 23–24. The margin of error is plus or minus 4 percentage points. "Don't know" and other responses not shown. The *Newsweek* Poll © 1990 by Newsweek, Inc.
Source: From *Newsweek*, September 10, 1990, p. 48.

(INS) cannot by themselves stop the vast number of aliens flooding illegally into this country, Congress has also passed a law that prohibits employers from hiring illegal aliens. This law has, in effect, forced the nation's 7 million employers to work for free as agents of the INS. They must ask for a job applicant's proof of citizenship or legal residency. They must further keep detailed new records documenting their efforts to maintain their workplace free of illegal aliens. Can this law successfully cut off the economic lure for illegal immigrants? According to two studies by the General Accounting Office, sanctions have failed to be an effective deterrent in the United States and 20 other nations. Moreover, the sanctions have produced widespread discrimination against minorities, particularly Hispanic-and Asian-Americans. Some employers practice "preventive discrimination" by refusing to hire any foreign-sounding job applicants in order to avoid the possibility of hiring illegal aliens. Other employers simply use the sanctions as an excuse for not hiring people who have a "foreign appearance or accent." Thus, many organizations, including the U.S. Civil Rights Commission and various Hispanic groups, have called for the sanctions to be repealed (Solis et al., 1987; Yoshihashi, 1990).

QUESTIONS FOR DISCUSSION AND REVIEW

1. What are the two basic strategies that governments can use to control population, and what are the pros and cons of each?
2. What has been the result of compulsory birth control programs in overpopulated countries like India and China?
3. How does U.S. population policy differ from that of other societies?
4. What roles might the birth dearth and immigration play in determining the composition of the American population in the future?

Ecology

To understand how the growth of population and consumption can damage the environment and thus endanger us, we look to **ecology.** It is a study of the interactions among organisms and between organisms and their physical environment.

ELEMENTS OF ECOLOGY

Like all organisms, humans exist within a thin layer of air, soil, and water known as the **biosphere.** Within the biosphere we can isolate countless **ecosystems,** communities of living things interacting with the physical environment. An ecosystem may be as small as a puddle in a forest or as large as the biosphere itself. But whatever ecosystem we choose to look at, we find that the organisms within it depend on one another and on the physical environment for their survival. They are bound together by mutual interdependence. Energy and matter are constantly being transformed and transferred by the components of an ecosystem, providing the organisms with the essentials of life. Plants, for example, take in carbon dioxide and give off oxygen, which humans and other animals require for survival, and animals exhale carbon dioxide. Plants, in turn, use carbon dioxide in photosynthesis, the process by which they convert solar energy into carbohydrates and become food for animals. When animals die, their decomposed bodies provide nutrients to the soil, which plants then use.

From an examination of ecosystems we can isolate two simple principles. First, natural resources are finite. Every ecosystem therefore has a limited *carrying capacity,* a limited number of living things that it can support. Second, we can never do just one thing, because everything is related to everything else. If we try to alter one aspect of an ecosystem, we end up changing others as well. When farmers used DDT, for example, they meant merely to kill pests. But DDT also got into the soil and water, from there into plankton, into fish that ate plankton, and into birds that ate the fish. The DDT eventually damaged the ability of some birds to reproduce. The chemical also found its way into our food. Some American women had so much DDT in their systems that their milk would have been legally prohibited from sale in interstate commerce (Ehrlich, Ehrlich, and Holdren, 1977).

Despite all the amazing things humans have managed to do, we are still limited by these ecological principles. We are still living organisms, dependent like other organisms on ecosystems. However, we have tried to ignore that dependence and act in defiance of nature's limits. An important result is environmental pollution.

ENVIRONMENTAL POLLUTION

To consume more, we must produce more and thereby create more wastes. These by-products of our consumption must go somewhere. Nature has many cycles for transforming wastes to be used in some other form, but we are overtaxing nature's recycling capacity. We put too much waste, such as automobile emissions, in one place at the same time, and we have created new toxic substances, such as dioxin, that cannot be recycled safely. The result is pollution.

Pollution of the air has many sources. Throughout the world, power-generating plants, oil refineries, chemical plants, steel mills, and the like spew about 140 million tons of pollutants into the air every year. The heaviest polluter is the automobile, which accounts for at least 80 percent of air pollution. The pollutants irritate our eyes, noses, and throats; damage buildings; lower the productivity of the soil; and may cause serious illnesses, such as bronchitis, emphysema, and lung cancer. Air pollution is especially bad in Eastern Europe. As many as 10 percent of the deaths in Hungary are attributed directly to air pollution; the problem is even worse in parts of Czechoslovakia, Poland, and former East Germany (Nelson, 1990). Throughout the world, a growing concentration of industrial gases (carbon dioxide, methane, nitrous oxides, and chlorofluorocarbons) in the atmosphere is retaining more and more radiation from sunlight and thus will substantially raise the temperature of the earth's surface in the next century. A

We have created new toxic substances, such as dioxin, that cannot be recycled safely. The result is pollution, as shown here at a site in North Carolina that has been polluted by dioxin from a paper mill.

number of scientists expect this global warming to cause worldwide flooding, climatic change, and social disruption (Shabecoff, 1990). Some of the industrial gases—especially chlorofluorocarbons, used in refrigeration and air conditioning—have already weakened the ozone layer in many areas of the globe, thereby letting in more of the sun's ultraviolet light, which may cause skin cancer, harm the human immune system, and damage some crops and wild plants (Lemonick, 1992).

Another kind of air pollution, called *acid rain,* has also aroused concern. When sulfur and nitrogen compounds are emitted by factories and automobiles, chemical reactions in the atmosphere may convert them to acidic compounds that can be carried hundreds of miles and then fall to the earth in rain and snow. Rain as acidic as vinegar has been recorded. This acid rain can kill fish and aquatic vegetation. It damages forests, crops, and soils. It corrodes buildings and water pipes and tanks because it can erode limestone, marble, and even metal surfaces. Because

of acid rain, thousands of lakes and rivers in North America and Europe are now "dead," unable to support fish and plant life. Worst is the acid rain in Russia's Siberia, which has ruined more than 1500 square miles of timber, an area half as large as Rhode Island (Feshbach and Friendly, 1992).

Lakes, rivers, underground wells, and even the oceans are further polluted by tons of garbage and oil spills. The greatest dumpers are industry and agriculture. An average paper mill, for example, produces as much organic waste as the human sewage of a large city. Chemical industries produce even more hazardous wastes. Careless disposal of these wastes has caused fires, contamination of food and drinking water, and harm to humans, animals, and plants. Modern farmers also apply huge quantities of nitrate and phosphate fertilizers to their land—chemicals that are often washed by rain and irrigation into lakes and rivers. In recent years, the number of oil spill accidents has increased sharply. It went up from 257 in 1987 to 368 in 1989 in New York and New Jersey alone. A few oil spills were huge, such as the ones in Alaska's Prince William Sound in March 1989 and in the Arthur Kill between Staten Island and New Jersey in January 1990. Most spills are small, rarely capturing the public's attention. They occur underground, with the oil leaking from storage tanks or their connecting pipes. Unlike the big spills in the sea, which disrupt the ecosystem by killing many species of fish and birds, the underground spills threaten our health directly because about half of all Americans rely on groundwater as a source of drinking water. Moreover, small spills are, cumulatively, more dangerous than the larger ones because they are not cleaned up for lack of publicity (Smith, 1984; Schmitt, 1990).

Nuclear pollution has also become a source of special concern. In 1986, the nuclear power plant in Chernobyl, the former Soviet Union, exploded, spreading a cloud of dangerous radioactivity over large parts of the country and much of Eastern and Western Europe. Although the Soviet government reported that only two died and fewer than 200 were injured, Western experts believe that "the disaster was catastrophic, possibly causing thousands of casualties and contaminating an area the size of Rhode Island" (Gabor, 1986). This accident made it clear that, contrary to all the assurances experts had given, serious nuclear disasters can happen. Even without a major accident, nuclear power poses environmental hazards. People living near a nuclear plant may be subject to routine releases of low-level radiation, and workers in the plants may receive dangerous doses of radioactivity. Transporting uranium to nuclear plants and disposing of radioactive wastes pose other problems. The mining and refining of uranium has produced millions of tons of radioactive tailings, which can be spread by the wind and contaminate drinking water. The nuclear power plants themselves are running out of storage space for their wastes. Some of this material will remain radioactive and very dangerous for thousands of years.

SAVING THE ENVIRONMENT

Since 1970 our federal and state governments have taken many steps to bring environmental problems under control. The main approaches to these problems include antipollution laws, conservation, alternative technologies, and limitations on economic and population growth.

Antipollution laws have attracted the most attention. Industry resisted them because of their expense. Unions sometimes opposed them because they feared jobs would be lost as a result of the cost to industry. Some consumers objected to these laws because they feared prices would rise too high once industry was forced to reduce pollution. State governments were often reluctant to make or enforce their own pollution-control laws for fear that companies would move their business elsewhere.

Despite all these concerns, laws regulating air and water pollution, pesticide use, and the disposal of hazardous wastes were passed in the last two decades, and now they enjoy wide public support. A recent poll asked a representative sample of Americans if they agreed that the environment must be protected regardless of cost; 74 percent said yes. This is quite a change from 10 years ago, when only 45 percent said yes. The antipollution laws have had some success, but problems persist or have gotten worse. Utilities that burn coal for electricity are emitting 15 percent less sulfur dioxide (the coal by-product that causes acid rain) than they did 20 years ago, but they are burning more than twice as much coal, so that some 4000 lakes in the United States and 164,000 in Canada are still acidified or threatened. New cars are spewing 96 percent less carbon monoxide and hydrocarbons and 76 percent less nitrogen oxides, but there are so many more cars and so much more congestion that the resulting air pollution affects half of all Americans. Fish have returned to the Cuyahoga River and to Lake Erie and other Great Lakes, but many of those fish carry toxic chemicals that make them dangerous to eat (Wald, 1990).

Recently, in late 1990, sweeping changes were made in the Clean Air Act. Coal-burning utilities will have to cut their sulfur-dioxide emissions in half by the year 2000. Auto and oil companies will have to develop emission-reducing cars and cleaner-burning gasolines. Most large manufacturers and many small businesses will have to invest heavily in new pollution-control equipment to achieve a 90 percent reduction in the output of 189 toxic and cancer-causing chemicals. Businesses have complained that the cost will be staggering—as much as $25 billion to $35 billion a year. But environmentalists point out that the cost of doing nothing could be higher—perhaps $50 billion a year, assuming that one can calculate the price of environmental destruction and its effects, such as the ruining of forests and lakes by acid rain and the suffering from pollution-related lung diseases and birth defects (Lemonick, 1990).

Conservation provides a second method of reducing our negative impact on the environment. Dur-

Recycling provides a means of conserving energy and raw materials and of combating pollution. In 1993, the Illinois Power Company began to burn 7.5 million used tires a year. Tires are cheaper to burn and produce lower sulfur emissions than the coal used in Illinois.

ing the late 1970s, the federal and state governments took many steps to encourage the conservation of energy. People were urged to insulate their homes, turn down the thermostat in cold months, drive smaller cars at lower speeds, and ride buses and trains. The government began to offer tax credits and direct subsidies to encourage energy conservation. Americans were reminded that most European countries use far less energy than the United States while maintaining a high standard of living. Conservation efforts combined with rising energy prices and economic recession to produce a drop in Americans' energy use from 1979 to 1982 that was greater than experts had thought possible. Recycling, aside from combating pollution, provided another means of conserving energy and raw materials.

Today, conservation is once again popular. According to one poll, more than 80 percent of Americans are willing to separate their trash for recycling, to give up plastic containers and superfluous packaging to reduce waste, and to favor a ban on disposable diapers (Rosewicz, 1990). Many schools now teach children to become environmentally conscious. Thus, second-graders may ask their parents to use brown paper bags instead of plastic bags for garbage, or to avoid using air conditioners to conserve energy (Alexander, 1990b). The federal government sup-

ports conservation by declaring the spotted owl an endangered species that needs to be protected, which requires preserving permanently some 8.4 million acres of over-150-year-old trees in the national forests of northern California, Oregon, and Washington, where the bird lives. To environmentalists, saving these ancient trees is not just for humans' enjoyment of esthetics and recreation. It is crucial for sustaining an ecosystem on which animals and plants, as well as people, depend. The forests provide a habitat and food for a multitude of species, including birds and deer. The forests also clean the air, regulate water levels and quality, enhance the productivity of fisheries, enrich the soil, and prevent soil erosion and landslides (Gup, 1990).

A third approach to dealing with environmental problems focuses on the development of new technology that is efficient, safe, and clean. Changes in automobiles illustrate this approach. Since the early 1970s, the fuel efficiency of cars has been increased and their polluting emissions have been reduced. Especially in the last 10 years, the widespread use of catalytic converters in cars has greatly reduced two types of pollutants emitted by tailpipes: carbon monoxide and nitrogen oxide. Industrial scrubbers have also been used to remove much of the sulfur dioxide—the major ingredient of acid rain—from the process of producing energy from coal. The scrubbers, however, produce huge quantities of waste, and they also consume about 5 percent of the energy produced by burning coal, which raises total coal consumption. But scientists have been trying to develop photovoltaic cells to produce electricity directly from the sun, without releasing any pollutants into the air. The solar cells are expected to be in widespread use in the sunny Southwest later this decade, when they become cheaper than conventional power sources. By using energy more efficiently and at less cost, the new technology would make American economy more productive and more competitive internationally (Wald, 1990; Stevens, 1992).

Limiting both population growth and traditional economic growth is a fourth way of solving environmental problems. As John Firor (1990) observes, nearly every environmental problem, be it acid rain, global warming, or ozone depletion, is driven in the first instance and then exacerbated by growth in the world's population. By stemming population growth, we will go a long way toward reducing environmental pollution and resource depletion. The West has done much better than poor countries in curbing population growth. This is achieved primarily by abandoning the traditional value that favors having many children. However, the West—and many other countries—have not abandoned the traditional value that favors economic growth with little regard to its cost to the environment. Many countries still measure their gross national product (GNP) the old-fashioned way—the total value of their goods and services—*without* subtracting the value of clean air, water, ground, trees, fish, animals, human health, and other ecological elements that have been harmed by the production process, as if these were free goods rather than assets that we are losing. Thus, a large economic growth measured as a great increase in GNP does not truly represent a country's wealth, the welfare of its citizens, or the prices of its goods and services (Simons, 1990). We should stop pursuing this old kind of economic growth, which harms the environment, and seek a "green," ecologically safe economic growth. This means replacing technologies that deplete natural resources or produce pollutants with technologies that do not (Commoner, 1990).

QUESTIONS FOR DISCUSSION AND REVIEW

1. What major environmental problems now challenge the ecosystems of modern industrial societies?
2. Which environmental policies might work best to bring environmental destruction under control?

Stages of Urbanization

In 1693 William Penn wrote that "the country life is to be preferred for there we see the works of God, but in cities little else than the work of man." Most people at the time probably agreed with him. Less than 2 percent of the world's population then were urban dwellers. By 1900, however, Great Britain had become the first predominantly urban society. By 1920 the United States had followed suit. Since then, urbanization around the world has been occurring at an increasingly rapid pace. Today, about 39 percent of the world's population lives in urban areas, and more than 50 percent will do so by the end of the century (Fischer, 1984).

While urban populations have grown, the cities themselves have changed. We can identify three periods in their history: the preindustrial, industrial, and metropolitan-megalopolitan stages.

THE PREINDUSTRIAL CITY

For more than 99 percent of the time since human beings appeared on earth, our ancestors roamed about in search of food. They were able to hunt, fish, and gather edible plants, but they could never find enough food in one place to sustain them for very long. They had to move on, traveling in small bands from one place to another.

Then, about 10,000 years ago, technological advances allowed people to stop their wandering. This was the dawn of what is called the Neolithic period. People now had the simple tools and the know-how to cultivate plants and domesticate animals. They could produce their food supplies in one locale, and they settled down and built villages. The villages were very small—only about 200 to 400 residents each. For the next 5000 years, villagers produced just enough food to feed themselves.

By about 5000 years ago, humans had developed more powerful technologies. Thanks to innovations like the ox-drawn plow, irrigation, and metallurgy, farmers could produce more food than they needed to sustain themselves and their families. Because of this food surplus, some people abandoned agriculture and made their living by weaving, pottery, and other specialized crafts. Methods of transporting and storing food were also improved. The result was the emergence of cities (Childe, 1952).

Cities first arose on the fertile banks of such rivers as the Nile of Egypt, the Euphrates and Tigris in the Middle East, the Indus in Pakistan, and the Yellow River in China. Similar urban settlements later appeared in other parts of the world. These *preindustrial cities* were very small compared with the cities of today. Most had populations of 5000 to 10,000 people. Only a very few cities had more than 100,000 people, and even Rome never had more than several hundred thousand.

Several factors prevented expansion of the preindustrial city. By modern standards, agricultural techniques were still very primitive. It took at least 75 farmers to produce enough of a surplus to support just one city dweller. For transportation, people had to depend on their own muscle power or that of animals. It was difficult to carry food supplies from farms to cities, and even more difficult to transport heavy materials for construction in the cities. Poor sanitation, lack of sewer facilities, and ineffective medicine kept death rates high. Epidemics regularly killed as much as half of a city's population. Moreover, families still had a strong attachment to the land, which discouraged immigration to the cities. All these characteristics of preindustrial society kept the cities small (Davis, 1955).

Preindustrial cities differed in other ways from their larger counterparts today. First, their role in society was different. The countryside, not the city, was the dominant social and cultural force. City people still lived like farmers, in the shadow of extended family and large kinship networks. Second, living patterns in the preindustrial city were strikingly different from those typical of modern cities. The commercial district and residential areas were not segregated as they tend to be today. Artisans and traders worked at home. But other types of segregation were very marked. People with different crafts or trades lived in different sections of the city. Blacksmiths made their living and their homes in one quarter; tailors in another. Each occupational group had its own quarter. In most cases, these areas were walled off from one another, with their gates locked at night. People were further segregated into classes or castes, with little or no opportunity for social mobility. Residents were geographically separated into ethnic or religious groups, with little or no interaction with one another (Sjoberg, 1966).

THE INDUSTRIAL CITY

For almost 5000 years, cities changed little. Then their growth, in size and number, was so rapid it has been called an urban revolution or urban explosion. In 1700 less than 2 percent of the population in Great Britain lived in cities, but by 1900 the majority of the British did so. Other European countries and the United States soon achieved the same level of urbanization in an even shorter period.

The major stimulus to this urban explosion was the Industrial Revolution. It triggered a series of related events that sociologist Philip Hauser (1981) has termed a population explosion, population displo-

Left: *Food surpluses, allowing some people to practice specialized crafts rather than agriculture, and improved methods of transporting and storing food allowed for the emergence of the preindustrial city, represented here by the Aztec's capital city of Tenochtitlán.*
Right: *The emergence of the industrial city came about largely as a result of the Industrial Revolution.*

sion, population implosion, and technoplosion. In-industrialization first causes a rise in production growth, and the mechanization of agriculture brings about a farm surplus. Fewer farmers can support more people—and thus larger urban populations *(population explosion)*. Workers no longer needed on the farms move to the city. There is, then, displacement of people from rural to urban areas *(population displosion)* and a greater concentration of people in a limited area *(population implosion)*. The development of other new technologies (a *technoplosion*) spurs urbanization on. Improved transportation, for example, speeds the movement of food and other materials to urban centers.

The outcome of these events was the *industrial city*. Compared with the preindustrial city, the industrial city was larger, more densely settled, and more diverse. It was a place where large numbers of people—with different skills, interests, and cultural backgrounds—could live and work together in a limited space. Also, unlike the preindustrial city, which had served primarily as a religious or governmental center, the industrial city was a commercial hub. In fact, its abundant job opportunities attracted so many rural migrants that migration accounted for the largest share of its population growth. Without these migrants, the city would not have grown at all, because of its high mortality rate brought about by extremely poor sanitary conditions.

The quick pace of urbanization can be seen in U.S. history. In 1790 only 5 percent of Americans lived in urban areas. In 1860, when industrialization was confined largely to the northeast coast, only about 20 percent did so. But by 1920 more than half of the population was urban. Today, urban areas take up only about 1.5 percent of the nation's land area, but about 75 percent of the population lives in them. By specializing in finance, the oil industry, or some other sector of the world economy, New York, Houston, and other American cities exert a powerful influence on the world. As global cities, they attract foreign migrant labor, engage in international commerce, and search out raw materials and markets in all parts of the world (Rodriguez and Feagin, 1986).

Urbanization of the developing nations of Africa, Asia, and Latin America has been even more dramatic. Between 1950 and 1960, the proportion of their populations living in cities rose twice as fast as in the industrialized countries. From 1960 to 1984, the population of Calcutta increased from 6 to 10 million, and Mexico City's population rose from 5 million to 17 million. Efforts to industrialize rapidly have helped produce what might be called premature urbanization or overurbanization in the third world. This is made possible by state policies on investment, pricing, and taxation that encourage economic development in urban areas. The resulting higher standard of living in the city draws migrants from poorer, rural areas. In addition, American and other foreign corporations, seeking cheap labor, invest heavily in urban manufacturing, which creates jobs that lure rural workers to the city (Bradshaw, 1987). Much of the urban growth, however, comes not entirely from migration to the city, but to a large extent from high birth rates coupled with declining death rates in the city itself. As a result, their cities are growing faster than the supply of jobs and housing. Makeshift squatters' settlements have proliferated in the cities. In India's largest city, Calcutta, most of the residents live in slums, and it is common to see other people—600,000 of them—living on the streets. Yet Calcutta continues to grow at an explosive rate.

METROPOLIS AND MEGALOPOLIS

Early in this century, the large cities of the industrialized nations began to spread outward. They formed **metropolises,** large urban areas that include a city and its surrounding suburbs. Some of these suburbs are politically separate from their central cities, but socially, economically, and geographically, the suburbs and city are tied together. The U.S. Census Bureau recognizes this unity by defining what is called a *Standard Metropolitan Statistical Area,* which cuts across political boundaries. Since 1990 most Americans have been living in metropolitan areas with a million residents or more (Suro, 1991).

In the United States, the upper and middle classes have usually sparked the expansion of cities outward. As migrants from rural areas moved into the central city, the better-off classes moved to the surrounding suburbs. The automobile greatly facilitated this development. It encouraged people to leave the crowded inner city for the more comfortable life of the suburbs, if they could afford it. As the number of cars increased, so did the size of suburbs and metropolises. In 1900 there were only 8000 cars in the United States, but by 1930 the number had soared to more than 26 million. Meanwhile, the percentage of Americans living in the suburbs grew from only 15.7 percent in 1910 to 48.6 percent in 1950 (Glaab and Brown, 1983).

Since 1950, virtually all the growth in metropolitan areas has occurred in the suburbs. During the 1960s, American suburbs grew four times faster than inner cities, and stores and entertainment facilities followed the people there. Suburban jobs increased 44 percent, while inner-city employment dropped 7 percent. This pattern of suburban growth at the expense of the urban core continued in the 1970s and 1980s. Today, suburbanites outnumber city residents three to two. Traditional sociologists have attributed this suburban growth to transport technology. But Marxists explain it as the result of capitalists moving their factories to suburban areas—to avoid labor unrest in central cities, high city taxes, or other financial costs (Jaret, 1983; Gottdiener, 1983).

As the suburbs expanded, they merged with the suburbs of adjacent metropolitan areas, creating a vast urban complex called a **megalopolis.** For hundreds of miles from one major city to the next, suburbs and cities have merged with one another to form a continuous region in which distinctions between suburban, urban, and rural areas are blurred. The hundreds of miles from Boston to Washington, D.C., form one such megalopolis, another stretches from Detroit through Chicago to Milwaukee in the Midwest, and another goes from San Francisco to San Diego.

Demographics of American Cities What kinds of people live in these urban areas? In general, the poor and minority groups concentrate in the inner cities and more affluent people live in the suburbs. A closer look, however, led sociologist Herbert Gans (1968) to find five types of people in many cities:

1. Cosmopolites—artists, intellectuals, professionals
2. Unmarried individuals and childless couples
3. "Ethnic villagers"—immigrants from other countries
4. The deprived—the poor, African-Americans, other minorities
5. The trapped—poor elderly people

These groups are not likely to feel strong ties to each other or to the city as a whole. The deprived and the trapped are too poor to move—they live in the city by necessity, not choice. The ethnic villagers are likely to be strongly tied only to fellow immigrants in their neighborhoods. The unmarried and childless have ties mostly to those who share their life-style. Cosmopolites associate primarily with those who share their interests.

The movement of African-Americans into the central city has been especially striking. Just 50 years ago, less than half of the black population was urban. Today, a large majority of African-Americans live in urban areas, and most of these in the inner cities. For years African-Americans entering the city have come from the rural South, but now most of these migrants come from other urban areas. Compared with the inner-city natives, they rank higher in education and employment and have lower rates of crime. Some middle-class African-Americans have joined the exodus to the suburbs, but they move mostly to black suburbs. Thus, the different black and white migration patterns reinforce segregation. Today, African-Americans are much more likely to live in central cities than in suburbs. Several large cities are already predominantly black.

The number of cosmopolites, young professionals, adult singles, and childless couples in the inner city has also grown significantly. Increasing numbers of these affluent people now choose to remain in the inner city. They buy run-down buildings and renovate them into elegant townhouses and expensive condominiums. This urban revival, called **gentrification,** has transformed slums into such stylish enclaves as Capitol Hill in Washington, Philadelphia's Queen Village, Boston's South End, Cincinnati's Mount Adams, and Chicago's New Town. To a large extent, urban rehabilitation programs have stimulated gentrification. They have turned over abandoned homes and stores for the price of a few dollars and offered low-interest mortgage loans. Ironically, though, gentrification tends to drive up rents and property taxes, forcing poor and elderly residents to give up their homes to the well-off gentrifiers. However, gentrification has not been extensive enough to transform most of the city. In the last decade, nearly twice as many people have been moving from central cities to suburbs as those moving in the opposite direction. Central cities continue to lose residents, a trend that began in the early 1970s.

The Growth of Suburban Cities Most suburbs still offer better schools, more living space, less pollution, and less crime than the central city, so people continue to "vote with their feet" and head for suburbia. More than a decade ago, most suburbs were largely bedroom communities; their residents commuted to the nearby cities to work. But in the last 10 years, a new kind of suburbanization has taken place—involving not only people and homes but offices and jobs—that has transformed many suburbs into economic centers. In these suburbs, new office buildings, factories, and warehouses have sprung up alongside the housing subdivisions and shopping malls. Developers have already created vast clusters of big buildings, people, and cars. Thus, many sub-

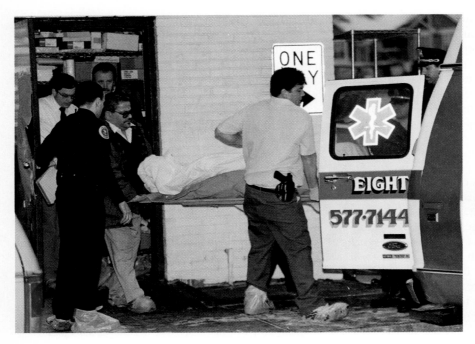

Many suburbs have developed problems once considered "urban," such as traffic jams and noise, air and water pollution, and crime. Shown here is the site of a mass killing that took place in a fast food chain restaurant in 1993 in a middle class suburb of Chicago.

urbs, in effect, have become cities in their own right. Unlike the traditional American city, where diverse businesses operate, the new suburban cities are typically focused on a principal activity, such as a collection of computer companies, a large regional medical center, or a sports or recreation complex. The growth of suburban cities, therefore, has taken away many jobs from the urban cores. Despite the arrival of some nonwhite residents, the suburbs are generally "whiter" than the inner cities (Suro, 1991).

Ironically, many suburbs have developed problems once considered "urban," such as congestion, pollution, and crime. Rapid, unregulated growth has created some of these problems. When industry and stores move to the suburbs to be near people's homes, they often bring with them traffic jams and noise, air and water pollution, not to mention landscape "pollution." Although most suburbs are prosperous, an increasing number are not. The Los Angeles suburbs have more poor families than the city, and there is more substandard housing in the suburbs of Pittsburgh than in the city itself. Poor suburbs tend to be predominantly black or Hispanic. Among the ten poorest suburbs, half are mostly black, such as Ford Heights, Illinois (outside Chicago), and Florida City, Florida (outside Miami). The other five poorest suburbs are predominantly Hispanic, such as Bell Gardens and Coachella, near Los Angeles (McCormick and McKillop, 1989).

As suburbs and cities have become more similar, many Americans have looked elsewhere for their homes. In the last 10 years, about one-third of our rural communities and small towns have grown quickly. This has taken place in the midst of a decline among large cities such as Detroit, Pittsburgh, Cleveland, Chicago, and Atlanta. Because most urban depopulation involves workers and consumers seeking good climate, more space, clean air, less crime, and other pleasant attributes of rural areas and small towns, industries tend to relocate into those places. By providing employment opportunities and a wide range of consumer goods, these industries further attract city folks out of the urban cores (Frey, 1987). Most of the nation's rural communities, however, have failed to lure people and industries. Examples are the mining communities in Wyoming and Kentucky and the cotton and catfish farms of the Mississippi Delta and the Great Plains. Such rural communities do not have an ocean view, a mountain resort, farmland only a short commute from urban areas, or some other natural attraction that would help entice urbanites to move there (Barringer, 1991b).

Recent Changes in American Cities   The 1990 U.S. census has revealed a number of significant changes in American cities over the last decade. As has long been expected by sociologists, many cities in the West and Southwest, particularly California, have grown significantly larger, while many north-eastern and midwestern cities have experienced a decline in population. However, there are some changes that have largely gone unnoticed.

First, older industrial cities in the South have fallen into the same cycle of decline as their northern counterparts. These cities include Atlanta, Georgia; Birmingham, Alabama; and Chattanooga, Tennessee. They represent half of all the big American cities that have lost population since 1980.

Second, immigration has served as a brake against population decline in major cities such as New York, Miami, and New Jersey's Elizabeth and Jersey City. In fact, these cities have registered modest population gains of 2 to 4 percent. But without a large influx of immigrants from countries such as India, China, the Philippines, and the Dominican Republic, they would have suffered a decline (Salins, 1991).

Third, although California's growth was expected to be significant, it has turned out to be astonishing. Of the 29 American cities that have surpassed the population mark of 100,000, most are in California. Seven of the ten fastest growing, large American cities are in Southern California: Bakersfield, Irvine, and Escondido, for example.

Fourth, a large majority (two-thirds) of state capitals have gained population, even though the states themselves have stagnated. North Dakota, for example, lost 1.7 percent of its population, but its capital, Bismarck, had a gain of 10.7 percent. Most cities that are within a declining state but that have a college or university have also grown larger. Examples are Lawrence, Kansas, home of the University of Kansas, and West Lafayette, Indiana, where Purdue University is (Barringer, 1991b).

QUESTIONS FOR DISCUSSION AND REVIEW
1. What stages give rise to urbanization, and why has it spread so rapidly in the twentieth century?
2. How does the industrial city differ from the preindustrial city?
3. What forces have led to the development of suburbs, metropolises, and, finally, megalopolises?
4. Why have many urbanites moved to suburbs and rural communities?

The Urban Environment

As we observed earlier, ecologists study the natural world and tell us that everything in it is related to everything else. Organisms affect other organisms, and they all affect the environment, which in turn affects them. During the 1920s and 1930s, some sociologists at the University of Chicago began to look at the urban world in a similar way. They initiated a new approach to the study of cities called **urban ecology,** the study of the relationship between people and the urban environment. A major issue here is how the urban environment affects the people living in it.

THE NATURE OF CITY LIFE

In 1964 Americans were horrified by a story that many took as typical of life in New York City—or any large city. A young woman named Kitty Genovese was walking home from work in the early morning hours when she was attacked. Her murderer stabbed her repeatedly for more than half an hour. Thirty-eight neighbors heard her screams or witnessed the attack. But no one helped or even called the police. Most of the neighbors later explained that they did not want to "get involved."

What could cause such cold-bloodedness? Many commentators of the time blamed the city. Living in a city, they believed, changes people for the worse. This charge echoed what some sociologists had long been saying. Louis Wirth, for example, contended in the 1930s that the conditions of the city produce a distinctive way of life, *urbanism,* and that the urban environment harms the people who live there. His analysis represented the ecological approach of the Chicago school. Since Wirth's time, some sociologists have supported his view. Richard Sennett (1991), for example, criticizes city life for insulating people from others who are racially, socially, or economically different. But many other sociologists have rejected Wirth's view. Some have argued that the city does not make much difference in people's lives, and others contend that the urban environment enriches people's lives by creating and strengthening subcultures. These three theories about the nature of urban life are called urban anomie theory, compositional theory, and subcultural theory.

Urban Anomie Theory Louis Wirth presented **urban anomie theory** in 1938 in his essay "Urbanism as a Way of Life." According to Wirth, the urban environment has three distinctive features: huge population size, high population density, and great social diversity. These characteristics, Wirth argued, have both a sociological and a psychological impact, producing social and personality disorders.

Wirth drew on the work of Ferdinand Tönnies (1855–1936) to analyze the sociological impact of the urban environment. As we discussed in Chapter 3 (Social Structure), Tönnies contrasted large industrial societies, which he called *Gesellschaft,* with small rural communities, which he called *Gemeinschaft.* In rural communities, according to Tönnies, people feel bound to each other and relate to each other in a personal way. In industrial societies, people are alienated from one another and their relationships are impersonal. In the country, people help their neighbors build a barn. In the city, they stand by passively while a neighbor is mugged, or even murdered.

Wirth essentially agreed with Tönnies' analysis and argued that the size, density, and diversity of the city create the anomie that marks industrial societies. In the city, people are physically close but socially distant. Every day they encounter strangers. They become accustomed to dealing with people only in terms of their roles. Their relationships tend to be impersonal. In other words, much of their lives are filled, not with primary relations with neighbors, who are also relatives and friends, but with secondary relations. Moreover, these people are separated by their diverse religious, ethnic, and racial backgrounds. It is difficult for people in the city to form friendships across these lines or to develop a moral consensus. Under these circumstances, people can no longer ensure social order by relying on informal controls such as tradition and gossip. Instead, they turn to formal controls, such as the police. Rather than talking to a young troublemaker's parents, they call the police. But formal controls, Wirth argued, are less effective than informal controls, so crimes and other forms of deviance are more frequent in the city than in the countryside.

The size, density, and diversity of the city, according to Wirth, also affect the psychological health of its residents. Drawing on the ideas of Georg Simmel (1858–1918), Wirth argued that because of these characteristics people in the city are bombarded with stimuli. Sights, sounds, and smells assault them virtually every minute of their waking hours. Wherever they turn, they must contend with the actions of others. They are jostled on the street and in the elevator. They wake to the sound of their neighbor's radio and fall asleep despite screaming sirens. Panhandlers, staggering inebriates, and soliloquizing mental patients are a common sight. To protect themselves from what Stanley Milgram (1970) called *psychic overload,* city people learn to shut out as many sensations as possible—sometimes even the call of a

neighbor for help. They deal with the unremitting assault of stimuli by becoming emotionally aloof from one another, concerned only with calculating their own interests. Despite this adaptation, the constant bombardment is still stressful. People become irritable, nervous, anxious. The result, Wirth claimed, is that mental disorders are more common in the city than in rural areas.

Compositional Theory   Wirth's description of the urban environment and its effects sounds reasonable. But is it accurate? Many empirical studies of cities have shown that his portrait amounts to an overdrawn stereotype. Some sociologists have therefore proposed a **compositional theory.** They argue that the urban environment does not fundamentally alter how people live their lives because most urbanites are enmeshed in a network of primary relations with people like themselves.

Perhaps the crucial difference between the urban anomie and compositional theorists concerns the influence of the urban environment on primary relations. Wirth argued that a city life is impersonal, that the city erodes primary relations. But compositional theorists contend that no matter how big, how dense, how diverse the city is, people continue to be deeply involved with a small circle of friends and relatives and others who have similar life-styles, backgrounds, or personalities. In this small social world, they find protection from the harsher, impersonal world of strangers. The streets of the city may seem cold and impersonal, but urban people's lives are not. As one exponent of compositional theory wrote:

> Social life is not a mass phenomenon. It occurs for the most part in small groups, within the family, within neighborhoods, within the church, formal and informal groups, and so on. The variables of number, density, and heterogeneity are, therefore, not crucial determinants of social life and personality (Lewis, 1965).

Many studies show that there is indeed a significant amount of social cohesion within cities, as compositional theorists contend. Herbert Gans (1982a) found that people in ethnic neighborhoods of large cities have a strong sense of community loyalty. He found the solidarity in these neighborhoods impressive enough to call them *ethnic villages.* When Scott Greer (1956) studied two Los Angeles neighborhoods, he discovered that the residents carried on their personal lives much as people in rural areas do,

People in ethnic neighborhoods in large cities have a strong sense of community loyalty. Sociologist Herbert Gans has found the solidarity in these neighborhoods impressive enough to call them "ethnic villages."

such as visiting relatives at least once a week. In their cross-cultural analysis of London, Los Angeles, and Sydney, Bartolomeo Palisi and Claire Canning (1983) also found that "people who live in more-urban settings visit friends as much or more frequently and share as much or more marriage companionship as people in less-urban environments." Even in slum neighborhoods, sociologists have found strong feelings of community solidarity.

It is true that rates of crime and mental illness are usually higher in urban than in rural areas. But compositional theorists argue that these disorders are not created by the urban environment itself. Instead, they result from the demographic makeup of the city—from the fact that the urban population includes a high percentage of those categories of people who are likely to suffer from social and mental disorders. Examples are young unmarried individuals, the lower classes, and minority groups.

Subcultural Theory   Claude Fischer (1982, 1984) has presented in his **subcultural theory** yet another view of city life. Like urban anomie theorists, he has argued that the urban ecology significantly affects city life, but, unlike them, he believes that the effect is positive. Instead of destroying social groups, the urban environment creates and strengthens them. These social groups are, in effect, *subcultures*—culturally distinctive groups, such as college students,

African-Americans, artists, corporate executives, and so forth. These subcultures are able to emerge because of the great population size, density, and diversity of the city, and the clash of subcultures within a city may strengthen each of them. When people come in contact with individuals from other subcultures, Fischer (1984) wrote, they "sometimes rub against one another only to recoil, with sparks flying. . . . People from one subculture often find people in another subculture threatening, offensive, or both. A common reaction is to embrace one's own social world all the more firmly, thus contributing to its further intensification."

Fischer has also argued that the urban experience brings some personal benefits to city dwellers. Urban housing, when compared to rural housing, generally has better plumbing facilities and is less crowded. Compared with people in the country, city people have access to far more facilities, services, and opportunities. As Harvey Cox (1966) noted, "Residents of a city of 10,000 may be limited to one or two theaters, while people who live in a city of a million can choose among perhaps 50 films on a given night. The same principle holds for restaurants, schools, and even in some measure for job opportunities or prospective marriage partners."

The three theories present partial truths about city life, and their conflicting judgments reflect the ambivalence most Americans feel toward the city. Migration has almost always been from country to city. But, as urban anomie theory suggests, residents of large cities are usually much less satisfied with their neighborhoods than are their counterparts in small towns (Lee and Guest, 1983). Why do people condemn the city but continue to live in it? Opportunity is the most important reason. The city provides a better chance than the farm or small town for jobs and economic advancement. As Fischer (1984) writes, "Most people see residence in cities as a necessary evil—necessary to achieve a desired standard of living, but not desirable in its own right."

All in all, however, city life is not as bad as popularly believed. People do lead a normal, pleasant life in the city, as compositional and subcultural theories suggest. Many urban people even enjoy what are often considered the city's negative features—large, busy, noisy, and impersonal downtown areas—which they find exciting (Reitzes, 1983). As urban sociologist William Whyte has found, city dwellers may complain about crowds, but they will mingle happily with others to watch a performer or buy food from a street vendor. They will even "chat in the middle of a teeming department store or stop to talk by a busy intersection, while avoiding quieter, emptier spaces nearby" (*Science Digest*, 1984). According to a survey, most New Yorkers consider their city an urban hellhole, with all its crime, poverty, homelessness, race riots, heavy taxes, exorbitant rents, filth, and official corruption. Nevertheless, they like living in the Big Apple very much. To them, "the pulse and pace and convenient, go-all-night action of the city, its rich ethnic and cultural stew, still outweigh its horrors" (Blundell, 1986). Indeed, many urbanites throughout the United States seem to consider the horrors a fair price for the freedom of expression they enjoy in the city. But many others find the price too high, choosing to leave the city for the suburb (Lapham, 1992).

THE SUBURBAN EXPERIENCE

About 2000 years ago, the poet Horace expressed feelings familiar to many Americans: "In Rome you long for the country; in the country—oh inconstant!—you praise the city to the stars." Many Americans have tried to solve this ancient dilemma by moving to the suburbs. They hope to leave noise, pollution, crowds, and crimes behind—but to keep their jobs in the city and their access to its stores and museums and nightlife. They hope in the suburbs to find the best of both worlds—the open space, quiet,

comfort, and wholesomeness of the country and the economic and recreational opportunities of the city.

Americans have expressed their preference for suburban life in many opinion polls and, more dramatically, by moving to the suburbs in droves. Today, more than half of all Americans live in the suburbs. Unlike the public at large, however, many intellectuals have seen little good in the suburbs. Particularly in the 1950s, it was common to criticize the suburbs as wastelands of bland, shallow conformity. Suburbanites, in this view, are a homogeneous lot, and their lives are ruled by the need to conform. They spend backbreaking hours trying to impress one another with their spic-and-span homes and perfect lawns, and their houses are all the same, inside and out. They seem very friendly, but form no deep friendships. They are bored, lonely, and depressed. The wives are domineering, the husbands absent, and the children spoiled. Behind the green lawns, barbecue pits, and two-car garages one finds marital friction, adultery, divorce, drunkenness, and mental breakdown (Gans, 1982b).

In the 1960s, these notions about suburbia were discredited as either gross exaggerations or totally unfounded. Suburbs are not all alike. There are predominantly white-collar suburbs, blue-collar suburbs, and various ethnic suburbs, much like the different neighborhoods within a central city. Even within a suburb, total homogeneity is very rare—there are almost always a few families of different ethnic, religious, or occupational backgrounds. Contrary to the old stereotypes, suburbanites are more likely than city residents to find their friends among their neighbors. Unwanted conformity to neighborhood pressures is rare. Suburbanites keep their houses and lawns clean and neat because of their social backgrounds and personal habits, not out of a slavish desire to conform (Berger, 1971).

Most Americans feel happier after they move out of the inner city into the suburbs. They are proud of their suburban homes, and they enjoy the open space that enables them to garden and their children to play safely. The move to the suburb tends to increase the time that parents spend with children and spouses spend with each other. Most suburbanites are less lonely and bored after their move. As we noted, however, many suburbs have become less "suburban" and more "urban." As they have grown, many suburbs have found themselves with problems once considered the special burden of cities. Especially in the larger, sprawling suburbs, the way of life has become much less centered on community, and much more on work, entrepreneurship, and the private life, with neighborhood groceries and gathering spots giving way to superstores and fast-food franchises. The potential for being lonely and friendless is therefore considerably greater (Morris, 1987). Still, suburban homes remain the overwhelming choice of most Americans. Moreover, those problems—suburban sprawl, traffic congestion, and lonely existence—may not haunt carefully planned suburbs of the future. Near Sacramento, California; Tacoma, Washington; and Tampa, Florida, preparations are under way to build new suburbs that resemble a small town. Single-family homes, rental apartments, townhouses, day-care centers, parks, and commercial buildings will be clustered around a town center, where residents can stroll, shop, relax, and socialize (Thomas, 1990).

QUESTIONS FOR DISCUSSION AND REVIEW
1. Why do the different theories about the nature of city life make such conflicting judgments?
2. How have the suburbs changed in recent years?

CHAPTER REVIEW

1. *Why is the modern census better than the earlier ones?* The modern census seeks to achieve its governmental, scientific, and commercial objectives by employing an enormous number of trained census takers and by making extra efforts to reach the typically hard-to-reach people, such as the homeless. *How fast are populations around the world growing?* Overall, global population is growing by about 1.7 percent a year, which means it should double in about 40 years. Most of this growth, however, is occurring in poor, nonindustrialized countries. *What elements determine a nation's growth rate?* It is the birth rate plus the net immigration rate minus the death rate.

2. *How can governments control population growth?* By encouraging voluntary family planning and setting up compulsory population programs. But family-planning programs work only if people prefer to have small families, and compulsory programs may meet stiff opposition. China, however, has reduced its birth rate through a basically compulsory program that combines rewards for small families and punishments for large families. *Does the U.S. government control population growth?* No, but it does give some aid to family-planning centers. Social and economic factors, not government action, keep birth rates low.

3. *Why are sociologists interested in ecology?* Humans, like other organisms, live within ecosystems, dependent on other organisms and on the physical environment. Thus, we are limited by two ecological principles. One, natural resources are finite. Two, if we alter one aspect of our environment, we end up changing others as well. *How is pollution related to consumption?* To consume we must produce, and both production and consumption create waste materials that must go somewhere. When our creation of wastes exceeds nature's capacity to recycle the material, pollution results. *What are the main methods of saving the environment?* Antipollution laws, conservation, development of more efficient, less polluting technology, and a slowing of traditional economic and population growth.

4. *What are the main stages in the history of cities?* Preindustrial, industrial, and metropolitan-megalopolitan. Preindustrial cities began developing about 5000 years ago. They were very small, with people living where they worked. The industrial city developed when the Industrial Revolution triggered urbanization. During the twentieth century the industrial city spread outward, and the city and its suburbs became interdependent, forming a metropolis. *Who usually lives in the city, and who lives in the suburbs?* Generally, more affluent people live in the suburbs. The poor and minority groups tend to concentrate in central cities. But typical urban residents also include immigrants, professionals, unmarried individuals, and childless couples. *Do the suburbs provide a refuge from urban problems?* To some extent, but many suburbs have become economic centers like cities. Thus, they have begun to suffer congestion, pollution, and crime. While most suburbs are pre-

dominantly white and prosperous, some are mostly nonwhite and poor. *How has urban America changed over the last 10 years?* Many western and southwestern cities have grown larger, while many northeastern, midwestern, and southern cities have lost population. Some large cities have been rescued from decline by substantial immigration from foreign countries. Most state capitals and college towns have grown larger even in the midst of their states' decline.

5. *Does the urban environment make city people different from other people?* Three prominent theories offer different answers. According to urban anomie theory, large population size, high population density, and great social diversity create a unique way of life. City life is filled with alienation, impersonal relations, and reliance on formal social control as well as psychic overload, emotional aloofness, and stress. In contrast, compositional theorists argue that city dwellers' social lives, centered in small groups of friends, relatives, and neighbors, are much like those of people outside the city. Subcultural theorists contend that the city enriches people's lives by offering them diverse opportunities and by promoting the development of subcultures. *What is the nature of suburban life?* A stereotype of suburbia holds that the suburbs are homogeneous places in which people are dominated by the need to conform and that social relations are shallow and short-lived. Research, however, does not support this stereotype, and most Americans who move from inner cities to suburbs are happier and less lonely after the move.

KEY TERMS

Biosphere A thin film of air, water, and soil surrounding the earth (p. 348).

Birth rate The number of births for every 1000 people in a given year (p. 341).

Census A periodic head count of the entire population of a country (p. 339).

Compositional theory The theory that city dwellers are as involved with small groups of friends, relatives, and neighbors as are noncity people (p. 358).

Death rate The number of deaths for every 1000 people in a given year (p. 342).

Demographic process An aspect of a population that is always changing, such as the birth rate, death rate, or net migration rate (p. 341).

Demography The scientific study of population (p. 338).

Ecology The study of the interrelationships among organisms and between organisms and their environment (p. 348).

Ecosystem A self-sufficient community of organisms depending for survival on one another and on the environment (p. 348).

Gentrification The movement of affluent people into urban neighborhoods, displacing poor and working-class residents (p. 355).

Infant mortality rate The number of deaths among infants less than 1 year old for every 1000 live births (p. 343).

Life expectancy The average number of years that a group of people can expect to live (p. 343).

Megalopolis A vast area in which many metropolises merge (p. 355).

Metropolis A large urban area including a city and its surrounding suburbs (p. 354).

Subcultural theory Fischer's theory that the city enriches people's lives by offering diverse opportunities and developing various subcultures (p. 359).

Urban ecology The study of the relationship between people and their urban environment (p. 357).

Urban anomie theory Wirth's theory that city people have a unique way of life, characterized by alienation, impersonal relations, and stress (p. 357).

Vital statistics Data about births, marriages, deaths, and migrations into and out of a country (p. 339.)

SUGGESTED READINGS

Commoner, Barry. 1990. *Making Peace with the Planet.* New York: Pantheon. Shows the importance of harmonizing our technologies with our environment to prevent pollution.

Firor, John, 1990. *The Changing Atmosphere: A Global Challenge.* New Haven, Conn.: Yale University Press. A clear analysis of various environmental problems, especially acid rain, global warming, and ozone holes.

Kelly, Barbara M. (ed.). 1989. *Suburbia Re-examined.* New York: Greenwood. A collection of articles presenting diverse views of suburban life.

Shelton, Beth Anne, et al. 1989. *Houston: Growth and Decline in a Sunbelt Boomtown.* Philadelphia: Temple University Press. An analysis of the social, political, and economic forces behind the eye-catching changes of an American metropolis.

Simon, Julian L. 1989. *The Economic Consequences of Immigration.* New York: Basil Blackwell. A data-packed analysis of how immigrants contribute to the U.S. economy in the late twentieth century.

15

COLLECTIVE
BEHAVIOR AND
SOCIAL CHANGE

MYTHS AND REALITIES

Myth: If you are watching a humorous movie in a theater, how often you laugh depends solely on how funny you think the movie is.

Reality: The size of the audience also has a significant impact. The larger the audience, the more frequent your laughter will be.

Myth: The violence in most riots is contagious—virtually all participants engage in the violence.

Reality: Not all participants in riots engage in violence. Many simply watch others commit the violence.

Myth: Don't listen to rumors, because they are always false.

Reality: Rumors are not necessarily false; they may turn out to be true. They are merely unverified stories spread from one person to another—unverified because people do not bother to check them against facts.

Myth: Discontent, if it is deep enough, can by itself bring about a social movement.

Reality: Discontent alone does not spark a movement; there also must be available resources for mobilization, such as strong organization, effective leadership, money, and media access.

Myth: Karl Marx's anticapitalist ideas are mere propaganda. It is no wonder that all of his predictions about capitalism have turned out to be false.

Reality: It is true that Marx's prediction of capitalism's demise has not come true, but he did accurately predict other outcomes of capitalism, such as the emergence of multinational corporations and the concentration of capital in a few giant companies.

Myth: With many years of development assistance from rich countries, poor countries must have increased their share in gross world product.

Reality: On the contrary, the 33 poorest countries that contain nearly half of the world's population have suffered a drop in their share of gross world product.

Myth: Modernization always threatens or destroys tradition.

Reality: Tradition and modernization can co-exist or even reinforce each other, as evidenced by the continuing traditional practices among India's Westernized elites or by the positive impact of group-oriented culture on modernization in Japan.

The long ideological conflict between the United States and the Soviet Union is finally over. But 42-year-old John Driscoll, like many Americans of his generation, still holds many memories of the Cold War. One of the things he most vividly remembers is the fear that came with the air raid drills at school. He and other students learned to crawl under their desks, practicing for the day when the Soviet hydrogen bombs were expected to fall. "It seems surreal now," he said recently, soon after the Soviet Union formally announced its end as a nation. "Every summer, when I heard heat lightning over the city and the sky would light up, I was convinced it was over. My whole childhood was built on the notion that the Soviets were a real threat." Today, Driscoll teaches economics and government at a high school just outside Washington, D.C. He is helping an organization to coordinate food shipments to Moscow, the capital of the "evil empire" that terrified him as a child. He found on a recent visit to Moscow that "these folks have absolutely no confidence in themselves" (Brinkley, 1992).

Like Driscoll, we are bound to witness great changes in our lives. The reason is that **social change**—the alteration of society over time—is nothing new. We can see it in the emergence of space travel, heart transplants, ubiquitous computers, omnipresent foreign cars, lower productivity growth, large shopping malls, the increased gap between rich and poor, widespread homelessness, and many other great events that have made our society different from what it was a decade or two ago. Where is all this social change taking us? Is there some general pattern behind the way societies change? Where can we expect future changes to come from, and can they be controlled?

To understand these issues better, we will look in this chapter at several theories of social change. We will also examine modernization—a particular social change that shaped many features of our society and is now reshaping many societies around the world. But let us first take a look at collective behavior, which can stimulate social change. **Collective behavior** is a relatively spontaneous, unorganized, and unpredictable social behavior. This contrasts with institutionalized behavior, which occurs in a well-organized, rather predictable way. Institutionalized behavior takes place frequently and routinely. Every weekday, masses of people hurry to work. On every campus, groups of students walk to classes during the week. Such predictable patterns of group action are basically governed by social norms. They are the bedrock of social order. Collective behavior, however, operates largely outside the confines of conventional norms.

Collective Behavior

Sociologists who study collective behavior face two special difficulties. First, collective behavior is relatively unstructured, spontaneous, and unpredictable, whereas scientific analysis seeks out predictable, regular patterns. Second, collective behavior includes a wide, varied range of social behavior. What, for example, do break dancing and a riot have in common? Is a social movement such as the pro-life, movement an example of collective behavior? Some sociologists say yes. Others say that social movements are a different, though related, category of human action.

Despite these difficulties, the sociological analysis of collective behavior has been fruitful. Although collective behavior is relatively unstructured compared with institutionalized behavior, it does have a structure, which sociologists have been able to illuminate. Even rumor, for example, involves some division of labor, as some people are its messengers while others are interpreters, skeptics, or merely an audience. The difference between institutionalized and collective behavior is not absolute. Instead, these are classifications based on the relative degree of control exercised by traditional norms. Thus, we can arrange social behaviors on a continuum like that shown in Figure 15.1. As we move from left to right in the figure, the behavior noted is increasingly subject to traditional norms. Thus, institutionalized behavior is at the far right of the continuum and collective behavior lies to the left.

Only the main forms of collective behavior are shown on the continuum. At the far left, for example, is panic, the least structured, most transitory, and rarest form of mass action. When people in a burning theater rush to the same exit, losing their capacity to cooperate and reducing their chance of escape, that is a panic. Next on the continuum are crowds, which are somewhat more structured than panics, more subject to the influence of social norms. As a result, members of a crowd can be persuaded to work toward a common goal. Moving further to the right on the continuum, we can see that social movements are even more structured than crowds. Their members

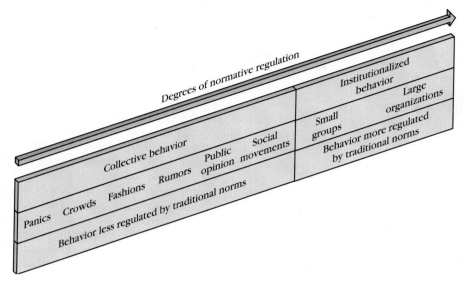

FIGURE 15.1 *A Continuum of Normative Regulation.* *There are two kinds of social behavior: collective and institutionalized. The difference is not absolute but relative to normative regulation. Collective behavior may further be divided into different forms, which vary from one another in the degree to which they are regulated by traditional norms.*

consciously work together to achieve a common objective.

PRECONDITIONS

Despite their diversity, all forms of collective behavior are basically an attempt to deal with a situation of strain, such as danger to life, threat of loss of money, or social injustice. The specific form such behavior takes depends largely on how the people involved define the problem. If they see it as a simple matter, they are likely to engage in such "clumsy" or "primitive" behavior as a panic or riot. If they believe the problem is complex enough to require an elaborate analysis, they are more prone to respond through a social movement. Thus, the more complex the situation of strain is believed to be, the more structured the collective behavior. Whatever the form of the collective behavior, six factors, according to Neil Smelser (1971), are necessary to produce the behavior. By itself, no one of these factors can generate collective behavior. Only the combination of all six factors, occurring in sequence, creates the conditions necessary for any kind of collective behavior to happen. Let us examine these six factors, fleshed out with some facts about the 1992 riot in South-Central Los Angeles.

1. *Structural conduciveness.* The social organization must permit collective action to occur. Individ-

uals by themselves cannot start a collective action. Some condition, such as living in the same neighborhood, must exist for them to assemble and communicate with each other before they can take part in collective behavior. In South-Central Los Angeles, the African-American residents who joined the riot were brought together by the media reporting that a nearly all-white jury had found four white policemen not guilty for savagely beating black motorist Rodney King.

2. *Social strain.* The strain may arise from a conflict between different groups, from the failure of a government to meet citizens' needs, or from the society's inability to solve a social problem. The strain that existed in the black community had stemmed from many cases of police brutality against blacks.

3. *The growth and spread of a generalized belief.* Participants in a collective action come to share some belief about the social strain. The rioters in South-Central Los Angeles shared the belief that the local police had often brutalized and mistreated blacks.

4. *A precipitating factor.* Some event brings the social strain to a high pitch and confirms the generalized belief about it. The King verdict clearly touched off the riot.

5. *The mobilization of participants for action.* Leaders emerge to move people to take a specific action. Some leaders in the Los Angeles riot urged people on the street to follow them, saying something

like "Come with us. Let's burn." Other leaders set an example for others by initiating the burning or looting of stores.

6. *Inadequate social control.* Agents of control such as the police fail to prevent the collective action. The Los Angeles police department was slow to respond to the riot. The police were virtually absent in the early hours of rioting, which led many looters to smash storefronts and burn buildings with impunity.

If we look at many other riots, such as those in the Liberty City section of Miami in 1980 and in the Overtown section in 1982, we can find a similar sequence of events (Porter and Dunn, 1984). In most riots, however, the violence is not "mutually inclusive"—not all participants engage in violence. Many simply watch (McPhail and Wohlstein, 1983).

PANICS

On a December afternoon in 1903, a fire broke out in Chicago's Iroquois Theater. According to an eyewitness,

> Somebody had of course yelled "Fire!" . . . The horror in the auditorium was beyond all description. . . . The fire-escape ladders could not accommodate the crowd, and many fell or jumped to death on the pavement below. Some were not killed only because they landed on the cushion of bodies of those who had gone before. But it was inside the house that the greatest loss of life occurred, especially on the stairways. Here most of the dead were trampled or smothered, though many jumped or fell to the floor. In places on the stairways, particularly where a turn caused a jam, bodies were piled seven or eight feet deep. . . . An occasional living person was found in the heap, but most of these were terribly injured. The heel prints on the dead faces mutely testified to the cruel fact that human animals stricken by terror are as mad and ruthless as stampeding cattle. Many bodies had the clothes torn from them, and some had the flesh trodden from their bones (Schultz, 1964).

The theater did not burn down. Firefighters arrived quickly after the alarm and extinguished the flames so promptly that no more than the seats' upholstery was burned. But 602 people died and many more were injured. Panic, not the fire itself, largely accounted for the tragedy. Similarly, on a July morning in 1990 in the holy city of Mecca, Saudi Arabia, when the lights went out accidentally in a 600-yard-long

In 1984, the Indian Army attacked the Sikh's holiest Golden Temple, shown here. The conflict that existed between the Hindu majority and the Sikh minority was one of the preconditions that led to the anti-Sikh riots, which resulted in the destruction of many Sikh homes and lives as well as Hindu lives.

tunnel through which thousands of Muslim pilgrims were walking, panic triggered a stampede, killing 1426 people.

The people in the Iroquois Theater and the tunnel in Mecca behaved as people often do when faced with unexpected threats such as fires, earthquakes, floods, and other disasters: they exhibited panic behavior. A **panic** is a type of collective behavior characterized by a maladaptive, fruitless response to a serious threat. That response generally involves flight, but it is a special kind of flight. In many situations, flight is a rational, adaptive response: it is perfectly sensible to flee a burning house or an oncoming car. In these cases, flight is the only appropriate way of achieving a goal—successful escape from danger. In panic behavior, however, the flight is irrational and uncooperative. It follows a loss of self-control, and it increases, rather than reduces, danger to oneself and others. If people in a burning theater panic, they stampede each other, rather than filing out in an orderly way, and produce the kind of unnecessary loss of life that occurred in the Iroquois Theater.

Preconditions When five knife-wielding hijackers took over a Chinese airplane bound for Shanghai in 1982, the passengers did not panic. Instead, they cooperated and, with mop handles, soda bottles, and other objects, overpowered the hijackers. About 20 years ago, during a performance of *Long Day's Journey into Night* in Boston, word spread through the audience that there was a fire. But the audience did not stampede to the exits. One of the actors "stepped to the footlights and calmly said, "Please be seated, ladies and gentlemen, nothing serious has happened. Just a little accident with a cigarette. . . . The fire is out now and if you will sit down again we can resume.' The audience laughed and sat down." In this case, as in the Iroquois fire, the audience had an impulse to flee for their lives. But, because the crisis had been defused, a contradictory impulse, to follow the norms of polite society and remain calm and quiet, won out.

In short, the existence of a crowd and a threat does not ensure that people will panic. There are several social-psychological preconditions for the development of a panic. First, there must be a *perception* that a crisis exists. Second, there must be *intense fear* of the perceived danger. This fear is typically compounded by a feeling of *possible* entrapment. If people believed they were *certainly* trapped, as in the case of prisoners who are about to be executed by a firing squad, they would give in to calm resigna-

tion rather than wild panic. Third, there must be some *panic-prone individuals*. Typically, they are very self-centered persons whose frantic desire to save themselves makes them oblivious to the fate of others and to the self-destructive consequences of their panic. Fourth, there must be *mutual emotional facilitation*. The people in the crowd must spread and enhance each other's terror. Finally, there must be a *lack of cooperation* among people. Cooperation typically breaks down in a panic because no norms exist to tell people how to behave appropriately in an unusual, unanticipated situation. But most crowds are made up of many small, primary groups of relatives or friends rather than strangers. Constrained by the bonds of these primary groups, members of crowds usually do not panic and stampede each other to death (Schultz, 1964; Johnson, 1987).

Mass Hysteria Panic sometimes takes the form of **mass hysteria,** in which numerous people engage in a frenzied activity without bothering to check the source of their anxiety. A classic case occurred in 1938, when the play *War of the Worlds* was broadcast on the radio. Many people thought that they were hearing a news report. While listening to music on the radio, they suddenly heard an announcement that Martians had invaded the earth:

Ladies and gentlemen, I have a grave announcement to make. Incredible as it may seem, both the observations of science and the evidence of our eyes lead to the inescapable assumption that those strange beings who landed in the New Jersey farmlands tonight are the vanguard of an invading army from the planet Mars. The battle which took place tonight . . . has ended in one of the most startling defeats ever suffered by an army in modern times; seven thousand men armed with rifles and machine guns pitted against a single fighting machine of the invaders from Mars. One hundred and twenty known survivors. The rest strewn over the battle area . . . and trampled to death under the metal feet of the monster, or burned to cinders by its heat ray (Cantril, 1982).

Long before the broadcast ended, at least a million of the 6 million listeners were swept away by panic. Many prayed, cried, or fled, frantic to escape death from the Martians. Some hid in cellars. Young men tried to rescue girlfriends. Parents woke their sleeping children. People telephoned friends to share the bad news or to say good-bye. Many called hospitals for ambulances, and others tried to summon police cars.

Why did the mass hysteria occur? As much as 42 percent of the audience tuned in to the program late and thus never heard the opening explanation that the broadcast was only a play. Moreover, the play was presented as a series of special news bulletins, and they were very believable. The actors were very convincing as news announcers, scientific and military experts, and witnesses to the Martian invasion. In addition, economic crisis and political turmoil abroad had created a great deal of insecurity and had accustomed Americans to bad news. Many were therefore ready to believe horrifying reports.

But not everyone who tuned in late to the broadcast panicked. Hadley Cantril directed a study to find out who panicked, who didn't, and why. Those who did not were found to have what Cantril called *critical ability.* Some of these people found the broadcast simply too fantastic to believe. As one of them reported, "I heard the announcer say that he saw a Martian standing in the middle of Times Square and he was as tall as a skyscraper. *That's all I had to hear*—just the word Martian was enough even without the fantastic and incredible description." Others with critical ability had sufficient specific knowledge to recognize the broadcast as a play. They were familiar with Orson Welles's story or recognized that he was acting the role of Professor Pierson. Still others tried to check the accuracy of the broadcast by looking up newspaper listings of radio schedules and programs. These people, on the whole, had more years of education than those who did panic. The less educated, aside from lacking critical ability, were found to have a feeling of personal inadequacy and emotional insecurity (Cantril, 1982).

CROWDS

A **crowd** is a collection of people temporarily doing something while in proximity to one another. They may be gathered on a street corner, watching a fire. They may be in a theater, watching an opera. They may be on a street, throwing rocks at police. Nearly all crowds share a few characteristics. One is *uncertainty:* the participants do not share clear expectations about how to behave or about the outcome of their collective behavior. Another element common to most crowds is a *sense of urgency.* The people in the crowd feel that something must be done right

A crowd is a collection of people temporarily doing something while in proximity to one another. One of the different kinds of crowds, the expressive crowd is one whose members plunge themselves into some unrestrained activity, such as a rock concert, releasing emotions and tensions.

away to solve a common problem. The third characteristic of crowds is the *communication* of mood, attitude, and idea among the members, which pressures them to conform. Crowds are also marked by *heightened suggestibility.* Those in the crowd tend to respond uncritically to the suggestions of others and to go along impulsively with their actions. Finally, crowds are characterized by *permissiveness,* by freedom from the constraint of conventional norms. Thus, people tend to express feelings and take actions that under ordinary circumstances they would suppress (Turner and Killian, 1987).

Beyond these similarities among crowds, there are significant differences. Sociologist Herbert Blumer (1978) has classified crowds into four types: casual, conventional, acting, and expressive. The *casual crowd* is the type with the shortest existence and loosest organization. It emerges spontaneously. "Its members," wrote Blumer, "come and go, giving but temporary attention to the object which has awakened the interest of the crowd, and entering into only feeble association with one another." People collecting at a street corner to watch a burning building, a traffic accident, or a street musician constitute a casual crowd. The *conventional crowd,* unlike the casual crowd, occurs in a planned, regularized manner. Examples include the audience in a theater and the spectators at a football game. Whereas the conventional crowd assembles to observe some activity, the *acting crowd* is involved in an activity that enables its members to focus their energy on one particular goal. Rioters, a lynch mob, and a revolutionary crowd are all acting crowds. The *expressive crowd* has no goal. Its members plunge themselves into some unrestrained activity, releasing emotions and tensions. Examples include people at a rock concert or at a religious revival.

Some acting and expressive crowds are irrational or destructive. Consider American lynch mobs. Before 1900 many thousands of whites and blacks were lynched. The number of lynchings dropped during this century, but still, between 1900 and 1950 there were more than 3000 victims, nearly all of them black. The alleged crimes of the black victims were often trivial, such as trying to act like a white man, making boastful remarks, winking at a white man's wife, or being too ambitious. For these "crimes" the blacks were hanged, shot, burned to death, or mutilated (Raper, 1970).

Why did the members of lynch mobs behave so irrationally and destructively? In particular, why did otherwise civilized whites act like beasts as members of a lynch mob? There are two prominent theories that try to explain this kind of crowd behavior. One, based on the classic work of Gustave Le Bon, describes a psychology unique to crowds. A second theory focuses on the social interactions within crowds.

Social Contagion and the Collective Mind The French social psychologist Gustave Le Bon proposed his theory of crowds in 1896. According to Le Bon, a crowd is homogeneous in thought and action. All the people in a crowd think, feel, and act alike. Regardless of who the individuals are, "however like or unlike be their mode of life, their occupations, their character, or their intelligence, the fact that they have been transformed into a crowd puts them in possession of a sort of collective mind" (Le Bon, 1976). If we assume that, as Le Bon claimed, a crowd does share a "collective mind," then we are left with two questions: what is this collective mind like, and how does it come about?

According to Le Bon, the collective mind of crowds is emotional and irrational. It represents the human personality stripped bare of all civilizing restraints. Beneath those restraints, Le Bon believed, hides a barbarian. All the members of a crowd bring to the situation this hiding barbarian with its primitive instincts. Normally, they suppress these instincts, wearing the mask of civilized behavior. But a crowd provides them with a different sort of mask: the large numbers of people give individuals a cloak of anonymity that weakens their restraining sense of responsibility and releases primitive emotions.

Individuals give up their individuality and are transformed into part of this collective mind, in Le Bon's view, as a result of **social contagion**—the spreading of a certain emotion and action from one member of the crowd to another. Many sociologists have identified processes that can produce this contagion. One is *imitation,* the tendency of an individual to imitate another person in a crowd, especially a leader. Another is *suggestibility,* the psychological readiness to be influenced by the images, feelings, and actions of others. Still another process that produces contagion is called a *circular reaction:* the members of a crowd intensify their emotional excitement further and further by stimulating one another's feelings. An interested crowd is likely to applaud heated rhetoric, for example, which is likely to encourage the speaker to yet more inflamed talk, which stimulates the crowd's emotions further (Turner and Killian, 1987). Research has further uncovered factors that can facilitate these processes of contagion. Among these factors are crowd size and noise. When people are viewing a humorous movie in a theater, the larger the audience, the more frequent the laughter. If a person coughs in a room full of people, others are more likely to cough than if there were only a few people around. In watching a videotaped arm-wrestling match, the subjects' tendency to imitate the wrestlers increases with higher levels of audience noise (Levy and Fenley, 1979; Pennebaker, 1980; Markovsky and Berger, 1983).

The Emergent-Norm Theory To most sociologists today, Le Bon's notion of a collective mind is valid only as a loose metaphor for what happens in crowds. Members of a crowd may appear homogeneous. They may seem to have given up their individuality and become absorbed into a "collective mind." But beneath these appearances, the members of a crowd are basically just individuals engaged in a particular kind of interaction. Whereas Le Bon set the behavior of crowds apart from normal social interaction as a sort of bizarre regression to almost subhuman behavior, other sociologists have found that routine and orderly behavior prevails in most crowds (McPhail and Wohlstein, 1983).

American sociologists Ralph Turner and Lewis Killian (1987), for example, accept Le Bon's fundamental idea that a crowd appears to act as a homogeneous group, but they have argued that Le Bon exaggerated its homogeneity. In a lynch mob, for example, not all the members think or act in the same way. Some individuals storm the jail, others drag out the prisoner, others bring ropes, others hang the victim, and some just stand by and watch. Even those engaged in the same act may have different feelings, attitudes, or beliefs, and they participate because of diverse motives. How, then, does the apparent unanimity among the participants develop?

Turner and Killian proposed the **emergent-norm theory** to answer this question. The crowd finds itself in an unconventional situation, in which existing norms provide inadequate guidelines. Eventually, through social interaction, members develop a new norm appropriate for the situation. This norm encourages the participants to behave in a certain way, such as praying loudly at a religious revival meeting. Because of the norm, people feel pressed to conform with the crowd's outward behavior, even if they disagree with the action. The result, according to Turner and Killian, is the appearance of unanimity, which may be more illusion than reality. Indeed, many studies have found the "illusion of unanimity" in most crowds (McPhail and Wohlstein, 1983).

FASHIONS

Compared with crowds, fashions are more subject to traditional norms. Practically all aspects of human life—clothes, hairstyles, architecture, philosophy, and the arts—are influenced by fashions. A **fashion** is a great though brief enthusiasm among a relatively large number of people for a particular innovation. Because their novelty wears off quickly, fashions are very short-lived. Most are related to clothes, but as long as there is something new about any artifact that strikes many people's fancy, it can become a fashion.

Why do fashions occur in the first place? One reason is that some cultures, like ours, value change: what is new is good. Thus, in many modern societies clothing styles change yearly, while people in traditional societies may wear the same style of clothing for many generations. Many industries promote quick changes in fashions to increase their sales. Although a new style occasionally originates from lower-status groups, as blue jeans did, most fashions trickle down from the top. Upper-class people adopt some style or artifact as a badge of their status, but they cannot monopolize most status symbols for long. The style is adopted by the middle class, maybe copied and modified for use by lower-status groups, providing people with the prestige of possessing a high-status symbol. By trickling down, however, the symbol eventually loses its prestige. The upper class adopts a new style, until it, too, "trickles down" and must be replaced by another (Turner and Killian, 1987).

Fads and **crazes** are similar to fashions, but they occur less predictably, have an even shorter life, and are less socially respectable. Examples of fads include hula hoops, goldfish-swallowing, telephone booth stuffing, streaking, pet rocks, yo-yos, and Air Jordans. (If these things mean nothing to you, that is

Most fashions, which are a great but brief enthusiasm among a large number of people for a particular innovation, are related to clothes. But any artifact that strikes people's fancy can become a fashion.

testimony to how fast the magic of fads can fade.) Fads are basically trivial, but they can be a source of status to some people. Nowadays, for example, carrying a beeper is a status symbol for teenagers in New York City, and wearing a Slap Wrap around the wrist makes preteens everywhere feel like a "cool kid" (Rabinovitz, 1991). Certain individuals get a sense of being part of an in-group by playing the game Trivial Pursuit or by wearing ripped jeans. They also like being part of something new, creative, or avant-garde, as shown by the current worldwide popularity of rap. Teenagers from France and Russia to Japan and Brazil not only get excited dancing to the fierce and proud music of the American black underclass., they also take to wearing rap-inspired outfits, such as baggy pants, pricey sneakers, hooded sweatshirts, and flashy jewelry (Cocks, 1992). Fads are basically less bizarre and less harmful than crazes, which are a kind of contagious folly with serious consequences. Usually crazes are economic in nature, including a *boom,* in which many people frantically try to buy something of madly exaggerated value, and a *bust,* in which many frantically try to sell a worthless thing.

The most famous craze is probably the tulip mania that swept Holland in 1634. For some unknown reason, the Dutch developed a passion for tulips. Eventually, one bulb would cost as much as a large house. Soon the Dutch were more interested in making a fortune out of tulips than in growing them. People bought bulbs only to sell them for a huge profit. The Dutch even expected to become wealthy by exporting bulbs to other countries, but to their great surprise, they discovered that other people found tulip bulbs less precious. They were astonished when people who returned from long trips abroad did not appreciate the tulip bulbs at all. It was widely known that a sailor mistook a valuable bulb for an onion and ate it with his herring. Eventually, people began to realize that the price of tulips could not keep rising forever. Thus, the boom was broken, and the price of tulips fell sharply, bankrupting thousands.

Like an epidemic disease, a fashion, fad, or craze usually goes through five phases. First, during the latent phase, the new idea exists in the minds of a few but shows little sign of spreading. Then the idea spreads rapidly. In the third phase, the idea reaches a peak and begins to go downhill. Then, its newness wearing thin, resistance to it develops, rather like immunity to an infectious disease. The final phase, quiescence, is much like the first phase. Most people no longer share the enthusiasm, but it is embedded in the lives of a few. The tulip craze, for example, is long gone, but the Dutch are still known for their fine tulips. Similarly, such American toy fads and crazes as Slinky, Silly Putty, Barbie dolls, and Pac-Man have died down, but some people still buy or play with them (Penrose, 1981; Simon, 1981).

RUMOR

A **rumor** is an unverified story that is spread from one person to another. As the story is circulating, each person distorts the account by dropping some items and adding his or her own interpretation. But a rumor is not necessarily false. It may turn out to be true. It is unverified *not* because it is necessarily a distortion but because people do not bother to check it against facts.

Indeed, we all act every day on the basis of unverified reports. Sociologists therefore view rumors as a normal form of communication. Tamotsu Shibutani (1966), for example, wrote that rumor is "a communication pattern that develops when people who are involved together in a situation in which something out of the ordinary has happened pool their intellectual resources in an effort to orient themselves." Rumor, then, is a process in which many individuals try together to construct a definition of an ambiguous situation.

Why do rumors emerge? According to Shibutani, a rumor is likely to develop and circulate if people's demand for news about an ambiguous situation is not met by institutionalized channels of communication, such as newspapers, government announcements, and television and radio newscasts. The more ambiguous a situation, the greater the chance for a rumor to develop. Thus, rumor is much more a part of interpersonal communications in police states and totalitarian societies. In such countries, people do not trust the media because the government controls them. Anxiety also plays a significant role. Not long ago, widespread anxiety over economic problems also made the United States ripe for the rumor mill. Americans who had lost or were afraid of losing their jobs, according to social psychologist Fredrick Koenig (1982), were especially likely to believe or pass on damaging rumors about big companies. Seeing a corporate giant in trouble seemed to make them feel better. All this provided fertile ground for the growth of the rumor in 1978 that McDonald's added earthworms to its hamburgers. In 1982 another rumor had it that Procter & Gamble's logo, showing

13 stars and a man in the moon, was a sign of devil worship. In 1991 it was rumored that Liz Claiborne, the clothing company, gave 30 percent of its profits to the Church of Satan. In that same year, Tropical Fantasy—a soft drink marketed to minorities in Northeastern cities, became the target of a rumor that the Ku Klux Klan owned the company and that they added to the drink an ingredient that would make black men sterile (Goleman, 1991). Although all these rumors were false, they spread like a prairie fire.

PUBLIC OPINION

When we talk about "the public," we usually mean the population at large. In sociology, however, **public** also has a different, more limited meaning. It is a dispersed collection of people who share some interest or concern, such as an interest in environmental issues, or in civil rights, or in outlawing pornography. Thus, there are a great many publics within the population at large.

Whenever a public comes into being, it forms an opinion. **Public opinion** is the collection of ideas and attitudes shared by the members of a particular public. As measured by polls and surveys, public opinion often seems fickle, changing easily even while values appear constant. This fickleness may reflect the difference between private and public opinion. "What a person says only to his wife, himself, or in his sleep," wrote Turner and Killian (1987), "constitutes his private opinion. What he will say to a stranger is public opinion." In private, many people will express doubts about an opinion. In public, they might state an opinion shared by others.

Most pollsters and researchers assume that the public consists of individuals only. To them, the public does not include groups, organizations, societies, or any other collectivity because they do not really have opinions—only individual members in a group do. Thus, in public opinion polling only individuals are interviewed. The summation of individual opinions is then taken to represent the opinion of the group. But sociologists Zvi Namenwirth, Randi Miller, and Robert Weber (1981) argued that it is unrealistic for pollsters to exclude organizations such as chambers of commerce, labor unions, corporations, and churches. Through their spokespersons, organizations may express opinions that differ from those of their individual members. Even if the opinions of organizations and individuals are the same, the social

consequences are not, because the opinion of organizations generally counts more. Being more influential or having more resources, "organizations are better able to translate opinions into effective action." However, organizations and individuals are equally subject to change or manipulation by the mass media. Newspapers, magazines, movies, television, and radio can reach millions of Americans very rapidly, and there is no doubt that they have some influence on public opinion. Let us take a close look at the nature and extent of that influence.

Propaganda For the most part, the American media share one overriding goal: to make a profit. But they are also the main instruments for manipulating public opinion. Politicians want to win our hearts and minds, and businesses want to win our dollars. Both use the media to try to gain mass support by manipulating public opinion. In other words, they generate **propaganda**—communication tailored to influence opinion. Propaganda may be true or false. What sets it apart from other communications is the intent to change opinion. Alfred and Elizabeth Lee (1979) identified seven methods that are frequently used to sway public opinion:

1. *Name calling,* or giving something a very negative label. This method is designed to make the audience reject an idea or person or product without analysis. If a candidate is "ultraconservative," "ultraliberal," "flaky," or a "big spender," why bother to consider his or her qualifications seriously? If abortion is "murder," who can support its legalization?

2. *Glittering generality,* which is the opposite of name calling. An idea or product is associated with a very general, ambiguous, but extremely popular concept or belief. If a war represents the defense of democracy and freedom, who can oppose it?

3. *Transfer,* or associating an idea or product with something else that is widely respected or admired. Beautiful, scantily clad actresses sell cars and mattresses on television commercials. Ed McMahon became a celebrity just by being associated with Johnny Carson on the old *Tonight* show. Presidents give television speeches with the American flag prominently displayed behind them.

4. *Testimonial,* or presenting a respected or at least famous person to endorse or oppose some idea or product. Top athletes tell us to use a certain shampoo or shaving cream. Famous politicians travel to towns they never heard of to urge people to vote for obscure candidates.

5. *Plain folks,* or identifying the propagandist with the average person. Former President Carter made sure people saw him playing softball and going fishing—doing what ordinary Americans do. He frequently presented himself as a mere peanut farmer, not much different from average-income Americans, even though he was a wealthy man.

6. *Card stacking,* in which one fact or falsehood supporting a point of view is piled on top of another. Commercials do not tell us both the strengths and the weaknesses of a product or a candidate. Instead, we read that a brand-new car, for example, is "Quiet. Smooth riding. Full size. With comfort and luxury for six passengers. . . . Rich velour fabrics, thick carpeting and warm woodtones. . . . A truly fine automobile."

7. *Bandwagon,* creating the impression that everyone is using a product or supporting an idea or person. Soft-drink companies have often used commercials in which a horde of young, happy people are shown drinking their product and singing its praises. Political candidates are usually quick to announce favorable poll results. Thus, the propagandist creates pressure to conform to a real or illusory norm.

Influence of the Media Despite such manipulations, the effect of propaganda, like the effect of any communication, is limited. Because we are not computers to be programmed or clay to be molded, neither propagandists nor the media can simply insert opinions into our heads or erase previously held beliefs.

In general, at least three factors limit the influence of the American media on public opinion (Turner and Killian, 1987). First, a multitude of independent organizations make up what we call the American media, and they present a variety of viewpoints. People select the media they will pay attention to, and thus the media that have the chance to influence them. Second, because most of the media are interested in making a profit, not in convincing the public, they often present what listeners or readers want to see or hear. They try to gauge and match public opinion, not mold it. Third, the effects of the media are often indirect because communication frequently occurs, not in only one step from the media to an individual, but through what is called the *two-step flow* of influence. A neighbor hears an analysis of an issue on television, and we hear about it from that neighbor. Often people are most influenced by communication received, not directly from the

Although there are limitations to the influence of the American media on public opinion, it does have the power to influence opinion. This power comes largely from the media's role as gatekeepers—determining what information will be passed on to large numbers of Americans.

media, but from **opinion leaders,** individuals whose opinions they respect.

The media do influence public opinion. Their power comes largely from their role as gatekeepers—determining what information will be passed on to large numbers of Americans. We can identify at least five ways in which the media affect opinion (Turner and Killian, 1987). First, they *authenticate* information, making it more credible to the audience. A news item reported in the mass media often seems more believable than one passed by word of mouth. Second, the media *validate* private opinions, preferences, and values. If a famous commentator offers a view similar to our own, we are likely to feel more confident of our own opinion. Third, the media *legitimize* unconventional viewpoints. The wildest idea may eventually sound reasonable, or at least worth considering, if we read it repeatedly on the editorial pages of newspapers or hear it from the mouths of 50-year-old men in pin-striped suits on the evening news. Fourth, the mass media *concretize* free-floating anxieties and ill-defined preferences. By supplying such labels as "the crime wave," "population explosion," and "pro-life," the media in effect create a world of objects against which feelings can be specifically expressed. Fifth, the mass media help *establish a hierarchy* of importance and prestige among persons, objects, and opinions. If the national media never interview the senators from your state, the public is not likely to consider them important, even if they are very influential among their colleagues in the Senate.

While the media can influence public opinion in these five ways, all people who appear on television do not have the same impact on the audience. News commentators, experts, and popular presidents influence public opinion much more strongly than do unpopular presidents and various interest groups, such as those representing big business, organized labor, and the poor. Those who have a greater influence on public opinion share a higher level of credibility (Page et al., 1987).

SOCIAL MOVEMENTS

A hundred years ago, American women could not vote. Fifty years ago, paid vacations for workers were almost unheard of. A little more than two decades ago, George Wallace took office as governor of Alabama, declaring "segregation now, segregation tomorrow, segregation forever." These features of American society were transformed through **social movements,** conscious efforts to bring about or prevent change.

Compared with the forms of collective behavior we have so far discussed, social movements are far more purposive. A bank run or stock market crash, for example, unfolds without plan, but a social movement develops as a result of purposeful effort. Social movements are also far more structured than other forms of collective behavior, even if they are not centrally coordinated. A lynch mob may develop a division of labor, but it is an informal division with a very short life. In contrast, although the civil rights movement does not have one headquarters or one set of officers, it does have within it numerous organizations, recognized leaders, and sets of roles and statuses. Finally, a social movement is also more enduring

than other forms of collective behavior. A crowd may stay together for a few hours, but a movement may endure for years. These characteristics give social movements the potential to build a membership in the thousands or even millions.

Types Most social movements aim to change society, but they seek varying degrees of change. If we classify them by their aims, we find four types of social movements.

1. *Revolutionary movements* seek total, radical change in society. Their goal is to overthrow the existing form of government and replace it with a new one. Revolutionary movements typically resort to violence or some other illegal action. Examples include the American revolution, the Bolshevik revolution in Russia, the Chinese Communist revolution, and the Castro-led revolution in Cuba.

2. *Reform movements* seek only a partial change in society. They support the existing social system as a whole and want to preserve it, but they aim to improve it by removing its blemishes, typically through legal methods. Each reform movement usually focuses on just one issue. The civil rights movement seeks to rid society of racial discrimination. The women's movement seeks to eliminate gender inequality. The ecology movement seeks to put a stop to environmental pollution.

3. *Resistance movements* cherish an existing system and try to reverse trends that threaten to change that system. The Ku Klux Klan and the American Nazi party, for example, try to stop racial integration. The Moral Majority aims to stop changes in family life and gender roles. In Muslim countries, the Islamic revolution seeks to protect the traditional Islamic ways of life against Western influences.

4. *Expressive movements* seek to change the individual, not society. Many are religious, aimed at converting individuals to a particular faith. These movements enable their members to express their sense of guilt, their joy of redemption, and their devotion to their religion. Examples include the Moonies, Hare Krishnas, and other sects. Sometimes, an expressive movement can turn into a revolutionary movement, as shown by the Islamic revolution in Iran. Expressive movements may also be secular, like the human potential movement of the 1970s. This movement included numerous groups advocating various therapies, from the outrageous to the commonplace, that promised to clear the path to self-fulfillment.

The resistance movement is a type of social movement that cherishes an existing system and tries to reverse trends that threaten to change that system. Pro-life groups have tried to resist the legalization of abortion.

Causes There are many things to do in this world. You can spend your time making money, or fishing, or whatever. Why would people instead spend their time pushing a social movement? Eric Hoffer (1966) argued that those who participate in social movements are frustrated and troubled. They use social movements as a diversion, enabling them to hide from themselves their personal problems, such as a sense of inadequacy and inferiority. Furthermore, through such a social movement they can gain a sense of being noble and magnanimous, as they fight a good cause beyond their own self-interest. A social movement can also provide a sense of belonging and a way of identifying oneself. According to Hoffer, members are therefore strongly dedicated to their movement's objective, following their leaders blindly as "true believers."

There are, however, some holes in Hoffer's psychological theory. For one thing, he in effect blames movement participants rather than society for their frustration. The fact is that it is often the unpleasant social conditions, such as social injustice or racial discrimination, that have brought about the discontent in the first place, as is obvious in the case of the civil rights movement. Another problem with Hoffer's view is that, although frustration may motivate people to join a social movement, it cannot explain why some participate in the *pro*-abortion movement,

while others take part in the *anti*-abortion movement.

Whatever the role of psychological variables in determining movement participation, we cannot explain this social phenomenon unless we also look at the role of social variables. As we have observed in the discussion of revolutions (see Chapter 12: Politics and the Economy), deprivation alone cannot explain people's participation in these movements. If it could, most of the world would be constantly at the barricades, seeking change. Instead, we can say that social movements are unlikely to arise unless social conditions produce frustration among masses of people. This appears to be the first condition necessary for the emergence of a movement. According to the traditional sociological perspective, social movements develop when discontented individuals identify a common frustration, work out a plan to change the offending conditions, and band together to carry out that plan (Turner and Killian, 1987).

Proponents of contemporary **resource mobilization theory,** however, argue that what sparks a movement is not discontent but the availability of resources for mobilization, such as strong organization, effective leadership, money, and media access. But these theorists have in turn been criticized for virtually ignoring the place of discontent in social movements. In fact, both resource mobilization and discontent can be found in practically all movements. But the importance of each varies from one movement to another. As Harold Kerbo (1982) notes, discontent plays a larger role in "crisis movements" involving blacks, the unemployed, or poor people, while resource mobilization figures more in "affluence movements," such as environmental movements, which involve mostly affluent Americans.

QUESTIONS FOR DISCUSSION AND REVIEW

1. What makes collective behavior different from institutionalized behavior, and why is it difficult to study its forms?
2. According to Smelser, what are the six factors that together can generate collective behavior?
3. How do panics differ from other types of crowd behavior, and what preconditions must exist before they occur?
4. Why do sociologists regard fashions and rumors as collective behavior?
5. How do people use propaganda and the media to mold public opinion?
6. How do sociologists define and categorize social movements and distinguish them from other types of collective behavior?

Social Change

Modern sociology was born in a period of great social tumult, and its founding fathers developed many of their ideas as a result of trying to understand the vast social changes of their time. Anthropologists and historians, too, were intrigued by the question of how societies change. To some, human society seemed like a one-way train, headed toward eventual Utopia. To others, it was like a human being, passing inevitably from innocent childhood to decrepit old age. To yet others, it was rather like an ocean tide, rising and falling and then rising again. No one theory has emerged that can adequately account for all social change. We look here at four views that have had great influence on sociology: the evolutionary, cyclical, equilibrium, and conflict theories.

EVOLUTIONARY THEORY

Human horizons expanded greatly during the nineteenth century, as Europeans "discovered" and studied peoples of other lands and of the distant past.

The early anthropologists believed that these peoples offered a portrait of their own ancestors. Most agreed that all societies progressed, or evolved, through three stages of development: savagery, barbarism, and civilization. Western societies, of course, were deemed civilized. All other peoples were considered savages or barbarians.

This was the origin of **evolutionary theory.** One of its early exponents was Herbert Spencer (1820–1903). He believed that all societies followed uniform, natural laws of evolution. These laws decreed "survival of the fittest": those aspects of society that worked well would survive; those that did not would die out. Thus, over time societies would naturally and inevitably improve.

This early version of evolutionary theory received a boost from its similarities to Darwin's theory of biological evolution. It was also buttressed by the fact that it justified the Europeans' exploitation of people in other lands. These people, after all, had supposedly not yet "evolved" to a "civilized" stage. It seemed therefore natural for them to be ruled by civilized whites and for their lands to be held as colonies.

Behind this simplistic form of evolutionary theory were three unsupported assumptions. First, it assumed that Western culture represents the height of human civilization—an extremely ethnocentric position. Second, it assumed that widely different non-Western societies could be lumped together. For example, peoples of Mexico who had developed empires, cities, astronomy, and mathematics were put in the same stage of barbarism as simple pueblo peasants. Third, the early evolutionists insisted that all societies independently went through an identical, unilinear process of evolution. But societies do not evolve independently. Most borrow many elements of their neighbors' culture. Moreover, evolution is multilinear, not unilinear. Societies evolve along different paths. Hunting societies, for example, make adaptations to their environments different from those made by agricultural societies (Steward, 1973).

Modern evolutionary theorists have discarded these assumptions. In general, they argue that societies tend to change gradually from simple to complex forms. Pastoral societies may be considered simple; modern industrial societies, complex. But evolutionary theorists no longer imply that the change represents an improvement. Neither do they assume that all societies change in the same way or at the same rate (Lenski et al., 1991). Evolving complexity can be seen in the change Durkheim described from mechanical solidarity to organic solidarity (see Chapter 3: Social Structure). But organic solidarity is not necessarily "better" than mechanical solidarity. A modern life-style is not always an improvement over a traditional one. Moreover, among developing countries today, some are industrializing at a snail's pace, while others are catching up with the West. As Gerhard Lenski and Patrick Nolan (1984) found, industrializing agricultural societies such as Mexico, Brazil, and South Korea show a higher level of technological and economic development than industrializing horticultural societies such as Ghana, Chad, and Uganda.

CYCLICAL THEORY

Evolutionists assume that social change has only one direction. They believe that when societies change they, in effect, burn their bridges behind them—they cannot return to their previous states. In contrast, proponents of **cyclical theory** believe that societies move forward and backward, up and down, in an endless series of cycles.

Spengler's "Majestic Cycles" German historian Oswald Spengler (1880–1936) was the first to make this assumption explicit. Like many of his contemporaries in the early twentieth century, Spengler was led by the savagery of World War I to question the belief in progress and the supremacy of Western civilization. As suggested by the title of his 1918 book, *The Decline of the West,* Spengler believed that Western civilization was headed downhill and would soon die out, just as the Greek and Egyptian civilizations had. "The great cultures," he wrote, "accomplish their majestic wave cycles. They appear suddenly, swell in splendid lines, flatten again, and vanish, and the face of the waters is once more a sleeping waste." More often, Spengler likened a culture to an organism. Like any living thing, a culture, he believed, went through a life cycle of birth, youth, maturity, old age, and death. Western civilization, as he saw it, had reached old age and was tottering toward death.

Spengler's theory was very popular for a time. But to modern sociologists, there is too much poetry and too little science in his argument, and the analogy between societies and biological organisms is more misleading than useful. Nevertheless, Spengler's basic idea that social change is cyclical has influenced social science. Arnold Toynbee, Pitirim Sorokin, and Paul Kennedy, for example, offered their famous theories based on this view.

Toynbee's "Challenge" and "Response" From 1934 to 1961 the British historian Arnold Toynbee (1889–1975) formulated a cyclical theory in his multivolume work *A Study of History.* Like Spengler, Toynbee believed that all civilizations rise and fall. But in his view, the rise and fall do not result from some inevitable, biologically determined life cycle. Instead, they depend both on human beings and on their environments. Environments present "challenges," and humans choose "responses" to those challenges. The fate of a civilization, according to Toynbee, depends on both the challenges presented to a civilization and the responses it devises.

The challenge may come from the natural environment or from human sources. Barren land, a frigid climate, and war, for example, all represent "challenges." A civilization declines if the challenge it faces is either too weak or too severe. Suppose food is extremely abundant; people may become lazy, and their civilization will decline. But if food is very scarce, starvation may kill the people, and their civilization as well. A moderate challenge is likely to stimulate a civilization to grow and flourish. The relatively large population and relatively scarce natural resources of Japan might represent a "moderate" challenge.

The fate of a civilization, however, depends not just on the challenge from the environment but also on the people's response. Whether a successful response comes about usually hinges on the actions of a creative minority. They develop new ideas and lead the masses to meet the challenge. The founders of the Chinese civilization, for example, emerged from among those who lived along the Yellow River rather than the far more numerous peoples occupying the vast region to the south and southwest of China. Toynbee called them the creative minority because they responded successfully to the challenge presented by the river. It was unnavigable most of the time. In the winter, it was either frozen or choked with floating ice. In the spring, the melting ice produced devastating floods. The people were compelled to devise means to navigate the river and control the flood. Thus, the rise and fall of a civilization depend both on the severity of the challenge offered by the environment and on the creativity of people's response to it.

Toynbee's theory provides an interesting way of looking at the history of civilizations, but it does not give us a means of predicting how societies will change. What, after all, is a "severe" challenge? Will the depletion of oil and minerals represent a "moderate" or an overly "severe" challenge for Western civilization? We know the answer only after the fact. If a civilization falls, we may assume that the challenge was too severe and the response was inadequate. *Before* a civilization rises or falls, we have no way of testing Toynbee's theory. But it still can be considered a useful theory. According to French sociologist Raymond Boudon (1983a, 1983b), social change is so complex that the best we can expect from a theory is whether it can help us understand what has happened rather than predict what will happen. That's what Toynbee's theory does.

Sorokin's Principle of Immanent Change Another cyclical theory was offered by Pitirim Sorokin (1889–1968), a Russian-American sociologist. In essence, Sorokin argued that societies fluctuate between two extreme forms of culture, which he called ideational and sensate. **Ideational culture** emphasizes faith or religion as the key to knowledge and encourages people to value spiritual life. **Sensate culture** stresses empirical evidence or science as the path to knowledge and urges people to favor a practical, materialistic, and hedonistic way of life.

External forces such as international conflict or contact with another culture may force change on a society, but Sorokin believed that internal forces—forces within the society itself—are more powerful in bringing about social change. As he wrote, "One of the most important 'determinators' of the course of any system lies within the system itself, is inherent in it. . . . Its life course is set down in its essentials when the system is born" (Sorokin, 1967). Hence, Sorokin called his theory the **principle of immanent change.** When the time has come for a society's "inwardly ordained change," all the main aspects of the culture change. Thus, society eventually reacts against one extreme form of culture, and swings to the other extreme. Sorokin regarded the Western culture of his time, for example, as sensate, and, like Spengler, he thought it was declining. In the widespread pursuit of pleasure, proliferation of fraud and crime, and deterioration of the family, Sorokin saw signs that Western culture was "overripe" and ready to swing to the other extreme—ideational culture.

To most sociologists today, Sorokin's theory is too speculative, impossible to test scientifically. Although Sorokin supported his theory with a mountain of historical data, he seems to have selected those facts that supported his view and ignored those

that did not. Nevertheless, Sorokin's theory, like Toynbee's, can help us understand some of the changes in our history, such as the rise of fundamentalist religion in the last decade (see Chapter 11: Religion). It can be interpreted as a reflection of the shift from a sensate to an ideational culture.

Is the United States in Decline? Like Spengler, American historian Paul Kennedy (1988) assumes that great civilizations can eventually suffer a decline. To support this assumption, Kennedy cites the examples of such formerly powerful nations as Spain, the Netherlands, France, and Britain, all of which, one after another, have finally lost their superpower status over the last 300 years. The reason for their decline is what Kennedy calls "imperial overstretch," a nation's hell-bent pursuit of great military power to the extent of bankrupting its economy. According to Kennedy, a nation that wants to remain number one for generation after generation requires not just military capability but also a flourishing and efficient economy, strong finances, and a healthy social fabric, because it is upon such foundations that the nation's military strength rests in the long term. By applying this insight to the United States today, Kennedy finds that this superpower is running the risk of imperial overstretch. With so much attention and effort geared toward maintaining its status as the world's strongest military power, the United States has for the last 30 years been neglecting its domestic problems. Unlike Spengler, though, Kennedy does not conclude that the West is doomed to cyclical decline. But he warns that "if the trends in national indebtedness, inadequate productivity increases, mediocre educational performance and decaying social fabric in the United States are allowed to continue at the same time that massive American commitments of men, money and materials are made in different parts of the globe" in order to maintain our international status as the foremost military power, we will lose that very power in a decade or so down the road (Kennedy, 1991).

This warning obviously implies that, to Kennedy, the United States is not in decline yet. After all, given its quick, easy victory in the Gulf War in 1991 and the unraveling of its rival superpower the former Soviet Union, the United States is now, more than ever, unquestionably the world's strongest military power. But Kennedy is concerned that the country will eventually decline because its political leaders may not take his warning seriously. He is afraid that the country cannot solve its economic problems, im-

The United States' position as a superpower derives from more than military and economic strength. It also comes from "soft power"—the ability to persuade rather than command—as shown by the worldwide popularity of American movies.

prove its public education, and eliminate its social problems, such as crime, drugs, and homelessness.

Kennedy's theory, however, has stirred up a storm of criticisms. Most critics erroneously assume that Kennedy believes the United States to be already in decline militarily. But they are more convincing in pointing out some holes in his argument that the United States is suffering an economic decline. As Joseph Nye (1990) observes, our country, for all its problems, continues to be the world's largest economy, with the highest level of absolute productivity, while our share of world product has remained constant for the last 15 years. Nye also criticizes Kennedy for comparing the position of the United States in today's post-Cold War world with the position of Spain, Britain, and others in the past. It used to be that a superpower's position was derived from its "hard" power—military and economic strength—alone. Today, the United States' position rests on both hard and soft power. Soft power—the ability to persuade rather than command—comes from intangible sources, such as the adoption of English as the new world language, the worldwide popularity of American movies, the use of the American dollar as the world's benchmark currency, and the admiration and good will that Americans often enjoy abroad. The 1991 Gulf War has shown how the United States possesses those two kinds of power. It succeeded in using its military's hard power to defeat Iraq swiftly and with remarkably few American casualties. It succeeded in using its soft power to persuade the United Nations to pass resolutions forcing Iraq to withdraw from Kuwait; the United States further used its soft power successfully to mobilize an international coalition to wage war against Iraq. Increasingly, the soft, noncoercive power will be more effective than the hard, military power in leading the world, and here Nye believes the United States has a clear edge over any other nation. Nye does agree with Kennedy that American decline will occur if such domestic issues as the large budget deficit, the poor educational system, and the deteriorating condition of our cities are not soundly addressed. But Nye is optimistic about Americans' ability to deal with these problems.

EQUILIBRIUM THEORY

American sociologist Talcott Parsons developed yet another theory of social change, one that remains influential today. According to **equilibrium theory,** which is a version of functionalist theory, all the parts of society serve some function and are interdependent (see Chapter 1: The Essence of Sociology). As a result, a change in one part produces compensatory changes elsewhere. It has recently become necessary, for example, for both parents to work in order to earn enough income to support a family. But if both parents must leave the home, who will care for their children? Society has responded with the increased availability of day-care services. Such changes keep the various parts of the social system in balance, ensuring social order and stability.

In this view of society, social change seems rather like an infection invading the body. Just as an infection triggers the body's immune system to fight it, so too a change in one part of the social system triggers other parts of the system to make adjustments.

Many sociologists have argued that the equilibrium theory may explain social stability but that it cannot explain social change. Parsons (1964), however, insisted that his theory is *"equally* applicable to the problems of change and to those of process within a stabilized system." To Parsons, social change is not the overthrow of the old and the creation of something wholly new. Instead, new elements are integrated with aspects of the old society through a "moving equilibrium," or movement toward a new equilibrium.

Like evolutionary theorists, Parsons (1966) believed that societies evolve from simpler to more complex forms. He argued that the most important type of change represents an "enhancement of adaptive capacity," and that evolutionary changes follow a common pattern. First, there is **differentiation,** in which one unit of society divides into two or more. In a simple society, for example, the family serves as the unit of residence *and* of production, of kinship and occupation (Chapter 10: The Family). But as a society evolves, production moves out of the household. An additional, separate social unit—an economic institution, such as the factory—is then formed, and the family itself is altered. Thus, the family has become differentiated from its original function as a production unit, which is now taken over by the economic institution. Differentiation, however, poses problems of **integration.** The new social units—such as the modern family and the economic institution—must be coordinated. As a result, other changes will occur within the society. Social status becomes more dependent on work than on family background. Young people are now more likely to choose the jobs they prefer than those their parents prefer. Families become smaller. Individuals tend more to identify with their country as opposed to their village. In short, traditionalism has given way to modernism, a new social equilibrium in which various parts, such

as the family, the economic institution, and nationhood, are integrated with each other (Inkeles, 1983).

Parsons's theory is useful for describing gradual change. According to its critics, however, it fails to explain why social change occurs, does not deal with *revolutionary* change, and portrays societies as far more stable and harmonious than they are.

CONFLICT THEORY

Whereas equilibrium theory portrays stability as the pervasive characteristic of societies, conflict theorists believe that societies are always marked by conflict and that conflict is the key to change. Karl Marx (1818–1883) is the father of **conflict theory.** We have discussed some aspects of his work several times in previous chapters, especially his prediction of the downfall of capitalism.

According to Marx, a capitalist society includes two classes: the owners of the means of production (the bourgeoisie or capitalists) and those who must sell their labor (the proletariat or workers). These classes are in constant conflict with each other. The capitalists are determined to keep wages low in order to maximize their profits, while the workers resist this exploitation. The capitalists have the upper hand, but they unwittingly sow the seeds of their own destruction. By completely controlling the labor of workers, capitalists further their alienation. By exploiting workers mercilessly, capitalists fuel rage and resentment among workers, and lead them to feel that they have nothing to gain from the present system. And through factories and improved transportation and communication, the capitalist society brings workers together and helps them share their sufferings with one another. As a result, the workers develop a consciousness of themselves as a class. According to Marx, the alienation, resentment, and class consciousness eventually lead workers to revolt against capitalist society.

History has not fulfilled these predictions. Marx failed to anticipate the emergence of a large middle class, made up largely of white-collar workers. He also failed to see that governments might respond to social conflict by improving the condition of workers. In fact, Marx's dire predictions about the future of capitalism helped spur governments to ease the suffering of workers. In a sense, by predicting that capitalism carried the seeds of its destruction, Marx sowed seeds that would help destroy his own prediction. Through the emergence of the welfare state as well as the growth of the middle class, workers in capitalist societies have grown richer, not poorer as Marx predicted. They have thus gained a stake in the system and are not likely to overthrow it by supporting revolution.

Other aspects of Marx's work have stood up better against the test of time. Marx did accurately predict the rise of large-scale industry, the emergence of multinational corporations, and the continuous squeeze of technology on employees. His analysis further implied the concentration of capital in a few giant corporations, which is evident in the United States today. Moreover, many social scientists agree with Marx that material conditions—economic production in particular—shape intellectual, political, and social life. They also accept his view that "the innermost nature of things" is dynamic and filled with conflict (Heilbroner, 1980).

QUESTIONS FOR DISCUSSION AND REVIEW

1. What are the four major theories of social change, and what factor does each consider to be the basic agency of change?
2. Why do only a few people still believe in the evolutionary theory of social change?
3. How do the separate versions of cyclical theory differ from each other, and how does each contribute to sociology's understanding of social change?
4. Why are differentiation and integration important processes in the equilibrium theory of social change?
5. What are the strengths and weaknesses of Marx's approach to social change?

Modernization

A typical American farmer and, say, a Guatemalan peasant seem to be separated not just by hundreds of miles but by hundreds of years. Behind this gap lies a set of social changes that goes by the name of **modernization.** Its key element is the change from an agricultural society to an industrial one. Whenever this transformation has occurred, many other changes have swept through various spheres of social life.

Societies that have undergone modernization are those that we have at various times called "developed," "industrialized," and "rich," as well as "modern." Examples are the United States, Japan, and Western European countries. Those societies that have not modernized or are still undergoing modernization we have previously described as "developing," "poor," "third world," or "traditional" societies. They are mostly in Africa, Asia, and Latin America. Here we look at the causes and consequences of modernization.

WHAT STIMULATES MODERNIZATION?

How does modernization come about? First, several economic developments must occur if a society is to modernize. According to a classical economic theory, modernization requires the following:

Modernization requires not only economic and psychological changes but also sociological changes. The emergence of entrepreneurs, shown here, and the desire to be modern are important, but education, the factory, urbanism, and mass communication are the strongest stimulants to modernization.

1. A technological revolution in agriculture, which permits, and even forces, workers to move off the farms and into industry.
2. An accumulation of capital and of money that can be loaned to exploit natural resources and manufacture consumer goods.
3. An expansion of foreign trade, which provides an export market for the country's manufactured goods as well as foreign funds and technology.
4. The emergence of entrepreneurs—people who are willing to take risks to invest in new business ventures (Rostow, 1960).

For modernization to occur, these economic factors must be accompanied by sociological and psychological changes. The people of a society must themselves become modern and committed to modernization. But this is not likely to happen without the influence of some social factors. Alex Inkeles (1983) has found four social factors—education, the factory, urbanism, and mass communication—to be the strongest stimulants to modernization. He discovered, for example, that the more years of formal schooling a person had, the higher he or she scored on the "modernity test." Industrial workers also scored higher on the test than peasants. Working in a factory apparently can increase "a man's sense of efficacy, make him less fearful of innovation, and impress on him the value of education as a general qualification for competence and advancement"— qualities typical of a modern person. Thus, Inkeles called the factory "a school of modernization."

Other researchers have found that nationalism has become the most powerful of the "ideologies of development" in the third world, replacing the Protestant ethic and individualistic values that have contributed to the economic success in the West (Germani, 1981). Nationalism can stimulate modernization because both are compatible. Nationalism involves a transfer of allegiance from tribes to a nation-state, and modernization requires participation of diverse groups in the national mainstream. This is why developing nations often try to promote modernization by appealing to nationalism. The leaders of Kenya, for example, have long adopted the policy of *harambee* ("let us pull together") in order to unify various tribes, blacks and whites, and villagers and urbanites (Segal, 1982).

Marxist analysts, however, argue that it is difficult for third-world countries to modernize because of their "inherited dependency" on or exploitation by rich nations. They cannot acquire enough loans or aid from industrial nations to finance their development projects. The level of development assistance that they need should be at least 2 percent of the rich nations' GNP, but they get less than 1 percent. They also find it difficult to export their manufactured goods to rich countries because of the latter's protectionist restrictions (Stone, 1983; Chilcote and Johnson, 1983).

TOWARD ONE WORLD SOCIETY?

Discussions about modernization often make three assumptions. One, all societies will, sooner or later, modernize and follow the path forged by Western industrial nations. Two, modernization destroys traditions. And three, as a result, eventually there will be just one worldwide society. All these assumptions are worth examining.

Barriers to Industrialization There is no certainty that developing countries will mimic the social history of nineteenth-century Western nations, or that if they do industrialize, they will also modernize in the same way Western nations did. In fact, developing nations face several barriers to industrialization, and there are significant differences between their situation today and the world in which Western societies industrialized.

In the West, the transformation of an **agricultural** society into an industrialized one using **high** technology took more than 300 years. The governments of most developing countries today believe that the needs of their people require that they achieve similar technological development within just a few decades. Their efforts are hindered, however, by a population explosion that Western nations did not face at a similar point in their development. As the population grows, economic gains must be used to sustain the increased numbers of people, rather than to fund investments for continued economic development. The economic pie may grow, but it must be divided into ever more slices. Little is left for the improved transportation or machinery or other capital that would aid future growth.

A second barrier to industrialization of the third world is **neocolonialism**—economic dependence on the West, which once held most of the developing world as colonies. While the Western nations were industrializing, they used their colonies as a source of cheap raw materials. Today, developing nations lack a comparable outside source of cheap raw materials. They also must compete with the modernized West in selling their manufactured goods. Many are still finding it difficult to break out of the pattern of a colonial economy, in which the colony exports raw materials and imports manufactured goods. Often developing nations must sell their raw materials cheaply and pay high prices for the manufactured goods they import. This makes it impossible for them to earn enough to build up their own countries.

Finally, the developing world faces dilemmas in choosing a path to modernization. The economic success of Western nations makes them an alluring model. But efforts to imitate the West can be counterproductive. Developing nations seeking to copy the mass education system of the United States, for example, may divert money badly needed for industrial investments into expensive education that has little practical value to their people and little relation to the job opportunities within their nations. They may also find that their people perceive modernization on the Western model as a betrayal of their own values and way of life, a new colonization by the West.

If, on the other hand, developing nations resist the temptation to mimic the West, they face another set of problems. One is that the United States in particular and Western investors in general may view their policies with suspicion, as a move toward socialism and perhaps anti-Americanism. They may then find it difficult to attract foreign investment and to secure favorable trade policies. Even if Western nations remain friendly, however, developing nations that spurn imitation of existing economic systems face the difficulty of being in largely uncharted waters, of having no good guide to tell them how else they might achieve economic development. During the 1960s, for example, China rejected both Soviet-style socialism and Western-style capitalism, seeking an ideologically pure socialism. One slogan declared, "We would prefer a poor society under socialism to a rich one under capitalism." The effort destroyed the economy and was abandoned in the 1970s.

Traditions and Modernization Many people assume that modernization inevitably destroys tradition. But some studies suggest that the traditions of developing societies are surviving the onslaught of modernization. Anthropologist Stephen Lansing (1978), for example, has found that economic development has not dismantled Balinese culture. Instead, economic development through tourism has stimulated the traditional Balinese art of woodcarving.

This survival of traditions is really not surprising. Even in the very modernized United States, after all, we find cultural elements, such as religion, that

Some developing nations are tempted to mimic the West as a path to modernization. But in some cases, imitation of the West can be counterproductive, as when copying the mass education system of the United States leads to the diversion of funds badly needed for industrial investments into expensive education that has little practical value to the people.

predated modernization. As Inkeles (1983) notes, we are by any measure one of the most modern nations in the world and yet we have one of the highest rates of church membership and attendance (see Chapter 11: Religion). When sociologist Theodore Caplow and his colleagues (1983) studied a midwestern community, they found that the cultural values of high school students were not significantly different from those of earlier generations. In any society, some people are likely to be more "modern" than others, but some aspects of society are more likely than others to endure.

Furthermore, traditions and industrialization do not always clash. As Joseph Gusfield (1967b) has pointed out, they may reinforce each other. In studying the impact of modernization on India, Gusfield found a reinforcement of traditions. When Indians of middle and lower levels seek upward mobility, they do so by "becoming more devoutly Hinduistic," by being as genuinely Indian as possible. Even among very Westernized elites, the native culture still exerts a powerful influence. Nearly all Indian intellectuals speak a regional language as their mother tongue, are steeped in classical Sanskrit literature, are strongly tied to an extended family, and are likely to find a spouse through parental arrangements. The men marry very traditional wives.

We can also see the impact of tradition on modernization in Japan. Without its traditional culture, Japan would not have become an industrial giant. The Japanese culture emphasizes the importance of social relations and collective welfare. It encourages consensus rather than conflict, deference to rather than disrespect for authority, and paternalism rather than indifference by those in authority. These cultural values saturate Japan's economic system. A business enterprise, no matter how large, is run like a household, with the accompanying interdependence and loyalty characteristic of the family. Since the company takes care of its workers by giving them lifetime employment, employees tend to identify strongly with employers and work as hard as they can. Moreover, the traditional emphasis on collective welfare serves more than just enhancing productivity through cooperation between managers and workers. It causes society to favor business and industry at the expense of individuals, transferring funds and wealth from individuals to industries. This can be seen in the fact that factories and company apartments are mostly grand and imposing, whereas private homes are cramped yet highly expensive.

Convergence Theory   Political scientist Zbigniew Brzezinski once predicted that exposure to supersonic aircraft, satellite communication, and multinational companies would eventually Westernize Asia. This reflects the view known as **convergence theory.** It assumes that modernization will break down the cultural barriers between the third world and the West and that the third world will adopt Western ways of living and virtually all the values of the West. Under the influence of modernization, technocrats and leaders in Asia, Africa, and South America will become a "cosmopolitan elite." They will abandon their own cultures and will be capable of dissolving the cultural differences between their countries and the West.

It is true that third-world countries have acquired many social and cultural characteristics of the West. But as we have noted, there is also evidence that non-Western traditions are surviving and that at least some elites remain closely tied to their native cultures. Convergence theory seems to assume that modernization is a uniform, all-embracing, all-powerful process. But when Selig Harrison (1979) evaluated the application of convergence theory to Asia, he found, instead of a convergence toward Western culture,

an altogether different prospect. Cultural divisions are hardening rather than dissolving. Economic and social change is generating unprecedented pressures for the democratization of cultural life and the reinforcement of cultural identities. While cosmopolitan elites are growing in absolute numbers, their ability to serve as effective mediators is steadily declining. Increasingly, these Westernized elites find themselves isolated and engulfed by rising tides of cultural nationalism.

Sociologist Wilbert Moore (1979) also failed to see the trend toward a common destination. Aside from the failures of most developing countries to catch up economically with the developed nations, Moore offered some instances where convergence is unlikely to happen. Saudi Arabia and other mideastern countries preserve their traditional Islamic way of life despite their embrace of modernization. Thus, in Saudi Arabia, gambling, movies, and dancing are forbidden, and Western videos, books, and publications are heavily censored. Islamic laws are also strictly enforced: thieves' hands are chopped off, adulterers are stoned to death, murderers and rapists are beheaded, and lesser offenders are flogged; all such punishments are carried out in the city squares for the public to see (Beyer, 1990). Nationalism, the antithesis of the world-society concept, has also become the "secular religion" of new nations while it continues to be alive in older nations.

If Harrison and Moore are correct, we can expect conflict and misunderstanding between cultures to continue and probably even increase. But we can also look forward to a far more diverse, more interesting, and richer world than the look-alike world predicted by convergence theory.

QUESTIONS FOR DISCUSSION AND REVIEW

1. What roles do entrepreneurs, technology, and nationalism play in helping a society become more modern?
2. How do population explosions and neocolonialism create barriers to industrialization in the third world?
3. Why do beliefs in traditions and nationalism challenge the assumptions of the convergence theory of modernization?

Major Changes in Our Future

What is in store for us in the remainder of this century? Demographic changes should have a marked impact on American society. Working adults and the elderly will each make up a larger share of the population, while the young will constitute a smaller share. With fewer youth, we can expect crime and competition for entry-level jobs to decrease. With more working and elderly adults, productivity and political conservatism will increase. The conservatism may find expression in toughness toward criminals, in heartlessness toward the poor, and in resistance to efforts by women and minorities to achieve social and economic equality. Brought up in such an environment, young people will also become more conservative. Political conflict between elderly and younger Americans may increase, as the interests of those receiving Social Security and those paying the taxes clash. People will continue to migrate from the Frostbelt to the Sunbelt, so that the West and Southwest will grow richer at the expense of the Northeast and Midwest. But Sunbelt cities, as a magnet for the unemployed from economically depressed areas, will eventually have higher unemployment, more crime, greater traffic congestion, and more pollution, while Frostbelt states would gradually strengthen their economies by offering tax benefits and other incentives to attract industry, especially electronics and other high-tech firms.

Technology will also stimulate change. Many social scientists and commentators have described how technology is moving us into a new era through a "revolution" as momentous as the Industrial Revolution. This new era has been called the *postindustrial age* by sociologist Daniel Bell (1973) and the *Third Wave era* by journalist Alvin Toffler (1980). According to Toffler, the First Wave era was launched by the agricultural revolution around 8000 B.C. and ended around A.D. 1750. Then the Second Wave, set off by the Industrial Revolution, shaped the world until about 1955. A new civilization then began to emerge out of the old, sparked by computers, jets, space exploration, genetic engineering, the electronic mass media, and other manifestations of high technology. While the industrial era revolved around the machine and the production of goods, this new era, which Toffler called the Third Wave, will revolve around computers and the production of information. Industrial societies, Bell noted, "are goods-producing societies. Life is a game against fabricated nature. . . . A postindustrial society is based on services. Life becomes a game between persons. What counts is not raw muscle power, or energy; what counts is information." Today, more than two-thirds of the American labor force already work in the information-related service industry, such as health care, retail trade, and financial services.

But the postindustrial era, due to its excessive emphasis on information and service jobs, has short-changed the production of goods. Consequently, the United States now imports more products than it exports. This trade deficit, which is bad for our economy, may eventually goad the United States to manufacture more goods and improve their quality, so that we will export more, as well as replace imports with our own goods. This may weaken the service-oriented character of the postindustrial era, because a majority of American service workers, who have never been as well paid as their foreign counterparts, will be lured into the manufacturing sector. But this new industrial age, with its reemphasis on production of goods, will differ from the old one. It will rely heavily on many labor-saving and productivity-

Computers and robotics will constitute labor-saving and productivity-enhancing technologies in a new industrial age. But whether producing goods or services, the computer-driven technologies have already begun and will continue to dismantle the traditional industrial principle of mass production aimed at a mass society.

enhancing technologies, such as robotics and computers (L. Thurow, 1989).

Whether producing services or goods, the computer-driven technologies have already begun and will continue to dismantle the traditional industrial principle of mass production aimed at a mass society. By using computers, companies are increasingly customizing their goods and services for niche markets. The new technologies are also making local production as competitive as national mass production. Many supermarkets, while selling bread of national brands, have begun to bake their own bread. Photos, which used to be sent to Rochester, New York, to be processed centrally by Kodak, can now be developed and printed anywhere in the United States. The same demassification process has taken away much of the audiences from the three giant TV networks, as cable and other media have proliferated to serve new niche markets. Similar changes have also weakened the mass-production labor unions (Toffler, 1990).

With demassification, however, our society will become more individualistic, more fragmented, and less cohesive. We will consequently have more social conflicts. There are already signs of how demassification has made us more aware of our individual rights. Our society has become awash with almost as many

different rights as there are many different individuals. There are criminal rights, victim rights, animal rights, pro-choice rights, pro-life rights, housing rights, privacy rights, the right to own AK-47s (powerful assault rifles) for hunting purposes, a damaged fetus's right not to be born, and airline pilots' right not to be randomly tested for alcohol, which presumably leaves passengers the right to crash every now and then (Leo, 1991). With many different groups demanding that only their rights be protected, social responsibility or civic obligation will decline, and national consensus will be harder to sustain. Thus, more social conflicts will occur.

Finally, the end of the cold war may temporarily make us less interested in foreign affairs because the Soviet threat to our national security no longer exists. But new international problems will goad our nation into action. The United States will help to contain the inter-ethnic conflict unleashed by the disintegration of the Soviet empire. Our nation will try to control the spread of missiles and nuclear technology, which the former members of the Soviet Union are eager to sell to third-world countries. And our government will make sure that American companies can more easily sell their products in foreign countries (Friedman, 1992).

CHAPTER REVIEW

1. *According to Smelser, what are the preconditions for the appearance of collective behavior?* Six conditions must appear, in the following sequence: (1) structural conduciveness, (2) social strain, (3) the spread of a generalized belief, (4) a precipitating factor, (5) mobilization of participants, and (6) inadequate social control.

2. *How does a panic come about?* There must be a perception of a crisis, intense fear of possible entrapment, some panic-prone individuals, mutual emotional facilitation, and a lack of cooperation among people. *Which type of people are most likely to succumb to mass hysteria?* Those with little critical ability and little education.

3. *Why do crowds sometimes act irrationally, even violently?* Le Bon argued that as a result of the anonymity of a crowd, people give up their individuality and release their primitive instincts. Then as a result of social contagion, they become part of a collective mind that is irrational. Many sociologists today believe that Le Bon's "collective mind" is a fiction and that crowds are not as homogeneous as they appear. Instead, as Turner and Killian have argued, crowds appear homogeneous because they conform to a new norm that emerges to deal with the unconventional situation in which the crowd finds itself.

4. *Do fashions affect many aspects of life?* Yes. In fact, almost all aspects of life are influenced by fashion. *How do fashions, fads, and crazes differ?* Fashions occur more predictably, last longer, and are more socially respectable than fads and crazes. Fads are less outrageous and less harmful than crazes.

5. *Are rumors always distortions?* No. They are merely unverified. They may turn out to be true. *When are rumors likely to develop?* If a situation is ambiguous and institutionalized channels of communication do not satisfy the demand for news about it, then a rumor is likely to emerge.

6. *How does propaganda differ from other types of communication?* It is designed to influence opinion. *Why is the influence of the American media limited?* There are several reasons: the multitude of viewpoints presented by the media; its tendency to try to match rather than mold opinion, telling people what they want to hear; and the frequency with which communication occurs by a two-step flow—from the media to opinion leaders and only then to the public. *What influence do the media have?* They frequently authenticate information; validate private opinions, preferences, and values; legitimize unconventional viewpoints and behavior; concretize ill-defined anxieties and preferences; and establish a hierarchy of importance and prestige among people, objects, or ideas.

7. *What are the aims of social movements?* Generally, they seek some sort of change. Revolutionary movements seek total, radical change of society. Reform movements seek a partial change in society. Resistance movements try to turn back some ongoing social change. Expressive movements seek to change individuals, not society. *What are the social causes of social movements?* According to the traditional perspective, social conditions must first frustrate masses of people; then people must identify a common frustration and work out a plan and band together to change the offending conditions. But resource mobilization theory emphasizes the importance of resources at the expense of discontent as the cause of social movements.

8. *How do modern evolutionary theorists describe social change?* They argue that societies tend to change gradually from simple to complex forms. *What is a primary difference between evolutionary and cyclical theorists?* Evolutionary theorists see social change as having one principal direction: toward increased complexity. Cyclical theorists portray social change as reversible: societies may move "forward" and "backward," they may rise and fall, in cycles. *What is equilibrium theory?* It holds that the various parts of society are all interdependent and that a change in any one part stimulates compensatory changes in other parts of the system. *What, in Parsons's view, are two basic processes in the evolution of societies?* Differentiation and integration. *How does conflict theory differ from equilibrium*

theory? Whereas equilibrium theory portrays stability as the pervasive characteristic of societies, conflict theorists believe that societies are always marked by conflict and that conflict is the key to change.

9. *What is modernization?* It is the set of social changes that has accompanied the transformation of agricultural societies into industrial ones. *What conditions are necessary for modernization to occur?* Several economic developments are necessary: (1) a technological revolution in agriculture, (2) an accumulation of capital, (3) an expansion of foreign trade, and (4) the emergence of entrepreneurs. The people of a society must also become modern, be committed to modernization, and harbor feelings of nationalism. *Will modernization produce one worldwide society?* Not necessarily. Modernization of the third world along Western lines is not inevitable, and modernization does not always destroy traditions. In some nations undergoing industrialization today, cultural differences with the West are increasing rather than decreasing.

10. *What effects are demographic changes in the United States likely to produce in the near future?* The aging of the population seems likely to lead to lower crime rates and increased productivity and conservatism. Political conflict between racial and ethnic groups, sexes, and generations may increase. Migration from the Frostbelt to the Sunbelt will continue. *How is technology changing the society?* It is carrying us into a "postindustrial age" or a "Third Wave" era in which information will be the most important product. Computer technology will produce goods and services more efficiently, but its tendency to demassify production for individual needs will encourage more social conflicts.

Key Terms

Collective behavior Relatively spontaneous, unorganized, and unpredictable social behavior (p. 366).

Conflict theory The theory that societies are always marked by conflict and that conflict is the key to change (p. 382).

Convergence theory The theory that modernization will bring the third world and the West together by breaking down their cultural barriers (p. 386).

Craze A fad with serious consequences (p. 372).

Crowd A collection of people who for a brief time do something in close proximity to one another (p. 370).

Cyclical theory The theory that societies change in an endless series of cycles, by growing, maturing, and declining and then starting over with a new form (p. 379).

Differentiation The process by which one unit of society divides into two or more (p. 382).

Emergent-norm theory Turner and Killian's theory that members of a crowd develop, through interaction, a new norm to deal with the unconventional situation facing them (p. 372).

Equilibrium theory The theory that various parts of a society are so interdependent that changes in one part produce compensatory changes in others, thereby ensuring social order and stability (p. 381).

Evolutionary theory The theory that societies change gradually from simple to complex forms (p. 378).

Fad A temporary enthusiasm for an innovation less respectable than a fashion (p. 372).

Fashion A great though brief enthusiasm among a relatively large number of people for some innovation (p. 372).

Ideational culture Sorokin's term for the culture that emphasizes faith as the key to knowledge (p. 380).

Integration The process by which various units of society are coordinated (p. 382).

Mass hysteria A form of collective behavior in which numerous people engage in a frenzied activity without checking the source of their fear (p. 369).

Modernization The set of social changes that has accompanied the transformation of agricultural societies into industrial societies (p. 383).

Neocolonialism The economic dependence of third-world countries on their former colonial rulers, the current Western industrial powers (p. 384).

Opinion leader A person whose opinion is respected by others and influences them (p. 375).

Panic A form of collective behavior characterized by a maladaptive, fruitless response to a serious threat (p. 369).

Principle of immanent change Sorokin's term for social change being the product of the social forces that exist within a society (p. 380).

Propaganda Communication tailored to influence opinion (p. 374).

Public A dispersed collection of people who share some interest or concern (p.374).

Public opinion The collection of ideas and attitudes shared by members of a particular public (p. 374).

Resource mobilization theory The theory that social movements result from the availability of resources for mobilization, such as strong organization, effective leadership, money, and media access (p. 377).

Rumor An unverified story passed from one person to another (p. 373).

Sensate culture Sorokin's term for the culture that emphasizes empiricism or science as the key to knowledge (p. 380).

Social change The alteration of society over time (p. 366).

Social contagion The spreading of a certain emotion and action from one member of a crowd to another (p. 371).

Social movement An activity in which many people jointly struggle to bring about or resist social change (p. 376).

SUGGESTED READINGS

Harris, Marvin. 1989. *Our Kind: Who We Are, Where We Came From, and Where We Are Going.* New York: Harper & Row. An interesting narration of how humans have been changing from prehistoric times to the present.

Inkeles, Alex. 1983. *Exploring Individual Modernity.* New York: Columbia University Press. A well-integrated collection of articles that reports and analyzes findings from the author's famous studies on becoming modern in developing countries.

Kennedy, Paul M. 1988. *The Rise and Fall of the Great Powers.* New York: Random House. A Spenglerian, cyclical analysis of how past great powers such as Spain and Britain eventually declined, spiced with a controversial comparison between those former superpowers and the United States of today.

Nye, Joseph, Jr. 1990. *Bound to Lead: The Changing Nature of American Power.* New York: Basic Books. An anticyclical analysis of how in the new international order the United States will lead the world with its social and cultural resources more than with its military power.

Toffler, Alvin. 1990. *Powershift.* New York: Bantam Books. Argues that industrialism is losing world dominance to new forces of power.

GLOSSARY

Absolute poverty The lack of minimum food and shelter necessary for maintaining life.

Achieved status A status that is attained through an individual's own action.

Acute disease A disease that lasts for a short time, during which the victim either recovers or dies.

Ad-hocracy Toffler's term for an organization that assembles temporary groups of experts for solving specific problems.

Ageism Prejudice and discrimination against people because of their age.

Agricultural society A society that produces food by relying on plows and draft animals.

Alienation of labor Marx's term for laborers' loss of control over their work process.

Amalgamation The process by which the subcultures of various groups are blended together, forming a new culture.

Animism The belief in spirits capable of helping or harming people.

Anomaly Kuhn's term for a research finding that cannot be fitted into the existing paradigm and thus cannot be explained by it.

Anomie A condition in which social norms are absent, weak, or in conflict.

Anticipatory socialization Socialization that prepares a person to assume a role in the future.

Anti-Semitism Prejudice or discrimination against Jews.

Aptitude The capacity for developing physical or social skills.

Ascribed status A status that one has no control over, such as status based on race, sex, or age.

Assimilation The process by which a minority adopts the dominant group's culture, blending into the larger society.

Authority Legitimate power that derives from traditions, a leader's charisma, or laws.

Behavioral assimilation A minority's adoption of the dominant group's language, values, and behavioral patterns.

Belief An idea that is relatively subjective, unreliable, or unverifiable.

Biosphere A thin film of air, water, and soil surrounding the earth.

Birth rate The number of births for every 1000 people in a given year.

Bureaucracy An organization characterized by a division of labor, hierarchy of authority, the hiring of employees on the basis of impersonal procedures and technical qualifications, and reliance on formal rules.

Capitalism An economic system based on private ownership of property and competition in producing and selling goods and services.

Caste system A relatively rigid stratification system in which one's position is ascribed and there is almost no mobility.

Census A periodic head count of the entire population of a country.

Charisma An exceptional personal quality popularly attributed to certain individuals.

Chromosomes The materials in a cell that transmit hereditary traits to the carrier from his or her parents.

Chronic disease A disease that lasts for a long time before the victim dies.

Church A relatively large, well-established religious organization that is integrated into the society and does not make strict demands on its members.

Civil religion A collection of beliefs, symbols, and rituals that sanctify the dominant values of society.

Class conflict Marx's term for the struggle between capitalists, who own the means of production, and the proletariat, who do not.

Class system A stratification system in which achieved characteristics play a large role in determining one's position and in which there is considerable social mobility.

Coercion Illegitimate use of force or threat of force to compel obedience.

Collective behavior Relatively spontaneous, unorganized, and unpredictable social behavior.

Communality The norm that requires scientists to share their knowledge freely with each other.

Competition A relationship in which two individuals or groups strive to achieve the same goal before the other does.

Compositional theory The theory that city dwellers are as involved with small groups of friends, relatives, and neighbors as are noncity people.

Conflict A relationship in which two individuals or groups struggle to achieve a goal by defeating each other without regard to rules.

Conflict perspective A theoretical perspective that focuses on conflict and change in society, particularly conflict between a dominant and a subordinate group, and emphasizes that conflict is a constant fact of social life.

Conflict theory The theory that societies are always marked by conflict and that conflict is the key to change.

Content analysis The analysis of a communication by searching for its specific words or ideas and then turning them into numbers.

Control group The subjects in an experiment who are not exposed to the independent variable.

Convergence theory The theory that modernization will bring the third world and the West together by breaking down their cultural barriers.

Cooperation A relationship in which two or more persons work together to achieve a common goal.

Craze A fad with serious consequences.

Crowd A collection of people who for a brief time do something in proximity to one another.

Crystalline intelligence Wisdom and insight into the human condition, as shown by one's skills in philosophy, language, music, or painting.

Cult A religious group that professes new religious beliefs, rejects society, and demands extreme loyalty from its members.

Cultural pluralism The peaceful coexistence of various racial and ethnic groups, with each retaining its own subculture.

Cultural relativism Evaluating other cultures on their own terms, with the result of not passing judgment on them.

Cultural transmission The process by which the values of crime and delinquency are transmitted from one group to another.

Culture A complex whole consisting of objects, values, and other characteristics that people have acquired as members of society.

Cyclical theory The theory that societies change in an endless series of cycles by growing, maturing, and declining, and then starting over with a new form.

Date rape Rape committed by a man against a woman he is out with.

Death rate The number of deaths for every 1000 people in a given year.

De facto segregation Segregation sanctioned by tradition and custom.

De jure segregation Segregation sanctioned by law.

Demographic process An aspect of a population that is always changing, such as the birth rate, death rate, or net migration rate.

Demography The scientific study of population.

Dependent variable A variable that is considered the effect of another variable.

Detached observation A method of observation in which the researcher stands apart from the subjects.

Developmental socialization The kind of socialization that teaches a person to be more adequate in playing his or her currently assumed role.

Deviant behavior An act that is considered by public consensus or the powerful at a given place and time to be a violation of some social rule.

Differential association The process by which potential deviants associate more with criminal elements than with noncriminal elements.

Differentiation The process by which one unit of society divides into two or more.

Discrimination An unfavorable action against individuals that is taken because they are members of some category.

Disintegrative shaming Punishing wrongdoers in such a way as to stigmatize, reject, or ostracize them.

Disinterestedness The norm that requires scientists to pursue truth rather than self-interest.

Double standard The social norm that allows males but not females to engage in nonmarital sex.

Ecology The study of the interrelationships among organisms and between organisms and their environments.

Economic institution A system for producing and distributing goods and services.

Ecosystem A self-sufficient community of organisms depending for survival on one another and on the environment.

Emergent-norm theory Turner and Killian's theory that members of a crowd develop, through interaction, a new norm to deal with the unconventional situation facing them.

Epidemiology The study of the origin and spread of disease within a population.

Equilibrium theory The theory that various parts of a society are so interdependent that changes in one part produce compensatory changes in others, thereby ensuring social order and stability.

Ethicalism The type of religion that emphasizes moral principles as guides for living a righteous life.

Ethnic group People who share a distinctive cultural heritage.

Ethnocentrism The attitude that one's own culture is superior to that of others.

Evolutionary theory The theory that societies change gradually from simple to complex forms.

Exchange A reciprocal transaction between individuals, groups, or societies.

Experiment A research method in which the researcher manipulates variables so that their influence can be determined.

Experimental group The subjects in an experiment who are exposed to the independent variables.

Expressive role Role that requires taking care of personal relationships.

Fad A temporary enthusiasm for an innovation less respectable than a fashion.

Fashion A great though brief enthusiasm among a relatively large number of people for some innovation.

Feminist perspective A theoretical perspective that views social life and human experience from the standpoint of women.

Feminization of poverty The significant increase in the number of women bearing the burden of poverty alone, mostly as single mothers or heads of families.

Fluid intelligence Ability to comprehend abstract relationships, as in mathematics, physics, or some other science.

Folk society Redfield's term for a society that is small, nonliterate, and homogeneous, with a strong group solidarity; used to distinguish preindustrial from industrial societies.

Folkways "Weak" norms that specify expectations about proper behavior.

Formal organization A group whose activities are rationally designed to achieve specific goals.

Gemeinschaft Tönnies's term for a type of society marked by a strong sense of community and by personal interactions among its members.

Gender role The pattern of attitudes and behaviors that a society expects of its members because of their being male or female.

Generalized others Mead's term for people whose names are unknown to the child but who influence the child's internalization of the values of society.

Genocide Wholesale killing of a racial or ethnic group.

Gentrification The movement of affluent people into urban neighborhoods, displacing poor and working-class residents.

Gesellschaft Tönnies's term for a type of society

characterized by individualism and by impersonal interactions.

Groupthink The tendency for members of a group to maintain consensus to the extent of ignoring the truth.

Hawthorne effect The unintended effect of the researcher's presence on the subjects' behavior.

Healing role A set of social expectations that defines the doctor's rights and obligations.

Homogamy Marriage that involves two people having similar characteristics, or norm that requires such a marriage.

Horizontal mobility The movement of a person from one job to another within the same status category.

Hormones Chemical substances that stimulate or inhibit vital biological processes.

Horticultural society A society that depends on growing plants in small gardens for its survival.

Hunting-gathering society A society that hunts animals and gathers plants to survive.

Hypothesis A tentative statement about how various events are related to one another.

Ideal type Weber's term for a description of what are theorized to be the essential characteristics of a phenomenon, with which actual phenomena can be compared.

Ideational culture Sorokin's term for a culture that emphasizes faith as the key to knowledge.

Impression management The act of presenting one's "self" in such a way as to make others form the desired impression.

Individual mobility Social mobility related to an individual's personal achievement and characteristics.

Industrial Revolution The dramatic economic change brought about by the introduction of machines into the work process about 200 years ago.

Infant mortality rate The number of deaths among infants less than one year old for every 1000 live births.

Influence The ability to control others' behavior through persuasion rather than coercion or authority.

Informal organization A group formed by the informal relations among members of an organization; based on personal interactions, not on any plan by the organization.

Informed consent The approval that a patient gives to a doctor for a treatment after receiving adequate information on it.

In-group The group to which an individual is strongly tied as a member.

Instincts Fixed traits that are biologically inherited and enable the carrier to perform complex tasks.

Institutional differentiation The process by which the functions of one institution are gradually taken over by other institutions.

Institutionalized discrimination The persistence of discrimination in social institutions, not necessarily known to everybody as discrimination.

Instrumental role Role that requires performing a task.

Integration The process by which various units of society are coordinated.

Intelligence The capacity for mental or intellectual achievement.

Interest group An organized collection of people who attempt to influence government policy.

Intergenerational mobility A change in social standing from one generation to the next.

Internalization The process by which individuals incorporate the values of society into their personalities, accepting the norms of society as their own.

Intragenerational mobility A change in an individual's social standing, also called *career mobility*.

Jim Crow The system of laws made in the late nineteenth century in the South for segregating blacks from whites in all kinds of public and private facilities.

Kinesics Use of body movements as a means of communication.

Knowledge A collection of relatively objective ideas and facts about the physical and social worlds.

Latent function A function that is unintended and thus often unrecognized.

Laws Norms that are specified formally in writing and backed by the power of the state.

Life chances Opportunities for living a good, long, or successful life in a society.

Life expectancy The average number of years that a group of people can expect to live.

Life-styles Tastes, preferences, and ways of living.

Living will Advance instructions on what people want their doctors to do in the event of a terminal illness.

Looking-glass self Cooley's term for the self-image that we develop from the way others treat us.

Manifest function A function that is intended and thus seems obvious.

Marginal surplus population Marxist term for unemployed workers who are useless to the capitalist economy.

Mass hysteria A form of collective behavior in which numerous people engage in a frenzied activity without checking the source of their fear.

Master status A status that dominates a relationship.

Material culture All the physical objects produced by humans as members of society.

Matthew effect The tendency to praise famous scientists and to ignore the contributions of those who are not well known.

Mechanical solidarity A form of social cohesion that develops when people do similar work and have similar beliefs and values, characteristic of simple, traditional societies.

Megalopolis A vast area in which many metropolises merge.

Metropolis A large urban area including a city and its surrounding suburbs.

Minority A racial or ethnic group that is subjected to prejudice and discrimination.

Mixed economy An economic system that includes both capitalist and socialist elements.

Modernization The set of social changes that has accompanied the transformation of agricultural societies into industrial societies.

Monotheism The belief in one god.

Mores "Strong" norms that specify normal behavior and constitute demands, not just expectations.

Multiculturalism The belief that all racial and ethnic cultures in the United States should be equally respected and cultivated.

Neocolonialism The economic dependence of third-world countries on their former colonial rulers, the current Western industrial powers.

Neurosis Mental problem characterized by a persistent fear, anxiety, or worry about trivial matters.

Nonmaterial culture Norms, values, and all the other intangible components of culture.

Norm A social rule that directs people to behave in a certain way.

Normal science Kuhn's term for routine research.

Objective method The method of identifying social classes by using occupation, income, and education to rank people.

Opinion leader A person whose opinion is respected by others and influences them.

Organic solidarity A form of social cohesion that develops when the differences among occupations make people depend on each other; characteristic of complex, industrialized societies.

Organized skepticism The norm that requires scientists to be critical of any scientific idea or finding.

Out-group The group of which an individual is not a member.

Panic A form of collective behavior characterized by a maladaptive, fruitless response to a serious threat.

Paradigm A model for defining, studying, and solving problems in accordance with certain basic assumptions.

Parkinson's Law Parkinson's observation—that "work expands to fill the time available for its completion"—for explaining why bureaucracy tends to keep growing.

Participant observation A method of observation in which the researcher takes part in the activities of the group being studied.

Pastoral society A society that domesticates and herds animals for food.

Patriarchy A system of domination in which men exercise power over women.

Personality A fairly stable configuration of feelings, attitudes, ideas, and behaviors that characterizes an individual.

Peter Principle Peter's observation—that "in a hierarchy, every employee tends to rise to his level of incompetence"—for explaining the prevalence of incompetence among bureaucrats.

Plea bargaining A pretrial negotiation in which the

defendant agrees to plead guilty to a lesser charge in exchange for a less severe penalty.

Political power The capacity to use the government to make decisions that affect the whole society.

Politics Process in which people acquire and exercise power, determining who gets what, when, and how.

Polytheism The belief in more than one god.

Popular culture A collection of relatively unsophisticated artistic creations that appeal to the masses of a society.

Population The entire group of people to be studied.

Postmarital sex The sexual experience of the divorced or widowed.

Power The ability to control the behavior of others, even against their wills.

Power elite A small group of individuals who hold top positions in the federal government, military, and corporations, having similar backgrounds, values, and interests.

Prejudice A negative attitude toward some category of people.

Prescribed role A set of expectations held by society regarding how an individual with a particular status should behave.

Primary deviance An isolated violation of a norm that is not considered deviant by the person committing the act.

Primary group A group whose members interact informally, relate to each other as whole persons, and enjoy their relationship for its own sake.

Principle of immanent change Sorokin's term for the idea that social change is the product of the social forces existing within a society.

Propaganda Communication tailored to influence opinion.

Proxemics Perception and use of space as a means of communication.

Psychosis Mental disorder typified by loss of touch with reality.

Public A dispersed collection of people who share some interest or concern.

Public opinion The collection of ideas and attitudes shared by members of a particular public.

Race A group of people who are perceived by a given society as biologically different from others.

Random sample A sample drawn in such a way that all members of the population had an equal chance of being selected.

Rationalization Weber's term for the tendency to replace traditional, spontaneous, informal, and diverse ways of doing things with a planned, formally unified method based on abstract rules.

Recidivism Repeated commission of crimes.

Reference group A group that is used as the frame of reference for evaluating one's own behavior.

Reintegrative shaming Making wrongdoers feel guilty while showing them understanding, forgiveness, or even respect.

Relative poverty A state of deprivation that results from having less than what the majority of the people have.

Religion A unified system of beliefs and practices regarding sacred things that unites its adherents into a single moral community.

Reputational method The method of identifying social classes by selecting a group of people and then asking them to rank others.

Resocialization The kind of socialization that is aimed at replacing one's old self with a new self.

Resource mobilization theory The theory that social movement results from the availability of resources for mobilization, such as strong organization, effective leadership, money, and media access.

Revolution The violent overthrow of an existing government and drastic change in the social and political order.

Ritual Behavioral expression of a religious belief.

Role A set of expectations of what individuals should do in accordance with a particular status of theirs.

Role conflict Conflict between two roles being played simultaneously.

Roleless role Being assigned no role in society's division of labor, a predicament of the elderly in industrial society.

Role performance Actual performance of a role.

Role strain Stress caused by incompatible demands built into a role.

Rumor An unverified story passed from one person to another.

Sacred Whatever transcends the everyday world and inspires awe and reverence.

Sample A relatively small number of people selected from a larger population.

Sanction Formal or informal rewards for conformity to norms, or punishments for violation of norms.

Scapegoat The minority that the dominant group's frustrated members blame for their own failures.

Science A body of knowledge about natural phenomena that is acquired through the systematic use of objective methods.

Scientific revolution Kuhn's term for the replacement of an old paradigm by a new one.

Secondary analysis The analysis of existing data collected by somebody else.

Secondary deviance Habitual norm violations that the person recognizes as deviant and commits in conformity with his or her self-image as a deviant.

Secondary group A group in which the individuals interact formally, relate to each other as players of particular roles, and expect to profit from each other.

Sect A relatively small religious group that sets itself apart from society and makes heavy demands on its members.

Segregation The spatial and social separation of a minority group from the dominant group, forcing the minority to live in inferior conditions.

Senescence The natural physical process of aging.

Senility An abnormal condition characterized by serious memory loss, confusion, and loss of the ability to reason; not a natural result of aging.

Sensate culture Sorokin's term for a culture that emphasizes empiricism or science as the key to knowledge.

Sexism Prejudice and discrimination based on the victim's gender.

Shamanism The belief that a spiritual leader can communicate with the spirits by acting as their mouthpiece or letting his soul leave his body and enter the spiritual world.

Sick role A pattern of expectation regarding how a sick person should behave.

Significant others Mead's term for specific persons, such as parents, who have a significant influence on the child because the child interacts mainly with them in his or her early years and plays at being these adults.

Social aggregate A collection of people who happen to be in one place but do not interact with one another.

Social category A number of people who happen to share some characteristics but do not interact with one another or gather in one place.

Social change The alteration of society over time.

Social class A category of people who have about the same amount of income, power, and prestige.

Social consensus Condition in which most members of society agree on what is good for everybody to have and cooperate to achieve it.

Social contagion The spreading of a certain emotion and action from one member of a crowd to another.

Social control Process by which individuals are pressured by others, such as teachers, peers, and police, to conform to social norms.

Social forces Forces that arise from the society we are part of.

Social institution A set of widely shared beliefs, norms, or procedures necessary for meeting the needs of a society.

Social integration The degree to which people are related to a social group.

Social interaction The process by which individuals act toward and react to one another.

Social mobility The movement from one social standing to another.

Social movement An activity in which many people jointly struggle to bring about or resist social change.

Social network A web of social relationships in which individuals or groups are tied to one another.

Social stratification A system in which people are ranked into categories, with some getting more rewards than others.

Social structure A recurrent pattern in the ways people relate to one another.

Socialism An economic system based on public ownership and government control of the economy.

Socialization The process by which a society transmits its cultural values to its members.

Society A collection of interacting individuals sharing the same culture and territory.

Sociological imagination C. Wright Mills's term for the ability to see the impact of social forces on individuals, especially on their private lives.

Sociology The scientific study of human social behavior.

State A political institution that regulates conflict and allocates resources among the citizens of a country.

Status A position in a group or society.

Status inconsistency The condition in which the individual is given a different ranking in various social categories, such as being high in occupation but low in income.

Status system System in which people are stratified according to their social prestige.

Stratified sampling The process of drawing a random sample in which various categories of people are represented in proportions equal to their presence in the population.

Structural assimilation Social condition in which minority groups cease to be minorities and are accepted on equal terms with the rest of society.

Structural functionalism A theoretical perspective that focuses on social order, which is assumed to be based on the positive functions performed by the interdependent parts of society.

Structural mobility A change in social standing that affects many people at the same time and results from changes in the structure of society.

Structured interview The interview in which the researcher asks standardized questions that require respondents to choose from among several standardized answers.

Subcultural theory Fischer's theory that the city enriches people's lives by offering diverse opportunities and developing various subcultures.

Subculture A culture within a larger culture.

Subjective method The method of identifying social classes by asking people to rank themselves.

Subordinate status A status that does not dominate a relationship; the opposite of master status.

Survey A research method that involves asking questions about opinions, beliefs, or behavior.

Symbol A thing that stands for some other thing.

Symbolic interactionism A theoretical perspective that focuses on the interaction between individuals and is based on the assumption that their subjective interpretations of each other's actions influence their interaction.

Systematic sampling The process of drawing a random sample systematically rather than haphazardly.

Technology The application of scientific knowledge for practical purposes.

Theism The type of religion that centers on the worship of a god or gods.

Theoretical perspective A set of broad assumptions, which cannot be proven true or false, about the nature of a subject.

Theory A set of logically related hypotheses that explains the relationship among various phenomena.

Totemism The belief that a kinship exists between humans and an animal or a plant.

Universalism The norm that requires scientists to evaluate ideas in accordance with impersonal criteria.

Unstructured interview The interview in which open-ended questions are asked and the respondent is allowed to answer freely.

Urban anomie theory Wirth's theory that city people have a unique way of life, characterized by alienation, impersonal relations, and stress.

Urban ecology The study of the relationship between people and their urban environment.

Urban society Redfield's term for societies that are large, literate, and heterogeneous, with little group solidarity.

Validity The extent to which a study measures what it is supposed to measure; popularly known as "accuracy."

Value A socially shared idea that something is good, desirable, or important.

Verstehen Weber's term for the subjective method, which requires sociologists to adopt an attitude of understanding or empathy toward their subjects.

Vertical mobility The movement of people up or down the status ladder.

Vital statistics Data about births, marriages, deaths, and migrations into and out of a country.

White ethnics Americans of Eastern and Southern European origins.

Women's ghettos Traditionally female low-paying occupations that are subordinate to positions held by men.

World system A capitalist network of relationships among all the members of the world's community.

REFERENCES

Abraham, A. S. 1984. "The north-south gap." *World Press Review,* 31, October, p. 39.

Achikson, William. 1990. *Lighting the Night: Revolution in Eastern Europe.* New York: Morrow.

Acton, H. B. 1967. *What Marx Really Said.* New York: Schocken.

Adler, Jerry. 1992. "Hey, I'm terrific!" *Newsweek,* February 17, pp. 46-51.

Ainsworth, Martha. 1984. "Population policy: Country experience." *Finance & Development,* 21, pp. 18-20.

Alba, Richard D. 1981. "The twilight of ethnicity among American Catholics of European ancestry." *The Annals,* 454, March, pp. 86-97.

———. 1985. "The twilight of ethnicity among Americans of European ancestry: The case of Italians." *Ethnic and Racial Studies,* 8, pp. 134-158.

———. 1990. *Ethnic Identity: The Transformation of White America.* New Haven, Conn.: Yale University Press.

Albrecht, Terrance, et al. 1982. "Integration in a communication network as a mediator of stress." *Social Work,* 27, pp. 229-234.

Alexander, Suzanne. 1990a. "Freshmen flood black colleges, defying trend." *Wall Street Journal,* July 9, p. B1.

———. 1990b. "Schools sow environmental seeds early." *Wall Street Journal,* June 26, p. B1.

Alonso, William. 1964. "The historic and the structural theories of urban form: Their implications for urban renewal." *Journal of Land Economics,* 40, pp. 227-231.

Alter, Jonathan. 1983. "Hispanic power at the polls." *Newsweek,* July 4, pp. 23-24.

Altman, Lawrence K. 1990. "Changes in medicine bring pain to healing profession." *New York Times,* February 18, pp. 1, 20-21.

———. 1991. "Many Hispanic Americans reported in ill health and lacking insurance." *New York Times,* January 9, p. A10.

Amir, Menachem. 1971. *Patterns in Forcible Rape.* Chicago: University of Chicago Press.

Andersen, Margaret L. 1993. *Thinking about Women: Sociological Perspectives on Sex and Gender,* 3rd ed. New York: Macmillan.

———, and Patricia Hill Collins (eds.). 1992. *Race, Class, and Gender: An Anthology.* Belmont, Calif.: Wadsworth.

Anderson, George M. 1981. "White-collar crime." *America,* May 30, pp. 446-447.

Anderson, Linda S., Theodore G. Chiricos, and Gordon P. Waldo. 1977. "Formal and informal sanctions: A comparison of deterrent effects." *Social Problems,* 25, pp. 103-114.

Angier, Natalie. 1990a. "Cancer rates rising steeply for those 55 or older." *New York Times,* August 24, p. A13.

———. 1990b. "Marriage is lifesaver for men after 45." *New York Times,* October 16, p. B11.

Archer, Margaret S. 1985. "The myth of cultural integration." *British Journal of Sociology,* 36, pp. 333-353.

Aronoff, Joel, and William D. Crano. 1975. "A re-examination of the cross-cultural principles of task segregation and sex role differentiation in the family." *American Sociological Review,* 40, pp. 12-20.

Asch, Solomon E. 1955. "Opinions and social pressure." *Scientific American,* 193, pp. 31-35.

Atchley, Robert C. 1988. *Social Forces and Aging,* 5th ed. Belmont, Calif.: Wadsworth.

Azmitia, Margarita. 1988. "Peer interaction and problem solving: When are two hands better than one?" *Child Development,* 59, pp. 87-96.

Babbie, Earl R. 1989. *The Practice of Social Research,* 5th ed. Belmont, Calif.: Wadsworth.

Bailey, Kenneth D. 1987. *Methods for Social Research,* 3rd ed. New York: Free Press.

Balkan, Sheila, Ronald J. Berger, and Janet Schmidt. 1980. *Crime and Deviance in America: A Critical Approach.* Belmont, Calif.: Wadsworth.

Banfield, Edward C. 1974. *The Unheavenly City Revisited.* Boston: Little, Brown.

Barber, Bernard. 1961. "Resistance by scientists to scientific discoveries." *Science,* 134, pp. 596-602.

Barden, J. C. 1987. "Marital rape: Drive for tougher laws is pressed." *New York Times,* May 13, p. 10.

Barker, Eileen. 1984. *The Making of a Moonie.* New York: Basil Blackwell.

Barlett, Donald L., and James B. Steele. 1992. *America: What Went Wrong?* Kansas City: Andrews and McMeel.

Barnes, Donald. 1983. "An overview on dioxin." *EPA Journal,* 9, November, pp. 16-19.

Barney, G. O., et al. 1982. *The Global 2000 Report to the President of the United States: Entering the 21st Century,* vol. 1. London: Penguin Books.

Barrett, Paul M. 1990. "Struggling Feds." *Wall Street Journal,* June 26, pp. A1, A10.

Barringer, Felicity. 1989. "Doubt on 'trial marriage' raised by divorce rates." *New York Times,* June 9, pp. 1, 23.

———. 1991a. "Census shows profound change in racial make-up of the nation." *New York Times,* March 11, pp. A1, A12.

———. 1991b. "Population grows in state capitals." *New York Times,* January 26, pp. 1, 10.

Bartley, Robert L. 1991. "Beyond the recession." *Wall Street Journal,* January 2, p. A6.

Basow, Susan A. 1986. *Sex-Role Stereotypes.* Monterey, Calif.: Brooks/Cole.

Beaty, Jonathan, and S.C. Gwynne. 1992. "The dirtiest bank of all." *Time,* July 29, pp. 42-47.

Beck, E. M., and Stewart E. Tolnay. 1990. "The killing fields of the deep South: The market for cotton and the lynching of blacks, 1882-1930." *American Sociological Review,* 55, pp. 526-539.

Beck, Lois. 1982. "Nomads and urbanites, involuntary hosts and uninvited guests." *Middle East Studies,* 18, pp. 426-444.

Beck, Melinda. 1978. "The world of cults." *Newsweek,* December 4, pp. 78-81.

———. 1990a. "Going for the gold." *Newsweek,* April 23, pp. 74-76.

———. 1990b. "Trading places." *Newsweek,* July 16, pp. 48-54.

Becker, George. 1984. "Pietism and science: A critique of Robert K. Merton's hypothesis." *American Journal of Sociology,* 89, pp. 1065-1090.

Becker, Howard S. 1963. *Outsiders.* New York: Free Press.

———. et al. 1961. *Boys in White: Student Culture in Medical School.* Chicago: University of Chicago Press.

Beer, William R. 1987. "The wages of discrimination." *Public Opinion,* July/August, pp. 17-19, 58.

Begley, Sharon. 1990. "The search for the fountain of youth." *Newsweek,* March 5, pp. 44-48.

Beilin, Robert. 1982. "Social functions of denial of death." *Omega,* 12(1), pp. 25-35.

Belkin, Lisa. 1990. "Many in medicine are calling rules a professional malaise." *New York Times,* February 19, pp. A1, A9.

Bell, Daniel, 1973. *The Coming of Post-Industrial Society.* New York: Basic Books.

Bellah, Robert N., and Phillip E. Hammond. 1980. *Varieties of Civil Religion.* New York: Harper & Row.

———, et al. 1986. *Habits of the Heart: Individualism and Commitment in American Life.* New York: Harper & Row.

Benderly, Beryl Lieff. 1989. "Don't believe everything you read. . . " *Psychology Today,* November, pp. 67-69.

Bendix, Reinhard. 1962. *Max Weber: An Intellectual Portrait.* Garden City, N.Y.: Anchor.

Bengston, Vern L., Jose B. Cuellar, and Pauline K. Ragan. 1977. "Stratum contrasts and similarities in attitudes toward death." *Journal of Gerontology,* 32, pp. 76-88.

Benjamin, Daniel, et al. 1992. "Shock of reform." *Time,* February 17, pp. 38-40.

Bennett, Stephen Earl, and David Resnick. 1990. "The implications of nonvoting for democracy in the United States." *American Journal of Political Science,* 34, pp. 771-802.

Bennett, William J. 1989. "A response to Milton Friedman." *Wall Street Journal,* September 19, p. A32.

Bennis, Warren. 1989. "The dilemma at the top." *New York Times,* December 31, p. F3.

———, and Philip E. Slater. 1968. *The Temporary Society.* New York: Harper Colophon.

Berger, Bennett M. 1971. *Working-Class Suburb: A Study of Auto Workers in Suburbia.* Berkeley: University of California Press.

Berger, Brigitte, and Peter L. Berger. 1983. *The War over the Family: Capturing the Middle Ground.* Garden City, N.Y.: Anchor/Doubleday.

Berger, Peter L. 1963. *Invitation to Sociology.* Garden City, N.Y.: Anchor/Doubleday.

———. 1967. "A sociological view of the secularization of theology." *Journal for the Scientific Study of Religion,* 6, pp. 3-16.

Berman, Paul. 1992. "Still sailing the lemonade sea." *New York Times Magazine,* October 27, pp. 32-34, 78-79.

Bernard, Jessie. 1981. *The Female World.* New York: Free Press.

Bernstein, Richard. 1990. "In U.S. schools a war of words." *New York Times Magazine,* October 14, pp. 34, 48–52.

Beyer, Lisa. 1990. "Lifting the veil." *Time,* September 24, pp. 38–44.

Bienen, Leigh, Alicia Ostriker, and J. P. Ostriker. 1977. "Sex discrimination in the universities," in Nona Glazer and Helen Youngelson Waehrer (eds.), *Women in a Man-Made World,* 2nd ed. Chicago: Rand McNally.

Bilge, Barbara, and Gladis Kaufman. 1983. "Children of divorce and one-parent families: Cross-cultural perspectives." *Family Relations,* 32, pp. 59–71.

Bilheimer Robert S. (ed.). 1983. *Faith and Ferment: An Interdisciplinary Study of Christian Beliefs and Practices.* Minneapolis, Minn.: Augsburg.

Binder, David. 1990. "Where fear and death went forth and multiplied." *New York Times,* January 24, p. A8.

Bird, Caroline. 1975. *The Case Against College.* New York: McKay.

Black, Donald. 1983. "Crime as social control." *American Sociological Review,* 48, pp. 34–45.

Blackman, Ann. 1992. "The war against feminism." *Time,* March 9, pp. 50–55.

Blalock, Hubert M., Jr. 1982. *Race and Ethnic Relations.* Englewood Cliffs, N.J.: Prentice-Hall.

———. 1984. *Basic Dilemmas in the Social Sciences.* Beverly Hills, Calif.: Sage.

Blau, Peter M. 1977. *Inequality and Heterogeneity: A Primitive Theory of Social Structure.* New York: Free Press.

———, and Otis Dudley Duncan. 1967. *The American Occupational Structure.* New York: Wiley.

Bloom, Harold. 1992. *The American Religion: The Emergence of the Post-Christian Nation.* New York: Simon & Schuster.

Blumer, Herbert. 1978. "Elementary collective groupings," in Louis E. Genevie (ed.), *Collective Behavior and Social Movements.* Itasca, Ill.: Peacock.

Blundell, William E. 1986. "Gripe session." *Wall Street Journal,* May 9, pp. 1, 9.

Bodard, Lucien. 1972. *Green Hell.* New York: Dutton.

Bossard, James. 1932. "Residential propinquity as a factor in marriage selection." *American Journal of Sociology,* 38, pp. 219–244.

Boudon, Raymond. 1983a. "Individual action and social change: A no-theory of social change." *British Journal of Sociology,* 34, pp. 1–18.

———. 1983b. "Why theories of social change fail: Some methodological thoughts." *Public Opinion Quarterly,* 47, pp. 143–160.

Boulding, Kenneth E. 1981. "On the virtues of muddling through." *Technology Review,* 83, pp. 6–7.

Bowen, Ezra. 1986. "Nakasone's world-class blunder." *Time,* October 6, pp. 66–67.

Bowles, Samuel, and Herbert Gintis. 1976. *Schooling in Capitalist America.* New York: Basic Books.

Brabant, Sarah, and Linda Mooney. 1986. "Sex role stereotyping in the Sunday comics: Ten years later." *Sex Roles,* 14, pp. 141–148.

Bradburd, Daniel. 1982. "Volatility of animal wealth among Southwest Asian pastoralists." *Human Ecology,* 10, pp. 85–106.

Bradburn, Norman M. 1969. *The Structure of Psychological Well-Being.* Chicago: Aldine.

Bradshaw, York W. 1987. "Urbanization and underdevelopment: A global study of modernization, urban bias, and economic dependency." *American Sociological Review,* 52, pp. 224–239.

Braithwaite, John. 1981. 1989. *Crime, Shame and Reintegration.* New York: Cambridge University Press.

Brandt, Anthony. 1982. "Avoiding couple karate." *Psychology Today,* October, pp. 38–43.

Breault, K. D., and Augustine J. Kposowa. 1987. "Explaining divorce in the United States: A study of 3,111 counties, 1980." *Journal of Marriage and the Family,* 49, pp. 549–558.

Bridges, William P., and Wayne J. Villemez. 1986. "Informal hiring and income in the labor market." *American Sociological Review,* 51, pp. 574–582.

Bridgewater, Carol Austin. 1984. "The work ethic lives." *Psychology Today,* February, p. 17.

Brim, John, et al. 1982. "Social network characteristics of hospitalized depressed patients." *Psychological Reports,* 50, pp. 423–433.

Brinkley, Joel. 1992. "U.S. looking for a new path as superpower conflict ends." *New York Times,* February 2, pp. 1, 8.

Broad, William J. 1990a. "Small-scale science feels the pinch from big projects." *New York Times,* September 4, pp. B5, B8.

———. 1990b. "Vast sums for new discoveries pose a threat to basic science." *New York Times,* May 27, pp. 1, 12.

———. 1992. "Japan seen passing U.S. in research by industry." *New York Times,* February 25, p. B5.

Broad, William J., and Nicholas Wade. 1983. *Betrayers of the Truth.* New York: Simon & Schuster.

Broadhead, Robert S. 1983. *The Private Lives and Professional Identity of Medical Students.* New Brunswick, N.J.: Transaction.

Brody, Jane E. 1992. "Personal health." *New York Times,* March 18, p. B8.

Bromley, David G. 1991. "The satanic cult scare." *Society,* May/June, pp. 67–72.

Brooke, James. 1987. "In Burundi, minority persists in control of nation." *New York Times,* June 5, p. 8.

Brown, Roger. 1965. *Social Psychology.* New York: Free Press.

Brownmiller, Susan. 1984. *Femininity.* New York: Simon & Schuster.

Budiansky, Stephen. 1988. "The numbers racket: How polls and statistics lie." *U.S. News & World Report,* July 11, pp. 44-47.

Buller, Mary Klein, and David B. Buller. 1987. "Physicians' communication style and patient satisfaction." *Journal of Health and Social Behavior,* 28, pp. 275-388.

Bumpass, Larry, and James Sweet. 1989. "National estimates of cohabitation." *Demography,* 26, pp. 615-625.

Burke, Ronald J., and Tamara Weir. 1976. "Relationship of wives' employment status to husband, wife, and pair satisfaction and performance." *Journal of Marriage and the Family,* 38, pp. 279-287.

Burkhead, Dan L. 1983. *Lifetime Earnings Estimates for Men and Women in the United States: 1979.* Current Population Reports, Series P-60, No. 139. Washington, D.C.: U.S. Government Printing Office.

Burns, John F. 1982. "An apron awaits Soviet cosmonaut." *New York Times,* August 29, p. 3.

Burstein, Paul. 1981. "The sociology of democratic politics and government." *Annual Review of Sociology,* 7, pp. 291-319.

Burt, Martha. 1980. "Cultural myths and supports for rape." *Journal of Personality and Social Psychology,* 38, pp. 217-230.

Burtless, Gary. 1990. "It's better than watching Oprah." *Wall Street Journal,* January 4, p. A14.

Busacca, Richard, and Mary P. Ryan. 1982. "Beyond the family crisis." *Democracy,* Fall, pp. 79-92.

Bush, Diane Mitsch, and Roberta G. Simmons. 1981. "Socialization processes over the life course," in Morris Rosenberg and Ralph H. Turner (eds.), *Social Psychology: Sociological Perspectives.* New York: Basic Books.

Butler, Robert. 1984. Interviewed in *U.S. News & World Report,* July 2, pp. 51-52.

Butterfield, Fox. 1991. "Asians spread across a land, and help change it." *New York Times,* February 24, p. 14.

Button, James, and Walter Rosenbaum. 1990. "Gray power, gray peril, or gray myth?: The political impact of the aging in local Sunbelt politics." *Social Science Quarterly,* 71, pp. 25-38.

Cantril, Hadley, with Hazel Gaudet and Herta Herzog. 1982/1940. *The Invasion from Mars.* Princeton, N.J.: Princeton University Press.

Caplow, Theodore, et al. 1983. *Middletown Families: Fifty Years of Change and Continuity.* Minneapolis: University of Minnesota Press.

Capron, Alexander Morgan. 1990. "The burden of decision." *Hastings Center Report,* May/June, pp. 36-41.

Carey, Joseph, and Joanne Silberner. 1987. "Fending off the leading killers." *U.S. News & World Report,* August 17, pp. 56-64.

Carlson, Elwood, and Kandi Stinson. 1982. "Motherhood, marriage timing, and marital stability: A research note." *Social Forces,* 61, pp. 258-267.

Carmody, Deirdre. 1990. "Identity crisis for "Seven Sisters.'" *New York Times,* August 6, p. C1.

Carnoy, Martin, and Henry M. Levin. 1985. *Schooling and Work in the Democratic State.* Stanford, Calif.: Stanford University Press.

Carter, Hodding. 1989. "We're losing the drug war because prohibition never works." *Wall Street Journal,* July 13, p. A15.

Carter, Stephen L. 1991. *Reflections of An Affirmative Action Baby.* New York: Basic Books.

Castro, Janice. 1993. "Disposable workers." *Time,* March 29, pp. 43-47.

Catalano, Ralph, and David Dooley. 1983. "Health effects of economic instability: A test of economic stress hypothesis." *Journal of Health and Social Behavior,* 24, pp. 46-60.

Celis, William. 1991. "Students trying to draw line between sex and an assault." *New York Times,* January 2, pp. A1, B7.

Census Bureau. 1993. *Statistical Abstract of the United States.* Washington, D.C.: U.S. Government Printing Office.

Chafetz, Janet Saltzman. 1978. *Masculine, Feminine or Human?* Itasca, Ill.: Peacock.

Chagnon, Napoleon A. 1968. *Yanomamo: The Fierce People.* New York: Holt, Rinehart and Winston.

Chambliss, William J. 1969. *Crime and the Legal Process.* New York: McGraw-Hill.

———. 1973. "The saints and the rough-necks." *Society,* November/December, pp. 24-31.

Champion, Dean J. 1975. *The Sociology of Organizations.* New York: McGraw-Hill.

Cherlin, Andrew. 1983. "Changing family and household: Contemporary lessons from historical research." *Annual Review of Sociology,* 9, pp. 51-66.

———, and Frank F. Furstenberg, Jr. 1983. "The American family in the year 2000." *Futurist,* 18, June, pp. 7-14.

Chilcote, Ronald H., and Dale L. Johnson (eds.). 1983. *Theories of Development: Mode of Production or Dependency?* Beverly Hills, Calif.: Sage.

Childe, Gordon. 1952. *Man Makes Himself.* New York: New American Library.

Chipello, Christopher J., and Neal Templin. 1992. "Two worlds: Work ethic aside, some U.S. employees still live very well." *Wall Street Journal,* February 24, pp. A1, A10.

Chira, Susan. 1992. "Bias against girls is found rife in schools, with lasting damage." *New York Times,* February 12, pp. A1, B6.

Christopher, Robert C. 1983. *The Japanese Mind: The Goliath Explained.* New York: Linden/Simon & Schuster.

Clark, Margaret S. 1981. "Noncomparability of benefits given and received: A cue to the existence of friendship." *Social Psychology Quarterly,* 44, pp. 375–381.

Clark, Ramsey. 1971. *Crime in America.* New York: Pocket Books.

Clifford, Margaret M., and Elaine Walster. 1973. "The effect of physical attractiveness on teacher expectation." *Sociology of Education,* 46, pp. 248–258.

Clymer, Adam. 1992. "Turnout on election day '92 was the largest in 24 years." *New York Times,* December 17, 1992, p. A13.

Cockerham, William C. 1989. *Medical Sociology,* 4th ed. Englewood Cliffs, N.J.: Prentice-Hall.

Cocks, Jay. 1992. "Rap around the globe." *Time,* October 19, pp. 70–71.

Cohen, Albert K. 1966. *Deviance and Control.* Englewood Cliffs, N.J.: Prentice-Hall.

———, and Harold M. Hodges. 1963. "Characteristics of the lower-blue-collar class." *Social Problems,* 10, pp. 303–334.

Cohen, Jere. 1980. "Rational capitalism in Renaissance Italy." *American Journal of Sociology,* 85, pp. 1340–1355.

———. 1983. "Reply to Holton." *American Journal of Sociology,* 89, pp. 181–187.

Cole, Stephen. 1976. *The Sociological Method.* Chicago: Rand McNally.

Coleman, Eli. 1982. "Developmental stages of the coming out process." *American Behavioral Scientist,* 25, pp. 269–482.

Coleman, James S. 1982. *The Asymmetric Society.* Syracuse, N.Y.: Syracuse University Press.

Coleman, James William, and Donald R. Cressey. 1993. *Social Problems,* 5th ed. New York: Harper & Row.

Collins, Randall. 1971. "Functional and conflict theories of educational stratification." *American Sociological Review,* 36, pp. 1002–1019.

———. 1975. *Conflict Sociology.* New York: Academic Press.

———. 1979. *The Credential Society: An Historical Sociology of Education and Stratification.* New York: Academic Press.

———. 1986. "Is 1980s sociology in the doldrums?" *American Journal of Sociology,* 91, pp. 1336–1355.

Collins, W. Andrew, and Megan R. Gunnar. 1990. "Social and personality development." *Annual Review of Psychology,* 41, pp. 387–416.

Comer, James P. 1983. "Single-parent black families." *Crisis,* 90, pp. 510–515.

Commoner, Barry. 1990. *Making Peace with the Planet.* New York: Pantheon.

Conant, Jennet. 1987. "What women want to read." *Newsweek,* February 23, p. 61.

Conklin, John E. 1977. *"Illegal but Not Criminal": Business Crime in America.* Englewood Cliffs, N.J.: Prentice-Hall.

Conrad, Peter, and Rochelle Kern (eds.). 1986. *Sociology of Health and Illness: Critical Perspectives,* 2nd ed. New York: St. Martin's.

Cook, Karen S., et al. 1983. "The distribution of power in exchange networks: Theory and experimental results." *American Journal of Sociology,* 89, pp. 275–304.

Cooley, Charles H. 1909. *Social Organization.* New York: Scribner's.

Cooper, Kristina, et al. 1986. "Correlates of mood and marital satisfaction among dual-worker and single-worker couples." *Social Psychology Quarterly,* 49, pp. 322–329.

Cornell, Stephen. 1986. "The new Indian politics." *The Wilson Quarterly,* New Year's 1986, pp. 113–131.

Corliss, Richard. 1993. "A few good women." *Time,* April 15, pp. 58–59.

Corsaro, William A., and Donna Eder. 1990. "Children's peer cultures." *Annual Review of Sociology,* 16, pp. 197–220.

———, and Thomas A. Rizzo. 1988. *"Discussione* and friendship: Socialization processes in the peer culture of Italian nursery school children." *American Sociological Review,* 53, pp. 879–894.

Cory, Christopher T. 1979. "Women smile less for success." *Psychology Today,* March, p. 16.

Coverman, Shelley. 1989. "Role overload, role conflict, and stress: Addressing consequences of multiple role demands." *Social Forces,* 67, pp. 965–982.

Cowgill, Donald O. 1974. "Aging and modernization: A revision of the theory," in J. F. Gubrium (ed.). *Late Life: Communities and Environmental Policy.* Springfield, Ill.: Thomas.

———, and Llewelyn Holmes. 1972. *Aging and Modernization.* New York: Appleton-Century-Crofts.

Cowley, Geoffrey. 1988. "The wisdom of animals." *Newsweek,* May 23, pp. 52–59.

Cox, Frank D. 1990. *Human Intimacy: Marriage, the Family, and Its Meaning,* 5th ed. St. Paul, Minn.: West.

Cox, Harold G. 1990. "Roles for aged individuals in post-industrial societies." *International Journal of Aging and Human Development,* 30, pp. 55–63.

Cox, Harvey. 1966. *The Secular City.* New York: Macmillan.

Cramer, Jerome. 1989. "Where did the gung-ho go?" *Time,* September 11, pp. 52–56.

Crane, L. Ben, Edward Yeager, and Randal L. Whitman. 1981. *An Introduction to Linguistics.* Boston: Little, Brown.

Creech, James C., Jay Corzine, and Lin Huff-Corzine. 1989.

"Theory testing and lynching: Another look at the power threat hypothesis." *Social Forces,* 67, pp. 626–630.

Crispell, Diane. 1990. "Workers in 2000." *American Demographics,* March, pp. 36–40.

Crossen, Cynthia. 1991. "Kids acting up? Don't yell, validate their tiny feelings." *Wall Street Journal,* December 10, pp. A1, A4.

Crossette, Barbara. 1990. "India to shake up birth-control bureaucracy." *New York Times,* March 14, p. A4.

Crovitz, L. Gordon. 1991. "How Bush outflanked Iraq and liberated the Constitution." *Wall Street Journal,* March 6, p. A9.

Cummings, Scott. 1980. "White ethnics, racial prejudice, and labor market segmentation." *American Journal of Sociology,* 85, pp. 938–950.

Curtin, Philip D., et al. 1978. *African History.* Boston: Little, Brown.

Dabbs, James M., Jr., and Neil A. Stokes. 1975. "Beauty is power: The use of space on the sidewalk." *Sociometry,* 38, pp. 551–557.

Dahl, Robert A. 1981. *Democracy in the United States: Promise and Performance,* 4th ed. Boston: Houghton Mifflin.

Dahrendorf, Ralf. 1984. "The new underclass." *World Press Review,* 31, April, pp. 21–23.

Daly, Kathleen, and Meda Chesney-Lind. 1988. "Feminism and criminology." *Justice Quarterly,* 5, pp. 497–538.

Daley, Susanne. 1991. "Girls' self-esteem is lost on way to adolescence, new study finds." *New York Times,* January 9, pp. B1, B6.

Dank, Barry M. 1971. "Coming out in the gay world." *Psychiatry,* 34, pp. 180–197.

Dannefer, Dale. 1984. "Adult development and social theory: A paradigmatic reappraisal." *American Sociological Review,* 49, pp. 100–116.

Dardis, Rachel, et al. 1981. "Cross-section studies of recreation expenditures in the United States." *Journal of Leisure Research,* 13, pp. 181–194.

Darling-Fisher, Cynthia S., and Nancy Kline Leidy. 1988. "Measuring Eriksonian development in the adult: The modified Erikson psychosocial stage inventory." *Psychological Reports,* 62, pp. 747–754.

Davies, Gordon K., and Kathleen F. Slevin. 1984. "Babel or opportunity?" *College Board Review,* No. 130, Winter, pp. 18–21, 37.

Davies, Mark, and Denise B. Kandel. 1981. "Parental and peer influences on adolescents' educational plans: Some further evidence." *American Journal of Sociology,* 87, pp. 363–387.

Davis, Bernard D. 1990. "Right to die: Living wills are inadequate." *Wall Street Journal,* July 31, p. A12.

Davis, Bob, and Dana Milbank. 1992. "Job blues." *Wall Street Journal,* February 7, pp. A1, A5.

Davis, Cary, Carl Haub, and JoAnne Willette. 1983. "U.S. Hispanics: Changing the face of America." *Population Bulletin,* 39, June, pp. 1–45.

Davis, James. 1982. "Up and down opportunity's ladder." *Public Opinion,* June/July, pp. 11–15, 48–51.

Davis, Kingsley. 1947. "Final note on a case of extreme isolation." *American Journal of Sociology,* 52, pp. 432–437.

———. 1955. "The origin and growth of urbanization in the world." *American Journal of Sociology,* 60, pp. 429–437.

———. 1974. "The urbanization of the human population," in Charles Tilly (ed.), *An Urban World.* Boston: Little, Brown.

———. 1976. "The world's population crises," in Robert K. Merton and Robert Nisbet (eds.), *Contemporary Social Problems,* 4th ed. New York: Harcourt Brace Jovanovich.

———, and Wilbert E. Moore. 1945. "Some principles of stratification." *American Sociological Review,* 10, pp. 242–249.

Davis, Simon. 1990. "Men as success objects and women as sex objects: A study of personal advertisements." *Sex Roles,* 23, pp. 43–50.

Deegan, Mary Jo. 1988. *Jane Addams and the Men of Chicago School.* New Brunswick, N.J.: Transaction.

Deford, Frank. 1992. "Jewel on ice." *Newsweek,* February 10, pp. 46–53.

de Leeuw, Frank, Anne B. Schnare, and Raymond J. Struyk. 1976. "Housing," in William Gorham and Nathan Glazer (eds.), *The Urban Predicament.* Washington, D.C.: The Urban Institute.

Deloria, Vine, Jr. 1981. "Native Americans: The American Indian today." *The Annals of the American Academy of Political and Social Science,* 454, March, pp. 139–149.

DeMaris, Alfred, and Gerald R. Leslie. 1984. "Cohabitation with the future spouse: Its influence upon marital satisfaction and communication." *Journal of Marriage and the Family,* 46, pp. 77–84.

DeMause, Lloyd. 1975. "Our forebears made childhood a nightmare." *Psychology Today,* April, pp. 85–86.

Denton, Nancy A., and Douglas S. Massey. 1989. "Racial identity among Caribbean Hispanics: The effect of double minority status on residential segregation." *American Sociological Review,* 54, pp. 790–808.

DeParle, Jason. 1990. "In debate over who is poor, fairness becomes the issue." *New York Times,* September 3, pp. 1, 10.

De Witt, Karen. 1992. "Test scores are up slightly for college-bound students." *New York Times,* August 27, p. A8.

Dickey, Christopher. 1991. "Not just a case of trying to save face." *Newsweek,* January 21, p. 22.

Diesenhouse, Susan. 1990. "More women are playing, but fewer call the shots." *New York Times,* December 11, pp. B11–B12.

DiPrete, Thomas A., and David Grusky. 1990. "Structure and

trend in the process of stratification for American men and women." *American Journal of Sociology*, 96, pp. 107–143.

DiVall, Linda. 1992. "Women of the year." *New York Times*, May 14, p. A15.

Dolan, Barbara. 1990. "What price love? Read carefully." *Time*, October 15, pp. 94–95.

Doleschal, Eugene. 1979. "Crime—some popular beliefs." *Crime and Delinquency*, 25, pp. 1–8.

Domhoff, G. William. 1978. *The Powers That Be: Processes of Ruling-Class Domination in America*. New York: Random House.

————. 1983. *Who Rules America Now? A View for the Eighties*. Englewood Cliffs, N.J.: Prentice-Hall.

Dowd, Maureen. 1983. "Rape: The sexual weapon." *Time*, September 5, pp. 27–29.

————. 1993. "Growing sorority in Congress edges into ol' boys' club." *New York Times*, March 5, p. A1.

Dowell, William. 1991. "Freedom is the best revenge." *Time*, Decemer 16, pp. 24–29.

Drucker, Peter. 1987. "Goodbye to the old personnel department." *Wall Street Journal*, May 22, p. 24.

Duchon, Dennis, et al. 1986. "Vertical dyad linkage: A longitudinal assessment of antecedents, measures, and consequences." *Journal of Applied Psychology*, 71, pp. 56–60.

Duncan, Lois. 1991. "Helpig friends who grieve." *Reader's Digest*, November, pp. 29–32.

Durkheim, Emile. 1965/1915. *The Elementary Forms of the Religious Life*. New York: Free Press.

————. 1951/1897. *Suicide*. New York: Free Press.

Dychtwald, Ken. 1989. *Age Wave: The Challenges and Opportunities of an Aging America*. Los Angeles: Jeremy Tarcher.

Dye, Thomas R. 1976. *Who's Running America? Institutional Leadership in the United States*. Englewood Cliffs, N.J.: Prentice-Hall.

Eagly, Alice H., and Antonio Mladinic. 1989. "Gender stereotypes and attitudes toward women and men." *Personality and Social Psychology Bulletin*, 15, pp. 543–558.

————, and Blair T. Johnson. 1990. "Gender and leadership style: A meta-analysis." *Psychological Bulletin*, 108, pp. 233–256.

Earley, P. Christopher. 1989. "Social loafing and collectivism: A comparison of the United States and the People's Republic of China." *Administrative Science Quarterly*, 34, pp. 565–581.

Earth Science. 1983. "Trends in acid-rain patterns have shifted across U.S.," 36, Winter, pp. 9–10.

Easterbrook, Gregg. 1987. "The revolution in medicine." *Newsweek*, January 26, pp. 40–74.

————. 1989. "Cleaning up." *Newsweek*, July 24, pp. 26–42.

Echikson, William. 1990. *Lighting the Night: Revolution in Eastern Europe*. New York: Morrow.

Egan, Timothy. 1991. "7 Indian tribes seeking end to shackles of dependency." *New York Times*, January 16, pp. A1, A11.

Ehrenreich, Barbara. 1990. "The warrior culture." *Time*, October 15, p. 100.

Ehrlich, Paul R., Anne H. Ehrlich, and John P. Holdren. 1977. *Ecoscience: Population, Resources, Environment*. San Francisco: Freeman.

Eichenwald, Kurt. 1990. "For Ivan Boesky, punishment was tax-deductible." *New York Times*, May 25, pp. 1, C15.

Ekerdt, David J. 1986. "The busy ethic: Moral continuity between work and retirement." *The Gerontologist*, 26, pp. 239–247.

Elkin, Frederick, and Gerald Handel. 1988. *The Child and Society*, 5th ed. New York: Random House.

Ellis, Godfrey J., Gary R. Lee, and Larry R. Petersen. 1978. "Supervision and conformity: A cross-cultural analysis of parental socialization values." *American Journal of Sociology*, 84, pp. 386–403.

Ellis, Lee. 1985. "Religiosity and criminality." *Sociological Perspectives*, 28, pp. 501–520.

Ellis, William N., and Margaret McMahon Ellis. 1989. "Cultures in transition." *Futurist*, March/April, pp. 22–25.

Ellul, Jacques. 1964. *The Technological Society*. Translated by John Wilkinson. New York: Vintage Books.

Elmer-DeWitt, Philip. 1991. "Why isn't our birth control better?" *Time*, August 12, pp. 52–53.

Elson, John. 1978. "Socialism: Trials and errors." *Time*, March 13, pp. 24–36.

Engels, Friedrich. 1942/1884. *The Origin of the Family, Private Property, and the State*. New York: International Publishing.

Enloe, Cynthia. 1983, *Does Khaki Become You? The Militarisation of Women's Lives*. London: South End Press.

————. 1989. *Bananas, Beaches and Bases: Making Feminist Sense of International Politics*. Berkeley, Calif.: University of California Press.

Epstein, Cynthia Fuchs. 1976. "Sex roles," in Robert K. Merton and Robert Nisbet (eds.), *Contemporary Social Problems*. New York: Harcourt Brace Jovanovich.

Erikson, Erik H. 1963. *Childhood and Society*. New York: Norton.

————. 1975. *Life History and Historical Moment*. New York: Norton.

Erikson, Kai T. 1966. *Wayward Puritans*. New York: Wiley.

Eshleman, J. Ross. 1981. *The Family*. Boston: Allyn and Bacon.

Espinosa, P. K. 1992. "Life in these United States." *Reader's Digest*, January, p, 68.

Etzioni, Amitai. 1991. "A new community of thinkers, both liberal and conservative." *Wall Street Journal,* October 8, p. 20.

———. 1993. *The Spirit of Community: Rights, Responsibilities and the Communitarian Agenda.* New York: Crown.

Falco, Mathea. 1992. *The Making of a Drug-Free America: Programs That Work.* New York: Times Books.

Fallows, James. 1990. *More Like Us: Making America Great Again.* Boston: Houghton Mifflin.

Faludi, Susan. 1991. *Backlash: The Undeclared War Against American Women.* New York: Crown

Falwell, Jerry. 1981. *Listen America!* New York: Bantam Books.

Farley, John E. 1987. *American Social Problems: An Institutional Analysis.* Englewood Cliffs, N.J.: Prentice-Hall.

Farley, Reynolds. 1985. "Three steps forward and two back? Recent changes in the social and economic status of blacks." *Ethnic and Racial Studies,* 8, pp. 4–28.

Farran, D. C., and R. Haskins. 1980. "Reciprocal influence in the social interactions of mothers and three-year-old children from different socioeconomic backgrounds." *Child Development,* 51, pp. 780–791.

FBI (Federal Bureau of Investigation). 1990. *Uniform Crime Reports.* Washington, D.C.: U.S. Government Printing Office.

Feagin, Joe R. 1991. "The continuing significance of race: Antiblack discrimination in public places." *American Sociological Review,* 56, pp. 101–116.

Feagin, Joe R., and Clairece Booher Feagin. 1990. *Social Problems: A Critical Power-Conflict Perspective,* 3rd ed. Englewood Cliffs, N.J.: Prentice-Hall.

Featherman, David L., and Robert M. Hauser. 1978. *Opportunity and Change.* New York: Academic Press.

Feeney, Floyd, and Adrianne Weir. 1975. "The prevention and control of robbery." *Criminology,* 13, pp. 87–92.

Feld, Scott L. 1982. "Social structural determinants of similarity among associates." *American Sociological Review,* 47, pp. 797–801.

Felson, Richard B., and Mark D. Reed. 1986. "Reference groups and self-appraisals of academic ability and performance." *Social Psychology Quarterly,* 49, pp. 103–109.

Ferro-Luzzi, Gabriella Eichinger. 1986. "Language, thought, and Tamil verbal humor." *Current Anthropology,* 27, pp. 265–272.

Feshbach, Murray, and Alfred Friendly Jr. 1992. *Ecocide in the U.S.S.R.* New York: Basic Books.

Festinger, Leon. 1957. *A Theory of Cognitive Dissonance.* Stanford, Calif.: Stanford University Press.

Fidell, Linda. 1970. "Empirical verification of sex discrimination in hiring practices in psychology." *American Psychologist,* 25, pp. 1094–1098.

Filer, Randall K. 1990. "What we really know about the homeless." *Wall Street Journal,* April 10, p. 22.

Finkelhor, David, and Kersti Yllo. 1982. "Forced sex in marriage: A preliminary research report." *Crime and Delinquency,* 28, pp. 459–478.

Fiorina, Morris P. 1983. "Flagellating the federal bureaucracy." *Society,* March/April, pp. 66–73.

Firor, John. 1990. *The Changing Atmosphere: A Global Challenge.* New Haven, Conn.: Yale University Press.

Fischer, Claude. 1982. *To Dwell Among Friends: Personal Networks in Town and City.* Chicago: University of Chicago Press.

———. 1984. *The Urban Experience,* 2nd ed. San Diego: Harcourt Brace Jovanovich.

Fischer, David Hackett. 1977. *Growing Old in America.* New York: Oxford University Press.

Fischman, Joshua. 1986. "What are friends for?" *Psychology Today,* September, pp. 70–71.

Fishwick, Lesley, and Diane Hayes. 1989. "Sport for whom? Differential participation patterns of recreational athletes in leisure-time physical activities." *Sociology of Sport Journal,* 6, pp. 269–277.

Fiske, Edward B. 1987. "Global focus on quality in education." *New York Times,* June 1, pp. 19, 23.

Fitzpatrick, Joseph P., and Lourdes Travieso Parker. 1981. "Hispanic-Americans in the Eastern United States." *Annals,* 454, March, pp. 98–110.

Fligstein, Neil. 1987. "The intraorganizational power struggle: Rise of finance personnel to top leadership in large corporations, 1919–1979." *American Sociological Review,* 52, pp. 44–58.

Florida, Richard, and Martin Kenney. 1991. "Transplanted organizations: The transfer of Japanese industrial organization to the U.S." *American Sociological Review,* 56, pp. 381–398.

Flygare, Thomas J. 1979. "Schools and the law." *Phi Delta Kappan,* 60, pp. 529–530.

Foner, Anne. 1979. "Ascribed and achieved bases of stratification." *Annual Review of Sociology,* 5, pp. 219–242.

Ford, Clellan S., and Frank A. Beach. 1951. *Patterns of Sexual Behavior.* New York: Harper & Row.

Form, William. 1982. "Self-employed manual workers: Petty bourgeois or working class?" *Social Forces,* 60, pp. 1050–1069.

Fossett, Mark A., and K. Jill Kiecolt. 1989. "The relative size of minority populations and white racial attitudes." *Social Science Quarterly,* 70, pp. 820–835.

Francis, David R. 1987. "Despite concern, black Africa's population picture grows worse." *Christian Science Monitor,* November 7, p. 22.

Frankl, Razelle. 1987. *Televangelism: The Making of Popular Religion.* Carbondale: Southern Illinois University Press.

Franklin, John Hope. 1981. "The land of room enough." *Daedalus,* 110, pp. 1–12.

Freedman, Alix M. 1990. "Deadly diet." *Wall Street Journal,* December 18, pp. A1, A4.

Freedman, Jonathan L. 1978. *Happy People: What Happiness Is, Who Has It, and Why.* New York: Harcourt Brace Jovanovich.

———. 1986. "Television violence and aggression: A rejoinder." *Psychological Bulletin,* 100, pp. 372–378.

French, Marilyn. 1985. *Beyond Power.* New York: Summit Books.

Frey, William H. 1987. "Migration and depopulation of the metropolis: Regional restructuring or rural renaissance?" *American Sociological Review,* 52, pp. 240–257.

Friedman, Milton. 1989a. "An open letter to Bill Bennett." *Wall Street Journal,* September 7, p. A18.

———. 1989b. "We have socialism, Q.E.D." *New York Times,* December 31, p. E11.

Friedman, Thomas L. 1992. "Rethinking foreign affairs: Are they still a U.S. affair?" *New York Times,* February 7, pp. A1, A7.

Friedrich, Otto. 1984. "A proud capital's distress." *Time,* August 6, pp. 26–39.

Fussell, Paul. 1983. *Class: A Guide Through the American Status System.* New York: Summit.

Gabor, Andrea. 1986. "Stark fallout from Chernobyl." *U.S. News & World Report,* May 12, pp. 18–23.

Galles, Gary M. 1989. "What colleges really teach." *New York Times,* June 8, p. 23.

Galloway, Joseph L. 1987. "Islam: Seeking the future in the past." *U.S. News & World Report,* July 6, pp. 33–35.

Gallup, George, Jr., and Jim Castelli. 1989. *The People's Religion: American Faith in the '90s.* New York: Macmillan.

Gambino, Richard. 1974. *Blood of My Blood.* Garden City, N.Y.: Doubleday.

Gamoran, Adam, and Robert D. Mare. 1989. "Secondary school tracking and educational inequality: Compensation, reinforcement, or neutrality?" *American Journal of Sociology,* 94, pp. 1146–1183.

Gamson, William A. 1975. *The Strategy of Social Protest.* Homewood, Ill.: Dorsey.

Gans, Herbert J. 1968. *People and Plans.* New York: Basic Books.

———. 1971. "The uses of poverty: The poor pay all." *Social Policy,* 2, pp. 20–24.

———. 1982a. *The Urban Villagers.* New York: Free Press.

———. 1982b. *The Levittowners: Ways of Life and Politics in a New Suburban Community.* New York: Columbia University Press.

———. 1989. "Sociology in America: The discipline and the public." *American Sociological Review,* 54, pp. 1–16.

Gargan, Edward A. 1991. "Tearful bride, just 10, touches India." *New York Times,* October 21, p. A7.

Gartner, Michael. 1990. "Indian tribes shouldn't bet their future on casinos." *Wall Street Journal,* June 28, p. A15.

Gartner, Rosemary. 1990. "The victims of homicide: A temporal and cross-national comparison." *American Sociological Review,* 55, pp. 92–106.

Gates, Henry Louis, Jr. 1991. "It's not just Anglo-Saxon." *New York Times,* May 4, p. 15.

Gecas, Viktor. 1981. "Contexts of Socialization," in Morris Rosenberg and Ralph H. Turner (eds.), *Social Psychology: Sociological Perspectives.* New York: Basic Books.

———. 1982. "The self-concept." *Annual Review of Sociology,* 8, pp. 1–33.

Gelman, David. 1986. "Why we age differently." *Newsweek,* October 20, pp. 60–61.

———. 1990a. "A much riskier passage." *Newsweek,* Summer/Fall, pp. 10–16.

———. 1990b. "The mind of the rapist." *Newsweek,* July 23, pp. 46–52.

Gerber, Gwendolyn L. 1989. "The more positive evaluation of men than women on the gender-stereotyped traits." *Psychological Reports,* 65, pp. 275–286.

Germani, Gino. 1981. *The Sociology of Modernization.* New Brunswick, N.J.: Transaction.

Gest, Ted. 1990. "Did Milken get off too lightly?" *U.S. News & World Report,* May 7, pp. 22–24.

Gibbs, Nancy R. 1990. "Love and let die." *Time,* March 19, pp. 62–71.

Gilbert, Dennis, and Joseph A. Kahl. 1987. *The American Class Structure: A New Synthesis,* 3rd ed. Homewood, Ill.: Dorsey.

Giles, Michael W., and Arthur Evans. 1986. "The power approach to intergroup hostility." *Journal of Conflict Resolution,* 30, pp. 469–486.

Gilleard, Christopher John, and Ali Aslan Gurkan. 1987. "Socioeconomic development and the status of elderly men in Turkey: A test of modernization theory." *Journal of Gerontology,* 42, pp. 353–357.

Gillespie, Dair L., and Ann Leffler. 1983. "Theories of nonverbal behavior: A critical review of proxemics research," in Randall Collins (ed.), *Sociological Theory 1983.* San Francisco, Calif.: Jossey-Bass.

Gimenez, Martha E. 1990. "The feminization of poverty: Myth or reality?" *Social Justice,* 17, pp. 43–69.

Ginzberg, Eli. 1982. "The mechanization of work." *Scientific American,* 247, September, pp. 66–75.

Giordano, Joseph. 1987. "The Mafia mystique." *U.S. News & World Report,* February 16, p. 6.

Glaab, Charles N., and A. Theodore Brown. 1983. *A History of Urban America,* 3rd ed. New York: Macmillan.

Glass, David, Peverill Squire, and Raymond Wolfinger. 1984. "Voter turnout: An international comparison." *Public Opinion,* December/January, pp. 49-55.

Glazer, Nona. 1980. "Overworking the working woman: The double day in a mass magazine." *Women's Studies International Quarterly,* 3, pp. 79-83.

Glenn, Norval D., and Ruth Hyland. 1967. "Religious preference and worldly success: Some evidence from national surveys." *American Sociological Review,* 32, pp. 73-75.

———, and Charles N. Weaver. 1982. "Enjoyment of work by full-time workers in U.S., 1955 and 1980. *Public Opinion Quarterly,* 46, pp. 459-470.

Glick, Paul C., and Sung-Ling Lin. 1986. "Recent changes in divorce and remarriage." *Journal of Marriage and the Family,* 48, pp. 737-747.

———, and Charles N. Weaver. 1982. "Enjoyment of work by full-time workers in the U.S., 1955 and 1980." *Public Opinion Quarterly,* 46, pp. 459-470.

Goffman, Erving. 1959. *The Presentation of Self in Everyday Life.* Garden City, N.Y.: Doubleday/Anchor.

———. 1961. *Asylums: Essays on the Social Situation of Mental Patients and Other Inmates.* Garden City, N.Y.: Anchor.

Goldberg, Gertrude S., and Eleanor Kremen. 1987. "The feminization of poverty: Only in America." *Social Policy,* Spring, pp. 3-14.

Goldberg, Phillip. 1968. "Are women prejudiced against women?" *Transaction,* 6, April, pp. 28-30.

Goldberger, Marvin L., and Wolfgang P.K. Panofsky. 1990. "All science, great and small." *New York Times,* December 22, p. 15.

Goldman, Ari L. 1991. "Portrait of religion in U.S. holds dozens of surprises." *New York Times,* April 10, pp. A1, A11.

———. 1992. "Catholics are at odds with bishops." *New York Times,* June 19, p. A8.

Goldstein, Jeffrey H., and Robert L. Arms. 1971. "Effects of observing athletic contests on hostility." *Sociometry,* 34, pp. 83-90.

Goldstein, Melvyn C., and Cynthia M. Beall. 1982. "Indirect modernization and the status of the elderly in a rural third-world setting." *Journal of Gerontology,* 37, pp. 743-748.

Goldstone, Jack A. 1982. "The comparative and historical study of revolutions." *Annual Review of Sociology,* 8, pp. 187-207.

Goleman, Daniel. 1988. "Physicians may bungle part of treatment: Medical interview." *New York Times,* January 21, p. 12.

———. 1990. "Stereotypes of the sexes said to persist in therapy." *New York Times,* April 10, pp. B1, B7.

———. 1991. "Anatomy of a rumor: Fear feeds it." *New York Times,* June 4, pp. B1, B7.

Goode, Erich. 1989. *Drugs in American Society,* 3rd ed. New York: Knopf.

Goode, William J. 1982. *The Family,* 2nd ed. Englewood Cliffs, N.J.: Prentice-Hall.

Goodlad, John I. 1984. *A Place Called School: Prospects for the Future.* New York: McGraw-Hill.

Goodman, Norman, and Gary T. Marx. 1982. *Sociology Today,* 4th ed. New York: Random House.

Gordon, David M. 1973. "Capitalism, class and crime in America." *Crime and Delinquency,* 19, pp. 163-186.

Gorman, Christine. 1992. "Sizing up the sexes." *Time,* January 20, pp. 42-51.

Gortmaker, Steven L. 1979. "Poverty and infant mortality in the U.S." *American Sociological Review,* 44, pp. 280-297.

Gory, Mark, et al. 1990. "Depression among the homeless." *Journal of Health and Social Behavior,* 31, pp. 87-101.

Gottdiener, Mark. 1983. "Understanding metropolitan deconcentration: A clash of paradigms." *Social Science Quarterly,* 64, pp. 227-246.

Goy, R. W., and B. S. McEwen. 1980. *Sexual Differentiation of the Brain.* Cambridge, Mass.: MIT Press.

Gracey, Harry L. 1975. "Learning the student role: Kindergarten as academic boot camp," in Holger R. Stub (ed.), *The Sociology of Education.* Homewood, Ill.: Dorsey.

Granovetter, Mark. 1983. "The strength of weak ties: A network theory revisited," in Randall Collins (ed.), *Sociological Theory 1983.* San Francisco: Jossey-Bass.

———. 1984. "Small is bountiful: Labor markets and establishment size." *American Sociological Review,* 49, 323-334.

Grant, W. Vance, and Thomas D. Snyder. 1984. *Digest of Education Statistics 1983-84.* Washington, D.C.: U.S. Government Printing Office.

Greeley, Andrew M. 1989. *Religious Change in America.* Cambridge, Mass.: Harvard University Press.

———, and William C. McCready. 1974. *Ethnicity in the United States: A Preliminary Reconnaissance.* New York: Wiley.

Green, Mark. 1982. "Political PAC-man." *New Republic,* December 13, pp. 18--25.

Greenberg, David. 1981. *Crime and Capitalism: Readings in Marxist Criminology.* Palo Alto, Calif.: Mayfield.

Greenberger, Ellen, and Wendy A. Goldberg. 1989. "Work, parenting, and the socialization of children." *Developmental Psychology,* 25, pp. 22-35.

Greer, Scott. 1956. "Urbanism reconsidered: A comparative study of local areas in a metropolis." *American Sociological Review,* 21, pp. 19-25.

Greider, William. 1992. *Who Will Tell the People: The Betrayal of American Democracy.* New York: Simon & Schuster.

Grellert, Edward A., et al. 1982. "Childhood play activities of male and female homosexuals and heterosexuals." *Archives of Sexual Behavior,* 11, pp. 451-478.

Griffith, Jeanne E., et al. 1989. "American education: The challenge of change." *Population Bulletin,* December, pp. 2-39.

Grobstein, Clifford. 1988. *Science and the Unborn: Choosing Human Futures.* New York: Basic Books.

Gross, Jane. 1991. "More young single men clinging to apron strings." *New York Times,* June 16, pp 1, 10.

Grusky, David B., and Robert M. Hauser. 1984. "Comparative social mobility revisited: Models of convergence and divergence in 16 countries." *American Sociological Review,* 49, pp. 19-38.

Gruson, Lindsey. 1990. "Political violence on the rise again in Guatemala, tarnishing civilian rule." *New York Times,* June 28, p. A3.

Gup, Ted. 1990. "Owl vs. man." *Time,* June 25, pp. 56-63.

Gusfield, Joseph R. 1967a. "Moral passage: The symbolic process in public designations of deviance." *Social Problems,* 15, pp. 175-188.

———. 1967b. "Tradition and modernity: Misplaced polarities in the study of social change." *American Journal of Sociology,* 72, pp. 351-362.

Gwartney-Gibbs, Patricia A. 1986. "The institutionalization of premarital cohabitation: Estimates from marriage license applications, 1970 and 1980." *Journal of Marriage and the Family,* 48, pp. 423-434.

Gwynne, S. C. 1990. "The right stuff." *Time,* October 29, pp. 74-84.

———. 1992. "The long haul." *Time,* September 28, pp. 34-38.

Hacker, Andrew. 1983. "What the very rich really think." *Forbes,* Fall, pp. 66-70.

———, 1992. *Two Nations: Black and White, Separate, Hostile, Unequal.* New York: Scribner's.

Hage, Jerald. 1980. *Theories of Organizations: Form, Process, and Transformation.* New York: Wiley.

Hall, Edward T. 1966. *The Hidden Dimension.* Garden City, N.Y.: Anchor/Doubleday.

———. 1976. "How cultures collide." *Psychology Today,* July, p. 66.

Hall, Wayne. 1986. "Social class and survival on the *S.S. Titanic.*" *Social Science and Medicine,* 22, pp. 687-690.

Haller, Archibald O., and David B. Bills. 1979. "Occupational prestige hierarchies: Theory and evidence." *Contemporary Sociology,* 8, pp. 721-734.

Haller, Max, et al. 1985. "Patterns of career mobility and structural positions in advanced capitalist societies: A comparison of men in Austria, France, and the United States." *American Sociological Review,* 50, pp. 579-603.

Hammond, Phillip E. 1985. "The curious path of conservative

Protestantism." *Annals of American Academy of Political and Social Science,* 480, July, pp. 53-62.

Hancock, R. Kelly. 1980. "The social life of the modern corporation: Changing resources and forms." *Journal of Applied Behavioral Science,* 16, pp. 279-298.

Handwerker, W. Penn, and Paul V. Crosbie. 1982. "Sex and dominance." *American Anthropologist,* 84, pp. 97-104.

Hanlon, Martin D. 1982. "Primary group assistance during unemployment." *Human Organization,* 41, pp. 156-161.

Harayda, Janice. 1986. *The Joy of Being Single.* Garden City, N.Y.: Doubleday.

Hare, A. Paul. 1962. *Handbook of Small Group Research.* Glencoe, Ill.: Free Press.

Harris, Anthony R., and Gary D. Hill. 1982. "The social psychology of deviance: Toward a reconciliation with social structure." *Annual Review of Sociology,* 8, pp. 161-186.

Harris, Louis. 1987. *Inside America.* New York: Vintage.

Harris, Marvin. 1974. *Cows, Pigs, Wars and Witches.* New York: Random House.

———. 1985. *Good to Eat: Riddles of Foods and Culture.* New York: Simon & Schuster.

Harrison, Selig S. 1979. "Why they won't speak our language in Asia." *Asia,* March/April, pp. 3-7.

Harwood, John, and Timothy Noah. 1992. "Candidates head down campaign trail. . ." *Wall Street Journal,* October 21, p. A18.

Hasenfeld, Yeheskel. 1987. "Is bureaucratic growth inevitable?" *Contemporary Sociology,* 16, pp. 316-318.

Hatch, Ruth C., Dorothy E. James, and Walter R. Schumm. 1986. "Spiritual intimacy and marital satisfaction." *Family Relations,* 35, pp. 539-545.

Haub, Carl V. 1991. "Populations and population movements." *Encyclopaedia Britannica: 1991 Book of the Year,* pp. 278-281.

Hauser, Philip M. 1981. "Chicago—urban crisis exemplar," in J. John Palen (ed.), *City Scenes,* 2nd ed. Boston: Little, Brown.

Hawkes, Kristen, and James F. O'Connell. 1981. "Affluent hunters? Some comments in light of the Alyawara case." *American Anthropologist,* 83, pp. 622-626.

Hawkins, Dana. 1992. "A very rich dessert." *U.S. News & World Report,* March 23, pp. 52-53.

Headland, Thomas N., and Lawrence A. Reid. 1989. "Hunter-gatherers and their neighbors from prehistory to the present." *Current Anthropology,* 30, pp. 43-51.

Hearn, John. 1978. "Rationality and bureaucracy: Maoist contributions to a Marxist theory of bureaucracy." *Sociological Quarterly,* 19, pp. 37-54.

Hearst, Norman, and Stephen B. Hulley. 1988. "Preventing the heterosexual spread of AIDS." *Journal of the American Medical Association,* 259, pp. 2428-2432.

Heilbroner, Robert L. 1972. *The Worldly Philosophers: The Lives, Times, and Ideas of the Great Economic Thinkers,* 4th ed. New York: Simon & Schuster.

———. 1980. *Marxism: For and Against.* New York: Norton.

Heilman, Samuel C. 1982. "The sociology of American Jewry: The last ten years." *Annual Review of Sociology,* 8, pp. 135-160.

Helgesen, Sally. 1990. "The pyramid and the web." *New York Times,* May 27, p. F13.

Henry, William A., III. 1990. "Beyond the melting pot." *Time,* April 9, pp. 28-31.

Hensley, Thomas R., and Glen W. Griffin. 1986. "Victims of groupthink: The Kent State University board of trustees and the 1977 gymnasium controversy." *Journal of Conflict Resolution,* 30, pp. 497-531.

Herberg, Will. 1983. *Protestant-Catholic-Jew: An Essay in American Religions.* Chicago: University of Chicago.

Heyl, Barbara. 1979. *The Madam as Entrepreneur: Career Management in House Prostitution.* New Brunswick, N.J.: Transaction.

Heyneman, Stephen P., and William A. Loxley. 1983. "The effect of primary-school quality on academic achievement across twenty-nine high- and low-income countries." *American Journal of Sociology,* 88, pp. 1162-1194.

Hill, Martha S. 1985. "The changing nature of poverty." *The Annals of the American Academy of Political and Social Sciences,* 479, pp. 31-47.

Hilts, Philip J. 1990. "AIDS bias grows faster than disease, study says." *New York Times,* July 17, pp. 1, 14.

Hippler, Arthur E. 1978. "Culture and personality perspective of the Yolngu of Northeastern Arnhem Land. Part I—Early socialization." *Journal of Psychological Anthropology,* 1, pp. 221-244.

Hirschi, Travis. 1969. *Causes of Delinquency.* Berkeley and Los Angeles: University of California Press.

Hirschman, Charles. 1983. "America's melting pot reconsidered." *Annual Review of Sociology,* 9, pp. 397-423.

Hite, Shere. 1976. *The Hite Report.* New York: Macmillan.

Hochschild, Arlie R. 1983. *The Managed Heart: Commercialization of Human Feeling.* Berkeley: University of California Press.

———. 1989. *The Second Shift.* New York: Viking.

Hodge, Robert W., Paul M. Siegel, and Peter H. Rossi. 1964. "Occupational prestige in the United States: 1925-1963." *American Journal of Sociology,* 70, pp. 286-302.

Hodson, Randy. 1989. "Gender differences in job satisfaction: Why aren't women more dissatisfied?" *Sociological Quarterly,* 30, pp. 385-399.

Hoetler, John W. 1982. "Race differences in selective credulity and self-esteem." *Sociological Quarterly,* 23, pp. 527-537.

Hoffer, Eric. 1966. *The True Believer: Thoughts on the Nature of Mass Movements.* New York: Harper & Row.

Hogan, Dennis P., et al. 1990. "Race, kin networks, and assistance to mother-headed families." *Social Forces,* 68, pp. 797-812.

Hollinger, Richard C., and John P. Clark. 1982. "Formal and informal social controls of employee deviance." *Sociological Quarterly,* 23, pp. 333-343.

Hollingsworth, J. Rogers. 1986. *A Political Economy of Medicine: Great Britain and the United States.* Baltimore, Md.: Johns Hopkins University Press.

Holton, R. J. 1983. "Max Weber, 'rational capitalism,' and Renaissance Italy: A critique of Cohen." *American Journal of Sociology,* 89, pp. 166-180.

Hopper, Earl. 1981. *Social Mobility: A Study of Social Control and Insatiability.* Oxford: Blackwell.

Horai, Joanne, Nicholas Naccari, and Elliot Fatoullan. 1974. "The effects of expertise and physical attractiveness upon opinion agreement and liking." *Sociometry,* 37, pp. 601-606.

Horner, Matina S. 1969. "Fail: Bright women." *Psychology Today,* November, pp. 36-38.

Hotz, Louis. 1984. "South Africa." *1984 Britannica Book of the Year,* pp. 621-624.

Hoult, Thomas Ford. 1974, 1979. *Sociology for a New Day,* 1st and 2nd eds. New York: Random House.

———. 1983. "Human sexuality in biological perspective: Theoretical and methodological considerations." *Journal of Homosexuality,* 9, pp. 138-139.

House, James S. 1981. "Social structure and personality," in Morris Rosenberg and Ralph H. Turner (eds.), *Social Psychology.* New York: Basic Books.

———, et al. 1988. "Social relationships and health." *Science,* 241, pp. 540-545.

Hout, Michael. 1988. "More universalism, less structural mobility." *American Journal of Sociology,* 93, pp. 1358-1400.

———, and Andrew M. Greeley. 1987. "The center doesn't hold: Church attendance in the United States, 1940-1984." *American Sociological Review,* 52, pp. 325-345.

Hoyt, Karen. 1987. *The New Age Rage.* Old Tappan, N.J.: Fleming Revell Co.

Hraba, Joseph. 1979. *American Ethnicity.* Itasca, Ill.: Peacock.

Hsu, Cheng-Kuang, Robert M. Marsh, and Hiroshi Mannari. 1983. "An examination of the determinants of organization structure." *American Journal of Sociology,* 88, pp. 975-996.

Hsu, Francis L. K. 1979. "The cultural problem of the cultural anthropologist." *American Anthropologist,* 81, pp. 517-532.

Huey, John. 1991. "What pop culture is tellin us." *Fortune,* June 17, pp. 90-92.

Humphreys, Laud. 1970. *Tearoom Trade: Impersonal Sex in Public Places.* Chicago: Aldine.

Huntley, Steve. 1983. "America's Indians: "Beggars in our own land.'" *U.S. News & World Report,* May 23, pp. 70-72.

Hyland, Michael E. 1989. "There is no motive to avoid success: The compromise explanation for success-avoiding behavior." *Journal of Personality,* 57, pp. 665-693.

Inkeles, Alex. 1983. *Exploring Individual Modernity.* New York: Columbia University Press.

Inwald, Robin Hurwitz, and N. Dale Bryant. 1981. "The effect of sex of participants on decision making in small teacher groups." *Psychology of Women Quarterly,* 5, pp. 532-542.

Jackson, Elton F., and Richard F. Curtis. 1972. "Effects of vertical mobility and status inconsistency: A body of negative evidence." *American Sociological Review,* 37, pp. 701-713.

Jacoby, Neil H., et al. 1977. *Bribery and Extortion in World Business: A Study of Corporate Political Payments Abroad.* New York: Macmillan.

Jacquard, Albert. 1983. "Myths under the microscope." *UNESCO Courier,* 36, November, pp. 25-27.

Jaggar, Alison M., and Paula Rothenberg Struhl. 1978. *Feminist Frameworks.* New York: McGraw-Hill.

Janis, Irving L. 1982. *Groupthink: Psychological Studies of Policy Decisions and Fiascos.* Boston: Houghton Mifflin.

Janman, Karen. 1989. "One step behind: Current stereotypes of women, achievement, and work." *Sex Roles,* 21, pp. 209-229.

Jaret, Charles. 1983. "Recent neo-Marxist urban analysis." *Annual Review of Sociology,* 9, pp. 499-525.

Jaynes, Gerald David, and Robin M. Williams, Jr. (eds.). 1989. *A Common Destiny: Blacks and American Society.* Washington, D.C.: National Academy Press.

Jencks, Christopher. 1992. *Rethinking Social Policy: Race, Poverty, and the Underclass.* Cambridge, Mass.: Harvard University Press.

Jencks, Christopher, et al. 1972. *Inequality: A Reassessment of the Effect of Family and Schooling in America.* New York: Basic Books.

Johnson, David W., and Roger T. Johnson. 1984. "The effects of intergroup cooperation and intergroup competition on ingroup and outgroup cross-handicap relationships." *Journal of Social Psychology,* 124, pp. 85-94.

Johnson, Dirk. 1990a. "Chastity organization: Starting over in purity." *New York Times,* January 28, p. 12.

———. 1990b. "Right to die: Second battle for abortion foes." *New York Times,* July 31, pp. A1, A6.

Johnson, Julie et al. 1991. "Why do blacks die young?" *Time,* September 16, pp. 50-52.

Johnson, Marguerite. 1984. "This is all so painful." *Time,* June 4, p. 36.

Johnson, Miriam M. 1982. "Fathers and 'femininity' in daughters: A review of the research." *Sociology and Social Research,* 67, pp. 1-17.

Johnson, Sterling, Jr. 1987. "This is the wrong message to give." *New York Times,* December 20, p. E20.

Josephson, Wendy L. 1987. "Television violence and children's aggression: Testing the priming, social script, and disinhibition predictions." *Journal of Personality and Social Psychology,* 53, pp. 882-890.

Joubert, Charles E. 1989. "The famous sayings test: Sex differences and some correlations with other variables." *Psychological Reports,* 64, pp. 763-766.

Judis, John B. 1989. "Rev. Moon's rising political influence." *U.S. News & World Report,* March 27, pp. 27-31.

Kagan, Donald. 1991. "Western values are central." *New York Times,* May 4, p. 15.

Kalick, S. Michael, and Thomas E. Hamilton III. 1986. "The matching hypothesis reexamined." *Journal of Personality and Social Psychology,* 51, pp. 673-682.

Kalisch, Philip A., and Beatrice J. Kalisch. 1984. "Sex-role stereotyping of nurses and physicians on prime-time television: A dichotomy of occupational portrayals." *Sex Roles,* 10, pp. 533-553.

Kalmuss, Debra. 1984. "The intergenerational transmission of marital aggression." *Journal of Marriage and the Family,* 46, pp. 11-19.

Kanin, Eugene J. 1983. "Rape as a function of relative sexual frustration." *Psychological Reports,* 52, pp. 133-134.

Kanter, Rosabeth Moss. 1977. *Men and Women of the Corporation.* New York: Basic Books.

Kantrowitz, Barbara. 1987. "How to stay married." *Time,* August, pp. 52-57.

———. 1991. "Falling further behind." *Newsweek,* August 19, p. 60.

———. 1992. "Breaking the divorce cycle." *Newsweek,* January 13, pp. 48-53.

Kasarda, John D., and John O. G. Billy. 1985. "Social mobility and fertility." *Annual Review of Sociology,* 11, pp. 305-328.

Kaufman, Herbert. 1977. *Red Tape.* Washington, D.C.: Brookings Institution.

Kaus, Mickey. 1992. *The End of Equality.* New York: Basic Books.

Keller, Helen. 1954. *The Story of My Life.* Garden City, N.Y.: Doubleday.

Kemper, Susan. 1984. "When to speak like a lady." *Sex Roles,* 10, pp. 435-443.

Kenna, John T. 1983. "The Latinization of the U.S." *1983 Britannica Book of the Year,* pp. 586-587.

Kennedy, Paul M. 1988. *The Rise and Fall of the Great Powers.* New York: Random House.

———. 1991. "A declining empire goes to war." *Wall Street Journal,* January 24, p. A10.

Kephart, William M., and Davor Jedlicka. 1988. *The Family, Society, and the Individual,* 6th ed. New York: Harper & Row.

Kerbo, Harold R. 1982. "Movements of 'crisis' and movements of 'affluence': A critique of deprivation and resource mobilization theories." *Journal of Conflict Resolution,* 26, pp. 645-663.

———. 1983. *Social Stratification and Inequality: Class Conflict in the United States.* New York: McGraw-Hill.

Kerckhoff, Alan C., Richard T. Campbell, and Idee Winfield-Laird. 1985. "Social mobility in Great Britain and the United States." *American Journal of Sociology,* 91, pp. 281-308.

Kessin, Kenneth. 1971. "Social and psychological consequences of intergenerational occupational mobility." *American Journal of Sociology,* 77, pp. 1-18.

Kessler, Ronald C., Richard H. Price, and Camille B. Wortman. 1985. "Social factors in psychopathology: Stress, social support, and coping processes." *Annual Review of Psychology,* 36, pp. 560-561.

Kilborn, Peter T. 1990a. "Wage gap between sexes is cut in test, but at a price." *New York Times,* May 31, pp. A1, A12.

———. 1990b. "Workers using computers find a supervisor inside." *New York Times,* December 23, pp. 1, 13.

Kilman, Scott, and Robert Johnson. 1991. "No haven." *Wall Street Journal,* March 5, pp. A1, A5.

Kim, Paul S. 1983. "Japan's bureaucratic decision-making on the textbook." *Public Administration,* 61, pp. 283-294.

Kimball, Meredith M. 1989. "A new perspective on women's math achievement." *Psychological Bulletin,* 105, pp. 198-214.

Kimmel, Michael S. 1986. "A prejudice against prejudice." *Psychology Today,* December, pp. 47-52.

———. 1992. "Reading men: Men, masculinity, and publishing." *Contemporary Sociology,* 21, pp. 162-171.December, pp. 47-52.

King, Anthony. 1985. "Transatlantic transgressions: A comparison of British and American scandals." *Public Opinion,* January, pp. 20-22, 64.

Kitagawa, Evelyn M., and Philip M. Hauser. 1968. "Education differentials in mortality by cause of death, United States 1960." *Demography,* 5, pp. 318-353.

Kitahara, Michio. 1982. "Menstrual taboos and the importance of hunting." *American Anthropologist,* 84, pp. 901-903.

Kitano, Harry H. L. 1981. "Asian-Americans: The Chinese, Japanese, Koreans, Filipinos, and Southeast Asians." *Annals,* 454, March, pp. 125-149.

Klag, Michael J., et al. 1991. "The association of skin color with blood pressure in U.S. blacks with low socioeconomic status." *Journal of the American Medical Association,* 265, pp. 599-640.

Klaus, Patsy A., and Michael R. Rand. 1984. "Family violence."

Bureau of Justice Statistics Special Report. U.S. Department of Justice.

Kluckhohn, Clyde. 1948. "As an anthropologist views it," in Albert Deutsch (ed.), *Sex Habits of American Men.* Englewood Cliffs, N.J.: Prentice-Hall.

Kluegel, James R. 1990. "Trends in whites' explanations of the black-white gap in socioeconomic status, 1977-1989." *American Sociological Review,* 55, pp. 512-525.

Knight, Robin. 1985. "The Marxist world: Lure of capitalism." *U.S. News & World Report,* February 4, pp. 36-42.

Knoke, David, and James H. Kuklinski. 1982. *Network Analysis.* Beverly Hills, Calif.: Sage.

Koenig, Fredrick. 1982. "Today's conditions make U.S. 'ripe for the rumor mill.'" *U.S. News & World Report,* December 6, p. 42.

Kohlberg, Lawrence. 1966. "A cognitive-developmental analysis of children's sex-role concepts and attitudes," in Eleanor E. Maccoby (ed.), *The Development of Sex Differences.* Stanford, Calif.: Stanford University Press.

Kohn, Alfie. 1988. "You know what they say. . . " *Psychology Today,* April, pp. 36-41.

Kohn, Melvin L. 1963. "Social class and parent-child relations: An interpretation." *American Journal of Sociology,* 68, pp. 471-480.

———. 1977. *Class and Conformity,* 2nd ed. Homewood, Ill. Dorsey.

———. 1980. "Job complexity and adult personality," in Neal Smelser and Erik Erikson (eds.), *Themes of Love and Work in Adulthood.* Cambridge, Mass.: Harvard University Press.

———. 1983. "The benefits of bureaucracy." In Melvin L. Kohn and Schooler (eds.), *Occupational Structure and Personality.* Norwood, N.J.: Ablex.

Kohn, Alfie. 1986. *No Contest: The Case Against Competition.* Boston: Houghton Mifflin.

Kolata, Gina. 1979. "Sex hormones and brain development." *Science,* September 7, pp. 985-987.

———. 1990. "Wariness is replacing trust between physician and patient." *New York Times,* February 20, pp. A1, A10.

———. 1991. "Are U.S. students the worst? Comparisons seen as flawed." *New York Times,* December 24, pp. A1, A6.

Koller, Marvin R., and Oscar W. Ritchie. 1978. *Sociology of Childhood,* 2nd ed. Englewood Cliffs, N.J.: Prentice-Hall.

Kosters, Marvin H. 1990. "Be cool, stay in school." *The American Enterprise,* March/April, pp. 60-67.

Kourvetaris, George A., and Betty A. Dobratz. 1982. "Political power and conventional political participation." *Annual Review of Sociology,* 8, pp. 289-317.

Krackhardt, David, and Robert N. Stern. 1988. "Informal networks and organizational crises: An experimental simulation." *Social Psychology Quarterly,* 51, pp. 123-140.

Kramon, Glenn. 1991. "Medical second-guessing—in advance." *New York Times,* February 24, p. F12.

Kraut, Robert E. 1976. "Deterrent and definitional influences on shoplifting." *Social Problems,* 23, pp. 358–368.

Krauthammer, Charles. 1990. "In praise of low voter turnout." *Time,* May 21, p. 88.

Kristof, Nicholas D. 1990. "More in China willingly rear one child." *New York Times,* May 9, pp. 1, B9.

———. 1991. "Chinese Relations." *New York Times Magazine,* August 18, pp. 8–10.

Krivo, Lauren. 1986. "Home ownership differences between Hispanics and Anglos in the United States." *Social Problems,* 33, pp. 319–334.

Krugman, Paul. 1990. *The Age of Diminished Expectations: U.S. Economic Policy in the 1990s.* Cambridge, Mass.: MIT Press.

Kruttschnitt, Candace. 1989. "A sociological, offender-based study of rape." *Sociological Quarterly,* 30, pp. 305–329.

Kübler-Ross, Elisabeth. 1969. *On Death and Dying.* New York: Macmillan.

Kuhn, Thomas S. 1970. *The Structure of Scientific Revolutions,* 2nd ed. Chicago: University of Chicago Press.

Kump, Theresa. 1992. "Moms' night out." *Parents,* February, pp. 58–63.

Lacayo, Richard. 1987. "Considering the alternatives." *Time,* February 2, pp. 60–61.

———. 1987. "Whose trial is it anyway?" *Time,* May 25, p. 62.

———. 1990. "Why no blue blood will flow." *Time,* November 26, p. 34.

Lader, Lawrence. 1983. "The China solution." *Science Digest,* April, p. 78.

La Gory, Mark, et al. 1990. "Depression among the homeless." *Journal of Health and Social Behavior,* 31, pp. 87–101.

Lamar, Jacob V. 1989. "I deserve punishment." *Time,* February 6, p. 34.

Landes, David S. 1969. *The Unbound Prometheus: Technological Change and Industrial Development in Western Europe from 1750 to the Present.* London: Cambridge University Press.

Landy, David, and Harold Sigall. 1974. "Beauty is talent—Task evaluation as a function of the performer's physical attractiveness." *Journal of Personality and Social Psychology,* 29, pp. 299–304.

Lane, Harlan. 1976. *The Wild Boy of Aveyron.* Cambridge, Mass.: Harvard University Press.

Laner, Mary Riege. 1989. *Dating: Delights, Discontents, and Dilemmas.* Salem, Wis.: Sheffield.

Langer, Gary. 1989. "Polling on prejudice: Questionable questions." *Public Opinion,* May/June, pp. 18–19, 57.

Lansing, J. Stephen. 1978. "Economic growth and traditional society: A cautionary tale from Bali." *Human Organization,* 37, pp. 391–394.

Lapham, Lewis H. 1992. "Fear of freedom." *New York Times,* June 6, p. 15.

Larsen, Otto. 1981. "Need for continuing support for social sciences." *ASA Footnotes,* 9, March, p. 8.

Lasch, Christopher. 1977. *Haven in a Heartless World: The Family Besieged.* New York. Basic Books.

———. 1979. *The Culture of Narcissism: American Life in an Age of Diminishing Expectations.* New York: Norton.

Latané, Bibb, and Steve Nida. 1981. "Ten years of research on group size and helping." *Psychological Bulletin,* 89, pp. 308–324.

Lawson, Carol. 1989. "Girls still apply makeup, boys fight wars." *New York Times,* June 15, pp. 15, 19.

Leakey, Richard E., and Roger Lewin. 1977. *Origins.* New York: Dutton.

Le Bon, Gustave. 1976/1896. *The Crowd: A Study of the Popular-Mind.* New York: Viking.

Lee, Alfred McClung, and Elizabeth Briant Lee. 1979. *The Fine Art of Propaganda.* San Francisco: International Society for General Semantics.

Lee, Barrett A., and Avery M. Guest. 1983. "Determinants of neighborhood satisfaction: A metropolitan-level analysis." *Sociological Quarterly,* 24, pp. 287–303.

Lee, Felicia R. 1990. "Crime up in New York in elementary schools." *New York Times,* April 24, p. A13.

Lee, John Alan. 1982. "Three paradigms of childhood." *Canadian Review of Sociology and Anthropology,* 19, pp. 591–608.

Lee, Richard B. 1979. *The !Kung San: Men, Women and Work in a Foraging Society.* New York: Cambridge University Press.

Lehner, Urban C. 1992. "Is it any surprise the Japanese make excellent loafers?" *Wall Street Journal,* February 28, pp. A1, A10.

Lemert, Edwin M. 1951. *Social Pathology.* New York: McGraw-Hill.

Lemonick, Michael D. 1990. "Forecast: Clear skies." *Time,* November 5, p. 33.

———. 1992."The ozone vanishes." *Time,* February 17, pp. 60–63.

Lengermann, Patricia Madoo, and Jill Niebrugge-Brantley. 1992. "Contemporary feminist theory." Pp. 447–496 in George Ritzer, *Sociological Theory,* 3rd ed. New York: McGraw-Hill.

Lenski, Gerhard. 1961. *The Religious Factor.* Garden City, N.Y.: Anchor/Doubleday.

———. 1966. *Power and Privilege.* New York: McGraw-Hill.

———, Jean Lenski, Patrick Nolan. 1991. *Human Societies,* 6th ed. New York: McGraw-Hill.

———, and Patrick D. Nolan. 1984. "Trajectories of development: A test of ecological-evolutionary theory." *Social Forces,* 63, pp. 1–23.

Leo, John. 1987. "Exploring the traits of twins." *Time,* January 12, p. 63.

———. 1991. "Community and personal duty." *U.S. News & World Report,* January 28, p. 17.

Lerner, Robert, Althea K. Nagai, and Stanley Rothman. 1989. "Marginality and liberalism among Jewish elites." *Public Opinion Quarterly,* 53, pp. 330–352.

Leslie, Gerald R., and Sheila K. Korman. 1989. *The Family in Social Context,* 7th ed. New York: Oxford University Press.

Levin, Jack, and William C. Levin. 1980. *Ageism: Prejudice and Discrimination against the Elderly.* Belmont, Calif.: Wadsworth.

———. 1990. "The second time around: Realities of remarriage." *U.S. News & World Report,* January 29, pp. 50–51.

Levine, John M., and Richard L. Moreland. 1990. "Progress in small group research." *Annual Review of Psychology,* 14, pp. 585–634.

Levine, Mark F., James C. Taylor, and Louis E. Davis. 1984. "Defining quality of working life." *Human Relations,* 37, pp. 81–104.

Levine, Saul V. 1984. *Radical Departures: Desperate Detours to Growing Up.* New York: Harcourt Brace Jovanovich.

Levitan, Sar A. 1984. "The changing workplace." *Society,* September/October, pp. 41–48.

———, and Richard S. Belous. 1981. *What's Happening to the American Family?* Baltimore, Md.: Johns Hopkins University Press.

Levy, S. G., and W. F. Fenley, Jr. 1979. "Audience size and likelihood and intensity of response during a humorous movie." *Bulletin of Psychonomic Society,* 13, pp. 409–412.

Lewin, Bo. 1982. "Unmarried cohabitation: A marriage form in a changing society." *Journal of Marriage and the Family,* 44, pp. 763–773.

Lewin, Tamar. 1990a. "Black children living with one parent put at 55%." *New York Times,* July 15, p. 10.

———. 1990b. "Father's vanishing act called common drama." *New York Times,* June 4, p. A15.

———. 1992a. "Rise in single parenthood is reshaping U.S." *New York Times,* October 5, pp. A1, A16.

Lewis, Lionel S. 1982. "Working at leisure." *Society,* July/August, pp. 27–32.

Lewis, Oscar. 1961. *The Children of Sanchez.* New York: Random House.

———. 1965. "Further observations on the folk-urban continuum and urbanization," in Philip M. Hauser and Leo F. Schnore (eds.), *The Study of Urbanization.* New York: Wiley.

Lightbourne, Robert, Jr., and Susheela Singh, with Cynthia P. Green. 1982. "The world fertility survey: Charting global childbearing." *Population Bulletin,* 37, March, pp. 1–54.

Lin, Nan. 1982. "Social resources and instrumental action." In Peter V. Marsden and Nan Lin (eds.), *Social Structure and Network Analysis.* Beverly Hills, Calif.: Sage, pp. 131–145.

Lincoln, C. Eric, and Lawrence H. Mamiya. 1990. *The Black Church in African American Experience.* Durham, N.C.: Duke University Press.

Lindberg, David C. 1992. *The Beginnings of Western Science: The European Scientific Tradition in Philosophical, Religious, and Institutional Context, 600 B.C. to A.D. 1450.* Chicago: University of Chicago Press.

Linn, Marcia C., and Janet S. Hyde. 1989. "Gender, mathematics, and science." *Educational Research,* 18, pp. 17–19, 22–27.

Lipset, Seymour Martin. 1982. "Social mobility in industrial societies." *Public Opinion,* June/July, pp. 41–44.

———. 1987. "Blacks and Jews: How much bias?" *Public Opinion,* July/August, pp. 4–5, 57–58.

———, and Earl Raab, 1978. *The Politics of Unreason,* 2nd ed. New York: Harper & Row.

———. 1990a. "A unique people in an exceptional country," in S. M. Lipset (ed.), *American Pluralism and the Jewish Community.* New Brunswick, N.J.: Transaction, pp. 3–29.

———. 1990b. "The work ethic—then and now." *Public Interest,* Winter, pp. 61–69.

Liska, Allen E., and Barbara D. Warner. 1991. "Functions of crime: A paradoxical process." *American Journal of Sociology,* 96, pp. 1441–1463.

Little, Stratton. 1991. "The 1990 U.S. census." *Encyclopaedia Britannica: 1991 Book of the Year,* pp. 279–280.

Littman, Mark S. 1989. "Reasons for not working: Poor and nonpoor householders." *Monthly Labor Review,* August, pp. 16–20.

Logan, John R., and Mark Schneider. 1984. "Racial segregation and racial change in American suburbs, 1970–1980." *American Journal of Sociology,* 89, pp. 874–888.

Long, Sharon K., Ann D. White, and Patrice Karr. 1983. "Family violence: A microeconomic approach." *Social Science Research,* 12, pp. 363–392.

Lopez, Julie Amparano. 1992. "Study says women face glass walls as well as ceilings." *Wall Street Journal,* March 3, pp. B1, B8.

Lord, Lewis J., and Miriam Horn. 1987. "The brain battle." *U.S. News & World Report,* January 19, pp. 58–64.

Lord, Walter. 1981. *A Night to Remember.* New York: Penguin.

Los, Maria. 1990. *The Second Economy in Marxist States.* New York: St. Martin's.

Mabry, Edward A., and Richard E. Barnes. 1980. *The Dynamics of Small Group Communication.* Englewood Cliffs, N.J.: Prentice-Hall.

Mack, Raymond W., and Calvin P. Bradford. 1979. *Transforming America.* New York: Random House.

Macrae, Norman. 1984. "Reducing medical costs." *World Press Review,* 31, July, pp. 27-29.

Madsen, Douglas, and Peter G. Snow. 1983. "The dispersion of charisma." *Comparative Political Studies,* 16, pp. 337-362.

Madsen, Jane M. 1982. "Racist images." *USA Today,* 111, p. 14.

Major, Brenda, et al. 1990. "Gender patterns in social touch: The impact of setting and age." *Journal of Personality and Social Psychology,* 58, pp. 634-643.

Malcolm, Andrew H. 1989. "More Americans are killing each other." *New York Times,* December 31, p. 14.

————. 1990. "States' prisons continue to bulge, overwhelming efforts at reform." *New York Times,* May 20, pp. 1, 18.

Malone, Janet H. 1982. "The questionable promise of enterprise zones: Lessons from England and Italy." *Urban Affairs Quarterly,* 18, pp. 19-30.

Maloney, Lawrence D. 1984. "Plague of religious wars around the globe." *U.S. News & World Report,* June 25, pp. 24-26.

Malson, Lucien. 1972. *Wolf Children and the Problem of Human Nature.* New York: Monthly Review.

Marden, Charles F., and Gladys Meyer. 1978. *Minorities in American Society.* New York: Van Nostrand.

Marini, Margaret Mooney. 1990. "Sex differences in earnings in the United States." *Annual Review of Sociology,* 15, pp. 343-380.

Markides, Kyriacos C., and Steven F. Cohn. 1982. "External conflict/internal cohesion: A reevaluation of an old theory." *American Sociological Review,* 47, pp. 88-98.

Markovsky, Barry, and Seymour M. Berger. 1983. "Crowd noise and mimicry." *Personality and Social Psychology Bulletin,* 9, pp. 90-96.

Marmor, Judd. 1980. "Overview: The multiple roots of homosexual behavior." In J. Marmor (ed.), *Homosexual Behavior.* New York: Basic Books, p. 13.

Marquand, Robert. 1986. "Speaking for teacher 'professionalism.'" *Christian Science Monitor,* October 6, pp. 27, 30.

Marriott, Michel. 1990. "Intense college recruiting drives lift black enrollment to a record." *New York Times,* April 15, pp. 1, 13.

Marsh, Barbara. 1991. "Women in the work force." *Wall Street Journal,* October 18, p. B3.

Martin, Teresa Castro, and Larry L. Bumpass. 1989. "Recent trends in marital disruption." *Demography,* 26, pp. 37-51.

Marty, Martin E. 1988. "Religion, television, and money." *Encyclopaedia Britannica,* pp. 294-295.

————. 1990. "Satan and the American spiritual underground." *Encyclopaedia Britannica: 1990 Book of the Year,* pp. 308-309.

————, and R. Scott Appleby (eds.) 1992. *Fundamentalisms Observed.* Chicago: University of Chicago Press.

Marx, Gary T. 1967. *Protest and Prejudice.* New York: Harper & Row.

Marx, Karl. 1967/1866. *Capital,* vol. 1. New York: International Publishers.

————. 1964. *Theories of Surplus Value,* vol. 1. London: Lawrence & Wishart.

Massey, Douglas S. 1983. "A research note on residential succession: The Hispanic case." *Social Forces,* 61, pp. 825-833.

Mathews, Tom. 1992a. "Secrets of a serial killer." *Newsweek,* February 3, pp. 44-49.

————. 1992b. "The siege of L.A." *Newsweek,* May 11, pp. 30-38.

Mathison, David L. 1986. "Sex differences in the perception of assertiveness among female managers." *Journal of Social Psychology,* 126, pp. 599-606.

Mazur, Allan. 1986. "U.S. trends in feminine beauty and overadaptation." *Journal of Sex Research,* 22, pp. 281-303.

McClearn, Gerald E. 1969. "Biological bases of social behavior with specific reference to violent behavior," in Donald J. Mulvihill et al. (eds.), *Crimes of Violence,* vol. 13. Washington, D.C.: U.S. Government Printing Office.

McCormick, John, and Peter McKillop. 1989. "The other suburb." *Newsweek,* June 26, pp. 22-24.

McHugh, Kevin E. 1989. "Hispanic migration and population redistribution in the United States." *Professional Geographer,* 41, pp. 429-439.

McIntosh, Peggy. 1993. "White privilege and male privilege: A personal account of coming to see correspondences through work in women's studies." Pp. 30-38 in Anne Minas (ed.), *Gender Basics: Feminist Perspectives on Women and Men.* Belmont, Cal.: Wadsworth.

McKinlay, John B., and Sonja M. McKinlay. 1987. "Medical measures and the decline of mortality," in Howard D. Schwartz (ed.), *Dominant Issues in Medical Sociology,* 2nd ed. New York: Random House.

McLanahan, Sara S. 1983. "Family structure and stress: A longitudinal comparison of two-parent and female-headed families." *Journal of Marriage and the Family,* 45, pp. 347-357.

McNeill, William H. 1963. *The Rise of the West: A History of the Human Community.* Chicago: University of Chicago Press.

McPhail, Clark, and Ronald T. Wohlstein. 1983. "Individual and collective behaviors within gatherings, demonstrations, and riots." *Annual Review of Sociology,* 9, pp. 579-600.

McTeer, William, and James E. Curtis. 1990. "Physical activity and psychological well-being: Testing alternative sociological interpretations." *Sociology of Sport Journal,* 7, pp. 329–346.

McWhirter, William. 1990. "Why can't a woman manage more like . . . a woman?" *Time,* Fall, p. 53.

McWilliams, Carey. 1948. *A Mask for Privilege.* Boston: Little, Brown.

Mead, Lawrence M. 1992. *The New Politics of Poverty: The Nonworking Poor in America.* New York: Basic Books.

Meadows, Donella H., et al. 1974. *The Limits to Growth,* 2nd ed. New York: Universe Books.

Medea, Andra, and Kathleen Thompson. 1974. *Against Rape.* New York: Farrar, Straus and Giroux.

Mednick, Sarnoff A., and J. Volavka. 1980. "Biology and crime," in N. Morris and M. Tonry (eds.), *Crime and Justice: An Annual Review of Research,* vol. 2. Chicago: University of Chicago Press.

Meer, Jeff. 1986. "The reason of age." *Psychology Today,* June, pp. 60–64.

Mendez, Juan E. 1990. "U.S. joins Peru's dirty war." *New York Times,* May 7, p. A15.

Mensch, Barbara. 1986. "Age differences between spouses in first marriages." *Social Biology,* 33, pp. 229–240.

Merton, Robert K. 1938. "Social structure and anomie." *American Sociological Review,* 3, pp. 672–682.

———. 1941. "Intermarriage and the social structure: Fact and theory." *Psychology,* 4, pp. 361– 374.

———. 1957. *Social Theory and Social Structure.* New York: Free Press.

———. 1973. *The Sociology of Science: Theoretical and Empirical Investigations.* Edited by Norman Storer. Chicago: University of Chicago Press.

———. 1976. *Sociological Ambivalence and Other Essays.* New York: Free Press.

———. 1984. "The fallacy of the last word: The case of "pietism and science.'" *American Journal of Sociology,* 89, pp. 1091–1121.

Meyer, Marshall W. 1985. *The Limits to Bureaucratic Growth.* New York: de Gruyter.

Michels, Robert. 1949/1915. *Political Parties.* Glencoe, Ill.: Free Press.

Mikulski, Barbara. 1970. "Who speaks for ethnic America?" *New York Times,* September 28, p. 72.

Milgram, Stanley. 1967. "The small-world problem." *Psychology Today,* 1, pp. 61–67.

———. 1970. "The experience of living in cities." *Science,* March, pp. 1461– 1468.

———. 1974. *Obedience to Authority.* New York: Harper & Row.

Miller, Arthur G. 1970. "Role of physical attractiveness in impression formation." *Psychonomic Science,* 19, pp. 241–243.

Miller, Karen A., Melvin L. Kohn, and Carmi Schooler. 1986. "Educational self-direction and personality." *American Sociological Review,* 51, pp. 372–390.

Mills, C. Wright. 1959a. *The Power Elite.* New York: Oxford University Press.

———. 1959b. *The Sociological Imagination.* New York: Grove.

Mills, Darrell K. 1989. "Alcohol and crime on the reservation: A 10-year perspective." *Federal Probation,* 53, pp. 12–15.

Mills, Theodore M. 1967. *The Sociology of Small Groups.* Englewood Cliffs, N.J.: Prentice-Hall.

Miner, Horace. 1956. "Body ritual among the Nacirema." *American Anthropologist,* 58, pp. 503–507.

Mintz, Beth. 1975. "The president's cabinet, 1897–1972: A contribution to the power structure debate." *Insurgent Sociologist,* 5, pp. 131–148.

Mitroff, Ian I. 1974. "Norms and counternorms in a select group of the Apollo moon scientists." *American Sociological Review,* 39, pp. 579–595.

Moberg, David O. 1984. "Review of James Hunter's *American Evangelicalism.*" *Contemporary Sociology,* 13, pp. 371, 372.

Molotsky, Irvin. 1988. "Senate votes to compensate Japanese-American internees." *New York Times,* April 21, pp. 1, 9.

Monagan, David. 1983. "The failure of coed sports." *Psychology Today,* March, pp. 58–63.

Money, John, and Anke A. Ehrhardt. 1972. *Man and Woman/Boy and Girl.* Baltimore, Md.: Johns Hopkins University Press.

Montana, Constanza. 1986. "Latino schism." *Wall Street Journal,* October 21, pp. 1, 25.

Montgomery, Robert L. 1980. "Reference groups as anchors in judgments of other groups: A biasing factor in "rating tasks'?" *Psychological Reports,* 47, pp. 967–975.

Moore, Wilbert E. 1979. *World Modernization: The Limits of Convergence.* New York: Elsevier.

Moran, Malcolm. 1992. "Title IX is now an irresistible force." New York Times, June 21, pp. 25, 27.

Morell, Marie A., et al. 1989. "Would a Type A date another Type A?: Influence of behavior type and personal attributes in the selection of dating partners." *Journal of Applied Social Psychology,* 19, pp. 918–931.

Morgan, Carolyn Stout, and Alexis J. Walker. 1983. "Predicting sex role attitudes." *Social Psychology Quarterly,* 46, pp. 148–151.

Morgan, S. Philip. 1983. "A research note on religion and morality: Are religious people nice people?" *Social Forces,* 61, pp. 683–692.

———. 1984. "Reply to King and Hunt." *Social Forces,* 62, pp. 1089–1090.

Morganthau, Tom. 1989. "Taking on the legalizers." *Newsweek,* December 25, pp. 46–48.

———. 1991. "The war at home: How to battle crime." *Newsweek,* March 25, pp. 35–38.

———. 1992. "It's not just New York. . ." *Newsweek,* March 9, pp. 25–29.

Morris, Allison. 1987. *Women, Crime, and Criminal Justice.* New York: Basil Blackwell.

Morris, Betsy. 1987. "Shallow roots." *Wall Street Journal,* March 27, pp. 1, 7.

Morrow, Lance. 1978. "The lure of doomsday." *Time,* December 4, p. 30.

Mortimer, Jeylan T., and Roberta G. Simmons. 1978. "Adult socialization." *Annual Review of Sociology,* 4, pp. 421–454.

Mortimore, Peter. 1988. *School Matters.* Berkeley: University of California Press.

Mullen, Brian, et al. 1989. "Group size, leadership behavior, and subordinate satisfaction." *Journal of General Psychology,* 116, pp. 155–169.

Mulvihill, Donald J., and Melvin M. Tumin, with Lynn A. Curtis. 1969. *Crimes of Violence,* vol. 11. Washington, D.C.: U.S. Government Printing Office.

Mumford, Lewis. 1963. *Technics and Civilization.* New York: Harcourt, Brace and World.

Münch, Richard. 1983. "Modern science and technology: Differentiation or interpenetration?" *International Journal of Comparative Sociology,* 24, pp. 157–175.

Murstein, Bernard I., et al. 1989. "Physical attractiveness and exchange theory in interracial dating." *Journal of Social Psychology,* 129, pp. 325–334.

Musto, David F. 1986. "Lessons of the first cocaine epidemic." *Wall Street Journal,* June 11, p. 30.

Myers, Mary Anne. 1990. "Success and the single woman." *New York Times,* March 22, p. A15.

Naisbitt, John, and Patricia Aburdene. 1990. *Megatrends 2000.* New York: Morrow.

Namenwirth, J. Zvi, Randi Lynn Miller, and Robert Philip Weber. 1981. "Organizations have opinions: A redefinition of publics." *Public Opinion Quarterly,* 45, pp. 463–476.

Nasar, Sylvia. 1992. "The 1980's: A very good time for the very rich." *New York Times,* March 5, pp. A1, C13.

National Commission on Excellence in Education. 1983. *A Nation at Risk: The Imperative for Educational Reform.* Washington, D.C.: U.S. Government Printing Office.

Nazario, Sonia L. 1990. "Fertility rights." *Wall Street Journal,* March 8, pp. A1, A6.

———. 1991. "Breakthrough in birth control may elude poor." *Wall Street Journal,* March 4, p. B1.

———. 1992. "Medical science seeks a cure for doctors suffering from boorish bedside manner." *Wall Street Journal,* March 17, pp. B1, B8.

Nelson, Candace, and Marta Tienda. 1985. "The structuring of Hispanic ethnicity: Historical and contemporary perspectives." *Ethnic and Racial Studies,* 8, pp. 49–74.

Nelson, Mark M. 1990. "Darkness at noon." *Wall Street Journal,* March 1, pp. A1, A13.

Nemy, Enid. 1991. "Numbers are up, status down for the family of one." *New York Times,* February 28, pp. B1, B5.

Newcomb, Michael D., and Peter M. Bentler. 1980. "Cohabitation before marriage: A comparison of married couples who did and did not cohabit." *Alternative Lifestyles,* 3, pp. 65–85.

Newcomb, Theodore. 1958. "Attitude development as a function of reference group: The Bennington study," in Guy E. Swanson et al. (eds.), *Readings in Social Psychology.* New York: Holt, Rinehart and Winston.

Newman, Maria. 1992. "Charismatic movement gains among Catholics." *New York Times,* March 1, p. 17.

Newman, William M. 1973. *American Pluralism: A Study of Minority Groups and Social Theory.* New York: Harper & Row.

Newton, George D., Jr., and Franklin E. Zimring. 1969. *Firearms and Violence in American Life.* Washington, D.C.: U.S. Government Printing Office.

New York Times. 1966. "Dr. King addresses an integrated junior chamber in Atlanta." October 21, p. 28.

Niebuhr, Gustav. 1992. "The lord's name." *Wall Street Journal,* April 27, pp. A1, A4.

Nisbet, Robert A. 1970. *The Social Bond.* New York: Knopf.

Nordheimer, Jon. 1990. "Stepfathers: The shoes rarely fit." *New York Times,* October 18, p. B6.

Novak, Michael. 1973. *The Rise of the Unmeltable Ethnics.* New York: Collier.

Nye, Joseph, Jr. 1990. *Bound to Lead: The Changing Nature of American Power.* New York: Basic Books.

Oakes, Russell C. 1985. "Individual Piagetian epistemological development of children from ages 6 to 11." *Journal of Genetic Psychology,* 146, pp. 367–377.

Oakley, Robert. 1987. "International terrorism." *Foreign Affairs,* 65, pp. 611–629.

Ochse, Rhona, and Cornelis Plug. 1986. "Cross-cultural investigation of the validity of Erikson's theory of personality development." *Journal of Personality and Social Psychology,* 50, pp. 1240–1252.

O'Dea, Thomas F., and Janet O'Dea Aviad. 1983. *The Sociology of Religion,* 2nd ed. Englewood Cliffs, N.J.: Prentice-Hall.

Orwell, George. *1984.* New York: Signet.

Ostling, Richard N. 1987. "John Paul's feisty flock." *Time,* September 7, pp. 46–51.

———. 1988. "Americans facing toward Mecca." *Time,* May 23, pp. 49–50.

———. 1991. "Superchurches and how they grow." *Time,* August 5, pp. 62–63.

———. 1992. "Cut from the wrong cloth." *Time,* June 22, pp. 64–65.

O'Toole, James. 1973. *Work in America.* Cambridge, Mass.: MIT Press.

Otten, Alan. 1990. "People patterns." *Wall Street Journal,* February 20, p. B1.

Page, Benjamin I. 1983. *Who Gets What from Government.* Berkeley: University of California Press.

———, Robert Y. Shapiro, and Glenn R. Dempsey. 1987. "What moves public opinion?" *American Political Science Review,* 81, pp. 23–43.

Palisi, Bartolomeo J., and Claire Canning. 1983. "Urbanism and social psychological well-being: A cross-cultural test of three theories." *Sociological Quarterly,* 24, pp. 527–543.

Palmore, Erdman, and Daisaku Maeda. 1985. *The Honorable Elders Revisited: A Revised Cross-Cultural Analysis of Aging in Japan.* Durham, N.C.: Duke University Press.

Parenti, Michael. 1977. *Democracy for the Few.* New York: St. Martin's.

Parker, Robert Nash. 1989. "Poverty, subculture of violence, and types of homicide." *Social Forces,* 67, pp. 983–1005.

Parkes, Peter. 1987. "Livestock symbolism and pastoral ideology among the Kafirs of the Hindu Kush." *Man,* 22, pp. 637–660.

Parkinson, C. Northcote. 1957. *Parkinson's Law.* Boston: Houghton Mifflin.

Parks, Malcolm, Charlotte M. Stan, and Leona L. Eggert. 1983. "Romantic involvement and social network involvement." *Social Psychology Quarterly,* 46, pp. 116–131.

Parsons, Talcott. 1964/1951. *The Social System.* Glencoe, Ill.: Free Press.

———. 1966. *Societies: Evolutionary and Comparative Perspectives.* Englewood Cliffs, N.J.: Prentice-Hall.

———, and Robert F. Bales. 1953. *Family, Socialization, and Interaction Process.* Glencoe, Ill. Free Press.

Patinkin, Don. 1983. "Multiple discoveries and the central message." *American Journal of Sociology,* 89, pp. 306–323.

Patterson, Orlando, quoted in Schlesinger, Arthur Jr. 1991. "A new era begins—but history remains." *Wall Street Journal,* December 11, p. A16.

Pauly, David, 1979. "Crime in the suites: On the rise." *Newsweek,* December 3, pp. 114–121.

Pear, Robert. 1992. "Ranks of U.S. poor reach 35.7 million, the most since '64." *New York Times,* September 4, pp. A1, A12.

Pearce, Diana M. 1993. "The feminization of poverty: Update. Pp. 290–296 in Alison M. Jaggar and Paula S. Rothenberg (eds.), *Feminist Frameworks, 3rd ed.* New York: McGraw-Hill.

Peek, Charles W., Evans W. Curry, and H. Paul Chalfant. 1985. "Religiosity and delinquency over time: Deviance deterrence and deviance amplification." *Social Science Quarterly,* 66, pp. 120–131.

Peirce, Kate. 1990. "A feminist theoretical perspective on the socialization of teenage girls through *Seventeen* magazine." *Sex Roles,* 23, pp. 491–500.

Pennebaker, J. W. 1980. "Perceptual and environmental determinants of coughing." *Basic Applied Social Psychology,* 1, pp. 83–91.

Penrose, L. S. 1981/1952. *On the Objective Study of Crowd Behavior.* London: H. K. Lewis.

Perlez, Jane. 1990. "Puberty rites for girls is bitter issue across Africa." *New York Times,* February 15, p. 6.

Persell, Caroline Hodges. 1984. *Understanding Society.* New York: Harper & Row.

Pescosolido, Bernice A., and Sharon Georgianna. 1989. "Durkheim, suicide, and religion: Toward a network theory of suicide." *American Sociological Review,* 54, pp. 33–48.

Peter, Laurence J., and Raymond Hull. 1969. *The Peter Principle.* New York: Morrow.

Peters, Thomas J., and Robert H. Waterman, Jr. 1982. *In Search of Excellence: Lessons from America's Best-Run Companies.* New York: Harper & Row.

Petersen, Larry R., Gary R. Lee, and Godfrey J. Ellis. 1982. "Social structure, socialization values, and disciplinary techniques: A cross-culture analysis." *Journal of Marriage and the Family,* 44, pp. 131–142.

Peterson, Iver. 1987. "Feminists discern a bias in Baby M. custody case." *New York Times,* March 20, p. 16.

Peterson, Janice. 1987. "The feminization of poverty." *Journal of Economic Issues,* March, pp. 329–337.

Pfost, Karen S., and Maria Fiore. 1990. "Pursuit of nontraditional occupations: Fear of success or fear of not being chosen?" *Sex Roles,* 23, pp. 15–24.

Phillips, Kevin. 1990. *The Politics of Rich and Poor: Wealth and the American Electorate in the Reagan Aftermath.* New York: Random House.

Pillemer, Karl, and David Finkelhor. 1989. "Causes of elder abuse: Caregiver stress versus problem relatives." *American Journal of Orthopsychiatry,* 59, pp. 179–187.

Pines, Maya. 1981. "The civilizing of Genie." *Psychology Today,* September, pp. 28–34.

Plog, Fred, and Daniel G. Bates. 1980. *Cultural Anthropology,* 2nd ed. New York: Knopf.

Pollak, Lauren Harte, and Peggy A. Thoits. 1989. "Processes in emotional socialization." *Social Psychology Quarterly,* 52, pp. 22–34.

Porter, Bruce, and Marvin Dunn. 1984. *The Miami Riot of 1980.* Lexington, Mass.: Lexington Books.

Porter, Judith R., and Robert E. Washington. 1979. "Black identity and self-esteem: A review of studies of black self-concept." *Annual Review of Sociology,* 5, pp. 53–74.

Porter, Michael. 1990. *The Competitive Advantage of Nations.* New York: Free Press.

Posner, Richard A. 1992. *Sex and Reason* Cambridge, Mass.: Harvard University Press.

Postman, Neil. 1985. *Amusing Ourselves to Death: Public Discourse in the Age of Show Business.* New York: Viking.

Power, Thomas G., and Josephine A. Shanks. 1989. "Parents and socializers: Maternal and paternal views." *Journal of Youth and Adolescence,* 18, pp. 203–217.

Prerost, Frank J., and Robert E. Brewer. 1980. "The appreciation of humor by males and females during conditions of crowding experimentally induced." *Psychology,* 17, pp. 15–17.

Prestowitz, Clyde V. 1989. *Trading Places.* New York: Basic Books.

Purvis, Andrew. 1992. "A day in the death of Somalia." *Time,* September 21, pp. 32–40.

Putka, Gary. 1990. "'Tracking' of minority pupils takes toll." *Wall Street Journal,* April 23, p. B1.

Quindlen, Anna. 1990. "A time to die." *New York Times,* June 3, p. 27.

Quinney, Richard. 1974. *Critique of Legal Order.* Boston: Little, Brown.

———. 1975. *Criminology.* Boston: Little, Brown.

Rabinovitz, Jonathan. 1991. "Teen-agers' beepers: Communications as fashions." *New York Times,* March 8, pp. A1, A4.

Radford, John. 1990. *Child Prodigies and Exceptional Early Achievers.* New York: Free Press.

Rainwater, Lee. 1974. *What Money Buys.* New York: Basic Books.

Ramirez, Francisco O., and John W. Meyer. 1980. "Comparative education: The social construction of the modern world system." *Annual Review of Sociology,* 6, pp. 369– 399.

Ranney, Austin. 1983. "Nonvoting is not a social disease." *Public Opinion,* October/November, pp. 16–19.

Ransford, H. Edward, and Jon Miller. 1983. "Race, sex, and feminist outlooks." *American Sociological Review,* 48, pp. 46–59.

Raper, Arthur F. 1970. *The Tragedy of Lynching.* New York: Dover.

Rau, William, and Dennis W. Roncek. 1987. "Industrialization and world inequality: The transformation of the division of labor in 59 nations, 1960 – 1981." *American Sociological Review,* 52, pp. 359–369.

Regier, Darrel A., et al. 1993. "The de facto US mental and ad-

dictive disorders service system: Epidemiologic catchment area prospective 1-year prevalence rates of disorders and services." *Archives of General Psychiatry,* 50, pp. 85–94.

Reich, Michael. 1981. *Racial Inequality: A Political-Economic Analysis.* Princeton, N.J.: Princeton University Press.

Reiman, Jeffrey H., and Sue Headlee. 1981. "Marxism and criminal justice policy." *Crime and Delinquency,* 27, pp. 24–47.

Reinisch, June M. 1990. *The Kinsey Institute New Report on Sex: What You Must Know to Be Sexually Literate.* New York: St. Martin's.

Reitzes, Donald C. 1981. "Role-identity correspondence in the college student role." *Sociological Quarterly,* 22, pp. 607–620.

———. 1983. "Urban images: A social psychological approach." *Sociological Inquiry,* 53, pp. 314–332.

Rensberger, Boyce. 1984. "What made humans human." *New York Times Magazine,* April 8, pp. 80–92.

Reser, Joseph. 1981. "Australian aboriginal man's inhumanity to man: A case of cultural distortion." *American Anthropologist,* 83, pp. 387–393.

Restak, Richard M. 1979. *The Brain: The Last Frontier.* Garden City, N.Y.: Doubleday. Retsinas, Joan. 1988. "A theoretical assessment of the applicability of Kübler-Ross's stages of dying." *Death Studies,* 12, pp. 207–216.

Reynolds, Paul Davidson. 1982. *Ethics and Social Science Research.* Englewood Cliffs, N.J.: Prentice-Hall.

Rheem, Donald L. 1986. "Free market system said to be more efficient than state planning." *Christian Science Monitor,* September 22, p. 7.

Rice, Mabel L., et al. 1990. "Words from 'Sesame Street': Learning vocabulary while viewing." *Developmental Psychology,* 26, pp. 421–428.

Rich, Adrienne. 1982. *Compulsory Heterosexuality and Lesbian Existence.* Denver, Co: Antelope Publications.

Richardson, Laurel. 1988. *The Dynamics of Sex and Gender: A Sociological Perspective.* New York: Harper & Row.

Ridgeway, Cecilia. 1982. "Status in groups: The importance of motivation." *American Sociological Review,* 47, pp. 76–88.

Riesman, David. 1950. *The Lonely Crowd.* New Haven, Conn.: Yale University Press.

Riley, John W., Jr. 1983. "Dying and the meanings of death: Sociological inquiries." *Annual Review of Sociology,* 9, pp. 191–216.

Rindos, David. 1986. "The evolution of the capacity for culture: Sociobiology, structuralism, and cultural selectionism." *Current Anthropology,* 27, pp. 315–332.

Roach, Jack L., Llewellyn Gross, and Orville R. Gursslin, eds. 1969. *Social Stratification in the United States.* Englewood Cliffs, N.J.: Prentice-Hall.

Robbins, William. 1990. "New decade finds new hope on the farm." *New York Times,* May 18, pp. A1, A10.

Roberts, Steven. 1990. "An all-American snapshot: How we count and why." *U.S. News & World Report,* April 2, p. 10.

Robinson, Ira E., and Davor Jedlicka. 1982. "Change in sexual attitudes and behavior of college students from 1965 to 1980: A research note." *Journal of Marriage and the Family,* 44, pp. 237–240.

Rodino, Peter W. 1986. "Will handgun foes be over a barrel?" *New York Times,* March 28, p. 27.

Rodriguez, Nestor P., and Joe R. Feagin. 1986. "Urban specialization in the world-system: An investigation of historical cases." *Urban Affairs Quarterly,* 22, pp. 187–220.

Roethlisberger, Fritz J., and William J. Dickson. 1939. *Management and the Worker.* Cambridge, Mass.: Harvard University Press.

Rogers, Richard G. 1989. "Ethnic and birth weight differences in cause-specific infant mortality." *Demography,* 26, pp. 335–343.

Roof, Wade Clark, and William McKinney. 1988. *American Mainline Religion: Its Changing Shape and Future.* New Brunswick, N.J.: Rutgers University Press.

Rosado, Lourdes. 1991. "Who's caring for grandma?" *Newsweek,* July 29, p. 47.

Rose, Arnold M. 1967. *The Power Structure.* New York: Oxford University Press.

Rose, Peter I. 1981. *They and We: Racial and Ethnic Relations in the United States.* New York: Random House.

———. 1983. *Mainstream and Margins: Jews, Blacks, and Other Americans.* New Brunswick, N.J.: Transaction.

Rosecrance, Richard. 1990. "Too many bosses, too few workers." *New York Times,* July 15, p. F11.

Rosenberg, Morris. 1990. "Reflexivity and emotions." *Social Psychology Quarterly,* 53, pp. 3–12.

Rosenblatt, Roger. 1992. *Life Itself: Abortion in the American Mind.* New York: Random House.

Rosenthal, Elisabeth. 1990. "U.S. is by far the leader in homicide." *New York Times,* June 27, p. A9.

Rosenthal, Robert. 1973. "The Pygmalion effect lives." *Psychology Today,* pp. 56–63.

Rosewicz, Barbara. 1990. "Friends of the earth." *Wall Street Journal,* April 20, pp. A1, A12.

Rosin, Hazel M. 1990. "The effects of dual career participation on men: Some determinants of variation in career and personal satisfaction." *Human Relations,* 43, pp. 169–182.

Ross, Dorothy. 1991. *The Origins of American Social Science.* New York: Cambridge University Press.

Rossi, Alice S. 1984. "Gender and parenthood." *American Sociological Review,* 49, pp. 1–19.

Rossi, Peter H. 1989. *Down and Out in America: The Origins of Homelessness.* Chicago: University of Chicago Press.

———, and William Foote Whyte. 1983. "The applied side of sociology," in Howard E. Freeman et al. (eds.), *Applied Sociology.* San Francisco: Jossey-Bass.

Rossides, Daniel W. 1976. *The American Class System.* Boston: Houghton Mifflin.

Rostow, Walt W. 1960. *The Process of Economic Growth.* New York: Norton.

Roth, Julius, and Robert Peck. 1951. "Social class and social mobility factors related to marital adjustment." *American Sociological Review,* 16, pp. 478–487.

Rothschild, Joyce, and Raymond Russell. 1986. "Alternatives to bureaucracy: Democratic participation in the economy." *Annual Review of Sociology,* 12, pp. 307–328.

Rothschild-Whitt, Joyce. 1982. "The collectivist organization: An alternative to bureaucratic models," in Frank Lindenfeld and Joyce Rothschild-Whitt (eds.), *Workplace Democracy and Social Change.* Boston: Porter Sargent.

Rubenstein, Carin. 1982. "Real men don't earn less than their wives." *Psychology Today,* November, pp. 36–41.

Rubin, Lillian Breslow. 1976. *Worlds of Pain: Life in the Working-Class Family.* New York: Basic Books.

———. 1990. *Erotic Wars: What Happened to the Sexual Revolution?* New York: Farrar, Stratus & Giroux.

Rubinson, Richard. 1986. "Class formation, politics, and institutions: Schooling in the United States." *American Journal of Sociology,* 92, pp. 519–548.

Rummel, R. J. 1986. "War isn't this century's biggest killer." *Wall Street Journal,* July 7, p. 10.

Russell, George. 1984. "People, people, people." *Time,* August 6, pp. 24–25.

Rutter, Michael. 1983. "School effects on pupil progress: Research findings and policy implications." *Child Development,* 54, pp. 1–29.

Sahlins, Marshall. 1972. *Stone Age Economics.* Chicago: Aldine.

Salins, Peter D. 1991. "In Living Colors," *The New Republic,* January 21, pp. 14–15.

Salholz, Eloise. 1986. "Too late for Prince Charming?" *Newsweek,* June 2, pp. 54–61.

———. 1990a. "The future of gay America." *Newsweek,* March 12, pp. 20–25.

———. 1990b. "The push for power." *Newsweek,* April 9, pp. 18–20.

———. 1990c. "Value judgments." *Newsweek,* June 25, pp. 16–18.

Sanday, Peggy Reeves. 1981. "The socio-cultural context of rape: A cross-cultural study." *Journal of Social Issues,* 37, pp. 5–27.

Sapir, Edward. 1929. "The status of linguistics as a science." *Language,* 5, pp. 207–214.

Sawhill, Isabel. 1989. "The underclass: An overview." *The Public Interest,* Summer, pp. 3- 15.

Sayle, Murray. 1982. "A textbook case of aggression." *Far Eastern Economic Review,* 117, August 20, pp. 36–38.

Scanzoni, Letha Dawson, and John Scanzoni. 1988. *Men, Women, and Change,* 3rd ed. New York: McGraw-Hill.

Schaefer, Richard T. 1988. *Racial and Ethnic Groups,* 3rd ed. Boston: Little, Brown.

Schanback, Mindy. 1987. "No patience for elder patients." *Psychology Today,* February, p. 22.

Schlesinger, Arthur, Jr. 1990. "Iraq, war and the Constitution." *Wall Street Journal,* November 12, p. A14.

———. 1991. "Toward a divisive diversity." *Wall Street Journal,* June 25, p. A18.

Schlossstein, Steven. 1990. "U.S. is the leader in decentralization." *New York Times,* June 3, p. F13.

Schmitt, Eric. 1990. "A spill a day, and hardly anyone has been checking." *New York Times,* February 25, p. E20.

Schor, Juliet B. 1991. *The Overworked American: The Unexpected Decline of Leisure.* New York: Basic Books.

Schultz, Duane P. 1964. *Panic Behavior.* New York: Random House.

Schulz, David A. 1982. *The Changing Family,* 3rd ed. Englewood Cliffs, N.J.: Prentice-Hall.

Schuman, Howard, Charlotte Steeh, and Lawrence Bobo. 1985. *Racial Attitudes in America: Trends and Interpretations.* Cambridge, Mass.: Harvard University Press.

Schur, Edwin M. 1984. *Labeling Women Deviant: Gender, Stigma, and Social Control.* New York: Random House.

Schwartz, John. 1987. "A 'superminority' tops out." *Newsweek,* May 11, pp. 48–49.

Schwochau, Susan. 1987. "Union effects on job attitudes." *Industrial and Labor Relations Review,* 40, pp. 209–224.

Science Digest. 1984. "Newscience/update: William H. Whyte observes the teeming tribes of urban jungles." March, p. 17.

Scott, Carlee. 1990. "As baby boomers age, fewer couples untie the knot." *Wall Street Journal,* November 7, pp. B1, B5.

Scott, David Clark. 1986. "How 'quality circles' move from the assembly line to the office." *Christian Science Monitor,* August 4, p. 18.

Scott, Jacqueline. 1989. "Conflicting beliefs about abortion: Legal approval and moral doubts." *Social Psychology Quarterly,* 52, pp. 319–326.

Scully, Diana, and Joseph Marolla. 1984. "Convicted rapists' vocabulary of motive: Excuses and justifications." *Social Problems,* 31, pp. 530–544.

Sebald, Hans. 1986. "Adolescents' shifting orientation toward parents and peers: A curvilinear trend over recent decades." *Journal of Marriage and the Family,* 48, pp. 5- 13.

Segal, Aaron. 1982. "Kenya," in Carol L. Thompson, Mary M. Anderberg, and Joan B. Antell (eds.), *The Current History of Developing Countries.* New York: McGraw-Hill.

Sellin, Thorsten. 1938. *Culture Conflict and Crime.* New York: Social Science Research Council.

Sennett, Richard. 1991. *The Conscience of the Eye: The Design and Social Life of Cities.* New York: Alfred A. Knopf.

Shabecoff, Philip. 1990. "Team of scientists sees substantial warming of earth." *New York Times,* April 16, p. A11.

Shah, Saleem A., and Loren H. Roth. 1974. "Biological and psychophysiological factors in criminality," in Daniel Glaser (ed.), *Handbook of Criminology.* Chicago: Rand McNally.

Shapiro, Joseph. 1992. "The elderly are not children." *U.S. News & World Report,* January 13, pp. 26–28.

Shapiro, Laura. 1990. "Guns and dolls." *Newsweek,* May 28, pp. 56–65.

Shariff, Zahid. 1979. "The persistence of bureaucracy." *Social Science Quarterly,* 60, pp. 3- 19.

Shaw, Clifford R., and Henry D. McKay. 1929. *Delinquency Areas.* Chicago: University of Chicago Press.

Sheldon, William H. 1949. *Varieties of Delinquent Youth.* New York: Harper.

Sheler, Jeffrey L. 1990. "Islam in America." *U.S. News & World Report,* October 8, pp. 69- 71.

Shellenbarger, Sue. 1991. "Work and family." *Wall Street Journal,* December 11, p. B1.

Shenon, Philip. 1990. "The score on drugs: It depends on how you see the figures." *New York Times,* April 22, p. E6.

Sherif, Muzafer. 1956. "Experiments in group conflict." *Scientific American,* 195, pp. 54–58.

Shibutani, Tamotsu. 1966. *Improvised News.* Indianapolis: Bobbs-Merrill.

Shipp, E. R. 1986. "Only 2 remain in dioxin ghost town." *New York Times,* April 8, p. 9.

———. 1991. "After scandals, TV's preachers see empty pews." *New York Times,* March 3, pp. 1, 17.

Shornack, Lawrence L., and Ellen McRoberts Shornack. 1982. "The new sex education and the sexual revolution: A critical view." *Family Relations,* 31, pp. 531–544.

Shrauger, J. Sidney, and Thomas J. Schoeneman. 1979. "Symbolic interactionist view of self-concept: Through the looking glass darkly." *Psychological Bulletin,* 86, pp. 549- 573.

Shrum, Wesley, and Neil H. Cheek, Jr. 1987. "Social structure during the school years: Onset of the degrouping process." *American Sociological Review,* 52, pp. 218–223.

Shupe, Anson. 1990. "Pitchmen of the Satan scare." *Wall Street Journal,* March 9, p. A12.

Sidel, Ruth. 1990. *On Her Own: Growing Up in the Shadow of the American Dream.* New York: Viking.

Silberman, Charles E. 1970. *Crisis in the Classroom.* New York: Vintage Books.

Simenauer, Jacqueline, and David Carroll. 1982. *Singles: The New Americans.* New York: Simon & Schuster.

Simmons, Jerry L. 1973. *Deviants.* Berkeley, Calif.: Glendessary Press.

Simon, Armando. 1981. "A quantitative, nonreactive study of mass behavior with emphasis on the cinema as behavioral catalyst." *Psychological Reports,* 48, pp. 775–785.

Simon, David R., and D. Stanley Eitzen. 1990. *Elite Deviance,* 3rd ed. Boston: Allyn and Bacon.

Simon, Julian. 1983. "Growth means progress." *Science Digest,* 91, April, pp. 76–79.

Simons, Marlise. 1990. "Europeans begin to calculate the price of pollution." *New York Times,* December 9, p. E3.

Simpson, Jeffry A., Bruce Campbell, and Ellen Berscheid. 1986. "The association between romantic love and marriage: Kephart (1967) twice revisited." *Personality and Social Psychology Bulletin,* 12, pp. 363–372.

Sizer, Theodore R. 1984. *Horace's Compromise: The Dilemma of the American High School.* Boston: Houghton Mifflin.

Sjoberg, Gideon. 1966. *The Preindustrial City: Past and Present.* New York: Free Press.

Skinner, B. F. 1983. "Creativity in old age." *Psychology Today,* September, pp. 28, 29.

Skinner, Denise. 1980. "Dual-career family stress and coping: A literature review." *Family Relations,* 29, pp. 473–480.

Skolnick, Arlene. 1987. *The Intimate Environment: Exploring Marriage and the Family,* 4th ed. Boston: Little, Brown.

Slaff, James, and John K. Brubaker. 1985. *The AIDS Epidemic.* New York: Warner Books.

Smelser, Neil J. 1971/1962. *Theory of Collective Behavior.* New York: Free Press.

Smith, Eleanor. 1984. "Midnight dumping." *Omni,* 6, March, p. 18.

Smith, Kevin B., and Lorene H. Stone. 1989. "Rags, riches, and bootstraps: Beliefs about the causes of wealth and poverty." *Sociological Quarterly,* 30, pp. 93–107.

Smolowe, Jill. 1990. "When jobs clash." *Time,* September 3, pp. 82–84.

Snow, David A., et al. 1990. "Examining homelessness." *Science,* March 23, pp. 1485–1486.

Snyder, Eldon E., and Elmer A. Spreitzer. 1989. *Social Aspects of Sport,* 3rd ed. Englewood Cliffs. N.J.: Prentice-Hall.

So, Alvin Y. 1990. *Social Change and Development: Modernization, Dependency, and World-System Theories.* Newbury Park, Cal.: Sage.

Solis, Dianna, et al. 1987. "Changing the rules." *Wall Street Journal,* June 5, pp. 1, 12.

Solomon, Jolie, 1989. "Firms grapple with language barriers." *Wall Street Journal,* November 7, pp. B1, B4.

Sorokin, Pitirim. 1967. "Causal-functional and logico-meaningful integration," in N.J. Demerath and Richard A. Peterson (eds.), *System, Change, and Conflict.* New York: Free Press.

Sorrentino, Constance. 1990. "The changing family in international perspective." *Monthly Labor Review,* March, pp. 41–55.

South, Scott J., and Glenna Spitze. 1986. "Determinants of divorce over the marital life course." *American Sociological Review,* 51, pp. 583–590.

Sowell, Thomas. 1981. *Ethnic America: A History.* New York: Basic Books.

————. 1983. *The Economics and Politics of Race: An International Perspective.* New York: Morrow.

Spanier, Graham B. 1983. "Married and unmarried cohabitation in the United States: 1980." *Journal of Marriage and the Family,* 45, pp. 277–288.

Spates, James L. 1983. "The sociology of values." *Annual Review of Sociology,* 9, pp. 27–49.

Spitz, René A. 1945. "Hospitalism." *Psychoanalytic Study of the Child,* 1, pp. 53–72.

Spreitzer, Elmer, and Eldon E. Snyder. 1983. "Correlates of participation in adult recreational sports." *Journal of Leisure Research,* 15, pp. 27–38.

Stack, Steven. 1983a. "The effect of the decline in institutionalized religion on suicide, 1954–1978." *Journal for the Scientific Study of Religion,* 22, pp. 239–252.

————. 1983b. "The effect of religious commitment on suicide: A cross-national analysis." *Journal of Health and Social Behavior,* 24, pp. 362–374.

Stark, Rodney, Lori Kent, and Daniel P. Doyle. 1982. "Religion and delinquency: The ecology of a 'lost' relationship." *Journal of Research in Crime and Delinquency,* 19, pp. 4–24.

————, and Charles Y. Glock. 1968. *American Piety.* Berkeley: University of California Press.

Steele, Shelby. 1990. *The Content of Our Character: A New Vision of Race in America.* New York: St. Martin's.

Steinberg, Laurence. 1987. "Why Japan's students outdo ours." *New York Times,* April 25, p. 15.

Steinberg, Stephen. 1981. *The Ethnic Myth: Race, Ethnicity, and Class in America.* New York: Atheneum.

Steinmetz, Susanne K., et al. 1990. *Marriage and Family Realities: Historical and Contemporary Perspectives.* New York: Harper & Row.

Stevens, Gillian, et al. 1990. "Education and attractiveness in marriage choices." *Social Psychology Quarterly,* 53, pp. 62–72.

Stevens, William K. 1992. "New studies predict profits in heading off warming." *New York Times,* March 17, pp. B5, B9.

Steward, Julian H. 1973. "A Neo-evolutionist approach," in Amitai Etzioni and Eva Etzioni-Halevy (eds.), *Social Change,* 2nd ed. New York: Basic Books.

Stoll, Clarice Stasz. 1978. *Female & Male.* Dubuque, Iowa: Brown.

Stolzenberg, Ross M. 1990. "Ethnicity, geography, and occupational achievement of Hispanic men in the United States." *American Sociological Review,* 55, pp. 143–154.

Stone, P. B. 1983. "Development at a crossroads." *World Press Review,* March, pp. 33–35.

Stone, Tim. 1990. "New free-market crime." *New York Times,* September 2, p. F12.

Straus, Murray A., et al. 1988. *Behind Closed Doors: Violence in the American Family.* Newbury Park, Calif.: Sage.

———. 1986. "Societal change and change in family violence from 1975 to 1985 as revealed by two national surveys." *Journal of Marriage and the Family,* 48, pp. 465–479.

Strong, Bryan, and Christine DeVault. 1989. *The Marriage and Family Experience,* 4th ed. St. Paul, Minn.: West.

Suro, Roberto. 1991. "Where America is growing: The suburban cities." *New York Times,* February 23, pp. 1, 10.

———. 1992. "Polls finds Hispanic desire to assimilate." *New York Times,* December 15, p. A18.

Sussman, Nan M., and Howard M. Rosenfeld. 1982. "Influence of culture, language, and sex on conversational distance." *Journal of Personality and Social Psychology,* 42, pp. 66–74.

Sutherland, Edwin E., and Donald R. Cressey. 1978. *Criminology,* 9th ed. Philadelphia: Lippincott.

Sweet, Ellen. 1985. "Date rape: The story of an epidemic and those who deny it." *Ms.,* October, p. 58.

Swigert, Victoria Lynn, and Ronald A. Farrell. 1976. *Murder, Inequality, and the Law.* Lexington, Mass.: Heath.

Swim, Janet, et al. 1989. "Joan McKay versus John McKay: Do gender stereotypes bias evaluations?" *Psychological Bulletin,* 105, pp. 409–429.

Syme, S. Leonard, and Lisa F. Berkman. 1987. "Social class, susceptibility, and sickness," in Howard D. Schwartz (ed.), *Dominant Issues in Medical Sociology,* 2nd ed. New York: Random House.

Szymanski, Albert. 1978. *The Capitalist State and the Politics of Class.* Cambridge, Mass.: Winthrop.

Tanfer, Koray. 1987. "Patterns of premarital cohabitation among never-married women in the United States." *Journal of Marriage and the Family,* 49, pp. 483–497.

Tannenbaum, Frank. 1938. *Crime and the Community.* New York: Columbia University Press.

Tanner, Deborah. 1991. *You Just Don't Understand: Women and Men in Conversation.* New York: Ballantine.

Tanner, Nancy Makepeace. 1983. "Hunters, gatherers, and sex roles in space and time." *American Anthropologist,* 85, pp. 335–341.

Tavris, Carol, and Carole Wade. 1984. *The Longest War: Sex Differences in Perspective,* 2nd ed. New York: Harcourt Brace Jovanovich.

Taylor, Alfred Maurice. 1967. *Imagination and the Growth of Science.* New York: Schocken.

Taylor, Frederick W. 1911. *Scientific Management.* New York: Harper.

Taylor, Ralph B., et al. 1979. "Sharing secrets: Disclosure and discretion in dyads and triads." *Journal of Personality and Social Psychology,* 37, pp. 1196–1203.

———, and Joseph C. Lanni. 1981. "Territorial dominance: The influence of the resident advantage in triadic decision making." *Journal of Personality and Social Psychology,* 41, pp. 909–915.

Taylor, Ronald A. 1987. "Why fewer blacks are graduating." *U.S. News & World Report,* June 8, 1987.

Taylor, Stuart, Jr. 1987. "High court deals setback to suit on Japanese-American detention." *New York Times,* June 2, p. 15.

Teachman, Jay D. 1987. "Family background, educational resources, and educational attainment." *American Sociological Review,* 52, pp. 548–557.

Terkel, Studs. 1974. *Working.* New York: Pantheon.

———. 1992. *Race: How Blacks and Whites Think and Feel About the American Obsession.* New York: The New Press.

Tharp, Mike. 1987. "Academic debate." *Wall Street Journal,* March 10, p. 1.

Thio, Alex. 1988. *Deviant Behavior,* 3rd ed. New York: Harper & Row.

Thoits, Peggy A. 1989. "The sociology of emotion." *Annual Review of Sociology,* 15, pp. 317–342.

Thomas, Laura. 1990. "Can a new suburb be like a small town?" *U.S. News & World Report,* March 5, p. 32.

Thompson, Dick. 1987. "A how-to guide on cholesterol." *Time,* October 19, p. 45.

Thornton, Arland. 1989. "Changing attitudes toward family issues in the United States." *Journal of Marriage and the Family,* 51, pp. 873–893.

———, Duane F. Alwin, and Donald Camburn. 1983. "Causes and consequences of sex-role attitudes and attitude change." *American Sociological Review,* 48, pp. 211–227.

———, and Deborah Freedman. 1983. "The changing American family." *Population Bulletin,* 38, October, pp. 1–43.

Thurow, Lester. 1989. "The post-industrial era is over." *New York Times,* September 4, p. 19.

Thurow, Roger. 1987. "Keeping control." *Wall Street Journal,* March 11, pp. 1, 26.

Tilly, Louise A., and Joan W. Scott. 1978. *Women, Work, and the Family.* New York: Holt, Rinehart and Winston.

Toffler, Alvin. 1980. *The Third Wave.* New York: Morrow.

———. 1990. *Powershift.* New York: Bantam Books.

Tolnay, Stewart E., E. M. Beck, and James L. Massey. 1989. "Black lynchings: The power threat hypothesis revisited." *Social Forces,* 67, pp. 605-623.

Toner, Robin. 1992. "Politics of Welfare: Focusing on the Problem." *New York Times,* July 5, pp. 1,13.

Train, John. 1986. "Parkinson's laws aren't by popular vote." *Wall Street Journal,* May 15, p. 28.

Travers, Jeffrey, and Stanley Milgram. 1969. "An experimental study of the small world problem." *Sociometry,* 32, pp. 425-443.

Treaster, Joseph B. 1991. "Cocaine use found on the way down among U.S. youths." *New York Times,* January 25, pp. A1, A10.

———. 1992. "20 years of war on drugs, and no victory yet." *New York Times,* June 14, E7.

Treiman, Donald J. 1977. *Occupational Prestige in Comparative Perspective.* New York: Academic Press.

Tresemer, David. 1974. "Fear of success: Popular but unproven." *Psychology Today,* March, pp. 82-85.

Troeltsch, Ernst. 1931. *The Social Teaching of the Christian Churches.* New York: Macmillan.

Trott, Stephen S. 1985. "Implementing criminal justice reform." *Public Administration Review,* 45, pp. 795-800.

Trotter, Robert J. 1987. "Mathematics: A male advantage?" *Psychology Today,* January, pp. 66-67.

Trussell, James, and K. Vaninadha Rao. 1989. "Premarital cohabitation and marital stability: A reassessment of the Canadian evidence." *Journal of Marriage and the Family,* 51, pp. 535-540.

Tumin, Melvin M. 1953. "Some principles of stratification: A critical analysis." *American Sociological Review,* 18, pp. 387-393.

———. 1967. *Social Stratification: The Forms and Functions of Inequality.* Englewood Cliffs, N.J.: Prentice-Hall.

Turner, Paul R. 1982. "Anthropological value positions." *Human Organization,* 41, pp. 76- 79.

Turner, Ralph H., and Lewis M. Killian. 1987. *Collective Behavior,* 4th ed. Englewood Cliffs, N.J.: Prentice-Hall.

Twaddle, Andrew, and Richard Hessler. 1987. *A Sociology of Health,* 2nd ed. New York: Macmillan.

Tynes, Sheryl R. 1990. "Educational heterogamy and marital satisfaction between spouses." *Social Science Research,* 19, pp. 153-174.

Tyree, Andrea, et al. 1979. "Gaps and glissandos: Inequality, economic development, and social mobility in 24 countries." *American Sociological Review,* 44, pp. 410-424.

———, and Moshe Semyonov. 1983. "Social mobility and immigrants or immigrants and social mobility." *American Sociological Review,* 48, pp. 583-584.

Udry, J. Richard. 1983. "The marital happiness/disruption relationship by level of marital alternatives." *Journal of Marriage and the Family,* 45, pp. 221-222.

Uhlig, Mark A. 1990. "Panama drug smugglers prosper as dictator's exit opens the door." *New York Times,* August 21, pp. A1, A4.

UN Chronicle. 1983. "State of the world environment." Vol. 20, May, pp. 33-46.

Unger, Irwin. 1982. *These United States: The Questions of Our Past,* vol. 1, 2nd ed. Boston: Little, Brown.

U.S. Department of Justice, Bureau of Justice Statistics. 1988. *Report to the Nation on Crime and Justice,* 2nd ed. Washington, D.C.: U.S. Government Printing Office.

Useem, Michael. 1979. "Which business leaders help govern?" *Insurgent Sociologist,* 9, Fall, pp. 107-120.

Valente, Judith. 1991. "A century later, Sioux still struggle, and still are losing." *Wall Street Journal,* March 25, pp. A1, A12.

Van Leeuwen, Mary Stewart. 1990. "Life after Eden." *Christianity Today,* July 16, pp. 19- 21.

Vandewiele, Michel. 1981. "Influence on family, peers, and school on Senegalese adolescents." *Psychological Reports,* 48, pp. 807-810.

Varghese, Raju. 1981. "An empirical analysis of the Eriksonian bipolar theory of personality." *Psychological Reports,* 49, pp. 819-822.

Verbrugge, Lois M. 1985. "Gender and health: An update on hypotheses and evidence." *Journal of Health and Social Behavior,* 26, pp. 156-182.

Verhovek, Sam Howe. 1990. "Whose law applies when lawlessness rules on Indian land?" *New York Times,* May 6, p. E6.

Veroff, Joseph, Elizabeth Douvan, and Richard A. Kulka. 1981. *The Inner American: A Self-Portrait from 1957 to 1976.* New York: Basic Books.

Vora, Erika. 1981. "Evolution of race: A synthesis of social and biological concepts." *Journal of Black Studies,* 12, pp. 182-192.

Voydanoff, Patricia, and Brenda W. Donnelly. 1989. "Work and family roles and psychological distress." *Journal of Marriage and the Family,* 51, pp. 923-932.

Wagner, David G., and Joseph Berger. 1985. "Do sociological theories grow?" *American Journal of Sociology,* 90, pp. 697-728.

Waitzkin, Howard. 1987. "A Marxian interpretation of the growth and development of coronary care technology," in Howard D. Schwartz (ed.), *Dominant Issues in Medical Sociology,* 2nd ed. New York: Random House.

Wald, Matthew L. 1990. "Guarding environment: A world of challenges." *New York Times,* April 22, pp. 1, 16-17.

Waldinger, Roger. 1989. "Structural opportunity or ethnic advantage? Immigrant business development in New York." *International Migration Review,* 23, pp. 48-72.

Waldrop, Judith. 1988. "The fashionable family." *American Demographics,* March, pp. 22- 26.

Wall Street Journal. 1986. "Das Kapital (revised ed.)," p. 32.

Wallerstein, Immanuel. 1987. "World-system analysis." Pp. 309–324 in Anthony Giddens and Jonathan H. Turner (eds.), *Social Theory Today.* Stanford, Cal.: Stanford University Press.

Wallerstein, James S., and Clement J. Wyle. 1947. "Our law-abiding law-breakers." *Probation,* 25, pp. 107–112.

Wallerstein, Judith S. 1989. *Second Chance: Men, Women, and Children a Decade after Divorce.* New York: Ticknor & Fields.

Walters, Pamela Barnhouse, and Richard Rubinson. 1983. "Educational expansion and economic output in the United States, 1890–1969: A production function analysis." *American Sociological Review,* 48, pp. 480–493.

Walton, John. 1982. "Cities and jobs and politics." *Urban Affairs Quarterly,* 18, pp. 5–17.

Walzer, Michael. 1978. "Must democracy be capitalist?" *New York Review of Books,* July 20, p. 41.

Wanner, Richard A., and Lionel S. Lewis. 1982. "Trends in education and earnings, 1950–70: A structural analysis." *Social Forces,* 61, pp. 436–455.

Warner, Carolyn. 1983. "Tuition tax credits: The death of private schooling." *College Board Review,* Fall, pp. 26–30.

Wartzman, Rick. 1992. "Sharing gains." *Wall Street Journal,* May 4, pp. A1, A4.

Waters, Harry F. 1982. "Life according to TV." *Newsweek,* December 6, pp. 136–140.

Watson, Roy E. L., and Peter W. DeMeo. 1987. "Premarital cohabitation vs. traditional courtship and subsequent marital adjustment: A replication and follow-up." *Family Relations,* 36, pp. 193–197.

Watson, Russell. 1989. "Small carrot, big stick." *Newsweek,* July 3, pp. 28–30.

———. 1992. "Ethnic cleansing." *Newsweek,* August 17, pp. 16–20.

Waxman, Chaim I. 1981. "The fourth generation grows up: The contemporary American Jewish community." *The Annals,* 454, March, pp. 70–85.

———. 1990. "Is the cup half-full or half-empty?: Perspectives on the future of the American Jewish community," in Seymour Martin Lipset (ed.), *American Pluralism and the Jewish Community.* New Brunswick, N.J.: Transaction, pp. 71–85.

Weaver, Charles N., and Michael D. Matthews. 1990. "Work satisfaction of females with full-time employment and full-time housekeeping: 15 years later." *Psychological Reports,* 66, pp. 1248–1250.

Weber, Max. 1954. *Max Weber on Law and Sociology.* Cambridge, Mass.: Harvard University Press.

———. 1957. *The Theory of Social and Economic Organization.* New York: Free Press.

Webster, Charles. 1975. *The Great Instauration: Science, Medicine and Reform, 1626–70.* London: Duckworth.

Webster, Murray, Jr., and James E. Driskell. 1983. "Beauty as status." *American Journal of Sociology,* 89, pp. 140–165.

Weinberg, Martin S., and Colin J. Williams. 1975. *Male Homosexuals.* New York: Penguin.

Weinraub, Bernard. 1989. "Bush urges educators to offer school choices." *New York Times,* January 11, p. 8.

Weinstein, Deena. 1979. "Fraud in science." *Social Science Quarterly,* 59, pp. 644–645.

Weis, Lois (ed.). 1988. *Class, Race, and Gender in American Education.* Albany, N.Y.: State University of New York Press.

Weitzman, Lenore. 1985. *The Divorce Revolution: The Unexpected Social and Economic Consequences for Women and Children in America.* New York: Free Press.

Wellborn, Stanley. 1987. "How genes shape personality." *U.S. News & World Report,* April 13, pp. 58–62.

Werner, Leslie Maitland. 1986. "Philosopher warns West of 'idolatry of politics.'" *New York Times,* May 13, p. 9.

Whitaker, Mark. 1984. "It was like breathing fire. . ." *Newsweek,* December 17, pp. 26–32.

White, James M. 1987. "Premarital cohabitation and marital stability in Canada." *Journal of Marriage and the Family,* 49, pp. 641–647.

White, Lynn K. 1983. "Determinants of spousal interaction: Marital structure or marital happiness." *Journal of Marriage and the Family,* 45, pp. 511–519.

———, and John N. Edwards. 1990. "Emptying the nest and parental well-being: An analysis of national panel data." *American Sociological Review,* 55, pp. 235–242.

White, Sheldon H. 1977. "The paradox of American education." *National Elementary Principal,* 56, May/June, pp. 9, 10.

Whitman, David. 1990. "The streets are filled with coke." *U.S. News & World Report,* March 5, pp. 24–26.

Whorf, Benjamin. 1956. *Language, Thought, and Reality.* New York: Wiley.

Whyte, Martin King. 1973. "Bureaucracy and modernization in China: The Maoist critique." *American Sociological Review,* 38, pp. 139–163.

———. 1992. "Choosing mates—The American way." *Society,* March/April, pp. 71–77.

Wicker, Tom. 1991. "The punitive society." *New York Times,* January 12, p. 17.

Widrick, Stanley, and Eugene Fram. 1984. "Is higher education a negative product?" *College Board Review,* 130, Winter, pp. 27–29.

Wierzbicka, Anna. 1986. "Human emotions: Universal or culture-specific?" *American Anthropology,* 88, pp. 584–594.

Wiley, Norbert. 1979. "Notes on self genesis: From me to we to I." *Studies in Symbolic Interaction*, 2, pp. 87-105.

Willhelm, Sidney M. 1980. "Can Marxism explain America's racism?" *Social Problems*, 29, pp. 98-112.

Williams, Dennis A. 1984. "Class conscious in Moscow." *Newsweek*, June 11, p. 73.

Williams, J. Allen, Jr., et al. 1987. "Sex role socialization in picture books: An update." *Social Science Quarterly*, 68, pp. 148-156.

Williams, Lena. 1989. "Teen-age sex: New codes amid the old anxiety." *New York Times*, February 27, pp. 1, 12.

———. 1992. "Girl's self-image is mother of the woman." *New York Times*, February 6, pp. A1, A12.

Williams, Robin M., Jr. 1970. *American Society: A Sociological Interpretation*, 3rd ed. New York: Knopf.

Wilson, John. 1978. *Religion in American Society*. Englewood Cliffs, N.J.: Prentice-Hall.

Wilson, Warner. 1989. "Brief resolution of the issue of similarity versus complementarity in mate selection using height preferences as a model." *Psychological Reports*, 65, pp. 387-393.

Wilson, William Julius. 1990. "Race-neutral programs and the Democratic coalition." *The American Prospect*, 1, pp. 75-81.

Wimberley, Dale W. 1984. "Socioeconomic deprivation and religious salience: A cognitive behavioral approach." *Sociological Quarterly*, 25, pp. 223-238.

Winch, Robert F. 1971. *The Modern Family*. New York: Holt, Rinehart and Winston.

———. 1974. "The functions of dating," in Robert Winch and Graham Spanier (eds.), *Selected Studies in Marriage and the Family*. New York: Holt, Rinehart and Winston.

Wines, Michael. 1993. "Senators approve a bill that eases vote registration." *New York Times*, March 18, pp. A1, 16.

Winslow, Ron. 1989. "Sometimes, talk is the best medicine." *Wall Street Journal*, October 5, p. B1.

Wolferen, Karel van. 1990. *The Enigma of Japanese Power*. New York: Vintage Books.

Wolfinger, Raymond E. 1986. "Registration creates an obstacle." *New York Times*, November 4, p. 31.

Wolfgang, Marvin E. 1958. *Patterns of Criminal Homicide*. Philadelphia: University of Pennsylvania Press.

Womack, Mari. 1978. "Sports magic." *Human Behavior*, September, pp. 43-44.

Wood, Michael, and Michael Hughes. 1984. "The moral basis of moral reform: Status discontent vs. culture and socialization as explanations of anti-pornography social movement adherence." *American Sociological Review*, 49, pp. 86-99.

Woodburn, James. 1982. "Egalitarian societies." *Man*, 17, pp. 431-451.

Woodward, Kenneth L. 1978. "Saving the family." *Newsweek*, May 15, pp. 63-73.

———. 1986. "From "mainline' to sideline." *Newsweek*, December 22, pp. 54-56.

———. 1987. "Saving souls—or a ministry?" *Newsweek*, July 13, pp. 52-53.

———. 1992. "Talking to God." *Newsweek*, January 6, pp. 39-44.

Wright, James D., et al. 1983. *Under the Gun: Weapons, Crime, and Violence in America*. New York: Aldine.

Wright, Stuart A., and Elizabeth S. Piper. 1986. "Families and cults: Familial factors related to youth leaving or remaining in deviant religious groups." *Journal of Marriage and the Family*, 48, pp. 15-25.

Wrong, Dennis H. 1990. *Population and Society*, 4th ed. New York: Random House.

Wuthnow, Robert. 1988. *The Restructuring of American Religion: Society and Faith since World War II*. Princeton, N.J.: Princeton University Press.

Yankelovich, Daniel. 1974. *The New Morality*. New York: McGraw-Hill.

———, and John Immerwahr. 1984. "Putting the work ethic to work. *Society*, 21, January/February, pp. 58-76.

Yeracaris, Constantine A., and Jay H. Kim. 1978. "Socioeconomic differentials in selected causes of death." *American Journal of Public Health*, 68, pp. 342-351.

Yoshihashi, Pauline. 1990. "Immigration law's employer sanctions prove to have little impact, study finds." *Wall Street Journal*, April 20, p. A16.

Young, T. R. 1984. "Crime and capitalism." Livermore, Colo.: Red Feather Institute.

Zangwill, Israel. 1909. *The Melting Pot*. New York: Macmillan.

Zenner, Walter P. 1985. "Jewishness in America: Ascription and choice." *Ethnic and Racial Studies*, 8, pp. 117-133.

Zimmer, Judith. 1984. "Courting the gods of sport." *Psychology Today*, July, pp. 36-39.

Zimmerman, Carle C. 1949. *The Family of Tomorrow*. New York: Harper & Brothers.

Zinsmeister, Karl. 1987. "Asians: Prejudice from top and bottom." *Public Opinion*, July/August, pp. 8-10, 59.

Zipp, John F., Richard Landerman, and Paul Luebke. 1982. "Political parties and political participation: A reexamination of the standard socioeconomic model." *Social Forces*, 60, pp. 1140-1153.

Zoglin, Richard. 1990. "Is TV ruining our children?" *Time,* October 15, pp. 75–76.

———. 1992. "Where fathers and mothers know best." *Time,* June 1, p. 33.

Zucker, Lynn. 1983. "Organizations as institutions." in Samuel B. Bacharach (ed.), *Research in the Sociology of Organizations,* vol. 2. Greenwich, Conn.: JAI Press.

Zur, Offer. 1987. "The psychohistory of warfare: The co-evolution of culture, psyche and enemy." *Journal of Peace Research,* 24, pp. 125–134.

Zurcher, Louis A. 1983. *Social Roles: Conformity, Conflict, and Creativity.* Beverly Hills, Calif.: Sage.

CREDITS

Unless otherwise acknowledged, all photographs are the property of Scott, Foresman and Company. Page abbreviations are as follows: (T) top, (C) center, (B) bottom, (L) left, (R) right.

Chapter 1   Page 2 Alan Berner; p. 5(T) M. Kelley/AlaskaStock Images; p. 5(B) Sarah Leen; p. 8 The Bettmann Archive; p. 9 The Bettmann Archive; p. 10 The University Library/University of Illinois at Chicago/Jane Addams Memorial Collection at Hull House; p. 14 AP/Wide World; p. 16 Barbara Kruger/Liz Claiborne, Inc.'s Women's Work program. Photo: PT and Co., Public Relations; p. 20 Schwadron; p. 22 R. Stott/The Image Works; p. 23 Copyright 1965 by Stanley Milgram, from the film *Obedience,* distributed by the Pennsylvania State University PCR.

Chapter 2   Page 30 Saunders/Leo de Wys; p. 33 Milt & Joan Mann/Cameramann International, Ltd.; p. 35 Stone/Sygma; p. 37 Azzi/Woodfin Camp & Associates; p. 39 © 1993 Warner Bros. All Rights Reserved.; p. 43 Napoleon Chagnon; p. 44 AP/Wide World.

Chapter 3   Page 48 Brent Jones; p. 51 Stone/Sygma; p. 53(T) Freeman/Grishaber/Photo Edit; p. 53(B) McCurry/Magnum Photos; p. 54 DeVore/Anthro-Photo; p. 56 Holland/Stock Boston; p. 57 Courtesy COMPAQ Computer Corp, TX/Milt & Joan Mann/Cameramann International, Ltd.; p. 60 Milt & Joan Mann/Cameramann International, Ltd.; p. 62 Pedrick/The Image Works; p. 64 AP/Wide World; p. 65 M. Peterson/JB Pictures Ltd.

Chapter 4   Page 70 Photo: Jon A. Rembold/*Insight* Magazine; p. 73 Drawing by Hamilton; © 1991/The New Yorker Magazine, Inc.; p. 74 Denny/Photo Edit; pp. 76, 78 Brent Jones; p. 79 Rick Browne/Stock Boston; p. 81 "Landscape with Figures" (detail) by George Tooker, The Marisa Del Re Gallery, New York; p. 83 Milt & Joan Mann/Cameramann International, Ltd.; p. 86 Joseph Nettis/Stock Boston.

Chapter 5   Page 90 Sam Abell; p. 92 Erika Stone; p. 94 AP/Wide World; p. 97 Freeman/Photo Edit; p. 99 Brent Jones; p. 100 Eiler/Stock Boston; p. 102 Drawing by Weber; © 1992/The New Yorker Magazine, Inc.; p. 104 Freeman/Photo Edit; p. 107 Oddie/Photo Edit.

Chapter 6   Page 110 J. P. Laffont/Sygma; p. 113 AP/Wide World; p. 115 Abbas/Magnum Photos; p. 118 Stephen Keller/

Visions Photographic; p. 120 David Young-Wolff/Photo Edit; p. 122 Starr/Picture Group; p. 125 Grecco/Stock Boston; p. 126 Paul Kuroda/*Orange County Register*; p. 129 J. P. Laffont/Sygma; p. 130 Cartoon Features Syndicate.

Chapter 7   Page 136 AP/Wide World; p. 138 Lewis Hine Photo/Library of Congress; p. 142 Neubauer/Photo Edit; p. 145(L) Jeff Dunn/The Picture Cube; p. 145(R) Timothy A. Murphy/*U.S. News & World Report*; p. 146(L) S. Katz/Black Star; p. 146(R) Andrew Holbrooke/Black Star; p. 154 G. Bellerose/Stock Boston; p. 156 Paul Conklin/Photo Edit; p. 158 Newman/Photo Edit.

Chapter 8   Page 164 Courtesy Benetton; p. 167 I. Berry/Magnum Photos; p. 169 Paul Dagys; p. 172 AP/Wide World; p. 174 Reuters/UPI/Bettmann; p. 176 J. Bergman/Gamma-Liaison; p. 179 John Running/Black Star; p. 182 Reuters/UPI/Bettmann; p. 186 N. Russell/Gamma-Liaison; p. 188 Hires/Gamma-Liaison; p. 190 California Institute of Technology.

Chapter 9   Page 196 Focus On Sports; p. 199 M. Ruiz/Picture Group; p. 200 Stephanie Maze/Woodfin Camp & Associates; p. 202 Used by permission of Johnny Hart and Creators Syndicate; p. 204 J. Forden/Sygma; p. 205 Monica Almeida/NYT Pictures; p. 208 Eastfoto/SOVFOTO; p. 209 J. Bernot/Stock Boston; p. 211 Maiman/Sygma; p. 214 P. Davies/SIPA-Press; p. 215 Nancy Coplon.

Chapter 10   Page 222 Bob Daemmrich; p. 225 Lila Abulughod/Anthro-Photo; p. 227 Culver Pictures; p. 230 Lerager/Sygma; p. 233 Dan Bosler/Tony Stone Images; p. 237 Schochet/Cartoon Features Syndicate; p. 238 Milt & Joan Mann/Cameramann International, Ltd.; p. 239 M. Forsyth/Monkmeyer Press Photo Service; p. 241 M. Ferguson/Photo Edit; p. 244 M. Ferguson Cate/Photo Edit.

Chapter 11   Page 248 Robert Frerck/Odyssey Productions, Chicago; p. 252(T) J. Rodriguez/Black Star; p. 252(B) Heiniger/Rapho/Photo Researchers; p. 254 Real to Reel Production; p. 257 Howard Simmons; p. 258 MacNelly/Reprinted by permission: Tribune Media Services; p. 259 Bouvet/Gamma-Liaison; p. 260(T) Sygma; p. 260(B) Fritz/Monkmeyer Press Photo Service; p. 267(L) Nine Network, Australia/Gamma-Liaison; p. 267(R) AP/Wide World; p. 272 Bryson/Sygma.

Name Index

SUBJECT INDEX